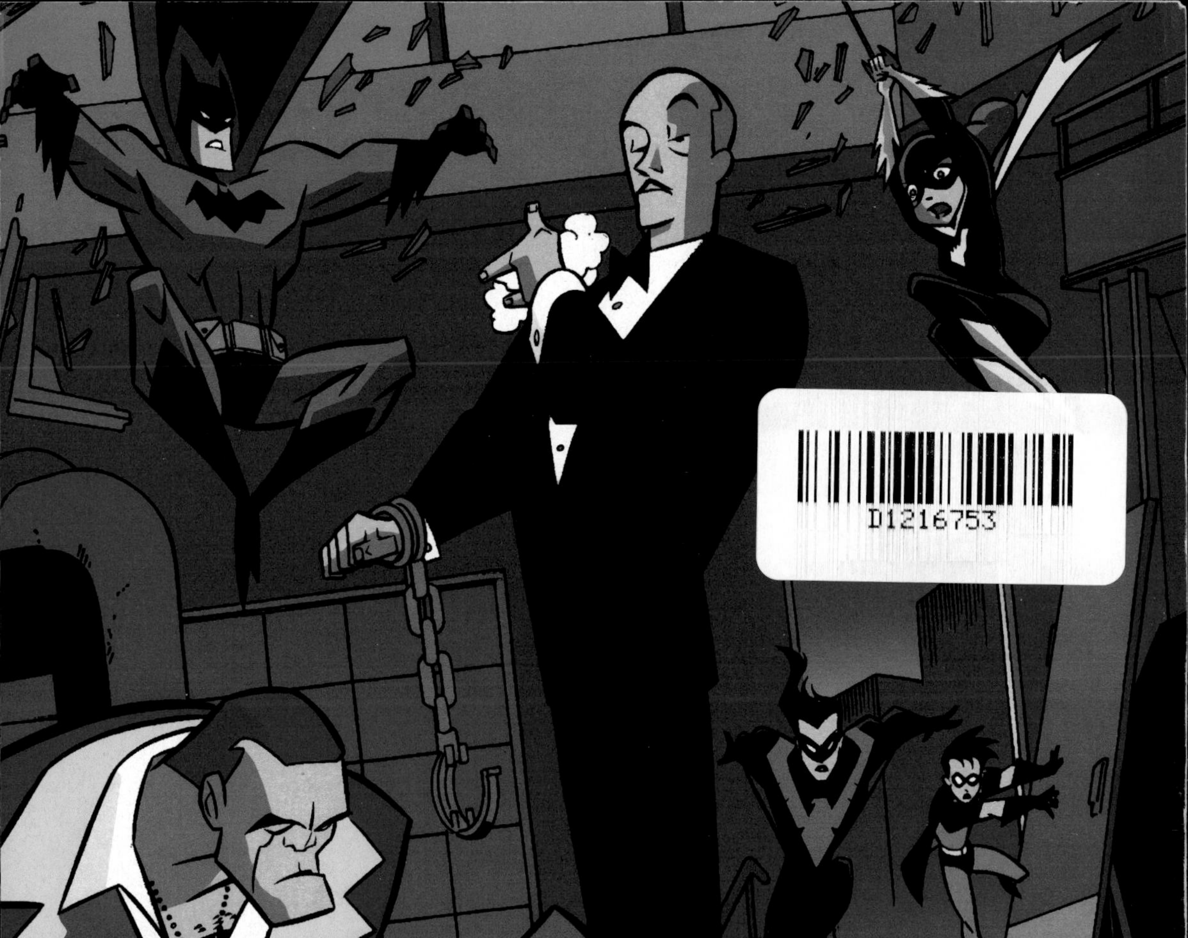



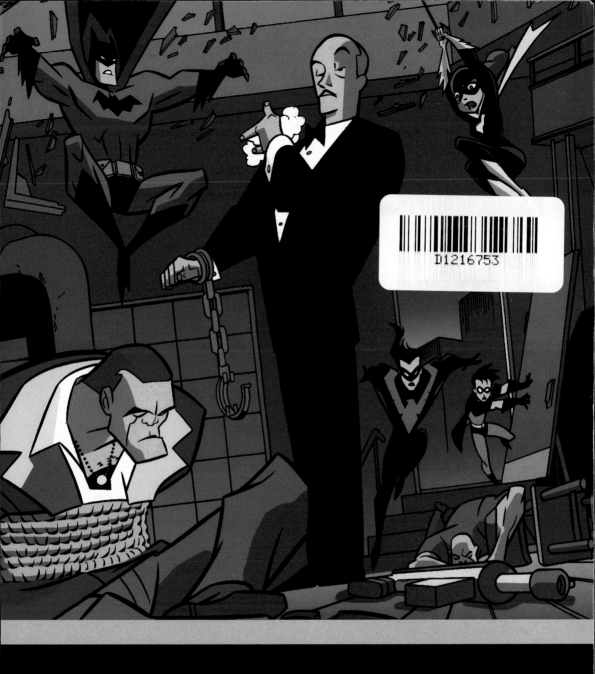

# BATMAN ALLIES

ALFRED PENNYWORTH

# TABLE OF CONTENTS

Front cover art by Alex Ross
Back cover art by Brian Bolland

Batman created by Bob Kane with Bill Finger

WHITNEY ELLSWORTH, PAUL LEVITZ,
DENNIS O'NEIL, DARREN VINCENZO, MICHAEL WRIGHT,
CHRIS CONROY, MARK DOYLE  Editors – Original Series
DAN RASPLER, JORDAN B. GORFINKEL, JOSEPH ILLIDGE,
REBECCA TAYLOR  Associate Editors – Original Series
DAVE WIELGOSZ  Assistant Editor – Original Series
JEB WOODARD  Group Editor – Collected Editions
ROBIN WILDMAN, ALEX GALER  Editors – Collected Edition
STEVE COOK  Design Director – Books
JOHN J. HILL  Publication Design
DANIELLE DIGRADO  Publication Production

BOB HARRAS  Senior VP – Editor-in-Chief, DC Comics
PAT McCALLUM  Executive Editor, DC Comics

DAN DiDIO  Publisher
JIM LEE  Publisher & Chief Creative Officer
BOBBIE CHASE  VP – New Publishing Initiatives & Talent Development
DON FALLETTI  VP – Manufacturing Operations & Workflow Management
LAWRENCE GANEM  VP – Talent Services
ALISON GILL  Senior VP – Manufacturing & Operations
HANK KANALZ  Senior VP – Publishing Strategy & Support Services
DAN MIRON  VP – Publishing Operations
NICK J. NAPOLITANO  VP – Manufacturing Administration & Design
NANCY SPEARS  VP – Sales
MICHELE R. WELLS  VP & Executive Editor, Young Reader

**BATMAN ALLIES: ALFRED PENNYWORTH**

Published by DC Comics. Compilation and all new material
Copyright © 2020 DC Comics. All Rights Reserved. Originally
published in single magazine form in *Batman* 16, 31, *Detective
Comics* 83, 356, 501, 502, 806, 807; *The Untold Legend of the
Batman* 2; *Batman Annual* (vol. 1) 13; *Batman: Shadow of the
Bat* 31; *Gotham Knights* 42; *Batman: Gotham Adventures* 16;
*Batman Eternal* 31; *Batman Annual* (vol. 3) 1, 3. Copyright ©
1943, 1944, 1945, 1966, 1980, 1981, 1989, 1994, 1999, 2003,
2005, 2015, 2016, 2018 DC Comics. All Rights Reserved. All
characters, their distinctive likenesses, and related elements
featured in this publication are trademarks of DC Comics. The
stories, characters, and incidents featured in this publication
are entirely fictional. DC Comics does not read or accept
unsolicited submissions of ideas, stories, or artwork.
DC – a WarnerMedia Company.

DC Comics, 2900 West Alameda Ave., Burbank, CA 91505
Printed by LSC Communications, Kendallville, IN, USA. 2/14/20.
First Printing.
ISBN: 978-1-4012-9894-4

Library of Congress Cataloging-in-Publication Data is
available.

PEFC Certified

This product is from
sustainably managed
forests and controlled
sources

PEFC/29-31-337    www.pefc.org

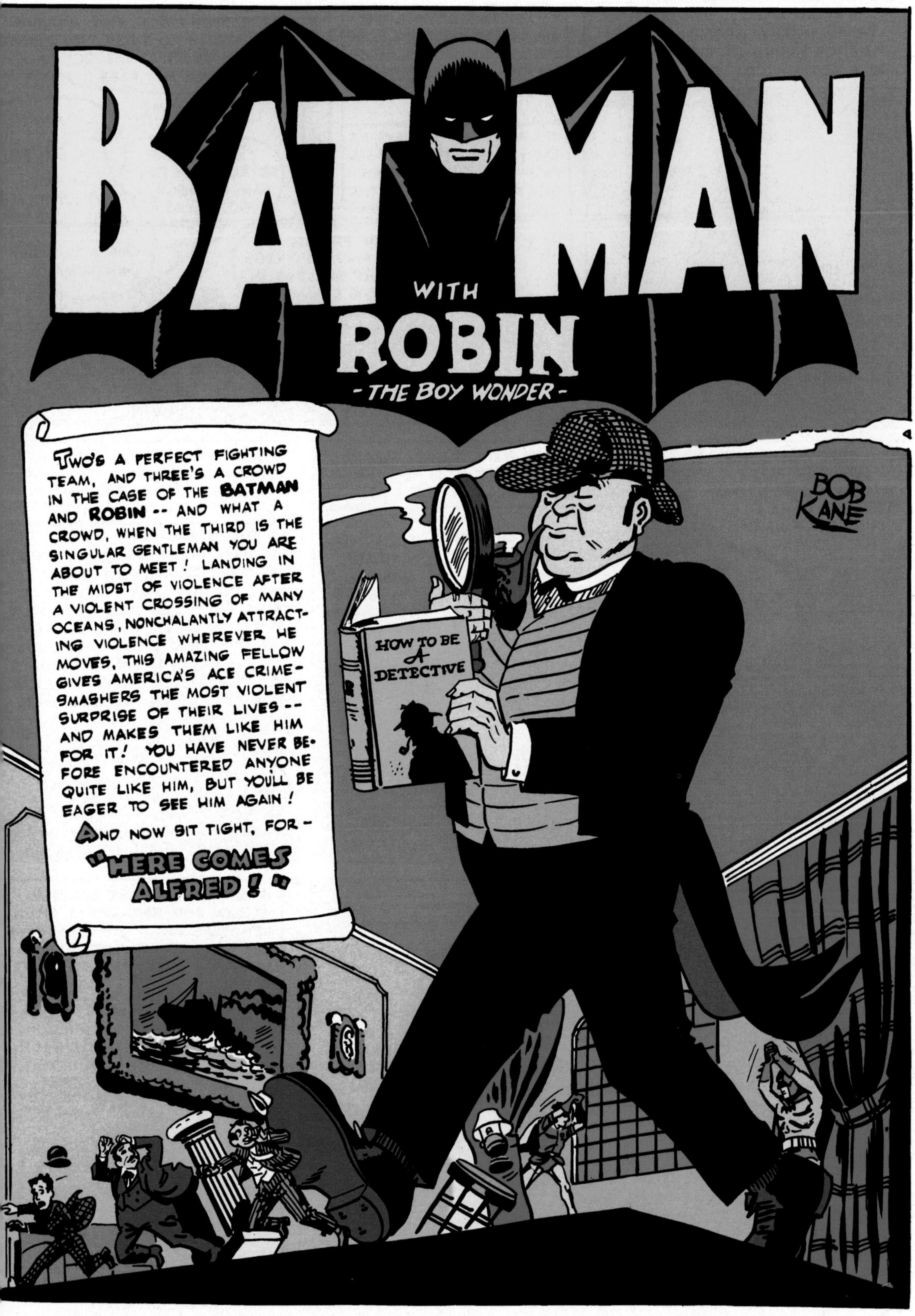
BATMAN
WITH
ROBIN
-THE BOY WONDER-
TWO'S A PERFECT FIGHTING TEAM, AND THREE'S A CROWD IN THE CASE OF THE BATMAN AND ROBIN -- AND WHAT A CROWD, WHEN THE THIRD IS THE SINGULAR GENTLEMAN YOU ARE ABOUT TO MEET! LANDING IN THE MIDST OF VIOLENCE AFTER A VIOLENT CROSSING OF MANY OCEANS, NONCHALANTLY ATTRACTING VIOLENCE WHEREVER HE MOVES, THIS AMAZING FELLOW GIVES AMERICA'S ACE CRIME-SMASHERS THE MOST VIOLENT SURPRISE OF THEIR LIVES -- AND MAKES THEM LIKE HIM FOR IT! YOU HAVE NEVER BEFORE ENCOUNTERED ANYONE QUITE LIKE HIM, BUT YOU'LL BE EAGER TO SEE HIM AGAIN!
AND NOW SIT TIGHT, FOR -
"HERE COMES ALFRED!"
BOB KANE
HOW TO BE A DETECTIVE

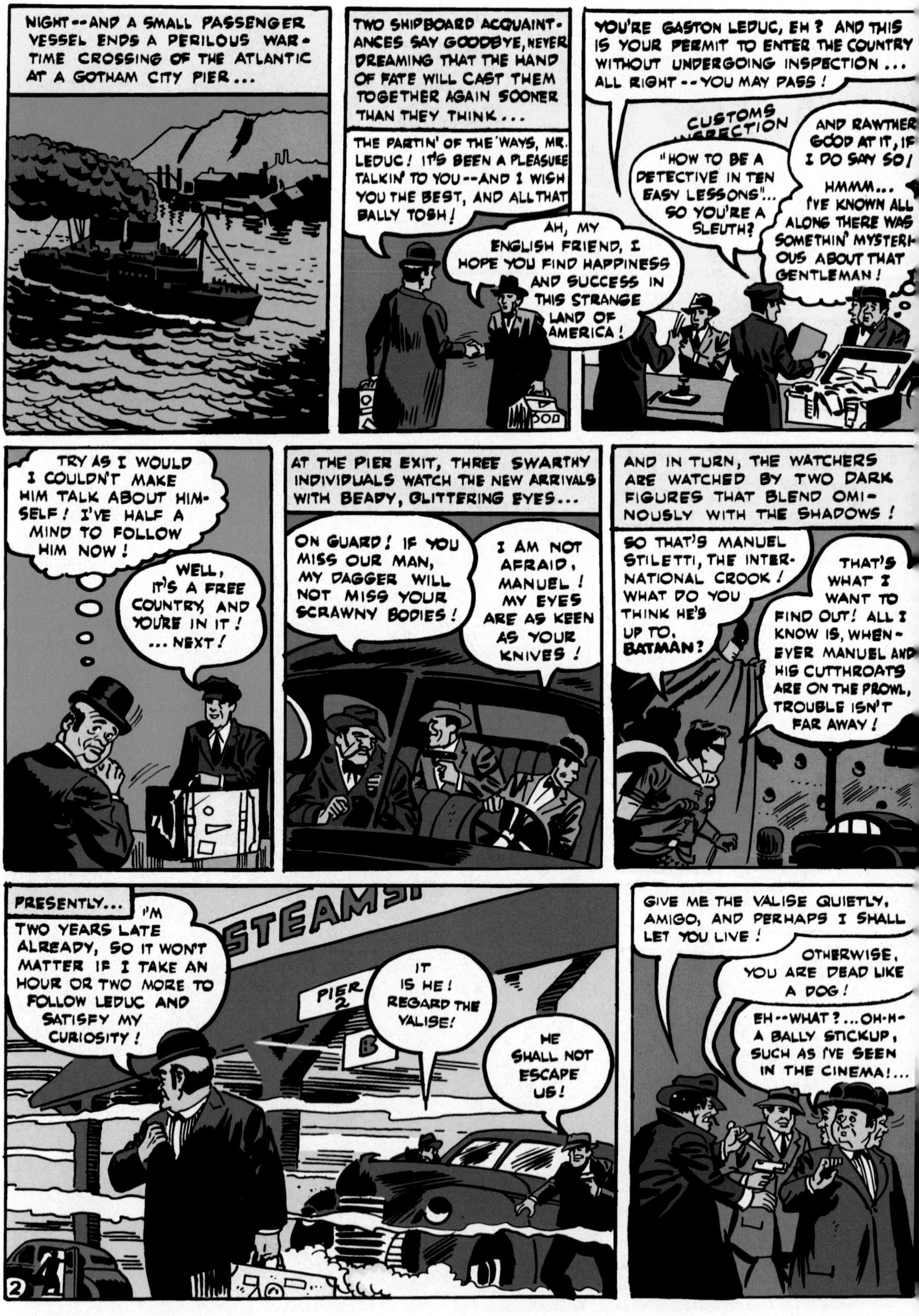
NIGHT--AND A SMALL PASSENGER VESSEL ENDS A PERILOUS WAR-TIME CROSSING OF THE ATLANTIC AT A GOTHAM CITY PIER...
TWO SHIPBOARD ACQUAINTANCES SAY GOODBYE, NEVER DREAMING THAT THE HAND OF FATE WILL CAST THEM TOGETHER AGAIN SOONER THAN THEY THINK...
THE PARTIN' OF THE 'WAYS, MR. LEDUC! IT'S BEEN A PLEASUEE TALKIN' TO YOU--AND I WISH YOU THE BEST, AND ALL THAT BALLY TOSH!
AH, MY ENGLISH FRIEND, I HOPE YOU FIND HAPPINESS AND SUCCESS IN THIS STRANGE LAND OF AMERICA!
YOU'RE GASTON LEDUC, EH? AND THIS IS YOUR PERMIT TO ENTER THE COUNTRY WITHOUT UNDERGOING INSPECTION... ALL RIGHT--YOU MAY PASS!
CUSTOMS
"HOW TO BE A DETECTIVE IN TEN EASY LESSONS"... SO YOU'RE A SLEUTH?
AND RAWTHER GOOD AT IT, IF I DO SAY SO!
HMMM... I'VE KNOWN ALL ALONG THERE WAS SOMETHIN' MYSTERIOUS ABOUT THAT GENTLEMAN!
TRY AS I WOULD I COULDN'T MAKE HIM TALK ABOUT HIMSELF! I'VE HALF A MIND TO FOLLOW HIM NOW!
WELL, IT'S A FREE COUNTRY, AND YOU'RE IN IT! ...NEXT!
AT THE PIER EXIT, THREE SWARTHY INDIVIDUALS WATCH THE NEW ARRIVALS WITH BEADY, GLITTERING EYES...
ON GUARD! IF YOU MISS OUR MAN, MY DAGGER WILL NOT MISS YOUR SCRAWNY BODIES!
I AM NOT AFRAID, MANUEL! MY EYES ARE AS KEEN AS YOUR KNIVES!
AND IN TURN, THE WATCHERS ARE WATCHED BY TWO DARK FIGURES THAT BLEND OMINOUSLY WITH THE SHADOWS!
SO THAT'S MANUEL STILETTI, THE INTERNATIONAL CROOK! WHAT DO YOU THINK HE'S UP TO, BATMAN?
THAT'S WHAT I WANT TO FIND OUT! ALL I KNOW IS, WHENEVER MANUEL AND HIS CUTTHROATS ARE ON THE PROWL, TROUBLE ISN'T FAR AWAY!
PRESENTLY...
I'M TWO YEARS LATE ALREADY, SO IT WON'T MATTER IF I TAKE AN HOUR OR TWO MORE TO FOLLOW LEDUC AND SATISFY MY CURIOSITY!
PIER 2
IT IS HE! REGARD THE VALISE!
HE SHALL NOT ESCAPE US!
GIVE ME THE VALISE QUIETLY, AMIGO, AND PERHAPS I SHALL LET YOU LIVE!
OTHERWISE, YOU ARE DEAD LIKE A DOG!
EH--WHAT?...OH-H-A BALLY STICKUP, SUCH AS I'VE SEEN IN THE CINEMA!...
2

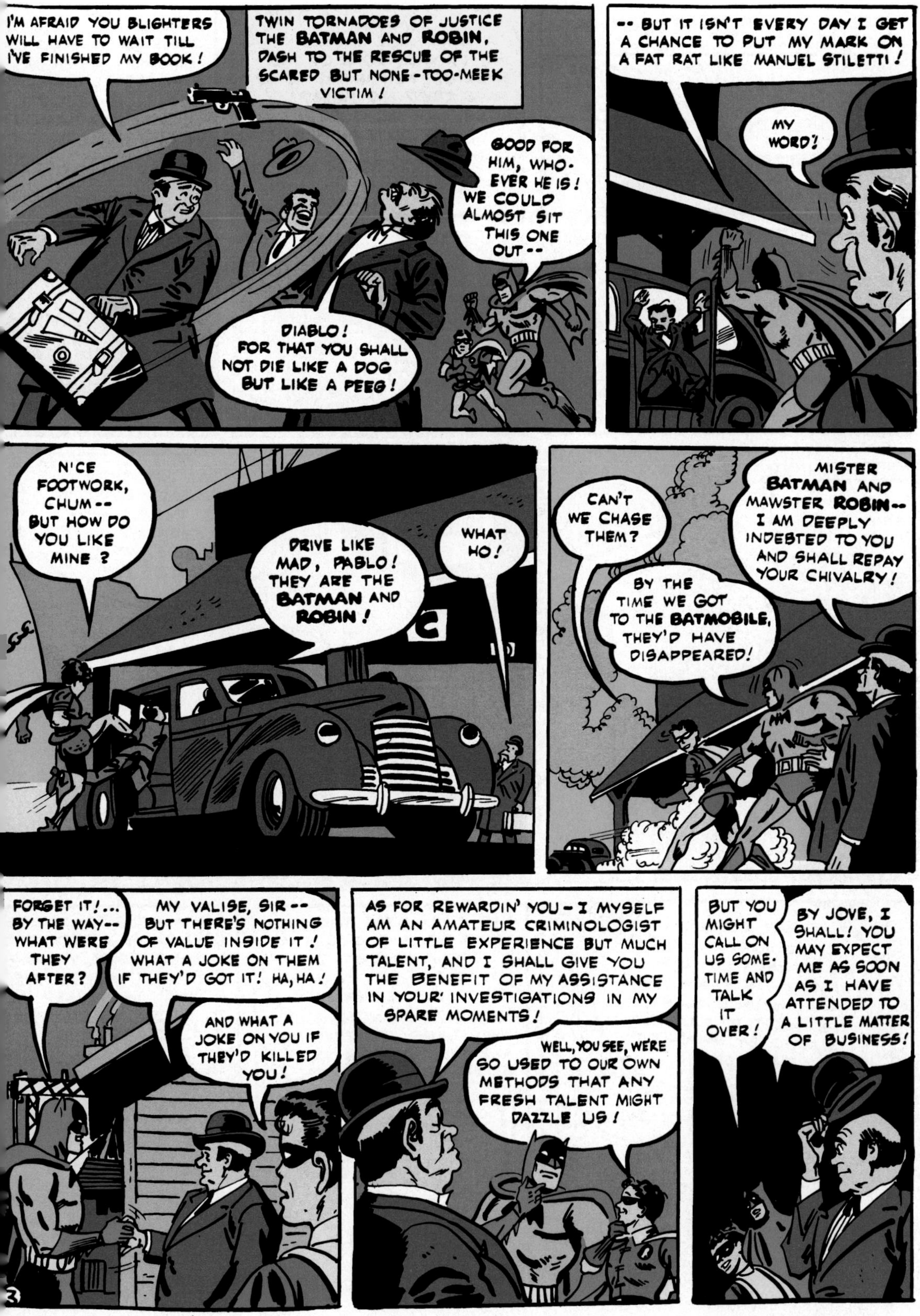
I'M AFRAID YOU BLIGHTERS WILL HAVE TO WAIT TILL I'VE FINISHED MY BOOK!
TWIN TORNADOES OF JUSTICE THE BATMAN AND ROBIN, DASH TO THE RESCUE OF THE SCARED BUT NONE-TOO-MEEK VICTIM!
GOOD FOR HIM, WHO-EVER HE IS! WE COULD ALMOST SIT THIS ONE OUT--
DIABLO! FOR THAT YOU SHALL NOT DIE LIKE A DOG BUT LIKE A PEEG!
--BUT IT ISN'T EVERY DAY I GET A CHANCE TO PUT MY MARK ON A FAT RAT LIKE MANUEL STILETTI!
MY WORD!
N'CE FOOTWORK, CHUM-- BUT HOW DO YOU LIKE MINE?
DRIVE LIKE MAD, PABLO! THEY ARE THE BATMAN AND ROBIN!
WHAT HO!
CAN'T WE CHASE THEM?
BY THE TIME WE GOT TO THE BATMOBILE, THEY'D HAVE DISAPPEARED!
MISTER BATMAN AND MAWSTER ROBIN-- I AM DEEPLY INDEBTED TO YOU AND SHALL REPAY YOUR CHIVALRY!
FORGET IT!... BY THE WAY-- WHAT WERE THEY AFTER?
MY VALISE, SIR-- BUT THERE'S NOTHING OF VALUE INSIDE IT! WHAT A JOKE ON THEM IF THEY'D GOT IT! HA, HA!
AND WHAT A JOKE ON YOU IF THEY'D KILLED YOU!
AS FOR REWARDIN' YOU - I MYSELF AM AN AMATEUR CRIMINOLOGIST OF LITTLE EXPERIENCE BUT MUCH TALENT, AND I SHALL GIVE YOU THE BENEFIT OF MY ASSISTANCE IN YOUR INVESTIGATIONS IN MY SPARE MOMENTS!
WELL, YOU SEE, WE'RE SO USED TO OUR OWN METHODS THAT ANY FRESH TALENT MIGHT DAZZLE US!
BUT YOU MIGHT CALL ON US SOME-TIME AND TALK IT OVER!
BY JOVE, I SHALL! YOU MAY EXPECT ME AS SOON AS I HAVE ATTENDED TO A LITTLE MATTER OF BUSINESS!
3

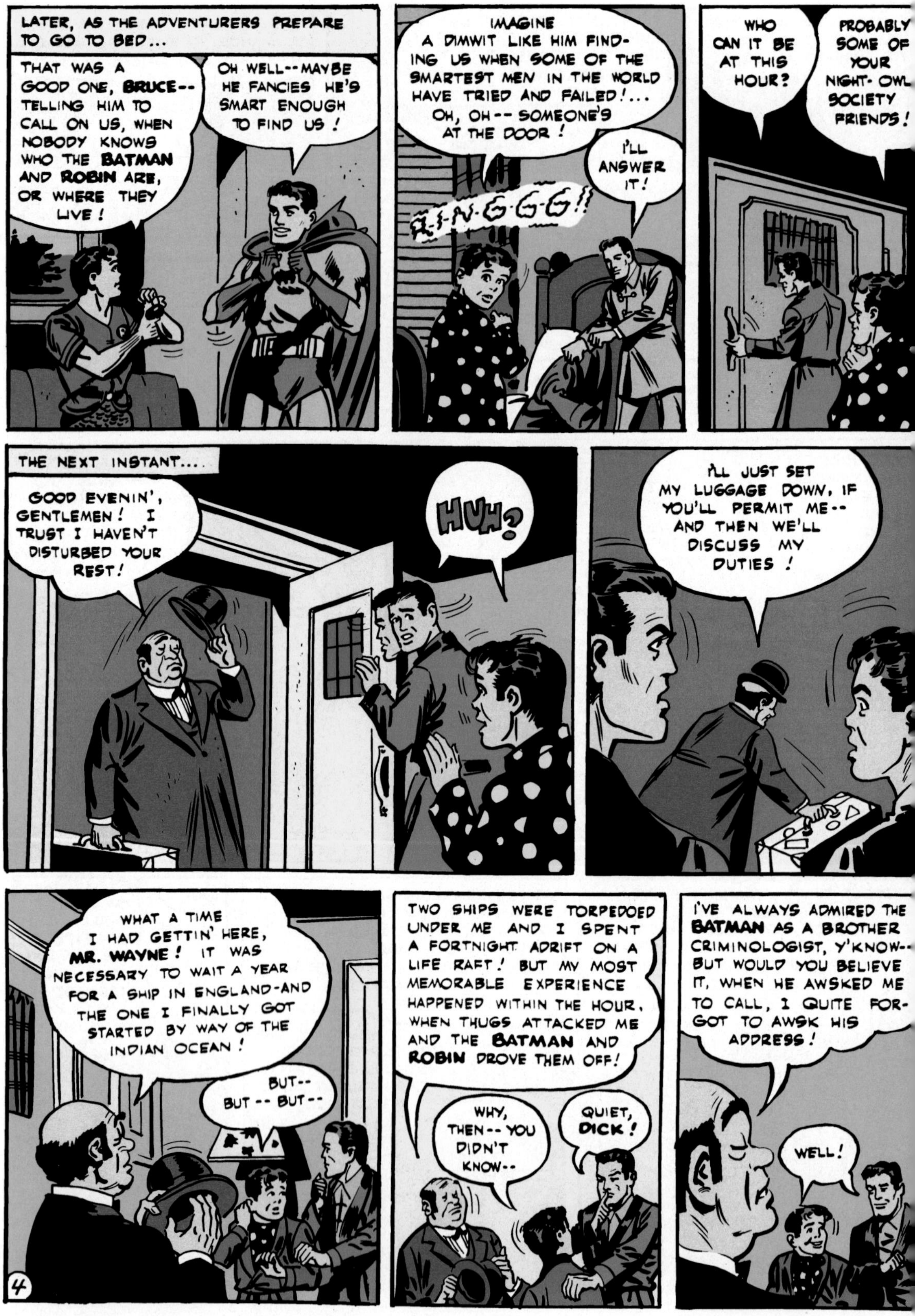

LATER, AS THE ADVENTURERS PREPARE TO GO TO BED...
THAT WAS A GOOD ONE, BRUCE-- TELLING HIM TO CALL ON US, WHEN NOBODY KNOWS WHO THE BATMAN AND ROBIN ARE, OR WHERE THEY LIVE!
OH WELL--MAYBE HE FANCIES HE'S SMART ENOUGH TO FIND US!
IMAGINE A DIMWIT LIKE HIM FINDING US WHEN SOME OF THE SMARTEST MEN IN THE WORLD HAVE TRIED AND FAILED!... OH, OH-- SOMEONE'S AT THE DOOR!
R-I-N-G-G-G!!
I'LL ANSWER IT!
WHO CAN IT BE AT THIS HOUR?
PROBABLY SOME OF YOUR NIGHT-OWL SOCIETY FRIENDS!
THE NEXT INSTANT....
GOOD EVENIN', GENTLEMEN! I TRUST I HAVEN'T DISTURBED YOUR REST!
HUH?
I'LL JUST SET MY LUGGAGE DOWN, IF YOU'LL PERMIT ME-- AND THEN WE'LL DISCUSS MY DUTIES!
WHAT A TIME I HAD GETTIN' HERE, MR. WAYNE! IT WAS NECESSARY TO WAIT A YEAR FOR A SHIP IN ENGLAND-AND THE ONE I FINALLY GOT STARTED BY WAY OF THE INDIAN OCEAN!
BUT-- BUT -- BUT--
4
TWO SHIPS WERE TORPEDOED UNDER ME AND I SPENT A FORTNIGHT ADRIFT ON A LIFE RAFT! BUT MY MOST MEMORABLE EXPERIENCE HAPPENED WITHIN THE HOUR, WHEN THUGS ATTACKED ME AND THE BATMAN AND ROBIN DROVE THEM OFF!
WHY, THEN-- YOU DIDN'T KNOW--
QUIET, DICK!
I'VE ALWAYS ADMIRED THE BATMAN AS A BROTHER CRIMINOLOGIST, Y'KNOW-- BUT WOULD YOU BELIEVE IT, WHEN HE AWSKED ME TO CALL, I QUITE FORGOT TO AWSK HIS ADDRESS!
WELL!

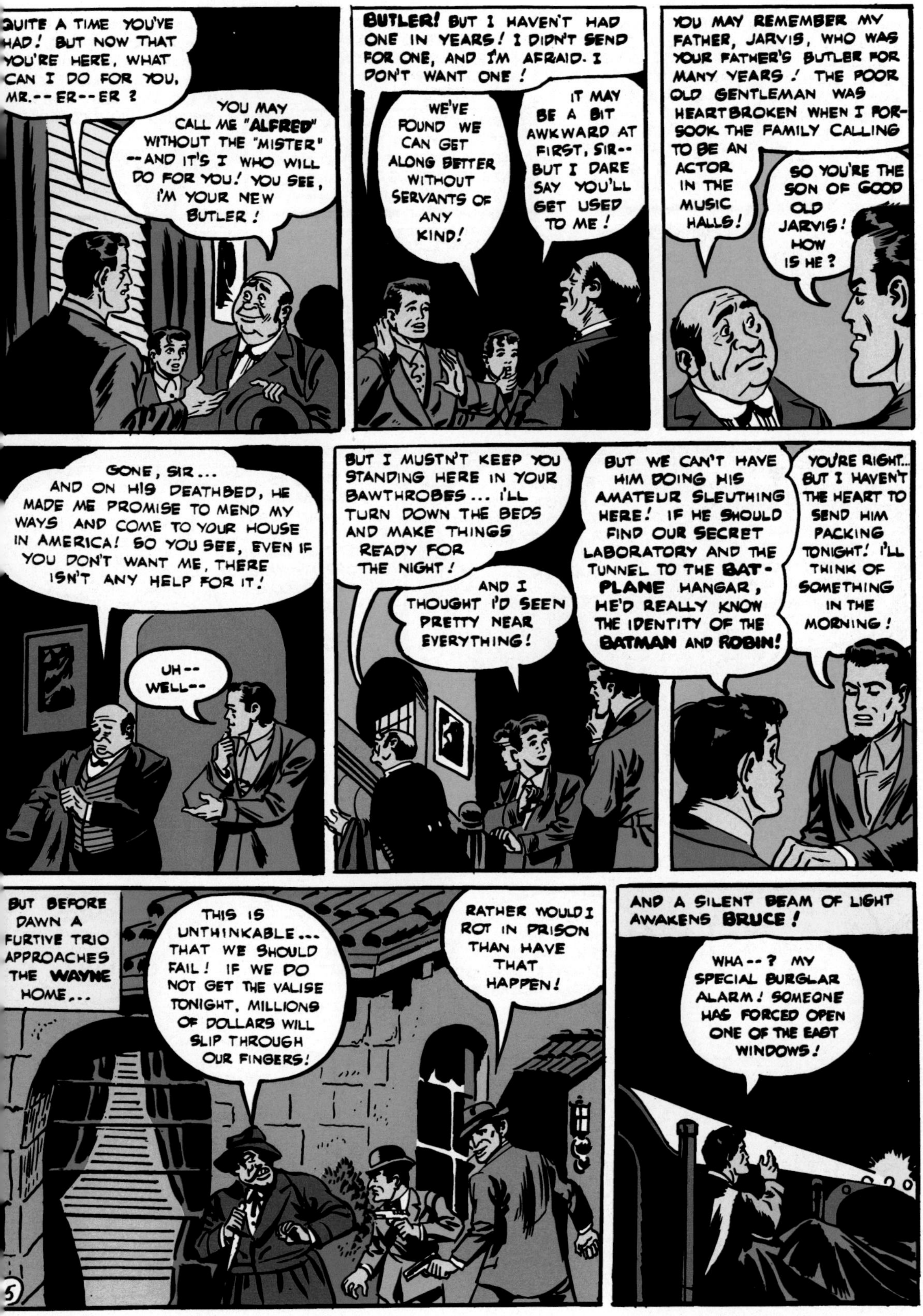
QUITE A TIME YOU'VE HAD! BUT NOW THAT YOU'RE HERE, WHAT CAN I DO FOR YOU, MR.--ER--ER ?
YOU MAY CALL ME "ALFRED" WITHOUT THE "MISTER" --AND IT'S I WHO WILL DO FOR YOU! YOU SEE, I'M YOUR NEW BUTLER!
BUTLER! BUT I HAVEN'T HAD ONE IN YEARS! I DIDN'T SEND FOR ONE, AND I'M AFRAID I DON'T WANT ONE!
WE'VE FOUND WE CAN GET ALONG BETTER WITHOUT SERVANTS OF ANY KIND!
IT MAY BE A BIT AWKWARD AT FIRST, SIR-- BUT I DARE SAY YOU'LL GET USED TO ME!
YOU MAY REMEMBER MY FATHER, JARVIS, WHO WAS YOUR FATHER'S BUTLER FOR MANY YEARS! THE POOR OLD GENTLEMAN WAS HEARTBROKEN WHEN I FORSOOK THE FAMILY CALLING TO BE AN ACTOR IN THE MUSIC HALLS!
SO YOU'RE THE SON OF GOOD OLD JARVIS! HOW IS HE?
GONE, SIR... AND ON HIS DEATHBED, HE MADE ME PROMISE TO MEND MY WAYS AND COME TO YOUR HOUSE IN AMERICA! SO YOU SEE, EVEN IF YOU DON'T WANT ME, THERE ISN'T ANY HELP FOR IT!
UH-- WELL--
BUT I MUSTN'T KEEP YOU STANDING HERE IN YOUR BAWTHROBES... I'LL TURN DOWN THE BEDS AND MAKE THINGS READY FOR THE NIGHT!
AND I THOUGHT I'D SEEN PRETTY NEAR EVERYTHING!
BUT WE CAN'T HAVE HIM DOING HIS AMATEUR SLEUTHING HERE! IF HE SHOULD FIND OUR SECRET LABORATORY AND THE TUNNEL TO THE BAT-PLANE HANGAR, HE'D REALLY KNOW THE IDENTITY OF THE BATMAN AND ROBIN!
YOU'RE RIGHT... BUT I HAVEN'T THE HEART TO SEND HIM PACKING TONIGHT! I'LL THINK OF SOMETHING IN THE MORNING!
BUT BEFORE DAWN A FURTIVE TRIO APPROACHES THE WAYNE HOME...
THIS IS UNTHINKABLE... THAT WE SHOULD FAIL! IF WE DO NOT GET THE VALISE TONIGHT, MILLIONS OF DOLLARS WILL SLIP THROUGH OUR FINGERS!
RATHER WOULD I ROT IN PRISON THAN HAVE THAT HAPPEN!
5
AND A SILENT BEAM OF LIGHT AWAKENS BRUCE!
WHA--? MY SPECIAL BURGLAR ALARM! SOMEONE HAS FORCED OPEN ONE OF THE EAST WINDOWS!

OH, YOU'RE AWAKE ... MY BURGLAR ALARM IS ON, AND I WONDERED IF YOU KNEW-- BUT I SEE YOU DO!
GET INTO YOUR UNIFORM, IN CASE WE HAVE TO GO OUT-- AND DON'T FORGET, WE'LL HAVE TO MAKE UP SOME EXPLANATION FOR THE BATMAN AND ROBIN APPEARING HERE IF WE DON'T WANT TO GIVE OURSELVES AWAY!
AND NOW LET US JOIN THE REMARKABLE ALFRED AS HIS ENTHUSIASM FOR HIS NEW JOB CARRIES HIM FAR INTO THE NIGHT...
MR WAYNE IS A NICE PERSON BUT A TYPICAL BACHELOR! LOOK AT THESE NEWSPAPERS, WEEKS OLD AND NOT YET TAKEN OUT!... HMMM-- THIS PICTURE...
IT IS HE, GASTON LE DUC! NO WONDER I SENSED SOMETHING MYSTERIOUS ABOUT HIM! I MUST LOOK HIM UP AND LET HIM KNOW I PIERCED HIS INCOGNITO!
The GOTHA
DUKE OF DORIAN, PREMIER, FLEES NAZI INVASION!
DUKE OF DORIAN
A MOMENT LATER...
SO-- YOU THOUGHT TO ESCAPE! YOU DID NOT THINK WE WOULD FOLLOW YOU, EH?
BLAWST IT! IF I RESIST IT WILL DISTURB THE MAWSTERS --AND A GOOD BUTLER NEVER LETS THAT HAPPEN!
THERE IS NO BATMAN TO SAVE YOU NOW, ENGLISH DOLT! LEAD US TO THE VALISE BEFORE MY TRIGGER FINGER BECOMES IMPATIENT!
IT'S IN THIS ROOM!... YOU CAN HAVE IT --B-BUT P-PLEASE DON'T KILL ME!
AH! AT LAST! THE TREASURE IS OURS!
BLESS ME-- I KNEW THAT VALISE WAS OLD, BUT I NEVER DREAMED IT WAS A VALUABLE ANTIQUE!
I SAY- IT'S BAD ENOUGH TO STEAL, BUT IT'S DOWNRIGHT CRIMINAL TO DESTROY A THING WHILE THERE'S STILL USE IN IT!
PABLO, HE ANNOYS ME! KILL HIM!
WITH THE GREATEST OF PLEASURE!

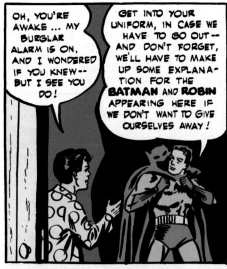

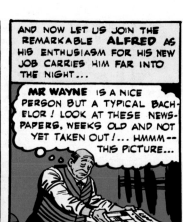

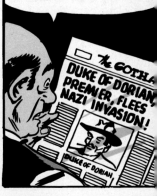

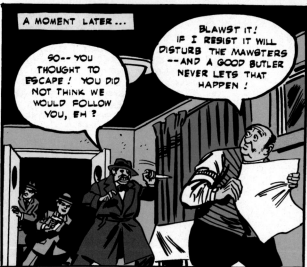

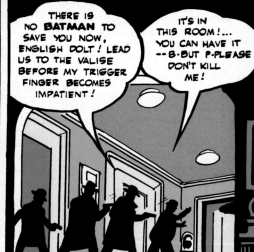

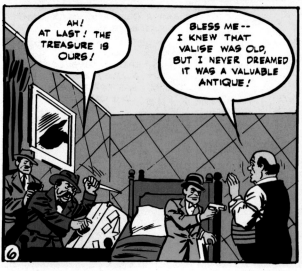

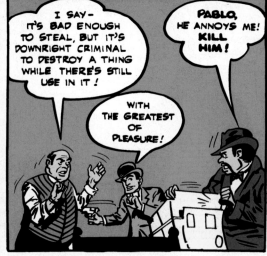

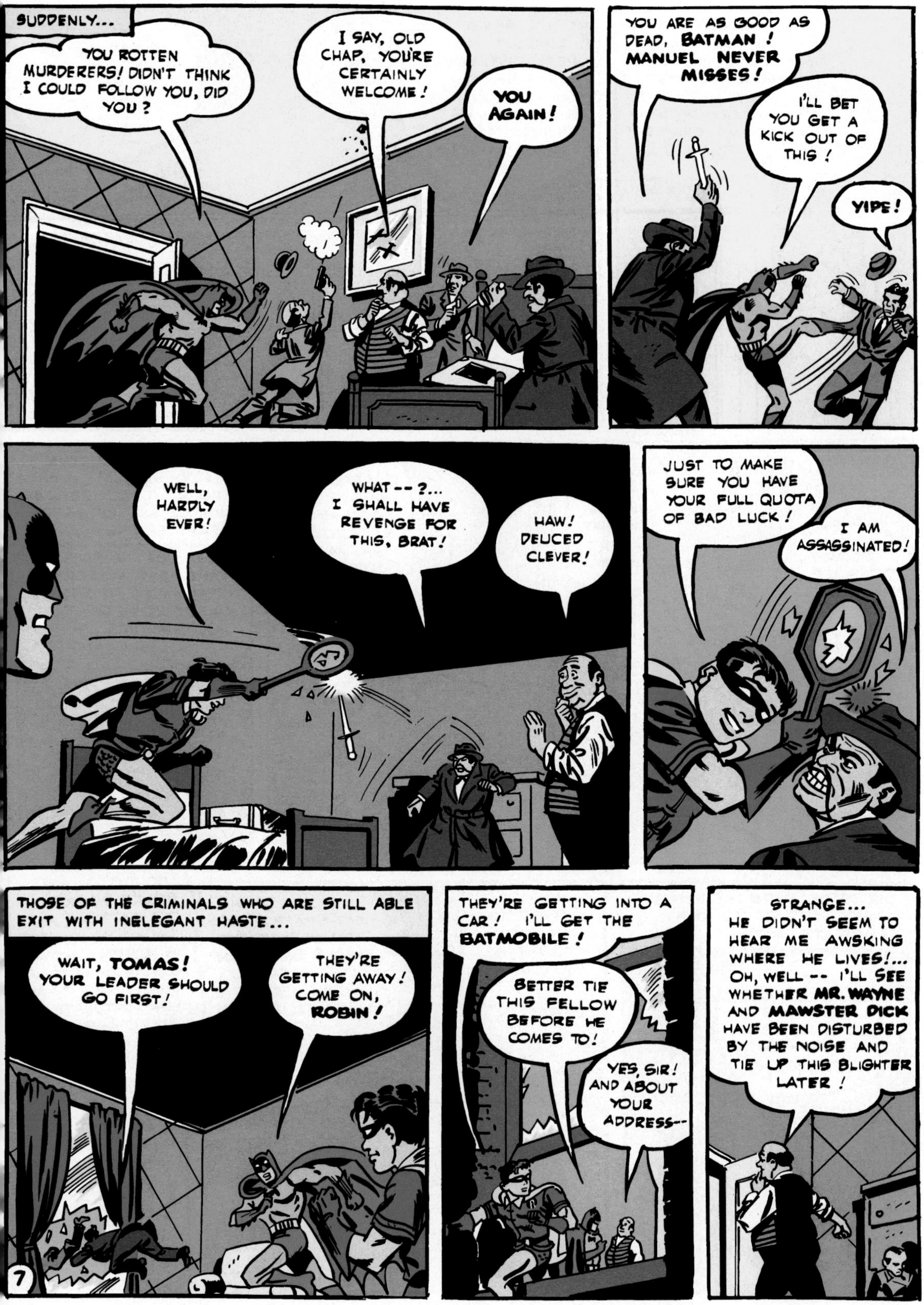
SUDDENLY...
YOU ROTTEN MURDERERS! DIDN'T THINK I COULD FOLLOW YOU, DID YOU?
I SAY, OLD CHAP, YOU'RE CERTAINLY WELCOME!
YOU AGAIN!
YOU ARE AS GOOD AS DEAD, BATMAN! MANUEL NEVER MISSES!
I'LL BET YOU GET A KICK OUT OF THIS!
YIPE!
WELL, HARDLY EVER!
WHAT -- ?... I SHALL HAVE REVENGE FOR THIS, BRAT!
HAW! DEUCED CLEVER!
JUST TO MAKE SURE YOU HAVE YOUR FULL QUOTA OF BAD LUCK!
I AM ASSASSINATED!
THOSE OF THE CRIMINALS WHO ARE STILL ABLE EXIT WITH INELEGANT HASTE...
WAIT, TOMAS! YOUR LEADER SHOULD GO FIRST!
THEY'RE GETTING AWAY! COME ON, ROBIN!
7
THEY'RE GETTING INTO A CAR! I'LL GET THE BATMOBILE!
BETTER TIE THIS FELLOW BEFORE HE COMES TO!
YES, SIR! AND ABOUT YOUR ADDRESS--
STRANGE... HE DIDN'T SEEM TO HEAR ME AWSKING WHERE HE LIVES!... OH, WELL -- I'LL SEE WHETHER MR. WAYNE AND MAWSTER DICK HAVE BEEN DISTURBED BY THE NOISE AND TIE UP THIS BLIGHTER LATER!

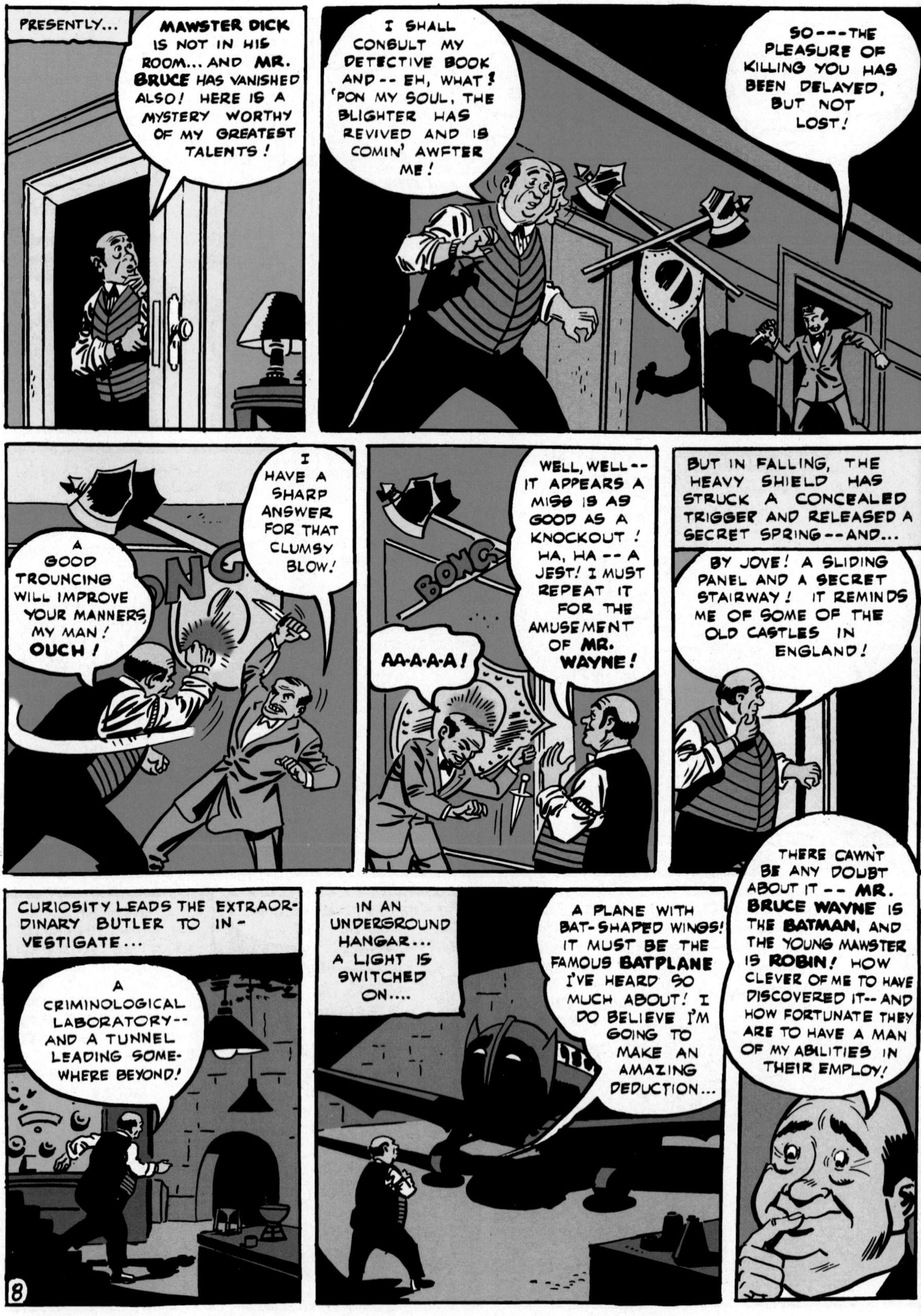
PRESENTLY...
MAWSTER DICK IS NOT IN HIS ROOM... AND MR. BRUCE HAS VANISHED ALSO! HERE IS A MYSTERY WORTHY OF MY GREATEST TALENTS!
I SHALL CONSULT MY DETECTIVE BOOK AND -- EH, WHAT! 'PON MY SOUL, THE BLIGHTER HAS REVIVED AND IS COMIN' AWFTER ME!
SO---THE PLEASURE OF KILLING YOU HAS BEEN DELAYED, BUT NOT LOST!
A GOOD TROUNCING WILL IMPROVE YOUR MANNERS, MY MAN! OUCH!
I HAVE A SHARP ANSWER FOR THAT CLUMSY BLOW!
AA-A-A-A!
WELL, WELL-- IT APPEARS A MISS IS AS GOOD AS A KNOCKOUT! HA, HA -- A JEST! I MUST REPEAT IT FOR THE AMUSEMENT OF MR. WAYNE!
BUT IN FALLING, THE HEAVY SHIELD HAS STRUCK A CONCEALED TRIGGER AND RELEASED A SECRET SPRING--AND...
BY JOVE! A SLIDING PANEL AND A SECRET STAIRWAY! IT REMINDS ME OF SOME OF THE OLD CASTLES IN ENGLAND!
CURIOSITY LEADS THE EXTRAORDINARY BUTLER TO INVESTIGATE...
A CRIMINOLOGICAL LABORATORY-- AND A TUNNEL LEADING SOMEWHERE BEYOND!
8
IN AN UNDERGROUND HANGAR... A LIGHT IS SWITCHED ON....
A PLANE WITH BAT-SHAPED WINGS! IT MUST BE THE FAMOUS BATPLANE I'VE HEARD SO MUCH ABOUT! I DO BELIEVE I'M GOING TO MAKE AN AMAZING DEDUCTION...
THERE CAWN'T BE ANY DOUBT ABOUT IT -- MR. BRUCE WAYNE IS THE BATMAN, AND THE YOUNG MAWSTER IS ROBIN! HOW CLEVER OF ME TO HAVE DISCOVERED IT-- AND HOW FORTUNATE THEY ARE TO HAVE A MAN OF MY ABILITIES IN THEIR EMPLOY!

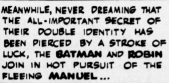

MEANWHILE, NEVER DREAMING THAT THE ALL-IMPORTANT SECRET OF THEIR DOUBLE IDENTITY HAS BEEN PIERCED BY A STROKE OF LUCK, THE BATMAN AND ROBIN JOIN IN HOT PURSUIT OF THE FLEEING MANUEL...

THERE THEY ARE-- TURNING THAT CORNER AHEAD!

STEP ON IT! IF WE DON'T CATCH THEM NOW, WE MAY NEVER HAVE ANOTHER CHANCE!

MOMENTS LATER...

THERE'S THEIR CAR-- BUT WHERE ARE THEY?

I CAN'T THINK OF ANY BETTER HIDEOUT THAN AN ABANDONED THEATER!

CLOSED

BUILDING FOR SALE

STAGE

STEEL MUSCLES FORCE A LOCKED DOOR, AND THE DYNAMIC DUO VENTURES INTO COBWEB-DRAPED DARKNESS...

SPOOKY PLACE, ISN'T IT? I'LL BET NOBODY'S BEEN HERE FOR YEARS!

YOU'D LOSE YOUR MONEY! EVEN ALFRED WOULD KNOW BETTER SEEING THESE FOOT-PRINTS IN THE DUST!

BRRR-R-R! I CAN HEAR THE GHOSTS OF DEAD PLAYS MOANING!

THERE'S A STRANGE WHIRRING SOUND COMING FROM SOMEWHERE!

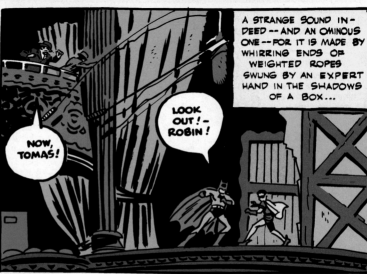

NOW, TOMAS!

LOOK OUT!- ROBIN!

A STRANGE SOUND INDEED -- AND AN OMINOUS ONE -- FOR IT IS MADE BY WHIRRING ENDS OF WEIGHTED ROPES SWUNG BY AN EXPERT HAND IN THE SHADOWS OF A BOX...

TOO LATE! THE NEXT INSTANT, HISSING COILS WHIP AROUND THE LIMBS AND BODIES OF THE STARTLED CRIME-CRUSHERS...

WHA--? A BOLA!

I CAN'T MOVE MY ARMS OR FEET! I'M FALLING!

AS FINE A CAST AS WAS EVER MADE! NOW TO FINISH THEM!

NOT YET! LET US DO ALL OUR KILLING AT ONCE, AND DIS-POSE OF THE BODIES TOGETHER! THESE STUPID ONES WILL BE SAFE IF WE TIE THEM TIGHTER AND HOIST THEM INTO THE AIR!

9

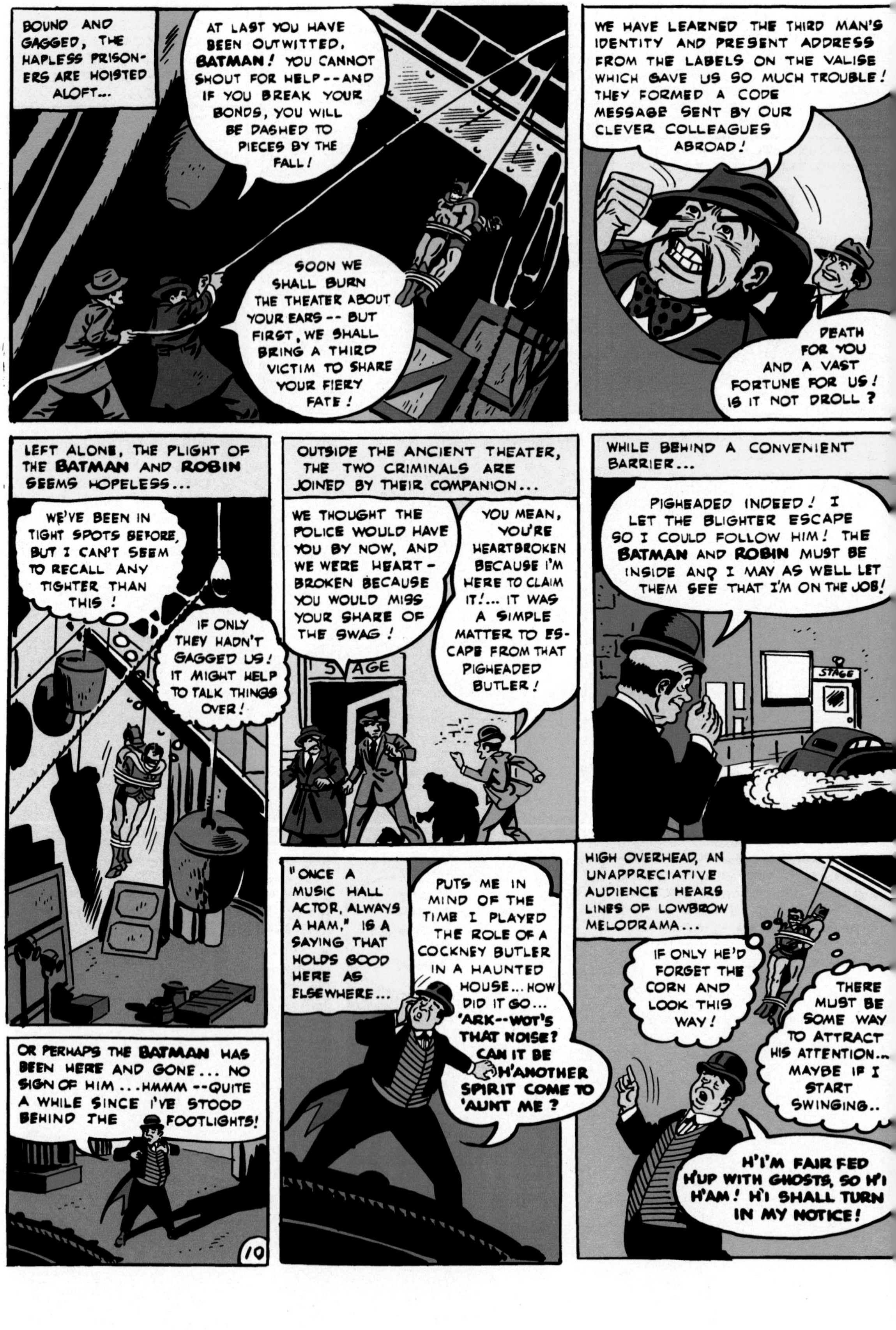
BOUND AND GAGGED, THE HAPLESS PRISONERS ARE HOISTED ALOFT...
AT LAST YOU HAVE BEEN OUTWITTED, BATMAN! YOU CANNOT SHOUT FOR HELP--AND IF YOU BREAK YOUR BONDS, YOU WILL BE DASHED TO PIECES BY THE FALL!
SOON WE SHALL BURN THE THEATER ABOUT YOUR EARS -- BUT FIRST, WE SHALL BRING A THIRD VICTIM TO SHARE YOUR FIERY FATE!
WE HAVE LEARNED THE THIRD MAN'S IDENTITY AND PRESENT ADDRESS FROM THE LABELS ON THE VALISE WHICH GAVE US SO MUCH TROUBLE! THEY FORMED A CODE MESSAGE SENT BY OUR CLEVER COLLEAGUES ABROAD!
DEATH FOR YOU AND A VAST FORTUNE FOR US! IS IT NOT DROLL?
LEFT ALONE, THE PLIGHT OF THE BATMAN AND ROBIN SEEMS HOPELESS...
WE'VE BEEN IN TIGHT SPOTS BEFORE, BUT I CAN'T SEEM TO RECALL ANY TIGHTER THAN THIS!
IF ONLY THEY HADN'T GAGGED US! IT MIGHT HELP TO TALK THINGS OVER!
OUTSIDE THE ANCIENT THEATER, THE TWO CRIMINALS ARE JOINED BY THEIR COMPANION...
WE THOUGHT THE POLICE WOULD HAVE YOU BY NOW, AND WE WERE HEART-BROKEN BECAUSE YOU WOULD MISS YOUR SHARE OF THE SWAG!
YOU MEAN, YOU'RE HEARTBROKEN BECAUSE I'M HERE TO CLAIM IT!... IT WAS A SIMPLE MATTER TO ESCAPE FROM THAT PIGHEADED BUTLER!
STAGE
WHILE BEHIND A CONVENIENT BARRIER...
PIGHEADED INDEED! I LET THE BLIGHTER ESCAPE SO I COULD FOLLOW HIM! THE BATMAN AND ROBIN MUST BE INSIDE AND I MAY AS WELL LET THEM SEE THAT I'M ON THE JOB!
STAGE
OR PERHAPS THE BATMAN HAS BEEN HERE AND GONE... NO SIGN OF HIM...HMMM --QUITE A WHILE SINCE I'VE STOOD BEHIND THE FOOTLIGHTS!
10
"ONCE A MUSIC HALL ACTOR, ALWAYS A HAM," IS A SAYING THAT HOLDS GOOD HERE AS ELSEWHERE...
PUTS ME IN MIND OF THE TIME I PLAYED THE ROLE OF A COCKNEY BUTLER IN A HAUNTED HOUSE... HOW DID IT GO... 'ARK--WOT'S THAT NOISE? CAN IT BE H'ANOTHER SPIRIT COME TO 'AUNT ME?
HIGH OVERHEAD, AN UNAPPRECIATIVE AUDIENCE HEARS LINES OF LOWBROW MELODRAMA...
IF ONLY HE'D FORGET THE CORN AND LOOK THIS WAY!
THERE MUST BE SOME WAY TO ATTRACT HIS ATTENTION... MAYBE IF I START SWINGING..
H'I'M FAIR FED H'UP WITH GHOSTS, SO H'I H'AM! H'I SHALL TURN IN MY NOTICE!

BACK AND FORTH, IN EVER-WIDEN-ING SWEEPS, THE BATMAN SWINGS HIS BODY-- UNTIL AT LAST HIS BOUND FEET CATCH ON A LOOSE ROPE...

HERE'S HOPING IT WORKS!

WONDER WHAT HE'S UP TO?

WRITHING LIKE A SERPENT, THE ROPE WHIPS ACROSS THE STAGE...

H'AWAY, H'AWAY, YE BLOOMIN' SPECTER! KEEP YER GHOSTLY FINGERS H'OFF ME!

OH-H-H-H! IT'S REALLY HAPPENIN'!

S-W-I-S-H

WELL! FOR A MOMENT I THOUGHT-- EH? ... WHY, THERE ARE THE BATMAN AND ROBIN IN DISTRESS!

AND AT THIS VERY MOMENT, MANUEL AND HIS THUGS ARE ENTERING AN APARTMENT IN AN EXCLUSIVE NEIGHBORHOOD...

AND THAT MIGHT BRING THE POLICE!

SOFTLY! IF WE AWAKEN THE OTHERS, WE SHALL HAVE TO USE OUR GUNS!

AND ALFRED'S MYSTERIOUS FRIEND OF THE SHIP HAS A RUDE AWAKENING...

NOT A SOUND, DUKE, OR YOU ARE A DEAD MAN!

BAH-- WHAT DO WE CARE FOR YOUR GOVERN-MENT? SILENCE HIM, PABLO!.

NO, YOU MUST NOT TAKE THE CROWN JEWELS! I BROUGHT THEM HERE TO ESTABLISH CREDITS FOR MY GOVERNMENT-IN-EXILE!

TO THINK HE BROUGHT THOSE JEWELS SECRETLY HALF AROUND THE WORLD, ONLY TO LOSE THEM AT THE END OF THE JOURNEY! IT SHOWS WHAT SHARP EYES AND EARS THE UNDERWORLD HAS!

AND IT SHOWS HOW PROMPTLY WE HAVE ACTED! ANOTHER TWO HOURS AND THE JEWELS WOULD HAVE BEEN IN A SAFE-DEPOSIT VAULT!

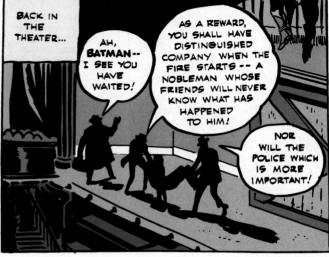

BACK IN THE THEATER...

AH, BATMAN-- I SEE YOU HAVE WAITED!

AS A REWARD, YOU SHALL HAVE DISTINGUISHED COMPANY WHEN THE FIRE STARTS -- A NOBLEMAN WHOSE FRIENDS WILL NEVER KNOW WHAT HAS HAPPENED TO HIM!

NOR WILL THE POLICE WHICH IS MORE IMPORTANT!

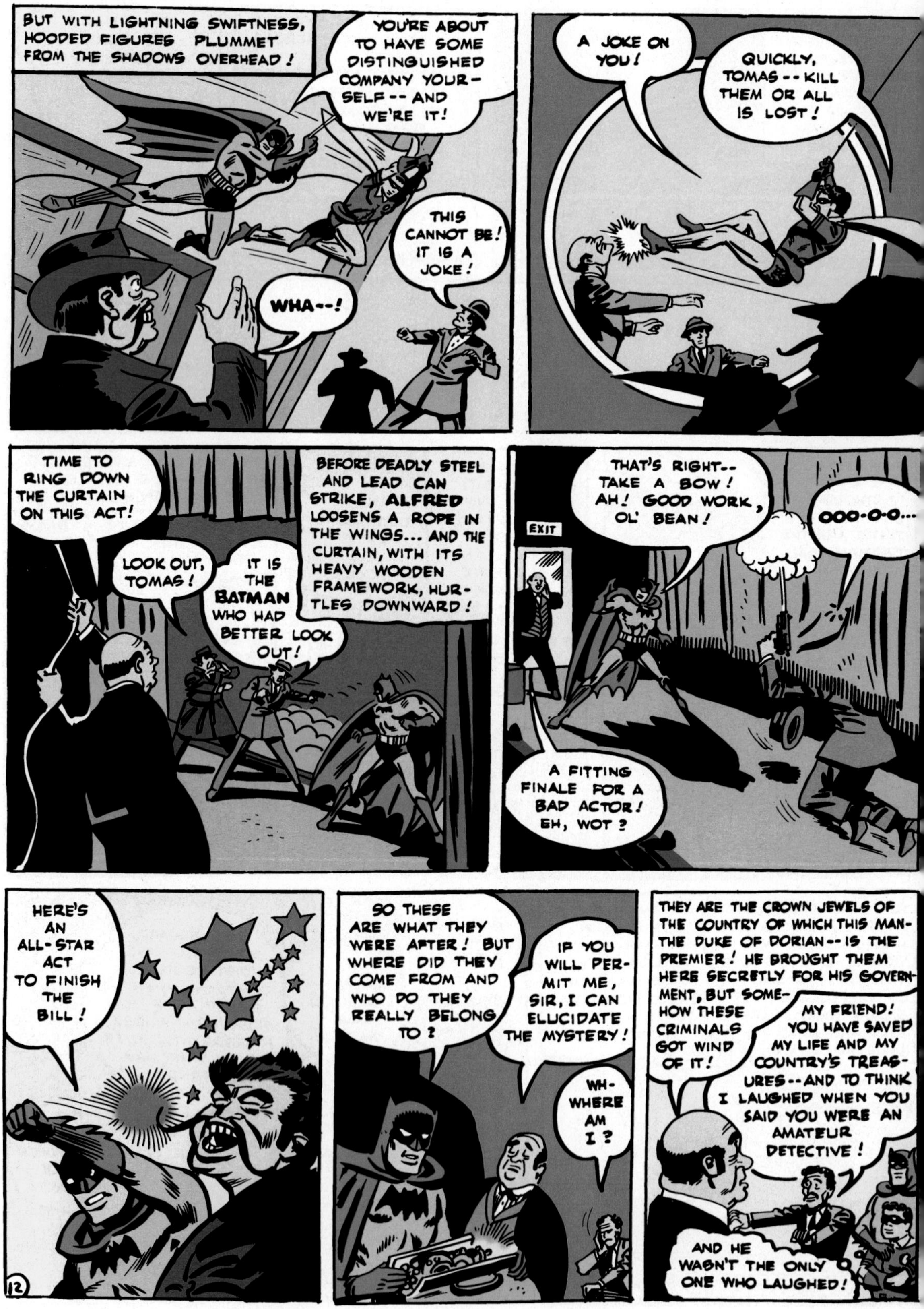
BUT WITH LIGHTNING SWIFTNESS, HOODED FIGURES PLUMMET FROM THE SHADOWS OVERHEAD!
YOU'RE ABOUT TO HAVE SOME DISTINGUISHED COMPANY YOUR-SELF -- AND WE'RE IT!
THIS CANNOT BE! IT IS A JOKE!
WHA--!
A JOKE ON YOU!
QUICKLY, TOMAS -- KILL THEM OR ALL IS LOST!
TIME TO RING DOWN THE CURTAIN ON THIS ACT!
LOOK OUT, TOMAS!
IT IS THE BATMAN WHO HAD BETTER LOOK OUT!
BEFORE DEADLY STEEL AND LEAD CAN STRIKE, ALFRED LOOSENS A ROPE IN THE WINGS... AND THE CURTAIN, WITH ITS HEAVY WOODEN FRAMEWORK, HURTLES DOWNWARD!
EXIT
THAT'S RIGHT-- TAKE A BOW! AH! GOOD WORK, OL' BEAN!
OOO-O-O...
A FITTING FINALE FOR A BAD ACTOR! EH, WOT?
HERE'S AN ALL-STAR ACT TO FINISH THE BILL!
12
SO THESE ARE WHAT THEY WERE AFTER! BUT WHERE DID THEY COME FROM AND WHO DO THEY REALLY BELONG TO?
IF YOU WILL PER-MIT ME, SIR, I CAN ELUCIDATE THE MYSTERY!
WH- WHERE AM I?
THEY ARE THE CROWN JEWELS OF THE COUNTRY OF WHICH THIS MAN-THE DUKE OF DORIAN -- IS THE PREMIER! HE BROUGHT THEM HERE SECRETLY FOR HIS GOVERN-MENT, BUT SOME-HOW THESE CRIMINALS GOT WIND OF IT!
MY FRIEND! YOU HAVE SAVED MY LIFE AND MY COUNTRY'S TREAS-URES -- AND TO THINK I LAUGHED WHEN YOU SAID YOU WERE AN AMATEUR DETECTIVE!
AND HE WASN'T THE ONLY ONE WHO LAUGHED!

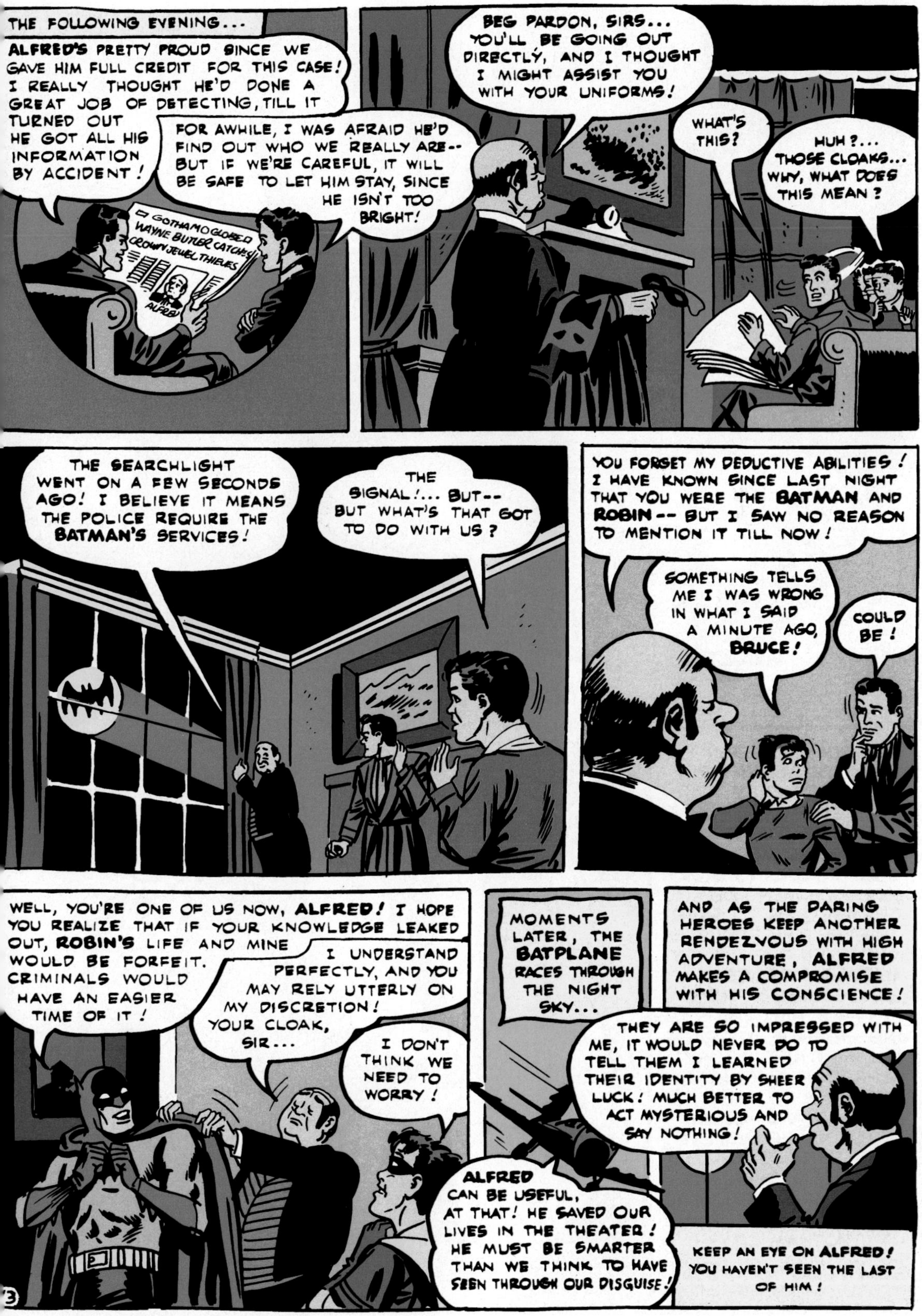
THE FOLLOWING EVENING...
ALFRED'S PRETTY PROUD SINCE WE GAVE HIM FULL CREDIT FOR THIS CASE! I REALLY THOUGHT HE'D DONE A GREAT JOB OF DETECTING, TILL IT TURNED OUT HE GOT ALL HIS INFORMATION BY ACCIDENT!
FOR AWHILE, I WAS AFRAID HE'D FIND OUT WHO WE REALLY ARE-- BUT IF WE'RE CAREFUL, IT WILL BE SAFE TO LET HIM STAY, SINCE HE ISN'T TOO BRIGHT!
GOTHAM GLOBE
WAYNE BUTLER CATCHES CROWN JEWEL THIEVES
ALFRED
BEG PARDON, SIRS... YOU'LL BE GOING OUT DIRECTLY, AND I THOUGHT I MIGHT ASSIST YOU WITH YOUR UNIFORMS!
WHAT'S THIS?
HUH?... THOSE CLOAKS... WHY, WHAT DOES THIS MEAN?
THE SEARCHLIGHT WENT ON A FEW SECONDS AGO! I BELIEVE IT MEANS THE POLICE REQUIRE THE BATMAN'S SERVICES!
THE SIGNAL!... BUT-- BUT WHAT'S THAT GOT TO DO WITH US?
YOU FORGET MY DEDUCTIVE ABILITIES! I HAVE KNOWN SINCE LAST NIGHT THAT YOU WERE THE BATMAN AND ROBIN-- BUT I SAW NO REASON TO MENTION IT TILL NOW!
SOMETHING TELLS ME I WAS WRONG IN WHAT I SAID A MINUTE AGO, BRUCE!
COULD BE!
WELL, YOU'RE ONE OF US NOW, ALFRED! I HOPE YOU REALIZE THAT IF YOUR KNOWLEDGE LEAKED OUT, ROBIN'S LIFE AND MINE WOULD BE FORFEIT. CRIMINALS WOULD HAVE AN EASIER TIME OF IT!
I UNDERSTAND PERFECTLY, AND YOU MAY RELY UTTERLY ON MY DISCRETION! YOUR CLOAK, SIR...
I DON'T THINK WE NEED TO WORRY!
MOMENTS LATER, THE BATPLANE RACES THROUGH THE NIGHT SKY...
ALFRED CAN BE USEFUL, AT THAT! HE SAVED OUR LIVES IN THE THEATER! HE MUST BE SMARTER THAN WE THINK TO HAVE SEEN THROUGH OUR DISGUISE!
AND AS THE DARING HEROES KEEP ANOTHER RENDEZVOUS WITH HIGH ADVENTURE, ALFRED MAKES A COMPROMISE WITH HIS CONSCIENCE!
THEY ARE SO IMPRESSED WITH ME, IT WOULD NEVER DO TO TELL THEM I LEARNED THEIR IDENTITY BY SHEER LUCK! MUCH BETTER TO ACT MYSTERIOUS AND SAY NOTHING!
KEEP AN EYE ON ALFRED! YOU HAVEN'T SEEN THE LAST OF HIM!
13

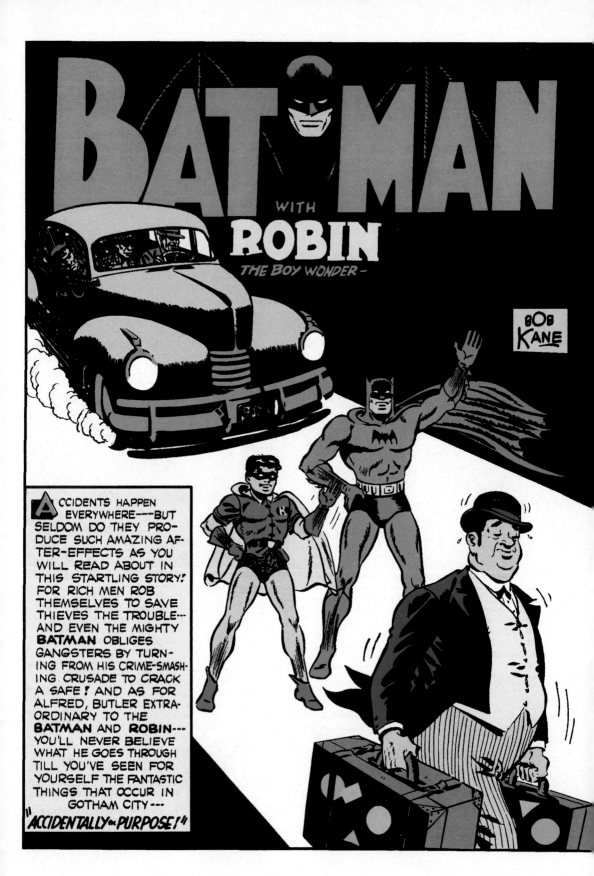

# BAT MAN

### WITH
## ROBIN
#### THE BOY WONDER –

BOB KANE

ACCIDENTS HAPPEN EVERYWHERE---BUT SELDOM DO THEY PRO-DUCE SUCH AMAZING AF-TER-EFFECTS AS YOU WILL READ ABOUT IN THIS STARTLING STORY! FOR RICH MEN ROB THEMSELVES TO SAVE THIEVES THE TROUBLE--- AND EVEN THE MIGHTY **BATMAN** OBLIGES GANGSTERS BY TURN-ING FROM HIS CRIME-SMASH-ING CRUSADE TO CRACK A SAFE! AND AS FOR ALFRED, BUTLER EXTRA-ORDINARY TO THE **BATMAN** AND **ROBIN**--- YOU'LL NEVER BELIEVE WHAT HE GOES THROUGH TILL YOU'VE SEEN FOR YOURSELF THE FANTASTIC THINGS THAT OCCUR IN GOTHAM CITY ---

*"ACCIDENTALLY ON PURPOSE!"*

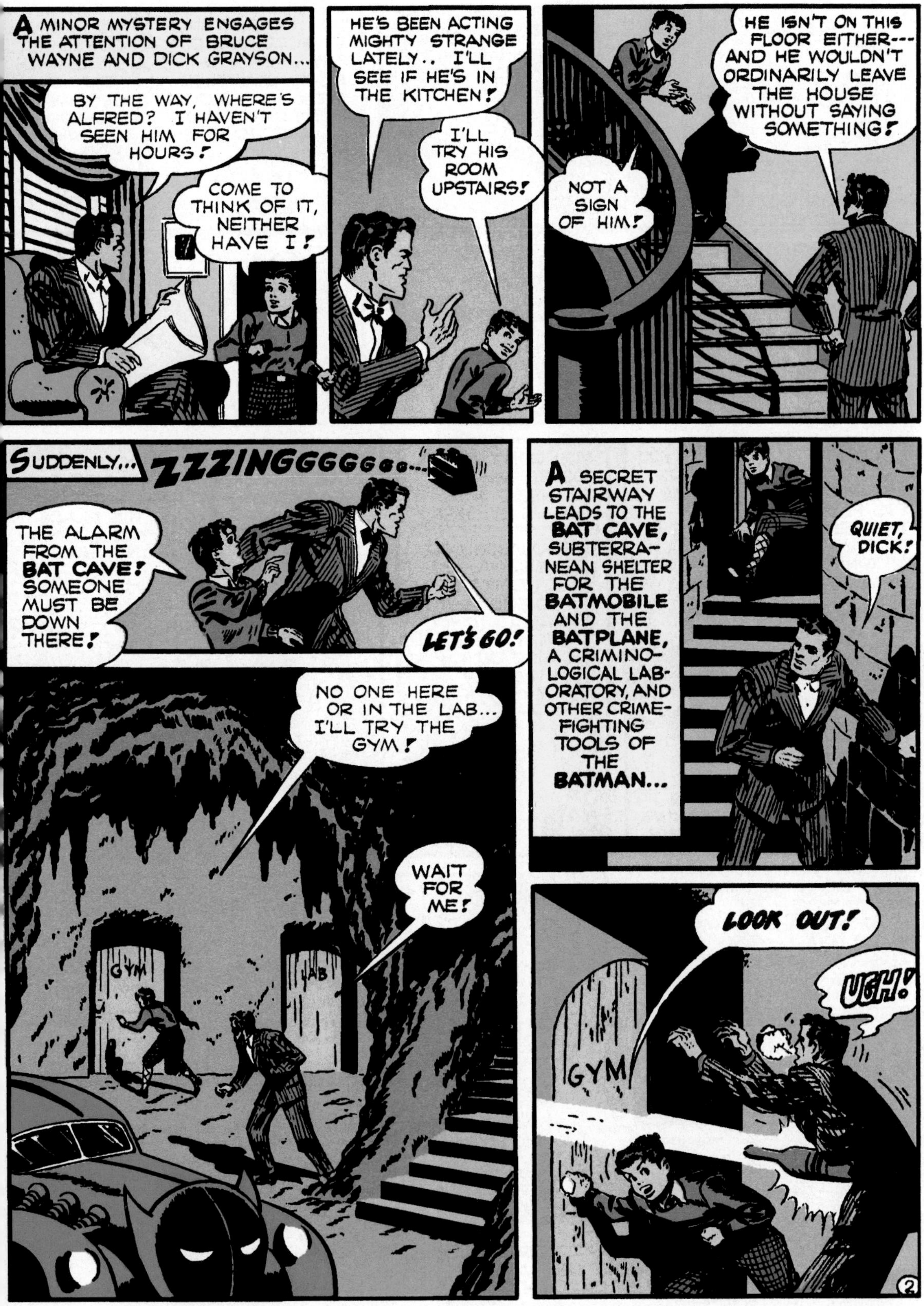
A MINOR MYSTERY ENGAGES THE ATTENTION OF BRUCE WAYNE AND DICK GRAYSON...
BY THE WAY, WHERE'S ALFRED? I HAVEN'T SEEN HIM FOR HOURS!
COME TO THINK OF IT, NEITHER HAVE I!
HE'S BEEN ACTING MIGHTY STRANGE LATELY.. I'LL SEE IF HE'S IN THE KITCHEN!
I'LL TRY HIS ROOM UPSTAIRS!
HE ISN'T ON THIS FLOOR EITHER--- AND HE WOULDN'T ORDINARILY LEAVE THE HOUSE WITHOUT SAYING SOMETHING!
NOT A SIGN OF HIM!
SUDDENLY...
ZZZINGGGGGGGG...
THE ALARM FROM THE BAT CAVE! SOMEONE MUST BE DOWN THERE!
LET'S GO!
A SECRET STAIRWAY LEADS TO THE BAT CAVE, SUBTERRANEAN SHELTER FOR THE BATMOBILE AND THE BATPLANE, A CRIMINOLOGICAL LABORATORY, AND OTHER CRIME-FIGHTING TOOLS OF THE BATMAN...
QUIET, DICK!
NO ONE HERE OR IN THE LAB... I'LL TRY THE GYM!
WAIT FOR ME!
GYM
LAB
LOOK OUT!
UGH!
GYM
2

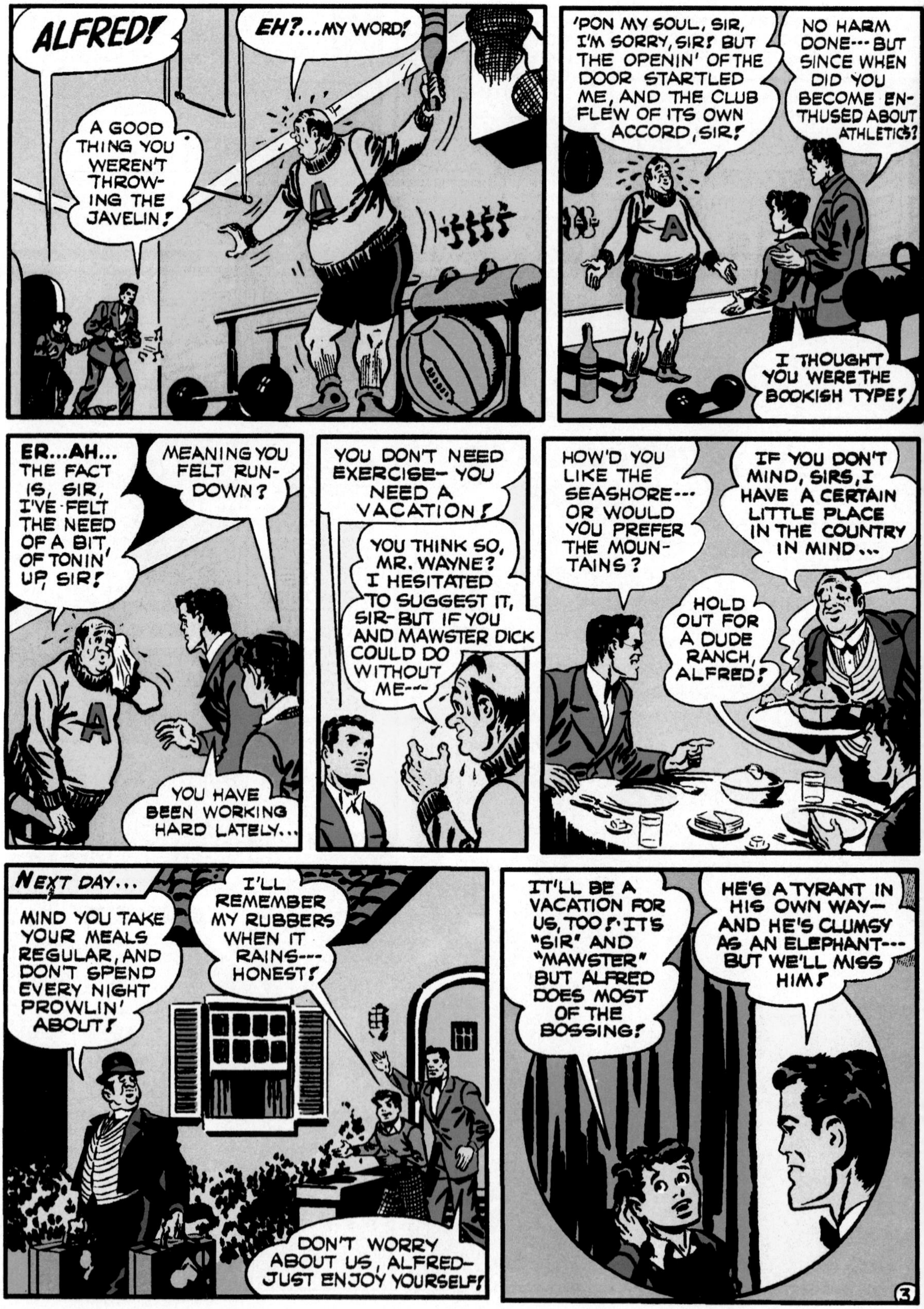
ALFRED!
EH?...MY WORD!
A GOOD THING YOU WEREN'T THROWING THE JAVELIN!
'PON MY SOUL, SIR, I'M SORRY, SIR! BUT THE OPENIN' OF THE DOOR STARTLED ME, AND THE CLUB FLEW OF ITS OWN ACCORD, SIR!
NO HARM DONE--- BUT SINCE WHEN DID YOU BECOME ENTHUSED ABOUT ATHLETICS?
I THOUGHT YOU WERE THE BOOKISH TYPE!
ER...AH... THE FACT IS, SIR, I'VE FELT THE NEED OF A BIT OF TONIN' UP, SIR!
MEANING YOU FELT RUN-DOWN?
YOU HAVE BEEN WORKING HARD LATELY...
YOU DON'T NEED EXERCISE- YOU NEED A VACATION!
YOU THINK SO, MR. WAYNE? I HESITATED TO SUGGEST IT, SIR- BUT IF YOU AND MAWSTER DICK COULD DO WITHOUT ME---
HOW'D YOU LIKE THE SEASHORE--- OR WOULD YOU PREFER THE MOUNTAINS?
HOLD OUT FOR A DUDE RANCH, ALFRED!
IF YOU DON'T MIND, SIRS, I HAVE A CERTAIN LITTLE PLACE IN THE COUNTRY IN MIND...
NEXT DAY...
MIND YOU TAKE YOUR MEALS REGULAR, AND DON'T SPEND EVERY NIGHT PROWLIN' ABOUT!
I'LL REMEMBER MY RUBBERS WHEN IT RAINS--- HONEST!
DON'T WORRY ABOUT US, ALFRED- JUST ENJOY YOURSELF!
IT'LL BE A VACATION FOR US, TOO! IT'S "SIR" AND "MAWSTER" BUT ALFRED DOES MOST OF THE BOSSING!
HE'S A TYRANT IN HIS OWN WAY— AND HE'S CLUMSY AS AN ELEPHANT--- BUT WE'LL MISS HIM!
3

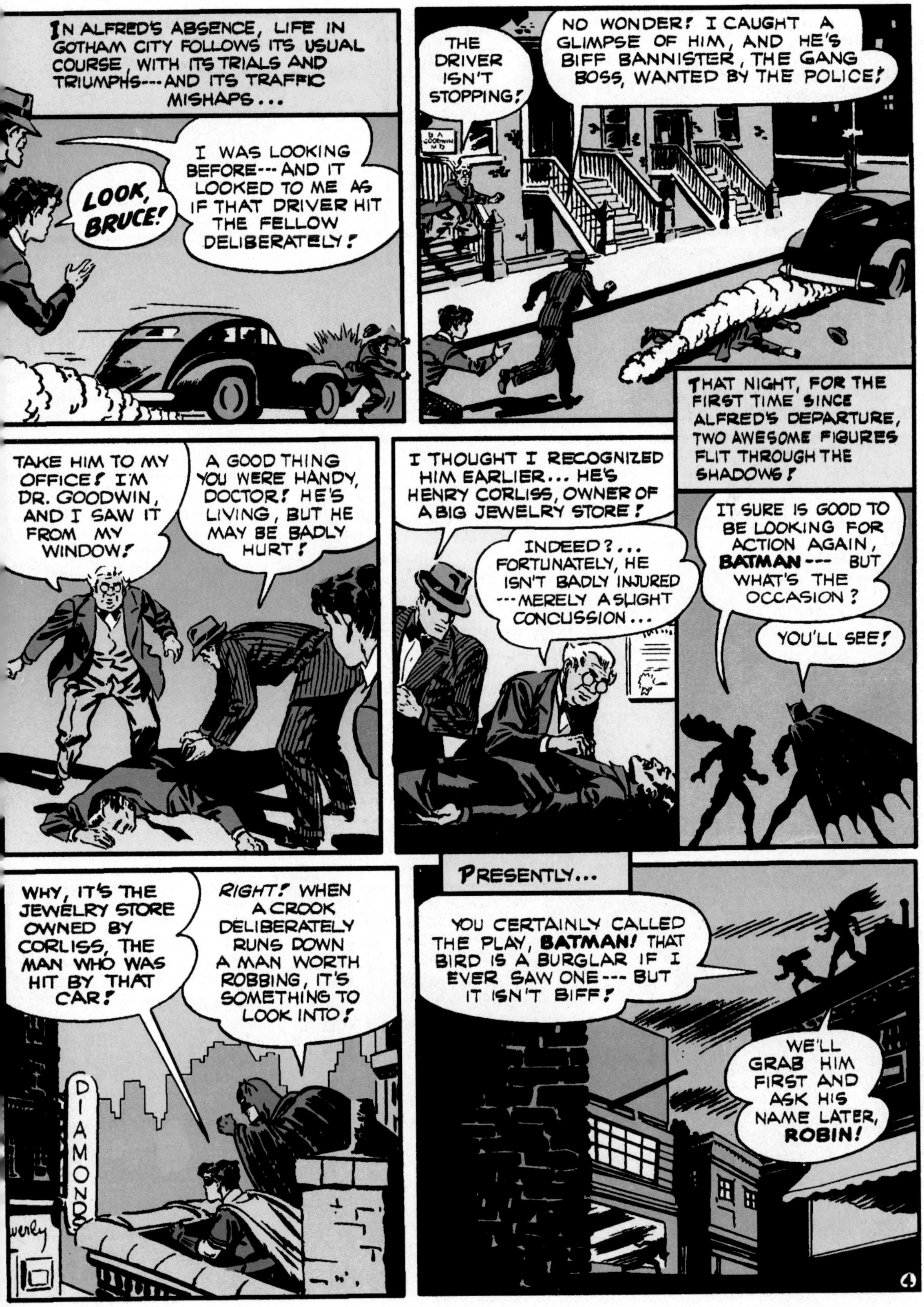
IN ALFRED'S ABSENCE, LIFE IN GOTHAM CITY FOLLOWS ITS USUAL COURSE, WITH ITS TRIALS AND TRIUMPHS--- AND ITS TRAFFIC MISHAPS...
LOOK, BRUCE!
I WAS LOOKING BEFORE--- AND IT LOOKED TO ME AS IF THAT DRIVER HIT THE FELLOW DELIBERATELY!
THE DRIVER ISN'T STOPPING!
NO WONDER! I CAUGHT A GLIMPSE OF HIM, AND HE'S BIFF BANNISTER, THE GANG BOSS, WANTED BY THE POLICE!
TAKE HIM TO MY OFFICE! I'M DR. GOODWIN, AND I SAW IT FROM MY WINDOW!
A GOOD THING YOU WERE HANDY, DOCTOR! HE'S LIVING, BUT HE MAY BE BADLY HURT!
I THOUGHT I RECOGNIZED HIM EARLIER... HE'S HENRY CORLISS, OWNER OF A BIG JEWELRY STORE!
INDEED?... FORTUNATELY, HE ISN'T BADLY INJURED ---MERELY A SLIGHT CONCUSSION...
THAT NIGHT, FOR THE FIRST TIME SINCE ALFRED'S DEPARTURE, TWO AWESOME FIGURES FLIT THROUGH THE SHADOWS!
IT SURE IS GOOD TO BE LOOKING FOR ACTION AGAIN, BATMAN--- BUT WHAT'S THE OCCASION?
YOU'LL SEE!
WHY, IT'S THE JEWELRY STORE OWNED BY CORLISS, THE MAN WHO WAS HIT BY THAT CAR!
RIGHT! WHEN A CROOK DELIBERATELY RUNS DOWN A MAN WORTH ROBBING, IT'S SOMETHING TO LOOK INTO!
DIAMONDS
PRESENTLY...
YOU CERTAINLY CALLED THE PLAY, BATMAN! THAT BIRD IS A BURGLAR IF I EVER SAW ONE--- BUT IT ISN'T BIFF!
WE'LL GRAB HIM FIRST AND ASK HIS NAME LATER, ROBIN!
4

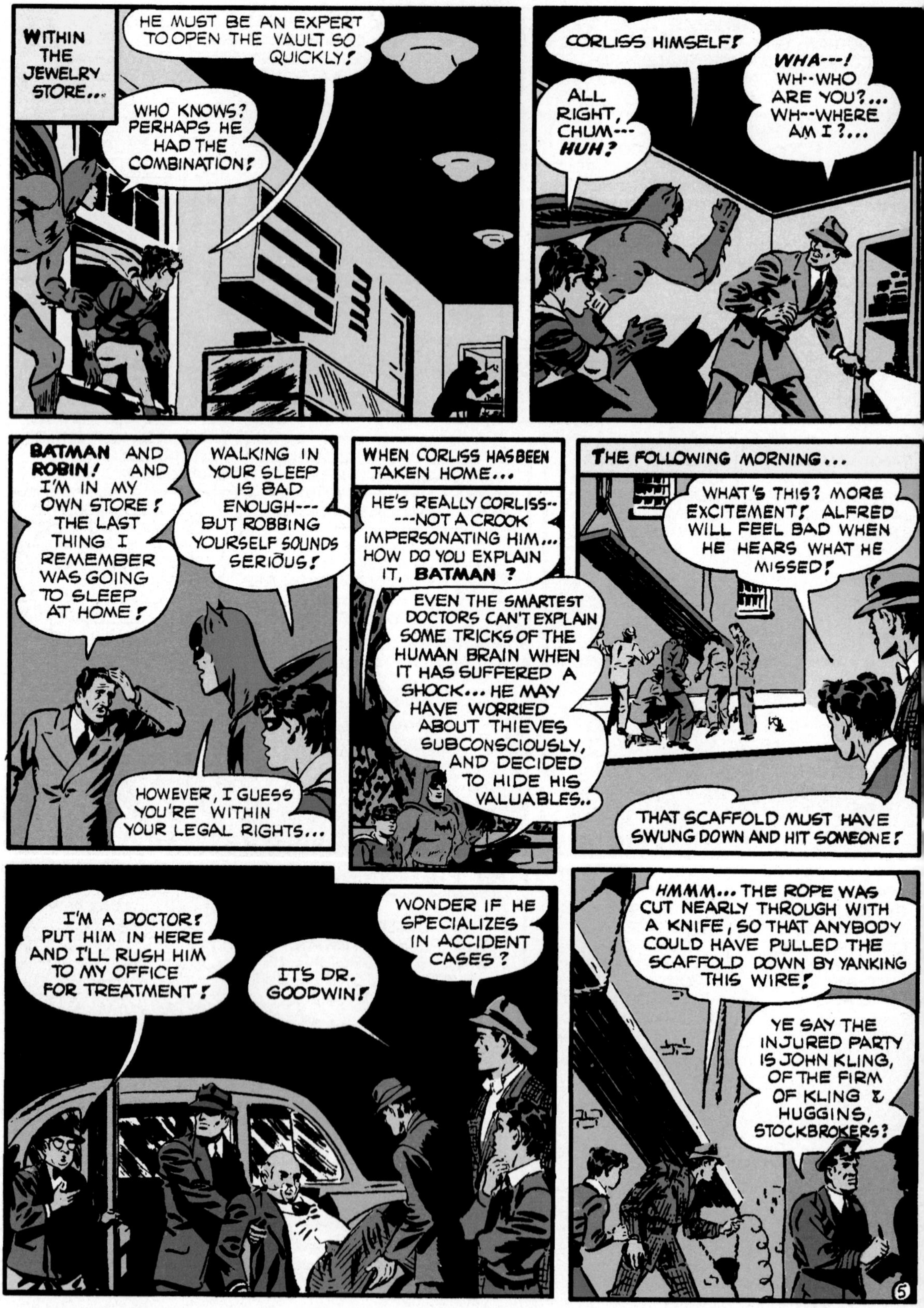

WITHIN THE JEWELRY STORE...
HE MUST BE AN EXPERT TO OPEN THE VAULT SO QUICKLY!
WHO KNOWS? PERHAPS HE HAD THE COMBINATION!
CORLISS HIMSELF!
ALL RIGHT, CHUM--- HUH?
WHA---! WH--WHO ARE YOU?... WH--WHERE AM I?...
BATMAN AND ROBIN! AND I'M IN MY OWN STORE! THE LAST THING I REMEMBER WAS GOING TO SLEEP AT HOME!
WALKING IN YOUR SLEEP IS BAD ENOUGH--- BUT ROBBING YOURSELF SOUNDS SERIOUS!
HOWEVER, I GUESS YOU'RE WITHIN YOUR LEGAL RIGHTS...
WHEN CORLISS HAS BEEN TAKEN HOME...
HE'S REALLY CORLISS-- ---NOT A CROOK IMPERSONATING HIM... HOW DO YOU EXPLAIN IT, BATMAN ?
EVEN THE SMARTEST DOCTORS CAN'T EXPLAIN SOME TRICKS OF THE HUMAN BRAIN WHEN IT HAS SUFFERED A SHOCK... HE MAY HAVE WORRIED ABOUT THIEVES SUBCONSCIOUSLY, AND DECIDED TO HIDE HIS VALUABLES..
THE FOLLOWING MORNING...
WHAT'S THIS? MORE EXCITEMENT! ALFRED WILL FEEL BAD WHEN HE HEARS WHAT HE MISSED!
THAT SCAFFOLD MUST HAVE SWUNG DOWN AND HIT SOMEONE!
I'M A DOCTOR! PUT HIM IN HERE AND I'LL RUSH HIM TO MY OFFICE FOR TREATMENT!
IT'S DR. GOODWIN!
WONDER IF HE SPECIALIZES IN ACCIDENT CASES ?
HMMM... THE ROPE WAS CUT NEARLY THROUGH WITH A KNIFE, SO THAT ANYBODY COULD HAVE PULLED THE SCAFFOLD DOWN BY YANKING THIS WIRE!
YE SAY THE INJURED PARTY IS JOHN KLING, OF THE FIRM OF KLING & HUGGINS, STOCKBROKERS?
5

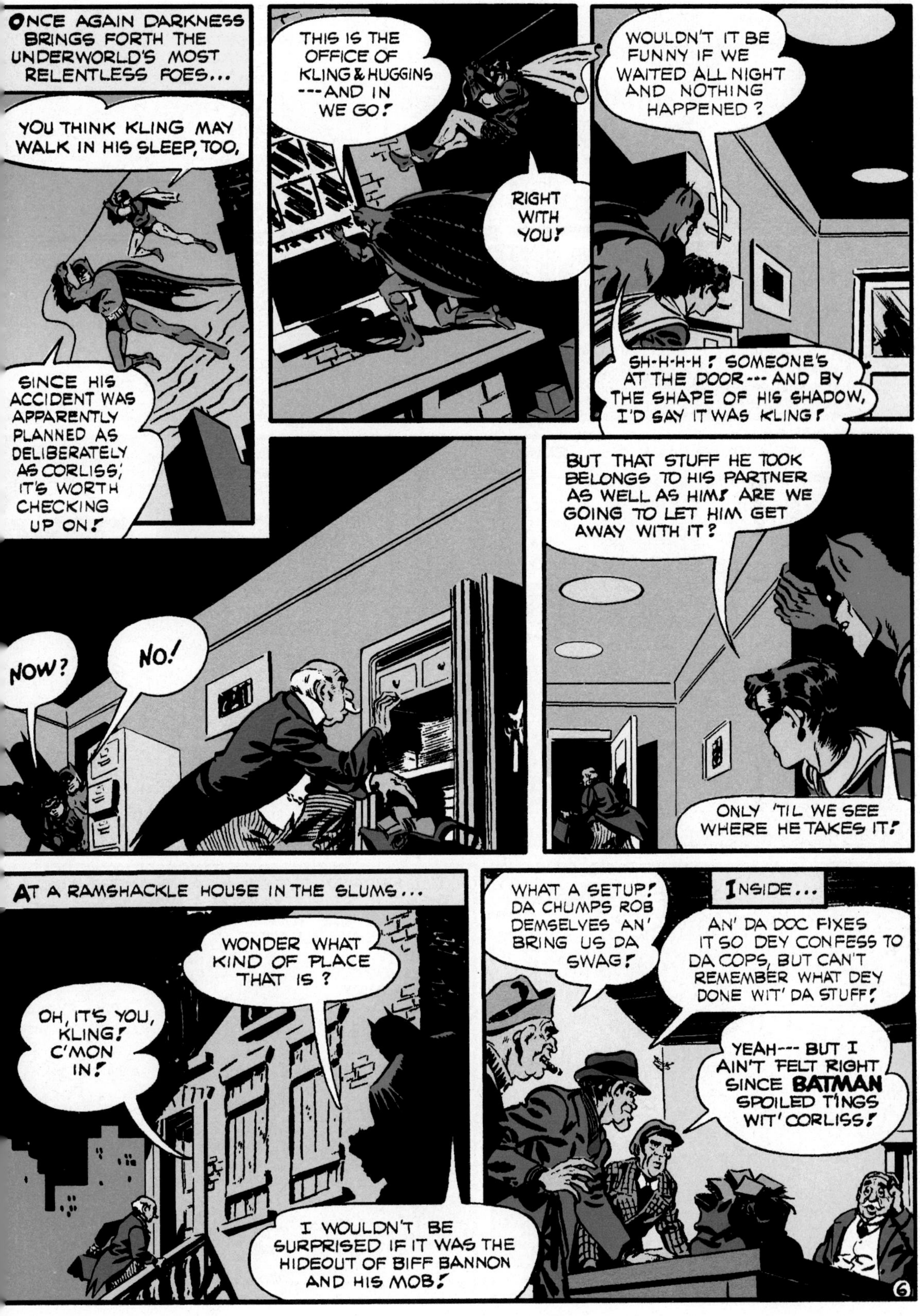

ONCE AGAIN DARKNESS BRINGS FORTH THE UNDERWORLD'S MOST RELENTLESS FOES...
YOU THINK KLING MAY WALK IN HIS SLEEP, TOO,
SINCE HIS ACCIDENT WAS APPARENTLY PLANNED AS DELIBERATELY AS CORLISS', IT'S WORTH CHECKING UP ON!
THIS IS THE OFFICE OF KLING & HUGGINS ---AND IN WE GO!
RIGHT WITH YOU!
WOULDN'T IT BE FUNNY IF WE WAITED ALL NIGHT AND NOTHING HAPPENED?
SH-H-H-H! SOMEONE'S AT THE DOOR --- AND BY THE SHAPE OF HIS SHADOW, I'D SAY IT WAS KLING!
NOW?
NO!
BUT THAT STUFF HE TOOK BELONGS TO HIS PARTNER AS WELL AS HIM! ARE WE GOING TO LET HIM GET AWAY WITH IT?
ONLY 'TIL WE SEE WHERE HE TAKES IT!
AT A RAMSHACKLE HOUSE IN THE SLUMS...
WONDER WHAT KIND OF PLACE THAT IS?
OH, IT'S YOU, KLING! C'MON IN!
I WOULDN'T BE SURPRISED IF IT WAS THE HIDEOUT OF BIFF BANNON AND HIS MOB!
WHAT A SETUP! DA CHUMPS ROB DEMSELVES AN' BRING US DA SWAG!
INSIDE...
AN' DA DOC FIXES IT SO DEY CONFESS TO DA COPS, BUT CAN'T REMEMBER WHAT DEY DONE WIT' DA STUFF!
YEAH--- BUT I AIN'T FELT RIGHT SINCE BATMAN SPOILED TINGS WIT' CORLISS!
6

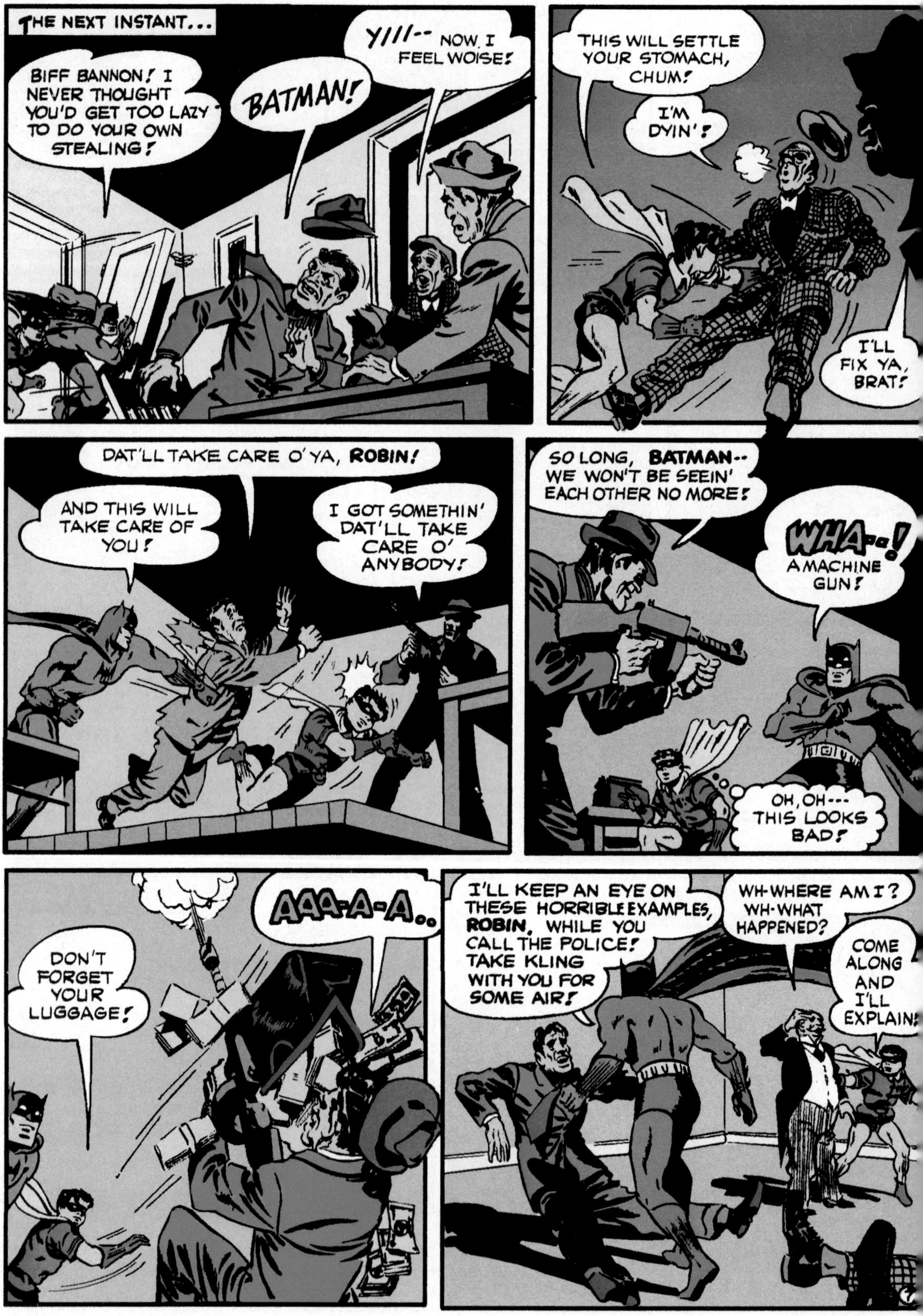
THE NEXT INSTANT...
BIFF BANNON! I NEVER THOUGHT YOU'D GET TOO LAZY TO DO YOUR OWN STEALING!
BATMAN!
Y///-- NOW I FEEL WOISE!
THIS WILL SETTLE YOUR STOMACH, CHUM!
I'M DYIN'!
I'LL FIX YA, BRAT!
DAT'LL TAKE CARE O'YA, ROBIN!
AND THIS WILL TAKE CARE OF YOU!
I GOT SOMETHIN' DAT'LL TAKE CARE O' ANYBODY!
SO LONG, BATMAN-- WE WON'T BE SEEIN' EACH OTHER NO MORE!
WHA--! A MACHINE GUN!
OH, OH--- THIS LOOKS BAD!
AAA-A-A..
DON'T FORGET YOUR LUGGAGE!
I'LL KEEP AN EYE ON THESE HORRIBLE EXAMPLES, ROBIN, WHILE YOU CALL THE POLICE! TAKE KLING WITH YOU FOR SOME AIR!
WH-WHERE AM I? WH-WHAT HAPPENED?
COME ALONG AND I'LL EXPLAIN!

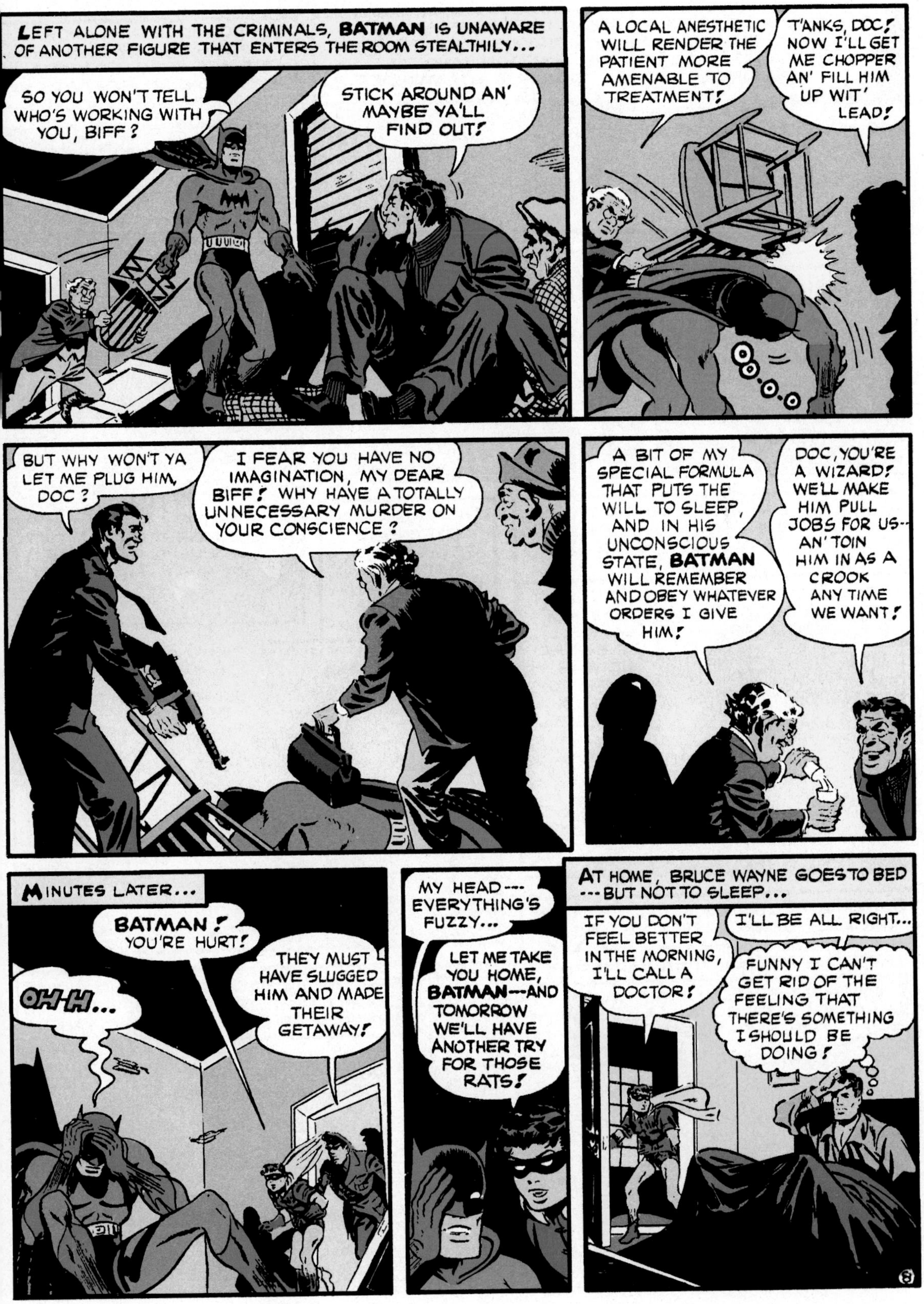
LEFT ALONE WITH THE CRIMINALS, BATMAN IS UNAWARE OF ANOTHER FIGURE THAT ENTERS THE ROOM STEALTHILY...
SO YOU WON'T TELL WHO'S WORKING WITH YOU, BIFF?
STICK AROUND AN' MAYBE YA'LL FIND OUT!
A LOCAL ANESTHETIC WILL RENDER THE PATIENT MORE AMENABLE TO TREATMENT!
T'ANKS, DOC! NOW I'LL GET ME CHOPPER AN' FILL HIM UP WIT' LEAD!
BUT WHY WON'T YA LET ME PLUG HIM, DOC?
I FEAR YOU HAVE NO IMAGINATION, MY DEAR BIFF! WHY HAVE A TOTALLY UNNECESSARY MURDER ON YOUR CONSCIENCE?
A BIT OF MY SPECIAL FORMULA THAT PUTS THE WILL TO SLEEP, AND IN HIS UNCONSCIOUS STATE, BATMAN WILL REMEMBER AND OBEY WHATEVER ORDERS I GIVE HIM!
DOC, YOU'RE A WIZARD! WE'LL MAKE HIM PULL JOBS FOR US--AN' TOIN HIM IN AS A CROOK ANY TIME WE WANT!
MINUTES LATER...
BATMAN! YOU'RE HURT!
THEY MUST HAVE SLUGGED HIM AND MADE THEIR GETAWAY!
OH-H...
MY HEAD--- EVERYTHING'S FUZZY...
LET ME TAKE YOU HOME, BATMAN---AND TOMORROW WE'LL HAVE ANOTHER TRY FOR THOSE RATS!
AT HOME, BRUCE WAYNE GOES TO BED ---BUT NOT TO SLEEP...
IF YOU DON'T FEEL BETTER IN THE MORNING, I'LL CALL A DOCTOR!
I'LL BE ALL RIGHT...
FUNNY I CAN'T GET RID OF THE FEELING THAT THERE'S SOMETHING I SHOULD BE DOING!
8

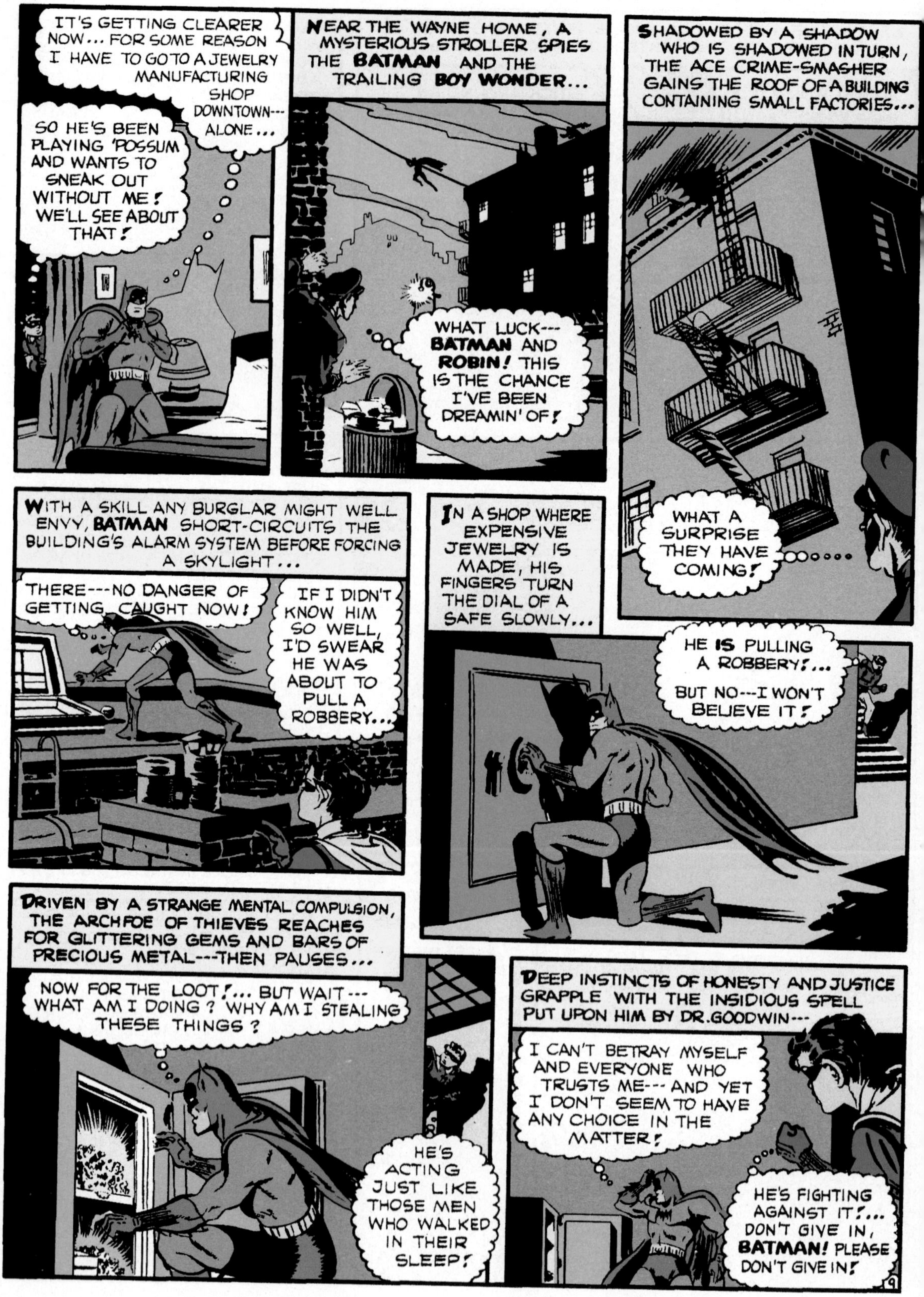
IT'S GETTING CLEARER NOW... FOR SOME REASON I HAVE TO GO TO A JEWELRY MANUFACTURING SHOP DOWNTOWN--- ALONE...
SO HE'S BEEN PLAYING 'POSSUM AND WANTS TO SNEAK OUT WITHOUT ME! WE'LL SEE ABOUT THAT!
NEAR THE WAYNE HOME, A MYSTERIOUS STROLLER SPIES THE BATMAN AND THE TRAILING BOY WONDER...
WHAT LUCK--- BATMAN AND ROBIN! THIS IS THE CHANCE I'VE BEEN DREAMIN' OF!
SHADOWED BY A SHADOW WHO IS SHADOWED IN TURN, THE ACE CRIME-SMASHER GAINS THE ROOF OF A BUILDING CONTAINING SMALL FACTORIES...
WHAT A SURPRISE THEY HAVE COMING!
WITH A SKILL ANY BURGLAR MIGHT WELL ENVY, BATMAN SHORT-CIRCUITS THE BUILDING'S ALARM SYSTEM BEFORE FORCING A SKYLIGHT...
THERE---NO DANGER OF GETTING CAUGHT NOW!
IF I DIDN'T KNOW HIM SO WELL, I'D SWEAR HE WAS ABOUT TO PULL A ROBBERY...
IN A SHOP WHERE EXPENSIVE JEWELRY IS MADE, HIS FINGERS TURN THE DIAL OF A SAFE SLOWLY...
HE IS PULLING A ROBBERY!... BUT NO---I WON'T BELIEVE IT!
DRIVEN BY A STRANGE MENTAL COMPULSION, THE ARCHFOE OF THIEVES REACHES FOR GLITTERING GEMS AND BARS OF PRECIOUS METAL---THEN PAUSES...
NOW FOR THE LOOT!... BUT WAIT--- WHAT AM I DOING? WHY AM I STEALING THESE THINGS?
HE'S ACTING JUST LIKE THOSE MEN WHO WALKED IN THEIR SLEEP!
DEEP INSTINCTS OF HONESTY AND JUSTICE GRAPPLE WITH THE INSIDIOUS SPELL PUT UPON HIM BY DR. GOODWIN---
I CAN'T BETRAY MYSELF AND EVERYONE WHO TRUSTS ME--- AND YET I DON'T SEEM TO HAVE ANY CHOICE IN THE MATTER!
HE'S FIGHTING AGAINST IT!... DON'T GIVE IN, BATMAN! PLEASE DON'T GIVE IN!
9

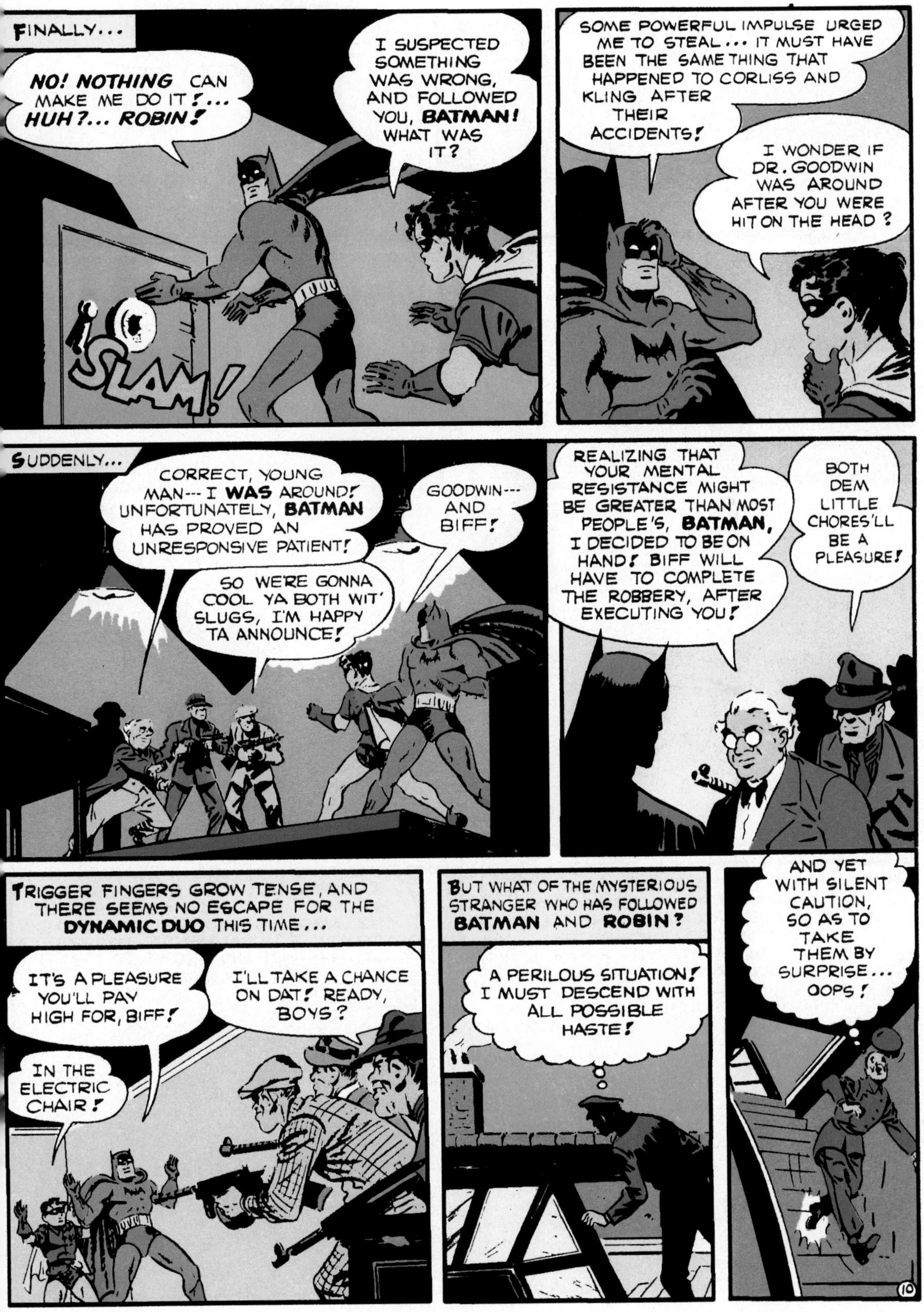
FINALLY...
NO! NOTHING CAN MAKE ME DO IT!... HUH?... ROBIN!
I SUSPECTED SOMETHING WAS WRONG, AND FOLLOWED YOU, BATMAN! WHAT WAS IT?
SLAM!
SOME POWERFUL IMPULSE URGED ME TO STEAL... IT MUST HAVE BEEN THE SAME THING THAT HAPPENED TO CORLISS AND KLING AFTER THEIR ACCIDENTS!
I WONDER IF DR. GOODWIN WAS AROUND AFTER YOU WERE HIT ON THE HEAD ?
SUDDENLY...
CORRECT, YOUNG MAN--- I WAS AROUND! UNFORTUNATELY, BATMAN HAS PROVED AN UNRESPONSIVE PATIENT!
SO WE'RE GONNA COOL YA BOTH WIT' SLUGS, I'M HAPPY TA ANNOUNCE!
GOODWIN--- AND BIFF!
REALIZING THAT YOUR MENTAL RESISTANCE MIGHT BE GREATER THAN MOST PEOPLE'S, BATMAN, I DECIDED TO BE ON HAND! BIFF WILL HAVE TO COMPLETE THE ROBBERY, AFTER EXECUTING YOU!
BOTH DEM LITTLE CHORES'LL BE A PLEASURE!
TRIGGER FINGERS GROW TENSE, AND THERE SEEMS NO ESCAPE FOR THE DYNAMIC DUO THIS TIME...
IT'S A PLEASURE YOU'LL PAY HIGH FOR, BIFF!
IN THE ELECTRIC CHAIR!
I'LL TAKE A CHANCE ON DAT! READY, BOYS?
BUT WHAT OF THE MYSTERIOUS STRANGER WHO HAS FOLLOWED BATMAN AND ROBIN?
A PERILOUS SITUATION! I MUST DESCEND WITH ALL POSSIBLE HASTE!
AND YET WITH SILENT CAUTION, SO AS TO TAKE THEM BY SURPRISE... OOPS!
10

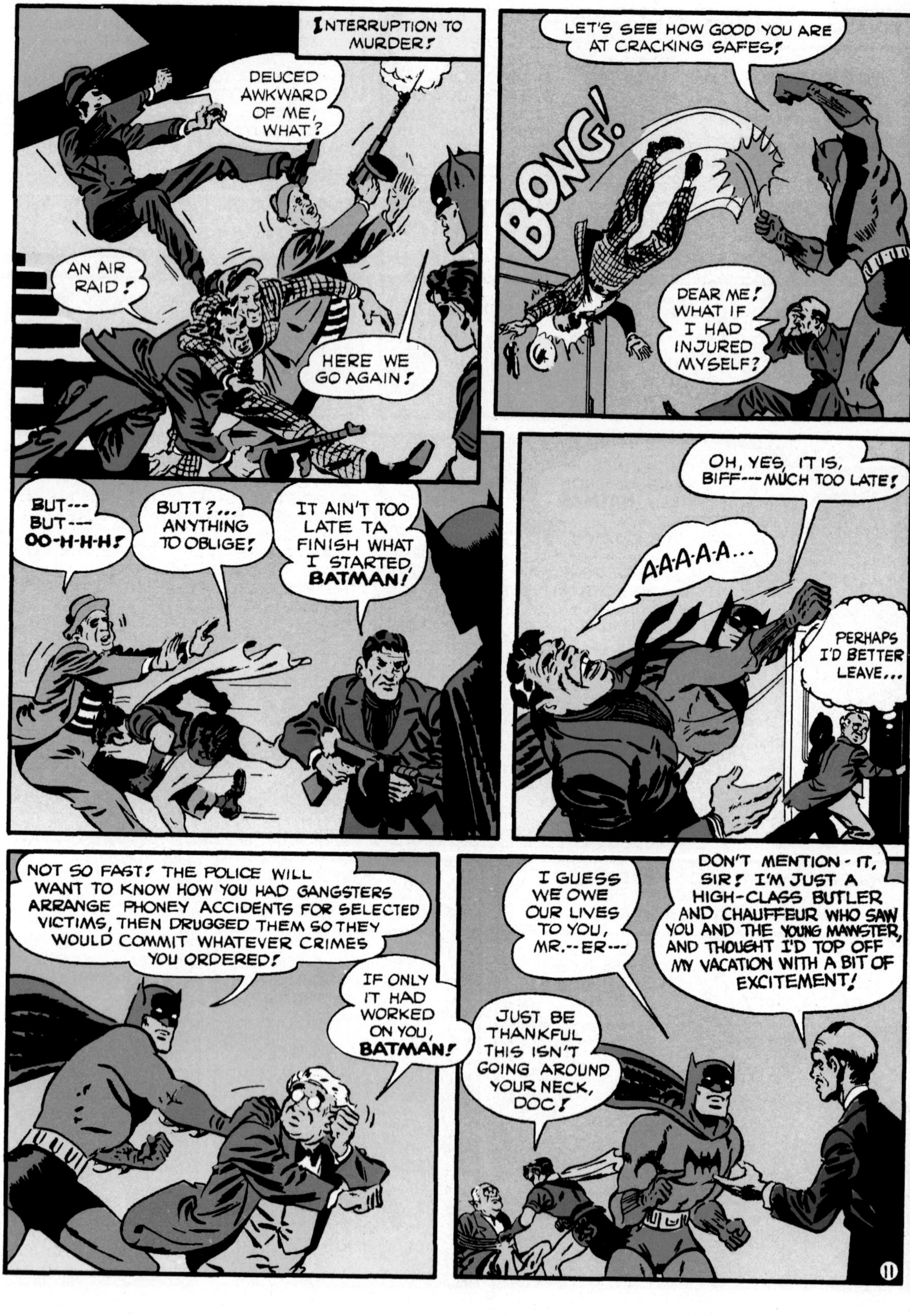
INTERRUPTION TO MURDER!
DEUCED AWKWARD OF ME, WHAT?
AN AIR RAID!
HERE WE GO AGAIN!
LET'S SEE HOW GOOD YOU ARE AT CRACKING SAFES!
BONG!
DEAR ME! WHAT IF I HAD INJURED MYSELF?
BUT--- BUT--- OO-H-H-H!
BUTT?... ANYTHING TO OBLIGE!
IT AIN'T TOO LATE TA FINISH WHAT I STARTED, BATMAN!
OH, YES, IT IS, BIFF---MUCH TOO LATE!
AAAAA...
PERHAPS I'D BETTER LEAVE...
NOT SO FAST! THE POLICE WILL WANT TO KNOW HOW YOU HAD GANGSTERS ARRANGE PHONEY ACCIDENTS FOR SELECTED VICTIMS, THEN DRUGGED THEM SO THEY WOULD COMMIT WHATEVER CRIMES YOU ORDERED!
IF ONLY IT HAD WORKED ON YOU, BATMAN!
I GUESS WE OWE OUR LIVES TO YOU, MR.--ER---
DON'T MENTION - IT, SIR! I'M JUST A HIGH-CLASS BUTLER AND CHAUFFEUR WHO SAW YOU AND THE YOUNG MAWSTER, AND THOUGHT I'D TOP OFF MY VACATION WITH A BIT OF EXCITEMENT!
JUST BE THANKFUL THIS ISN'T GOING AROUND YOUR NECK, DOC!
11

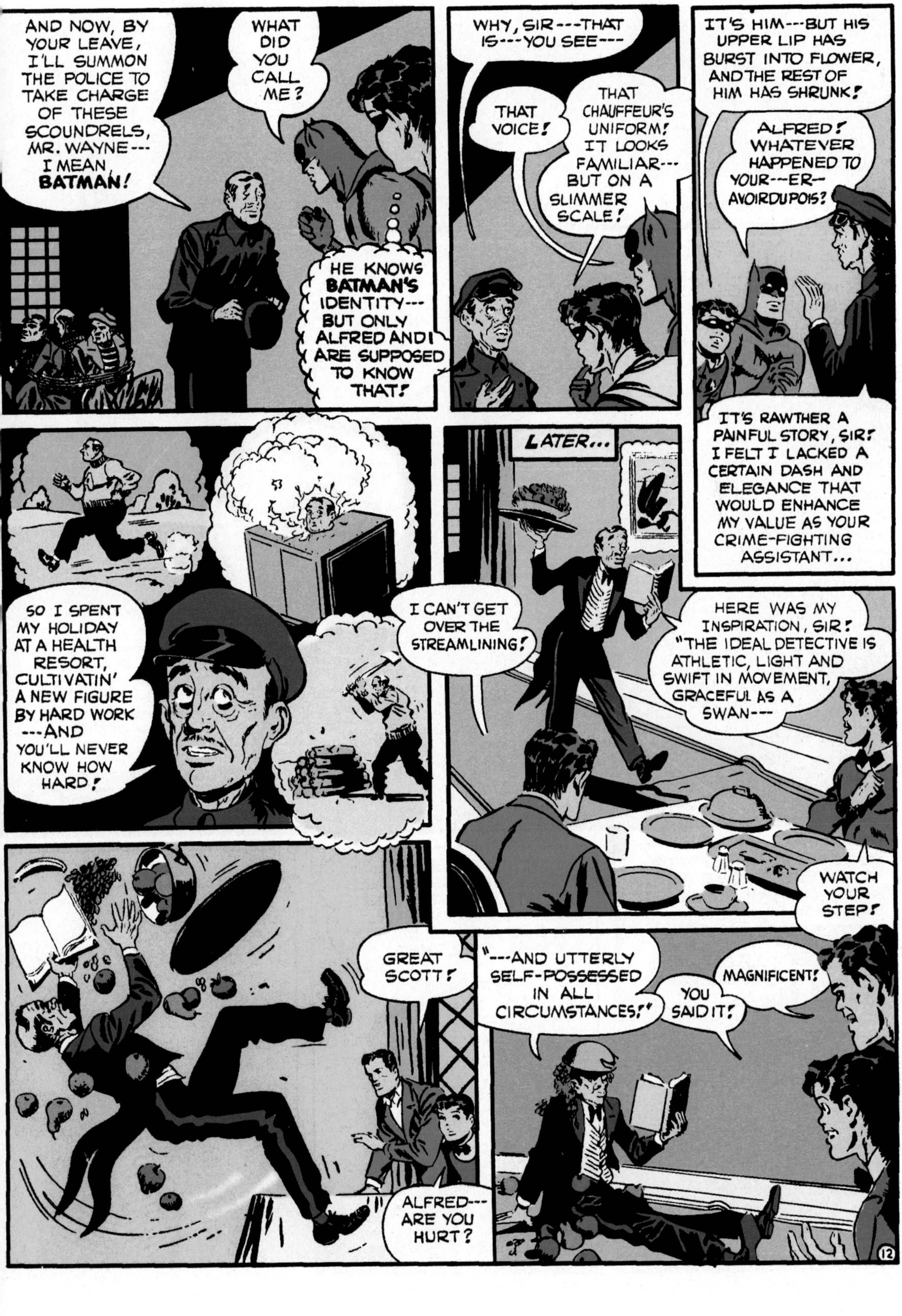
AND NOW, BY YOUR LEAVE, I'LL SUMMON THE POLICE TO TAKE CHARGE OF THESE SCOUNDRELS, MR. WAYNE--- I MEAN **BATMAN**!
WHAT DID YOU CALL ME?
HE KNOWS **BATMAN'S** IDENTITY--- BUT ONLY ALFRED AND I ARE SUPPOSED TO KNOW THAT!
WHY, SIR---THAT IS---YOU SEE---
THAT VOICE!
THAT CHAUFFEUR'S UNIFORM! IT LOOKS FAMILIAR--- BUT ON A SLIMMER SCALE!
IT'S HIM---BUT HIS UPPER LIP HAS BURST INTO FLOWER, AND THE REST OF HIM HAS SHRUNK!
ALFRED! WHATEVER HAPPENED TO YOUR---ER-- AVOIRDUPOIS?
IT'S RAWTHER A PAINFUL STORY, SIR! I FELT I LACKED A CERTAIN DASH AND ELEGANCE THAT WOULD ENHANCE MY VALUE AS YOUR CRIME-FIGHTING ASSISTANT...
SO I SPENT MY HOLIDAY AT A HEALTH RESORT, CULTIVATIN' A NEW FIGURE BY HARD WORK ---AND YOU'LL NEVER KNOW HOW HARD!
LATER...
I CAN'T GET OVER THE STREAMLINING!
HERE WAS MY INSPIRATION, SIR! "THE IDEAL DETECTIVE IS ATHLETIC, LIGHT AND SWIFT IN MOVEMENT, GRACEFUL AS A SWAN---
WATCH YOUR STEP!
GREAT SCOTT!
ALFRED--- ARE YOU HURT?
"---AND UTTERLY SELF-POSSESSED IN ALL CIRCUMSTANCES!"
YOU SAID IT!
MAGNIFICENT!
12

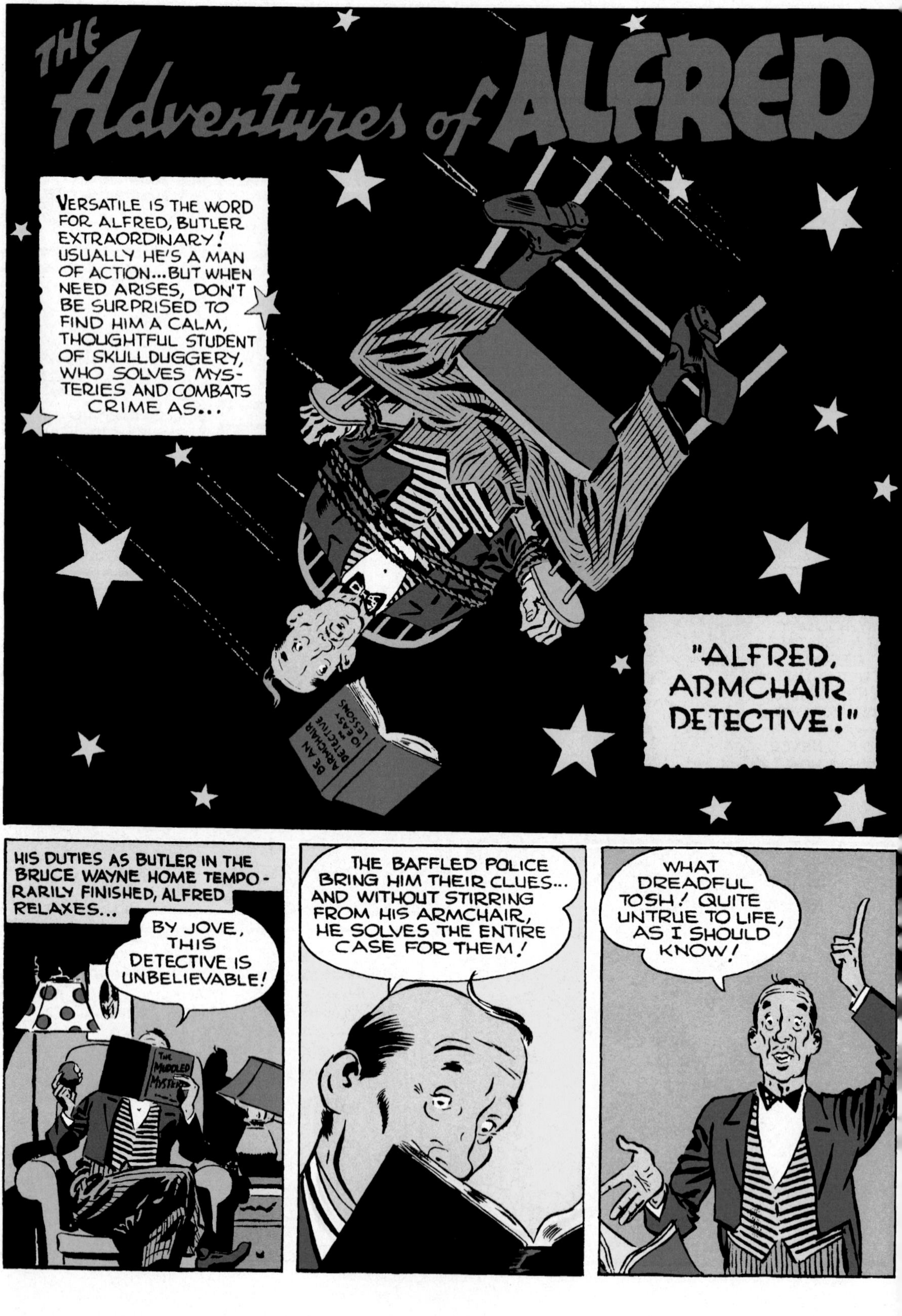
THE Adventures of ALFRED
VERSATILE IS THE WORD FOR ALFRED, BUTLER EXTRAORDINARY! USUALLY HE'S A MAN OF ACTION...BUT WHEN NEED ARISES, DON'T BE SURPRISED TO FIND HIM A CALM, THOUGHTFUL STUDENT OF SKULLDUGGERY, WHO SOLVES MYSTERIES AND COMBATS CRIME AS...
BE AN ARMCHAIR DETECTIVE IN 10 EASY LESSONS
"ALFRED, ARMCHAIR DETECTIVE!"
HIS DUTIES AS BUTLER IN THE BRUCE WAYNE HOME TEMPORARILY FINISHED, ALFRED RELAXES...
BY JOVE, THIS DETECTIVE IS UNBELIEVABLE!
THE MUDDLED MYSTERY
THE BAFFLED POLICE BRING HIM THEIR CLUES... AND WITHOUT STIRRING FROM HIS ARMCHAIR, HE SOLVES THE ENTIRE CASE FOR THEM!
WHAT DREADFUL TOSH! QUITE UNTRUE TO LIFE, AS I SHOULD KNOW!

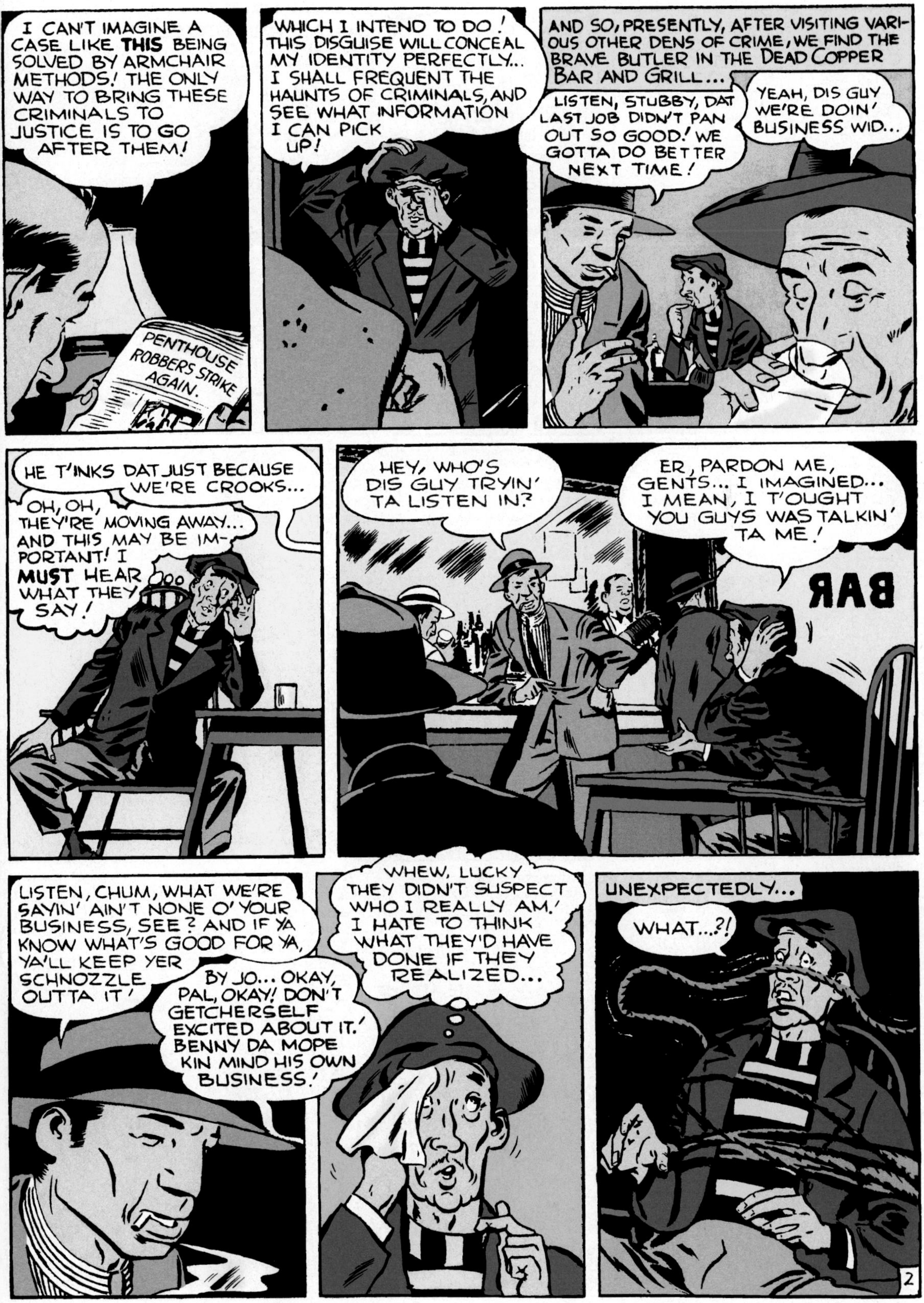
I CAN'T IMAGINE A CASE LIKE THIS BEING SOLVED BY ARMCHAIR METHODS! THE ONLY WAY TO BRING THESE CRIMINALS TO JUSTICE IS TO GO AFTER THEM!
PENTHOUSE ROBBERS STRIKE AGAIN.
WHICH I INTEND TO DO! THIS DISGUISE WILL CONCEAL MY IDENTITY PERFECTLY.. I SHALL FREQUENT THE HAUNTS OF CRIMINALS, AND SEE WHAT INFORMATION I CAN PICK UP!
AND SO, PRESENTLY, AFTER VISITING VARIOUS OTHER DENS OF CRIME, WE FIND THE BRAVE BUTLER IN THE DEAD COPPER BAR AND GRILL...
LISTEN, STUBBY, DAT LAST JOB DIDN'T PAN OUT SO GOOD! WE GOTTA DO BETTER NEXT TIME!
YEAH, DIS GUY WE'RE DOIN' BUSINESS WID...
HE T'INKS DAT JUST BECAUSE WE'RE CROOKS...
OH, OH, THEY'RE MOVING AWAY... AND THIS MAY BE IMPORTANT! I MUST HEAR WHAT THEY SAY!
HEY, WHO'S DIS GUY TRYIN' TA LISTEN IN?
ER, PARDON ME, GENTS... I IMAGINED... I MEAN, I T'OUGHT YOU GUYS WAS TALKIN' TA ME!
BAR
LISTEN, CHUM, WHAT WE'RE SAYIN' AIN'T NONE O' YOUR BUSINESS, SEE? AND IF YA KNOW WHAT'S GOOD FOR YA, YA'LL KEEP YER SCHNOZZLE OUTTA IT!
BY JO... OKAY, PAL, OKAY! DON'T GETCHERSELF EXCITED ABOUT IT! BENNY DA MOPE KIN MIND HIS OWN BUSINESS!
WHEW, LUCKY THEY DIDN'T SUSPECT WHO I REALLY AM! I HATE TO THINK WHAT THEY'D HAVE DONE IF THEY REALIZED...
UNEXPECTEDLY...
WHAT...?!
2

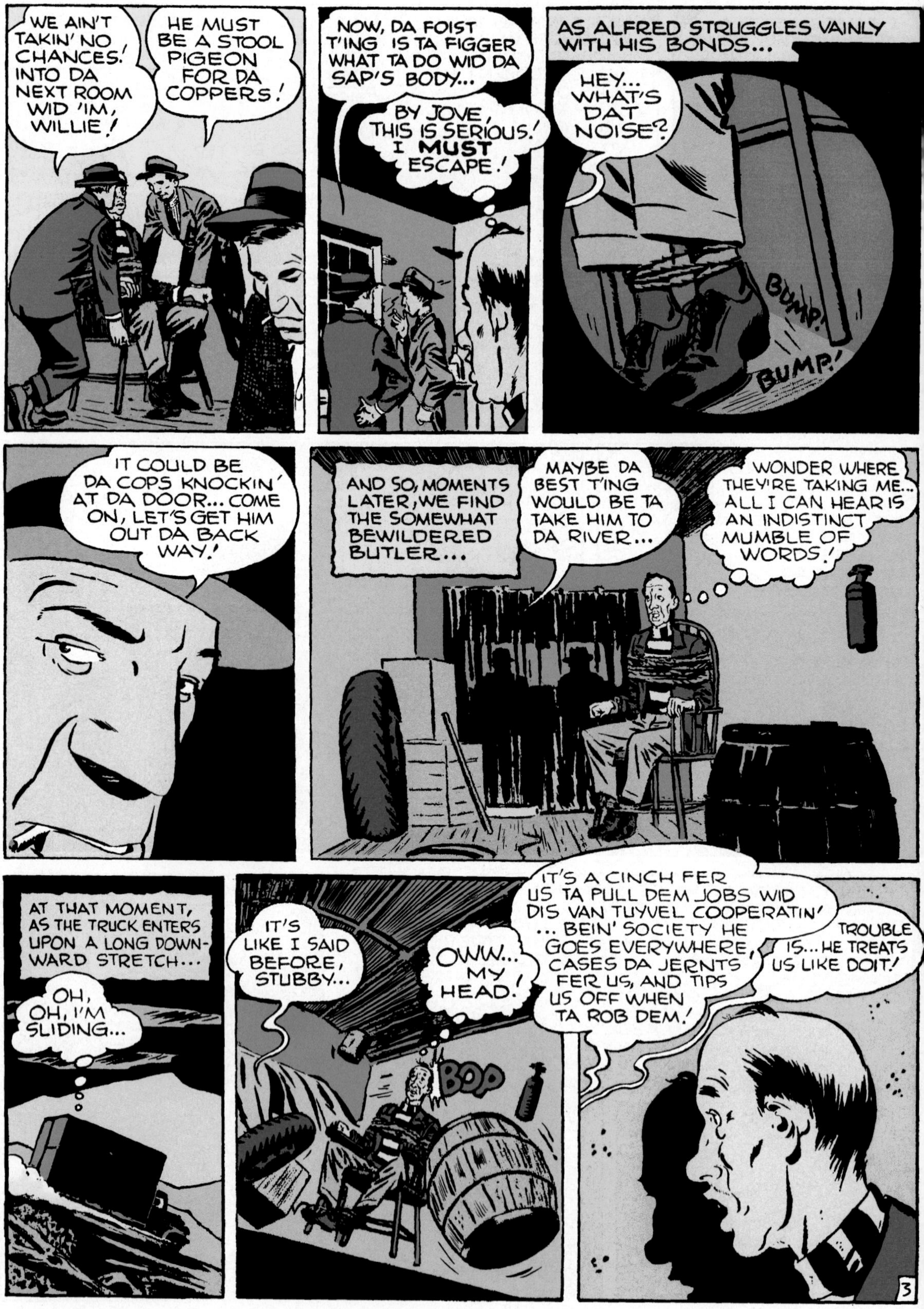
WE AIN'T TAKIN' NO CHANCES! INTO DA NEXT ROOM WID 'IM, WILLIE!
HE MUST BE A STOOL PIGEON FOR DA COPPERS!
NOW, DA FOIST T'ING IS TA FIGGER WHAT TA DO WID DA SAP'S BODY...
BY JOVE, THIS IS SERIOUS! I MUST ESCAPE!
AS ALFRED STRUGGLES VAINLY WITH HIS BONDS...
HEY... WHAT'S DAT NOISE?
BUMP!
BUMP!
IT COULD BE DA COPS KNOCKIN' AT DA DOOR... COME ON, LET'S GET HIM OUT DA BACK WAY!
AND SO, MOMENTS LATER, WE FIND THE SOMEWHAT BEWILDERED BUTLER...
MAYBE DA BEST T'ING WOULD BE TA TAKE HIM TO DA RIVER...
WONDER WHERE THEY'RE TAKING ME... ALL I CAN HEAR IS AN INDISTINCT MUMBLE OF WORDS!
AT THAT MOMENT, AS THE TRUCK ENTERS UPON A LONG DOWNWARD STRETCH...
OH, OH, I'M SLIDING...
IT'S LIKE I SAID BEFORE, STUBBY...
OWW... MY HEAD!
BOP
IT'S A CINCH FER US TA PULL DEM JOBS WID DIS VAN TUYVEL COOPERATIN' ... BEIN' SOCIETY HE GOES EVERYWHERE, CASES DA JERNTS FER US, AND TIPS US OFF WHEN TA ROB DEM!
TROUBLE IS... HE TREATS US LIKE DOIT!
3

YEAH, HE WANTS ALL DA GRAVY!

GREAT SCOTT! I'VE LEARNED THE WHOLE SECRET OF THOSE PENT-HOUSE ROBBERIES... IF I CAN ONLY LIVE LONG ENOUGH TO TELL IT TO THE POLICE!

PERHAPS IF I CAN CRASH TO THE FLOOR AND BREAK THE CHAIR, MY BONDS WILL LOOSEN! I'LL TRY TO LEAN TO THE SIDE...

BUT UNEXPECTEDLY, THE LUMBERING VEHICLE STRIKES A DEEP RUT IN THE ROAD...

HEY... WHAT...

CRASH

HONK

HELP!

CRASH!

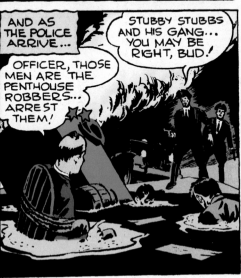

AND AS THE POLICE ARRIVE...

OFFICER, THOSE MEN ARE THE PENTHOUSE ROBBERS... ARREST THEM!

STUBBY STUBBS AND HIS GANG... YOU MAY BE RIGHT, BUD!

LATER, IN THE BRUCE WAYNE HOME ONCE MORE...

ALFRED, YOU'RE WONDERFUL! IT'S OBVIOUS NOW THAT THOSE PENTHOUSE ROBBERS HAD INSIDE HELP...

HOW DID YOU MANAGE TO PUT THE CLUES TO-GETHER?

IT WAS SIMPLY A MATTER OF USING THE OLD BEAN, MAWSTER DICK. I THOUGHT IT COULDN'T BE DONE... BUT I SOLVED THE CASE WITHOUT STIRRING FROM MY ARMCHAIR!

ThE End

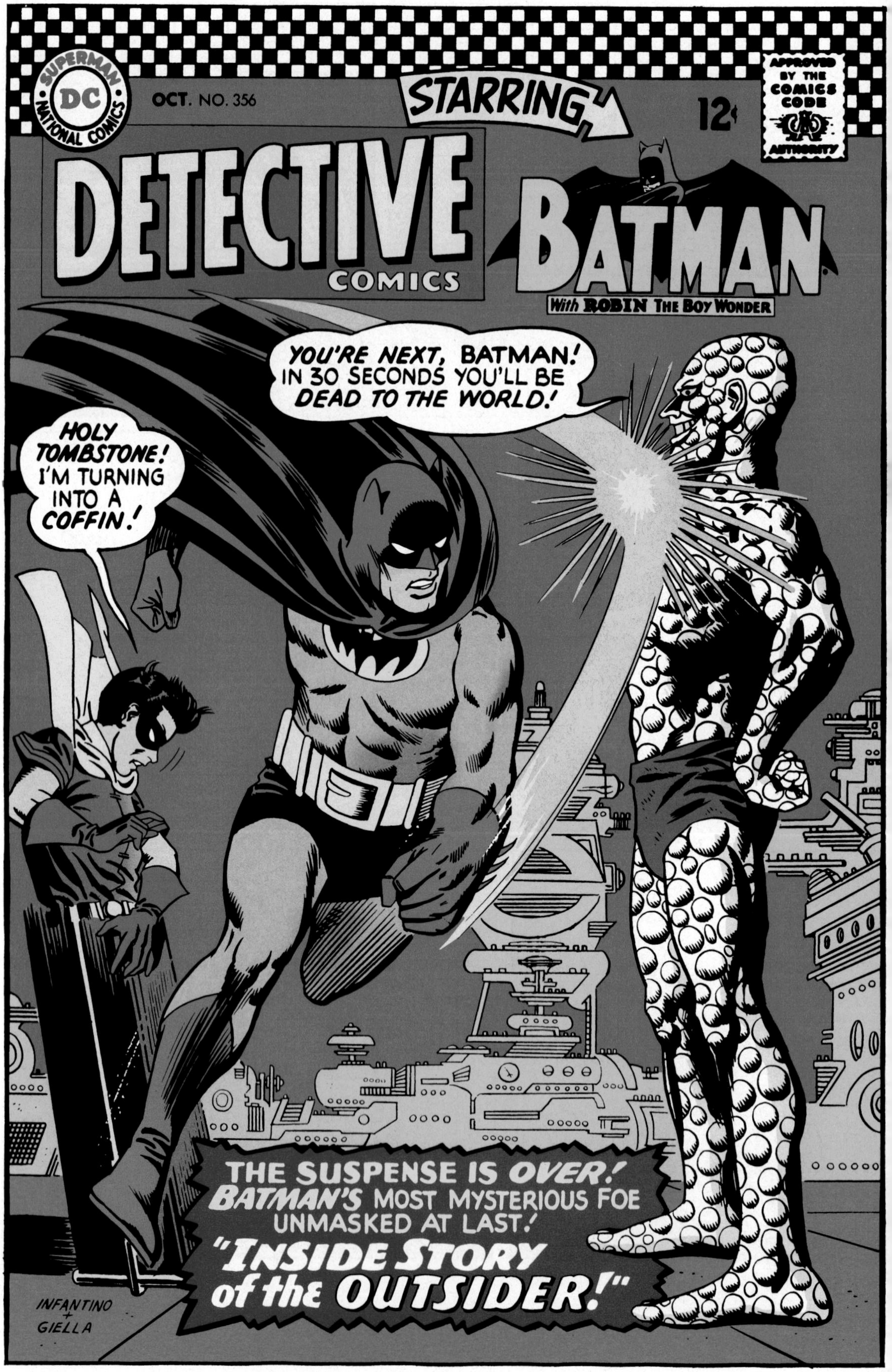

SUPERMAN DC NATIONAL COMICS
OCT. NO. 356
STARRING
12¢
APPROVED BY THE COMICS CODE AUTHORITY
DETECTIVE COMICS
BATMAN
With ROBIN THE BOY WONDER
YOU'RE NEXT, BATMAN! IN 30 SECONDS YOU'LL BE DEAD TO THE WORLD!
HOLY TOMBSTONE! I'M TURNING INTO A COFFIN!
THE SUSPENSE IS OVER! BATMAN'S MOST MYSTERIOUS FOE UNMASKED AT LAST! "INSIDE STORY of the OUTSIDER!"
INFANTINO + GIELLA

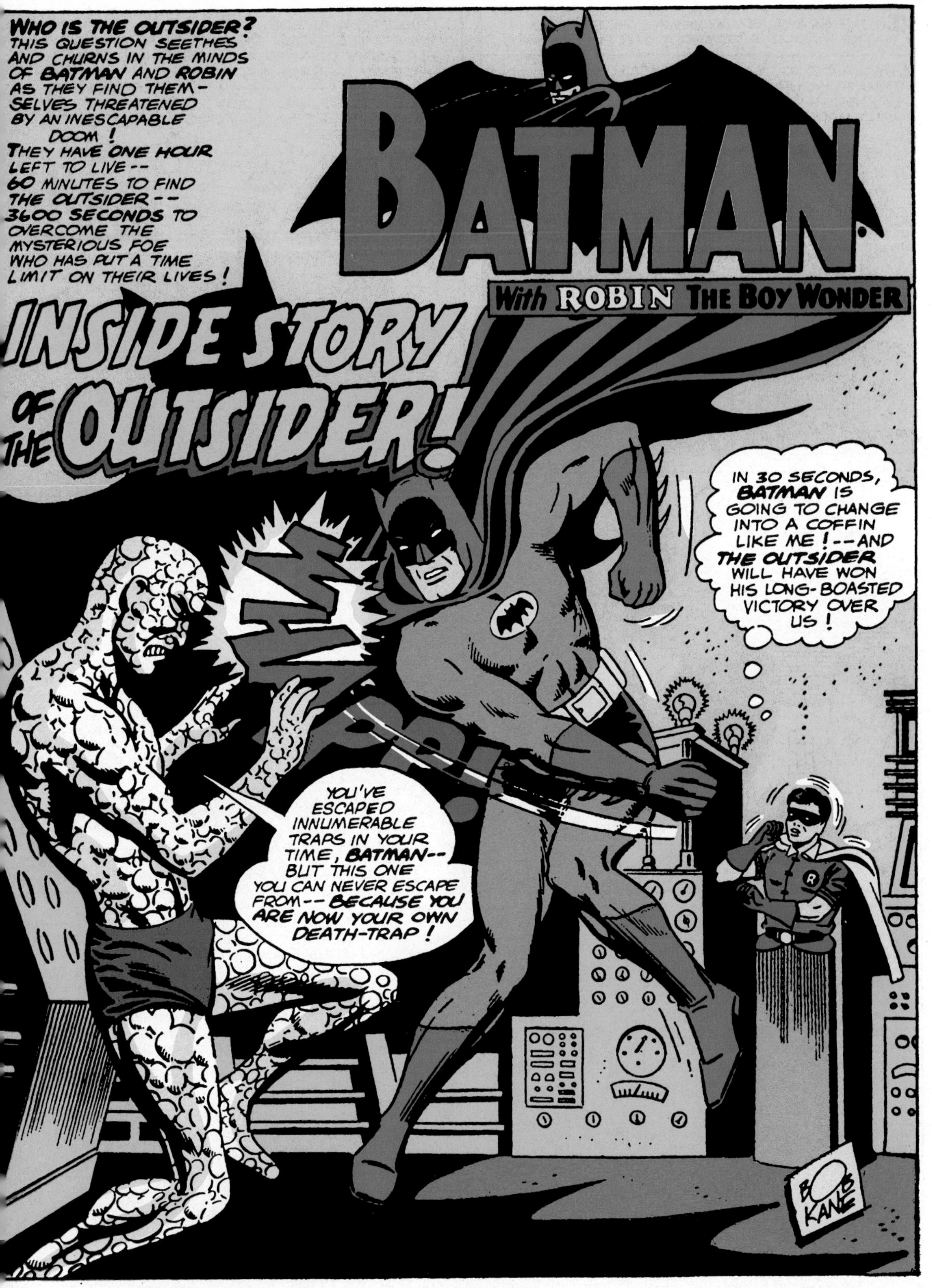
WHO IS THE OUTSIDER? THIS QUESTION SEETHES AND CHURNS IN THE MINDS OF BATMAN AND ROBIN AS THEY FIND THEMSELVES THREATENED BY AN INESCAPABLE DOOM! THEY HAVE ONE HOUR LEFT TO LIVE -- 60 MINUTES TO FIND THE OUTSIDER -- 3600 SECONDS TO OVERCOME THE MYSTERIOUS FOE WHO HAS PUT A TIME LIMIT ON THEIR LIVES!
BATMAN
With ROBIN THE BOY WONDER
INSIDE STORY OF THE OUTSIDER!
IN 30 SECONDS, BATMAN IS GOING TO CHANGE INTO A COFFIN LIKE ME!--AND THE OUTSIDER WILL HAVE WON HIS LONG-BOASTED VICTORY OVER US!
YOU'VE ESCAPED INNUMERABLE TRAPS IN YOUR TIME, BATMAN--BUT THIS ONE YOU CAN NEVER ESCAPE FROM--BECAUSE YOU ARE NOW YOUR OWN DEATH-TRAP!
BOB KANE

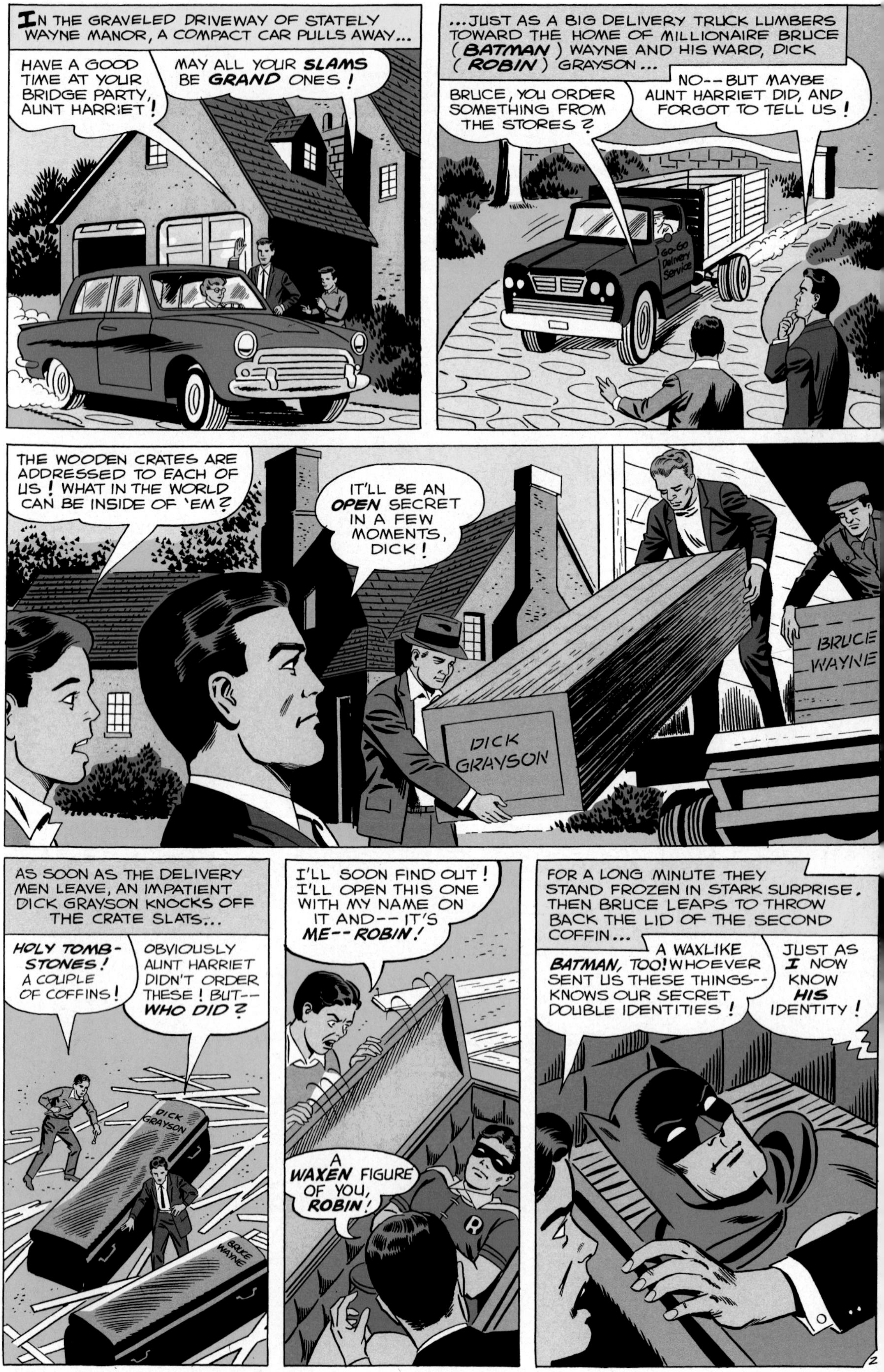
IN THE GRAVELED DRIVEWAY OF STATELY WAYNE MANOR, A COMPACT CAR PULLS AWAY...
HAVE A GOOD TIME AT YOUR BRIDGE PARTY, AUNT HARRIET!
MAY ALL YOUR SLAMS BE GRAND ONES!
...JUST AS A BIG DELIVERY TRUCK LUMBERS TOWARD THE HOME OF MILLIONAIRE BRUCE (BATMAN) WAYNE AND HIS WARD, DICK (ROBIN) GRAYSON...
BRUCE, YOU ORDER SOMETHING FROM THE STORES?
NO--BUT MAYBE AUNT HARRIET DID, AND FORGOT TO TELL US!
Go-Go Delivery Service
THE WOODEN CRATES ARE ADDRESSED TO EACH OF US! WHAT IN THE WORLD CAN BE INSIDE OF 'EM?
IT'LL BE AN OPEN SECRET IN A FEW MOMENTS, DICK!
BRUCE WAYNE
DICK GRAYSON
AS SOON AS THE DELIVERY MEN LEAVE, AN IMPATIENT DICK GRAYSON KNOCKS OFF THE CRATE SLATS...
HOLY TOMB-STONES! A COUPLE OF COFFINS!
OBVIOUSLY AUNT HARRIET DIDN'T ORDER THESE! BUT-- WHO DID?
DICK GRAYSON
BRUCE WAYNE
I'LL SOON FIND OUT! I'LL OPEN THIS ONE WITH MY NAME ON IT AND-- IT'S ME--ROBIN!
A WAXEN FIGURE OF YOU, ROBIN!
FOR A LONG MINUTE THEY STAND FROZEN IN STARK SURPRISE. THEN BRUCE LEAPS TO THROW BACK THE LID OF THE SECOND COFFIN...
A WAXLIKE BATMAN, TOO! WHOEVER SENT US THESE THINGS-- KNOWS OUR SECRET DOUBLE IDENTITIES!
JUST AS I NOW KNOW HIS IDENTITY!
2

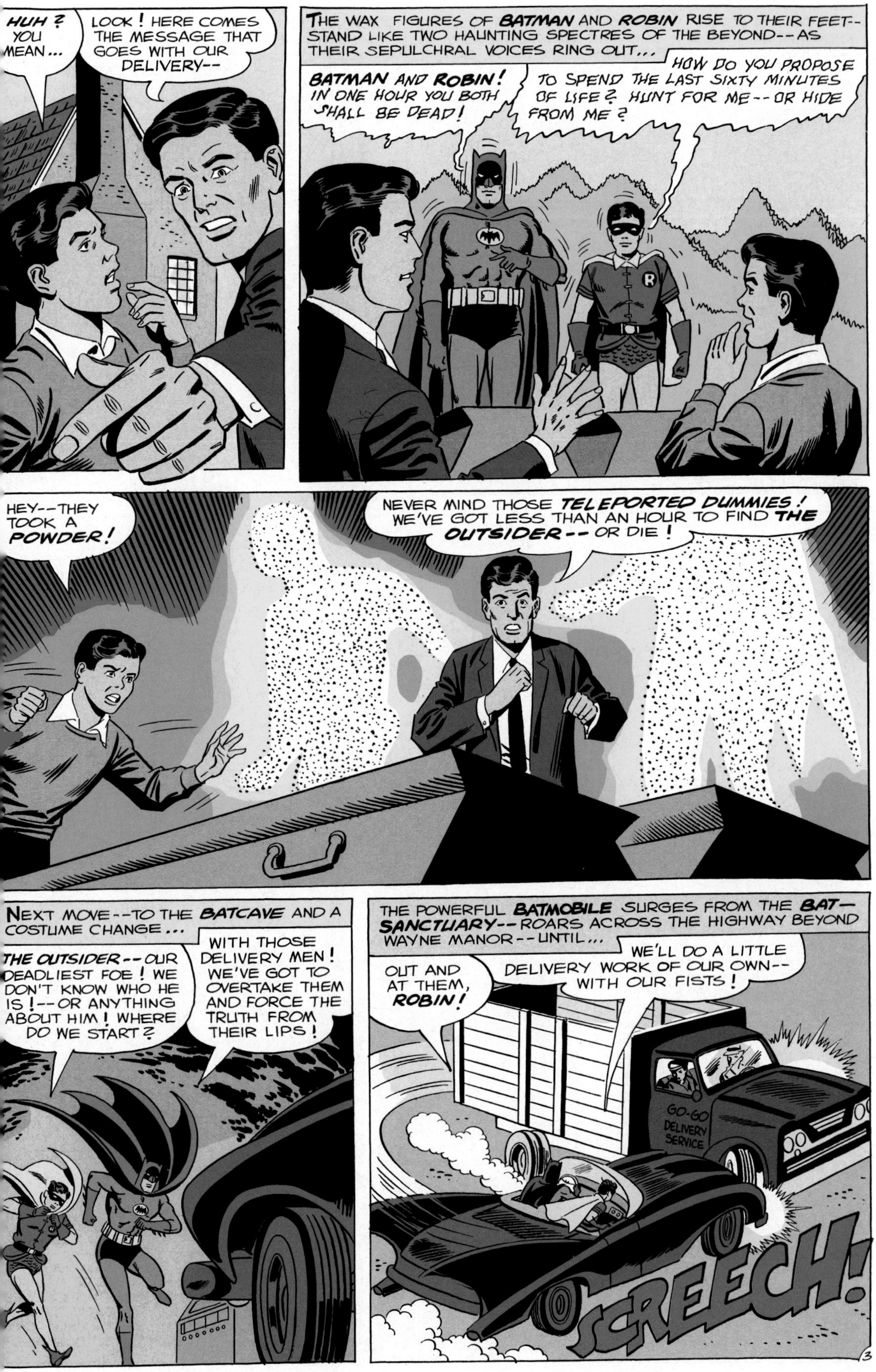
HUH ? YOU MEAN...
LOOK ! HERE COMES THE MESSAGE THAT GOES WITH OUR DELIVERY--
THE WAX FIGURES OF BATMAN AND ROBIN RISE TO THEIR FEET-- STAND LIKE TWO HAUNTING SPECTRES OF THE BEYOND--AS THEIR SEPULCHRAL VOICES RING OUT...
BATMAN AND ROBIN! IN ONE HOUR YOU BOTH SHALL BE DEAD!
HOW DO YOU PROPOSE TO SPEND THE LAST SIXTY MINUTES OF LIFE? HUNT FOR ME--OR HIDE FROM ME?
HEY--THEY TOOK A POWDER!
NEVER MIND THOSE TELEPORTED DUMMIES! WE'VE GOT LESS THAN AN HOUR TO FIND THE OUTSIDER--OR DIE!
NEXT MOVE--TO THE BATCAVE AND A COSTUME CHANGE...
THE OUTSIDER--OUR DEADLIEST FOE! WE DON'T KNOW WHO HE IS!--OR ANYTHING ABOUT HIM! WHERE DO WE START?
WITH THOSE DELIVERY MEN! WE'VE GOT TO OVERTAKE THEM AND FORCE THE TRUTH FROM THEIR LIPS!
THE POWERFUL BATMOBILE SURGES FROM THE BAT-SANCTUARY--ROARS ACROSS THE HIGHWAY BEYOND WAYNE MANOR--UNTIL...
OUT AND AT THEM, ROBIN!
WE'LL DO A LITTLE DELIVERY WORK OF OUR OWN--WITH OUR FISTS!
GO-GO DELIVERY SERVICE
SCREECH!
3

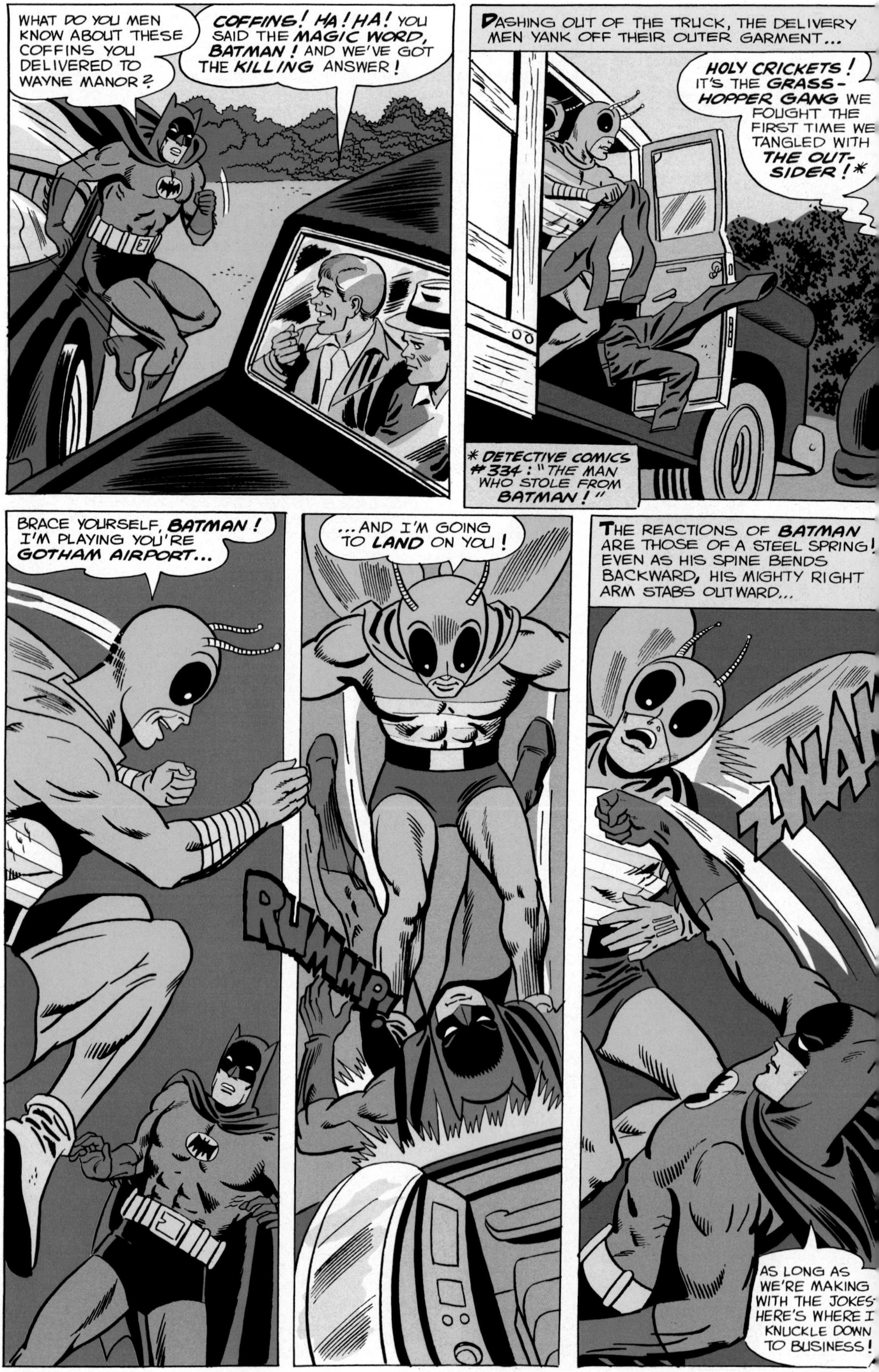
WHAT DO YOU MEN KNOW ABOUT THESE COFFINS YOU DELIVERED TO WAYNE MANOR?
COFFINS! HA! HA! YOU SAID THE MAGIC WORD, BATMAN! AND WE'VE GOT THE KILLING ANSWER!
DASHING OUT OF THE TRUCK, THE DELIVERY MEN YANK OFF THEIR OUTER GARMENT...
HOLY CRICKETS! IT'S THE GRASS-HOPPER GANG WE FOUGHT THE FIRST TIME WE TANGLED WITH THE OUT-SIDER!*
* DETECTIVE COMICS #334: "THE MAN WHO STOLE FROM BATMAN!"
BRACE YOURSELF, BATMAN! I'M PLAYING YOU'RE GOTHAM AIRPORT...
...AND I'M GOING TO LAND ON YOU!
RUMMP!
THE REACTIONS OF BATMAN ARE THOSE OF A STEEL SPRING! EVEN AS HIS SPINE BENDS BACKWARD, HIS MIGHTY RIGHT ARM STABS OUTWARD...
AS LONG AS WE'RE MAKING WITH THE JOKES-- HERE'S WHERE I KNUCKLE DOWN TO BUSINESS!

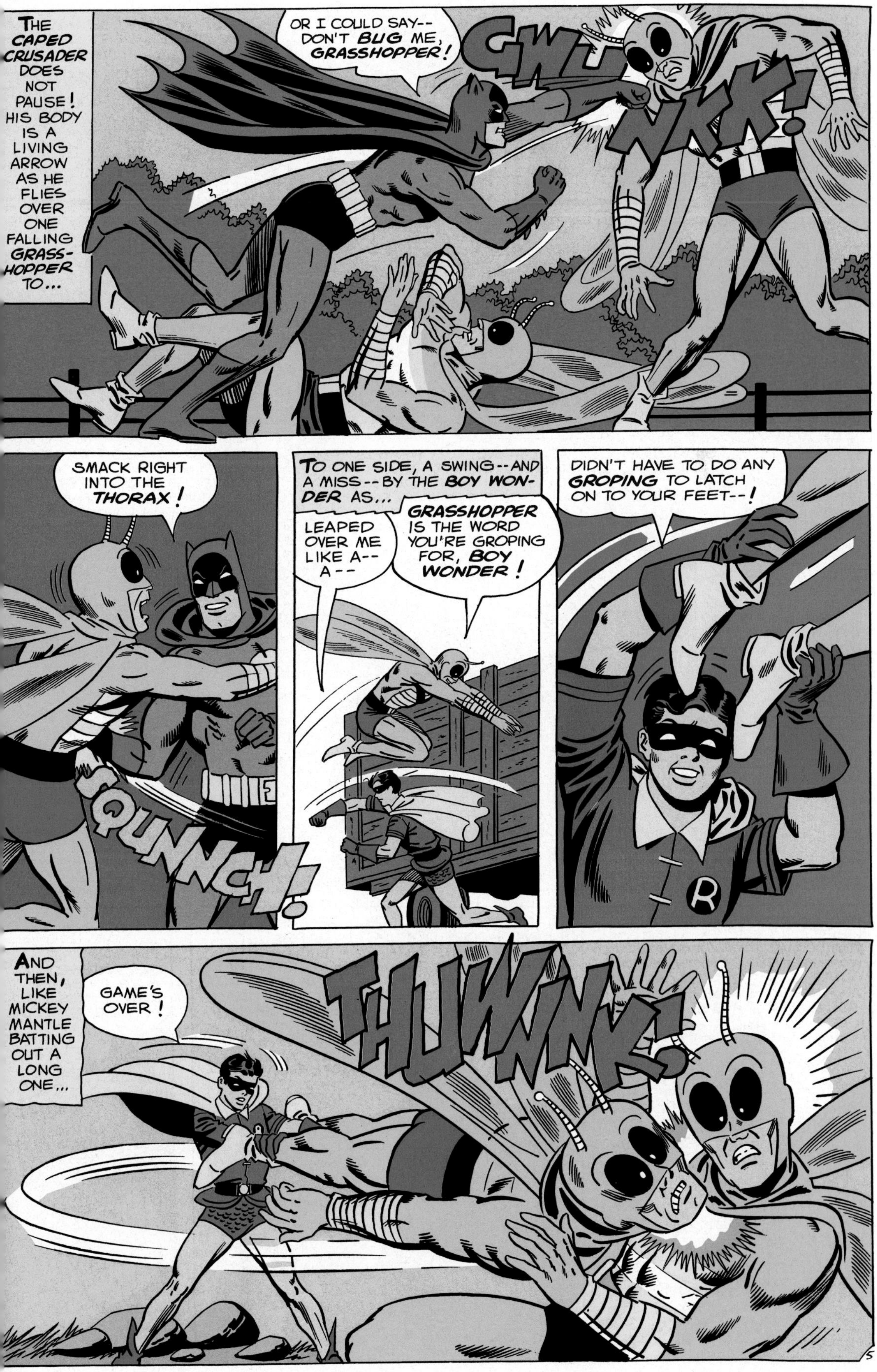
THE CAPED CRUSADER DOES NOT PAUSE! HIS BODY IS A LIVING ARROW AS HE FLIES OVER ONE FALLING GRASSHOPPER TO...
OR I COULD SAY-- DON'T BUG ME, GRASSHOPPER!
GWUNKK!
SMACK RIGHT INTO THE THORAX!
SQUNNCH!
TO ONE SIDE, A SWING--AND A MISS--BY THE BOY WONDER AS...
LEAPED OVER ME LIKE A-- A--
GRASSHOPPER IS THE WORD YOU'RE GROPING FOR, BOY WONDER!
DIDN'T HAVE TO DO ANY GROPING TO LATCH ON TO YOUR FEET--!
AND THEN, LIKE MICKEY MANTLE BATTING OUT A LONG ONE...
GAME'S OVER!
THWWNK!
5

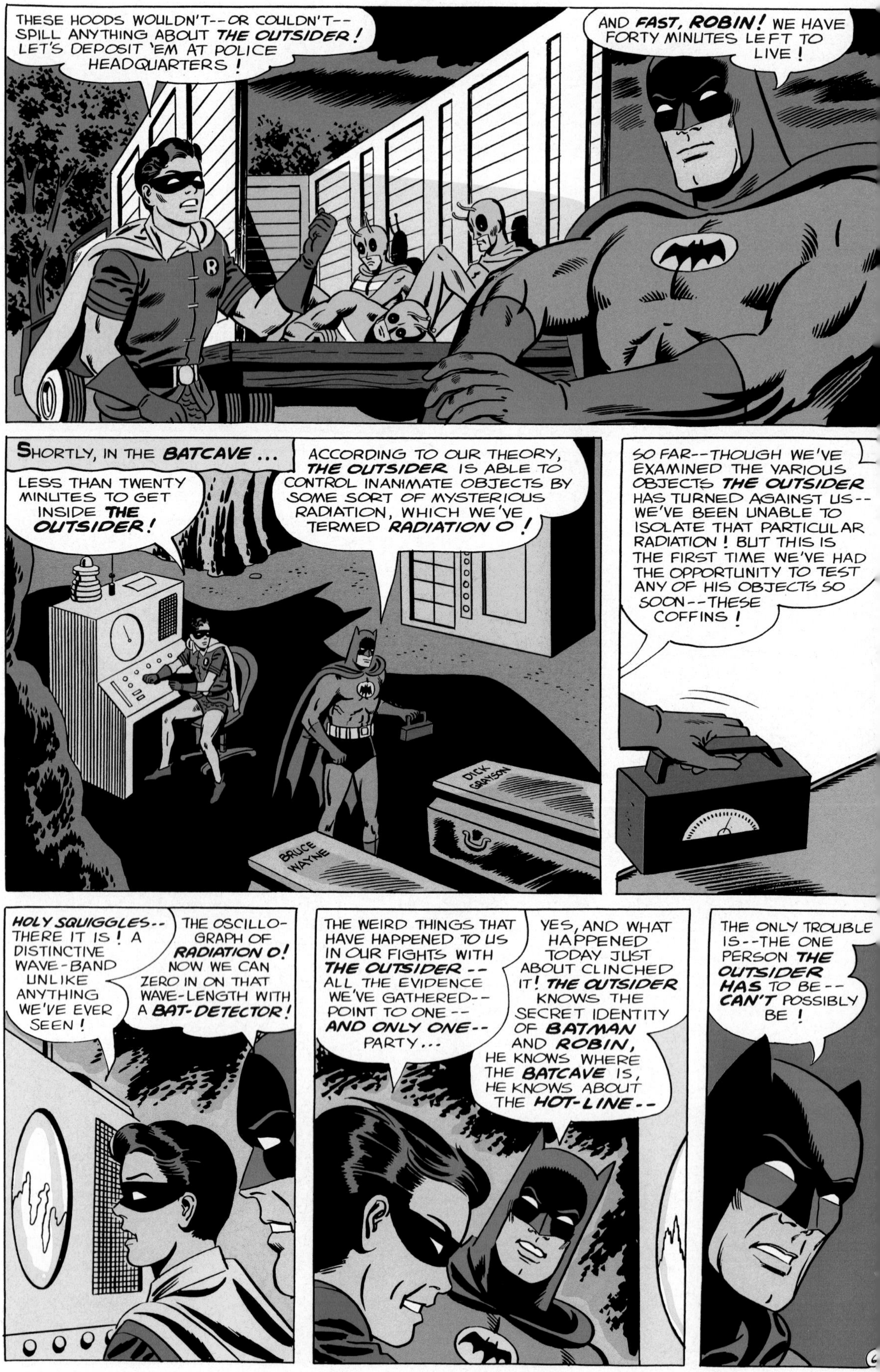
THESE HOODS WOULDN'T--OR COULDN'T--SPILL ANYTHING ABOUT THE OUTSIDER! LET'S DEPOSIT 'EM AT POLICE HEADQUARTERS!
AND FAST, ROBIN! WE HAVE FORTY MINUTES LEFT TO LIVE!
SHORTLY, IN THE BATCAVE...
LESS THAN TWENTY MINUTES TO GET INSIDE THE OUTSIDER!
ACCORDING TO OUR THEORY, THE OUTSIDER IS ABLE TO CONTROL INANIMATE OBJECTS BY SOME SORT OF MYSTERIOUS RADIATION, WHICH WE'VE TERMED RADIATION O!
DICK GRAYSON
BRUCE WAYNE
SO FAR--THOUGH WE'VE EXAMINED THE VARIOUS OBJECTS THE OUTSIDER HAS TURNED AGAINST US--WE'VE BEEN UNABLE TO ISOLATE THAT PARTICULAR RADIATION! BUT THIS IS THE FIRST TIME WE'VE HAD THE OPPORTUNITY TO TEST ANY OF HIS OBJECTS SO SOON--THESE COFFINS!
HOLY SQUIGGLES--THERE IT IS! A DISTINCTIVE WAVE-BAND UNLIKE ANYTHING WE'VE EVER SEEN!
THE OSCILLO-GRAPH OF RADIATION O! NOW WE CAN ZERO IN ON THAT WAVE-LENGTH WITH A BAT-DETECTOR!
THE WEIRD THINGS THAT HAVE HAPPENED TO US IN OUR FIGHTS WITH THE OUTSIDER--ALL THE EVIDENCE WE'VE GATHERED--POINT TO ONE--AND ONLY ONE--PARTY...
YES, AND WHAT HAPPENED TODAY JUST ABOUT CLINCHED IT! THE OUTSIDER KNOWS THE SECRET IDENTITY OF BATMAN AND ROBIN, HE KNOWS WHERE THE BATCAVE IS, HE KNOWS ABOUT THE HOT-LINE--
THE ONLY TROUBLE IS--THE ONE PERSON THE OUTSIDER HAS TO BE--CAN'T POSSIBLY BE!

YES, *THE OUTSIDER* HAS TO BE *ALFRED*-- OUR BUTLER! BUT-- ALFRED IS *DEAD*!

WE CHECKED THAT OUT AFTER EACH *OUTSIDER* ADVENTURE -- BUT WE'VE GOT TO DO IT ONCE MORE! TO CONVINCE OURSELVES IT CAN'T POSSIBLY BE ALFRED!

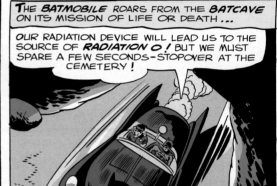

*THE BATMOBILE* ROARS FROM THE *BATCAVE* ON ITS MISSION OF LIFE OR DEATH ...

OUR RADIATION DEVICE WILL LEAD US TO THE SOURCE OF *RADIATION O*! BUT WE MUST SPARE A FEW SECONDS--STOPOVER AT THE CEMETERY!

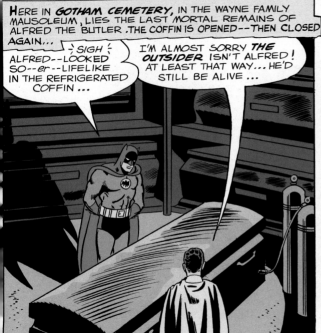

HERE IN *GOTHAM CEMETERY*, IN THE WAYNE FAMILY MAUSOLEUM, LIES THE LAST MORTAL REMAINS OF ALFRED THE BUTLER. THE COFFIN IS OPENED--THEN CLOSED AGAIN...

-SIGH- ALFRED--LOOKED SO--*er*--LIFELIKE IN THE REFRIGERATED COFFIN ...

I'M ALMOST SORRY *THE OUTSIDER* ISN'T ALFRED! AT LEAST THAT WAY... HE'D STILL BE ALIVE ...

TO DISPEL ANY LINGERING DOUBT, THE *WORLD'S GREATEST DETECTIVE* TAKES A SET OF FINGERPRINTS ...

THESE ARE ALFRED'S TRUE PRINTS! I'D KNOW THEM ANYWHERE!

OKAY! SINCE *THE OUTSIDER ISN'T* ALFRED-- WHO IN THE NAME OF SANITY--IS HE?

ARE YOU AS PUZZLED AS *BATMAN AND ROBIN?* IF YOU ARE--LET'S GO BACK IN TIME TO THAT CRITICAL MOMENT WHEN THE BRAVE BUTLER GAVE HIS LIFE THAT THE *DYNAMIC DUO* MIGHT LIVE!*...

MUST RISK MY LIFE TO SAVE THEIRS--SHOVE THEM OUT OF THE WAY OF THAT GIANT BOULDER!

*Detective Comics #328: "GOTHAM CITY LINE-UP!"

THREE DAYS LATER, BRUCE WAYNE AND DICK GRAYSON SLOW-FOOTED AWAY FROM THE MAUSOLEUM THAT HELD THE BODY OF THEIR FAITHFUL SERVITOR ...

WE'VE LOST THE BEST FRIEND WE'VE EVER HAD!

THERE'LL NEVER BE ANOTHER ALFRED!

WAYNE

7

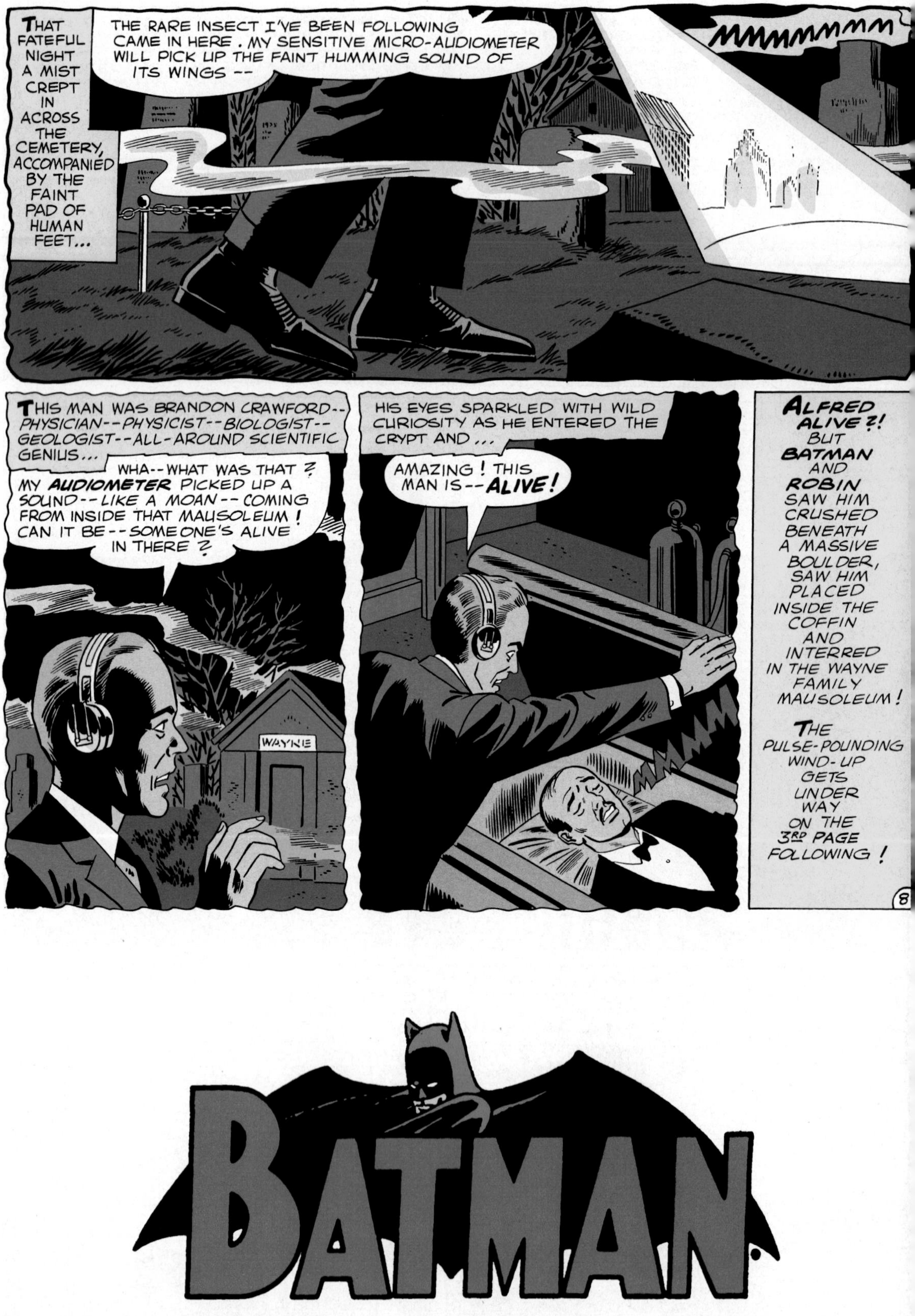
THAT FATEFUL NIGHT A MIST CREPT IN ACROSS THE CEMETERY, ACCOMPANIED BY THE FAINT PAD OF HUMAN FEET...
THE RARE INSECT I'VE BEEN FOLLOWING CAME IN HERE. MY SENSITIVE MICRO-AUDIOMETER WILL PICK UP THE FAINT HUMMING SOUND OF ITS WINGS --
MMMMMMMM
THIS MAN WAS BRANDON CRAWFORD-- PHYSICIAN--PHYSICIST--BIOLOGIST-- GEOLOGIST--ALL-AROUND SCIENTIFIC GENIUS...
WHA--WHAT WAS THAT? MY AUDIOMETER PICKED UP A SOUND--LIKE A MOAN--COMING FROM INSIDE THAT MAUSOLEUM! CAN IT BE--SOMEONE'S ALIVE IN THERE?
WAYNE
HIS EYES SPARKLED WITH WILD CURIOSITY AS HE ENTERED THE CRYPT AND...
AMAZING! THIS MAN IS--ALIVE!
ALFRED ALIVE?! BUT BATMAN AND ROBIN SAW HIM CRUSHED BENEATH A MASSIVE BOULDER, SAW HIM PLACED INSIDE THE COFFIN AND INTERRED IN THE WAYNE FAMILY MAUSOLEUM!
THE PULSE-POUNDING WIND-UP GETS UNDER WAY ON THE 3RD PAGE FOLLOWING!
8

# BATMAN

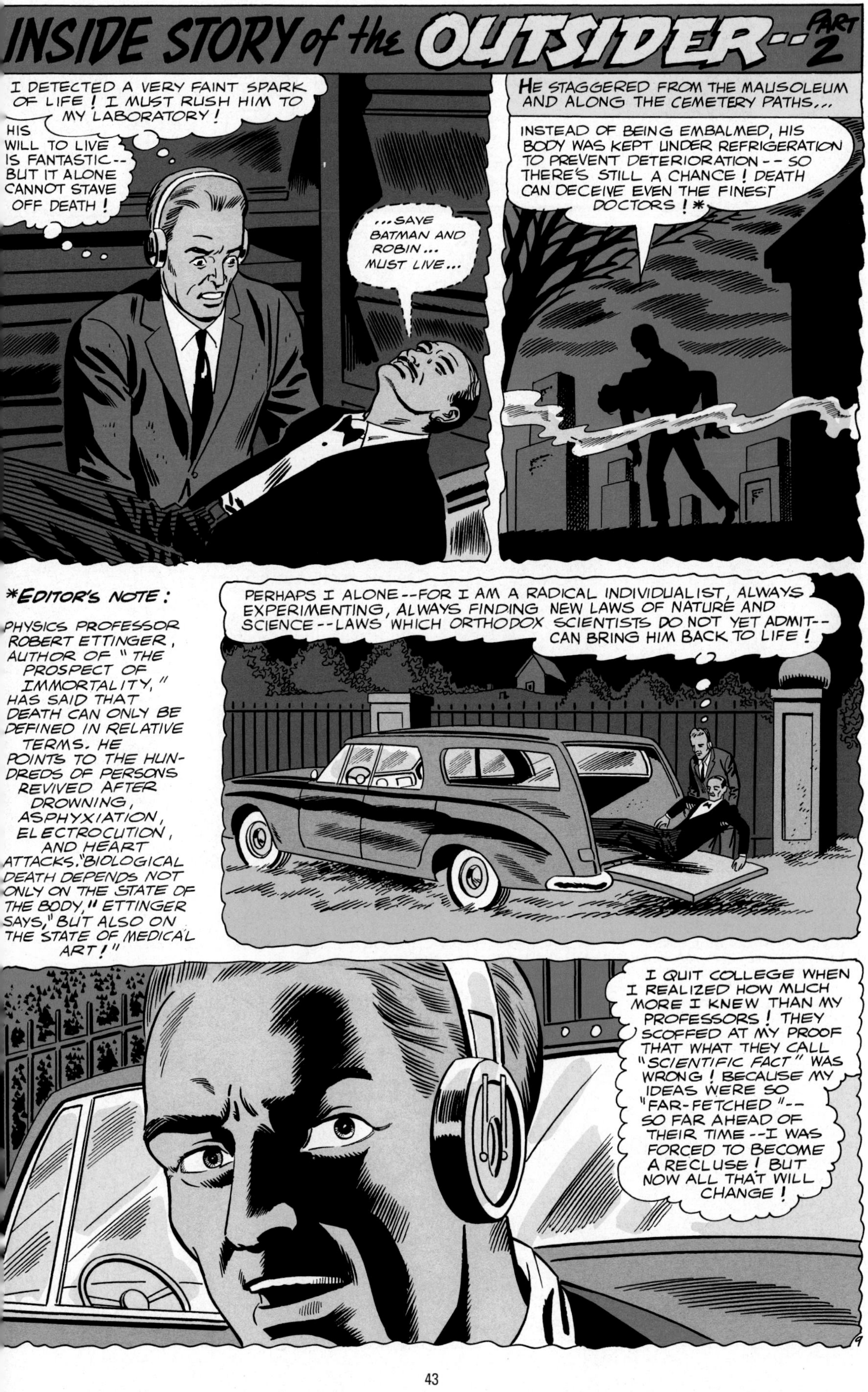
INSIDE STORY of the OUTSIDER -- PART 2
I DETECTED A VERY FAINT SPARK OF LIFE ! I MUST RUSH HIM TO MY LABORATORY !
HIS WILL TO LIVE IS FANTASTIC -- BUT IT ALONE CANNOT STAVE OFF DEATH !
...SAVE BATMAN AND ROBIN... MUST LIVE...
HE STAGGERED FROM THE MAUSOLEUM AND ALONG THE CEMETERY PATHS...
INSTEAD OF BEING EMBALMED, HIS BODY WAS KEPT UNDER REFRIGERATION TO PREVENT DETERIORATION -- SO THERE'S STILL A CHANCE ! DEATH CAN DECEIVE EVEN THE FINEST DOCTORS ! *
*EDITOR'S NOTE : PHYSICS PROFESSOR ROBERT ETTINGER, AUTHOR OF "THE PROSPECT OF IMMORTALITY," HAS SAID THAT DEATH CAN ONLY BE DEFINED IN RELATIVE TERMS. HE POINTS TO THE HUNDREDS OF PERSONS REVIVED AFTER DROWNING, ASPHYXIATION, ELECTROCUTION, AND HEART ATTACKS. "BIOLOGICAL DEATH DEPENDS NOT ONLY ON THE STATE OF THE BODY," ETTINGER SAYS, "BUT ALSO ON THE STATE OF MEDICAL ART !"
PERHAPS I ALONE -- FOR I AM A RADICAL INDIVIDUALIST, ALWAYS EXPERIMENTING, ALWAYS FINDING NEW LAWS OF NATURE AND SCIENCE -- LAWS WHICH ORTHODOX SCIENTISTS DO NOT YET ADMIT -- CAN BRING HIM BACK TO LIFE !
I QUIT COLLEGE WHEN I REALIZED HOW MUCH MORE I KNEW THAN MY PROFESSORS ! THEY SCOFFED AT MY PROOF THAT WHAT THEY CALL "SCIENTIFIC FACT" WAS WRONG ! BECAUSE MY IDEAS WERE SO "FAR-FETCHED" -- SO FAR AHEAD OF THEIR TIME -- I WAS FORCED TO BECOME A RECLUSE ! BUT NOW ALL THAT WILL CHANGE !
9

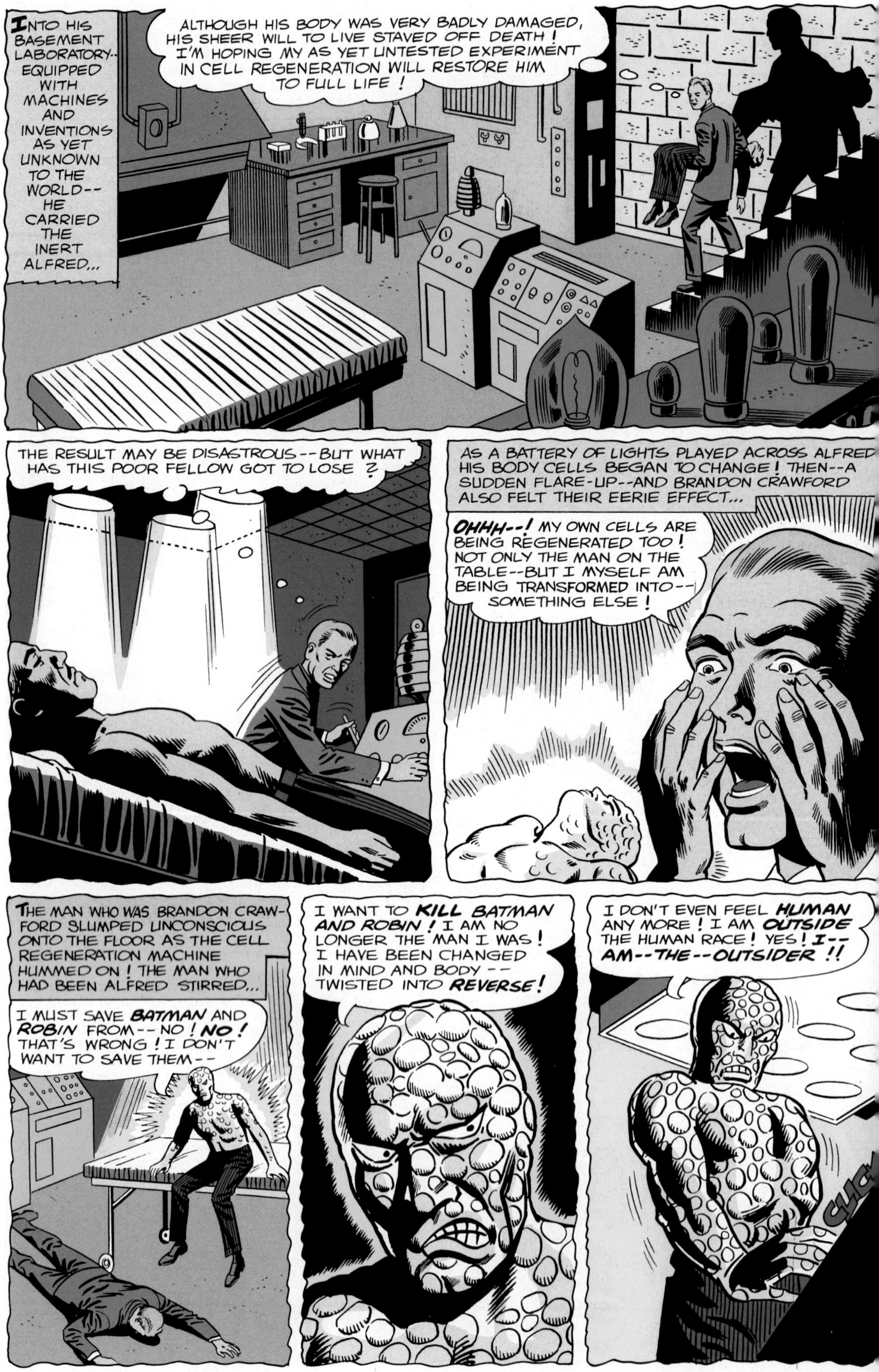
INTO HIS BASEMENT LABORATORY-- EQUIPPED WITH MACHINES AND INVENTIONS AS YET UNKNOWN TO THE WORLD-- HE CARRIED THE INERT ALFRED...
ALTHOUGH HIS BODY WAS VERY BADLY DAMAGED, HIS SHEER WILL TO LIVE STAVED OFF DEATH! I'M HOPING MY AS YET UNTESTED EXPERIMENT IN CELL REGENERATION WILL RESTORE HIM TO FULL LIFE!
THE RESULT MAY BE DISASTROUS--BUT WHAT HAS THIS POOR FELLOW GOT TO LOSE?
AS A BATTERY OF LIGHTS PLAYED ACROSS ALFRED HIS BODY CELLS BEGAN TO CHANGE! THEN--A SUDDEN FLARE-UP--AND BRANDON CRAWFORD ALSO FELT THEIR EERIE EFFECT...
OHHH--! MY OWN CELLS ARE BEING REGENERATED TOO! NOT ONLY THE MAN ON THE TABLE--BUT I MYSELF AM BEING TRANSFORMED INTO-- SOMETHING ELSE!
THE MAN WHO WAS BRANDON CRAWFORD SLUMPED UNCONSCIOUS ONTO THE FLOOR AS THE CELL REGENERATION MACHINE HUMMED ON! THE MAN WHO HAD BEEN ALFRED STIRRED...
I MUST SAVE BATMAN AND ROBIN FROM--NO! NO! THAT'S WRONG! I DON'T WANT TO SAVE THEM--
I WANT TO KILL BATMAN AND ROBIN! I AM NO LONGER THE MAN I WAS! I HAVE BEEN CHANGED IN MIND AND BODY-- TWISTED INTO REVERSE!
I DON'T EVEN FEEL HUMAN ANY MORE! I AM OUTSIDE THE HUMAN RACE! YES! I--AM--THE--OUTSIDER!!

TO PREVENT ANYONE FROM KNOWING WHAT HAS HAPPENED HERE, I MUST PUT THIS MAN WHO NOW LOOKS EXACTLY AS I USED TO LOOK--AND WHO IS IN A CATATONIC TRANCE BECAUSE OF SOME ACCIDENT OF HIS CELL REGENERATION MACHINE--BACK INTO THE COFFIN FROM WHICH HE TOOK ME!

AFTER THE BODY-SUBSTITUTION HAS BEEN MADE, THE *CHANGED ALFRED* RETURNS TO THE LABORATORY OF BRANDON CRAWFORD...

ODDLY ENOUGH, I FEEL AT HOME HERE! MY ALTERED BRAIN UNDERSTANDS THE PRINCIPLES OF THESE ULTRA-SCIENTIFIC MACHINES! WITH MY INCREASED MENTAL POWER I CAN OPERATE THEM--USE THEM TO DESTROY *BATMAN AND ROBIN!*

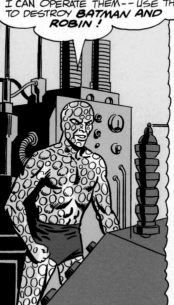

NOW--AS THE *DYNAMIC DUO* SPEEDS TOWARD A REMOTE AREA OF *GOTHAM CITY...*

BATMAN-- OUR *O RADIATION* FINDER IS GLOWING LIKE MAD!

WE'RE ABOUT TO MEET *THE OUTSIDER* AT LAST!

THEIR COUNTDOWN TO DEATH HAS REACHED TWO MINUTES AS THEY PEER INTO THE BASEMENT WINDOW OF A LONELY, OLD-FASHIONED HOUSE...

HOLY COMPUTERS! TAKE A GANDER AT ALL THAT SCIENTIFIC APPARATUS IN THERE!

I'M MORE INTERESTED IN TAKING *THE OUTSIDER*--AND THERE HE IS--THE MAN WHO SET A TIME LIMIT ON OUR LIVES!

CRASH!

BATMAN AND ROBIN! SO YOU FINALLY FOUND ME! BUT IT'S TOO LATE--TOO LATE! ALREADY DEATH IS SURGING THROUGH YOUR BODY!

THERE'S ENOUGH LIFE IN ME YET--TO KNOCK YOU *OUT, OUTSIDER!*

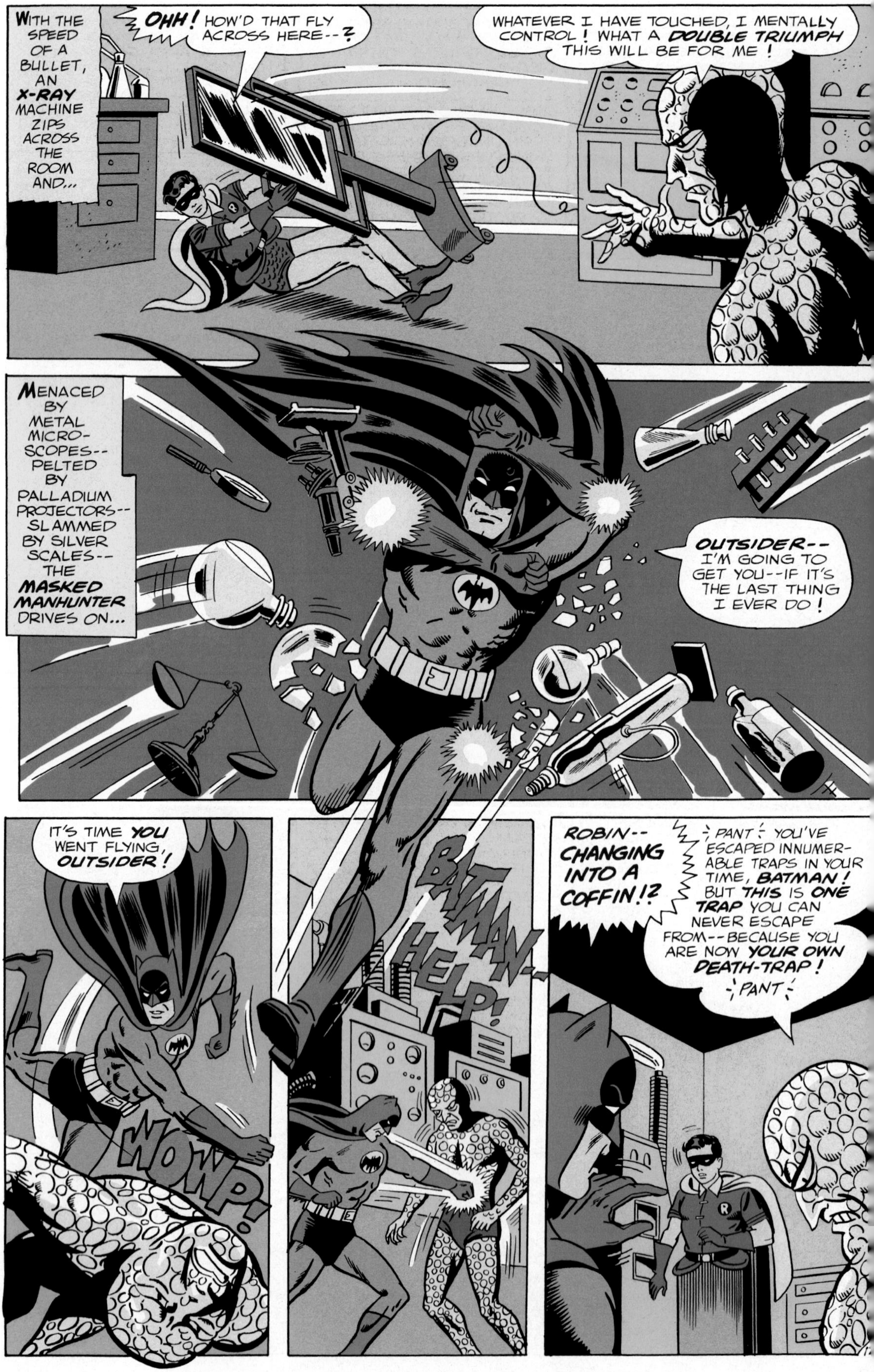
WITH THE SPEED OF A BULLET, AN X-RAY MACHINE ZIPS ACROSS THE ROOM AND...
OHH! HOW'D THAT FLY ACROSS HERE--?
WHATEVER I HAVE TOUCHED, I MENTALLY CONTROL! WHAT A DOUBLE TRIUMPH THIS WILL BE FOR ME!
MENACED BY METAL MICRO-SCOPES--PELTED BY PALLADIUM PROJECTORS--SLAMMED BY SILVER SCALES--THE MASKED MANHUNTER DRIVES ON...
OUTSIDER--I'M GOING TO GET YOU--IF IT'S THE LAST THING I EVER DO!
IT'S TIME YOU WENT FLYING, OUTSIDER!
WOWP!
BATMAN--HELP!
ROBIN--CHANGING INTO A COFFIN!?
-PANT- YOU'VE ESCAPED INNUMER-ABLE TRAPS IN YOUR TIME, BATMAN! BUT THIS IS ONE TRAP YOU CAN NEVER ESCAPE FROM--BECAUSE YOU ARE NOW YOUR OWN DEATH-TRAP! -PANT-

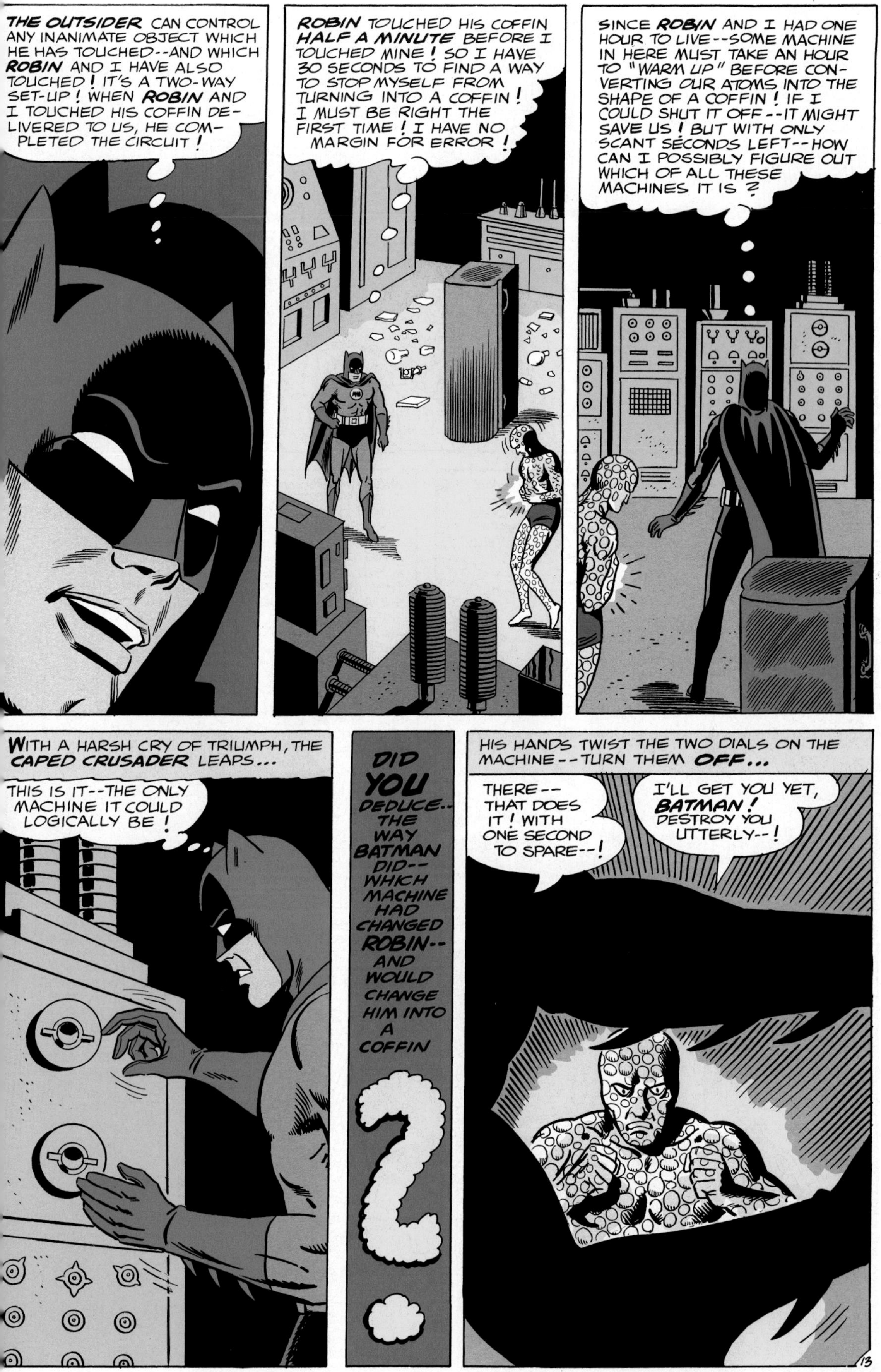
THE OUTSIDER CAN CONTROL ANY INANIMATE OBJECT WHICH HE HAS TOUCHED--AND WHICH ROBIN AND I HAVE ALSO TOUCHED! IT'S A TWO-WAY SET-UP! WHEN ROBIN AND I TOUCHED HIS COFFIN DELIVERED TO US, HE COMPLETED THE CIRCUIT!
ROBIN TOUCHED HIS COFFIN HALF A MINUTE BEFORE I TOUCHED MINE! SO I HAVE 30 SECONDS TO FIND A WAY TO STOP MYSELF FROM TURNING INTO A COFFIN! I MUST BE RIGHT THE FIRST TIME! I HAVE NO MARGIN FOR ERROR!
SINCE ROBIN AND I HAD ONE HOUR TO LIVE--SOME MACHINE IN HERE MUST TAKE AN HOUR TO "WARM UP" BEFORE CONVERTING OUR ATOMS INTO THE SHAPE OF A COFFIN! IF I COULD SHUT IT OFF--IT MIGHT SAVE US! BUT WITH ONLY SCANT SECONDS LEFT--HOW CAN I POSSIBLY FIGURE OUT WHICH OF ALL THESE MACHINES IT IS?
WITH A HARSH CRY OF TRIUMPH, THE CAPED CRUSADER LEAPS...
THIS IS IT--THE ONLY MACHINE IT COULD LOGICALLY BE!
DID YOU DEDUCE.. THE WAY BATMAN DID--WHICH MACHINE HAD CHANGED ROBIN--AND WOULD CHANGE HIM INTO A COFFIN ?
HIS HANDS TWIST THE TWO DIALS ON THE MACHINE--TURN THEM OFF...
THERE--THAT DOES IT! WITH ONE SECOND TO SPARE--!
I'LL GET YOU YET, BATMAN! DESTROY YOU UTTERLY--!
13

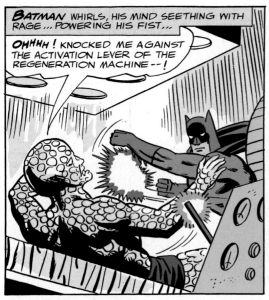

**BATMAN** WHIRLS, HIS MIND SEETHING WITH RAGE...POWERING HIS FIST...

OHHHH! KNOCKED ME AGAINST THE ACTIVATION LEVER OF THE REGENERATION MACHINE--!

REELING BACK BEFORE THE INTENSE FLARE OF THE REGENERATOR MACHINE LIGHTS, THE **CAPED CRUSADER** STARES DOWN AT...

GREAT THUNDER! HIS FACE-- CHANGING UNDER THE LIGHTS-- BECOMING MORE HUMAN-- MORE FAMILIAR...

ALFRED--**YOU** WERE **THE OUTSIDER!** BUT YOUR BODY--IN THE MAUSOLEUM--

PLEASE, SIR--LET ME TALK--TELL YOU WHAT HAPPENED--BEFORE MY MEMORY OF **THE OUTSIDER** COMPLETELY FADES AWAY...

**B**REATHLESSLY THE **EX-OUTSIDER** POURS OUT HIS STORY--AND THEN COLLAPSES WHEN THE CHANGE-OVER TO **ALFRED** IS COMPLETED...

POOR ALFRED! HIS VERY LOVE FOR AND DEVOTION TO **ROBIN** AND MYSELF BECAME WARPED AND TWISTED BY THIS MALEVOLENT MACHINE! BUT HIS STORY SHALL BE MY SECRET-- **ALFRED** MUST NEVER LEARN THE TRUTH!

I SAVED ALFRED-- BUT HAVE I LOST **ROBIN**--?

A MOAN TURNS HIS ATTENTION TO...

OOOOH! I HAD THE PECULIAR FEELING THAT I'D BEEN CHANGED INTO A COFFIN--

YOU **WERE** CHANGED, ROBIN--JUST AS **ALFRED** WAS...

WITH A SOB IN HIS THROAT THE **BOY WONDER** LEAPS FORWARD...

ALFRED?? HERE-- ALIVE?!

YES--BUT HE MUST NEVER KNOW HE WAS **THE OUTSIDER!** I THINK THE NEWS OF HIS TREACHERY MIGHT KILL HIM, SO GREAT WAS HIS DEVOTION TO US! WE'LL HAVE TO COVER UP HIS ABSENCE AS BEST AS WE CAN...

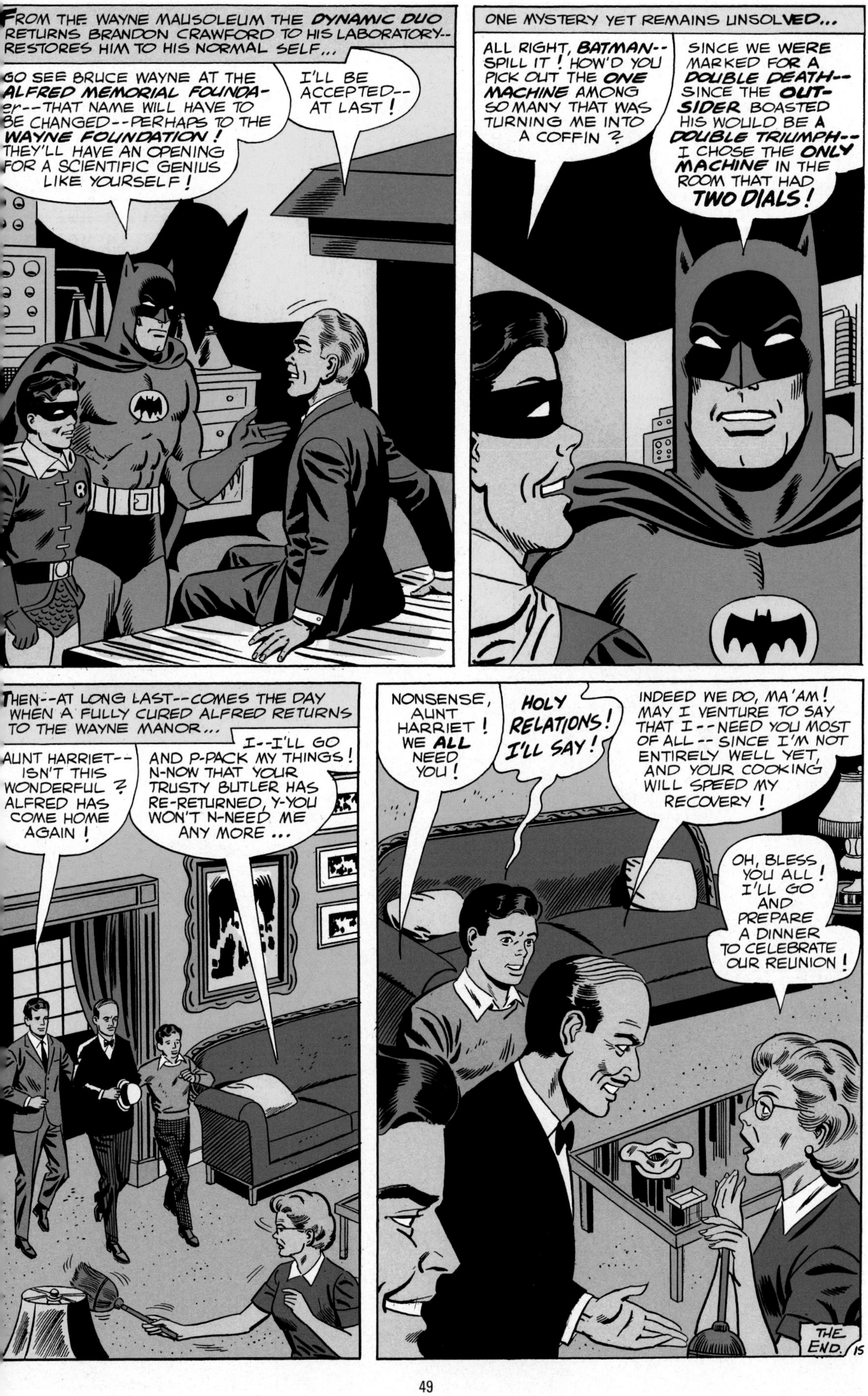

FROM THE WAYNE MAUSOLEUM THE DYNAMIC DUO RETURNS BRANDON CRAWFORD TO HIS LABORATORY--RESTORES HIM TO HIS NORMAL SELF...
GO SEE BRUCE WAYNE AT THE ALFRED MEMORIAL FOUNDA-er--THAT NAME WILL HAVE TO BE CHANGED--PERHAPS TO THE WAYNE FOUNDATION! THEY'LL HAVE AN OPENING FOR A SCIENTIFIC GENIUS LIKE YOURSELF!
I'LL BE ACCEPTED--AT LAST!
ONE MYSTERY YET REMAINS UNSOLVED...
ALL RIGHT, BATMAN--SPILL IT! HOW'D YOU PICK OUT THE ONE MACHINE AMONG SO MANY THAT WAS TURNING ME INTO A COFFIN?
SINCE WE WERE MARKED FOR A DOUBLE DEATH--SINCE THE OUTSIDER BOASTED HIS WOULD BE A DOUBLE TRIUMPH--I CHOSE THE ONLY MACHINE IN THE ROOM THAT HAD TWO DIALS!
THEN--AT LONG LAST--COMES THE DAY WHEN A FULLY CURED ALFRED RETURNS TO THE WAYNE MANOR...
AUNT HARRIET--ISN'T THIS WONDERFUL? ALFRED HAS COME HOME AGAIN!
I--I'LL GO AND P-PACK MY THINGS! N-NOW THAT YOUR TRUSTY BUTLER HAS RE-RETURNED, Y-YOU WON'T N-NEED ME ANY MORE...
NONSENSE, AUNT HARRIET! WE ALL NEED YOU!
HOLY RELATIONS! I'LL SAY!
INDEED WE DO, MA'AM! MAY I VENTURE TO SAY THAT I--NEED YOU MOST OF ALL--SINCE I'M NOT ENTIRELY WELL YET, AND YOUR COOKING WILL SPEED MY RECOVERY!
OH, BLESS YOU ALL! I'LL GO AND PREPARE A DINNER TO CELEBRATE OUR REUNION!
THE END.
15

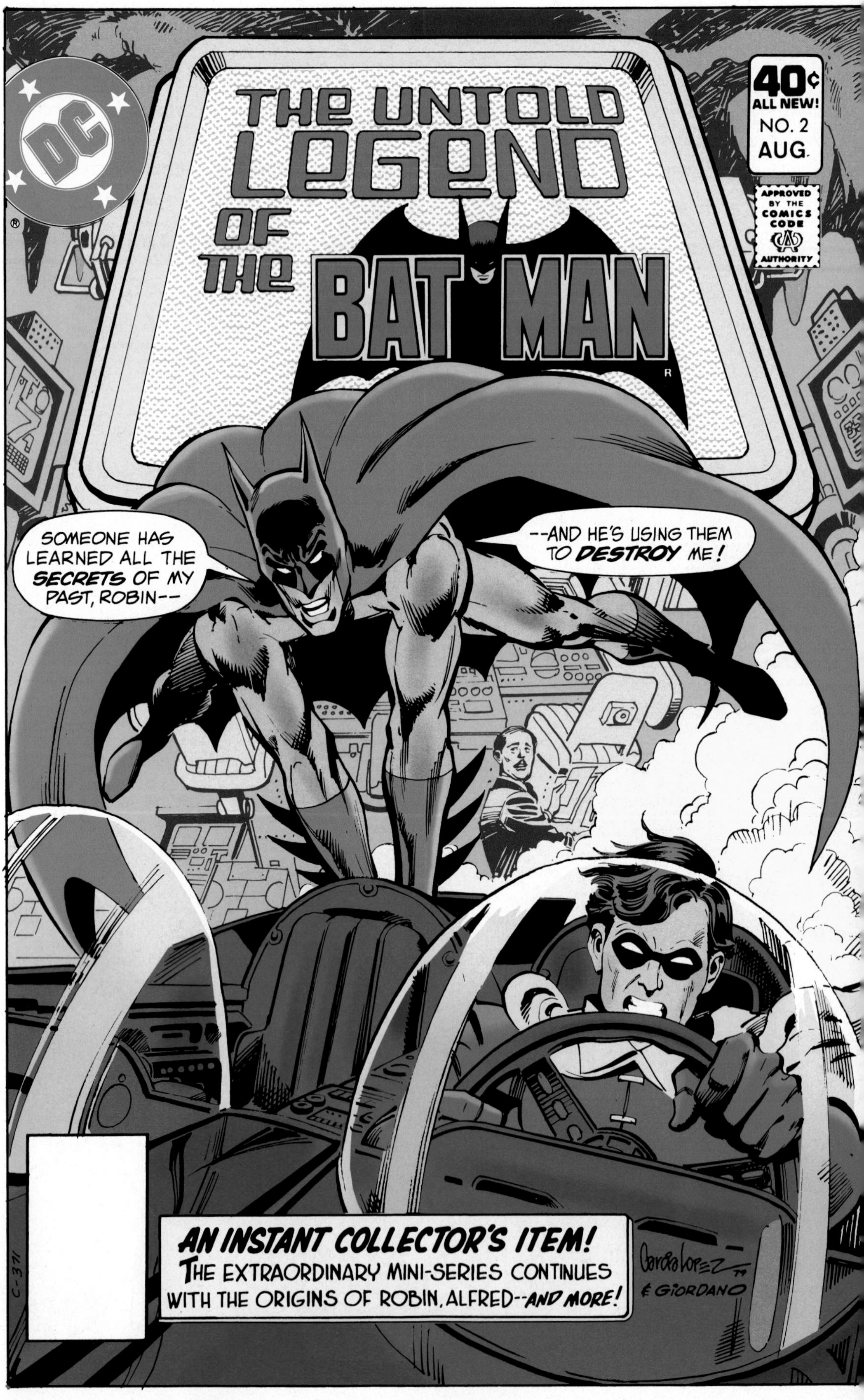
THE UNTOLD LEGEND OF THE BATMAN
40¢
ALL NEW!
NO. 2
AUG.
APPROVED BY THE COMICS CODE AUTHORITY
SOMEONE HAS LEARNED ALL THE SECRETS OF MY PAST, ROBIN--
--AND HE'S USING THEM TO DESTROY ME!
AN INSTANT COLLECTOR'S ITEM!
THE EXTRAORDINARY MINI-SERIES CONTINUES WITH THE ORIGINS OF ROBIN, ALFRED--AND MORE!
Garcia Lopez '79
& GIORDANO
C-371

FOR YEARS, IT HAS BEEN *WHISPERED* -- IN THE DARK DENS OF THE *WICKED* -- IN THE BRIGHT HALLS OF THE *JUST!* NOW, AT LAST, IT CAN BE *TOLD*...

The *UNTOLD LEGEND* OF THE BAT MAN

CREATED BY BOB KANE

YOU CAN ALMOST *SEE* THE AIR HERE, DIRTY GREY WITH *CIGARETTE SMOKE*, AND THICK WITH THE SMELL OF THE *SEA*...

THE BAR IS CALLED *THE LAST RESORT*, A GATHERING PLACE FOR THOSE WITH *NOWHERE ELSE TO GO* -- AND IT HAS BEEN A *SAFE HAVEN* FOR THOSE WHO SKIRT THE EDGES OF THE *LAW*...

...THAT IS, UNTIL *TONIGHT!*

*CRIPES* -- IT'S *HIM!*

WHAT IN BLAZES IS *HE* DOIN' *HERE?*

"WITH FRIENDS LIKE THESE..."

LEN WEIN | JIM APARO | GLYNIS WEIN | PAUL LEVITZ | WITH THANKS TO ALL THOSE WHO
WRITER | ARTIST | COLORIST | EDITOR | WALKED THIS PATH *BEFORE* US!

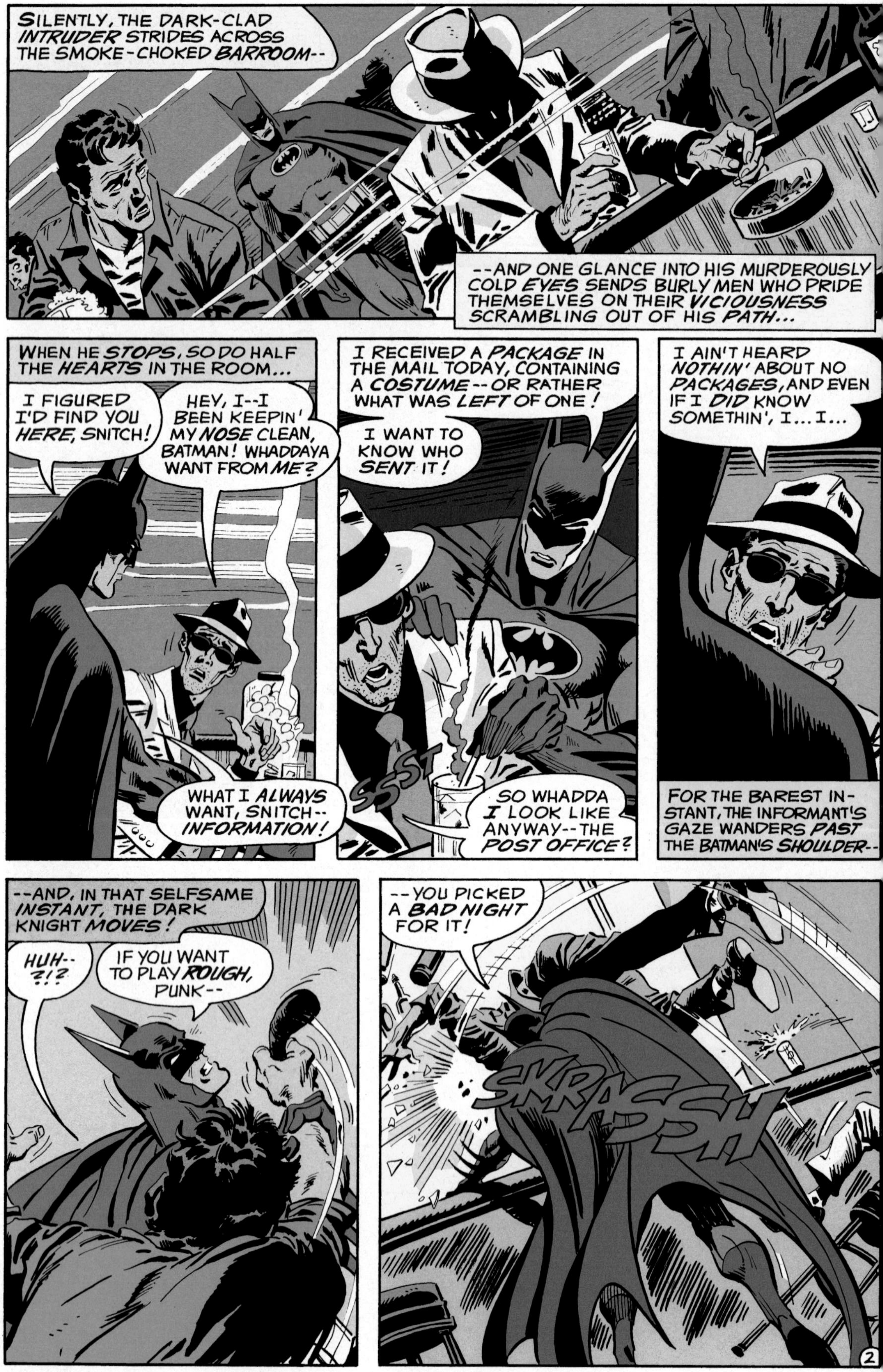
SILENTLY, THE DARK-CLAD INTRUDER STRIDES ACROSS THE SMOKE-CHOKED BARROOM--
--AND ONE GLANCE INTO HIS MURDEROUSLY COLD EYES SENDS BURLY MEN WHO PRIDE THEMSELVES ON THEIR VICIOUSNESS SCRAMBLING OUT OF HIS PATH...
WHEN HE STOPS, SO DO HALF THE HEARTS IN THE ROOM...
I FIGURED I'D FIND YOU HERE, SNITCH!
HEY, I--I BEEN KEEPIN' MY NOSE CLEAN, BATMAN! WHADDAYA WANT FROM ME?
WHAT I ALWAYS WANT, SNITCH-- INFORMATION!
I RECEIVED A PACKAGE IN THE MAIL TODAY, CONTAINING A COSTUME--OR RATHER WHAT WAS LEFT OF ONE!
I WANT TO KNOW WHO SENT IT!
SSSST
SO WHADDA I LOOK LIKE ANYWAY--THE POST OFFICE?
I AIN'T HEARD NOTHIN' ABOUT NO PACKAGES, AND EVEN IF I DID KNOW SOMETHIN', I... I...
FOR THE BAREST INSTANT, THE INFORMANT'S GAZE WANDERS PAST THE BATMAN'S SHOULDER--
--AND, IN THAT SELFSAME INSTANT, THE DARK KNIGHT MOVES!
HUH-- ?!?
IF YOU WANT TO PLAY ROUGH, PUNK--
--YOU PICKED A BAD NIGHT FOR IT!
SKRASSH
2

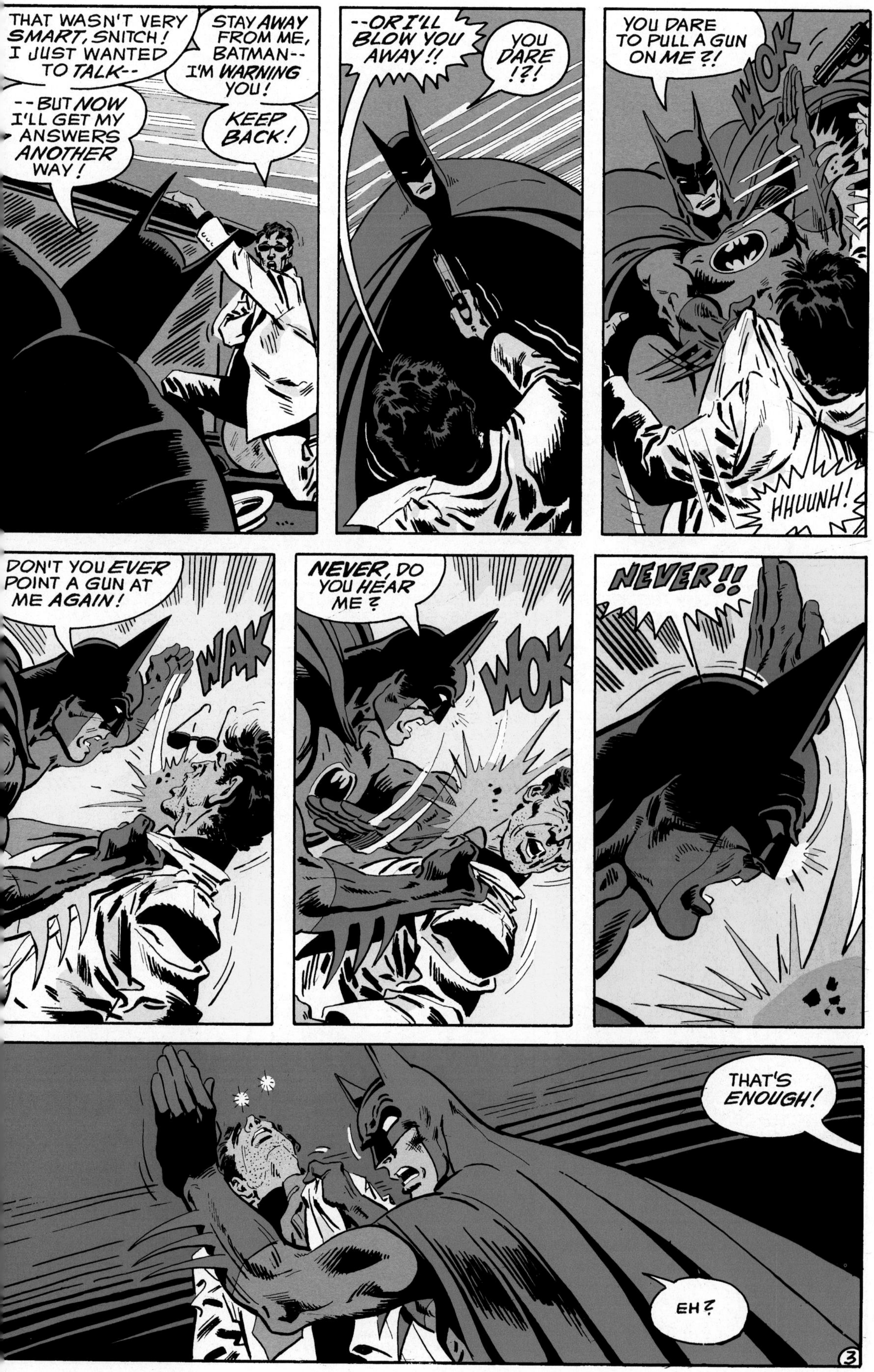
THAT WASN'T VERY SMART, SNITCH! I JUST WANTED TO TALK--
STAY AWAY FROM ME, BATMAN-- I'M WARNING YOU!
--BUT NOW I'LL GET MY ANSWERS ANOTHER WAY!
KEEP BACK!
--OR I'LL BLOW YOU AWAY!!
YOU DARE !?!
YOU DARE TO PULL A GUN ON ME ?!
WOK
HHUUNH!
DON'T YOU EVER POINT A GUN AT ME AGAIN!
WAK
NEVER, DO YOU HEAR ME?
WOK
NEVER!!
THAT'S ENOUGH!
EH?
3

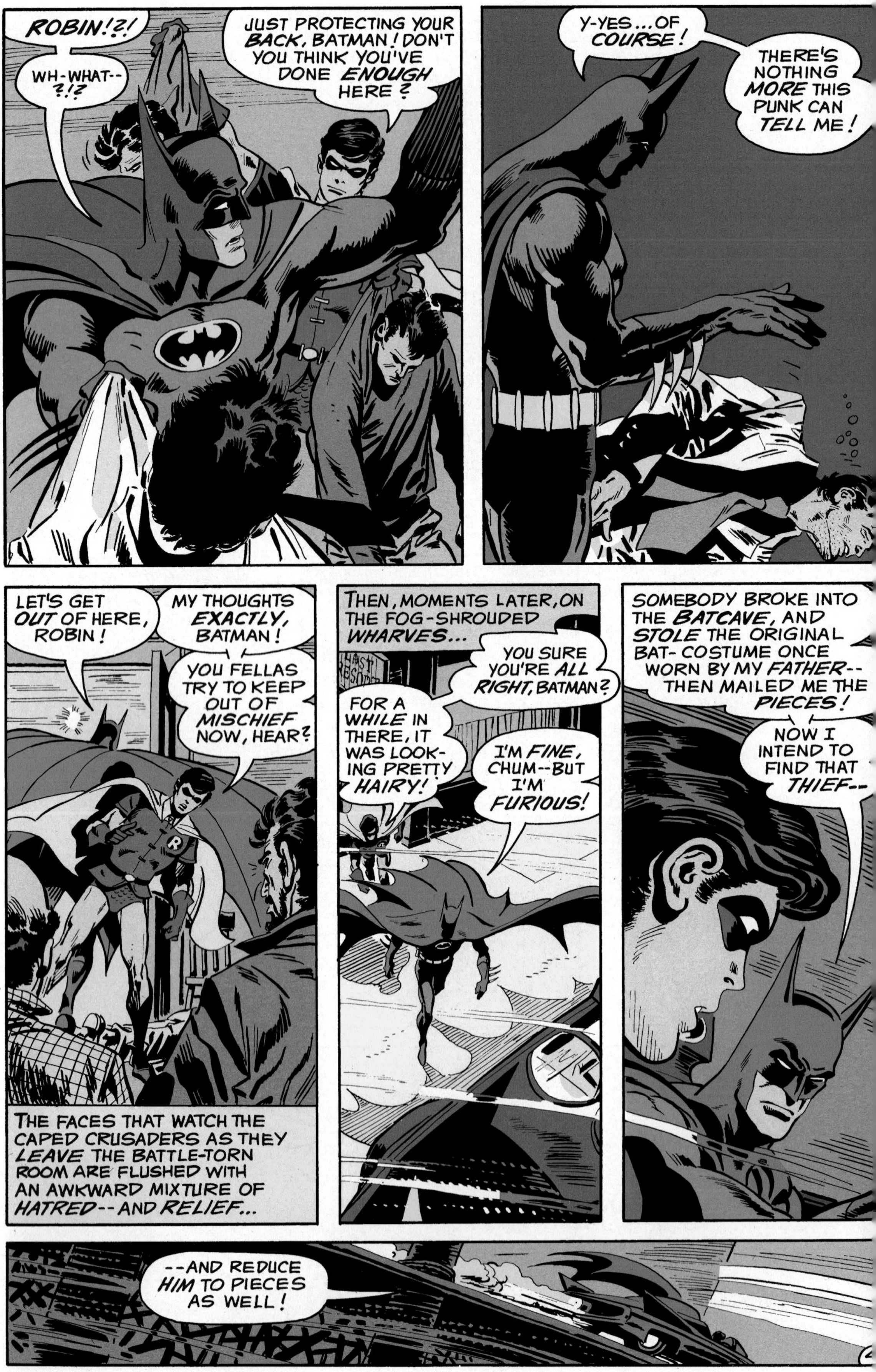
ROBIN!?!
WH-WHAT-- ?!?
JUST PROTECTING YOUR BACK, BATMAN! DON'T YOU THINK YOU'VE DONE ENOUGH HERE?
Y-YES...OF COURSE!
THERE'S NOTHING MORE THIS PUNK CAN TELL ME!
LET'S GET OUT OF HERE, ROBIN!
MY THOUGHTS EXACTLY, BATMAN!
YOU FELLAS TRY TO KEEP OUT OF MISCHIEF NOW, HEAR?
THE FACES THAT WATCH THE CAPED CRUSADERS AS THEY LEAVE THE BATTLE-TORN ROOM ARE FLUSHED WITH AN AWKWARD MIXTURE OF HATRED--AND RELIEF...
THEN, MOMENTS LATER, ON THE FOG-SHROUDED WHARVES...
YOU SURE YOU'RE ALL RIGHT, BATMAN?
FOR A WHILE IN THERE, IT WAS LOOKING PRETTY HAIRY!
I'M FINE, CHUM--BUT I'M FURIOUS!
SOMEBODY BROKE INTO THE BATCAVE, AND STOLE THE ORIGINAL BAT-COSTUME ONCE WORN BY MY FATHER--THEN MAILED ME THE PIECES!
NOW I INTEND TO FIND THAT THIEF--
--AND REDUCE HIM TO PIECES AS WELL!

AND AS THE POWERFUL *BATMOBILE* ROARS THROUGH THE WINDING STREETS OF *GOTHAM CITY...*

HE'S TAKING THIS *HARD*--AND I CAN UNDERSTAND *WHY!* HE AND I ARE SO MUCH *ALIKE* IN SO MANY WAYS...

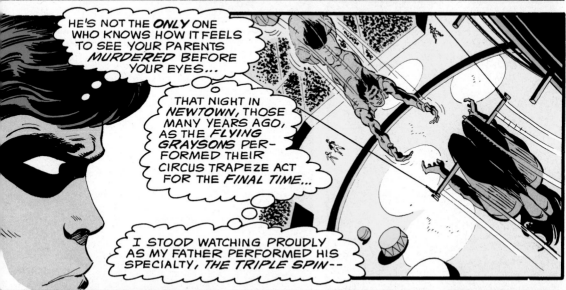

HE'S NOT THE *ONLY* ONE WHO KNOWS HOW IT FEELS TO SEE YOUR PARENTS *MURDERED* BEFORE YOUR EYES...

THAT NIGHT IN *NEWTOWN*, THOSE MANY YEARS AGO, AS THE *FLYING GRAYSONS* PER-FORMED THEIR CIRCUS TRAPEZE ACT FOR THE *FINAL TIME...*

I STOOD WATCHING PROUDLY AS MY FATHER PERFORMED HIS SPECIALTY, *THE TRIPLE SPIN*--

"--BUT MY HEART STOPPED IN MY CHEST AS THE TRAPEZE SUPPORTING MY PARENTS SUDDENLY *SNAPPED*--

"--SENDING THEM *PLUNGING* TO THE SAWDUST SO VERY FAR *BELOW!*"

MOM! DAD!

OH NO-- *NO!!*

LET ME *THROUGH!* THEY'RE *NOT*--

I'M AFRAID THEY *ARE*, SON! FOR YOUR OWN SAKE, STAY *BACK!*

THERE'S NOTHING MORE YOU CAN *DO* FOR THEM-- EXCEPT *MOURN!*

"MY PARENTS WERE *GONE*, AND FOR THE FIRST TIME IN MY LIFE, I WAS *ALONE*--

"--SO TERRIBLY, TERRIBLY *ALONE!*"

5

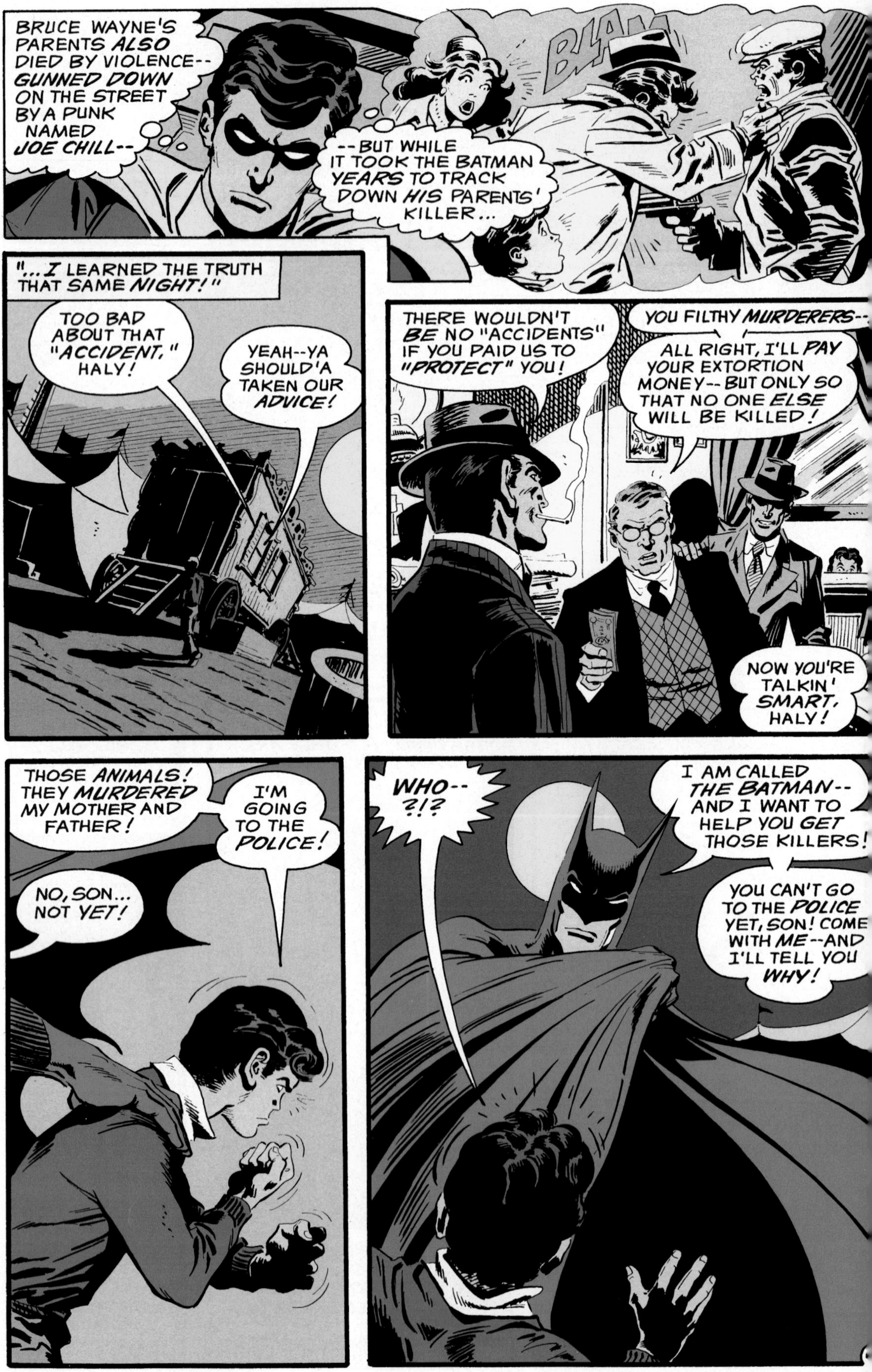
BRUCE WAYNE'S PARENTS ALSO DIED BY VIOLENCE-- GUNNED DOWN ON THE STREET BY A PUNK NAMED JOE CHILL--
BLAM
--BUT WHILE IT TOOK THE BATMAN YEARS TO TRACK DOWN HIS PARENTS' KILLER...
"...I LEARNED THE TRUTH THAT SAME NIGHT!"
TOO BAD ABOUT THAT "ACCIDENT," HALY!
YEAH--YA SHOULD'A TAKEN OUR ADVICE!
THERE WOULDN'T BE NO "ACCIDENTS" IF YOU PAID US TO "PROTECT" YOU!
YOU FILTHY MURDERERS--
ALL RIGHT, I'LL PAY YOUR EXTORTION MONEY-- BUT ONLY SO THAT NO ONE ELSE WILL BE KILLED!
NOW YOU'RE TALKIN' SMART, HALY!
THOSE ANIMALS! THEY MURDERED MY MOTHER AND FATHER!
I'M GOING TO THE POLICE!
NO, SON... NOT YET!
WHO-- ?!?
I AM CALLED THE BATMAN-- AND I WANT TO HELP YOU GET THOSE KILLERS!
YOU CAN'T GO TO THE POLICE YET, SON! COME WITH ME--AND I'LL TELL YOU WHY!

"I DON'T KNOW *WHY* I TRUSTED HIM THEN, THIS TERRIFYING FIGURE, LIKE SOMETHING OUT OF A *NIGHTMARE* -- BUT THERE WAS SOMETHING IN HIS *EYES*, SOMETHING IN THE TONE OF HIS *VOICE*..."

"HE LED ME TO A TANK-LIKE MACHINE HE CALLED THE *BATMOBILE*, AND SOON AFTER, ON A LONELY COUNTRY *ROAD*..."

OKAY -- WHY *CAN'T* I TELL THE POLICE?

BECAUSE THIS ENTIRE *TOWN* IS RUN BY A MAN CALLED *"BOSS"* ZUCCO, SON! IF YOU *TALKED*, YOU'D BE *DEAD* WITHIN THE HOUR!

I'M TAKING YOU TO *SAFETY* -- UNTIL I GET ENOUGH EVIDENCE TO *NAIL* ZUCCO!

I HAVE A *SPECIAL* INTEREST IN YOU -- BECAUSE MY *OWN* PARENTS WERE ALSO KILLED BY A *CRIMINAL!*

THAT'S WHY I'VE DEDICATED MY *LIFE* TO FIGHTING CRIME!

THEN *HELP* ME! GIVE ME A CHANCE TO *AVENGE* MY PARENTS!

"I KEPT *PLEADING* WITH HIM, *BEGGING* -- AND SOMETHING IN MY *VOICE* MUST HAVE TOUCHED SOMETHING IN THE BATMAN'S *SOUL*..."

ALL RIGHT, DICK -- I'LL GIVE YOU A *CHANCE!* BUT I *WARN* YOU -- I LEAD A *PERILOUS* LIFE!

I'M NOT *AFRAID!*

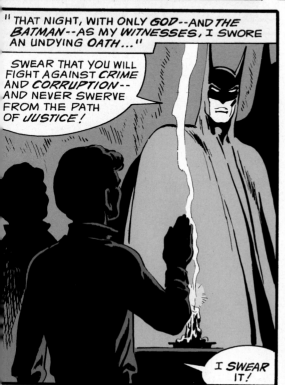

"THAT NIGHT, WITH ONLY *GOD* -- AND *THE BATMAN* -- AS MY *WITNESSES*, I SWORE AN UNDYING *OATH*..."

SWEAR THAT YOU WILL FIGHT AGAINST *CRIME* AND *CORRUPTION* -- AND NEVER SWERVE FROM THE PATH OF *JUSTICE!*

I SWEAR IT!

"AND THE FOLLOWING DAY, IN A GOTHAM CITY *COURTHOUSE*..."

I CAN'T LET YOU *ADOPT* THE BOY, MR. WAYNE -- BECAUSE YOU'RE A *BACHELOR!*

BUT SINCE YOU'VE OBTAINED THE CONSENT OF HIS NEAREST RELATIVES, I HEARBY APPOINT YOU *DICK GRAYSON'S* LEGAL GUARDIAN!

7

"AS SIMPLY AS *THAT*, A LIFE-LONG *BOND* WAS FORMED BETWEEN US--AND MY *TRAINING* FOR MY CHOSEN CAREER BEGAN IN *EARNEST*...

"ACROBATICS... CRIMINOLOGY... THE MARTIAL ARTS... I LEARNED ALL THAT I *NEEDED* TO KNOW--

"--AND *THEN SOME!*

"AND, FINALLY, AFTER MONTHS OF EXHAUSTIVE *EFFORT*..."

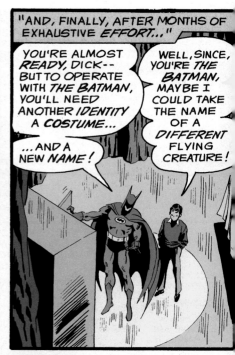

YOU'RE ALMOST *READY*, DICK-- BUT TO OPERATE WITH *THE BATMAN*, YOU'LL NEED ANOTHER *IDENTITY* A COSTUME...

... AND A NEW *NAME!*

WELL, SINCE, YOU'RE *THE BATMAN*, MAYBE I COULD TAKE THE NAME OF A *DIFFERENT* FLYING CREATURE!

I WAS THINKING PRECISELY THE SAME *THING!* HOW DO YOU LIKE THE NAME...

...*ROBIN!*

IT'S *PERFECT!* THE LEGENDARY *ROBIN HOOD* WAS ALWAYS ONE OF MY FAVORITE *HEROES!*

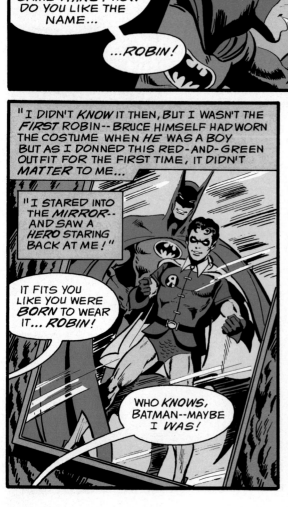

"I DIDN'T *KNOW* IT THEN, BUT I WASN'T THE *FIRST* ROBIN--BRUCE HIMSELF HAD WORN THE COSTUME WHEN *HE* WAS A BOY BUT AS I DONNED THIS RED-AND-GREEN OUTFIT FOR THE FIRST TIME, IT DIDN'T *MATTER* TO ME...

"I STARED INTO THE *MIRROR*-- AND SAW A *HERO* STARING BACK AT ME!"

IT FITS YOU LIKE YOU WERE *BORN* TO WEAR IT... *ROBIN!*

WHO *KNOWS*, BATMAN--MAYBE I *WAS!*

"24 HOURS LATER, WE WERE BACK IN *NEWTOWN*, ON THE TRAIL OF *"BOSS" ZUCCO*--SO WE WERE *THERE* WHEN THE MOBSTER *MURDERED* HIS OWN HENCHMAN...

"...AND *I* TOOK THE PHOTO THAT SENT ZUCCO TO THE *ELECTRIC CHAIR!*

KLIK

B

"BUT IF BEING THE *SIDEKICK* OF THE LEGENDARY *BATMAN* WAS LIKE A *DREAM COME TRUE*, BEING THE *WARD* OF MILLIONAIRE PLAYBOY *BRUCE WAYNE* WAS SOMETIMES MORE LIKE A *NIGHTMARE...*

"AT *PARTIES*, FOR EXAMPLE, I WAS LOOKED ON AS SOME KIND OF *PET...*"

OH, AREN'T YOU JUST THE *CUTEST* LITTLE THING?

SHAME ON YOU, BRUCIE-- FOR NOT INTRODUCING US TO THIS ANGEL SOONER!

"AND, AT *SCHOOL*, IT WAS EVEN *WORSE...*"

YOUR OLD MAN'S *MONEY* CAN'T BUY YA OUTTA *THIS* ONE, RICH BOY!

YOU GONNA PUT UP YER *DUKES*-- OR ARE YA TOO *CHICKEN*?

LEAVE ME *ALONE*, WALLY-- --I *CAN'T* FIGHT YOU!

CHICKEN... CHICKEN... GRAYSON IS A CHICKEN...

HA HA HA

THEY'RE *WRONG*-- THEY DON'T KNOW *HOW* WRONG! I JUST *COULDN'T* FIGHT WALLY--

--NOT WHEN I COULD *CRIPPLE* HIM WITH BOTH HANDS TIED BEHIND MY *BACK!*

HA HA

WHY? WHY DO THEY MAKE IT SO *HARD?* WHY DON'T THEY *UNDERSTAND?*

WHY CAN'T I JUST BE LIKE EVERY- ONE *ELSE?*

"BUT I *WASN'T* LIKE EVERYONE ELSE -- AND I *KNEW* IT!"

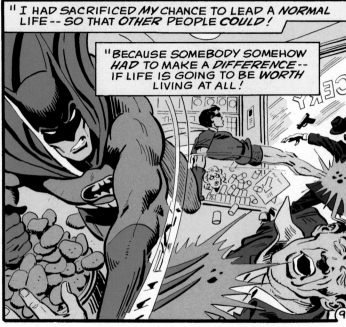

" I HAD SACRIFICED *MY* CHANCE TO LEAD A *NORMAL* LIFE -- SO THAT *OTHER* PEOPLE *COULD!*

"BECAUSE SOMEBODY SOMEHOW *HAD* TO MAKE A *DIFFERENCE* -- IF LIFE IS GOING TO BE *WORTH* LIVING AT ALL!"

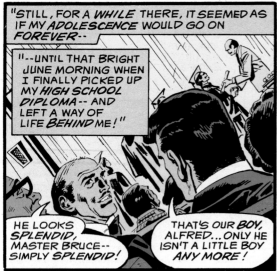

"STILL, FOR A *WHILE* THERE, IT SEEMED AS IF MY *ADOLESCENCE* WOULD GO ON *FOREVER*--

"--UNTIL THAT BRIGHT *JUNE* MORNING WHEN I FINALLY PICKED UP MY *HIGH SCHOOL DIPLOMA*-- AND LEFT A WAY OF LIFE *BEHIND* ME!"

HE LOOKS *SPLENDID*, MASTER BRUCE-- SIMPLY *SPLENDID*!

THAT'S OUR *BOY*, ALFRED...ONLY HE ISN'T A LITTLE BOY *ANY MORE*!

"THAT FALL, I LEFT WAYNE MANOR FOR *HUDSON UNIVERSITY*-- AND THAT SPRAWLING OLD MANSION SUDDENLY CEASED TO BE A *HOME*..."

THIS PLACE IS TOO *BIG* FOR JUST THE *TWO* OF US, ALFRED-- IT'S TIME FOR A *CHANGE*!

"WITHIN THE WEEK, BRUCE HAD *CLOSED* WAYNE MANOR --AND MOVED LOCK, STOCK, AND ALFRED INTO THE *PENTHOUSE* CROWNING THE OFFICES OF THE *WAYNE FOUNDATION*..."

ONCE AGAIN, THE *BATMAN* BECAME A VITAL *PART* OF THE CITY THAT HE *LOVED*!

THE *DARKNIGHT AVENGER* HAD FINALLY COME *HOME*!

FOR A MOMENT THE TEEN WONDER *PAUSES* IN HIS REVERIE, AS THE SLEEK BATMOBILE SLIPS *UNSEEN* INTO THE SECLUDED CUL-DE-SAC CALLED *FINGER ALLEY*--

--THEN ALONG A HIDDEN *TUNNEL*--

--WHICH LEADS TO THE SPRAWLING *BATCAVE* HIDDEN BENEATH THE TOWERING *WAYNE FOUNDATION BUILDING*...

WELCOME *HOME*, SIRS!

WOULD YOU CARE FOR SOMETHING TO *DRINK*?

SKREEEEEE

10

NOT *NOW*, ALFRED -- I'M *BUSY*!

AS YOU *WISH*, SIR!

MASTER DICK, PERHAPS *YOU*--?

I'LL TAKE A *DR. PEPPER*, ALFRED -- IF YOU'VE *GOT* ONE!

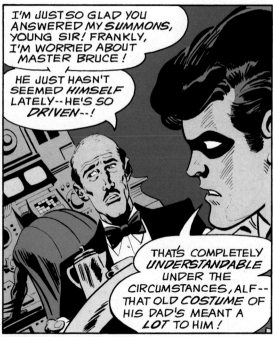

I'M JUST SO GLAD YOU ANSWERED MY *SUMMONS*, YOUNG SIR! FRANKLY, I'M WORRIED ABOUT MASTER BRUCE!

HE JUST HASN'T SEEMED *HIMSELF* LATELY -- HE'S SO *DRIVEN*--!

THAT'S COMPLETELY *UNDERSTANDABLE* UNDER THE CIRCUMSTANCES, ALF -- THAT OLD *COSTUME* OF HIS DAD'S MEANT A *LOT* TO HIM!

BUT THERE'S *MORE* TO IT THAN THAT, YOUNG *ROBIN*! EVER SINCE THAT *WAREHOUSE EXPLOSION* A FEW DAYS PAST, MASTER BRUCE HAS BEEN A *DIFFERENT MAN*--

--AS IF HE'S SUDDENLY REALIZED HIS OWN *MORTALITY*, AND IS STRUGGLING TO *DENY* IT!

I KNOW WHAT YOU *MEAN*, ALFRED -- I SAW AN *EXAMPLE* OF IT A LITTLE BIT *EARLIER* TONIGHT!

I GUESS THAT'S THE *MAJOR* DIFFERENCE BETWEEN ME AND BRUCE -- TO *ME*, CRIME-FIGHTING HAS ALWAYS BEEN AN *ADVENTURE* -- BUT TO *HIM*, IT'S A *HOLY MISSION*!

STILL, I SUPPOSE YOU CAN'T REALLY *BLAME* THE MAN! HE'S KNOWN A LOT OF *PAIN* IN HIS LIFE!

SO HAVE WE *ALL*, MASTER ROBIN... SO HAVE WE *ALL*!

11

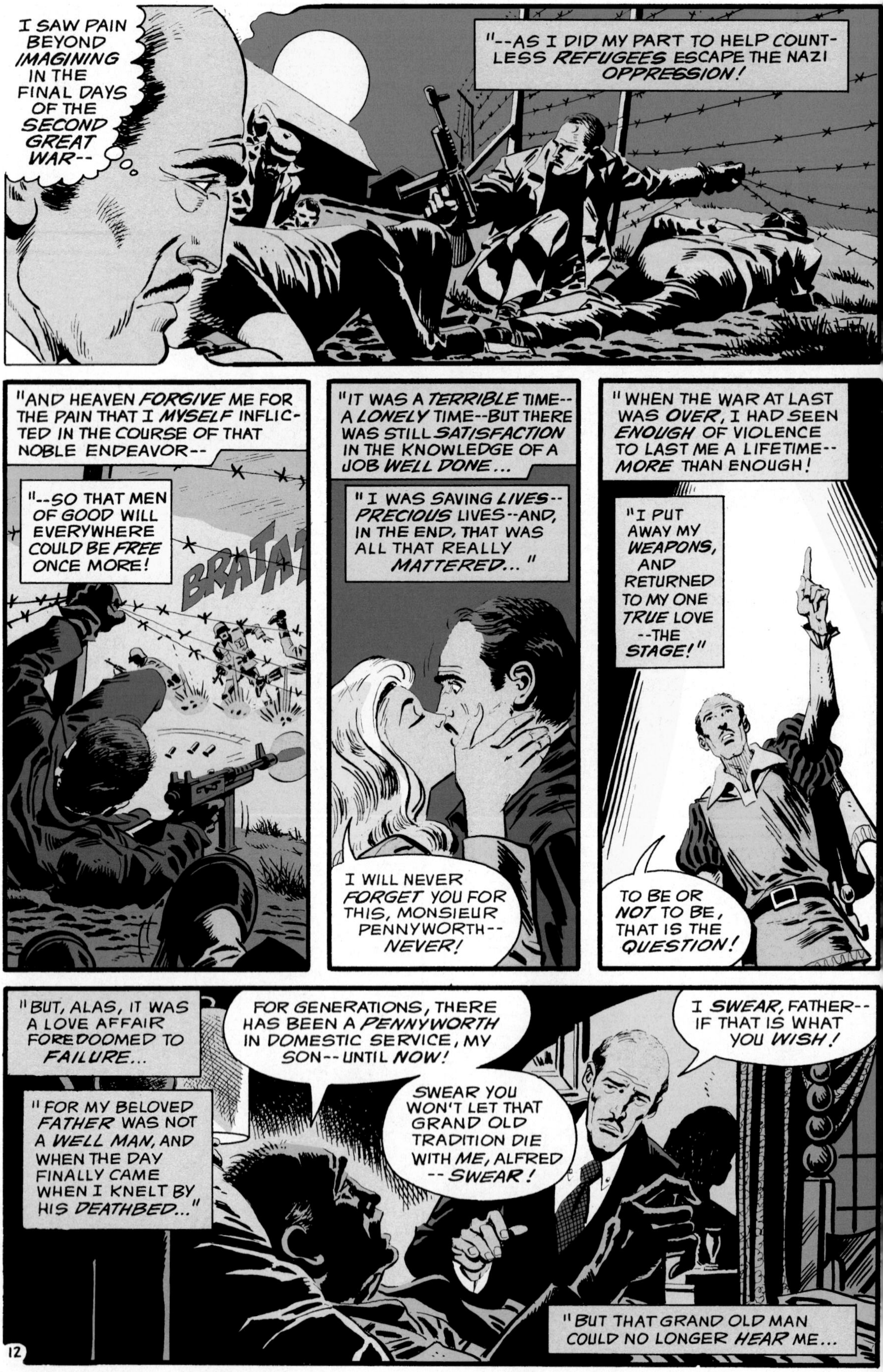

I SAW PAIN BEYOND IMAGINING IN THE FINAL DAYS OF THE SECOND GREAT WAR--
"--AS I DID MY PART TO HELP COUNTLESS REFUGEES ESCAPE THE NAZI OPPRESSION!
"AND HEAVEN FORGIVE ME FOR THE PAIN THAT I MYSELF INFLICTED IN THE COURSE OF THAT NOBLE ENDEAVOR--
"--SO THAT MEN OF GOOD WILL EVERYWHERE COULD BE FREE ONCE MORE!
BRATAT
"IT WAS A TERRIBLE TIME-- A LONELY TIME--BUT THERE WAS STILL SATISFACTION IN THE KNOWLEDGE OF A JOB WELL DONE...
"I WAS SAVING LIVES-- PRECIOUS LIVES--AND, IN THE END, THAT WAS ALL THAT REALLY MATTERED..."
I WILL NEVER FORGET YOU FOR THIS, MONSIEUR PENNYWORTH-- NEVER!
"WHEN THE WAR AT LAST WAS OVER, I HAD SEEN ENOUGH OF VIOLENCE TO LAST ME A LIFETIME-- MORE THAN ENOUGH!
"I PUT AWAY MY WEAPONS, AND RETURNED TO MY ONE TRUE LOVE --THE STAGE!"
TO BE OR NOT TO BE, THAT IS THE QUESTION!
"BUT, ALAS, IT WAS A LOVE AFFAIR FOREDOOMED TO FAILURE...
"FOR MY BELOVED FATHER WAS NOT A WELL MAN, AND WHEN THE DAY FINALLY CAME WHEN I KNELT BY HIS DEATHBED..."
FOR GENERATIONS, THERE HAS BEEN A PENNYWORTH IN DOMESTIC SERVICE, MY SON-- UNTIL NOW!
SWEAR YOU WON'T LET THAT GRAND OLD TRADITION DIE WITH ME, ALFRED --SWEAR!
I SWEAR, FATHER-- IF THAT IS WHAT YOU WISH!
"BUT THAT GRAND OLD MAN COULD NO LONGER HEAR ME...
12

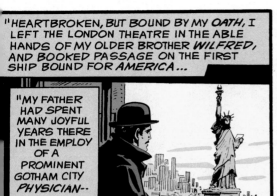

"HEARTBROKEN, BUT BOUND BY MY *OATH*, I LEFT THE LONDON THEATRE IN THE ABLE HANDS OF MY OLDER BROTHER *WILFRED*, AND BOOKED PASSAGE ON THE FIRST SHIP BOUND FOR *AMERICA*..."

"MY FATHER HAD SPENT MANY JOYFUL YEARS THERE IN THE EMPLOY OF A PROMINENT GOTHAM CITY *PHYSICIAN*--"

"--AND, ASSUMING HIS *HEIR* MIGHT WELL HAVE *NEED* OF ME, I MADE MY WAY DIRECTLY TO *WAYNE MANOR*..."

GOOD EVENING, GENTLEMEN! I TRUST I HAVEN'T *DISTURBED* YOU!

HUH--?!?

I'LL JUST SET MY LUGGAGE *DOWN*, IF YOU'LL PERMIT ME-- AND THEN WE CAN DISCUSS MY *DUTIES!*

NOW WAIT JUST ONE *MINUTE!* EXACTLY WHAT CAN I *DO* FOR YOU, MISTER--?

YOU MAY CALL ME *ALFRED*, WITHOUT THE *"MISTER"*-- AND IT IS *I* WHO WILL DO FOR *YOU*, SIR! I TRUST YOU'LL FIND MY *REFERENCES* IN GOOD ORDER!

YOU SEE-- I'M YOUR NEW *BUTLER!*

*BUTLER?* BUT I HAVEN'T HAD ONE IN *YEARS!* I DIDN'T *SEND* FOR ONE-- AND I'M AFRAID I DON'T REALLY *WANT* ONE!

WE'VE FOUND WE CAN GET ALONG BETTER *WITHOUT* SERVANTS OF *ANY* KIND!

IT MAY BE A BIT *AWKWARD* AT FIRST, SIR--BUT I DARE SAY YOU'LL GET *USED* TO ME!

MY FATHER FAITHFULLY SERVED *YOUR* FATHER-- AND NOW *I* SHALL SERVE *YOU!* IT'S THE WAY OF THE *WORLD*, SIR!

*BREAKFAST* SHALL BE SERVED PROMPTLY AT *SEVEN!* I WOULD APPRECIATE *PUNCTUALITY!*

GOOD EVENING, SIRS -- I SHALL FIND MY OWN WAY TO MY *ROOM!*

BUT... BUT...BUT...

13

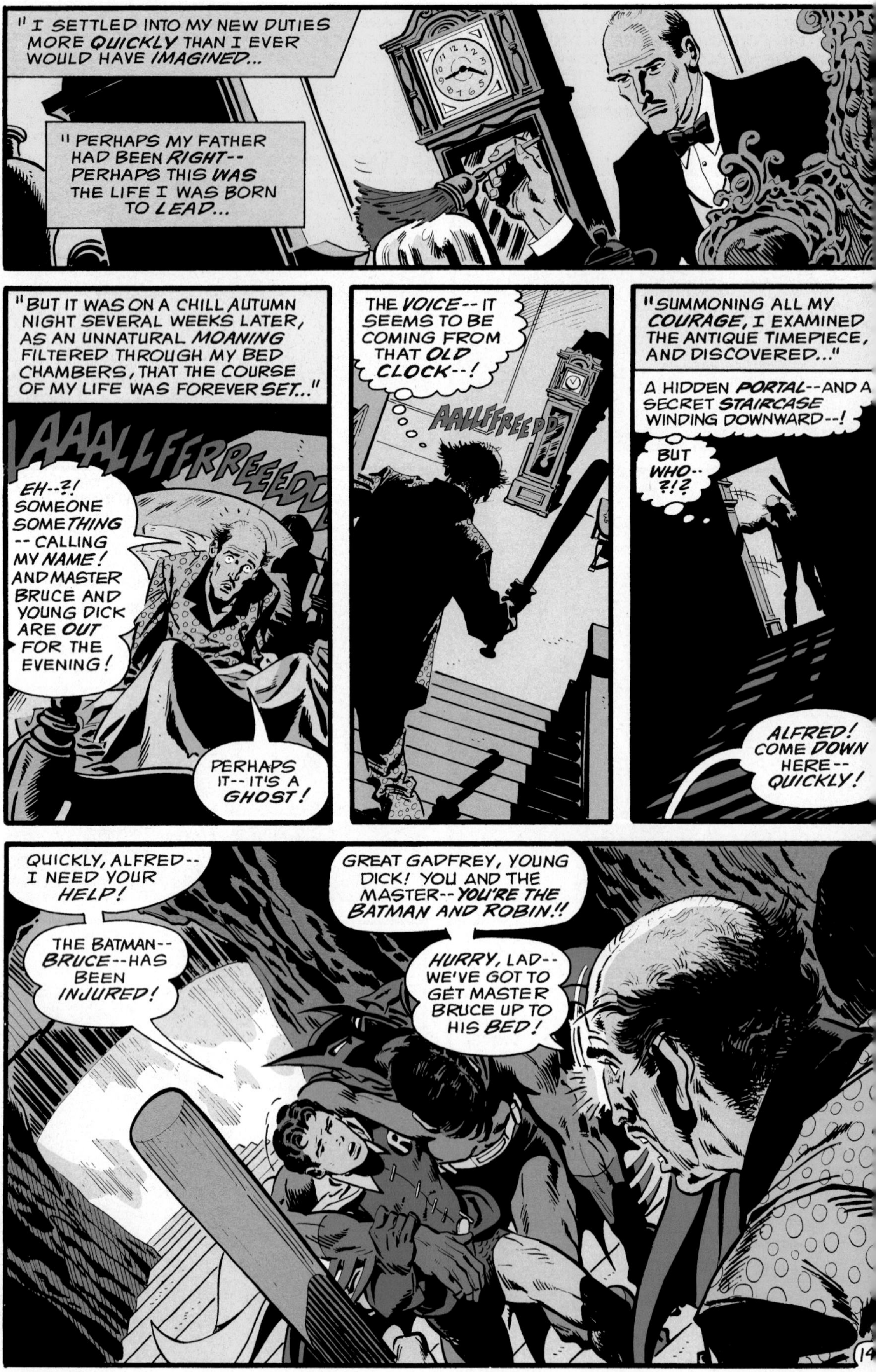
"I SETTLED INTO MY NEW DUTIES MORE QUICKLY THAN I EVER WOULD HAVE IMAGINED...
"PERHAPS MY FATHER HAD BEEN RIGHT-- PERHAPS THIS WAS THE LIFE I WAS BORN TO LEAD...
"BUT IT WAS ON A CHILL AUTUMN NIGHT SEVERAL WEEKS LATER, AS AN UNNATURAL MOANING FILTERED THROUGH MY BED CHAMBERS, THAT THE COURSE OF MY LIFE WAS FOREVER SET..."
AAAALLFFRREEEDD
EH--?! SOMEONE SOMETHING -- CALLING MY NAME! AND MASTER BRUCE AND YOUNG DICK ARE OUT FOR THE EVENING!
PERHAPS IT-- IT'S A GHOST!
THE VOICE-- IT SEEMS TO BE COMING FROM THAT OLD CLOCK--!
AALLFFREEDD
"SUMMONING ALL MY COURAGE, I EXAMINED THE ANTIQUE TIMEPIECE, AND DISCOVERED..."
A HIDDEN PORTAL--AND A SECRET STAIRCASE WINDING DOWNWARD--!
BUT WHO-- ?!?
ALFRED! COME DOWN HERE-- QUICKLY!
QUICKLY, ALFRED-- I NEED YOUR HELP!
THE BATMAN-- BRUCE--HAS BEEN INJURED!
GREAT GADFREY, YOUNG DICK! YOU AND THE MASTER-- YOU'RE THE BATMAN AND ROBIN!!
HURRY, LAD-- WE'VE GOT TO GET MASTER BRUCE UP TO HIS BED!
14

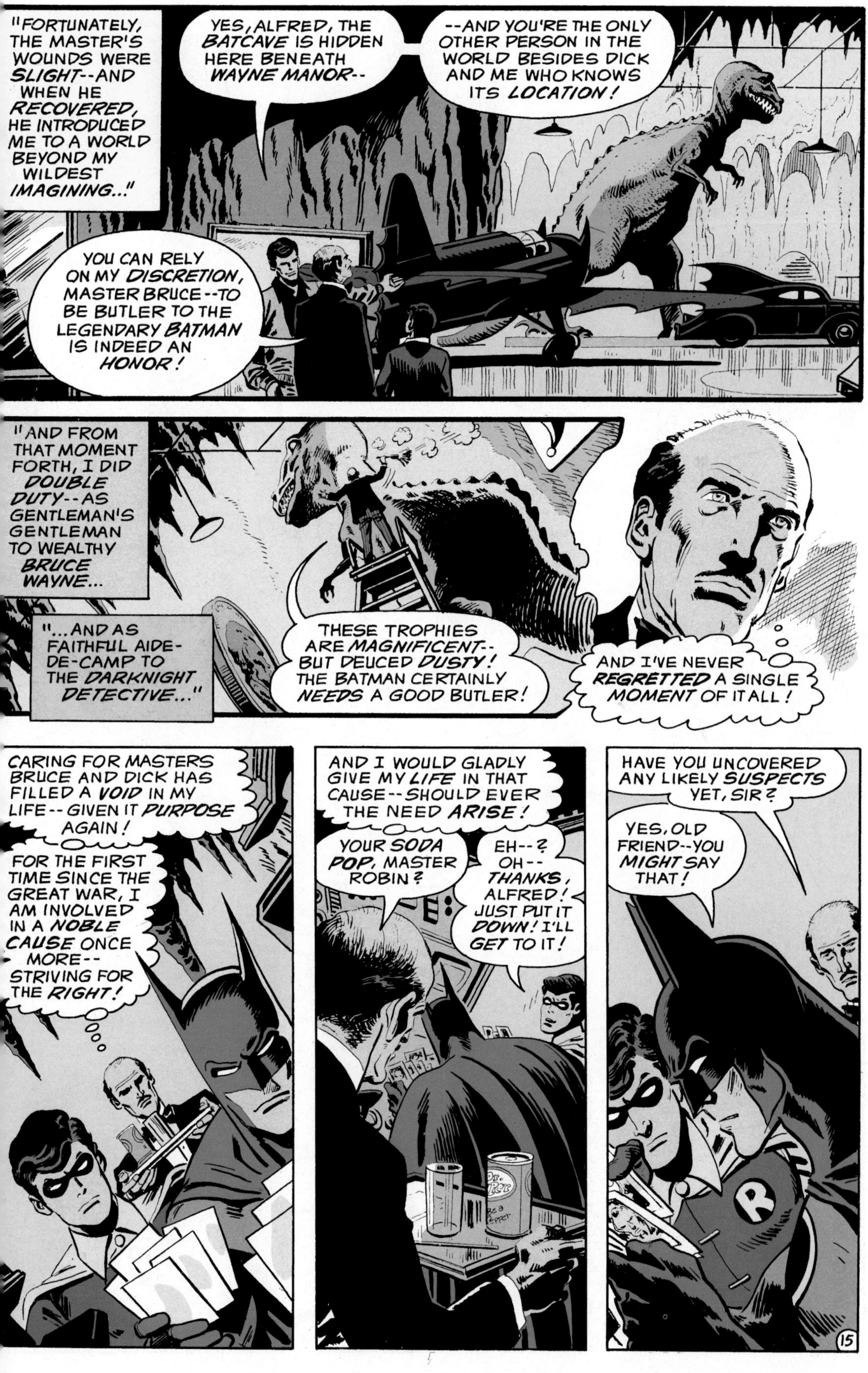
"FORTUNATELY, THE MASTER'S WOUNDS WERE SLIGHT--AND WHEN HE RECOVERED, HE INTRODUCED ME TO A WORLD BEYOND MY WILDEST IMAGINING..."
YES, ALFRED, THE BATCAVE IS HIDDEN HERE BENEATH WAYNE MANOR--
--AND YOU'RE THE ONLY OTHER PERSON IN THE WORLD BESIDES DICK AND ME WHO KNOWS ITS LOCATION!
YOU CAN RELY ON MY DISCRETION, MASTER BRUCE--TO BE BUTLER TO THE LEGENDARY BATMAN IS INDEED AN HONOR!
"AND FROM THAT MOMENT FORTH, I DID DOUBLE DUTY--AS GENTLEMAN'S GENTLEMAN TO WEALTHY BRUCE WAYNE...
"...AND AS FAITHFUL AIDE-DE-CAMP TO THE DARKNIGHT DETECTIVE..."
THESE TROPHIES ARE MAGNIFICENT--BUT DEUCED DUSTY! THE BATMAN CERTAINLY NEEDS A GOOD BUTLER!
AND I'VE NEVER REGRETTED A SINGLE MOMENT OF IT ALL!
CARING FOR MASTERS BRUCE AND DICK HAS FILLED A VOID IN MY LIFE--GIVEN IT PURPOSE AGAIN!
FOR THE FIRST TIME SINCE THE GREAT WAR, I AM INVOLVED IN A NOBLE CAUSE ONCE MORE--STRIVING FOR THE RIGHT!
AND I WOULD GLADLY GIVE MY LIFE IN THAT CAUSE--SHOULD EVER THE NEED ARISE!
YOUR SODA POP, MASTER ROBIN?
EH--? OH--THANKS, ALFRED! JUST PUT IT DOWN! I'LL GET TO IT!
HAVE YOU UNCOVERED ANY LIKELY SUSPECTS YET, SIR?
YES, OLD FRIEND--YOU MIGHT SAY THAT!
15

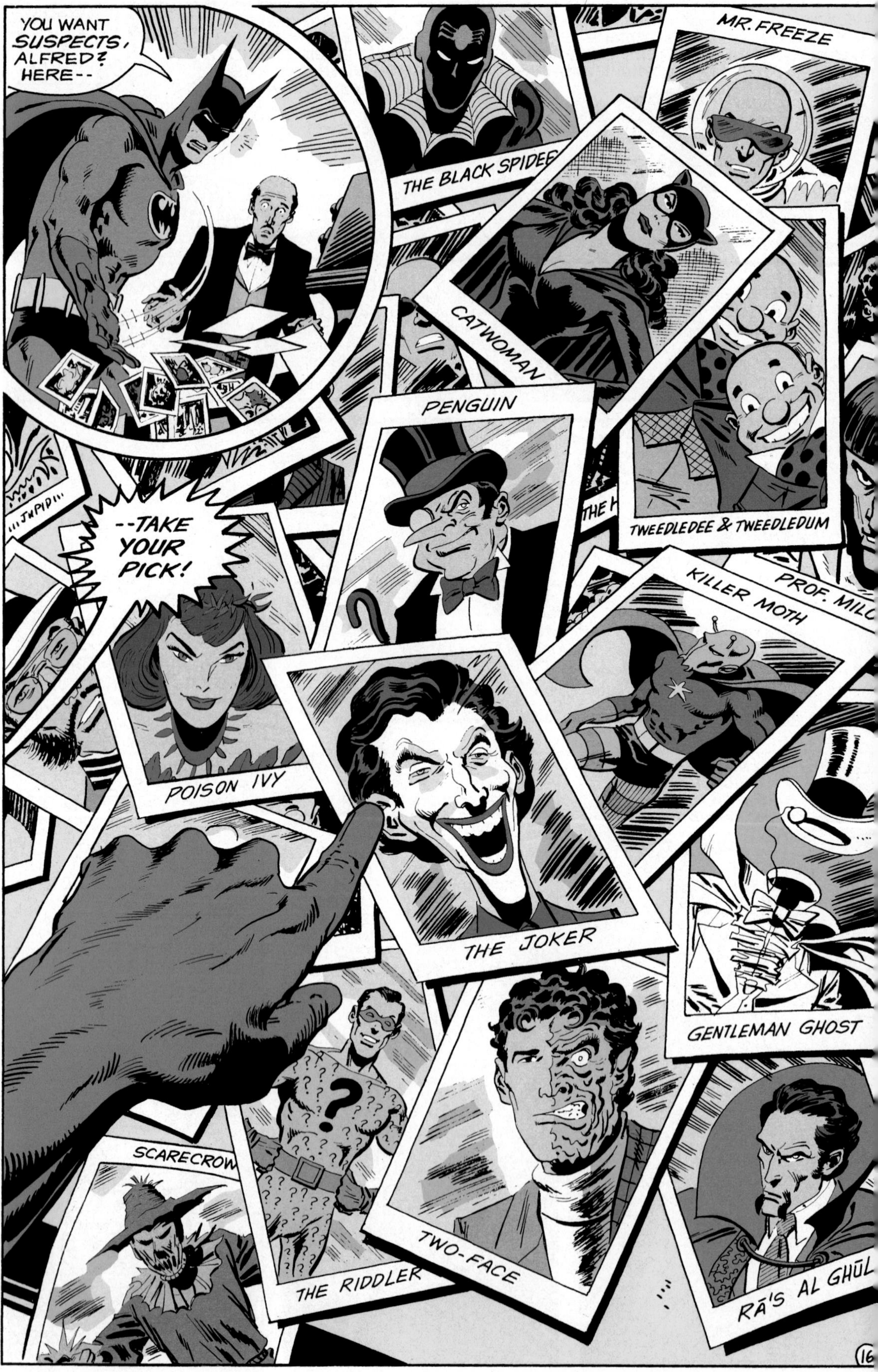
YOU WANT SUSPECTS, ALFRED? HERE--
MR. FREEZE
CATWOMAN
PENGUIN
TWEEDLEDEE & TWEEDLEDUM
--TAKE YOUR PICK!
KILLER MOTH
POISON IVY
THE JOKER
GENTLEMAN GHOST
SCARECROW
THE RIDDLER
TWO-FACE
RĀ'S AL GHŪL
16

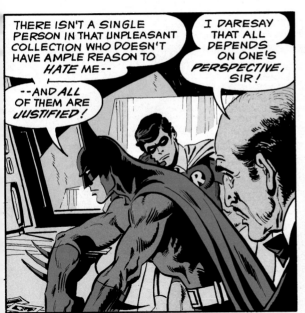

THERE ISN'T A SINGLE PERSON IN THAT UNPLEASANT COLLECTION WHO DOESN'T HAVE AMPLE REASON TO *HATE* ME--

--AND *ALL* OF THEM ARE *JUSTIFIED!*

I DARESAY THAT ALL DEPENDS ON ONE'S *PERSPECTIVE,* SIR!

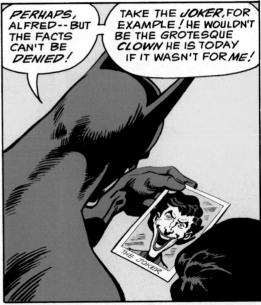

PERHAPS, ALFRED--BUT THE FACTS CAN'T BE *DENIED!*

TAKE THE *JOKER,* FOR EXAMPLE! HE WOULDN'T BE THE GROTESQUE *CLOWN* HE IS TODAY IF IT WASN'T FOR *ME!*

THE JOKER

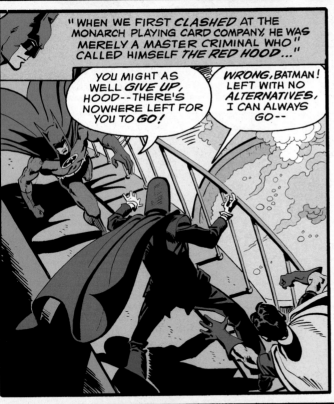

"WHEN WE FIRST *CLASHED* AT THE MONARCH PLAYING CARD COMPANY, HE WAS MERELY A MASTER CRIMINAL WHO" CALLED HIMSELF *THE RED HOOD...*

YOU MIGHT AS WELL *GIVE UP,* HOOD--THERE'S NOWHERE LEFT FOR YOU TO *GO!*

WRONG, BATMAN! LEFT WITH NO *ALTERNATIVES,* I CAN ALWAYS GO--

--DOWN!

*GREAT SCOTT!* HE'S DIVING INTO THE PLANT'S *CATCH BASIN* FOR ALL THE *CHEMICAL WASTES!*

MONARCH PLAYING CARD CO.

THE LIQUID EMPTIES OUT INTO THE *RIVER*-- BUT HE'LL NEVER *MAKE IT!* THAT DEADLY CHEMICAL MIXTURE WILL *FINISH* HIM FIRST!

"BUT I HAD *RECKONED* WITHOUT THE SPECIAL *OXYGEN SYSTEM* BUILT INTO THAT *BIZARRE CRIMSON HELMET...*

"THE RED HOOD *SURVIVED* HIS SWIM THROUGH THE VERY *THICK* OF THOSE NOXIOUS *CHEMICAL WASTES* --"

17

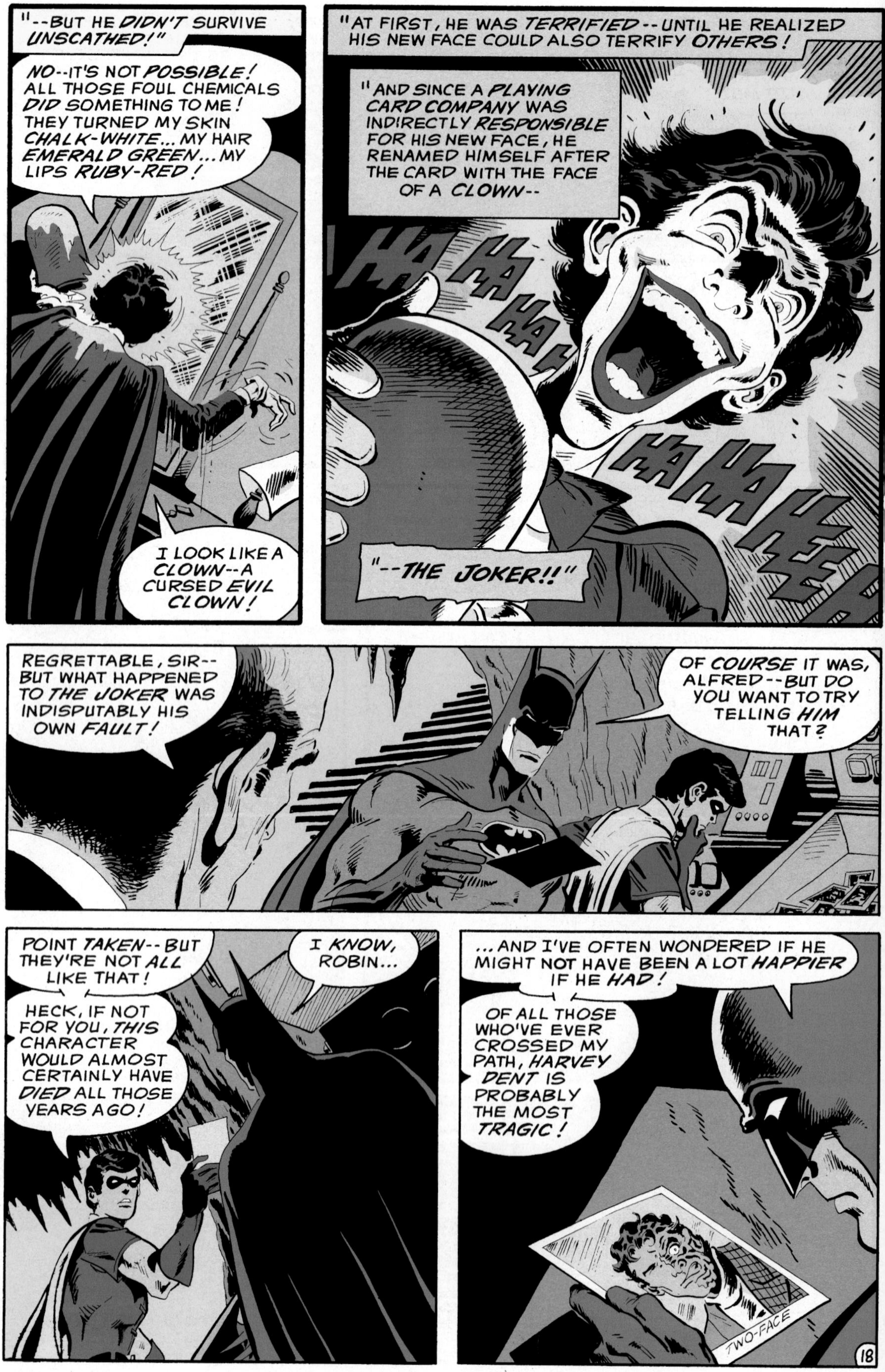
"--BUT HE DIDN'T SURVIVE UNSCATHED!"
NO--IT'S NOT POSSIBLE! ALL THOSE FOUL CHEMICALS DID SOMETHING TO ME! THEY TURNED MY SKIN CHALK-WHITE... MY HAIR EMERALD GREEN... MY LIPS RUBY-RED!
I LOOK LIKE A CLOWN--A CURSED EVIL CLOWN!
"AT FIRST, HE WAS TERRIFIED--UNTIL HE REALIZED HIS NEW FACE COULD ALSO TERRIFY OTHERS!
"AND SINCE A PLAYING CARD COMPANY WAS INDIRECTLY RESPONSIBLE FOR HIS NEW FACE, HE RENAMED HIMSELF AFTER THE CARD WITH THE FACE OF A CLOWN--
HA HA HA HA
HA HA HE HE
"--THE JOKER!!"
REGRETTABLE, SIR--BUT WHAT HAPPENED TO THE JOKER WAS INDISPUTABLY HIS OWN FAULT!
OF COURSE IT WAS, ALFRED--BUT DO YOU WANT TO TRY TELLING HIM THAT?
POINT TAKEN--BUT THEY'RE NOT ALL LIKE THAT!
HECK, IF NOT FOR YOU, THIS CHARACTER WOULD ALMOST CERTAINLY HAVE DIED ALL THOSE YEARS AGO!
I KNOW, ROBIN...
...AND I'VE OFTEN WONDERED IF HE MIGHT NOT HAVE BEEN A LOT HAPPIER IF HE HAD!
OF ALL THOSE WHO'VE EVER CROSSED MY PATH, HARVEY DENT IS PROBABLY THE MOST TRAGIC!
TWO-FACE
18

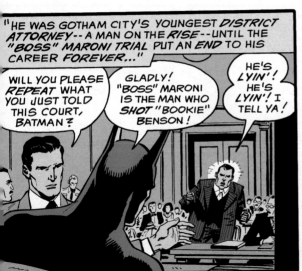

"HE WAS GOTHAM CITY'S YOUNGEST *DISTRICT ATTORNEY* -- A MAN ON THE *RISE* -- UNTIL THE *"BOSS" MARONI TRIAL* PUT AN *END* TO HIS CAREER *FOREVER...*"

WILL YOU PLEASE *REPEAT* WHAT YOU JUST TOLD THIS COURT, BATMAN?

GLADLY! *"BOSS" MARONI* IS THE MAN WHO *SHOT* "BOOKIE" BENSON!

HE'S *LYIN'*! HE'S *LYIN'*! I TELL YA!

IS HE, MARONI? THEN EXPLAIN *THIS!*

BLAST YOU, PRETTY-BOY -- I'LL *FIX* YA FOR THAT!

MARONI'S OWN *LUCKY PIECE* -- A *TWO-HEADED SILVER DOLLAR* -- FOUND AT THE SCENE OF THE CRIME WITH MARONI'S *FINGERPRINTS* ALL OVER IT!

"MARONI MOVED *FAST* FOR A FAT MAN, BUT I MOVED *FASTER* -- I JUST DIDN'T MOVE FAST *ENOUGH...*"

LOOK OUT, DENT! HE'S THROWING ACID!

AARRRGGH!! M-MY FACE--!?!

SSS SSS

"FOR MORE THAN A MONTH, DENT'S TORTURED FACE WAS SWATHED IN *BANDAGES*, AND THEN AT LAST..."

YOU WERE *LUCKY*, MR. DENT, THAT BATMAN'S HAND *DEFLECTED* THAT ACID -- SO IT ONLY STRUCK *ONE* SIDE OF YOUR FACE!

I *APPRECIATE* THAT, DOC! NOW PLEASE FINISH *UNRAVELLING* ME -- AND HAND ME A *MIRROR!*

NO! MY FACE--! WHAT HAVE YOU *DONE* TO IT--?!?

I'VE BECOME *HIDEOUS* -- *HIDEOUS!!*

"THE *SHOCK* OF THAT MOMENT WAS MORE THAN HARVEY DENT'S *FRAGILE* MIND COULD *STAND* -- AND IT SENT HIM SCREAMING OVER THE *EDGE...*"

"MARONI'S TWO-HEADED LUCKY PIECE BECAME HIS NEW *TRADEMARK* -- AND DENT HIMSELF BECAME *...TWO-FACE!*"

19

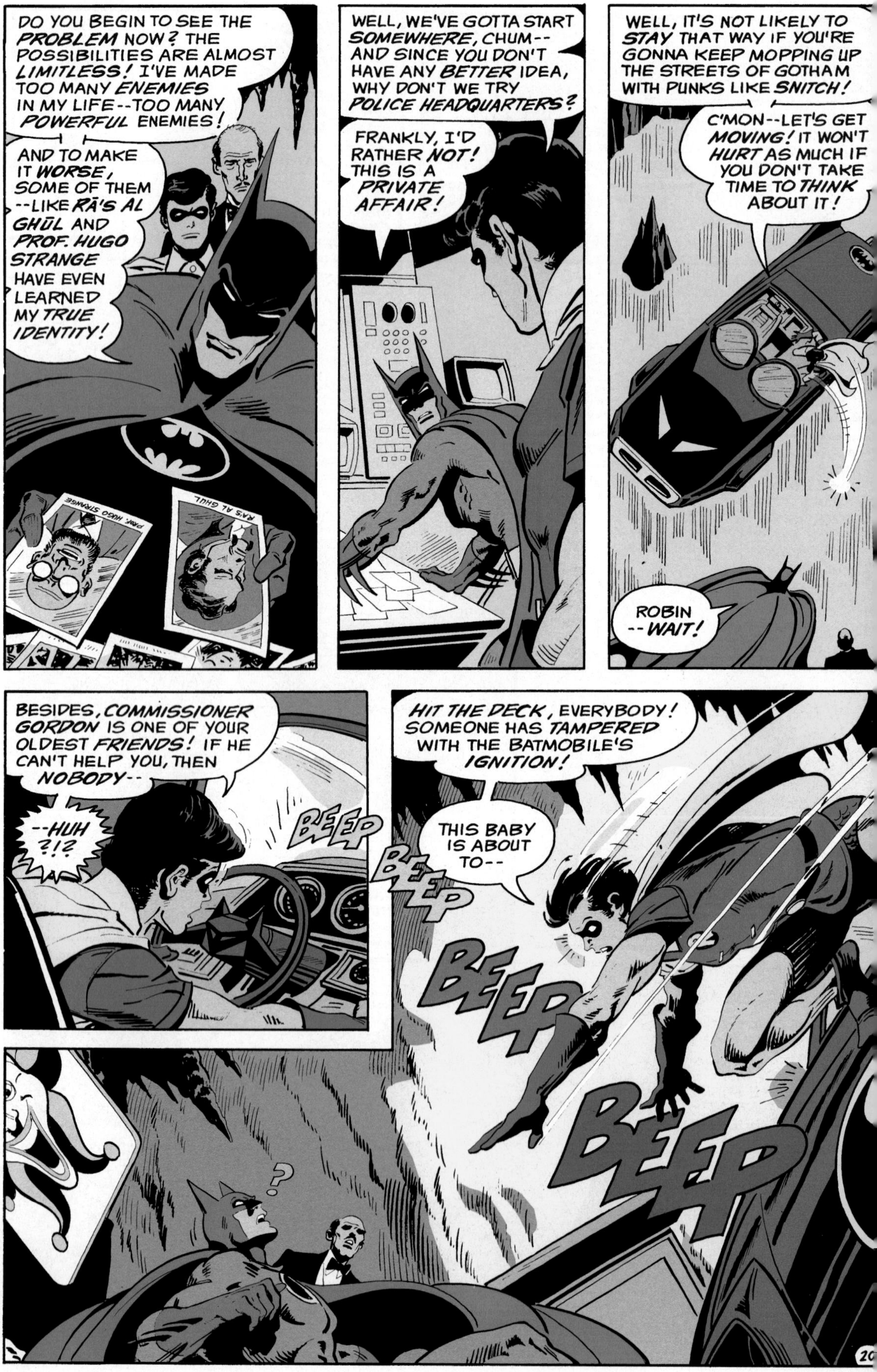
DO YOU BEGIN TO SEE THE PROBLEM NOW? THE POSSIBILITIES ARE ALMOST LIMITLESS! I'VE MADE TOO MANY ENEMIES IN MY LIFE--TOO MANY POWERFUL ENEMIES!
AND TO MAKE IT WORSE, SOME OF THEM --LIKE RĀ'S AL GHŪL AND PROF. HUGO STRANGE HAVE EVEN LEARNED MY TRUE IDENTITY!
PROF. HUGO STRANGE
RA'S AL GHUL
WELL, WE'VE GOTTA START SOMEWHERE, CHUM-- AND SINCE YOU DON'T HAVE ANY BETTER IDEA, WHY DON'T WE TRY POLICE HEADQUARTERS?
FRANKLY, I'D RATHER NOT! THIS IS A PRIVATE AFFAIR!
WELL, IT'S NOT LIKELY TO STAY THAT WAY IF YOU'RE GONNA KEEP MOPPING UP THE STREETS OF GOTHAM WITH PUNKS LIKE SNITCH!
C'MON--LET'S GET MOVING! IT WON'T HURT AS MUCH IF YOU DON'T TAKE TIME TO THINK ABOUT IT!
ROBIN --WAIT!
BESIDES, COMMISSIONER GORDON IS ONE OF YOUR OLDEST FRIENDS! IF HE CAN'T HELP YOU, THEN NOBODY--
--HUH ?!?
BEEP
BEEP
HIT THE DECK, EVERYBODY! SOMEONE HAS TAMPERED WITH THE BATMOBILE'S IGNITION!
THIS BABY IS ABOUT TO--
BEEP
BEEP
?

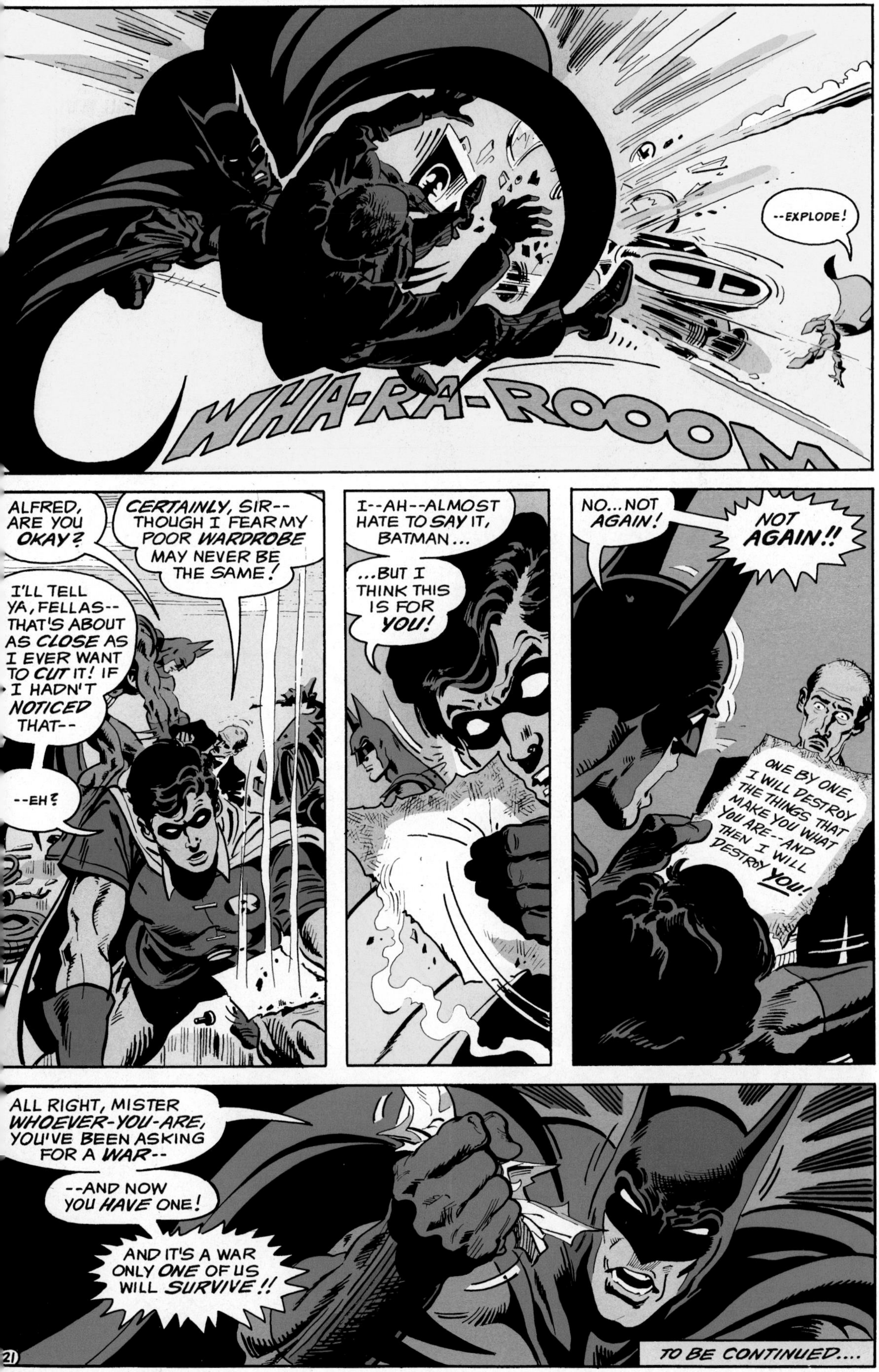
--EXPLODE!
WHA-RA-ROOOOM
ALFRED, ARE YOU OKAY?
CERTAINLY, SIR-- THOUGH I FEAR MY POOR WARDROBE MAY NEVER BE THE SAME!
I'LL TELL YA, FELLAS-- THAT'S ABOUT AS CLOSE AS I EVER WANT TO CUT IT! IF I HADN'T NOTICED THAT--
--EH?
I--AH--ALMOST HATE TO SAY IT, BATMAN...
...BUT I THINK THIS IS FOR YOU!
NO...NOT AGAIN!
NOT AGAIN!!
ONE BY ONE, I WILL DESTROY THE THINGS THAT MAKE YOU WHAT YOU ARE--AND THEN I WILL DESTROY YOU!
ALL RIGHT, MISTER WHOEVER-YOU-ARE, YOU'VE BEEN ASKING FOR A WAR--
--AND NOW YOU HAVE ONE!
AND IT'S A WAR ONLY ONE OF US WILL SURVIVE!!
21
TO BE CONTINUED....

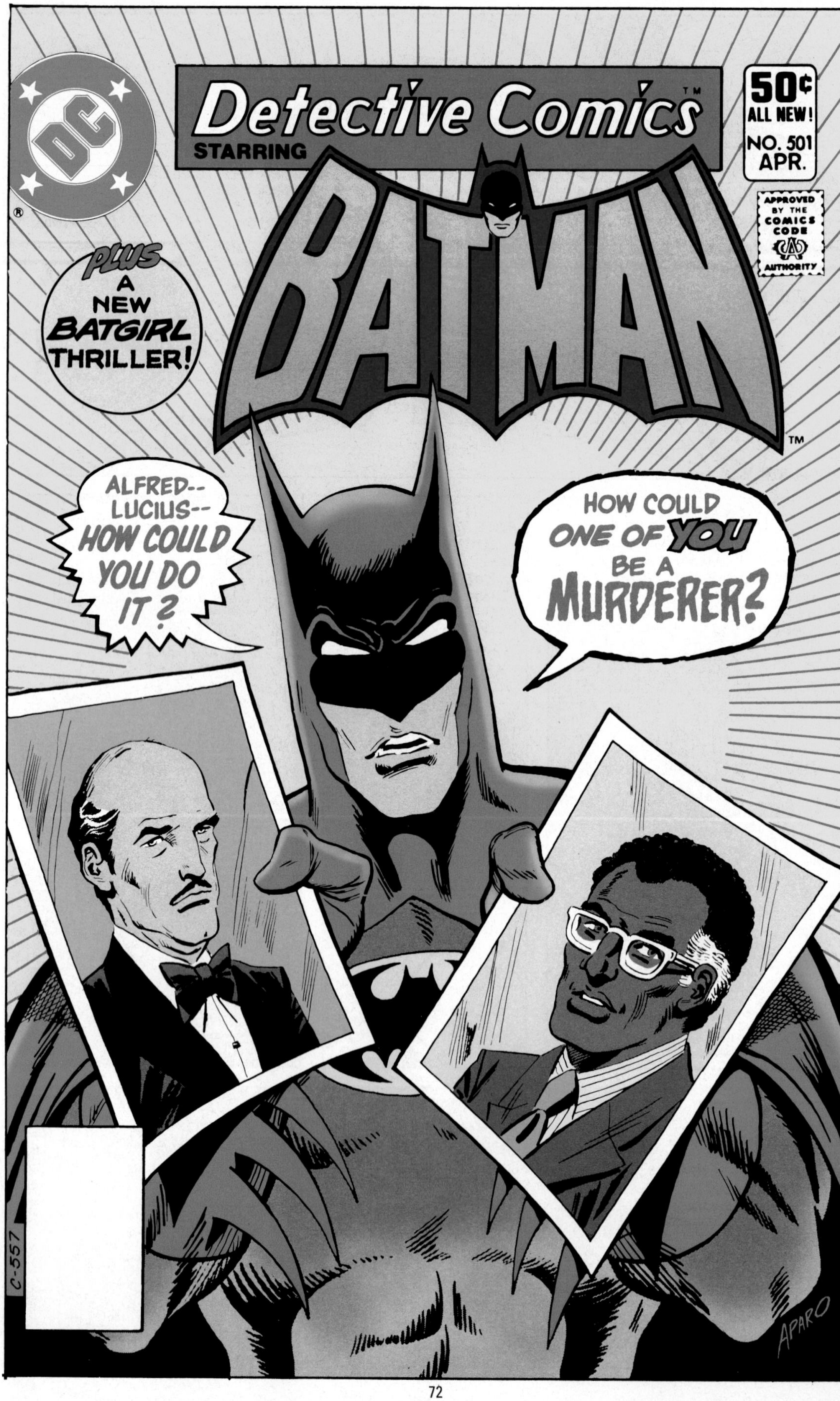
Detective Comics
STARRING
BATMAN
50¢
ALL NEW!
NO. 501
APR.
APPROVED BY THE COMICS CODE AUTHORITY
PLUS A NEW BATGIRL THRILLER!
ALFRED-- LUCIUS-- HOW COULD YOU DO IT?
HOW COULD ONE OF YOU BE A MURDERER?
C-557
APARO

ORPHANED AS A CHILD WHEN HIS PARENTS WERE MURDERED BEFORE HIS EYES, *BRUCE WAYNE* HAS TRAINED HIMSELF TO WAGE RELENTLESS WAR AGAINST CRIME AS THE DREAD *AVENGER OF THE NIGHT...*

BAT MAN

GOTHAM INTERNATIONAL AIRPORT IS ON A SPIT OF FORMER MARSHLAND OVERLOOKING *GOTHAM BAY,* AND TONIGHT, AS ON MOST NIGHTS, THERE IS A TANG OF SALTY *SEA BREEZE* IN THE AIR...

... THAT *MIXES* WITH THE ODOR OF *MACHINE OIL* AND *JET FUEL,* STIRRING THOUGHTS OF *DISTANT LANDS* AND *TIMES...*

I CAN'T *BELIEVE* IT. THE *TWO MEN* I TRUST MOST, NEXT TO DICK GRAYSON...

...LEAVING ON SOME *SECRET MISSION* TO *EUROPE -- TOGETHER!*

IN HEAVEN'S NAME -- *WHY??*

# "The Man Who Killed MLLE. MARIE!"

| GERRY CONWAY WRITER | DON NEWTON & DAN ADKINS ARTISTS | |
|---|---|---|
| BEN ODA LETTERER | ADRIENNE ROY COLORIST | PAUL LEVITZ EDITOR |

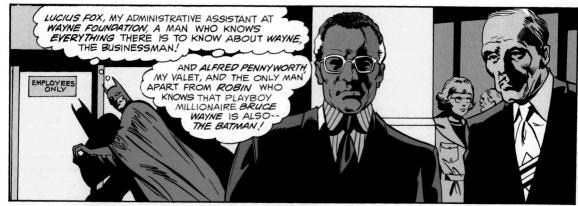

LUCIUS FOX, MY ADMINISTRATIVE ASSISTANT AT *WAYNE FOUNDATION*, A MAN WHO KNOWS *EVERYTHING* THERE IS TO KNOW ABOUT *WAYNE*, THE BUSINESSMAN!

AND *ALFRED PENNYWORTH*, MY VALET, AND THE ONLY MAN APART FROM *ROBIN* WHO KNOWS THAT PLAYBOY MILLIONAIRE *BRUCE WAYNE* IS ALSO-- THE BATMAN!

EMPLOYEES ONLY

AS FAR AS I *KNEW*, THEY BARELY *KNEW* EACH OTHER...

...AND NOW HERE THEY ARE, FLYING OFF TO *PARIS*, WITHOUT LEAVING ANY WORD AS TO *WHY*... WITHOUT LEAVING ANY WORD AT *ALL*!

THE STRANGE THING IS, I WAS THERE WHEN THIS MYSTERY *BEGAN*, NOT THAT IT *HELPS*...

"IT STARTED THIS MORNING, AT *BREAKFAST*...

YOU'RE *SLIPPING*, ALFRED. THIS TELEGRAM SHOULDN'T BE WITH *MY* MAIL--

--IT'S FOR *YOU*.

WHO DO YOU KNOW IN *PARIS*, ALFRED?

"HE *PALED* AS HE READ THE MESSAGE... IT WAS ONE OF THE FEW TIMES I'D SEEN HIM LOSE HIS STIFF-UPPER-LIP *COMPOSURE*...

②

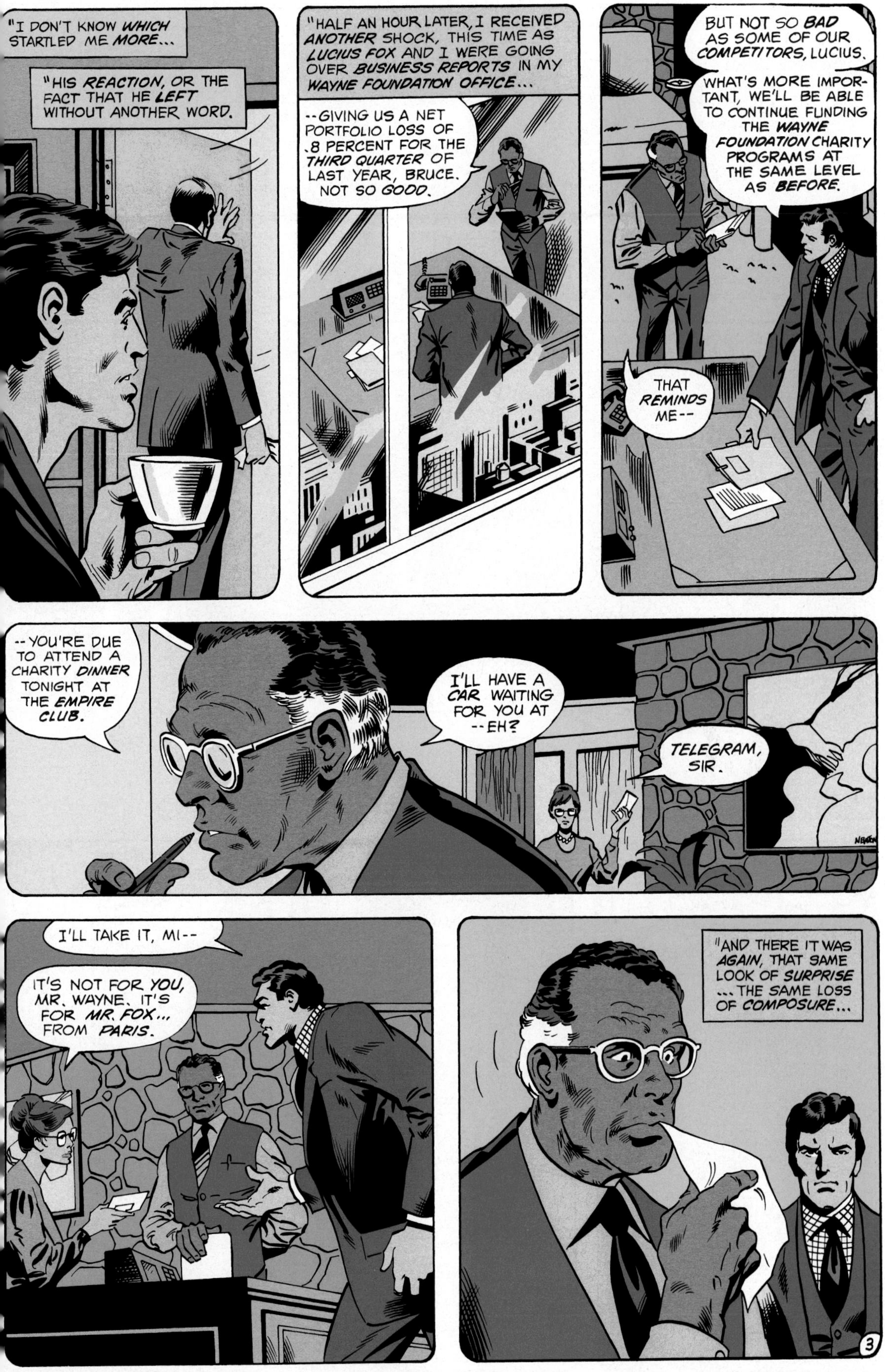
"I DON'T KNOW WHICH STARTLED ME MORE...
"HIS REACTION, OR THE FACT THAT HE LEFT WITHOUT ANOTHER WORD.
"HALF AN HOUR LATER, I RECEIVED ANOTHER SHOCK, THIS TIME AS LUCIUS FOX AND I WERE GOING OVER BUSINESS REPORTS IN MY WAYNE FOUNDATION OFFICE...
--GIVING US A NET PORTFOLIO LOSS OF .8 PERCENT FOR THE THIRD QUARTER OF LAST YEAR, BRUCE. NOT SO GOOD.
BUT NOT SO BAD AS SOME OF OUR COMPETITORS, LUCIUS.
WHAT'S MORE IMPORTANT, WE'LL BE ABLE TO CONTINUE FUNDING THE WAYNE FOUNDATION CHARITY PROGRAMS AT THE SAME LEVEL AS BEFORE.
THAT REMINDS ME--
--YOU'RE DUE TO ATTEND A CHARITY DINNER TONIGHT AT THE EMPIRE CLUB.
I'LL HAVE A CAR WAITING FOR YOU AT --EH?
TELEGRAM, SIR.
I'LL TAKE IT, MI--
IT'S NOT FOR YOU, MR. WAYNE. IT'S FOR MR. FOX... FROM PARIS.
"AND THERE IT WAS AGAIN, THAT SAME LOOK OF SURPRISE ... THE SAME LOSS OF COMPOSURE...
3

I...I'M NOT *FEELING* VERY WELL, BRUCE. I THINK I'D BETTER TAKE THE REST OF THE DAY *OFF*...

OF *COURSE*, LUCIUS.

FIRST *ALFRED* ...NOW *LUCIUS*? WHAT'S GOING *ON*?

"I WONDERED ABOUT IT *ALL DAY*, AND DURING THE CHARITY DINNER THAT EVENING, MY CURIOSITY BECAME *OVERWHELMING*...

"BY THE TIME THE DINNER WAS OVER, I *HAD* TO KNOW WHAT WAS HAPPENING TO THE TWO MEN I CONSIDERED MY *FRIENDS*...

IT COULD TAKE AN *HOUR* FOR THAT LIMOUSINE TRAFFIC-JAM TO BREAK UP.

SOME *INSTINCT* TELLS ME ANOTHER HOUR MIGHT BE *TOO LATE*.

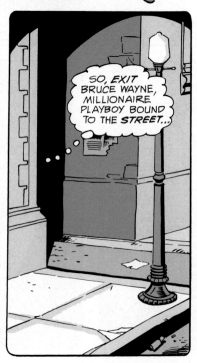

SO, *EXIT* BRUCE WAYNE, MILLIONAIRE PLAYBOY BOUND TO THE *STREET*...

...AND *ENTER* BATMAN, WHO HAS *OTHER WAYS* TO TRAVEL THAN BY *CAR*...

BOXING

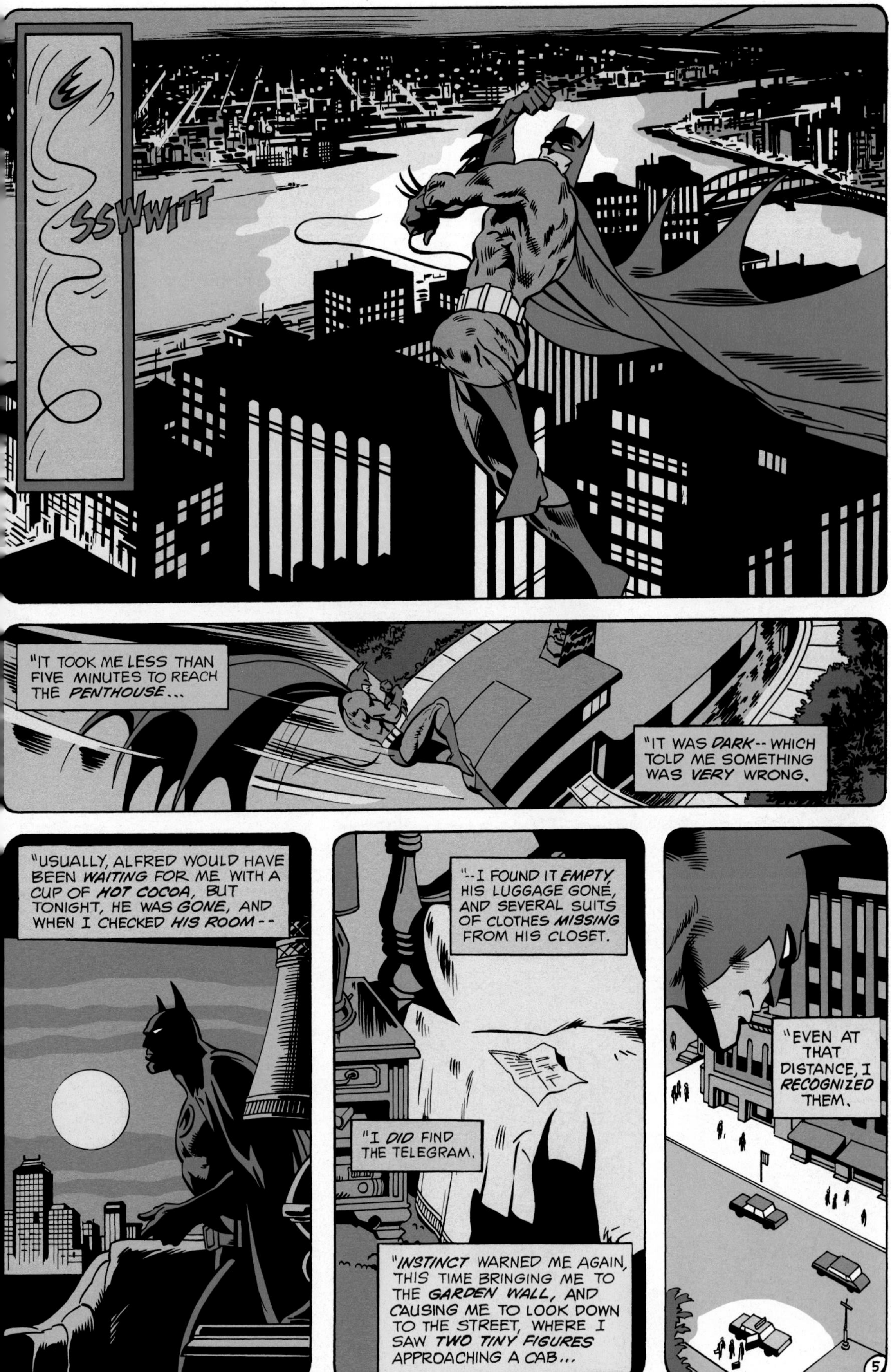
SSWWITT
"IT TOOK ME LESS THAN FIVE MINUTES TO REACH THE PENTHOUSE...
"IT WAS DARK-- WHICH TOLD ME SOMETHING WAS VERY WRONG.
"USUALLY, ALFRED WOULD HAVE BEEN WAITING FOR ME WITH A CUP OF HOT COCOA, BUT TONIGHT, HE WAS GONE, AND WHEN I CHECKED HIS ROOM--
"--I FOUND IT EMPTY, HIS LUGGAGE GONE, AND SEVERAL SUITS OF CLOTHES MISSING FROM HIS CLOSET.
"I DID FIND THE TELEGRAM.
"INSTINCT WARNED ME AGAIN, THIS TIME BRINGING ME TO THE GARDEN WALL, AND CAUSING ME TO LOOK DOWN TO THE STREET, WHERE I SAW TWO TINY FIGURES APPROACHING A CAB...
"EVEN AT THAT DISTANCE, I RECOGNIZED THEM.
5

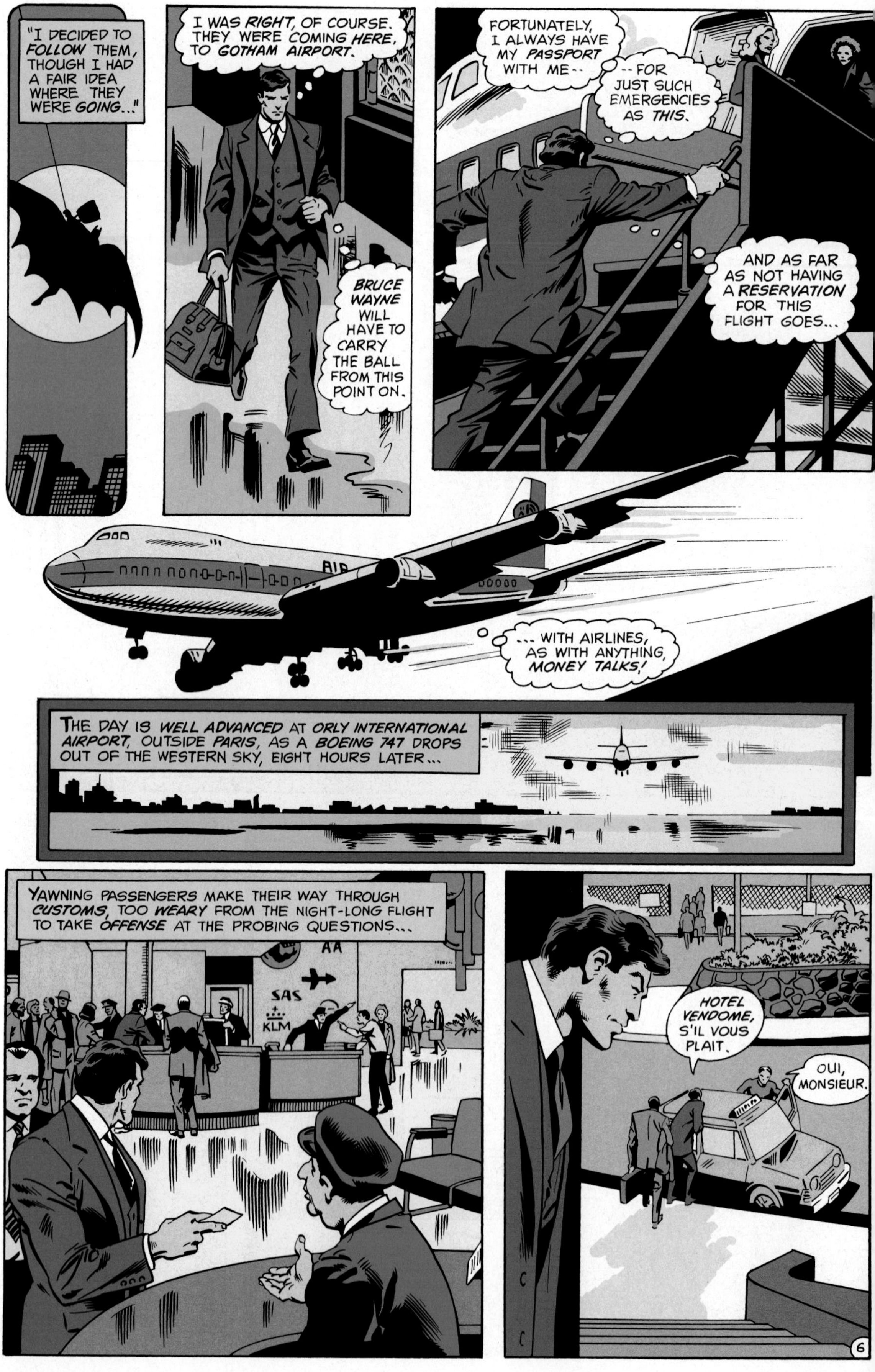
"I DECIDED TO FOLLOW THEM, THOUGH I HAD A FAIR IDEA WHERE THEY WERE GOING..."
I WAS RIGHT, OF COURSE. THEY WERE COMING HERE, TO GOTHAM AIRPORT.
BRUCE WAYNE WILL HAVE TO CARRY THE BALL FROM THIS POINT ON.
FORTUNATELY, I ALWAYS HAVE MY PASSPORT WITH ME--
--FOR JUST SUCH EMERGENCIES AS THIS.
AND AS FAR AS NOT HAVING A RESERVATION FOR THIS FLIGHT GOES...
...WITH AIRLINES, AS WITH ANYTHING, MONEY TALKS!
THE DAY IS WELL ADVANCED AT ORLY INTERNATIONAL AIRPORT, OUTSIDE PARIS, AS A BOEING 747 DROPS OUT OF THE WESTERN SKY, EIGHT HOURS LATER...
YAWNING PASSENGERS MAKE THEIR WAY THROUGH CUSTOMS, TOO WEARY FROM THE NIGHT-LONG FLIGHT TO TAKE OFFENSE AT THE PROBING QUESTIONS...
AA
SAS
KLM
HOTEL VENDOME, S'IL VOUS PLAIT.
OUI, MONSIEUR.
6

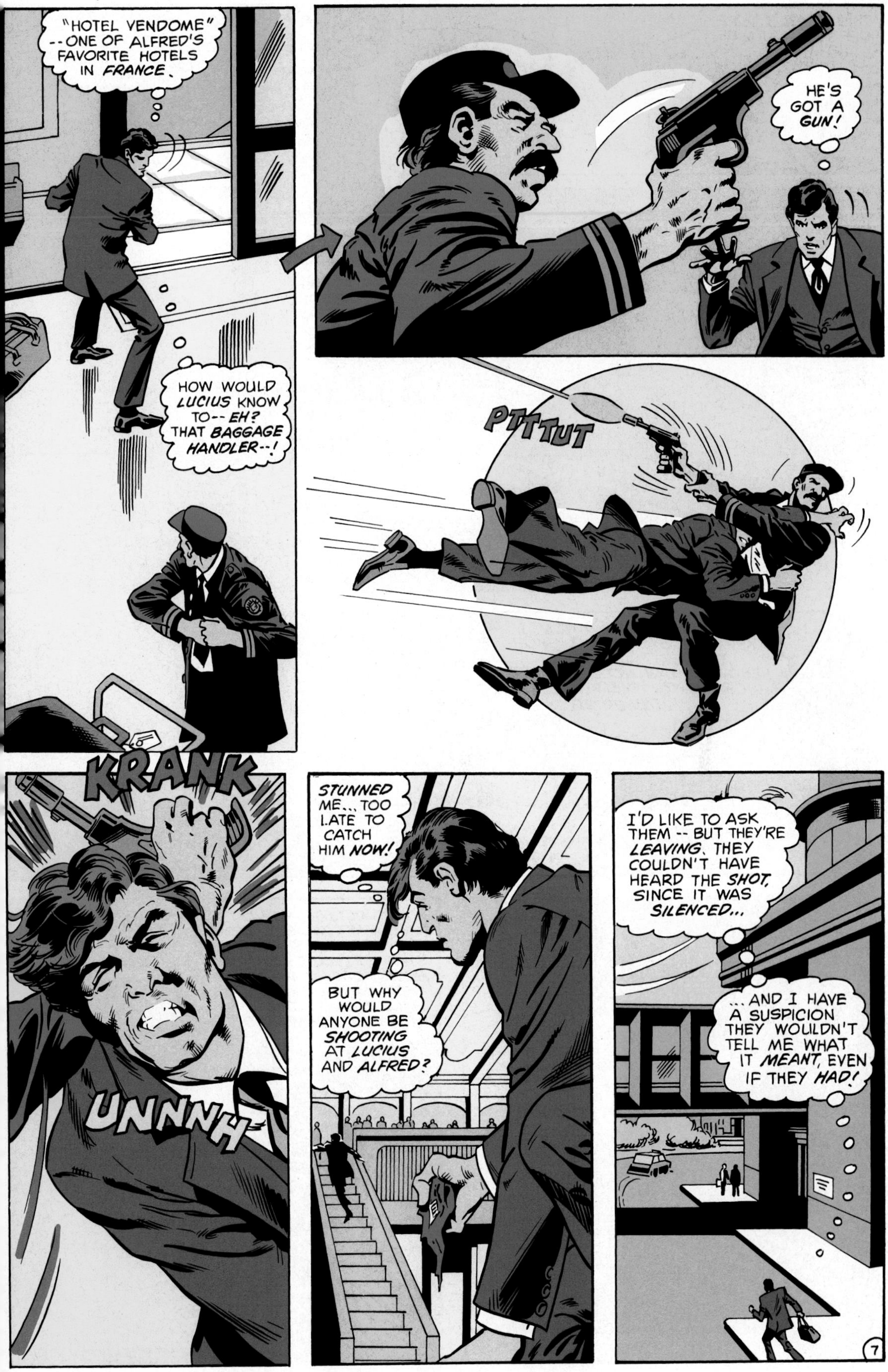
"HOTEL VENDOME" --ONE OF ALFRED'S FAVORITE HOTELS IN FRANCE.
HOW WOULD LUCIUS KNOW TO-- EH? THAT BAGGAGE HANDLER--!
HE'S GOT A GUN!
PTTTUT
KRANK
UNNNH
STUNNED ME... TOO LATE TO CATCH HIM NOW!
BUT WHY WOULD ANYONE BE SHOOTING AT LUCIUS AND ALFRED?
I'D LIKE TO ASK THEM -- BUT THEY'RE LEAVING. THEY COULDN'T HAVE HEARD THE SHOT, SINCE IT WAS SILENCED...
...AND I HAVE A SUSPICION THEY WOULDN'T TELL ME WHAT IT MEANT, EVEN IF THEY HAD!
7

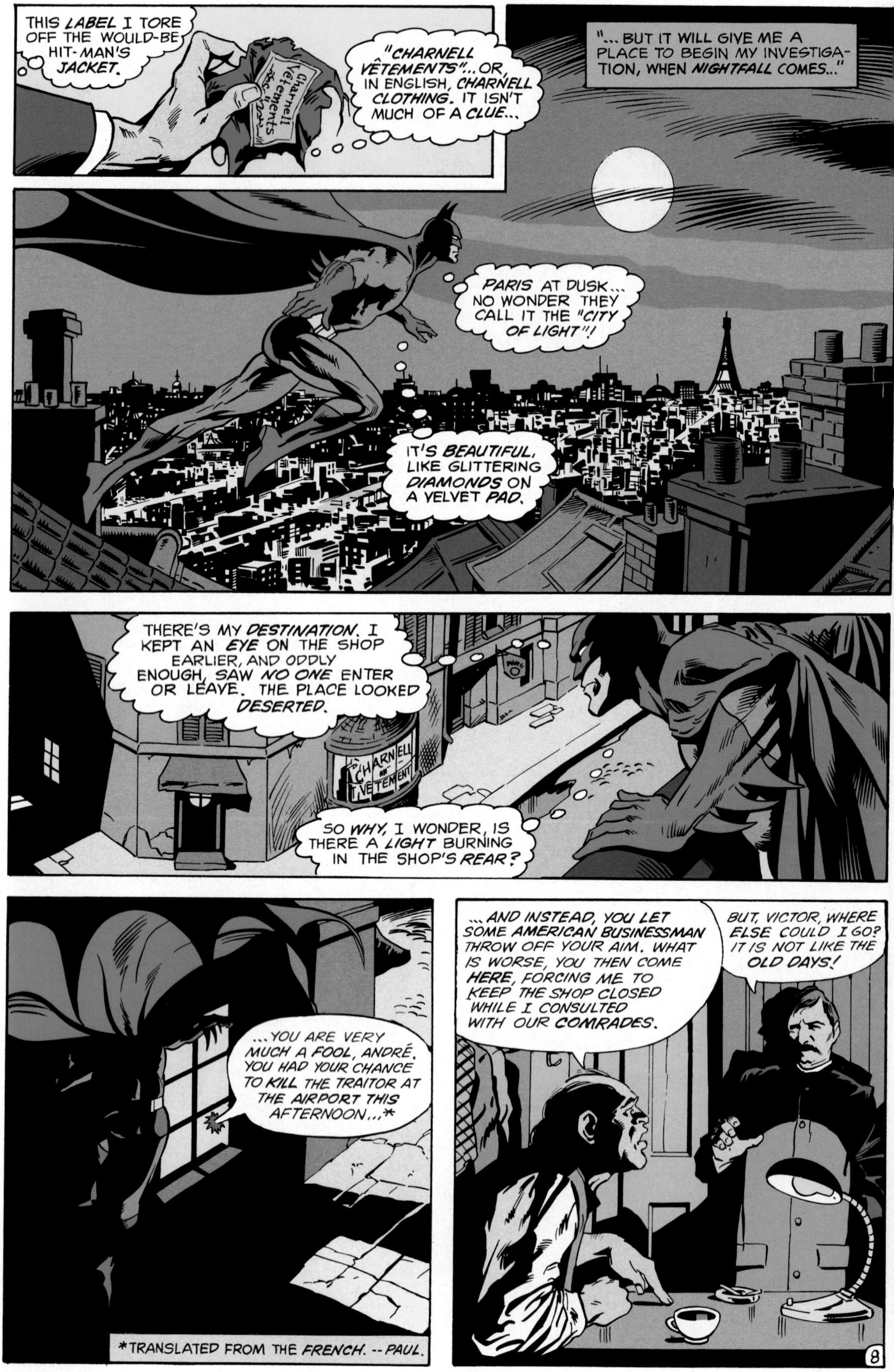

THIS LABEL I TORE OFF THE WOULD-BE HIT-MAN'S JACKET.
"CHARNELL VÊTEMENTS"... OR, IN ENGLISH, CHARNELL CLOTHING. IT ISN'T MUCH OF A CLUE...
"... BUT IT WILL GIVE ME A PLACE TO BEGIN MY INVESTIGATION, WHEN NIGHTFALL COMES..."
PARIS AT DUSK... NO WONDER THEY CALL IT THE "CITY OF LIGHT"!
IT'S BEAUTIFUL, LIKE GLITTERING DIAMONDS ON A VELVET PAD.
THERE'S MY DESTINATION. I KEPT AN EYE ON THE SHOP EARLIER, AND ODDLY ENOUGH, SAW NO ONE ENTER OR LEAVE. THE PLACE LOOKED DESERTED.
CHARNELL VETEMENT
SO WHY, I WONDER, IS THERE A LIGHT BURNING IN THE SHOP'S REAR?
...YOU ARE VERY MUCH A FOOL, ANDRÉ. YOU HAD YOUR CHANCE TO KILL THE TRAITOR AT THE AIRPORT THIS AFTERNOON...*
*TRANSLATED FROM THE FRENCH. -- PAUL.
...AND INSTEAD, YOU LET SOME AMERICAN BUSINESSMAN THROW OFF YOUR AIM. WHAT IS WORSE, YOU THEN COME HERE, FORCING ME TO KEEP THE SHOP CLOSED WHILE I CONSULTED WITH OUR COMRADES.
BUT, VICTOR, WHERE ELSE COULD I GO? IT IS NOT LIKE THE OLD DAYS!
8

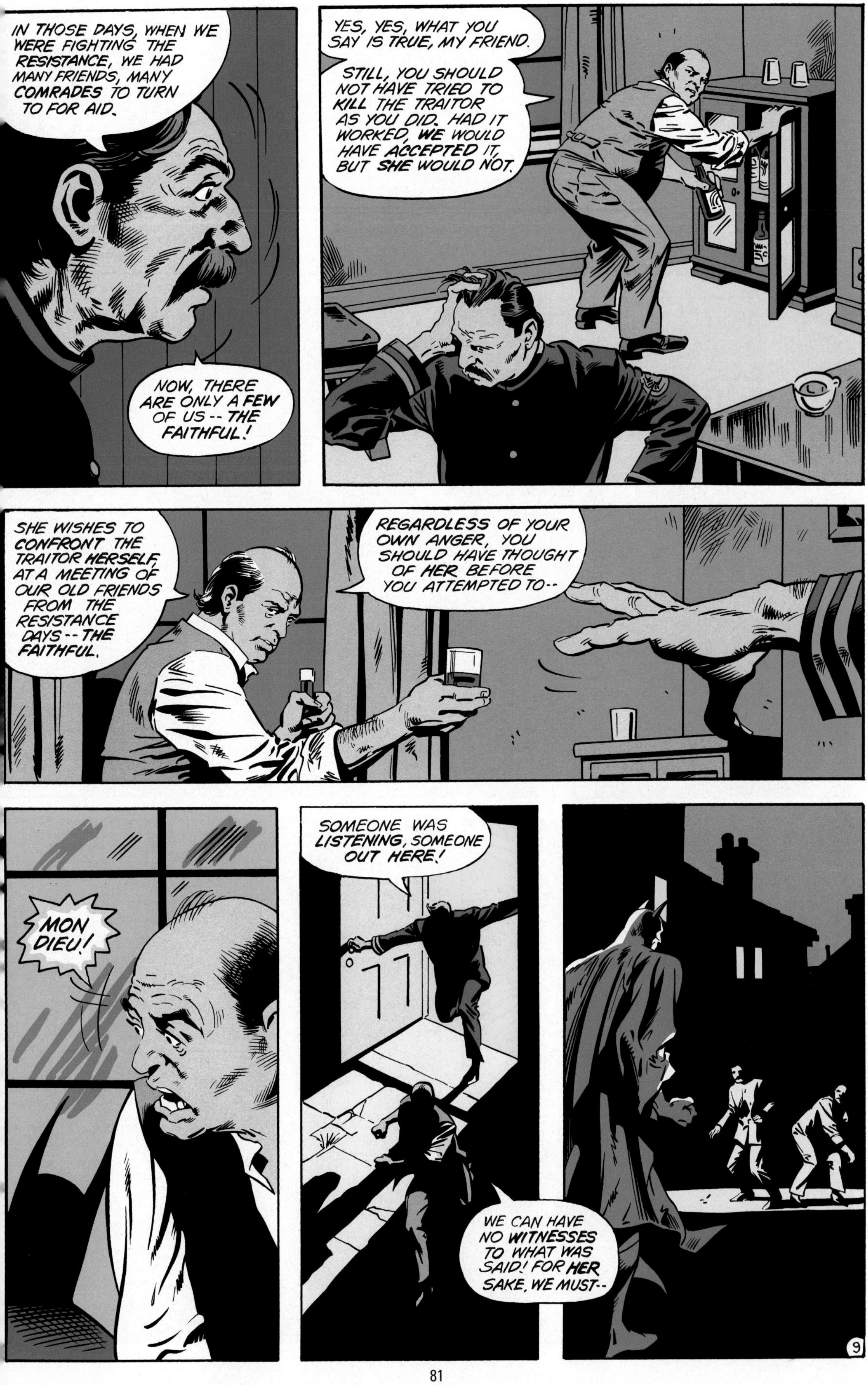
IN THOSE DAYS, WHEN WE WERE FIGHTING THE RESISTANCE, WE HAD MANY FRIENDS, MANY COMRADES TO TURN TO FOR AID.
NOW, THERE ARE ONLY A FEW OF US -- THE FAITHFUL!
YES, YES, WHAT YOU SAY IS TRUE, MY FRIEND.
STILL, YOU SHOULD NOT HAVE TRIED TO KILL THE TRAITOR AS YOU DID. HAD IT WORKED, WE WOULD HAVE ACCEPTED IT, BUT SHE WOULD NOT.
SHE WISHES TO CONFRONT THE TRAITOR HERSELF, AT A MEETING OF OUR OLD FRIENDS FROM THE RESISTANCE DAYS -- THE FAITHFUL.
REGARDLESS OF YOUR OWN ANGER, YOU SHOULD HAVE THOUGHT OF HER BEFORE YOU ATTEMPTED TO--
MON DIEU!
SOMEONE WAS LISTENING, SOMEONE OUT HERE!
WE CAN HAVE NO WITNESSES TO WHAT WAS SAID! FOR HER SAKE, WE MUST--
9

LIKE SOME GRAY-AND-BLACK *MATADOR*, THE TALL FIGURE *LEANS ASIDE*, LETTING THE GUNFIRE RIP *HARMLESSLY* THROUGH HIS FLUTTERING *CAPE* --

PFOOF  PFOOF

--AND THEN *LEANS BACK*, SITTING WITH A BLOW AS SHARP AS A MATADOR'S *ÉPÉE!*

KRAK

*NON, NON! C'EST IRRÉEL* --

PFOOF

*UNNNH!*

CLO-ONG

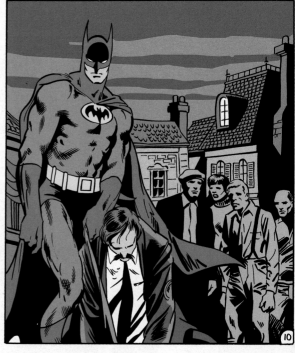

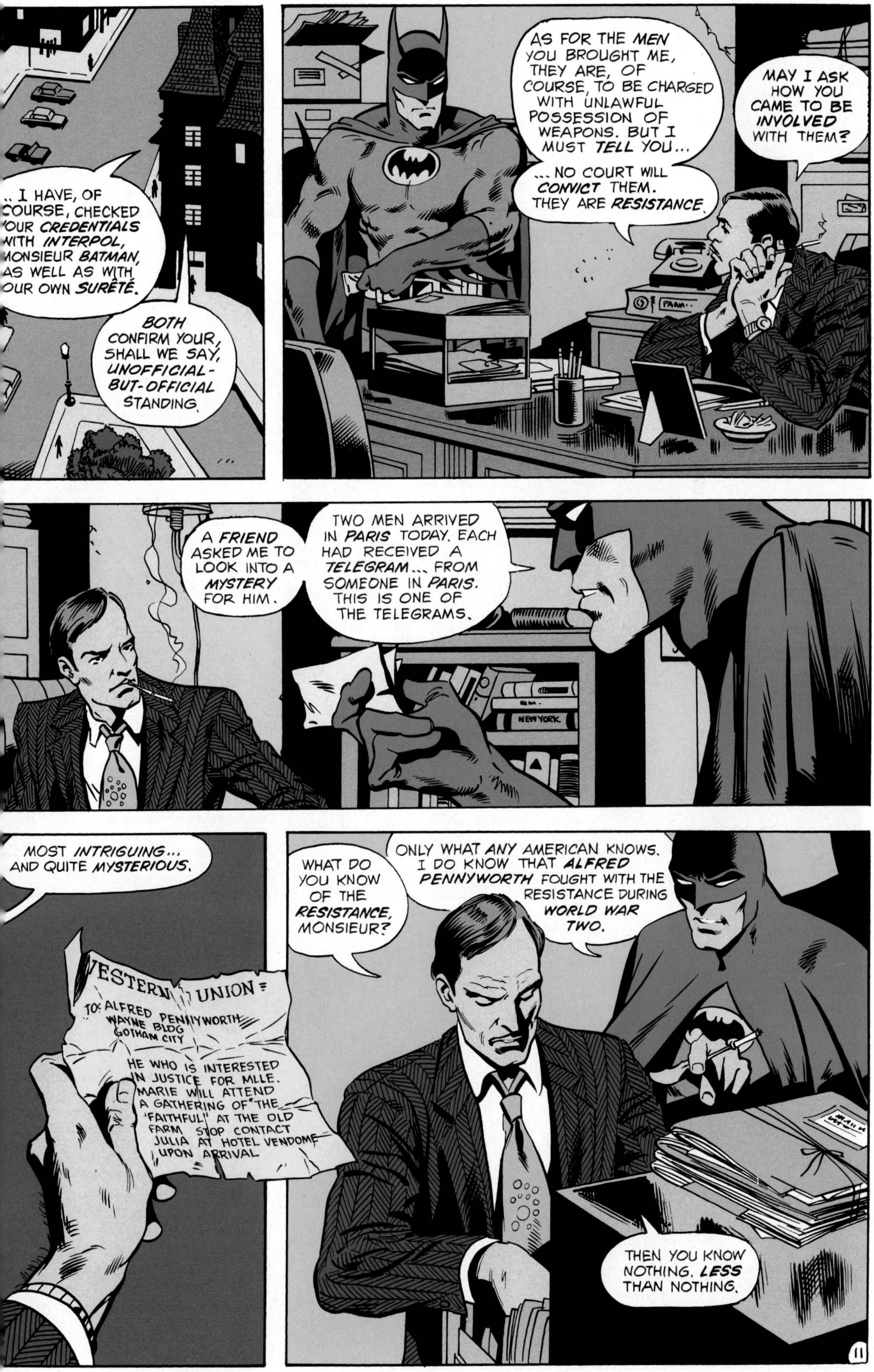
.. I HAVE, OF COURSE, CHECKED YOUR CREDENTIALS WITH INTERPOL, MONSIEUR BATMAN, AS WELL AS WITH OUR OWN SURÊTÉ.
BOTH CONFIRM YOUR, SHALL WE SAY, UNOFFICIAL-BUT-OFFICIAL STANDING.
AS FOR THE MEN YOU BROUGHT ME, THEY ARE, OF COURSE, TO BE CHARGED WITH UNLAWFUL POSSESSION OF WEAPONS. BUT I MUST TELL YOU...
... NO COURT WILL CONVICT THEM. THEY ARE RESISTANCE.
MAY I ASK HOW YOU CAME TO BE INVOLVED WITH THEM?
A FRIEND ASKED ME TO LOOK INTO A MYSTERY FOR HIM.
TWO MEN ARRIVED IN PARIS TODAY. EACH HAD RECEIVED A TELEGRAM... FROM SOMEONE IN PARIS. THIS IS ONE OF THE TELEGRAMS.
NEW YORK
MOST INTRIGUING... AND QUITE MYSTERIOUS.
WESTERN UNION
TO: ALFRED PENNYWORTH
WAYNE BLDG
GOTHAM CITY
HE WHO IS INTERESTED IN JUSTICE FOR MLLE. MARIE WILL ATTEND A GATHERING OF "THE 'FAITHFUL'" AT THE OLD FARM STOP CONTACT JULIA AT HOTEL VENDOME UPON ARRIVAL
WHAT DO YOU KNOW OF THE RESISTANCE, MONSIEUR?
ONLY WHAT ANY AMERICAN KNOWS. I DO KNOW THAT ALFRED PENNYWORTH FOUGHT WITH THE RESISTANCE DURING WORLD WAR TWO.
THEN YOU KNOW NOTHING. LESS THAN NOTHING.
11

THE *RESISTANCE* WAS THE BURNING *SOUL* OF OCCUPIED *FRANCE.*

IT WAS NOT *ONE* MOVEMENT, BUT A *DOZEN* MOVEMENTS, WELDED TOGETHER BY MUTUAL *HATRED* OF *NAZI* OPPRESSION.

THERE WERE *COMMUNISTS...* *RADICALS... MILITIA... CAPITALISTS... BOURGEOISIE,*

...ALL FIGHTING FOR *ONE* GOAL: THE FREEDOM OF *FRANCE!*

IT HAS BEEN SAID, SINCE THE *LIBERATION,* THAT IF EVERYONE WHO CLAIMED TO HAVE BEEN WITH THE *RESISTANCE* HAD INDEED BEEN WITH THEM--

*FLUMP*

--THEN THERE WOULD HAVE BEEN NO ONE LEFT TO *COLLABORATE.*

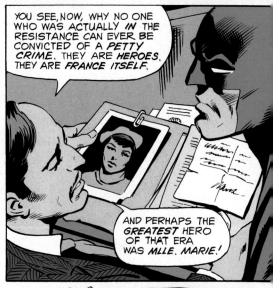

YOU SEE, NOW, WHY NO ONE WHO WAS ACTUALLY *IN* THE RESISTANCE CAN EVER BE CONVICTED OF A *PETTY CRIME.* THEY ARE *HEROES.* THEY ARE *FRANCE ITSELF.*

AND PERHAPS THE *GREATEST* HERO OF THAT ERA WAS *MLLE. MARIE!*

"SHE WAS THE LIVING *SPIRIT* OF THE RESISTANCE, A YOUNG FARM GIRL WHO COMMANDED THE *BOLDEST* GUERRILLA FORCE IN THE MOVEMENT...

"FOR FIVE YEARS, FROM JUNE 1940, UNTIL THE *END OF THE WAR,* SHE FOUGHT THE *NAZI OCCUPIERS* AS ANOTHER GIRL WOULD PURSUE A *LOVER\*...* "

\*AS TOLD IN INNUMERABLE ISSUES OF *STAR SPANGLED WAR STORIES.* -- PAUL.

12

"SHE BECAME A *LEGEND*, A SYMBOL OF GALLIC *COURAGE*.

"IN TIME, SHE DREW TO HER SIDE GUERRILLAS FROM A DOZEN OTHER GROUPS, AS WELL AS *FREEDOM FIGHTERS* FROM *BRITAIN* AND *AMERICA*.

"...AND THEN, IN THE LAST DAYS OF *LA GUERRE*..."

"...*MLLE. MARIE* WAS *SHOT* BY AN *UNKNOWN HAND*..."

"...AND THOUGH HER BODY WAS *NEVER FOUND*..."

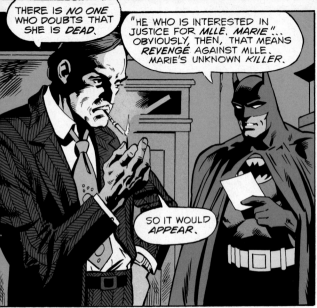

THERE IS *NO ONE* WHO DOUBTS THAT SHE IS *DEAD*.

"HE WHO IS INTERESTED IN JUSTICE FOR *MLLE. MARIE*"... OBVIOUSLY, THEN, THAT MEANS *REVENGE* AGAINST MLLE. MARIE'S UNKNOWN *KILLER*.

SO IT WOULD *APPEAR*.

AND FROM WHAT YOU *TELL* ME YOU OVERHEARD AT THE *CLOTHING SHOP*, THESE PEOPLE BELIEVE THAT *ONE* OF YOUR *TWO* FRIENDS IS *MLLE. MARIE'S MURDERER!*

13

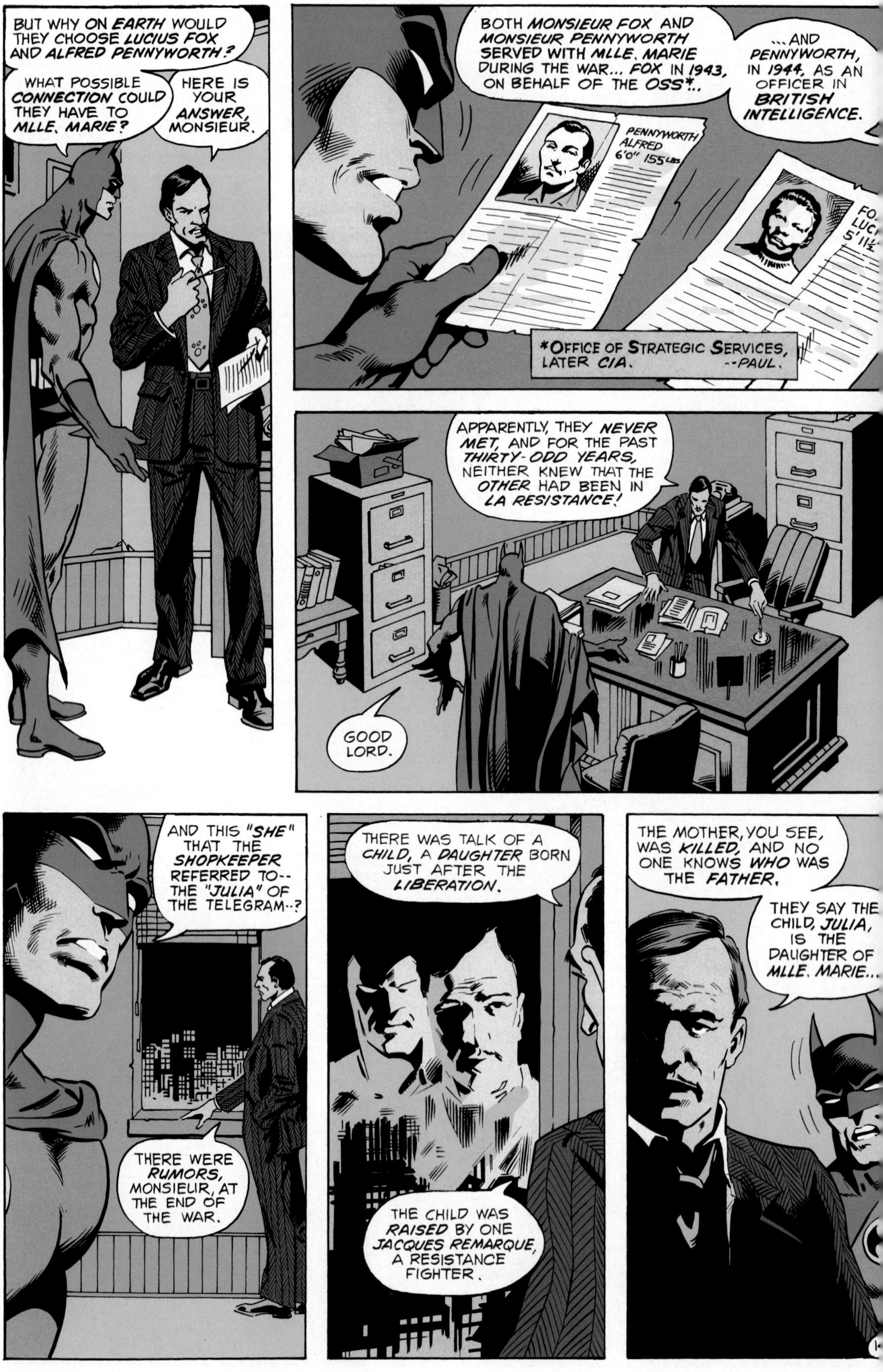

BUT WHY ON EARTH WOULD THEY CHOOSE LUCIUS FOX AND ALFRED PENNYWORTH?
WHAT POSSIBLE CONNECTION COULD THEY HAVE TO MLLE. MARIE?
HERE IS YOUR ANSWER, MONSIEUR.
BOTH MONSIEUR FOX AND MONSIEUR PENNYWORTH SERVED WITH MLLE. MARIE DURING THE WAR... FOX IN 1943, ON BEHALF OF THE OSS*...
...AND PENNYWORTH, IN 1944, AS AN OFFICER IN BRITISH INTELLIGENCE.
PENNYWORTH ALFRED 6'0" 155 LBS
*OFFICE OF STRATEGIC SERVICES, LATER CIA. --PAUL.
APPARENTLY, THEY NEVER MET, AND FOR THE PAST THIRTY-ODD YEARS, NEITHER KNEW THAT THE OTHER HAD BEEN IN LA RESISTANCE!
GOOD LORD.
AND THIS "SHE" THAT THE SHOPKEEPER REFERRED TO-- THE "JULIA" OF THE TELEGRAM--?
THERE WERE RUMORS, MONSIEUR, AT THE END OF THE WAR.
THERE WAS TALK OF A CHILD, A DAUGHTER BORN JUST AFTER THE LIBERATION.
THE CHILD WAS RAISED BY ONE JACQUES REMARQUE, A RESISTANCE FIGHTER.
THE MOTHER, YOU SEE, WAS KILLED, AND NO ONE KNOWS WHO WAS THE FATHER.
THEY SAY THE CHILD, JULIA, IS THE DAUGHTER OF MLLE. MARIE...

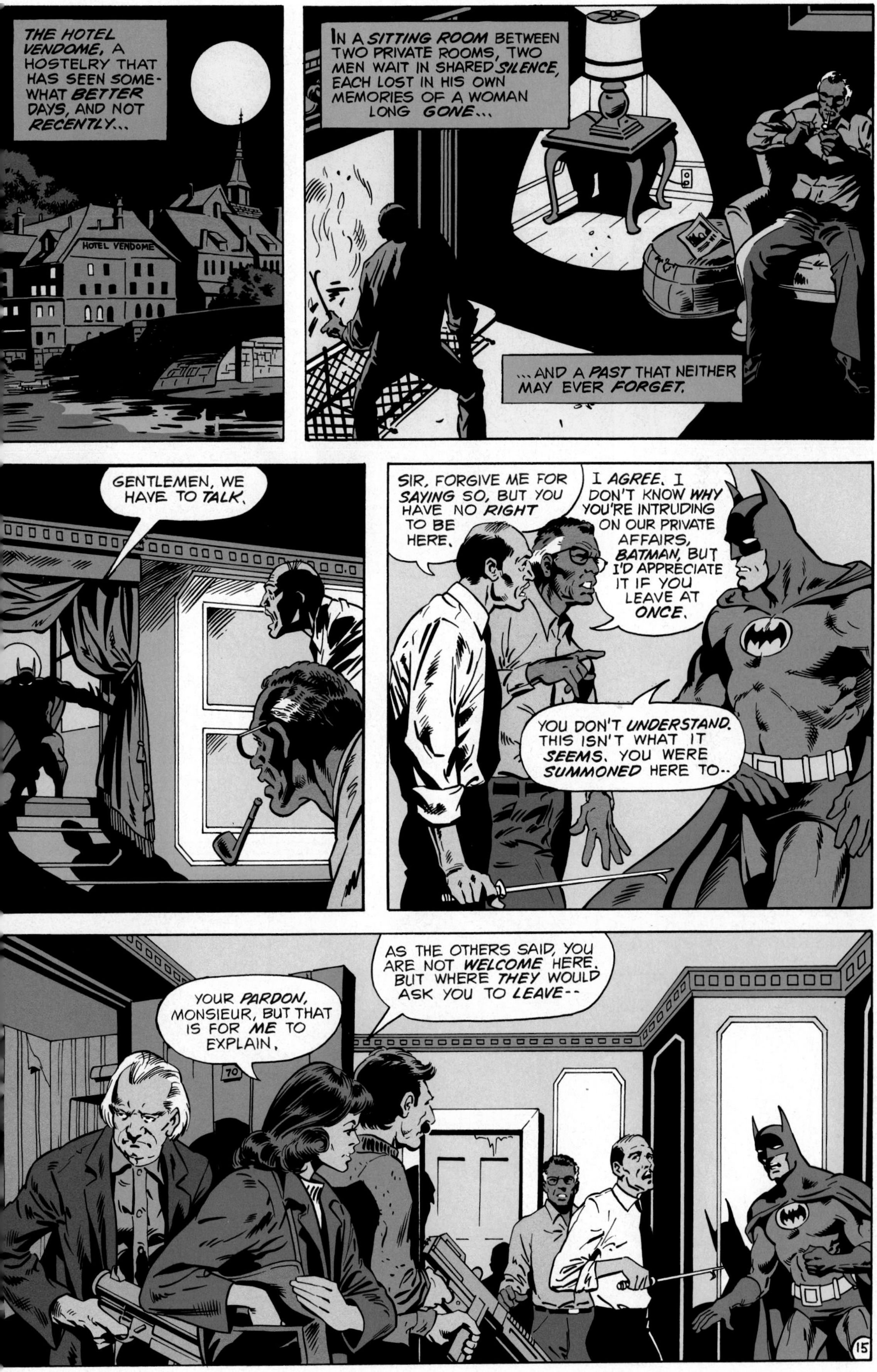
THE HOTEL VENDOME, A HOSTELRY THAT HAS SEEN SOME-WHAT BETTER DAYS, AND NOT RECENTLY...
HOTEL VENDOME
IN A SITTING ROOM BETWEEN TWO PRIVATE ROOMS, TWO MEN WAIT IN SHARED SILENCE, EACH LOST IN HIS OWN MEMORIES OF A WOMAN LONG GONE...
...AND A PAST THAT NEITHER MAY EVER FORGET.
GENTLEMEN, WE HAVE TO TALK.
SIR, FORGIVE ME FOR SAYING SO, BUT YOU HAVE NO RIGHT TO BE HERE.
I AGREE. I DON'T KNOW WHY YOU'RE INTRUDING ON OUR PRIVATE AFFAIRS, BATMAN, BUT I'D APPRECIATE IT IF YOU LEAVE AT ONCE.
YOU DON'T UNDERSTAND. THIS ISN'T WHAT IT SEEMS. YOU WERE SUMMONED HERE TO--
AS THE OTHERS SAID, YOU ARE NOT WELCOME HERE. BUT WHERE THEY WOULD ASK YOU TO LEAVE--
YOUR PARDON, MONSIEUR, BUT THAT IS FOR ME TO EXPLAIN.
70
15

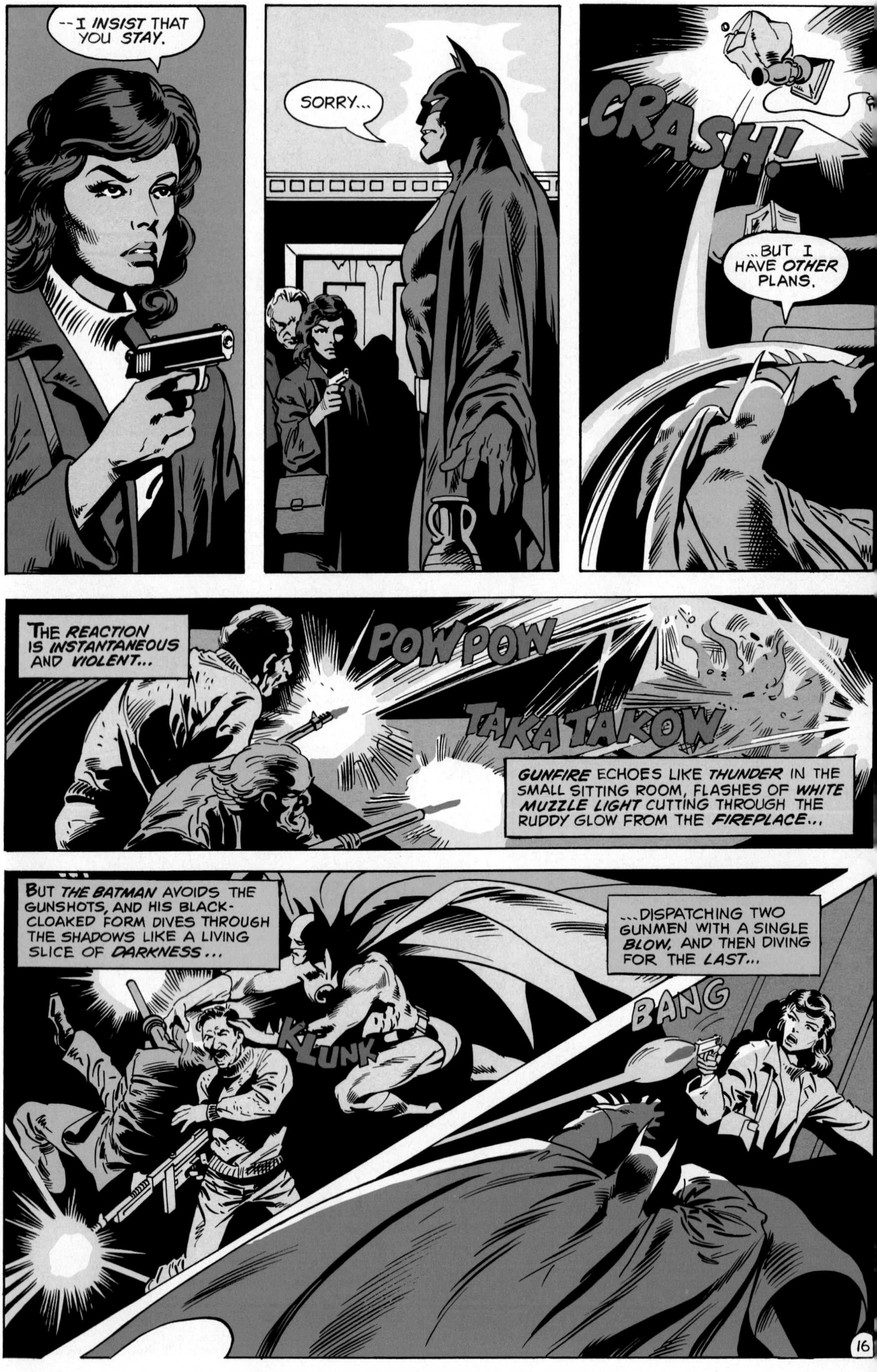
--I INSIST THAT YOU STAY.
SORRY...
CRASH!
...BUT I HAVE OTHER PLANS.
THE REACTION IS INSTANTANEOUS AND VIOLENT...
POWPOW
TAKATAKOW
GUNFIRE ECHOES LIKE THUNDER IN THE SMALL SITTING ROOM, FLASHES OF WHITE MUZZLE LIGHT CUTTING THROUGH THE RUDDY GLOW FROM THE FIREPLACE...
BUT THE BATMAN AVOIDS THE GUNSHOTS, AND HIS BLACK-CLOAKED FORM DIVES THROUGH THE SHADOWS LIKE A LIVING SLICE OF DARKNESS...
...DISPATCHING TWO GUNMEN WITH A SINGLE BLOW, AND THEN DIVING FOR THE LAST...
KLUNK
BANG
16

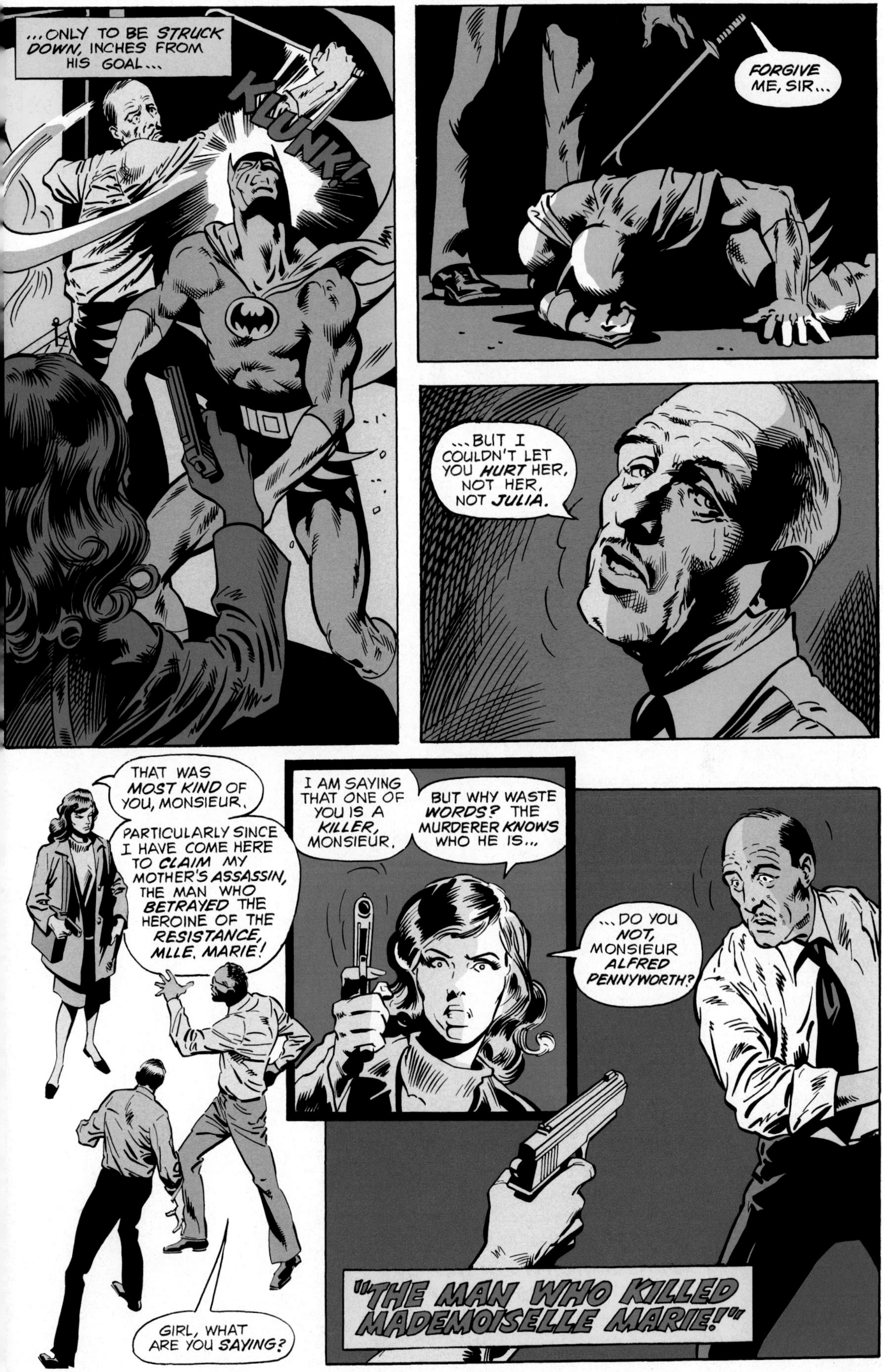
...ONLY TO BE STRUCK DOWN, INCHES FROM HIS GOAL...
KLUNK!
FORGIVE ME, SIR...
...BUT I COULDN'T LET YOU HURT HER, NOT HER, NOT JULIA.
THAT WAS MOST KIND OF YOU, MONSIEUR.
PARTICULARLY SINCE I HAVE COME HERE TO CLAIM MY MOTHER'S ASSASSIN, THE MAN WHO BETRAYED THE HEROINE OF THE RESISTANCE, MLLE. MARIE!
GIRL, WHAT ARE YOU SAYING?
I AM SAYING THAT ONE OF YOU IS A KILLER, MONSIEUR.
BUT WHY WASTE WORDS? THE MURDERER KNOWS WHO HE IS...
...DO YOU NOT, MONSIEUR ALFRED PENNYWORTH?
"THE MAN WHO KILLED MADEMOISELLE MARIE!"

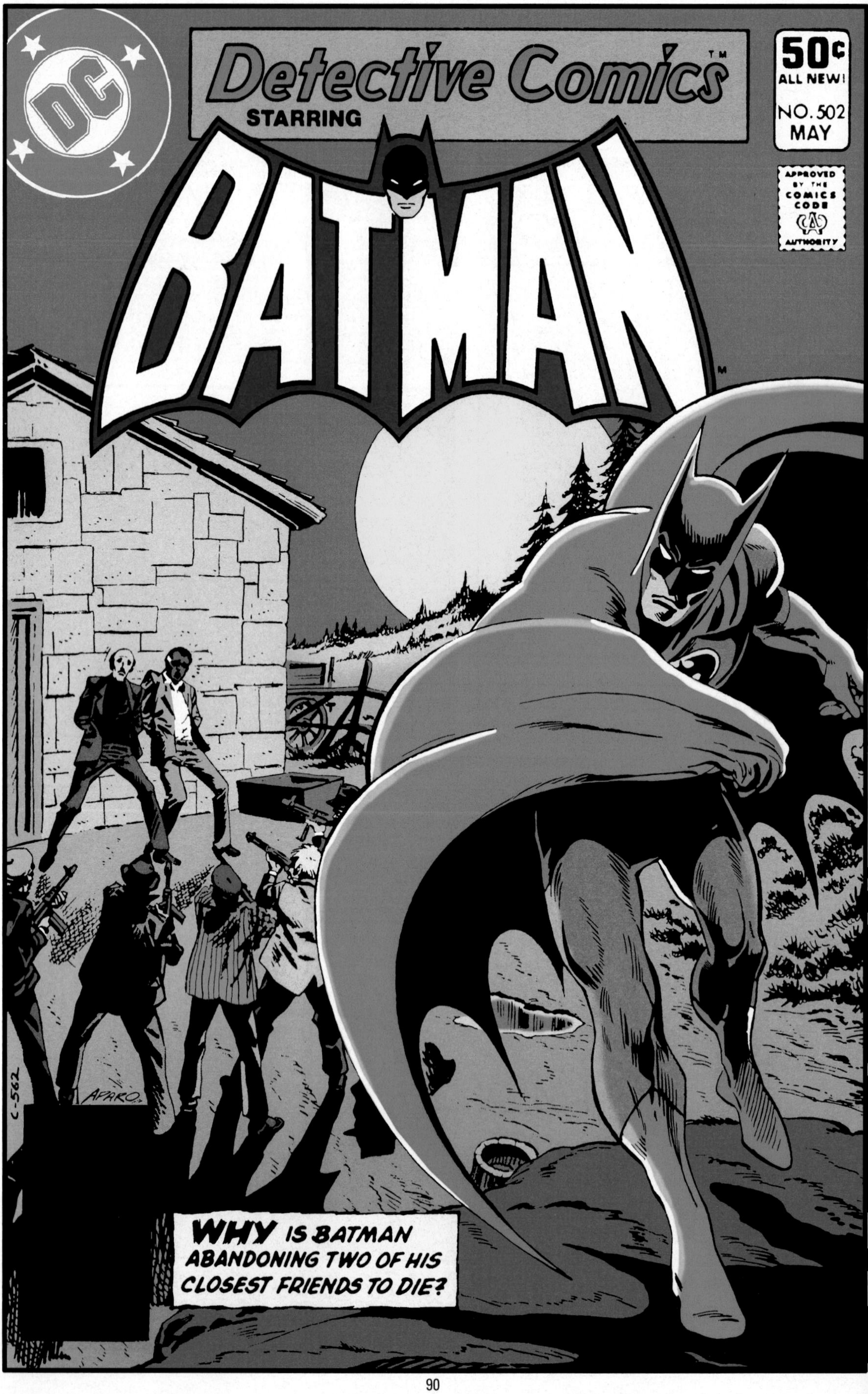
Detective Comics
STARRING
BATMAN
50¢
ALL NEW!
NO. 502
MAY
APPROVED BY THE COMICS CODE AUTHORITY
C-562
APARO
WHY IS BATMAN ABANDONING TWO OF HIS CLOSEST FRIENDS TO DIE?

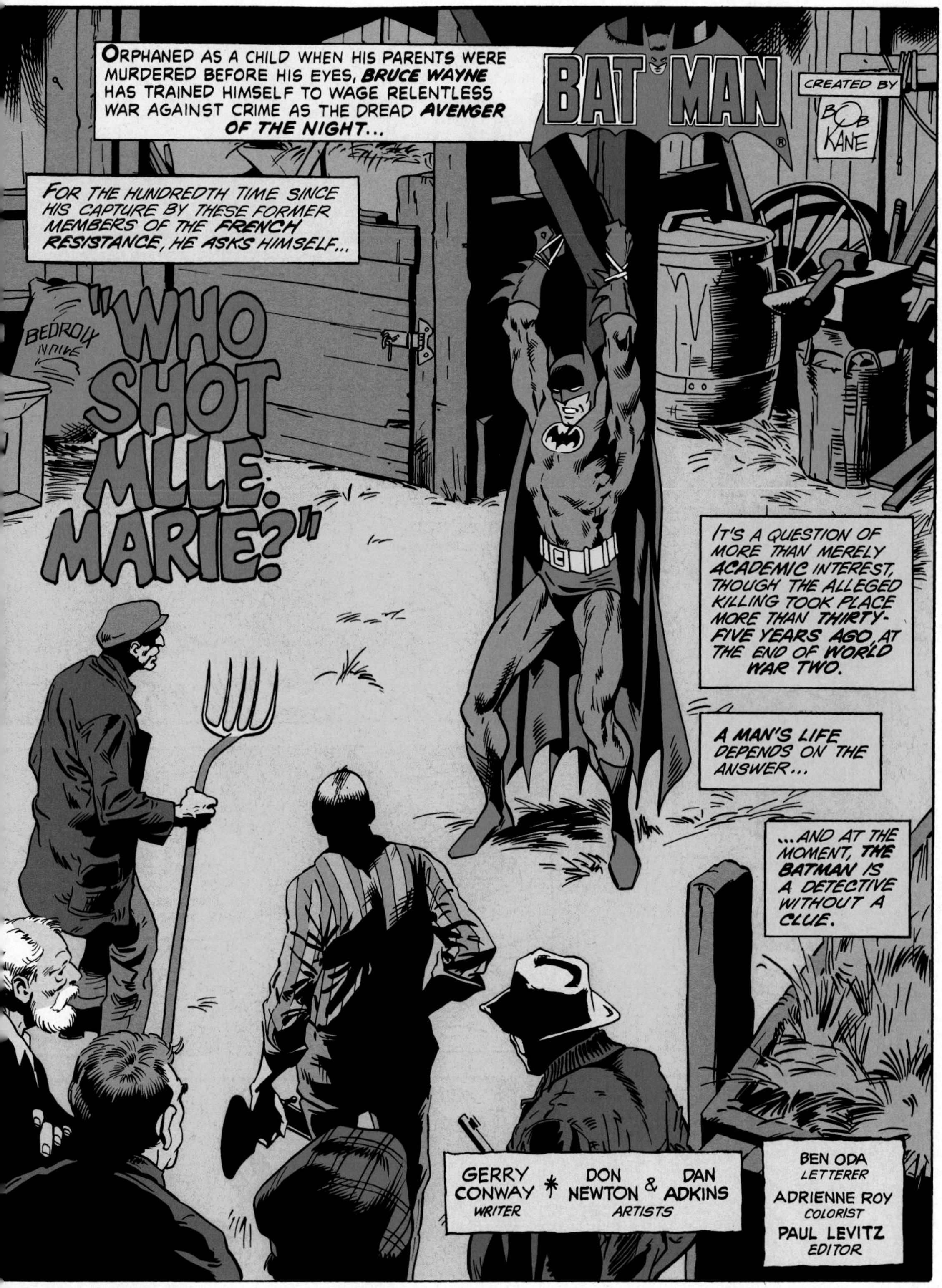
ORPHANED AS A CHILD WHEN HIS PARENTS WERE MURDERED BEFORE HIS EYES, BRUCE WAYNE HAS TRAINED HIMSELF TO WAGE RELENTLESS WAR AGAINST CRIME AS THE DREAD AVENGER OF THE NIGHT...
BATMAN
CREATED BY BOB KANE
FOR THE HUNDREDTH TIME SINCE HIS CAPTURE BY THESE FORMER MEMBERS OF THE FRENCH RESISTANCE, HE ASKS HIMSELF...
"WHO SHOT MLLE. MARIE?"
BEDROIX
IT'S A QUESTION OF MORE THAN MERELY ACADEMIC INTEREST, THOUGH THE ALLEGED KILLING TOOK PLACE MORE THAN THIRTY-FIVE YEARS AGO, AT THE END OF WORLD WAR TWO.
A MAN'S LIFE DEPENDS ON THE ANSWER...
...AND AT THE MOMENT, THE BATMAN IS A DETECTIVE WITHOUT A CLUE.
GERRY CONWAY WRITER
DON NEWTON & DAN ADKINS ARTISTS
BEN ODA LETTERER
ADRIENNE ROY COLORIST
PAUL LEVITZ EDITOR

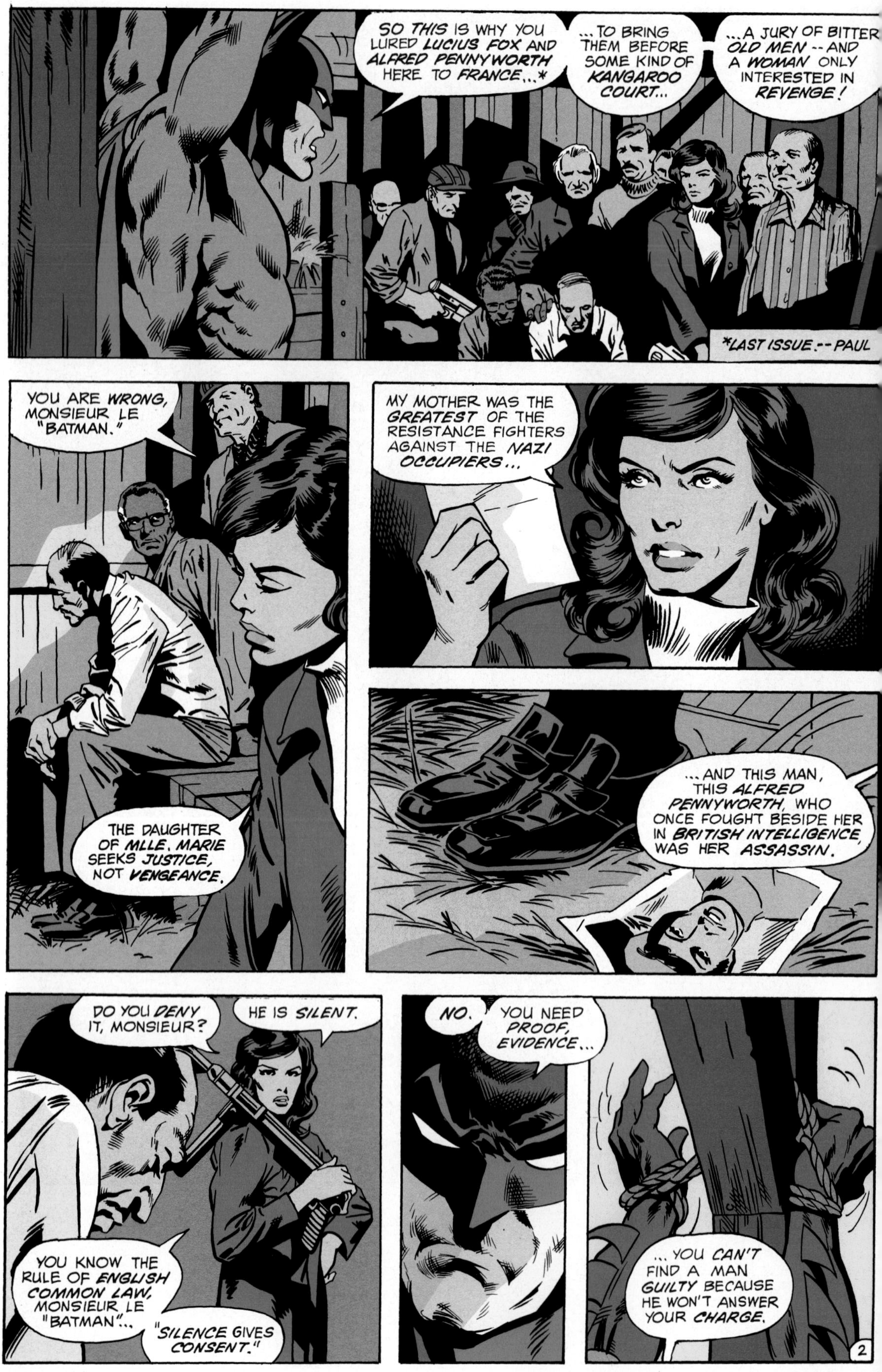
SO THIS IS WHY YOU LURED LUCIUS FOX AND ALFRED PENNYWORTH HERE TO FRANCE...*
...TO BRING THEM BEFORE SOME KIND OF KANGAROO COURT...
...A JURY OF BITTER OLD MEN -- AND A WOMAN ONLY INTERESTED IN REVENGE!
*LAST ISSUE.-- PAUL
YOU ARE WRONG, MONSIEUR LE "BATMAN."
THE DAUGHTER OF MLLE. MARIE SEEKS JUSTICE, NOT VENGEANCE.
MY MOTHER WAS THE GREATEST OF THE RESISTANCE FIGHTERS AGAINST THE NAZI OCCUPIERS...
...AND THIS MAN, THIS ALFRED PENNYWORTH, WHO ONCE FOUGHT BESIDE HER IN BRITISH INTELLIGENCE, WAS HER ASSASSIN.
DO YOU DENY IT, MONSIEUR?
HE IS SILENT.
YOU KNOW THE RULE OF ENGLISH COMMON LAW, MONSIEUR LE "BATMAN"...
"SILENCE GIVES CONSENT."
NO.
YOU NEED PROOF, EVIDENCE...
...YOU CAN'T FIND A MAN GUILTY BECAUSE HE WON'T ANSWER YOUR CHARGE.
2

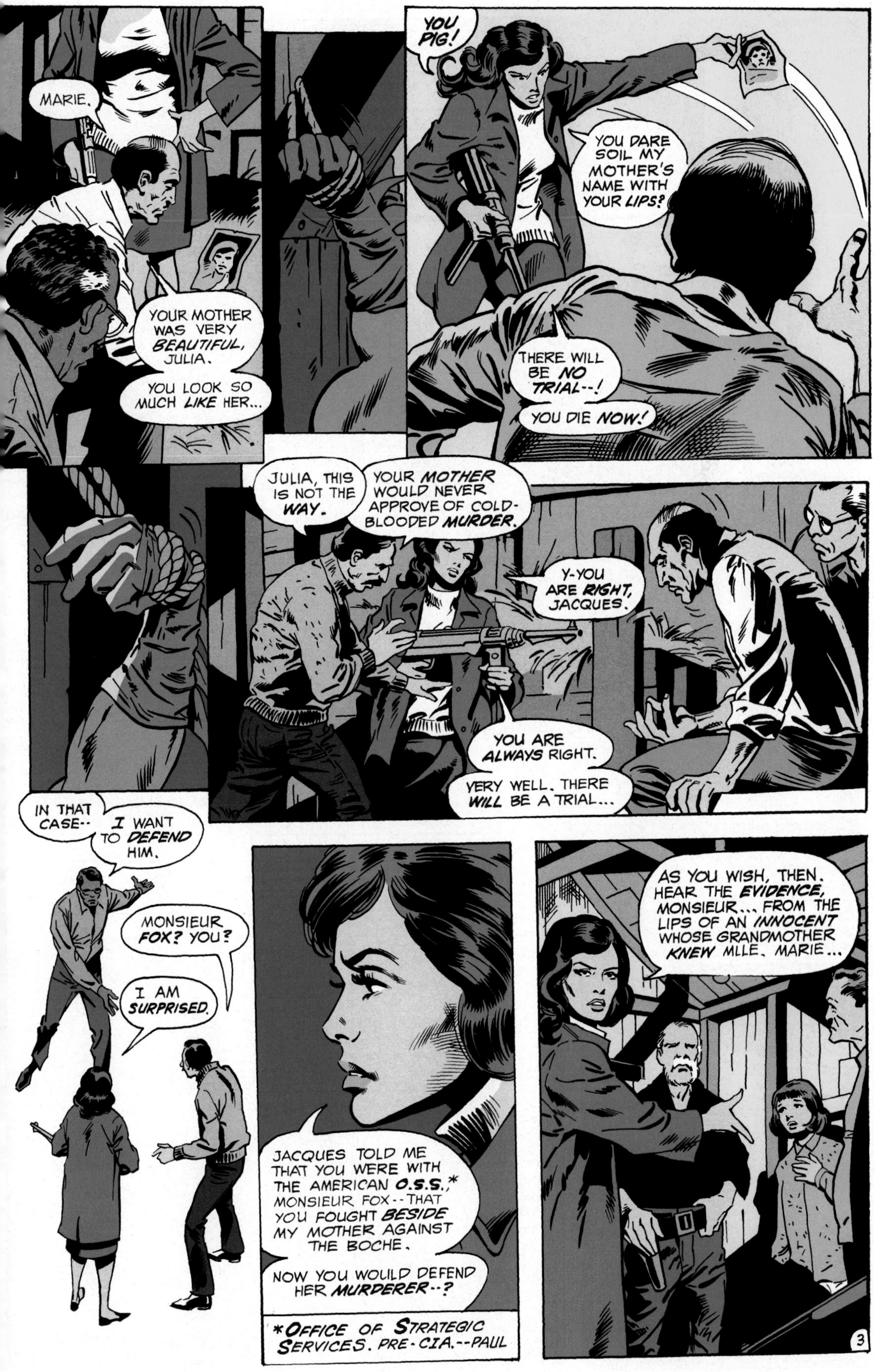
MARIE.
YOUR MOTHER WAS VERY BEAUTIFUL, JULIA.
YOU LOOK SO MUCH LIKE HER...
YOU PIG!
YOU DARE SOIL MY MOTHER'S NAME WITH YOUR LIPS?
THERE WILL BE NO TRIAL--!
YOU DIE NOW!
JULIA, THIS IS NOT THE WAY.
YOUR MOTHER WOULD NEVER APPROVE OF COLD-BLOODED MURDER.
Y-YOU ARE RIGHT, JACQUES.
YOU ARE ALWAYS RIGHT.
VERY WELL. THERE WILL BE A TRIAL...
IN THAT CASE--
I WANT TO DEFEND HIM.
MONSIEUR FOX? YOU?
I AM SURPRISED.
JACQUES TOLD ME THAT YOU WERE WITH THE AMERICAN O.S.S.,* MONSIEUR FOX--THAT YOU FOUGHT BESIDE MY MOTHER AGAINST THE BOCHE.
NOW YOU WOULD DEFEND HER MURDERER--?
*OFFICE OF STRATEGIC SERVICES. PRE-CIA.--PAUL
AS YOU WISH, THEN. HEAR THE EVIDENCE, MONSIEUR... FROM THE LIPS OF AN INNOCENT WHOSE GRANDMOTHER KNEW MLLE. MARIE...
3

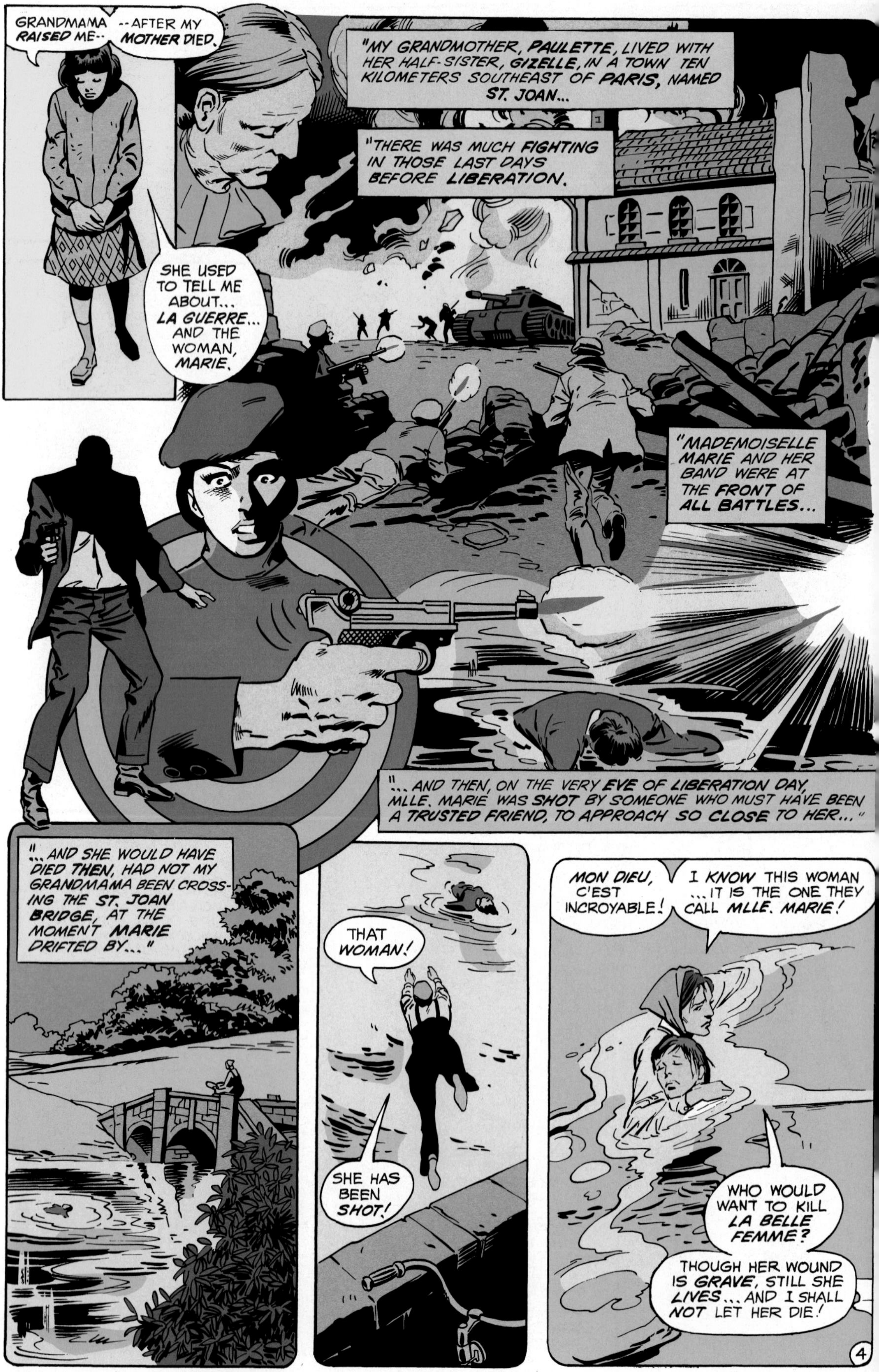
GRANDMAMA RAISED ME--
--AFTER MY MOTHER DIED.
"MY GRANDMOTHER, PAULETTE, LIVED WITH HER HALF-SISTER, GIZELLE, IN A TOWN TEN KILOMETERS SOUTHEAST OF PARIS, NAMED ST. JOAN...
"THERE WAS MUCH FIGHTING IN THOSE LAST DAYS BEFORE LIBERATION.
SHE USED TO TELL ME ABOUT... LA GUERRE... AND THE WOMAN, MARIE.
"MADEMOISELLE MARIE AND HER BAND WERE AT THE FRONT OF ALL BATTLES...
"... AND THEN, ON THE VERY EVE OF LIBERATION DAY, MLLE. MARIE WAS SHOT BY SOMEONE WHO MUST HAVE BEEN A TRUSTED FRIEND, TO APPROACH SO CLOSE TO HER..."
"... AND SHE WOULD HAVE DIED THEN, HAD NOT MY GRANDMAMA BEEN CROSSING THE ST. JOAN BRIDGE, AT THE MOMENT MARIE DRIFTED BY..."
THAT WOMAN!
SHE HAS BEEN SHOT!
MON DIEU, C'EST INCROYABLE!
I KNOW THIS WOMAN ... IT IS THE ONE THEY CALL MLLE. MARIE!
WHO WOULD WANT TO KILL LA BELLE FEMME?
THOUGH HER WOUND IS GRAVE, STILL SHE LIVES... AND I SHALL NOT LET HER DIE!
4

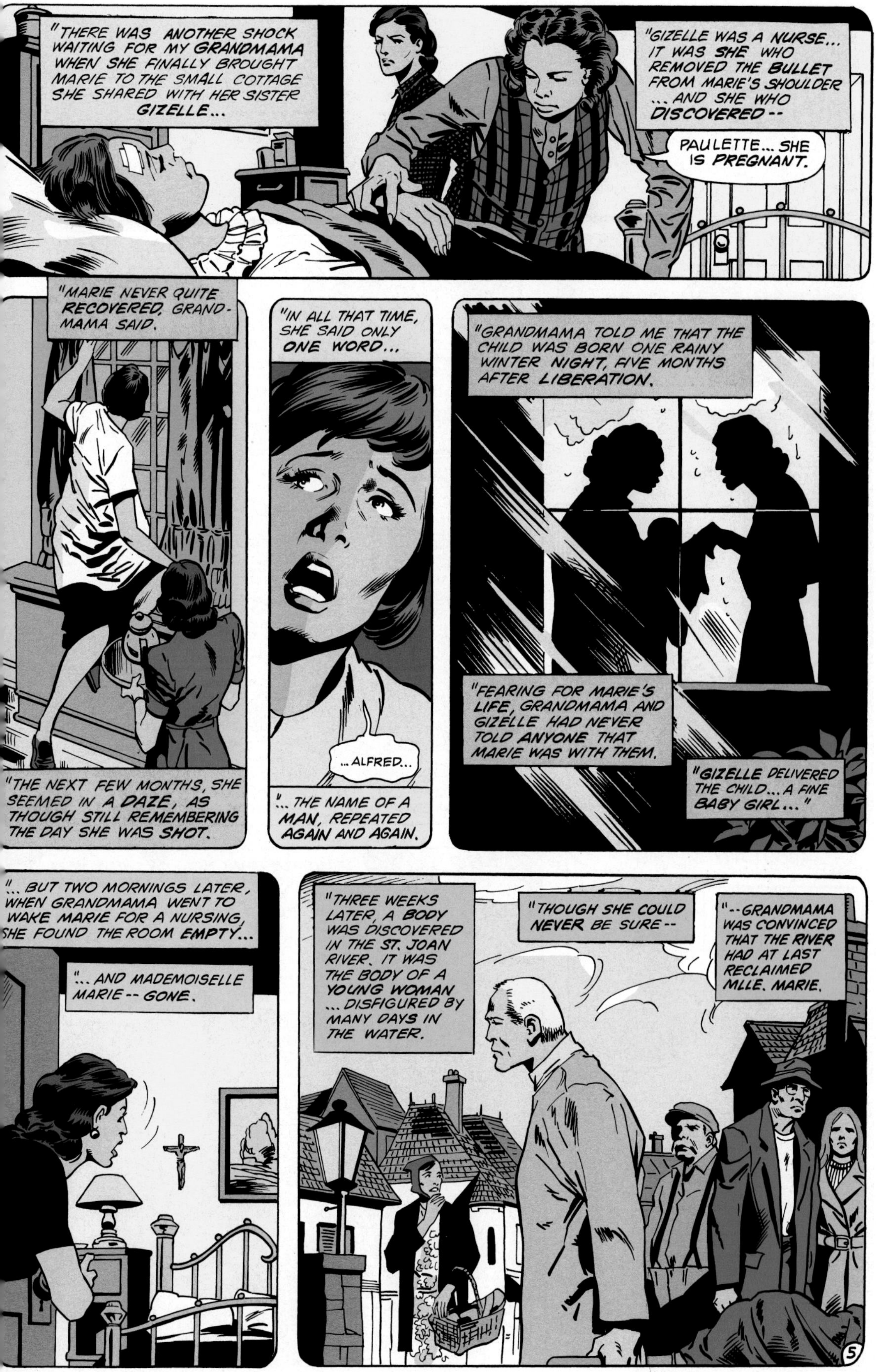
"THERE WAS ANOTHER SHOCK WAITING FOR MY GRANDMAMA WHEN SHE FINALLY BROUGHT MARIE TO THE SMALL COTTAGE SHE SHARED WITH HER SISTER GIZELLE...
"GIZELLE WAS A NURSE... IT WAS SHE WHO REMOVED THE BULLET FROM MARIE'S SHOULDER ...AND SHE WHO DISCOVERED --
PAULETTE... SHE IS PREGNANT.
"MARIE NEVER QUITE RECOVERED, GRAND-MAMA SAID.
"THE NEXT FEW MONTHS, SHE SEEMED IN A DAZE, AS THOUGH STILL REMEMBERING THE DAY SHE WAS SHOT.
"IN ALL THAT TIME, SHE SAID ONLY ONE WORD...
...ALFRED...
"...THE NAME OF A MAN, REPEATED AGAIN AND AGAIN.
"GRANDMAMA TOLD ME THAT THE CHILD WAS BORN ONE RAINY WINTER NIGHT, FIVE MONTHS AFTER LIBERATION.
"FEARING FOR MARIE'S LIFE, GRANDMAMA AND GIZELLE HAD NEVER TOLD ANYONE THAT MARIE WAS WITH THEM.
"GIZELLE DELIVERED THE CHILD... A FINE BABY GIRL..."
"...BUT TWO MORNINGS LATER, WHEN GRANDMAMA WENT TO WAKE MARIE FOR A NURSING, SHE FOUND THE ROOM EMPTY...
"...AND MADEMOISELLE MARIE -- GONE.
"THREE WEEKS LATER, A BODY WAS DISCOVERED IN THE ST. JOAN RIVER. IT WAS THE BODY OF A YOUNG WOMAN ...DISFIGURED BY MANY DAYS IN THE WATER.
"THOUGH SHE COULD NEVER BE SURE --
"--GRANDMAMA WAS CONVINCED THAT THE RIVER HAD AT LAST RECLAIMED MLLE. MARIE.
5

"IT WAS STRANGE, GRANDMAMA SAID, AS THOUGH THE RIVER HAD GIVEN THEM MARIE ONLY LONG ENOUGH FOR THE CHILD TO BE BORN...

"IN A WAY, GRANDMAMA SAID, THIS WAS LIKE LIFE ITSELF.

"SHE AND GIZELLE NAMED THE GIRL JULIA.

"THROUGH WHAT WAS LEFT OF THE RESISTANCE, THEY MADE CONTACT WITH ONE OF MARIE'S OLD COMRADES IN-ARMS...

"HIS NAME WAS JACQUES REMARQUE.

"HE PROMISED TO RAISE JULIA AS A MEMBER OF HIS OWN FAMILY, AND TO KEEP THE SECRET OF HER BIRTH --"

--WHICH HE DID, UNTIL JULIA PRESSED HIM FOR THE TRUTH ONLY A FEW WEEKS AGO.

JACQUES TOLD ME ABOUT THE WOMEN WHO TRIED TO SAVE MY MOTHER--

--AND FROM THIS CHILD, I LEARNED ABOUT YOU.

YOU'RE ACCUSING THIS MAN ON HEARSAY?

ALFRED, YOU CAN CLEAR THIS UP RIGHT NOW...

...TELL THEM YOU KNOW NOTHING ABOUT ANY OF THIS.

BUT ALFRED PENNYWORTH CANNOT ANSWER.

BOTH HIS SILENCE -- AND HIS TEARS -- ARE DAMNING.

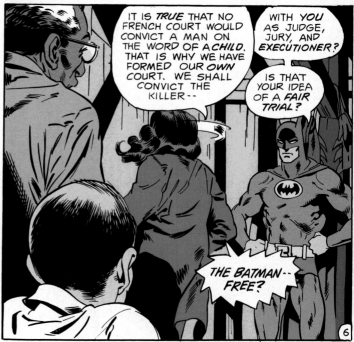

IT IS TRUE THAT NO FRENCH COURT WOULD CONVICT A MAN ON THE WORD OF A CHILD. THAT IS WHY WE HAVE FORMED OUR OWN COURT. WE SHALL CONVICT THE KILLER--

WITH YOU AS JUDGE, JURY, AND EXECUTIONER?

IS THAT YOUR IDEA OF A FAIR TRIAL?

THE BATMAN-- FREE?

6

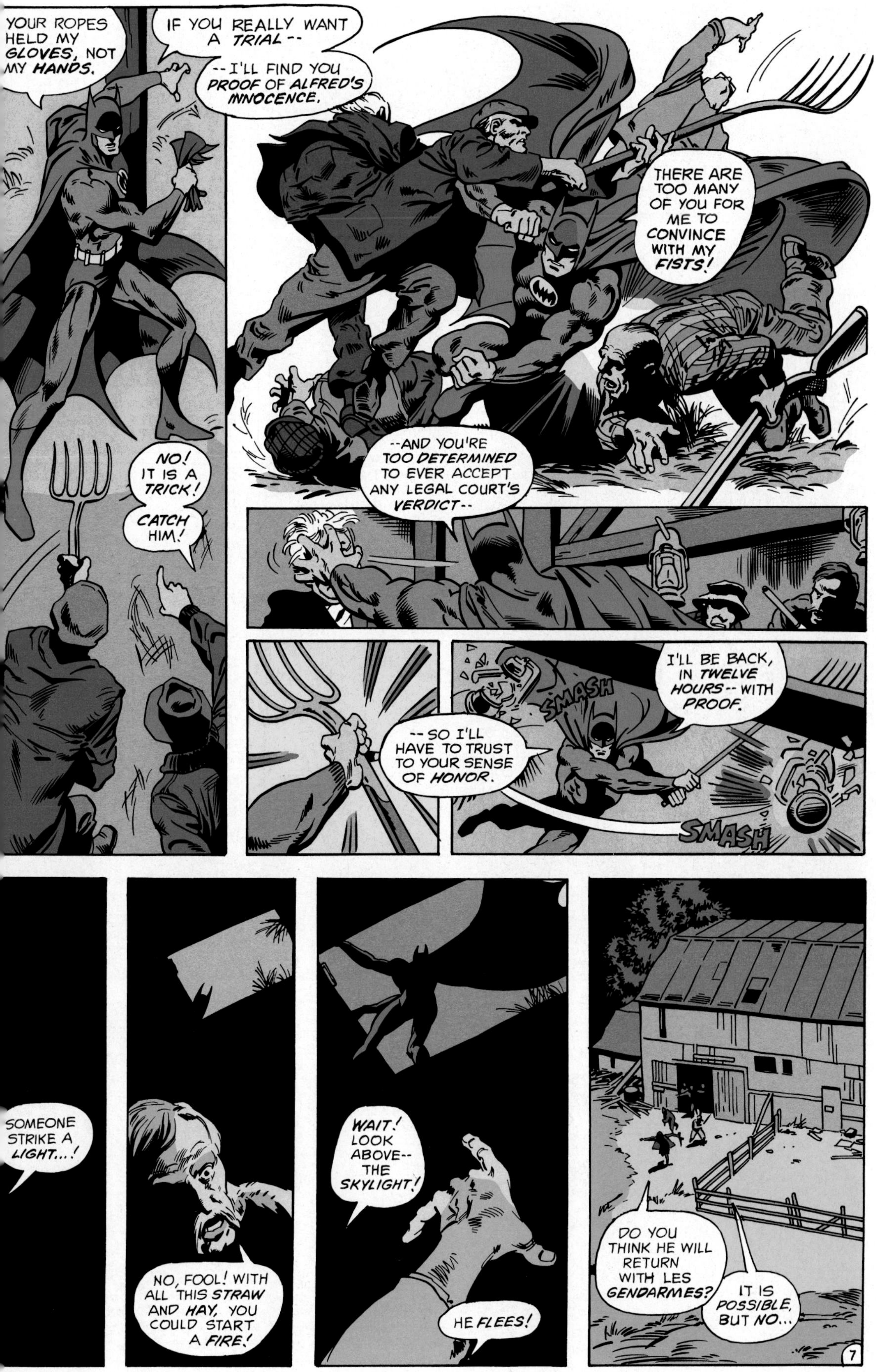
YOUR ROPES HELD MY GLOVES, NOT MY HANDS.
IF YOU REALLY WANT A TRIAL --
-- I'LL FIND YOU PROOF OF ALFRED'S INNOCENCE.
THERE ARE TOO MANY OF YOU FOR ME TO CONVINCE WITH MY FISTS!
--AND YOU'RE TOO DETERMINED TO EVER ACCEPT ANY LEGAL COURT'S VERDICT--
NO! IT IS A TRICK!
CATCH HIM!
--SO I'LL HAVE TO TRUST TO YOUR SENSE OF HONOR.
I'LL BE BACK, IN TWELVE HOURS--WITH PROOF.
SMASH
SMASH
SOMEONE STRIKE A LIGHT...!
NO, FOOL! WITH ALL THIS STRAW AND HAY, YOU COULD START A FIRE!
WAIT! LOOK ABOVE-- THE SKYLIGHT!
HE FLEES!
DO YOU THINK HE WILL RETURN WITH LES GENDARMES?
IT IS POSSIBLE, BUT NO...
7

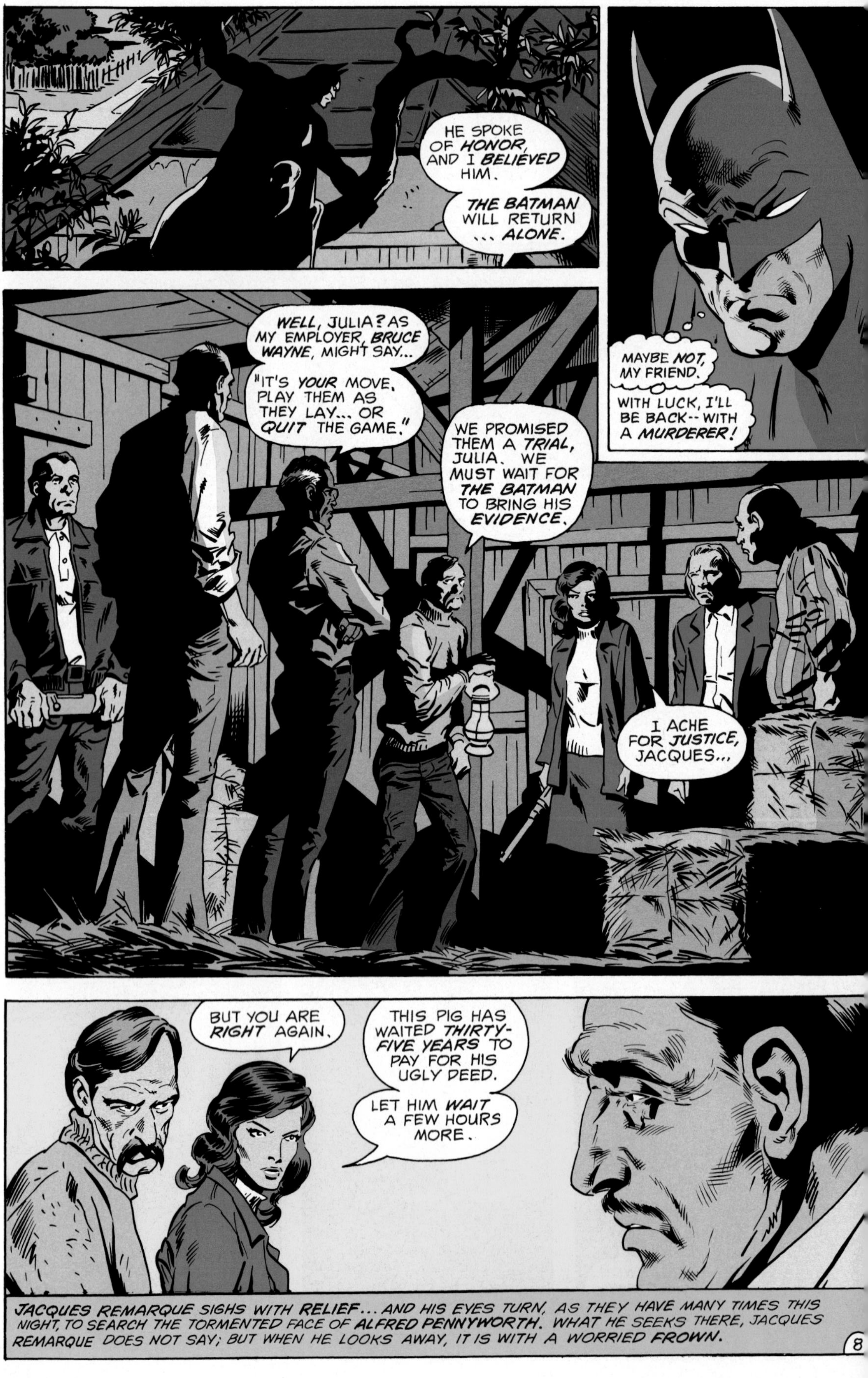
HE SPOKE OF HONOR, AND I BELIEVED HIM.
THE BATMAN WILL RETURN ... ALONE.
MAYBE NOT, MY FRIEND.
WITH LUCK, I'LL BE BACK-- WITH A MURDERER!
WELL, JULIA? AS MY EMPLOYER, BRUCE WAYNE, MIGHT SAY...
"IT'S YOUR MOVE. PLAY THEM AS THEY LAY... OR QUIT THE GAME."
WE PROMISED THEM A TRIAL, JULIA. WE MUST WAIT FOR THE BATMAN TO BRING HIS EVIDENCE.
I ACHE FOR JUSTICE, JACQUES...
BUT YOU ARE RIGHT AGAIN.
THIS PIG HAS WAITED THIRTY-FIVE YEARS TO PAY FOR HIS UGLY DEED.
LET HIM WAIT A FEW HOURS MORE.
JACQUES REMARQUE SIGHS WITH RELIEF... AND HIS EYES TURN, AS THEY HAVE MANY TIMES THIS NIGHT, TO SEARCH THE TORMENTED FACE OF ALFRED PENNYWORTH. WHAT HE SEEKS THERE, JACQUES REMARQUE DOES NOT SAY; BUT WHEN HE LOOKS AWAY, IT IS WITH A WORRIED FROWN.
8

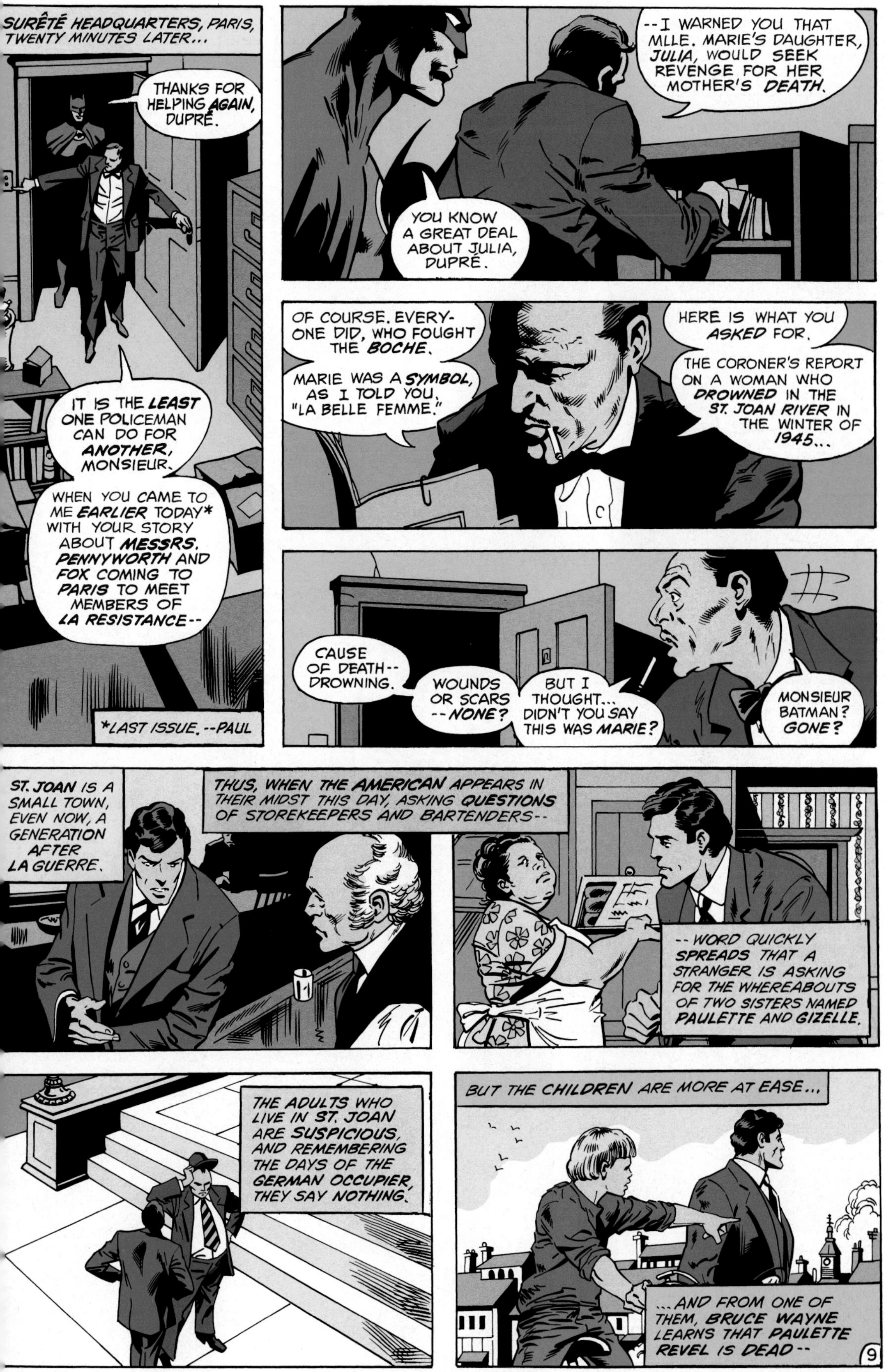
SURÊTÉ HEADQUARTERS, PARIS, TWENTY MINUTES LATER...
THANKS FOR HELPING AGAIN, DUPRÉ.
--I WARNED YOU THAT MLLE. MARIE'S DAUGHTER, JULIA, WOULD SEEK REVENGE FOR HER MOTHER'S DEATH.
YOU KNOW A GREAT DEAL ABOUT JULIA, DUPRÉ.
IT IS THE LEAST ONE POLICEMAN CAN DO FOR ANOTHER, MONSIEUR.
WHEN YOU CAME TO ME EARLIER TODAY* WITH YOUR STORY ABOUT MESSRS. PENNYWORTH AND FOX COMING TO PARIS TO MEET MEMBERS OF LA RESISTANCE--
*LAST ISSUE. --PAUL
OF COURSE. EVERYONE DID, WHO FOUGHT THE BOCHE.
MARIE WAS A SYMBOL, AS I TOLD YOU. "LA BELLE FEMME."
HERE IS WHAT YOU ASKED FOR.
THE CORONER'S REPORT ON A WOMAN WHO DROWNED IN THE ST. JOAN RIVER IN THE WINTER OF 1945...
CAUSE OF DEATH-- DROWNING.
WOUNDS OR SCARS --NONE?
BUT I THOUGHT... DIDN'T YOU SAY THIS WAS MARIE?
MONSIEUR BATMAN? GONE?
ST. JOAN IS A SMALL TOWN, EVEN NOW, A GENERATION AFTER LA GUERRE.
THUS, WHEN THE AMERICAN APPEARS IN THEIR MIDST THIS DAY, ASKING QUESTIONS OF STOREKEEPERS AND BARTENDERS--
--WORD QUICKLY SPREADS THAT A STRANGER IS ASKING FOR THE WHEREABOUTS OF TWO SISTERS NAMED PAULETTE AND GIZELLE.
THE ADULTS WHO LIVE IN ST. JOAN ARE SUSPICIOUS, AND REMEMBERING THE DAYS OF THE GERMAN OCCUPIER, THEY SAY NOTHING.
BUT THE CHILDREN ARE MORE AT EASE...
...AND FROM ONE OF THEM, BRUCE WAYNE LEARNS THAT PAULETTE REVEL IS DEAD--
9

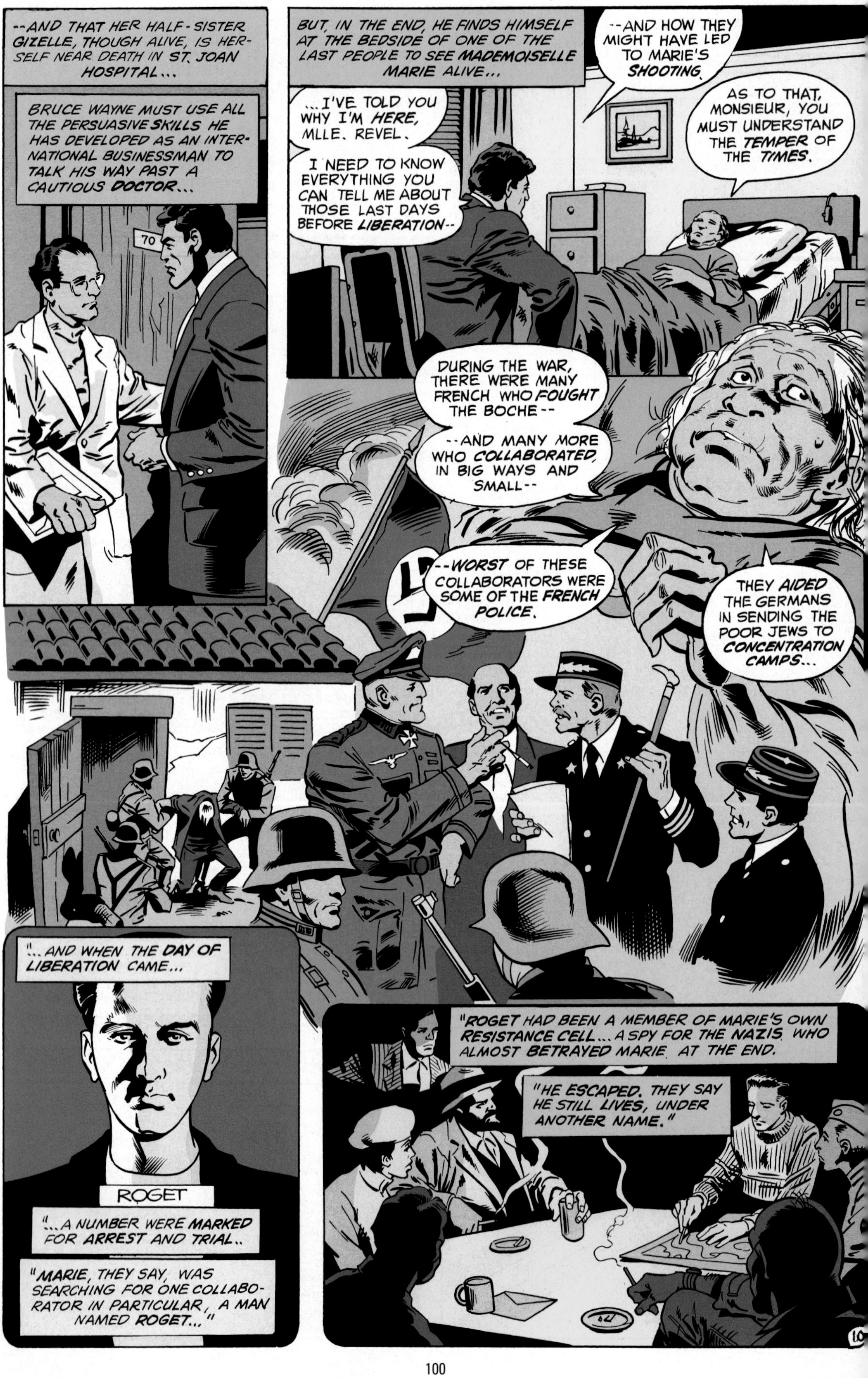
--AND THAT HER HALF-SISTER GIZELLE, THOUGH ALIVE, IS HERSELF NEAR DEATH IN ST. JOAN HOSPITAL...
BRUCE WAYNE MUST USE ALL THE PERSUASIVE SKILLS HE HAS DEVELOPED AS AN INTERNATIONAL BUSINESSMAN TO TALK HIS WAY PAST A CAUTIOUS DOCTOR...
70
BUT, IN THE END, HE FINDS HIMSELF AT THE BEDSIDE OF ONE OF THE LAST PEOPLE TO SEE MADEMOISELLE MARIE ALIVE...
...I'VE TOLD YOU WHY I'M HERE, MLLE. REVEL.
I NEED TO KNOW EVERYTHING YOU CAN TELL ME ABOUT THOSE LAST DAYS BEFORE LIBERATION--
--AND HOW THEY MIGHT HAVE LED TO MARIE'S SHOOTING.
AS TO THAT, MONSIEUR, YOU MUST UNDERSTAND THE TEMPER OF THE TIMES.
DURING THE WAR, THERE WERE MANY FRENCH WHO FOUGHT THE BOCHE--
--AND MANY MORE WHO COLLABORATED, IN BIG WAYS AND SMALL--
--WORST OF THESE COLLABORATORS WERE SOME OF THE FRENCH POLICE.
THEY AIDED THE GERMANS IN SENDING THE POOR JEWS TO CONCENTRATION CAMPS...
"...AND WHEN THE DAY OF LIBERATION CAME...
ROGET
"...A NUMBER WERE MARKED FOR ARREST AND TRIAL..
"MARIE, THEY SAY, WAS SEARCHING FOR ONE COLLABORATOR IN PARTICULAR, A MAN NAMED ROGET..."
"ROGET HAD BEEN A MEMBER OF MARIE'S OWN RESISTANCE CELL... A SPY FOR THE NAZIS WHO ALMOST BETRAYED MARIE AT THE END.
"HE ESCAPED. THEY SAY HE STILL LIVES, UNDER ANOTHER NAME."
10

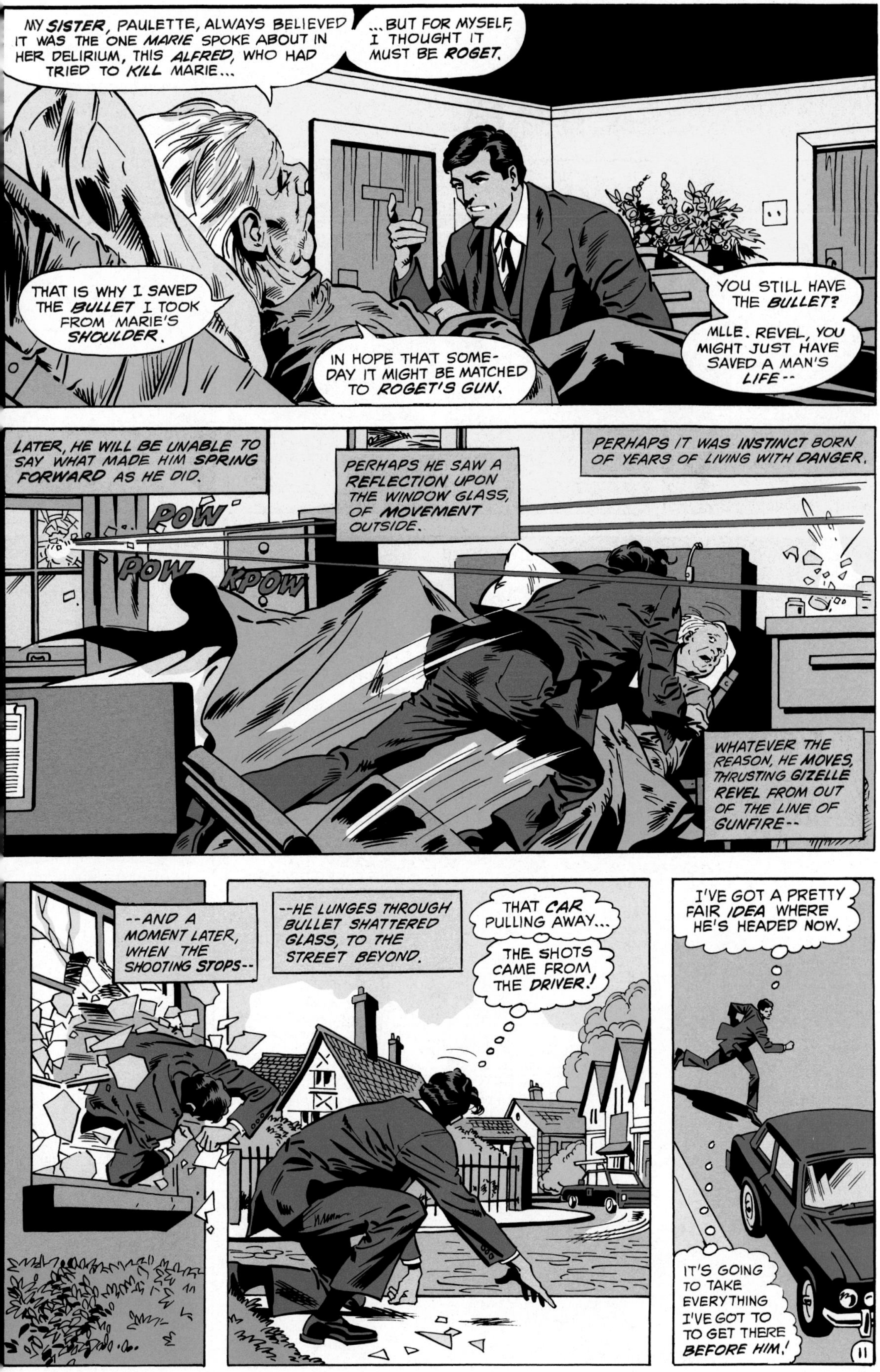
MY SISTER, PAULETTE, ALWAYS BELIEVED IT WAS THE ONE MARIE SPOKE ABOUT IN HER DELIRIUM, THIS ALFRED, WHO HAD TRIED TO KILL MARIE...
...BUT FOR MYSELF, I THOUGHT IT MUST BE ROGET.
THAT IS WHY I SAVED THE BULLET I TOOK FROM MARIE'S SHOULDER.
IN HOPE THAT SOMEDAY IT MIGHT BE MATCHED TO ROGET'S GUN.
YOU STILL HAVE THE BULLET?
MLLE. REVEL, YOU MIGHT JUST HAVE SAVED A MAN'S LIFE--
LATER, HE WILL BE UNABLE TO SAY WHAT MADE HIM SPRING FORWARD AS HE DID.
PERHAPS HE SAW A REFLECTION UPON THE WINDOW GLASS, OF MOVEMENT OUTSIDE.
PERHAPS IT WAS INSTINCT BORN OF YEARS OF LIVING WITH DANGER.
POW
POW
KPOW
WHATEVER THE REASON, HE MOVES, THRUSTING GIZELLE REVEL FROM OUT OF THE LINE OF GUNFIRE--
--AND A MOMENT LATER, WHEN THE SHOOTING STOPS--
--HE LUNGES THROUGH BULLET SHATTERED GLASS, TO THE STREET BEYOND.
THAT CAR PULLING AWAY...
THE SHOTS CAME FROM THE DRIVER!
I'VE GOT A PRETTY FAIR IDEA WHERE HE'S HEADED NOW.
IT'S GOING TO TAKE EVERYTHING I'VE GOT TO TO GET THERE BEFORE HIM!
11

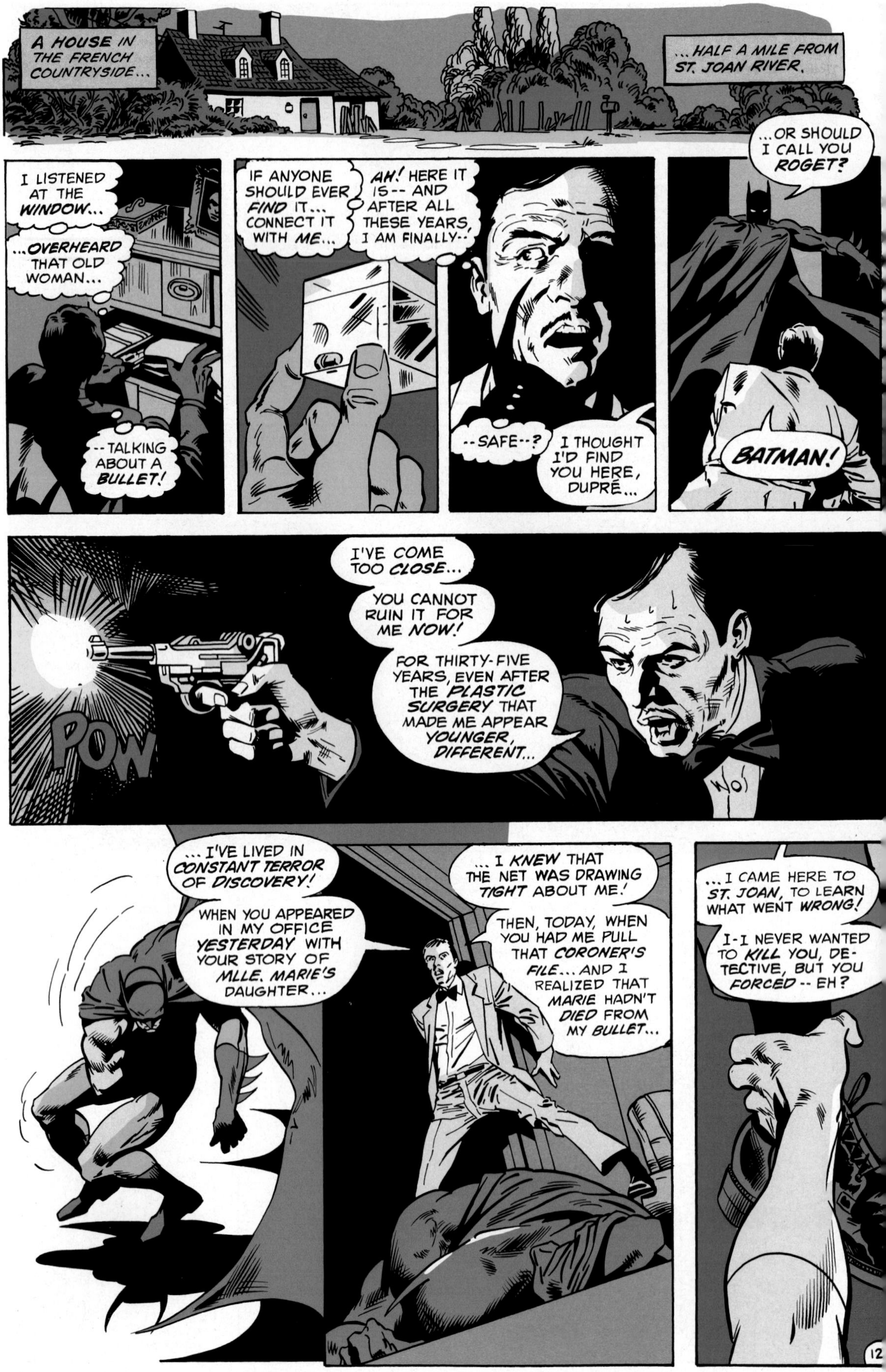

A HOUSE IN THE FRENCH COUNTRYSIDE...
...HALF A MILE FROM ST. JOAN RIVER.
I LISTENED AT THE WINDOW...
...OVERHEARD THAT OLD WOMAN...
--TALKING ABOUT A BULLET!
IF ANYONE SHOULD EVER FIND IT... CONNECT IT WITH ME...
AH! HERE IT IS-- AND AFTER ALL THESE YEARS, I AM FINALLY--
--SAFE--?
I THOUGHT I'D FIND YOU HERE, DUPRÉ...
...OR SHOULD I CALL YOU ROGET?
BATMAN!
POW
I'VE COME TOO CLOSE...
YOU CANNOT RUIN IT FOR ME NOW!
FOR THIRTY-FIVE YEARS, EVEN AFTER THE PLASTIC SURGERY THAT MADE ME APPEAR YOUNGER, DIFFERENT...
...I'VE LIVED IN CONSTANT TERROR OF DISCOVERY!
WHEN YOU APPEARED IN MY OFFICE YESTERDAY WITH YOUR STORY OF MLLE. MARIE'S DAUGHTER...
...I KNEW THAT THE NET WAS DRAWING TIGHT ABOUT ME!
THEN, TODAY, WHEN YOU HAD ME PULL THAT CORONER'S FILE... AND I REALIZED THAT MARIE HADN'T DIED FROM MY BULLET...
...I CAME HERE TO ST. JOAN, TO LEARN WHAT WENT WRONG!
I-I NEVER WANTED TO KILL YOU, DETECTIVE, BUT YOU FORCED-- EH?
12

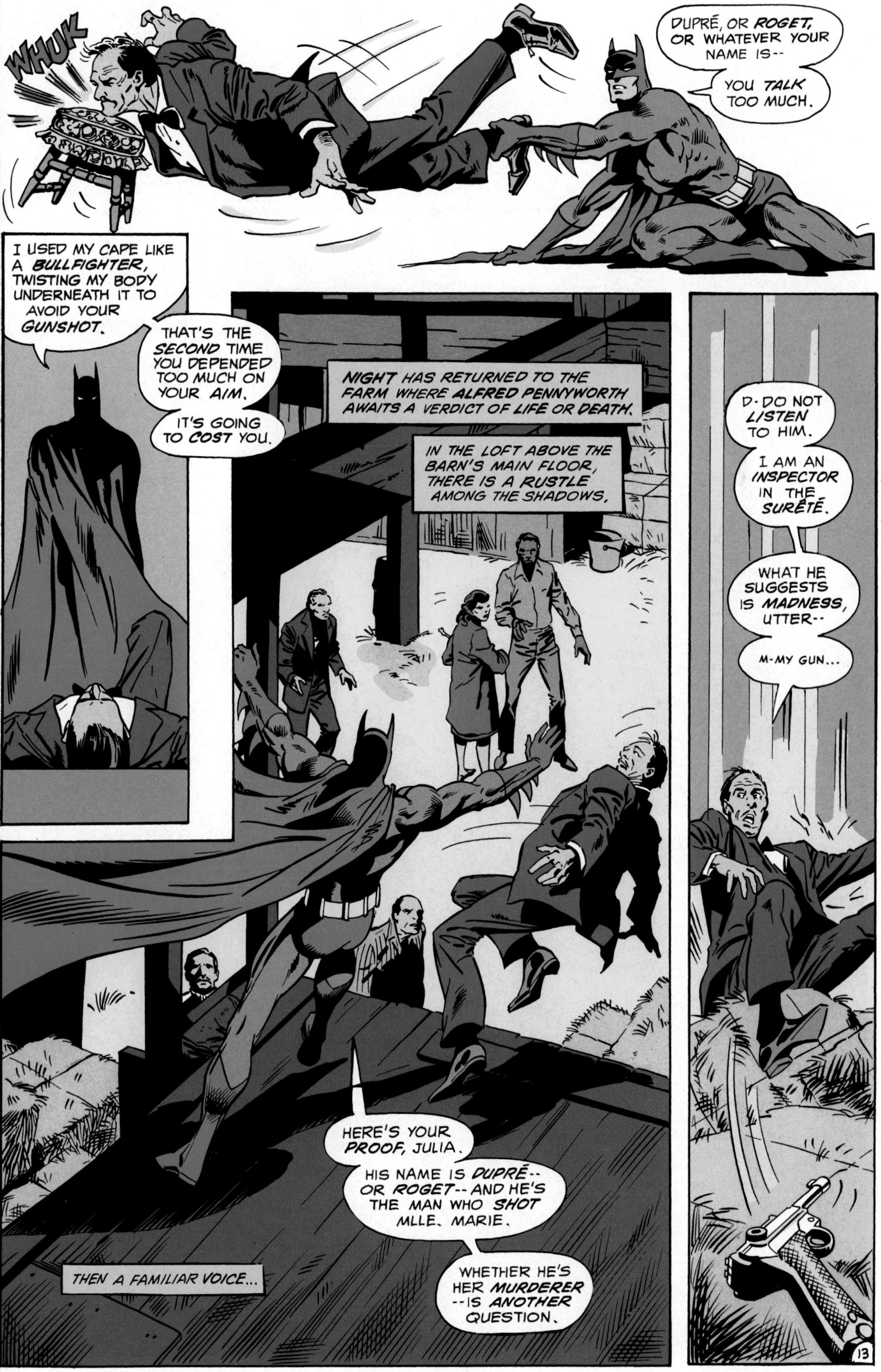

WHUK
DUPRÉ, OR ROGET, OR WHATEVER YOUR NAME IS--
YOU TALK TOO MUCH.
I USED MY CAPE LIKE A BULLFIGHTER, TWISTING MY BODY UNDERNEATH IT TO AVOID YOUR GUNSHOT.
THAT'S THE SECOND TIME YOU DEPENDED TOO MUCH ON YOUR AIM.
IT'S GOING TO COST YOU.
NIGHT HAS RETURNED TO THE FARM WHERE ALFRED PENNYWORTH AWAITS A VERDICT OF LIFE OR DEATH.
IN THE LOFT ABOVE THE BARN'S MAIN FLOOR, THERE IS A RUSTLE AMONG THE SHADOWS.
THEN A FAMILIAR VOICE...
HERE'S YOUR PROOF, JULIA.
HIS NAME IS DUPRÉ-- OR ROGET-- AND HE'S THE MAN WHO SHOT MLLE. MARIE.
WHETHER HE'S HER MURDERER --IS ANOTHER QUESTION.
D-DO NOT LISTEN TO HIM.
I AM AN INSPECTOR IN THE SURÊTÉ.
WHAT HE SUGGESTS IS MADNESS, UTTER--
M-MY GUN...
13

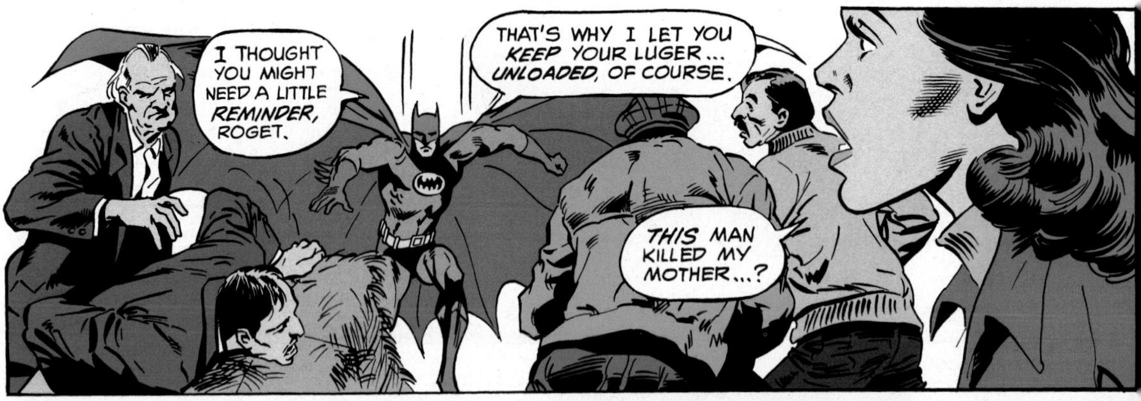
I THOUGHT YOU MIGHT NEED A LITTLE REMINDER, ROGET.
THAT'S WHY I LET YOU KEEP YOUR LUGER... UNLOADED, OF COURSE.
THIS MAN KILLED MY MOTHER...?

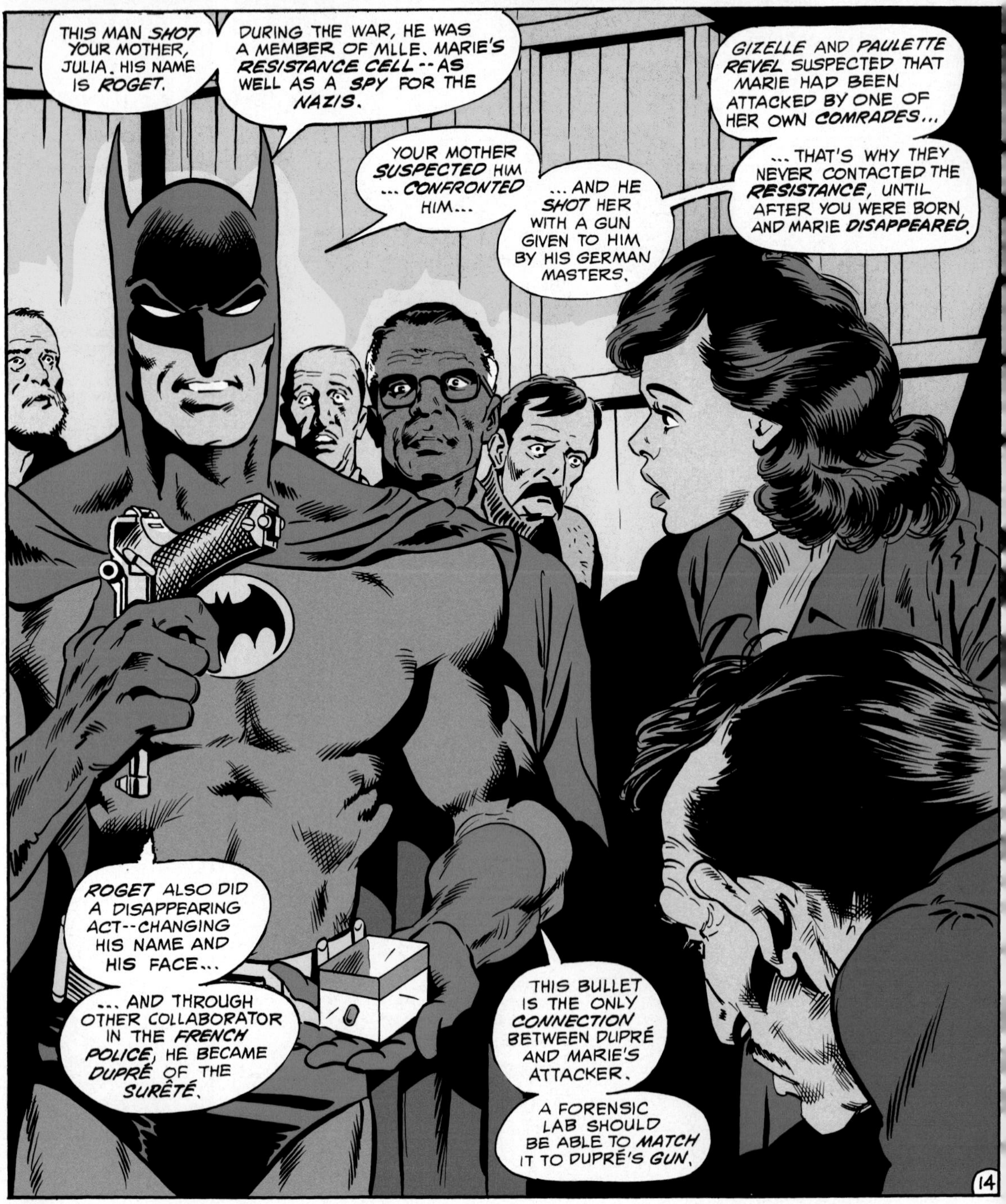
THIS MAN SHOT YOUR MOTHER, JULIA. HIS NAME IS ROGET.
DURING THE WAR, HE WAS A MEMBER OF MLLE. MARIE'S RESISTANCE CELL--AS WELL AS A SPY FOR THE NAZIS.
YOUR MOTHER SUSPECTED HIM ...CONFRONTED HIM...
...AND HE SHOT HER WITH A GUN GIVEN TO HIM BY HIS GERMAN MASTERS.
GIZELLE AND PAULETTE REVEL SUSPECTED THAT MARIE HAD BEEN ATTACKED BY ONE OF HER OWN COMRADES...
...THAT'S WHY THEY NEVER CONTACTED THE RESISTANCE, UNTIL AFTER YOU WERE BORN, AND MARIE DISAPPEARED.
ROGET ALSO DID A DISAPPEARING ACT--CHANGING HIS NAME AND HIS FACE...
...AND THROUGH OTHER COLLABORATOR IN THE FRENCH POLICE, HE BECAME DUPRÉ OF THE SURÊTÉ.
THIS BULLET IS THE ONLY CONNECTION BETWEEN DUPRÉ AND MARIE'S ATTACKER.
A FORENSIC LAB SHOULD BE ABLE TO MATCH IT TO DUPRÉ'S GUN.
14

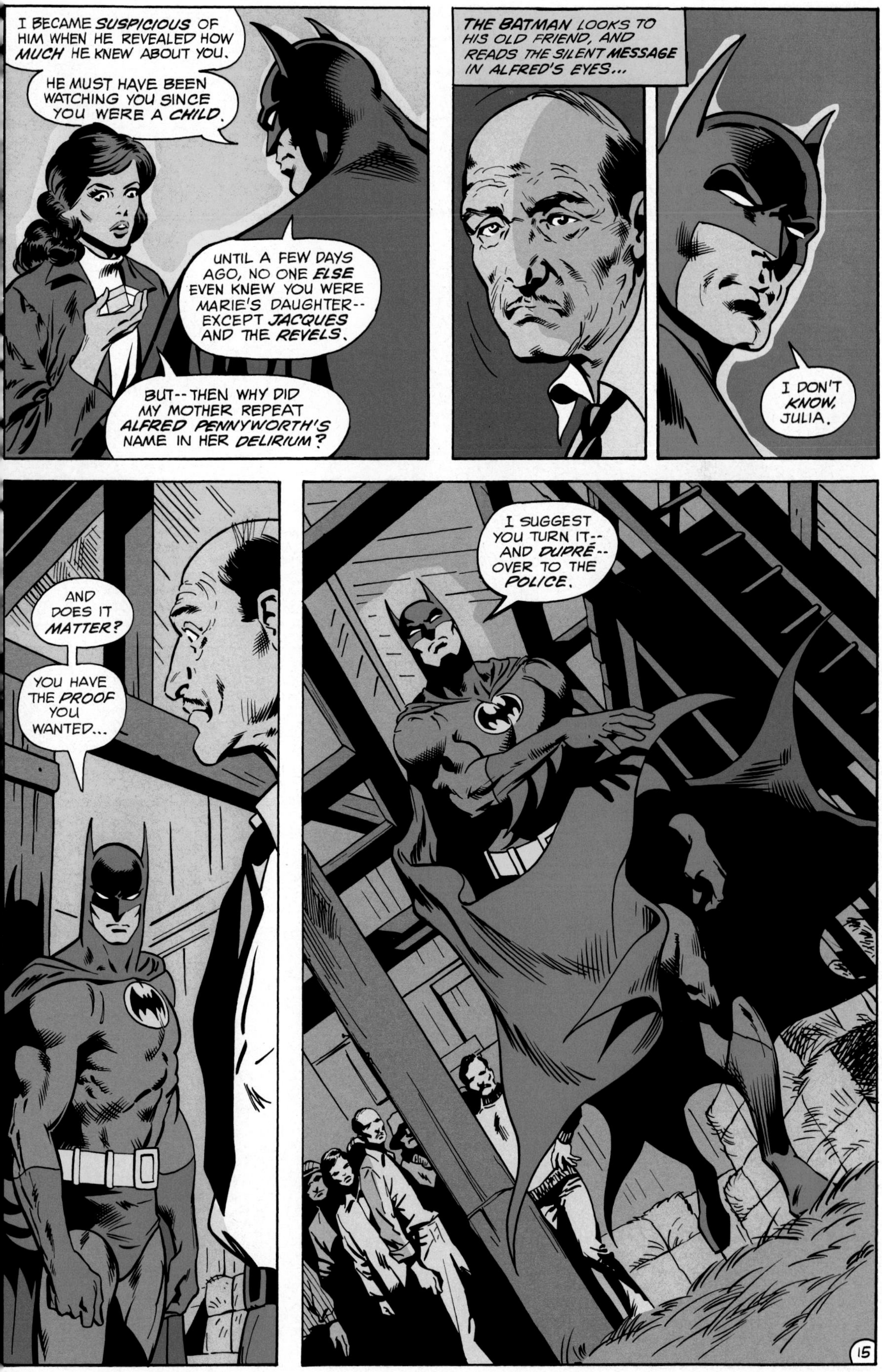
I BECAME SUSPICIOUS OF HIM WHEN HE REVEALED HOW MUCH HE KNEW ABOUT YOU.
HE MUST HAVE BEEN WATCHING YOU SINCE YOU WERE A CHILD.
UNTIL A FEW DAYS AGO, NO ONE ELSE EVEN KNEW YOU WERE MARIE'S DAUGHTER-- EXCEPT JACQUES AND THE REVELS.
BUT-- THEN WHY DID MY MOTHER REPEAT ALFRED PENNYWORTH'S NAME IN HER DELIRIUM?
THE BATMAN LOOKS TO HIS OLD FRIEND, AND READS THE SILENT MESSAGE IN ALFRED'S EYES...
I DON'T KNOW, JULIA.
AND DOES IT MATTER?
YOU HAVE THE PROOF YOU WANTED...
I SUGGEST YOU TURN IT-- AND DUPRÉ-- OVER TO THE POLICE.
15

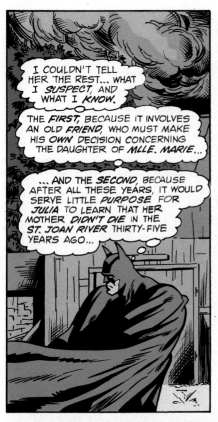

I COULDN'T TELL HER THE REST... WHAT I *SUSPECT*, AND WHAT I *KNOW*.

THE *FIRST*, BECAUSE IT INVOLVES AN OLD *FRIEND*, WHO MUST MAKE HIS *OWN* DECISION CONCERNING THE DAUGHTER OF *MLLE. MARIE*...

...AND THE *SECOND*, BECAUSE AFTER ALL THESE YEARS, IT WOULD SERVE LITTLE *PURPOSE* FOR *JULIA* TO LEARN THAT HER MOTHER *DIDN'T DIE* IN THE *ST. JOAN RIVER* THIRTY-FIVE YEARS AGO...

RAIN FALLS HARD ON ORLY INTERNATIONAL AIRPORT, THE NEXT MORNING...

..., LIKE TEARS OF MOURNING, *LONG DELAYED*...

STRANGE OF JULIA AND JACQUES REMARQUE TO SEE US *OFF*.

I *KNEW* JACQUES WHEN I SERVED AS OSS LIAISON TO THE *RESISTANCE*, OF COURSE, AND *ALFRED* SPENT TIME WITH THEM AS WELL, WHEN HE WAS IN *BRITISH INTELLIGENCE*...

"...YET THE WAY HE AND *REMARQUE* ARE LOOKING AT EACH OTHER, IT'S AS THOUGH THERE WERE SOMETHING *MORE* BETWEEN THEM THAN FRIEND-SHIP BORN IN A *WAR*..."

JACQUES... THANK YOU FOR NOT *SPEAKING OUT*.

THERE WERE MOMENTS WHEN I FELT THAT I *MUST*, MY FRIEND...

...BUT THE *OATH* I SWORE TO YOU OVER THREE DECADES AGO KEPT ME *SILENT*.

I HAVE ALWAYS DONE AS YOU *ASKED* WITHOUT *QUESTIONING*--

--BUT DON'T YOU THINK IT'S TIME YOU FINALLY *TOLD* HER?

TELL HER *WHAT*, JACQUES? THAT I *LOVED* HER MOTHER ...AND THAT I WOULD HAVE *MARRIED* MARIE, IF THE WAR HADN'T FORCED US *APART*?

SHOULD I TELL HER THAT I DIDN'T EVEN *KNOW* SHE WAS *ALIVE*--

--UNTIL YOU WROTE ME IN *AMERICA*, TWO YEARS AFTER SHE WAS *BORN*?

CAN I TELL HER HOW I SENT YOU *MONEY* ALL THESE YEARS...

16

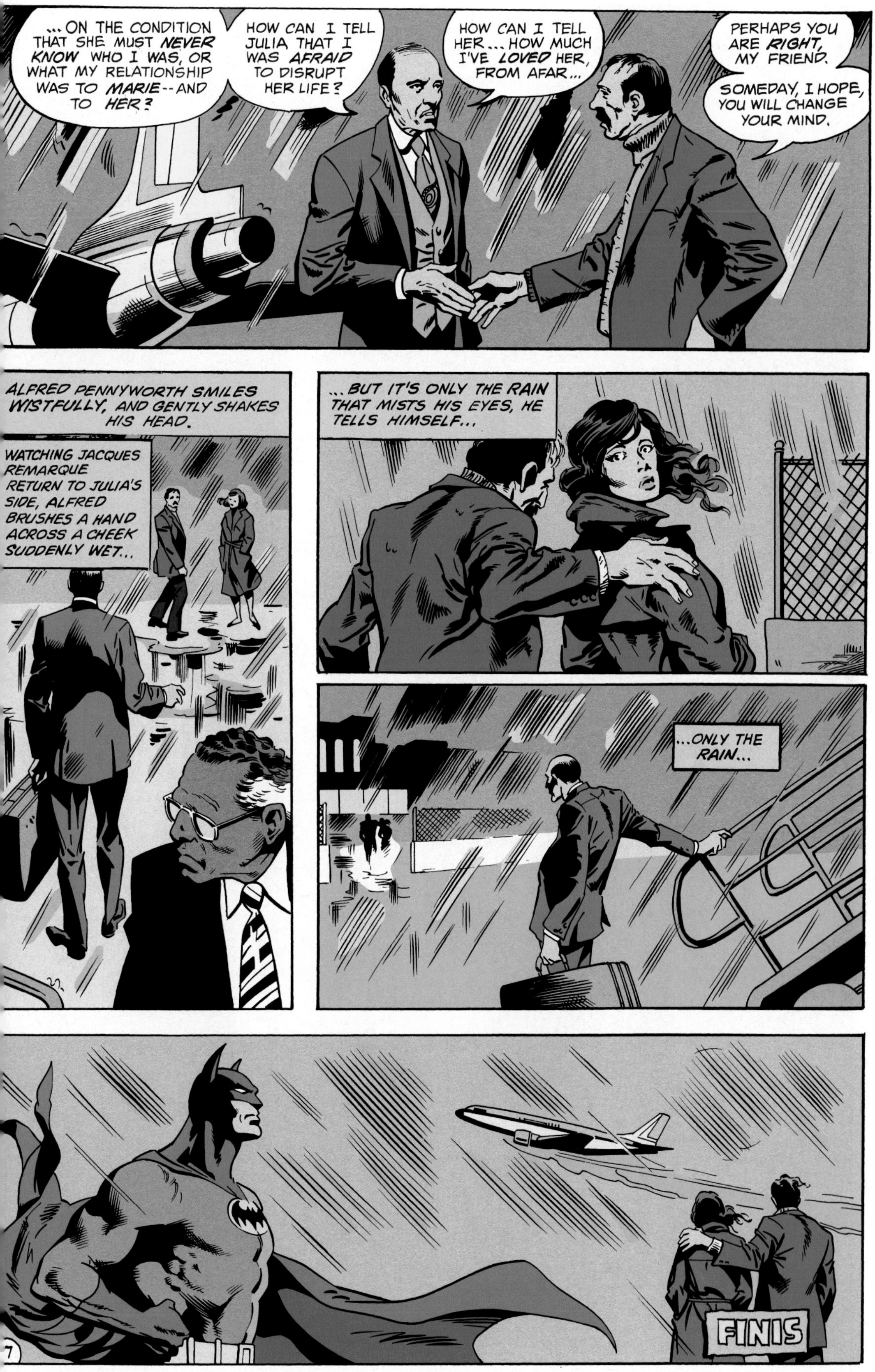
...ON THE CONDITION THAT SHE MUST NEVER KNOW WHO I WAS, OR WHAT MY RELATIONSHIP WAS TO MARIE--AND TO HER?
HOW CAN I TELL JULIA THAT I WAS AFRAID TO DISRUPT HER LIFE?
HOW CAN I TELL HER... HOW MUCH I'VE LOVED HER, FROM AFAR...
PERHAPS YOU ARE RIGHT, MY FRIEND.
SOMEDAY, I HOPE, YOU WILL CHANGE YOUR MIND.
ALFRED PENNYWORTH SMILES WISTFULLY, AND GENTLY SHAKES HIS HEAD.
WATCHING JACQUES REMARQUE RETURN TO JULIA'S SIDE, ALFRED BRUSHES A HAND ACROSS A CHEEK SUDDENLY WET...
...BUT IT'S ONLY THE RAIN THAT MISTS HIS EYES, HE TELLS HIMSELF...
...ONLY THE RAIN...
FINIS
7

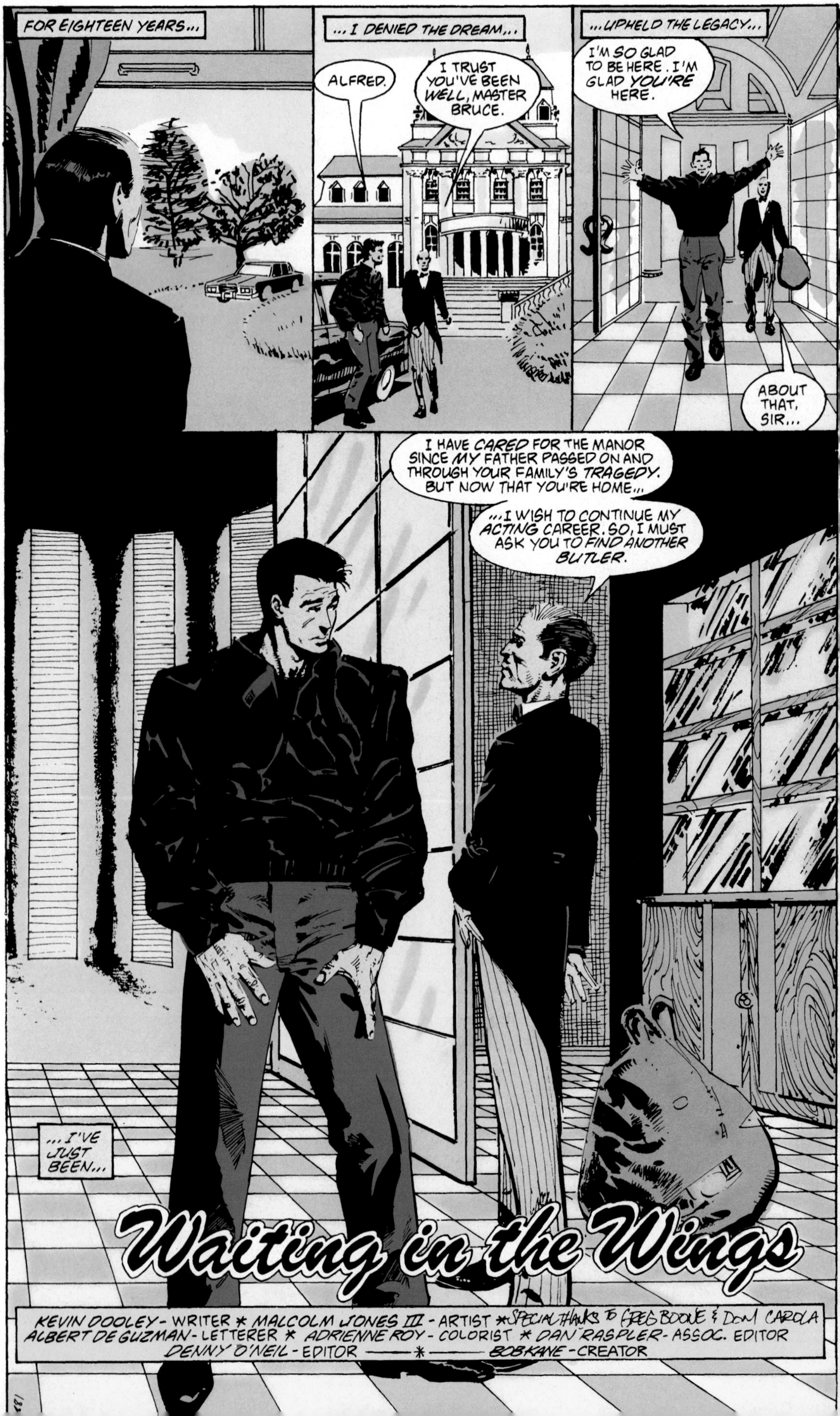

FOR EIGHTEEN YEARS...
...I DENIED THE DREAM...
ALFRED.
I TRUST YOU'VE BEEN WELL, MASTER BRUCE.
...UPHELD THE LEGACY...
I'M SO GLAD TO BE HERE. I'M GLAD YOU'RE HERE.
ABOUT THAT, SIR...
I HAVE CARED FOR THE MANOR SINCE MY FATHER PASSED ON AND THROUGH YOUR FAMILY'S TRAGEDY. BUT NOW THAT YOU'RE HOME...
...I WISH TO CONTINUE MY ACTING CAREER. SO, I MUST ASK YOU TO FIND ANOTHER BUTLER.
...I'VE JUST BEEN...
Waiting in the Wings
KEVIN DOOLEY - WRITER * MALCOLM JONES III - ARTIST * SPECIAL THANKS TO GREG BOONE & DON CAROLA
ALBERT DE GUZMAN - LETTERER * ADRIENNE ROY - COLORIST * DAN RASPLER - ASSOC. EDITOR
DENNY O'NEIL - EDITOR * BOB KANE - CREATOR

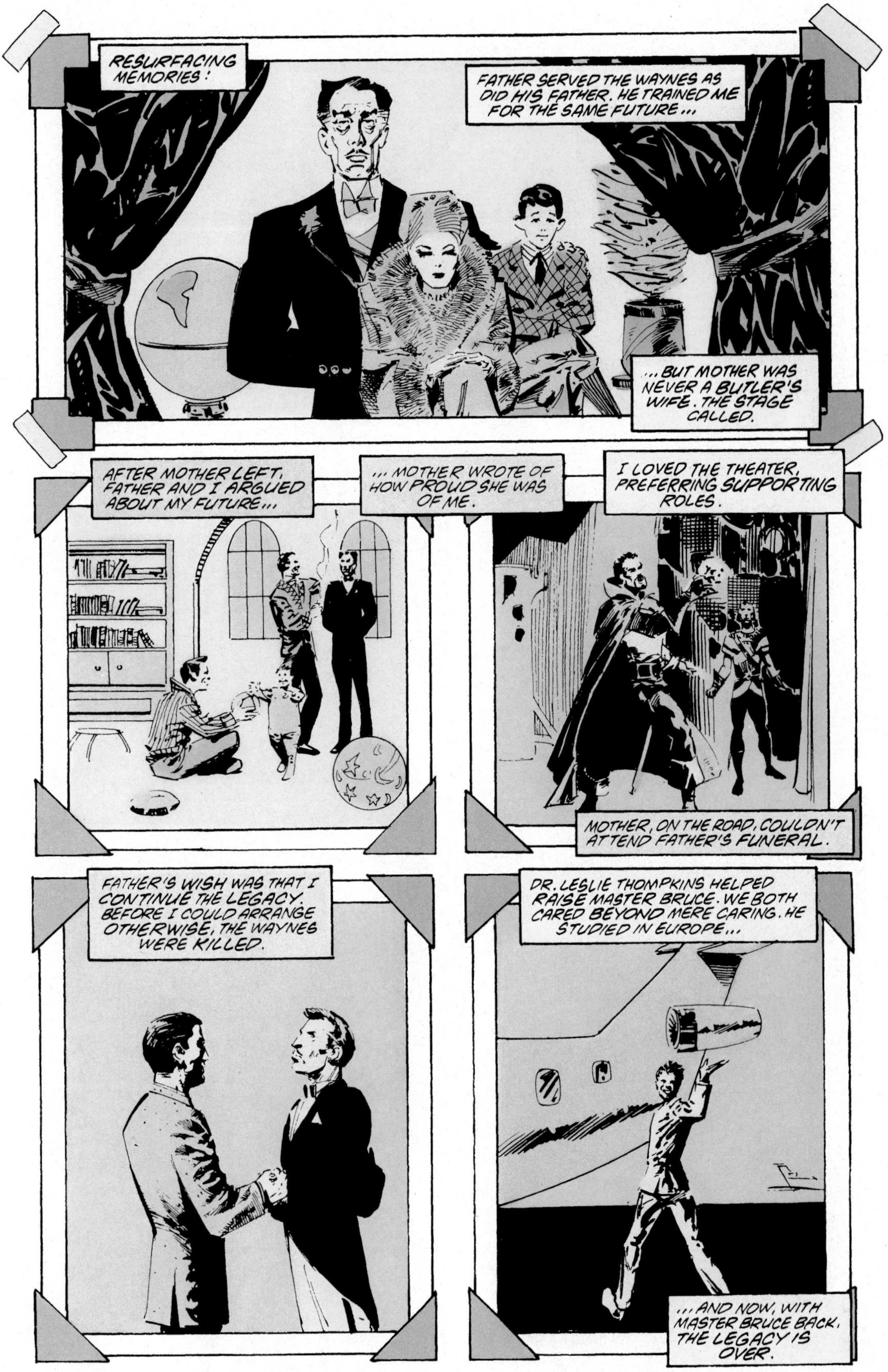
RESURFACING MEMORIES:
FATHER SERVED THE WAYNES AS DID HIS FATHER. HE TRAINED ME FOR THE SAME FUTURE...
...BUT MOTHER WAS NEVER A BUTLER'S WIFE. THE STAGE CALLED.
AFTER MOTHER LEFT, FATHER AND I ARGUED ABOUT MY FUTURE...
...MOTHER WROTE OF HOW PROUD SHE WAS OF ME.
I LOVED THE THEATER, PREFERRING SUPPORTING ROLES.
MOTHER, ON THE ROAD, COULDN'T ATTEND FATHER'S FUNERAL.
FATHER'S WISH WAS THAT I CONTINUE THE LEGACY. BEFORE I COULD ARRANGE OTHERWISE, THE WAYNES WERE KILLED.
DR. LESLIE THOMPKINS HELPED RAISE MASTER BRUCE. WE BOTH CARED BEYOND MERE CARING. HE STUDIED IN EUROPE...
...AND NOW, WITH MASTER BRUCE BACK, THE LEGACY IS OVER.

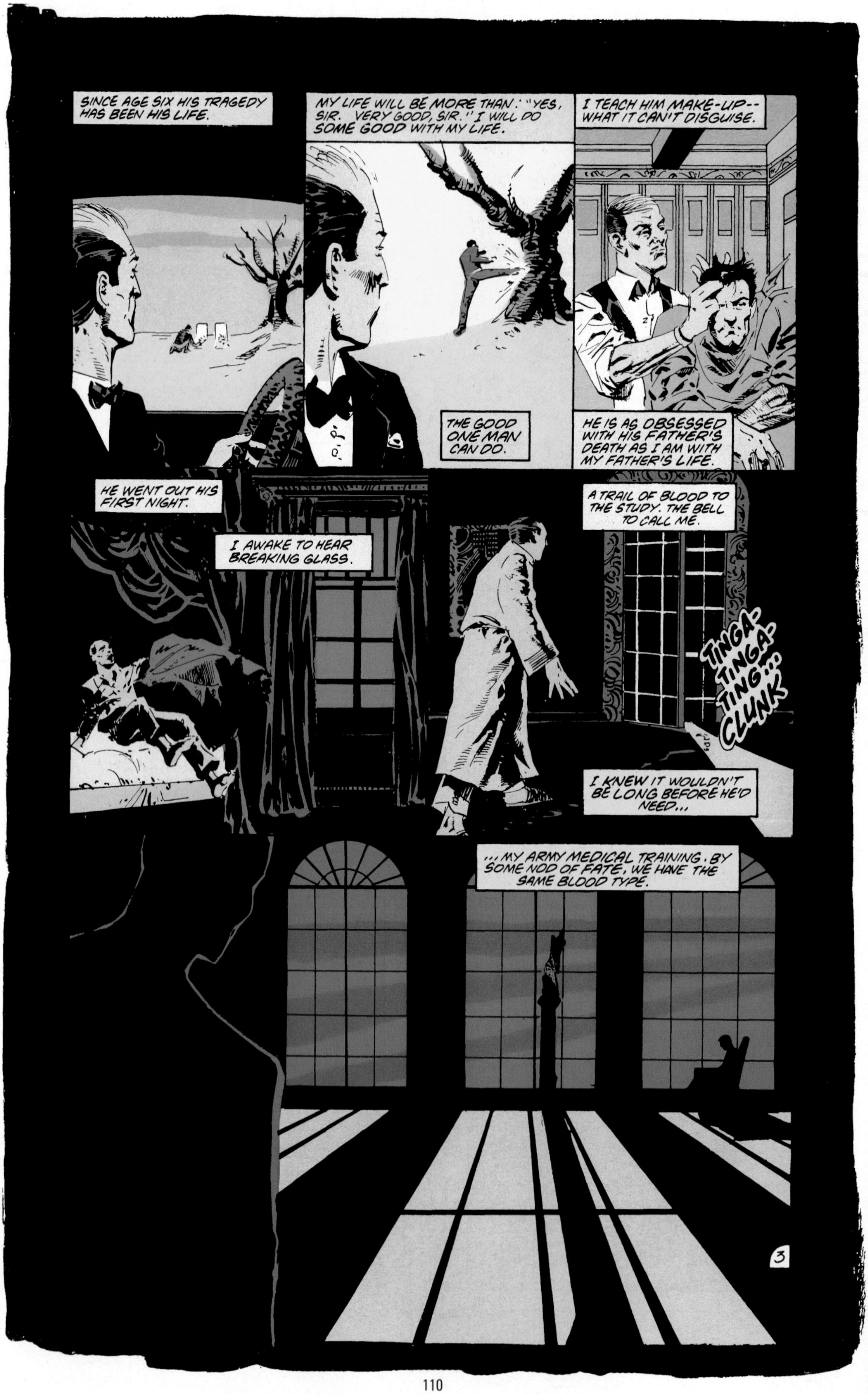
SINCE AGE SIX HIS TRAGEDY HAS BEEN HIS LIFE.
MY LIFE WILL BE MORE THAN: "YES, SIR. VERY GOOD, SIR." I WILL DO SOME GOOD WITH MY LIFE.
THE GOOD ONE MAN CAN DO.
I TEACH HIM MAKE-UP--WHAT IT CAN'T DISGUISE.
HE IS AS OBSESSED WITH HIS FATHER'S DEATH AS I AM WITH MY FATHER'S LIFE.
HE WENT OUT HIS FIRST NIGHT.
I AWAKE TO HEAR BREAKING GLASS.
A TRAIL OF BLOOD TO THE STUDY. THE BELL TO CALL ME.
TINGA-TINGA-TING.. CLUNK
I KNEW IT WOULDN'T BE LONG BEFORE HE'D NEED...
...MY ARMY MEDICAL TRAINING. BY SOME NOD OF FATE, WE HAVE THE SAME BLOOD TYPE.
3

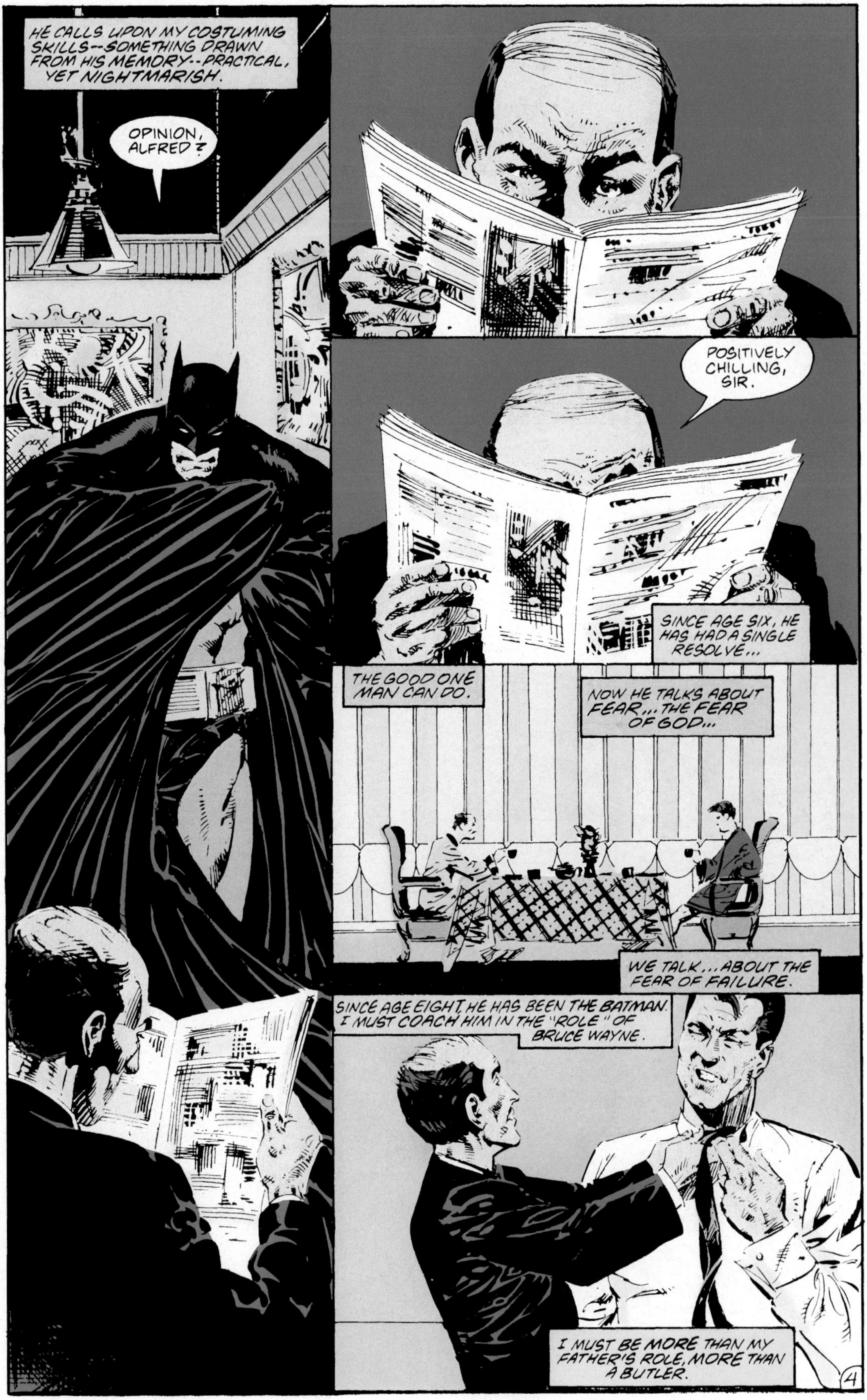
HE CALLS UPON MY COSTUMING SKILLS--SOMETHING DRAWN FROM HIS MEMORY--PRACTICAL, YET NIGHTMARISH.
OPINION, ALFRED?
POSITIVELY CHILLING, SIR.
SINCE AGE SIX, HE HAS HAD A SINGLE RESOLVE...
THE GOOD ONE MAN CAN DO.
NOW HE TALKS ABOUT FEAR... THE FEAR OF GOD...
WE TALK... ABOUT THE FEAR OF FAILURE.
SINCE AGE EIGHT, HE HAS BEEN THE BATMAN. I MUST COACH HIM IN THE "ROLE" OF BRUCE WAYNE.
I MUST BE MORE THAN MY FATHER'S ROLE, MORE THAN A BUTLER.
4

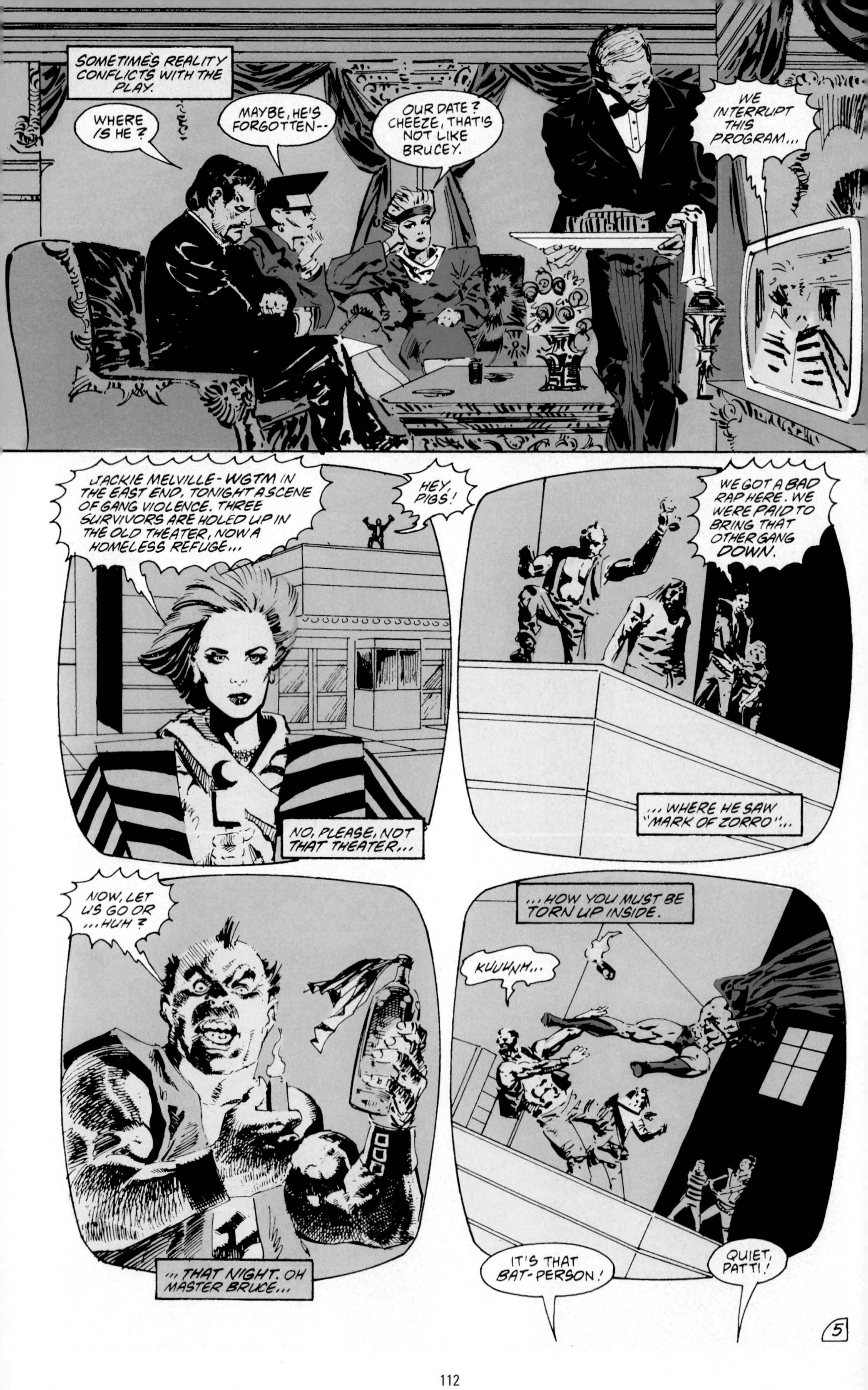
SOMETIMES REALITY CONFLICTS WITH THE PLAY.
WHERE IS HE ?
MAYBE, HE'S FORGOTTEN--
OUR DATE ? CHEEZE, THAT'S NOT LIKE BRUCEY.
WE INTERRUPT THIS PROGRAM...
JACKIE MELVILLE - WGTM IN THE EAST END. TONIGHT A SCENE OF GANG VIOLENCE. THREE SURVIVORS ARE HOLED UP IN THE OLD THEATER, NOW A HOMELESS REFUGE...
HEY, PIGS !
NO, PLEASE, NOT THAT THEATER...
WE GOT A BAD RAP HERE. WE WERE PAID TO BRING THAT OTHER GANG DOWN.
...WHERE HE SAW "MARK OF ZORRO"...
NOW, LET US GO OR ...HUH ?
...THAT NIGHT. OH MASTER BRUCE...
...HOW YOU MUST BE TORN UP INSIDE.
KUUUNH...
IT'S THAT BAT-PERSON !
QUIET, PATTI !
5

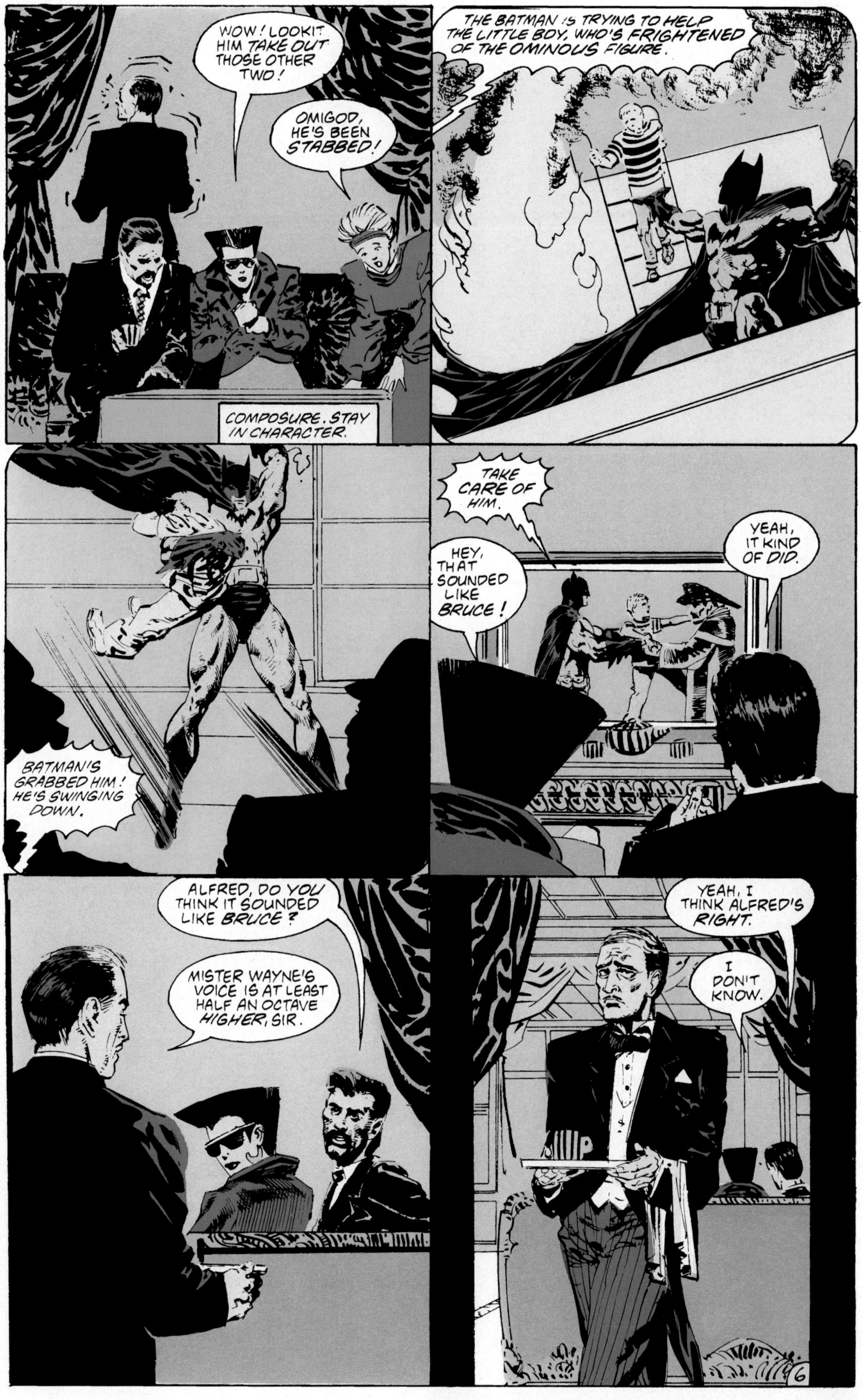
WOW! LOOKIT HIM TAKE OUT THOSE OTHER TWO!
OMIGOD, HE'S BEEN STABBED!
COMPOSURE. STAY IN CHARACTER.
THE BATMAN IS TRYING TO HELP THE LITTLE BOY, WHO'S FRIGHTENED OF THE OMINOUS FIGURE.
BATMAN'S GRABBED HIM! HE'S SWINGING DOWN.
TAKE CARE OF HIM.
HEY, THAT SOUNDED LIKE BRUCE!
YEAH, IT KIND OF DID.
ALFRED, DO YOU THINK IT SOUNDED LIKE BRUCE?
MISTER WAYNE'S VOICE IS AT LEAST HALF AN OCTAVE HIGHER, SIR.
YEAH, I THINK ALFRED'S RIGHT.
I DON'T KNOW.
6

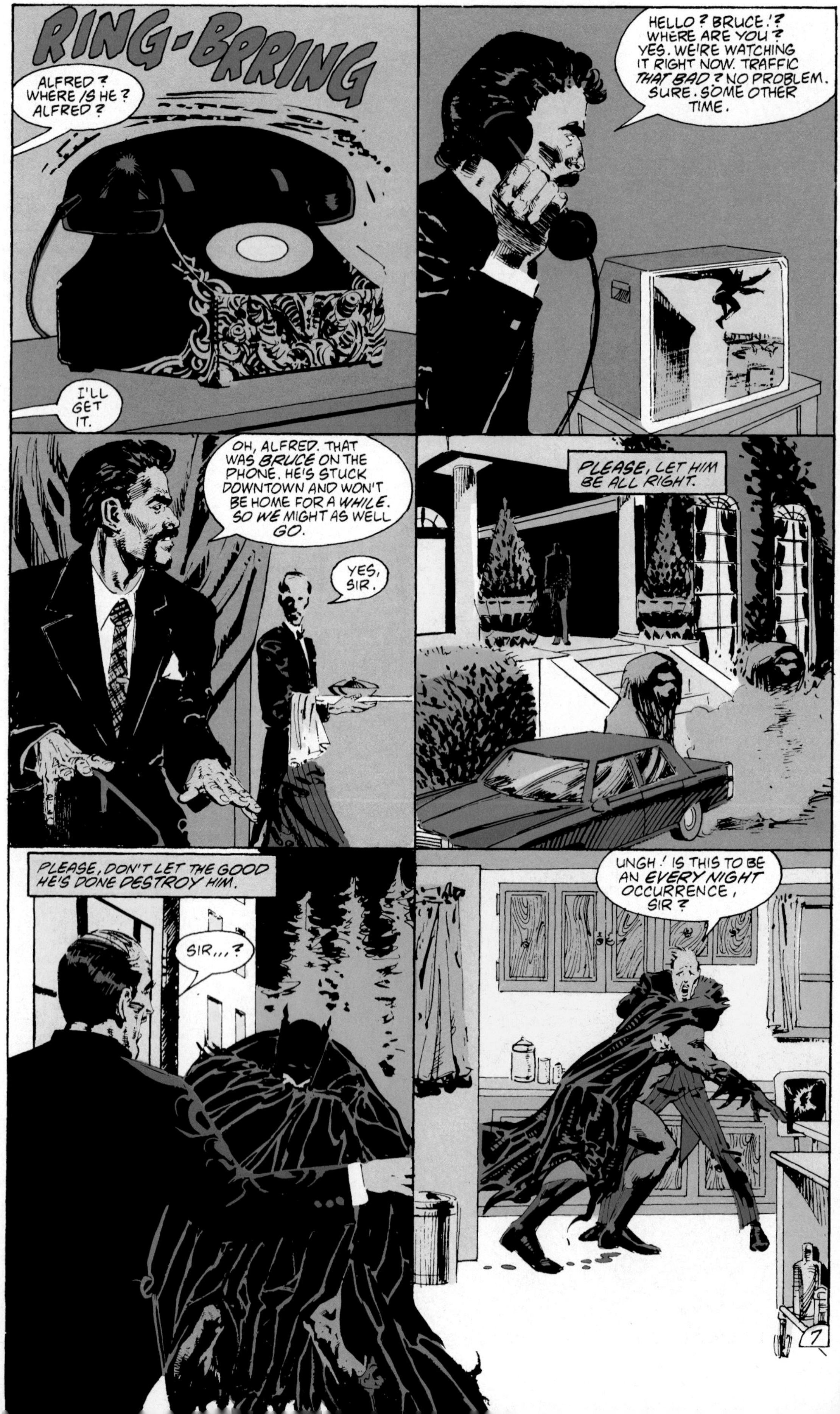
RING-BRRING
ALFRED? WHERE IS HE? ALFRED?
I'LL GET IT.
HELLO? BRUCE!? WHERE ARE YOU? YES. WE'RE WATCHING IT RIGHT NOW. TRAFFIC THAT BAD? NO PROBLEM. SURE. SOME OTHER TIME.
OH, ALFRED. THAT WAS BRUCE ON THE PHONE. HE'S STUCK DOWNTOWN AND WON'T BE HOME FOR A WHILE. SO WE MIGHT AS WELL GO.
YES, SIR.
PLEASE, LET HIM BE ALL RIGHT.
PLEASE, DON'T LET THE GOOD HE'S DONE DESTROY HIM.
SIR...?
UNGH! IS THIS TO BE AN EVERY NIGHT OCCURRENCE, SIR?

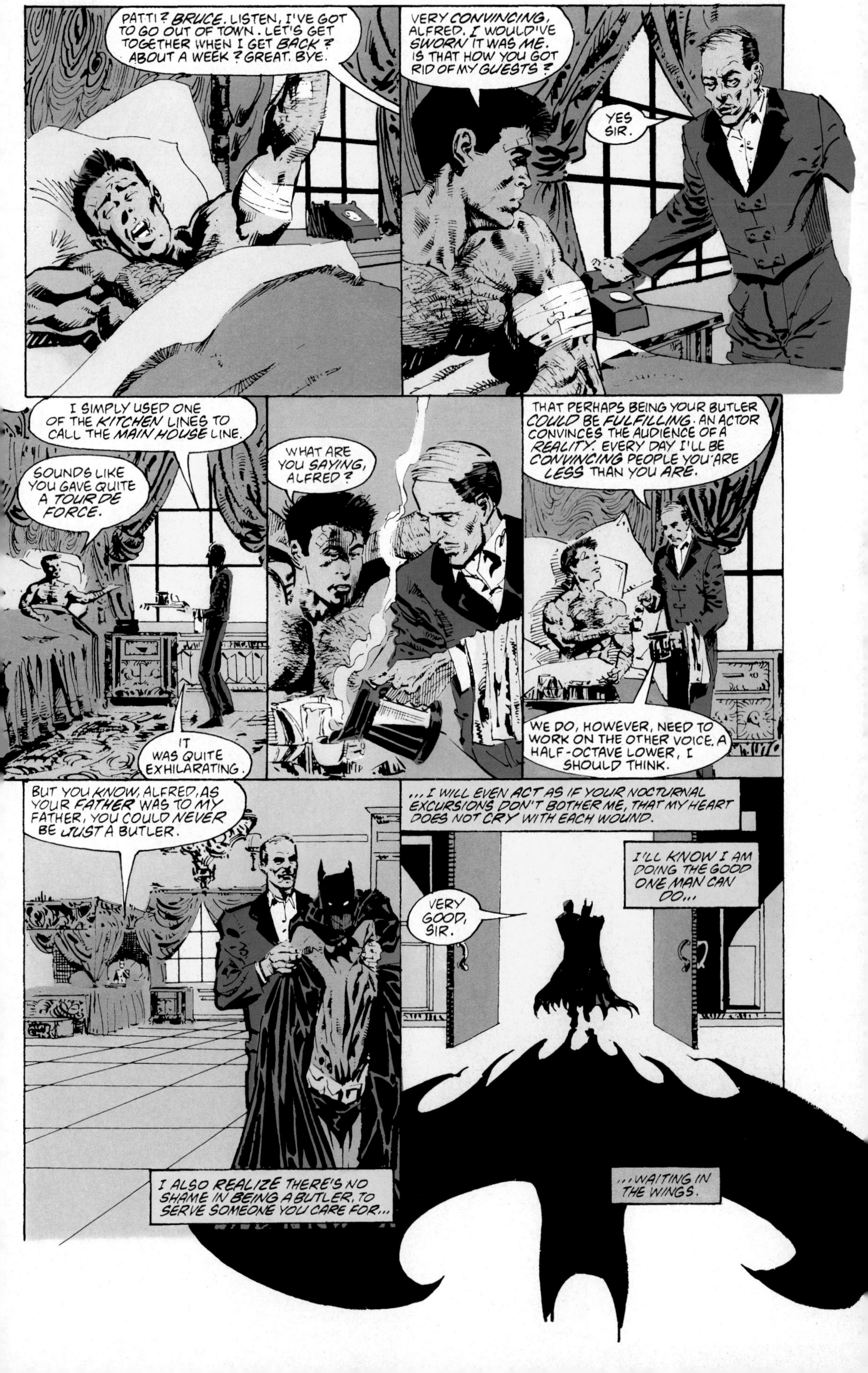
PATTI? BRUCE. LISTEN, I'VE GOT TO GO OUT OF TOWN. LET'S GET TOGETHER WHEN I GET BACK? ABOUT A WEEK? GREAT. BYE.
VERY CONVINCING, ALFRED. I WOULD'VE SWORN IT WAS ME. IS THAT HOW YOU GOT RID OF MY GUESTS?
YES SIR.
I SIMPLY USED ONE OF THE KITCHEN LINES TO CALL THE MAIN HOUSE LINE.
SOUNDS LIKE YOU GAVE QUITE A TOUR DE FORCE.
IT WAS QUITE EXHILARATING.
WHAT ARE YOU SAYING, ALFRED?
THAT PERHAPS BEING YOUR BUTLER COULD BE FULFILLING. AN ACTOR CONVINCES THE AUDIENCE OF A REALITY. EVERY DAY I'LL BE CONVINCING PEOPLE YOU'ARE LESS THAN YOU ARE.
WE DO, HOWEVER, NEED TO WORK ON THE OTHER VOICE. A HALF-OCTAVE LOWER, I SHOULD THINK.
BUT YOU KNOW, ALFRED, AS YOUR FATHER WAS TO MY FATHER, YOU COULD NEVER BE JUST A BUTLER.
I ALSO REALIZE THERE'S NO SHAME IN BEING A BUTLER, TO SERVE SOMEONE YOU CARE FOR...
...I WILL EVEN ACT AS IF YOUR NOCTURNAL EXCURSIONS DON'T BOTHER ME, THAT MY HEART DOES NOT CRY WITH EACH WOUND.
VERY GOOD, SIR.
I'LL KNOW I AM DOING THE GOOD ONE MAN CAN DO...
...WAITING IN THE WINGS.

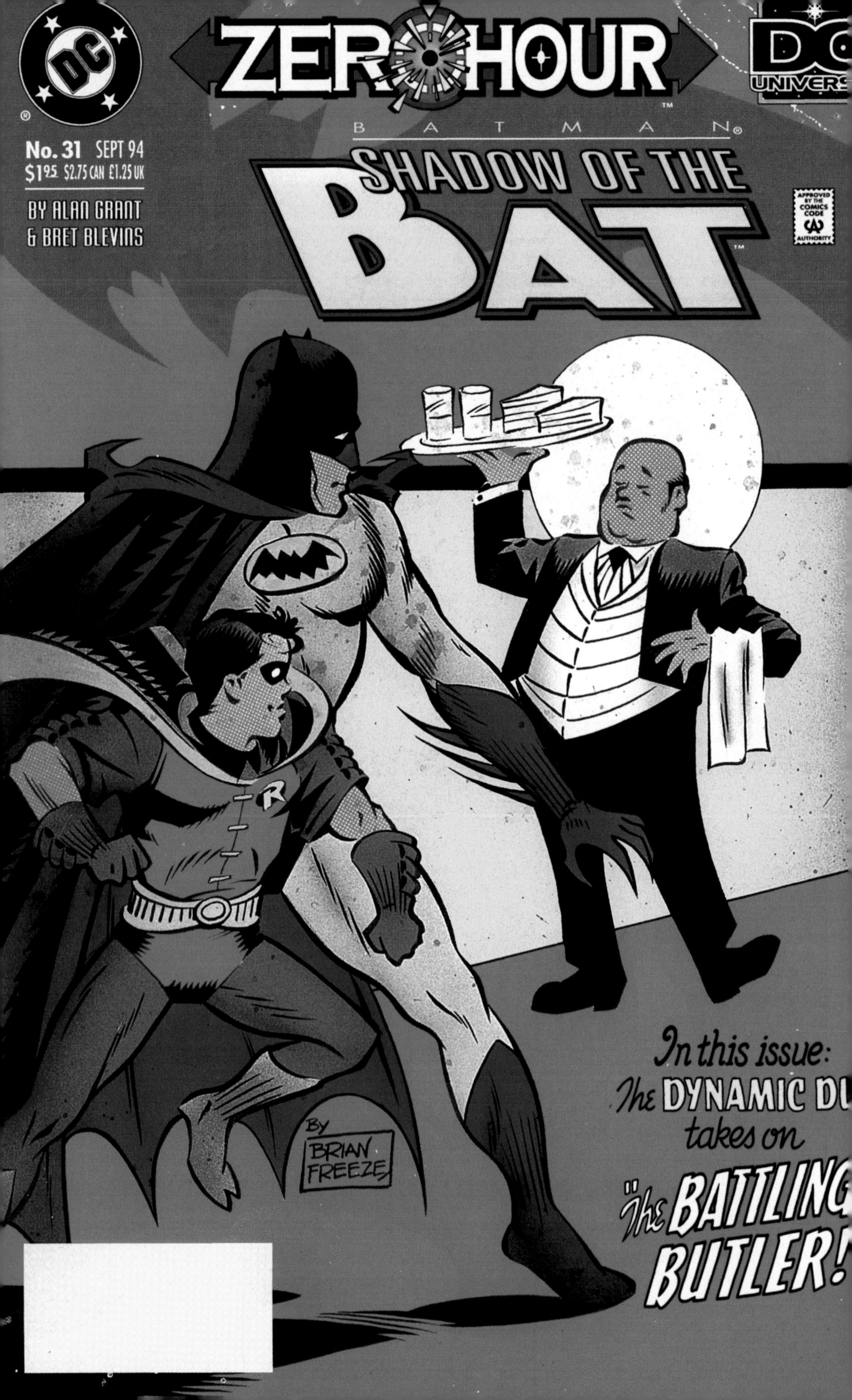

DC
ZERO HOUR
DC UNIVERSE
No. 31 SEPT 94
$1.95 $2.75 CAN £1.25 UK
BY ALAN GRANT
& BRET BLEVINS
BATMAN
SHADOW OF THE BAT
APPROVED BY THE COMICS CODE AUTHORITY
R
By BRIAN FREEZE
In this issue:
The DYNAMIC DU
takes on
"The BATTLING
BUTLER!"

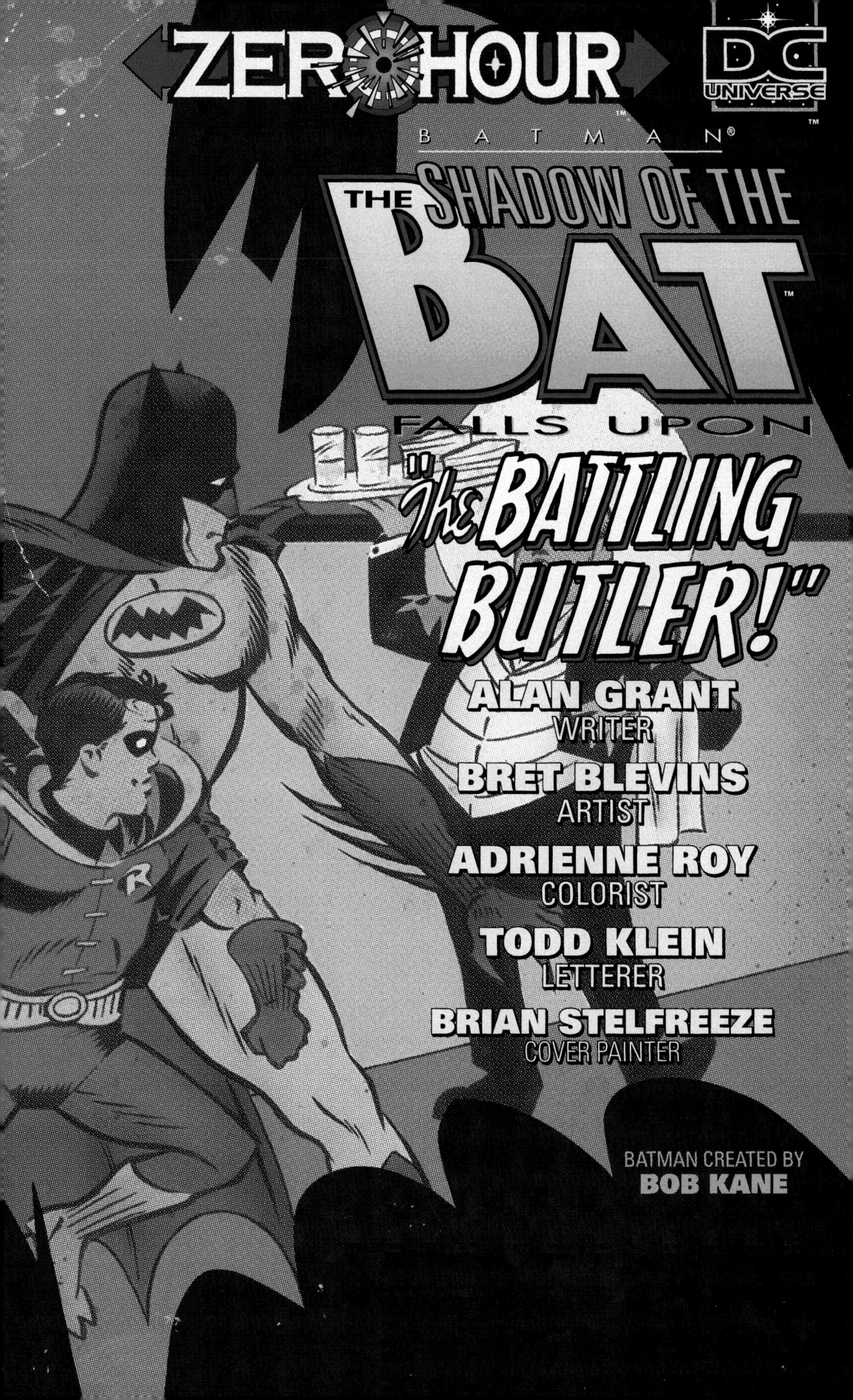

ZERO HOUR
DC UNIVERSE
BATMAN
THE SHADOW OF THE BAT
FALLS UPON
"The BATTLING BUTLER!"
ALAN GRANT
WRITER
BRET BLEVINS
ARTIST
ADRIENNE ROY
COLORIST
TODD KLEIN
LETTERER
BRIAN STELFREEZE
COVER PAINTER
BATMAN CREATED BY
BOB KANE

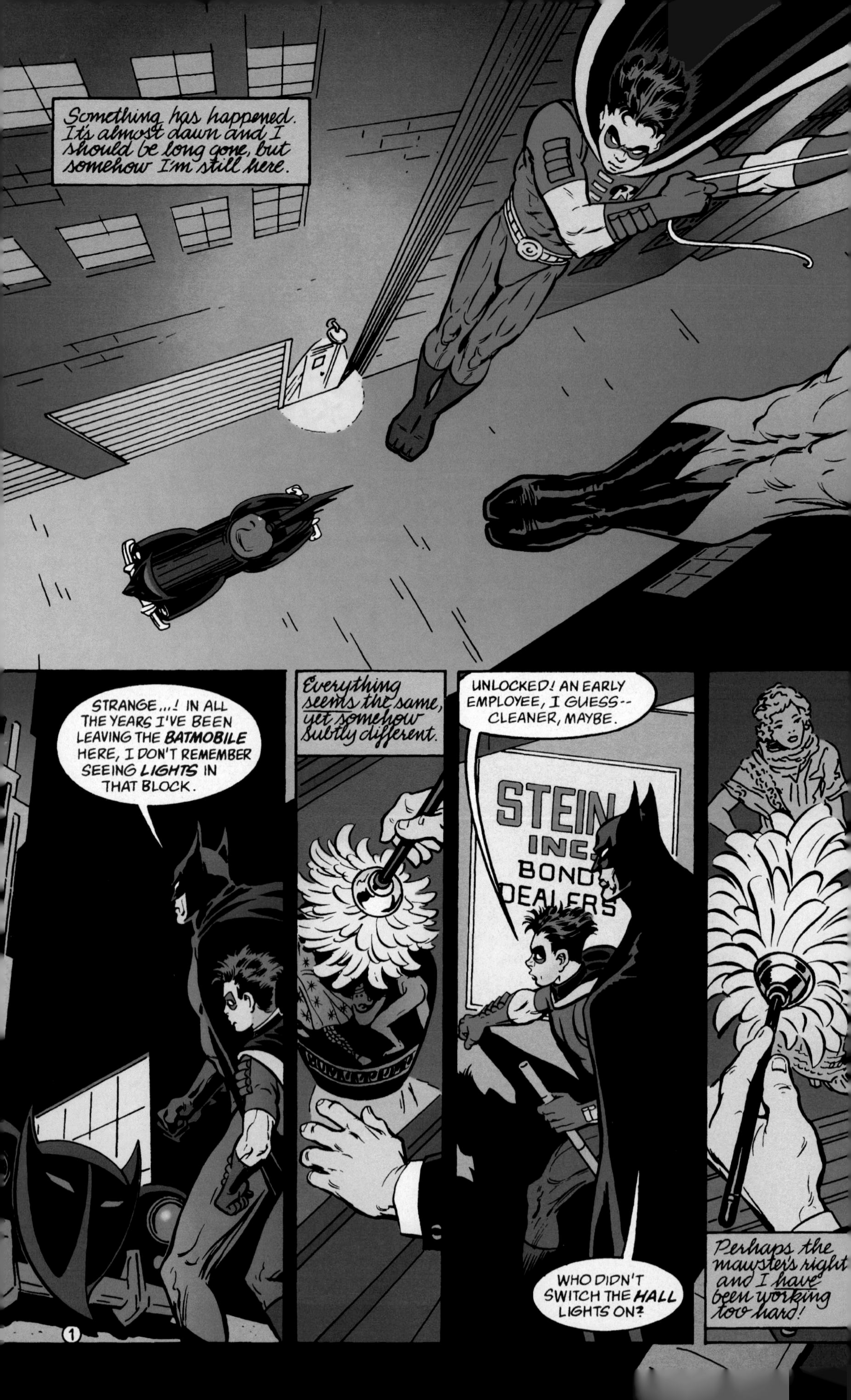
Something has happened. It's almost dawn and I should be long gone, but somehow I'm still here.
STRANGE...! IN ALL THE YEARS I'VE BEEN LEAVING THE BATMOBILE HERE, I DON'T REMEMBER SEEING LIGHTS IN THAT BLOCK.
Everything seems the same, yet somehow subtly different.
UNLOCKED! AN EARLY EMPLOYEE, I GUESS-- CLEANER, MAYBE.
STEIN INC. BOND DEALERS
WHO DIDN'T SWITCH THE HALL LIGHTS ON?
Perhaps the mauster's right and I have been working too hard!
1

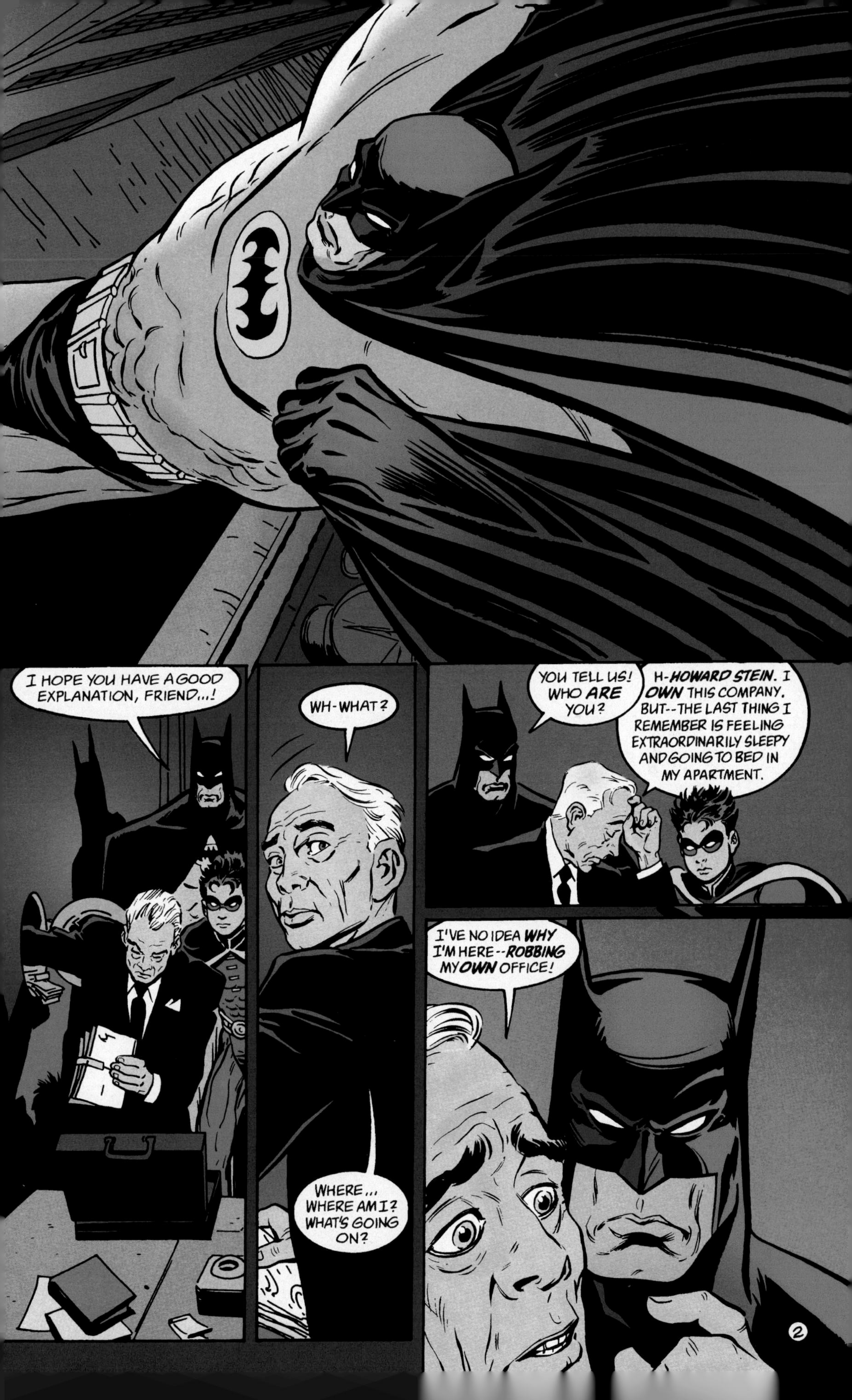

I HOPE YOU HAVE A GOOD EXPLANATION, FRIEND...!
WH-WHAT?
WHERE... WHERE AM I? WHAT'S GOING ON?
YOU TELL US! WHO ARE YOU?
H-HOWARD STEIN. I OWN THIS COMPANY. BUT--THE LAST THING I REMEMBER IS FEELING EXTRAORDINARILY SLEEPY AND GOING TO BED IN MY APARTMENT.
I'VE NO IDEA WHY I'M HERE--ROBBING MY OWN OFFICE!

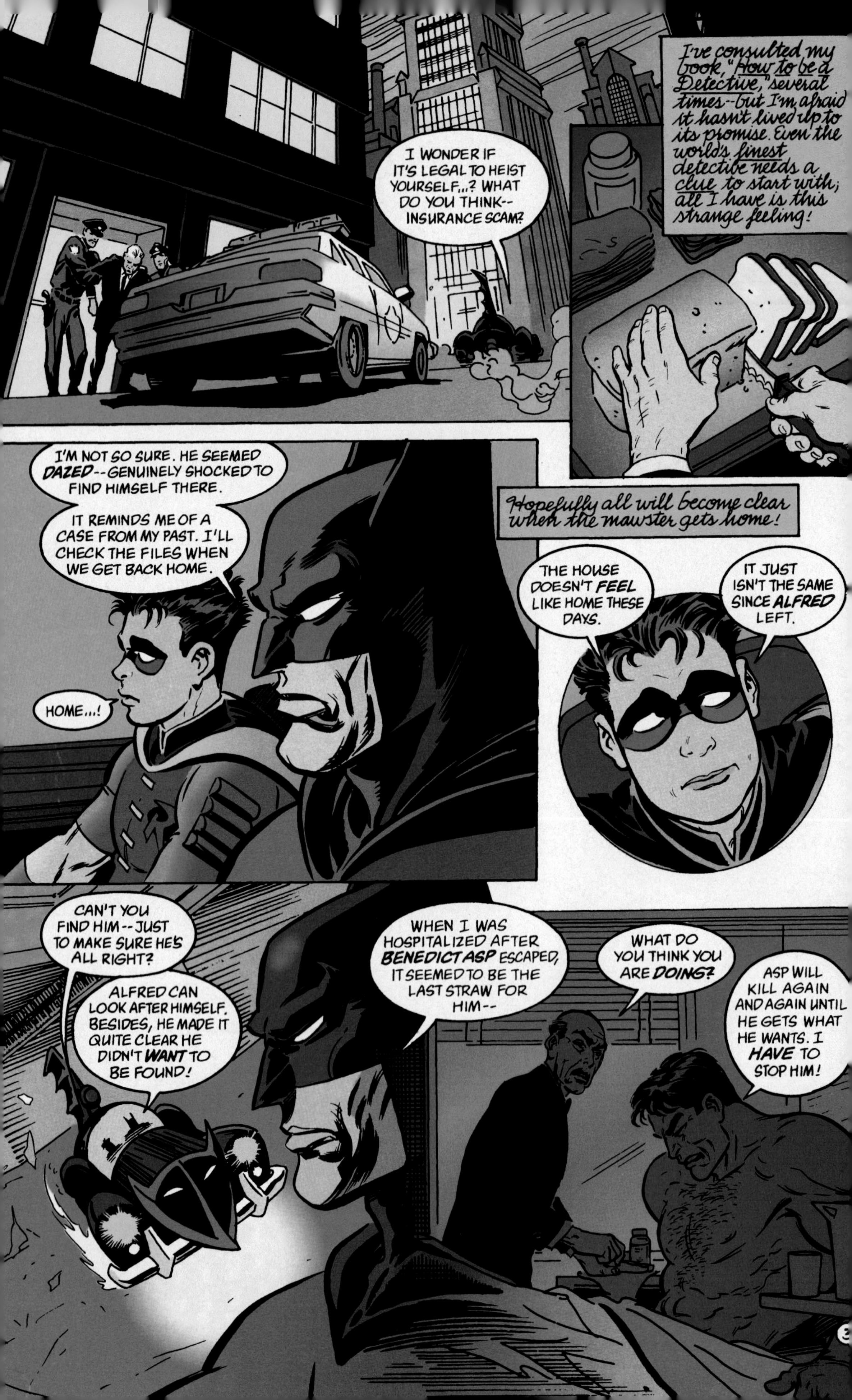
I WONDER IF IT'S LEGAL TO HEIST YOURSELF...? WHAT DO YOU THINK-- INSURANCE SCAM?
I've consulted my book, "How to be a Detective," several times--but I'm afraid it hasn't lived up to its promise. Even the world's finest detective needs a clue to start with; all I have is this strange feeling!
I'M NOT SO SURE. HE SEEMED DAZED--GENUINELY SHOCKED TO FIND HIMSELF THERE.
IT REMINDS ME OF A CASE FROM MY PAST. I'LL CHECK THE FILES WHEN WE GET BACK HOME.
HOME...!
Hopefully all will become clear when the mawster gets home!
THE HOUSE DOESN'T FEEL LIKE HOME THESE DAYS.
IT JUST ISN'T THE SAME SINCE ALFRED LEFT.
CAN'T YOU FIND HIM--JUST TO MAKE SURE HE'S ALL RIGHT?
ALFRED CAN LOOK AFTER HIMSELF. BESIDES, HE MADE IT QUITE CLEAR HE DIDN'T WANT TO BE FOUND!
WHEN I WAS HOSPITALIZED AFTER BENEDICT ASP ESCAPED, IT SEEMED TO BE THE LAST STRAW FOR HIM--
WHAT DO YOU THINK YOU ARE DOING?
ASP WILL KILL AGAIN AND AGAIN UNTIL HE GETS WHAT HE WANTS. I HAVE TO STOP HIM!

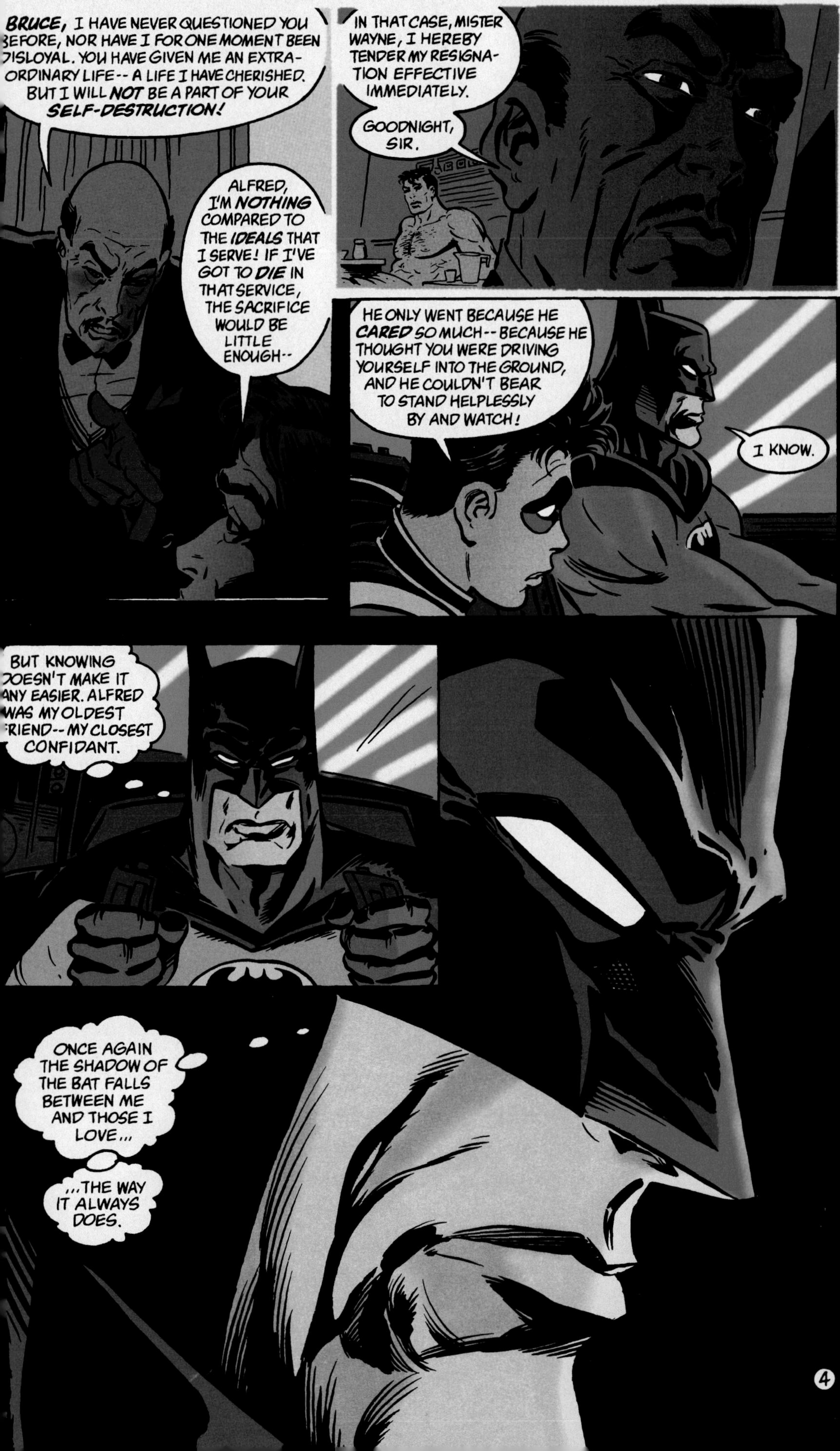
BRUCE, I HAVE NEVER QUESTIONED YOU BEFORE, NOR HAVE I FOR ONE MOMENT BEEN DISLOYAL. YOU HAVE GIVEN ME AN EXTRAORDINARY LIFE -- A LIFE I HAVE CHERISHED. BUT I WILL NOT BE A PART OF YOUR SELF-DESTRUCTION!
ALFRED, I'M NOTHING COMPARED TO THE IDEALS THAT I SERVE! IF I'VE GOT TO DIE IN THAT SERVICE, THE SACRIFICE WOULD BE LITTLE ENOUGH--
IN THAT CASE, MISTER WAYNE, I HEREBY TENDER MY RESIGNATION EFFECTIVE IMMEDIATELY.
GOODNIGHT, SIR.
HE ONLY WENT BECAUSE HE CARED SO MUCH -- BECAUSE HE THOUGHT YOU WERE DRIVING YOURSELF INTO THE GROUND, AND HE COULDN'T BEAR TO STAND HELPLESSLY BY AND WATCH!
I KNOW.
BUT KNOWING DOESN'T MAKE IT ANY EASIER. ALFRED WAS MY OLDEST FRIEND -- MY CLOSEST CONFIDANT.
ONCE AGAIN THE SHADOW OF THE BAT FALLS BETWEEN ME AND THOSE I LOVE...
...THE WAY IT ALWAYS DOES.

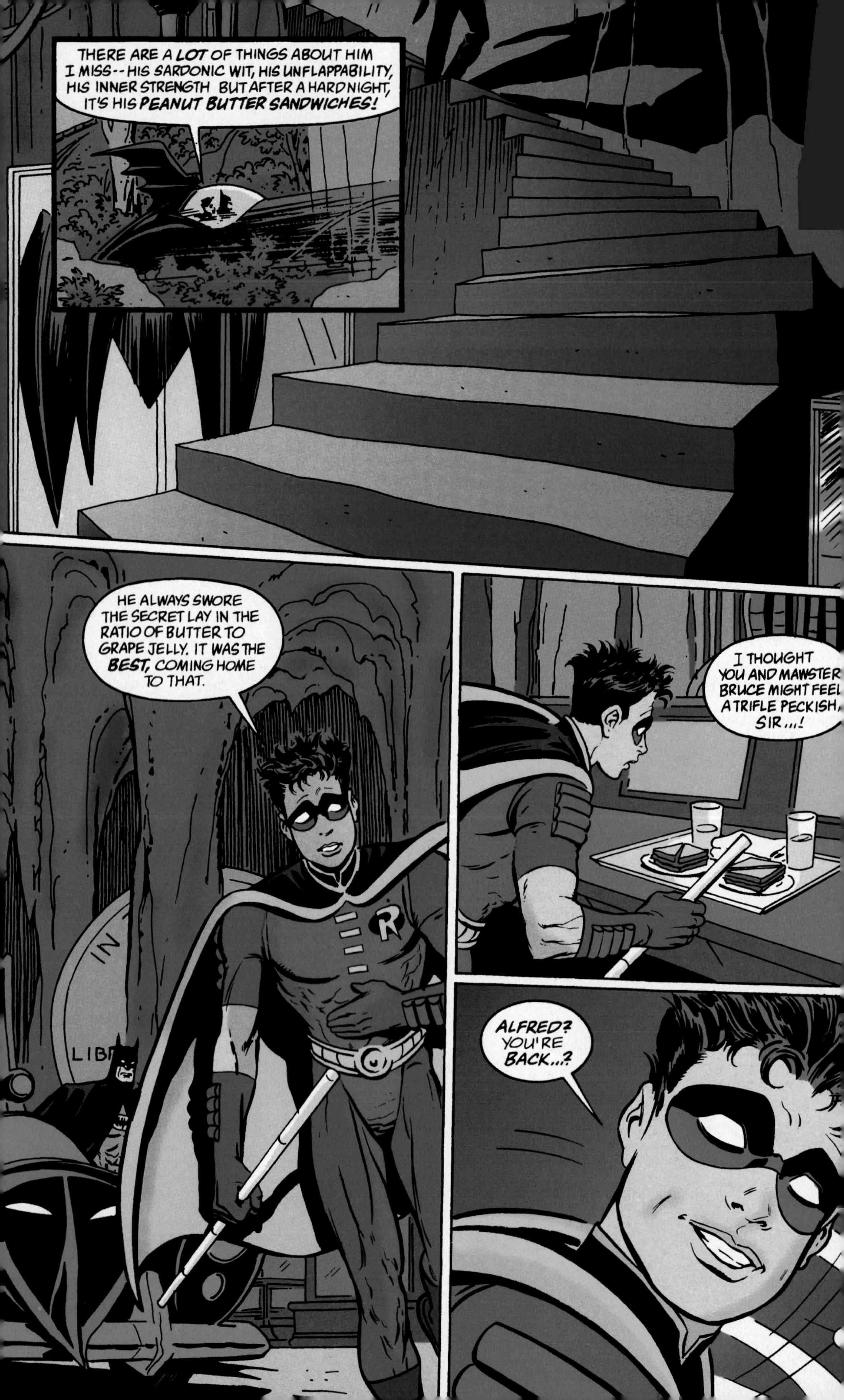
THERE ARE A LOT OF THINGS ABOUT HIM I MISS--HIS SARDONIC WIT, HIS UNFLAPPABILITY, HIS INNER STRENGTH BUT AFTER A HARD NIGHT, IT'S HIS PEANUT BUTTER SANDWICHES!
HE ALWAYS SWORE THE SECRET LAY IN THE RATIO OF BUTTER TO GRAPE JELLY. IT WAS THE BEST, COMING HOME TO THAT.
I THOUGHT YOU AND MAWSTER BRUCE MIGHT FEEL A TRIFLE PECKISH, SIR...!
ALFRED? YOU'RE BACK...?
LIB

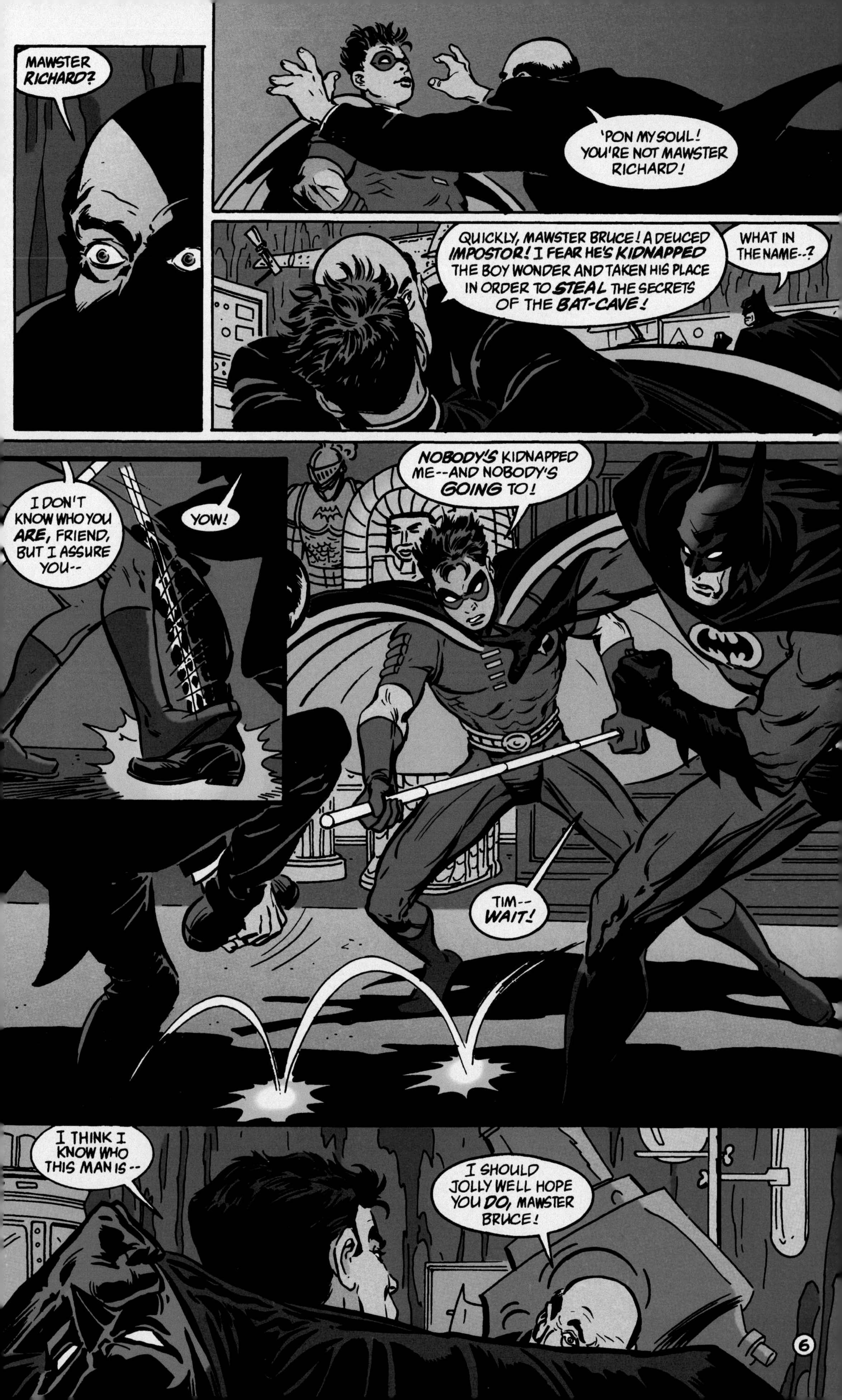

MAWSTER RICHARD?
'PON MY SOUL! YOU'RE NOT MAWSTER RICHARD!
QUICKLY, MAWSTER BRUCE! A DEUCED IMPOSTOR! I FEAR HE'S KIDNAPPED THE BOY WONDER AND TAKEN HIS PLACE IN ORDER TO STEAL THE SECRETS OF THE BAT-CAVE!
WHAT IN THE NAME--?
I DON'T KNOW WHO YOU ARE, FRIEND, BUT I ASSURE YOU--
YOW!
NOBODY'S KIDNAPPED ME--AND NOBODY'S GOING TO!
TIM--WAIT!
I THINK I KNOW WHO THIS MAN IS--
I SHOULD JOLLY WELL HOPE YOU DO, MAWSTER BRUCE!
6

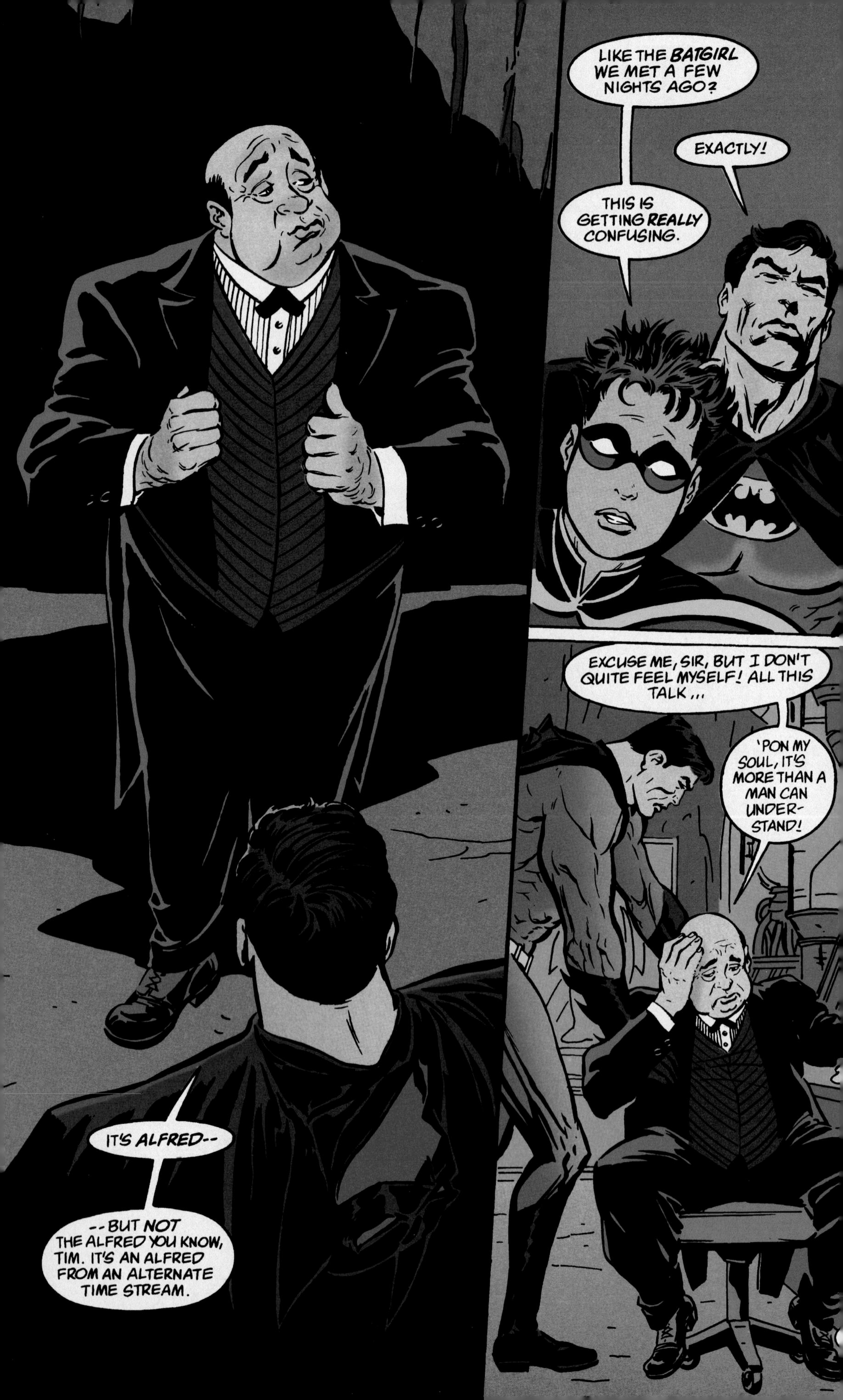
IT'S ALFRED--
--BUT NOT THE ALFRED YOU KNOW, TIM. IT'S AN ALFRED FROM AN ALTERNATE TIME STREAM.
LIKE THE BATGIRL WE MET A FEW NIGHTS AGO?
EXACTLY!
THIS IS GETTING REALLY CONFUSING.
EXCUSE ME, SIR, BUT I DON'T QUITE FEEL MYSELF! ALL THIS TALK...
'PON MY SOUL, IT'S MORE THAN A MAN CAN UNDER-STAND!

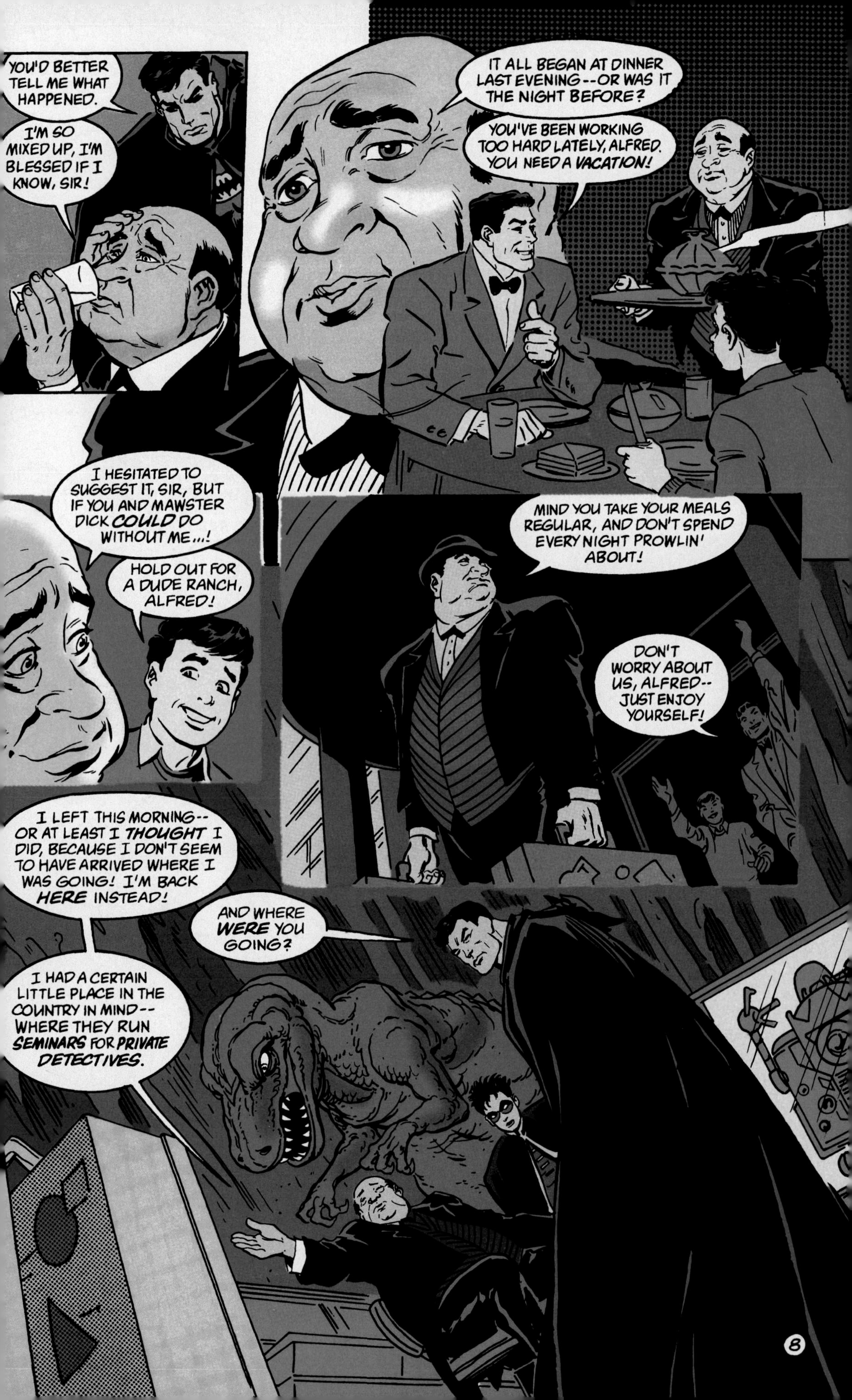
YOU'D BETTER TELL ME WHAT HAPPENED.
I'M SO MIXED UP, I'M BLESSED IF I KNOW, SIR!
IT ALL BEGAN AT DINNER LAST EVENING--OR WAS IT THE NIGHT BEFORE?
YOU'VE BEEN WORKING TOO HARD LATELY, ALFRED. YOU NEED A VACATION!
I HESITATED TO SUGGEST IT, SIR, BUT IF YOU AND MAWSTER DICK COULD DO WITHOUT ME...!
HOLD OUT FOR A DUDE RANCH, ALFRED!
MIND YOU TAKE YOUR MEALS REGULAR, AND DON'T SPEND EVERY NIGHT PROWLIN' ABOUT!
DON'T WORRY ABOUT US, ALFRED-- JUST ENJOY YOURSELF!
I LEFT THIS MORNING-- OR AT LEAST I THOUGHT I DID, BECAUSE I DON'T SEEM TO HAVE ARRIVED WHERE I WAS GOING! I'M BACK HERE INSTEAD!
AND WHERE WERE YOU GOING?
I HAD A CERTAIN LITTLE PLACE IN THE COUNTRY IN MIND-- WHERE THEY RUN SEMINARS FOR PRIVATE DETECTIVES.
8

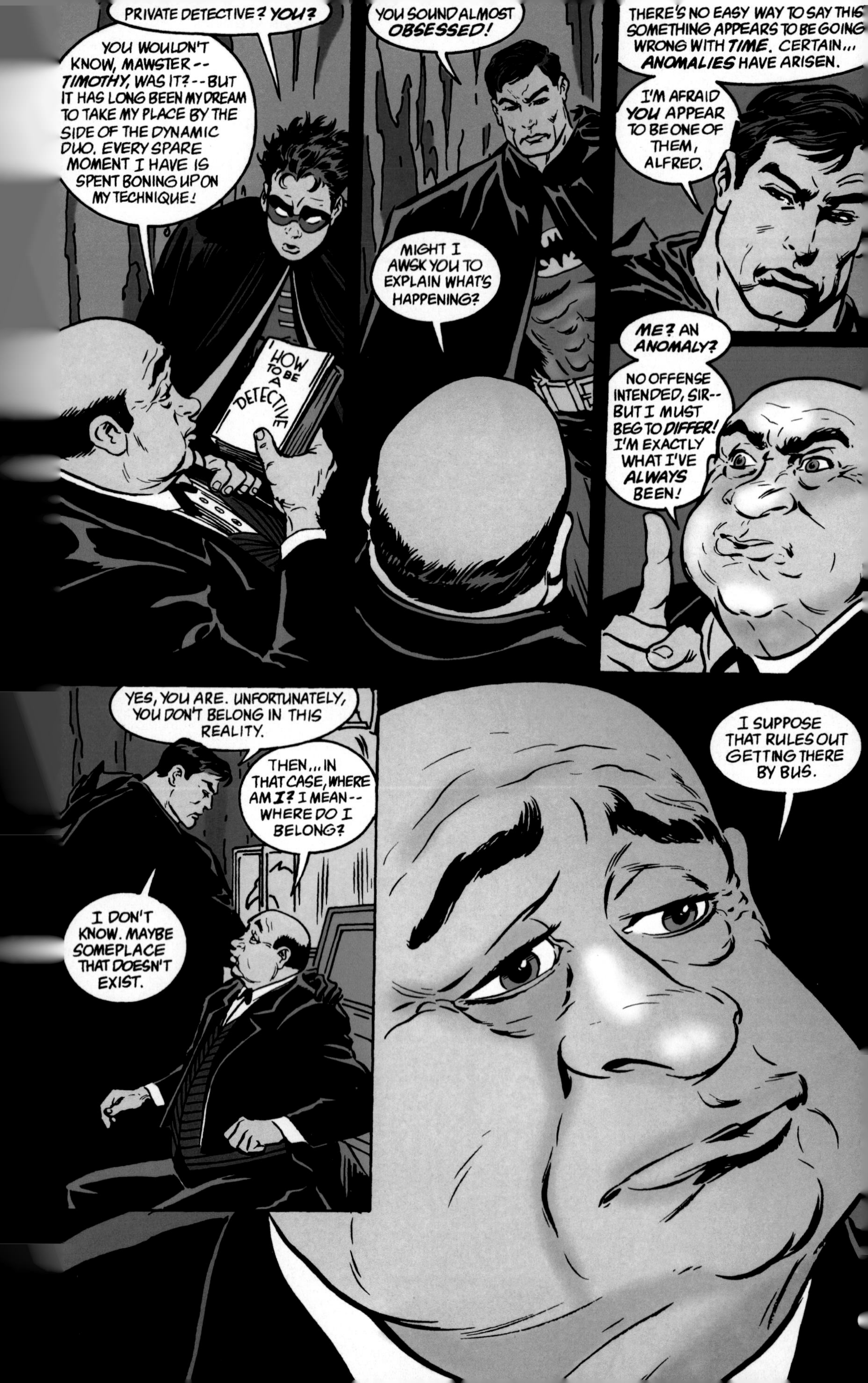
PRIVATE DETECTIVE? YOU?
YOU WOULDN'T KNOW, MAWSTER -- TIMOTHY, WAS IT? -- BUT IT HAS LONG BEEN MY DREAM TO TAKE MY PLACE BY THE SIDE OF THE DYNAMIC DUO. EVERY SPARE MOMENT I HAVE IS SPENT BONING UP ON MY TECHNIQUE!
HOW TO BE A DETECTIVE
YOU SOUND ALMOST OBSESSED!
MIGHT I AWSK YOU TO EXPLAIN WHAT'S HAPPENING?
THERE'S NO EASY WAY TO SAY THIS. SOMETHING APPEARS TO BE GOING WRONG WITH TIME. CERTAIN... ANOMALIES HAVE ARISEN.
I'M AFRAID YOU APPEAR TO BE ONE OF THEM, ALFRED.
ME? AN ANOMALY?
NO OFFENSE INTENDED, SIR-- BUT I MUST BEG TO DIFFER! I'M EXACTLY WHAT I'VE ALWAYS BEEN!
YES, YOU ARE. UNFORTUNATELY, YOU DON'T BELONG IN THIS REALITY.
THEN... IN THAT CASE, WHERE AM I? I MEAN-- WHERE DO I BELONG?
I DON'T KNOW. MAYBE SOMEPLACE THAT DOESN'T EXIST.
I SUPPOSE THAT RULES OUT GETTING THERE BY BUS.

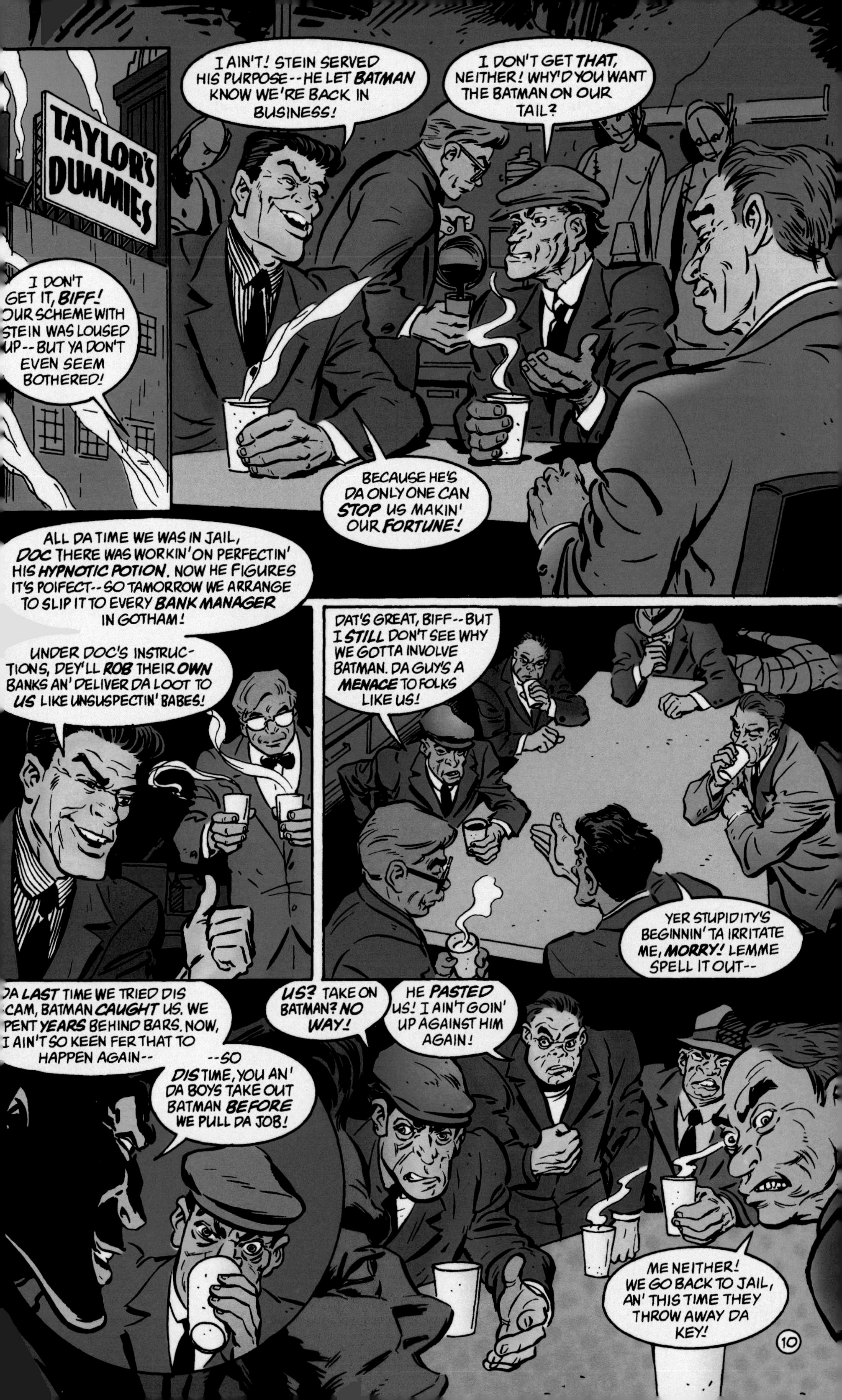

TAYLOR'S DUMMIES
I DON'T GET IT, BIFF! OUR SCHEME WITH STEIN WAS LOUSED UP-- BUT YA DON'T EVEN SEEM BOTHERED!
I AIN'T! STEIN SERVED HIS PURPOSE--HE LET BATMAN KNOW WE'RE BACK IN BUSINESS!
I DON'T GET THAT, NEITHER! WHY'D YOU WANT THE BATMAN ON OUR TAIL?
BECAUSE HE'S DA ONLY ONE CAN STOP US MAKIN' OUR FORTUNE!
ALL DA TIME WE WAS IN JAIL, DOC THERE WAS WORKIN' ON PERFECTIN' HIS HYPNOTIC POTION. NOW HE FIGURES IT'S POIFECT--SO TAMORROW WE ARRANGE TO SLIP IT TO EVERY BANK MANAGER IN GOTHAM!
UNDER DOC'S INSTRUCTIONS, DEY'LL ROB THEIR OWN BANKS AN' DELIVER DA LOOT TO US LIKE UNSUSPECTIN' BABES!
DAT'S GREAT, BIFF--BUT I STILL DON'T SEE WHY WE GOTTA INVOLVE BATMAN. DA GUY'S A MENACE TO FOLKS LIKE US!
YER STUPIDITY'S BEGINNIN' TA IRRITATE ME, MORRY! LEMME SPELL IT OUT--
DA LAST TIME WE TRIED DIS SCAM, BATMAN CAUGHT US. WE SPENT YEARS BEHIND BARS. NOW, I AIN'T SO KEEN FER THAT TO HAPPEN AGAIN--
--SO DIS TIME, YOU AN' DA BOYS TAKE OUT BATMAN BEFORE WE PULL DA JOB!
US? TAKE ON BATMAN? NO WAY!
HE PASTED US! I AIN'T GOIN' UP AGAINST HIM AGAIN!
ME NEITHER! WE GO BACK TO JAIL, AN' THIS TIME THEY THROW AWAY DA KEY!
10

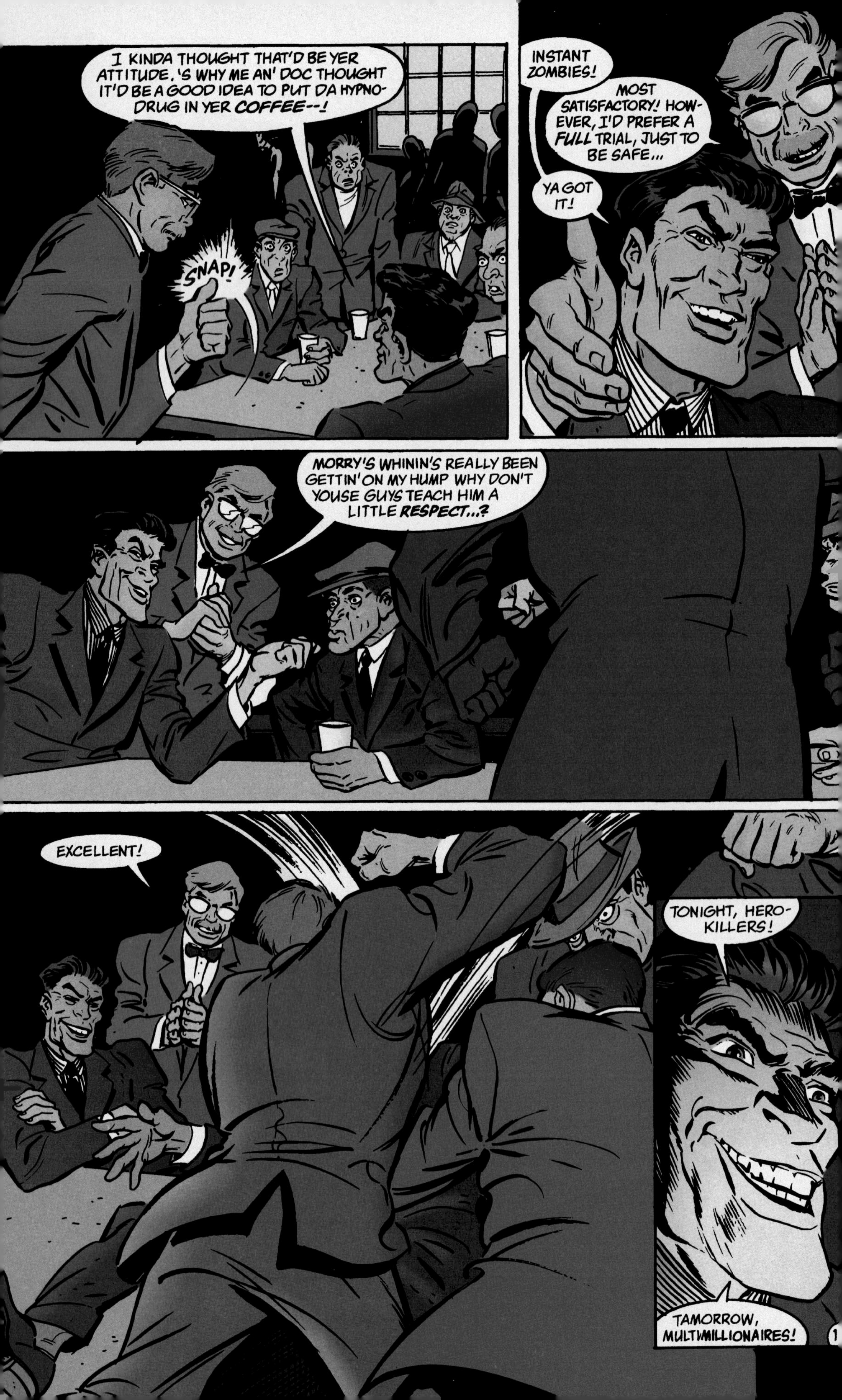
I KINDA THOUGHT THAT'D BE YER ATTITUDE. 'S WHY ME AN' DOC THOUGHT IT'D BE A GOOD IDEA TO PUT DA HYPNO-DRUG IN YER COFFEE--!
SNAP!
INSTANT ZOMBIES!
MOST SATISFACTORY! HOWEVER, I'D PREFER A FULL TRIAL, JUST TO BE SAFE...
YA GOT IT!
MORRY'S WHININ'S REALLY BEEN GETTIN' ON MY HUMP WHY DON'T YOUSE GUYS TEACH HIM A LITTLE RESPECT...?
EXCELLENT!
TONIGHT, HERO-KILLERS!
TAMORROW, MULTIMILLIONAIRES!
1

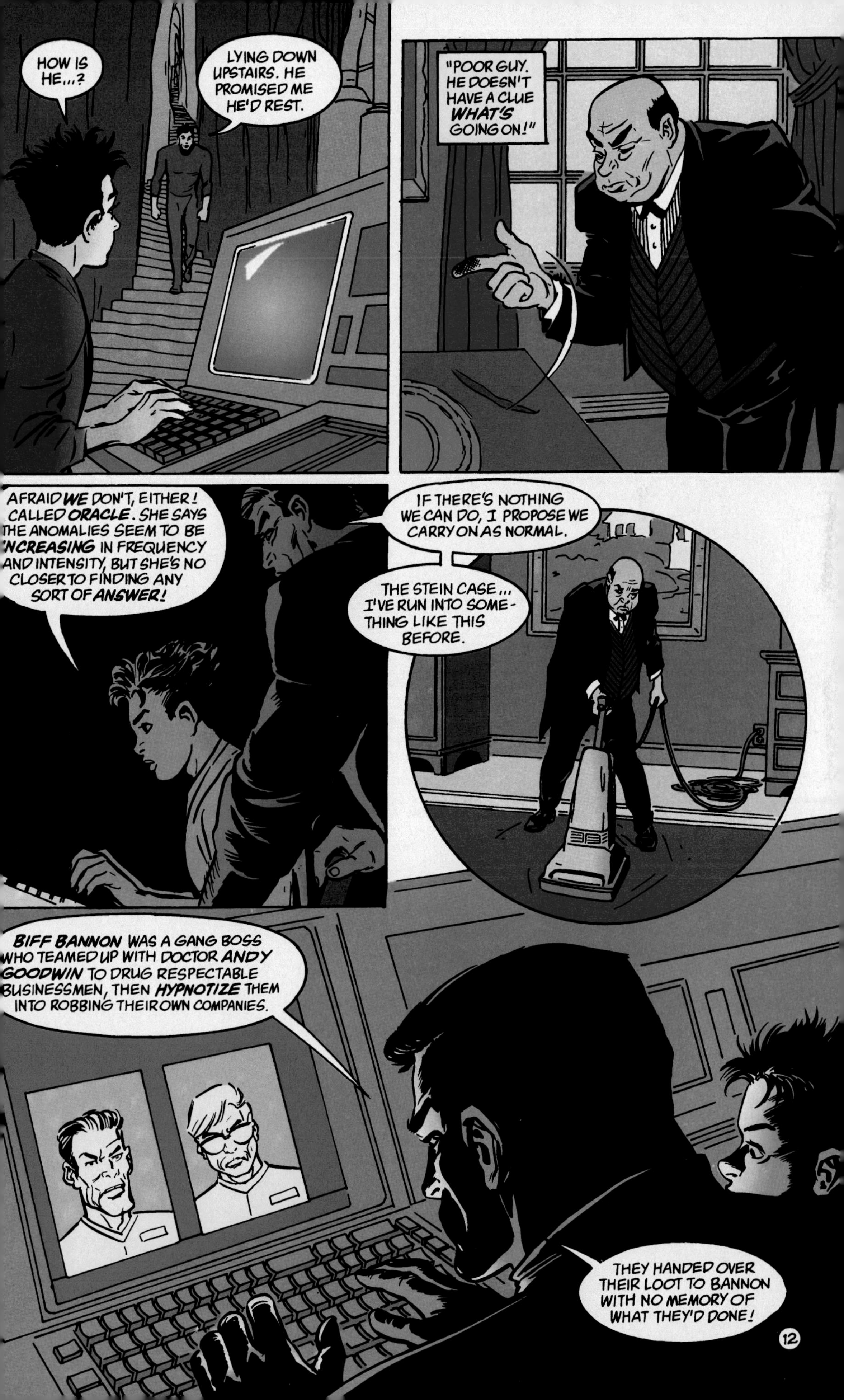
HOW IS HE...?
LYING DOWN UPSTAIRS. HE PROMISED ME HE'D REST.
"POOR GUY. HE DOESN'T HAVE A CLUE WHAT'S GOING ON!"
AFRAID WE DON'T, EITHER! CALLED ORACLE. SHE SAYS THE ANOMALIES SEEM TO BE INCREASING IN FREQUENCY AND INTENSITY, BUT SHE'S NO CLOSER TO FINDING ANY SORT OF ANSWER!
IF THERE'S NOTHING WE CAN DO, I PROPOSE WE CARRY ON AS NORMAL.
THE STEIN CASE... I'VE RUN INTO SOMETHING LIKE THIS BEFORE.
BIFF BANNON WAS A GANG BOSS WHO TEAMED UP WITH DOCTOR ANDY GOODWIN TO DRUG RESPECTABLE BUSINESSMEN, THEN HYPNOTIZE THEM INTO ROBBING THEIR OWN COMPANIES.
THEY HANDED OVER THEIR LOOT TO BANNON WITH NO MEMORY OF WHAT THEY'D DONE!
12

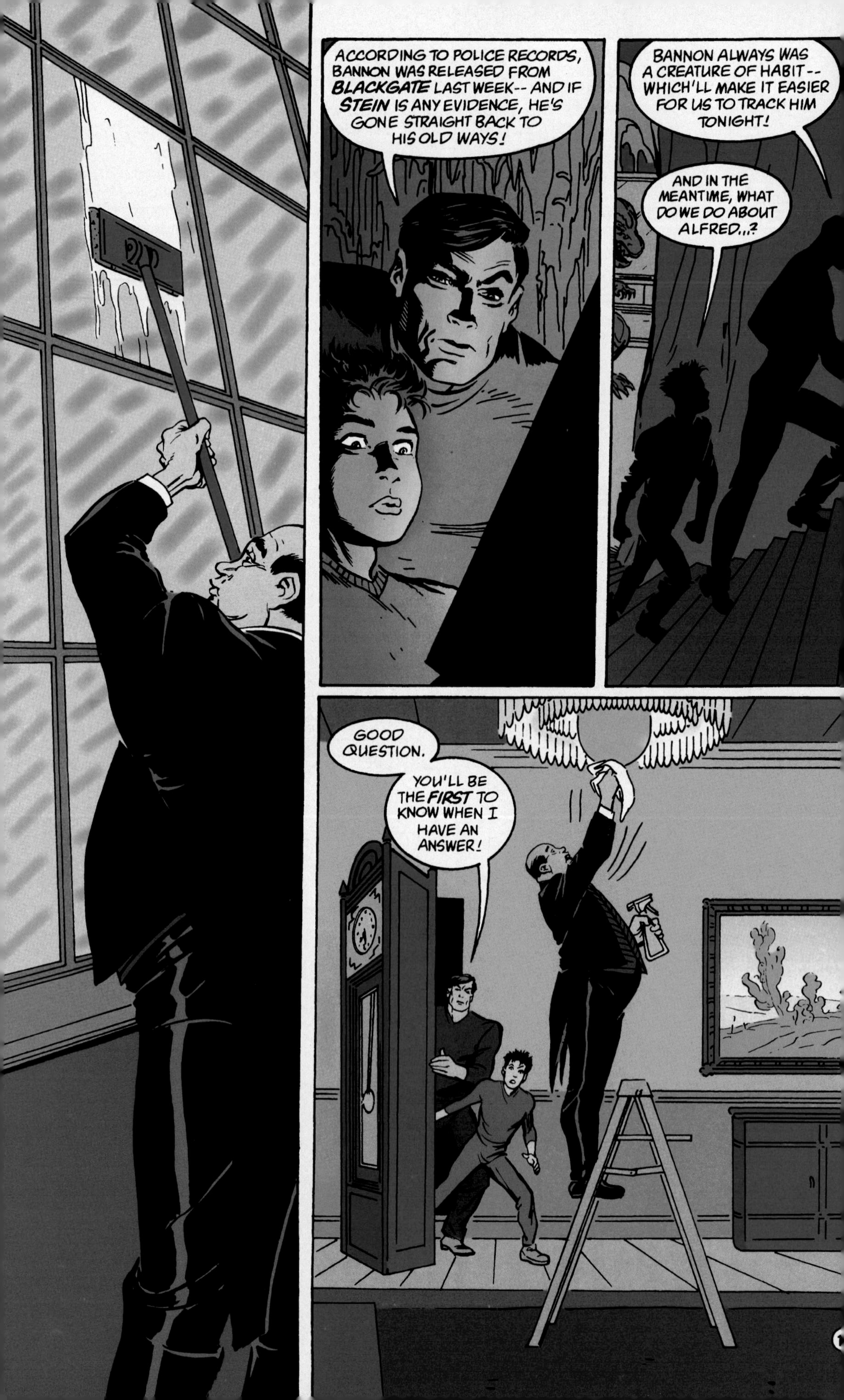
ACCORDING TO POLICE RECORDS, BANNON WAS RELEASED FROM BLACKGATE LAST WEEK-- AND IF STEIN IS ANY EVIDENCE, HE'S GONE STRAIGHT BACK TO HIS OLD WAYS!
BANNON ALWAYS WAS A CREATURE OF HABIT-- WHICH'LL MAKE IT EASIER FOR US TO TRACK HIM TONIGHT!
AND IN THE MEANTIME, WHAT DO WE DO ABOUT ALFRED...?
GOOD QUESTION.
YOU'LL BE THE FIRST TO KNOW WHEN I HAVE AN ANSWER!

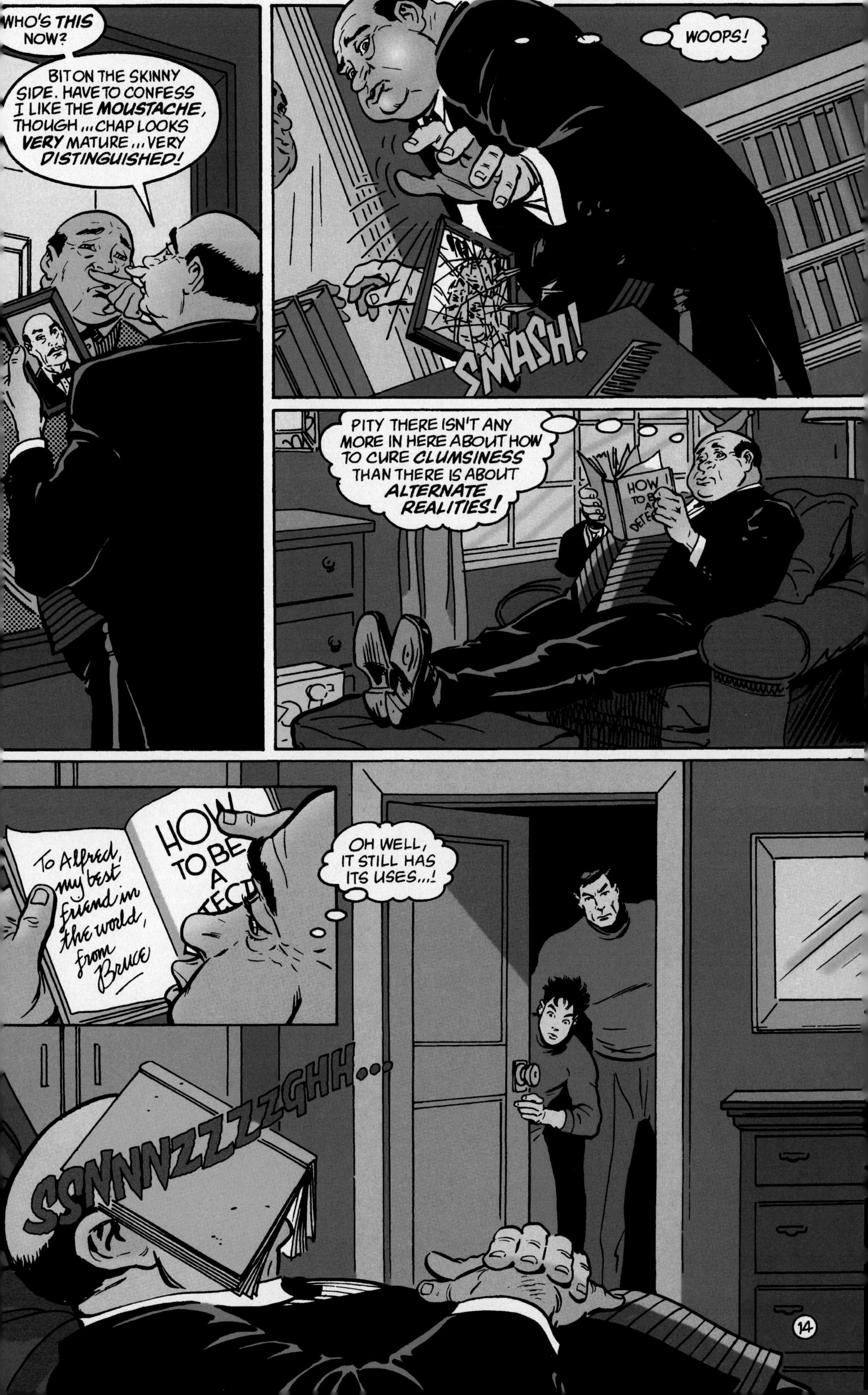
WHO'S THIS NOW?
BIT ON THE SKINNY SIDE. HAVE TO CONFESS I LIKE THE MOUSTACHE, THOUGH ... CHAP LOOKS VERY MATURE ... VERY DISTINGUISHED!
WOOPS!
SMASH!
PITY THERE ISN'T ANY MORE IN HERE ABOUT HOW TO CURE CLUMSINESS THAN THERE IS ABOUT ALTERNATE REALITIES!
HOW TO BE A DETEC
To Alfred, my best friend in the world, from Bruce
HOW TO BE A DETECT
OH WELL, IT STILL HAS ITS USES...!
SSNNNZZZZZGHH...

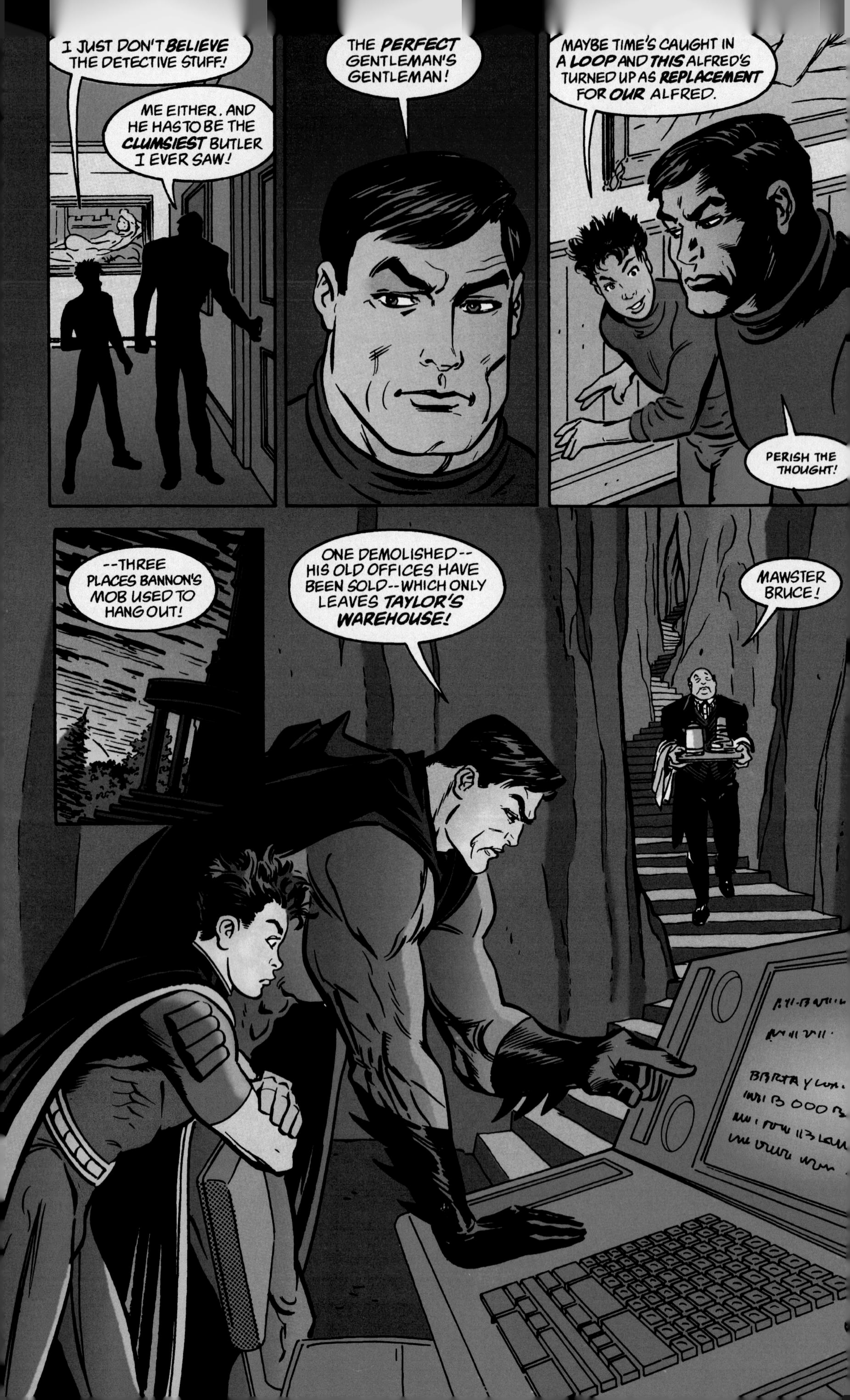
I JUST DON'T BELIEVE THE DETECTIVE STUFF!
ME EITHER. AND HE HAS TO BE THE CLUMSIEST BUTLER I EVER SAW!
THE PERFECT GENTLEMAN'S GENTLEMAN!
MAYBE TIME'S CAUGHT IN A LOOP AND THIS ALFRED'S TURNED UP AS REPLACEMENT FOR OUR ALFRED.
PERISH THE THOUGHT!
--THREE PLACES BANNON'S MOB USED TO HANG OUT!
ONE DEMOLISHED-- HIS OLD OFFICES HAVE BEEN SOLD--WHICH ONLY LEAVES TAYLOR'S WAREHOUSE!
MAWSTER BRUCE!

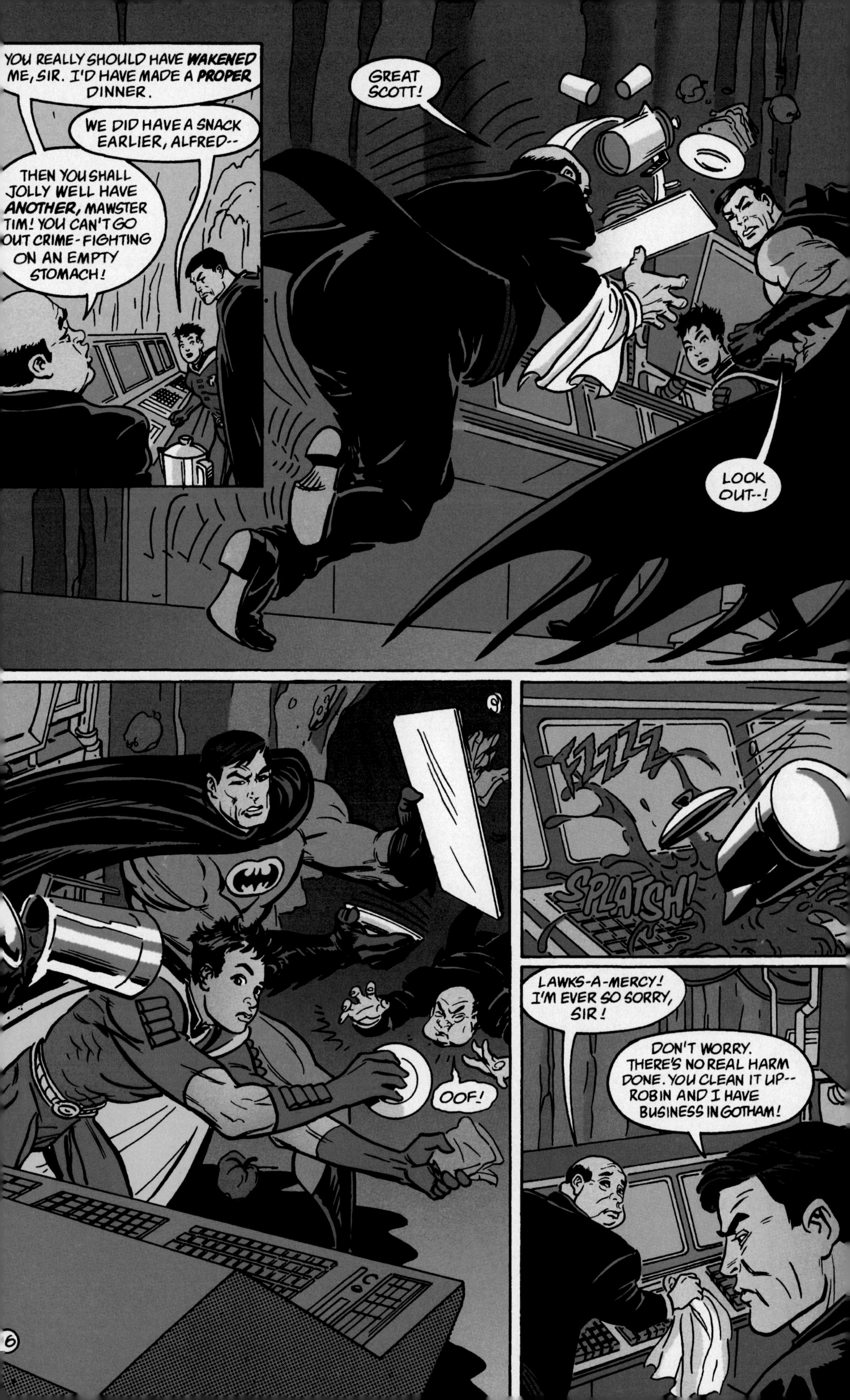
YOU REALLY SHOULD HAVE WAKENED ME, SIR. I'D HAVE MADE A PROPER DINNER.
WE DID HAVE A SNACK EARLIER, ALFRED--
THEN YOU SHALL JOLLY WELL HAVE ANOTHER, MAWSTER TIM! YOU CAN'T GO OUT CRIME-FIGHTING ON AN EMPTY STOMACH!
GREAT SCOTT!
LOOK OUT--!
FZZZZ
SPLATSH!
OOF!
LAWKS-A-MERCY! I'M EVER SO SORRY, SIR!
DON'T WORRY. THERE'S NO REAL HARM DONE. YOU CLEAN IT UP-- ROBIN AND I HAVE BUSINESS IN GOTHAM!
6

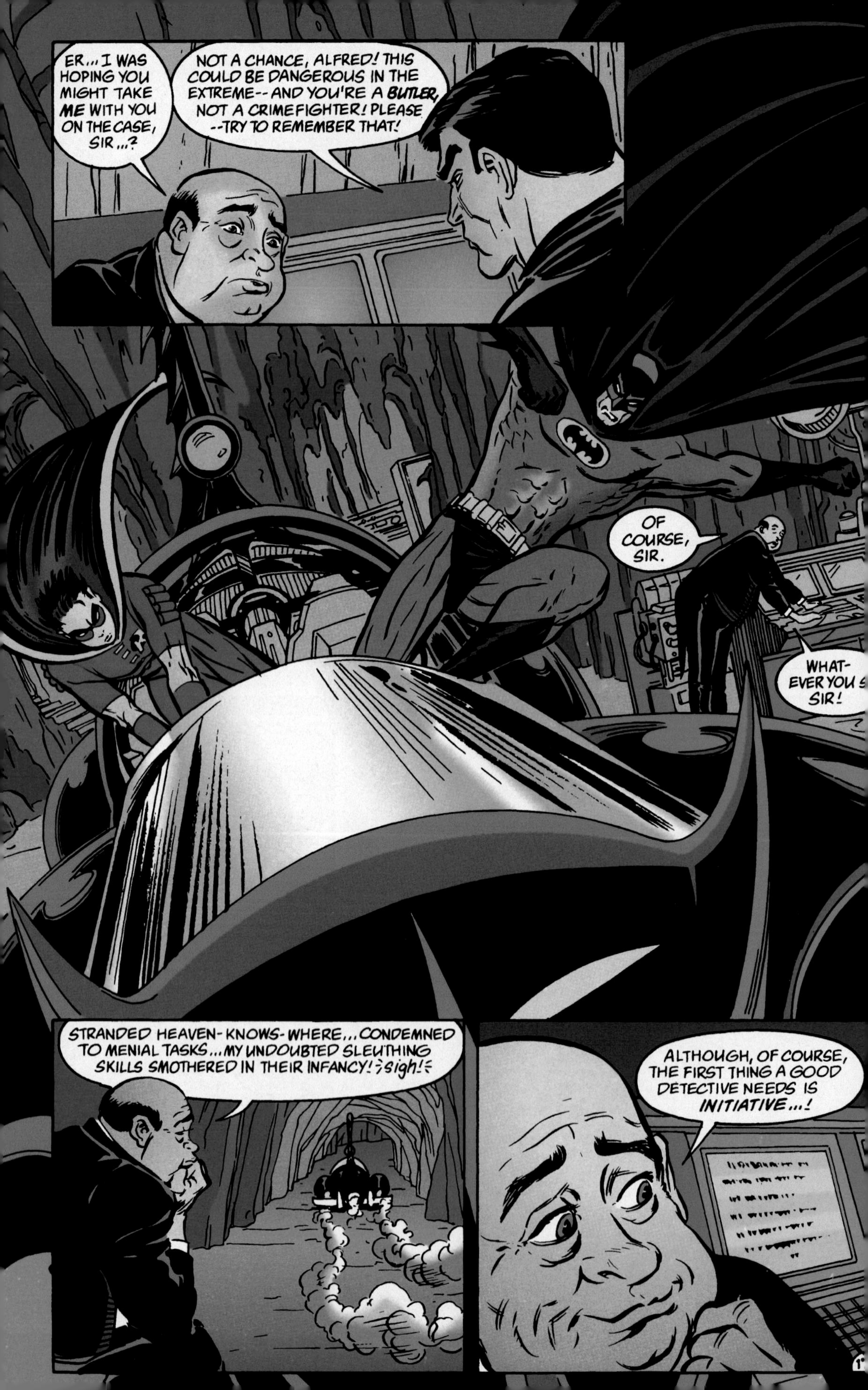
ER... I WAS HOPING YOU MIGHT TAKE ME WITH YOU ON THE CASE, SIR...?
NOT A CHANCE, ALFRED! THIS COULD BE DANGEROUS IN THE EXTREME-- AND YOU'RE A BUTLER, NOT A CRIMEFIGHTER! PLEASE --TRY TO REMEMBER THAT!
OF COURSE, SIR.
WHAT-EVER YOU S SIR!
STRANDED HEAVEN-KNOWS-WHERE... CONDEMNED TO MENIAL TASKS... MY UNDOUBTED SLEUTHING SKILLS SMOTHERED IN THEIR INFANCY! ~sigh!~
ALTHOUGH, OF COURSE, THE FIRST THING A GOOD DETECTIVE NEEDS IS INITIATIVE...!

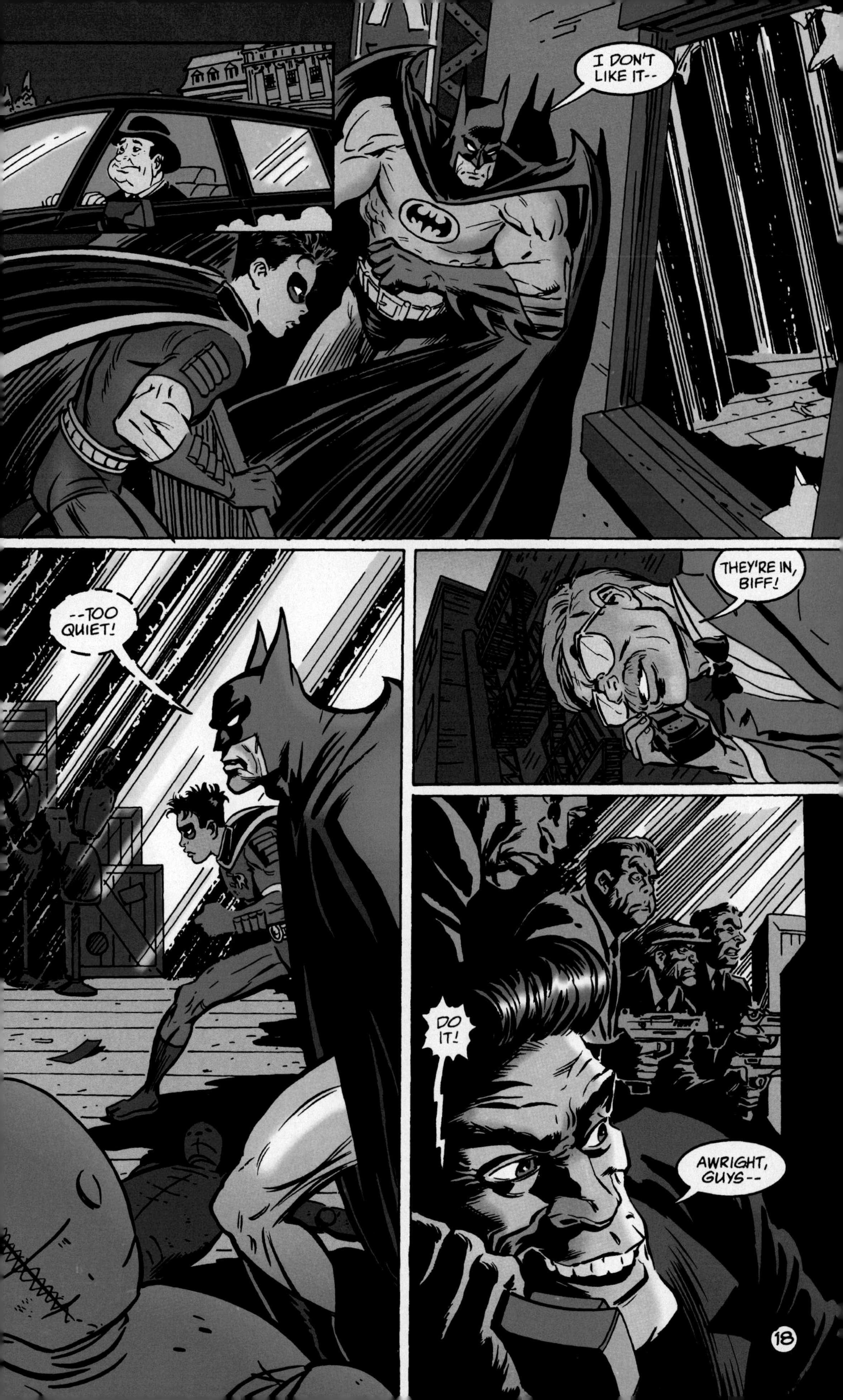
I DON'T LIKE IT--
--TOO QUIET!
THEY'RE IN, BIFF!
DO IT!
AWRIGHT, GUYS--
18

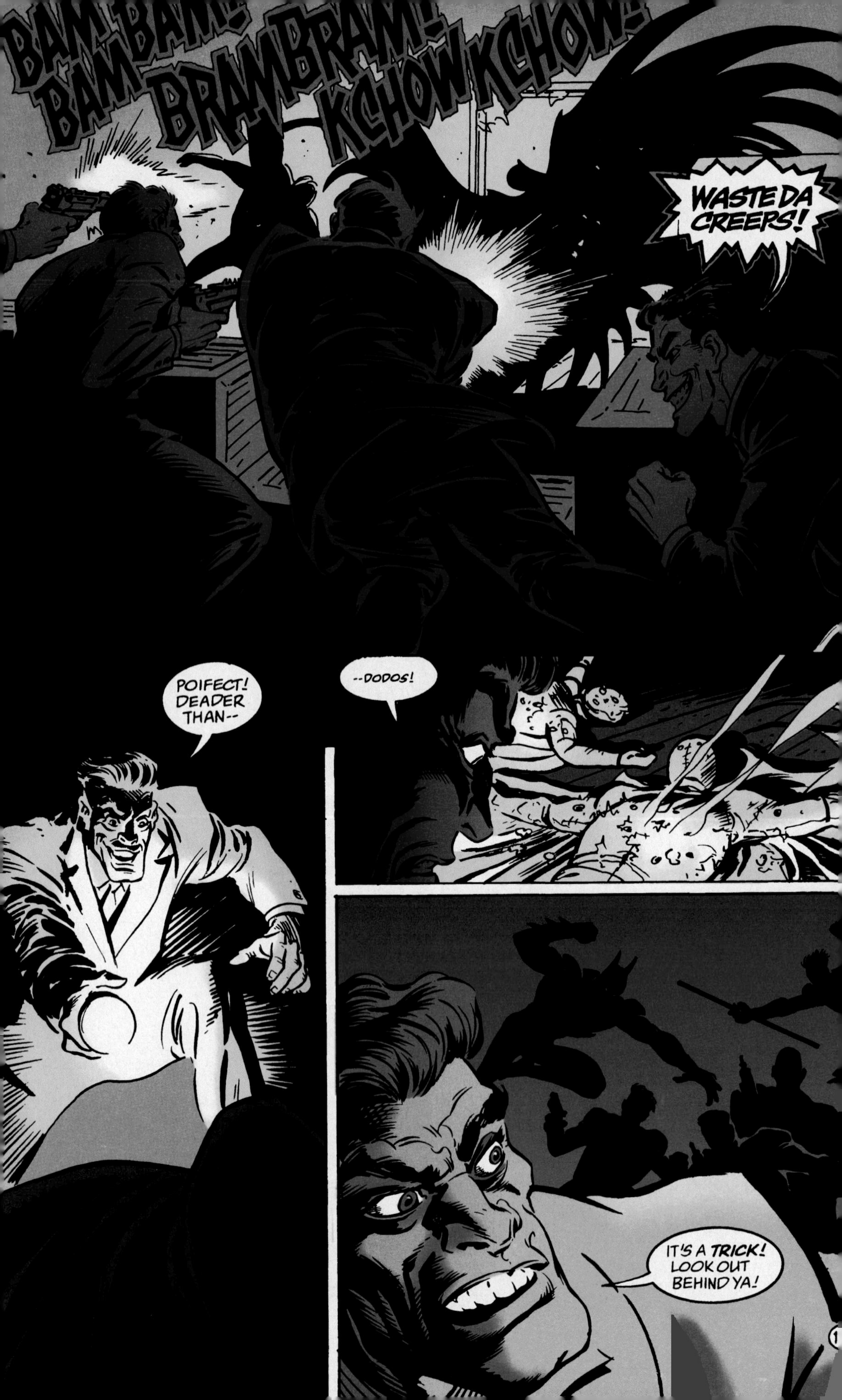
BAM BAM! BAM BAM!
BRAMBRAM! BRAMBRAM!
KCHOW KCHOW! KCHOW KCHOW!
WASTE DA CREEPS!
POIFECT! DEADER THAN--
--DODOS!
IT'S A TRICK! LOOK OUT BEHIND YA!

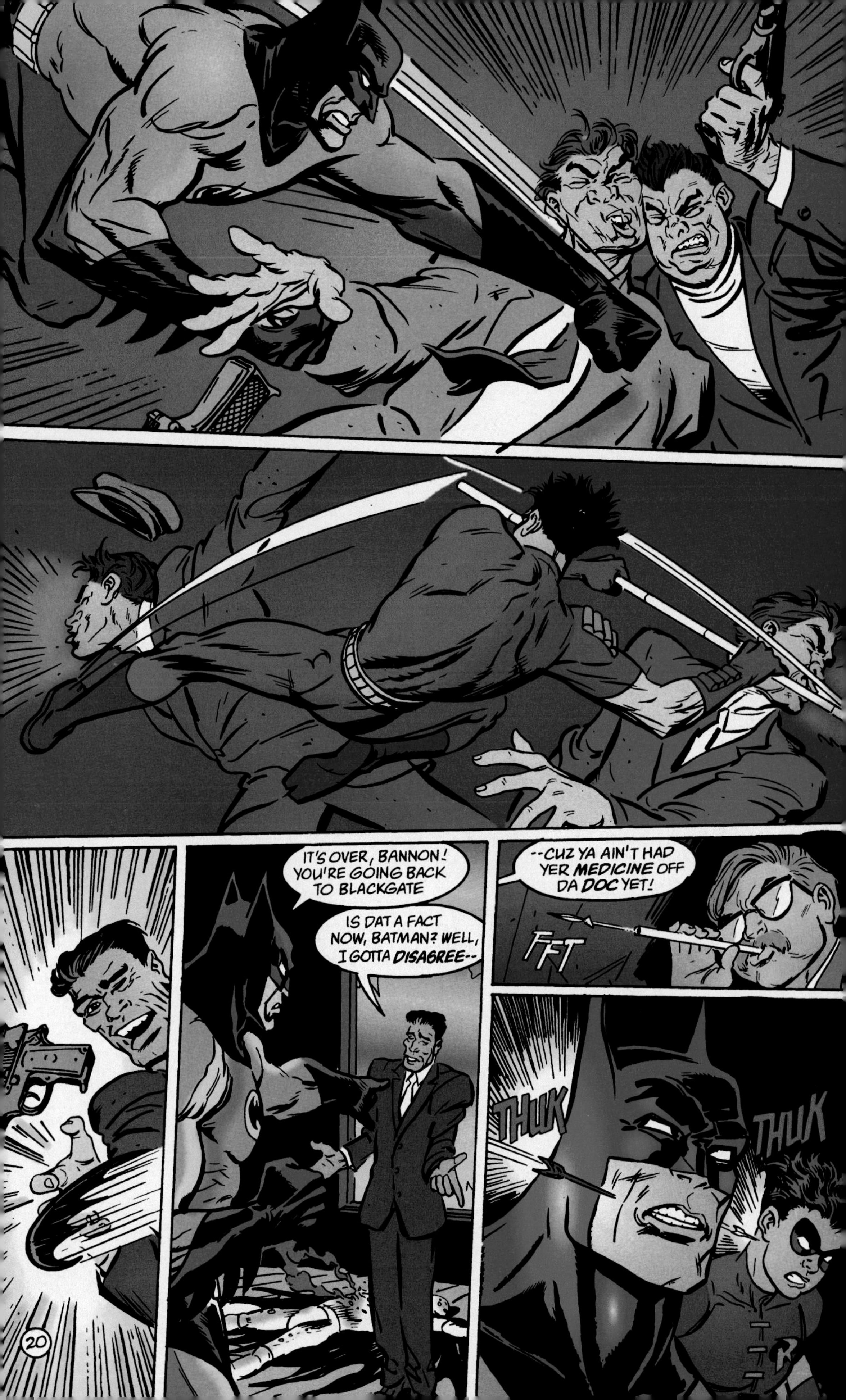
IT'S OVER, BANNON! YOU'RE GOING BACK TO BLACKGATE
IS DAT A FACT NOW, BATMAN? WELL, I GOTTA DISAGREE--
--CUZ YA AIN'T HAD YER MEDICINE OFF DA DOC YET!
FFT
THUK
THUK

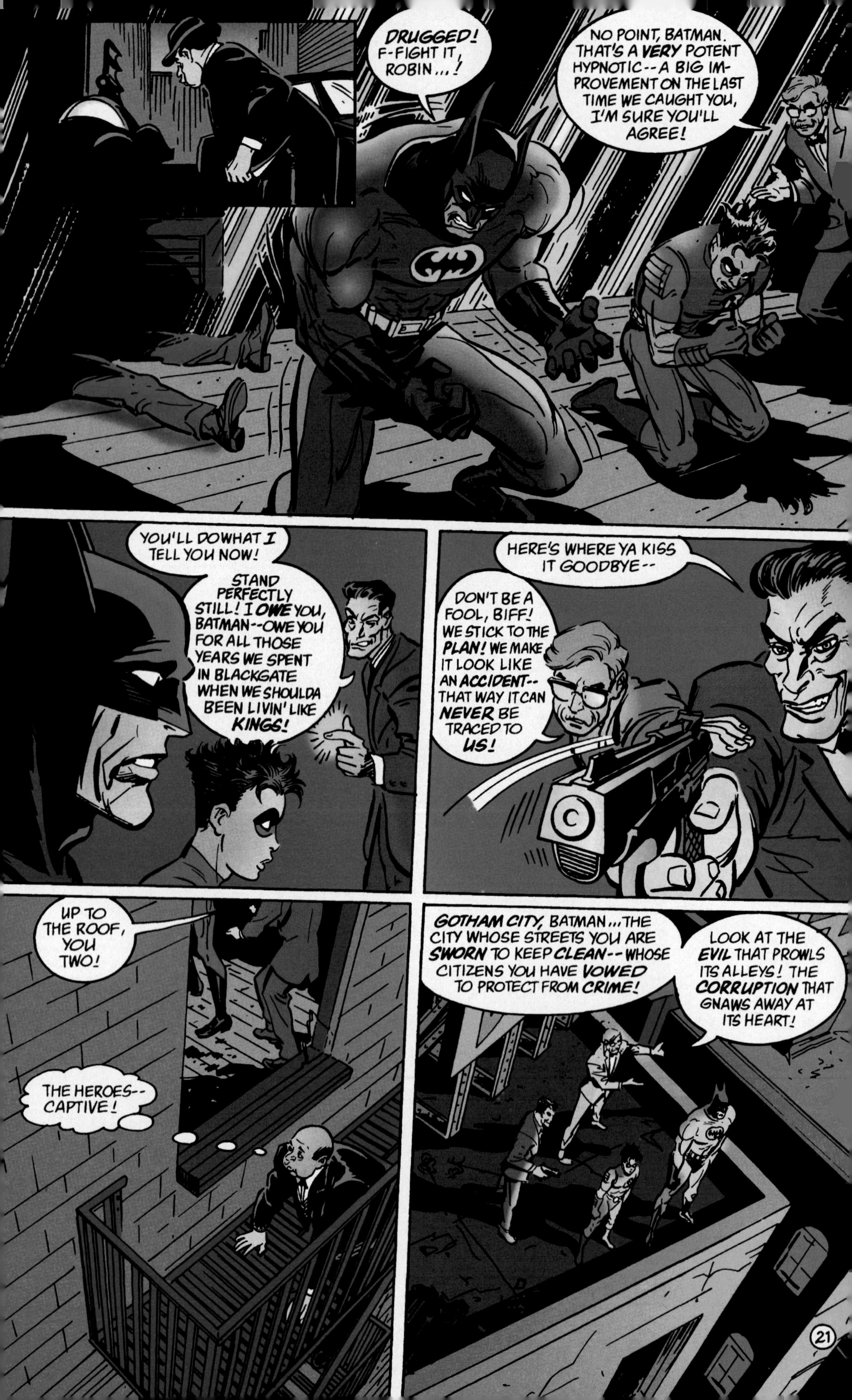
DRUGGED! F-FIGHT IT, ROBIN...!
NO POINT, BATMAN. THAT'S A VERY POTENT HYPNOTIC--A BIG IMPROVEMENT ON THE LAST TIME WE CAUGHT YOU, I'M SURE YOU'LL AGREE!
YOU'LL DO WHAT I TELL YOU NOW!
STAND PERFECTLY STILL! I OWE YOU, BATMAN--OWE YOU FOR ALL THOSE YEARS WE SPENT IN BLACKGATE WHEN WE SHOULDA BEEN LIVIN' LIKE KINGS!
HERE'S WHERE YA KISS IT GOODBYE--
DON'T BE A FOOL, BIFF! WE STICK TO THE PLAN! WE MAKE IT LOOK LIKE AN ACCIDENT--THAT WAY IT CAN NEVER BE TRACED TO US!
UP TO THE ROOF, YOU TWO!
THE HEROES--CAPTIVE!
GOTHAM CITY, BATMAN...THE CITY WHOSE STREETS YOU ARE SWORN TO KEEP CLEAN--WHOSE CITIZENS YOU HAVE VOWED TO PROTECT FROM CRIME!
LOOK AT THE EVIL THAT PROWLS ITS ALLEYS! THE CORRUPTION THAT GNAWS AWAY AT ITS HEART!
21

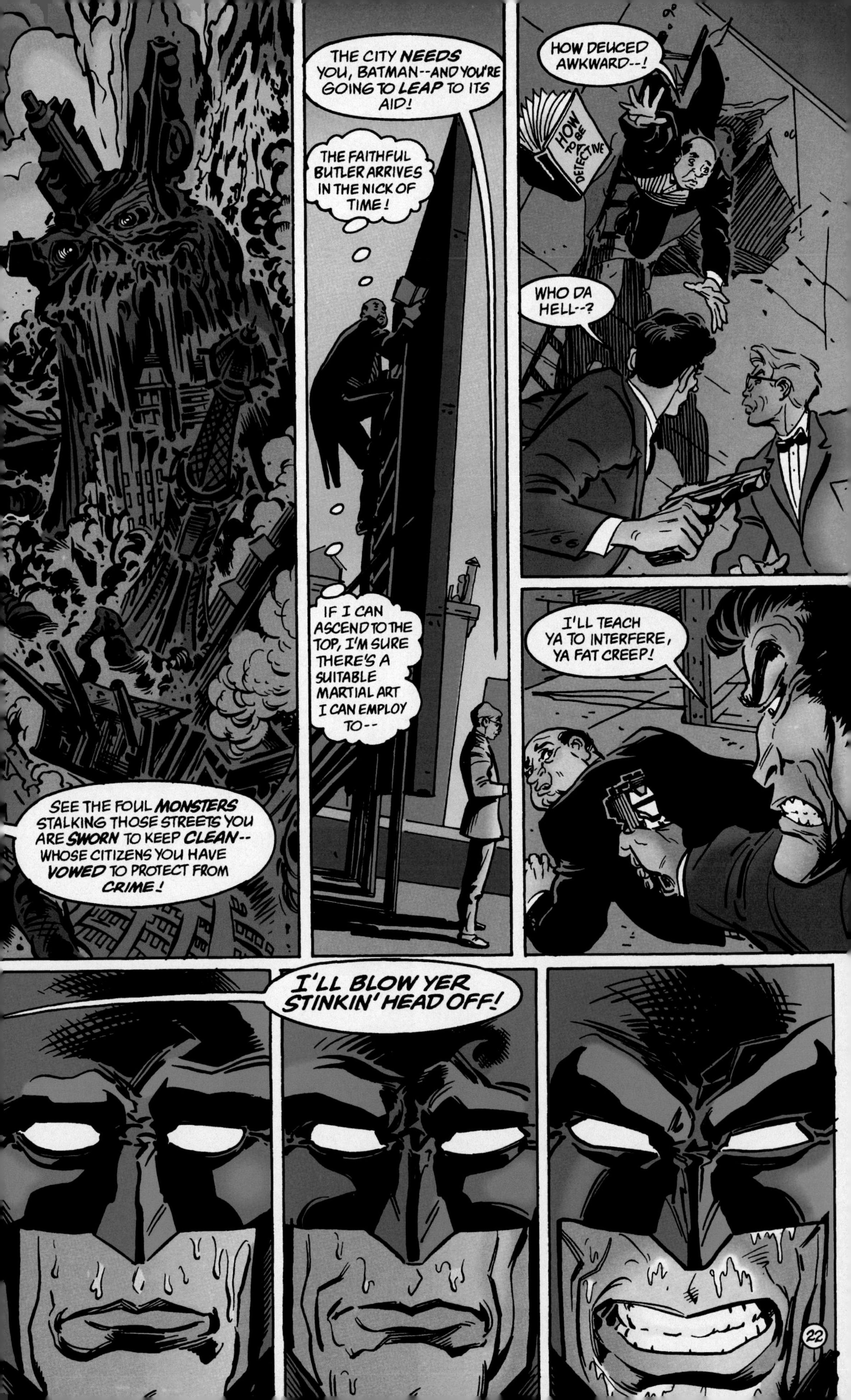
SEE THE FOUL MONSTERS STALKING THOSE STREETS YOU ARE SWORN TO KEEP CLEAN-- WHOSE CITIZENS YOU HAVE VOWED TO PROTECT FROM CRIME!
THE CITY NEEDS YOU, BATMAN--AND YOU'RE GOING TO LEAP TO ITS AID!
THE FAITHFUL BUTLER ARRIVES IN THE NICK OF TIME!
IF I CAN ASCEND TO THE TOP, I'M SURE THERE'S A SUITABLE MARTIAL ART I CAN EMPLOY TO--
HOW DEUCED AWKWARD--!
HOW TO BE A DETECTIVE
WHO DA HELL--?
I'LL TEACH YA TO INTERFERE, YA FAT CREEP!
I'LL BLOW YER STINKIN' HEAD OFF!
22

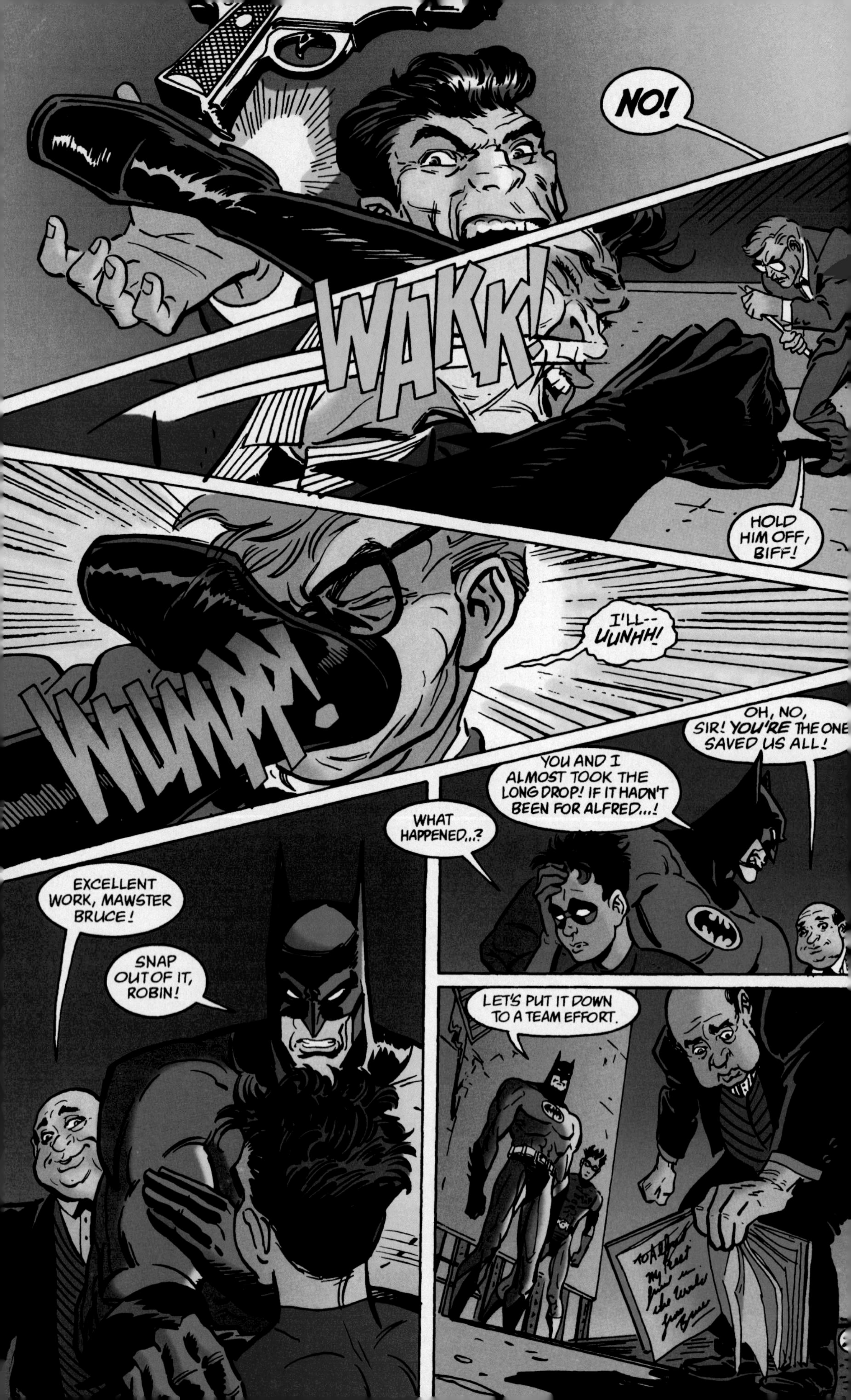
NO!
WAKK!
HOLD HIM OFF, BIFF!
I'LL-- UUNHH!
WUMPP!
EXCELLENT WORK, MAWSTER BRUCE!
SNAP OUT OF IT, ROBIN!
WHAT HAPPENED...?
YOU AND I ALMOST TOOK THE LONG DROP! IF IT HADN'T BEEN FOR ALFRED...!
OH, NO, SIR! YOU'RE THE ONE SAVED US ALL!
LET'S PUT IT DOWN TO A TEAM EFFORT.

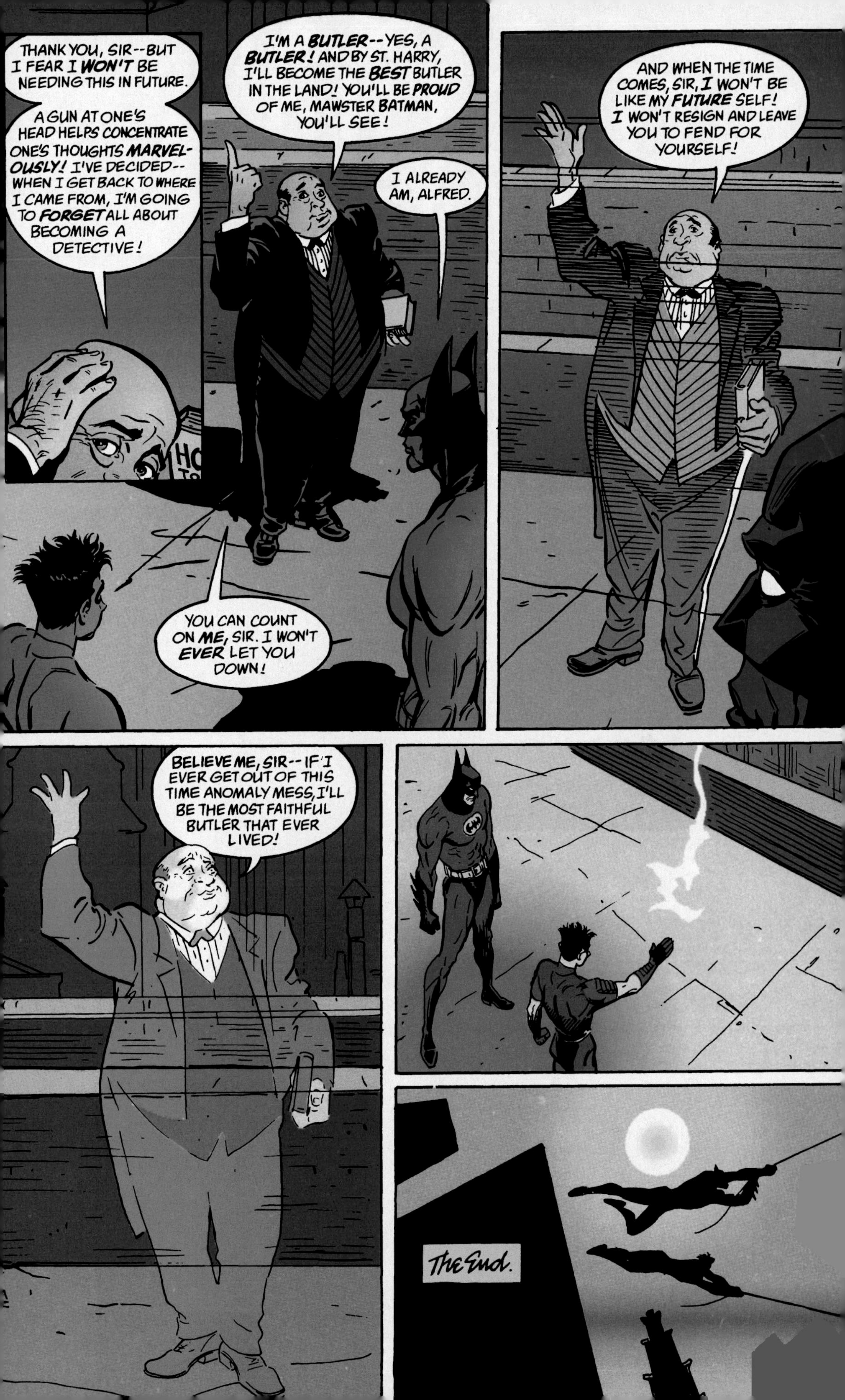
THANK YOU, SIR--BUT I FEAR I WON'T BE NEEDING THIS IN FUTURE.
A GUN AT ONE'S HEAD HELPS CONCENTRATE ONE'S THOUGHTS MARVEL-OUSLY! I'VE DECIDED-- WHEN I GET BACK TO WHERE I CAME FROM, I'M GOING TO FORGET ALL ABOUT BECOMING A DETECTIVE!
I'M A BUTLER--YES, A BUTLER! AND BY ST. HARRY, I'LL BECOME THE BEST BUTLER IN THE LAND! YOU'LL BE PROUD OF ME, MAWSTER BATMAN, YOU'LL SEE!
I ALREADY AM, ALFRED.
YOU CAN COUNT ON ME, SIR. I WON'T EVER LET YOU DOWN!
AND WHEN THE TIME COMES, SIR, I WON'T BE LIKE MY FUTURE SELF! I WON'T RESIGN AND LEAVE YOU TO FEND FOR YOURSELF!
BELIEVE ME, SIR--IF I EVER GET OUT OF THIS TIME ANOMALY MESS, I'LL BE THE MOST FAITHFUL BUTLER THAT EVER LIVED!
The End.

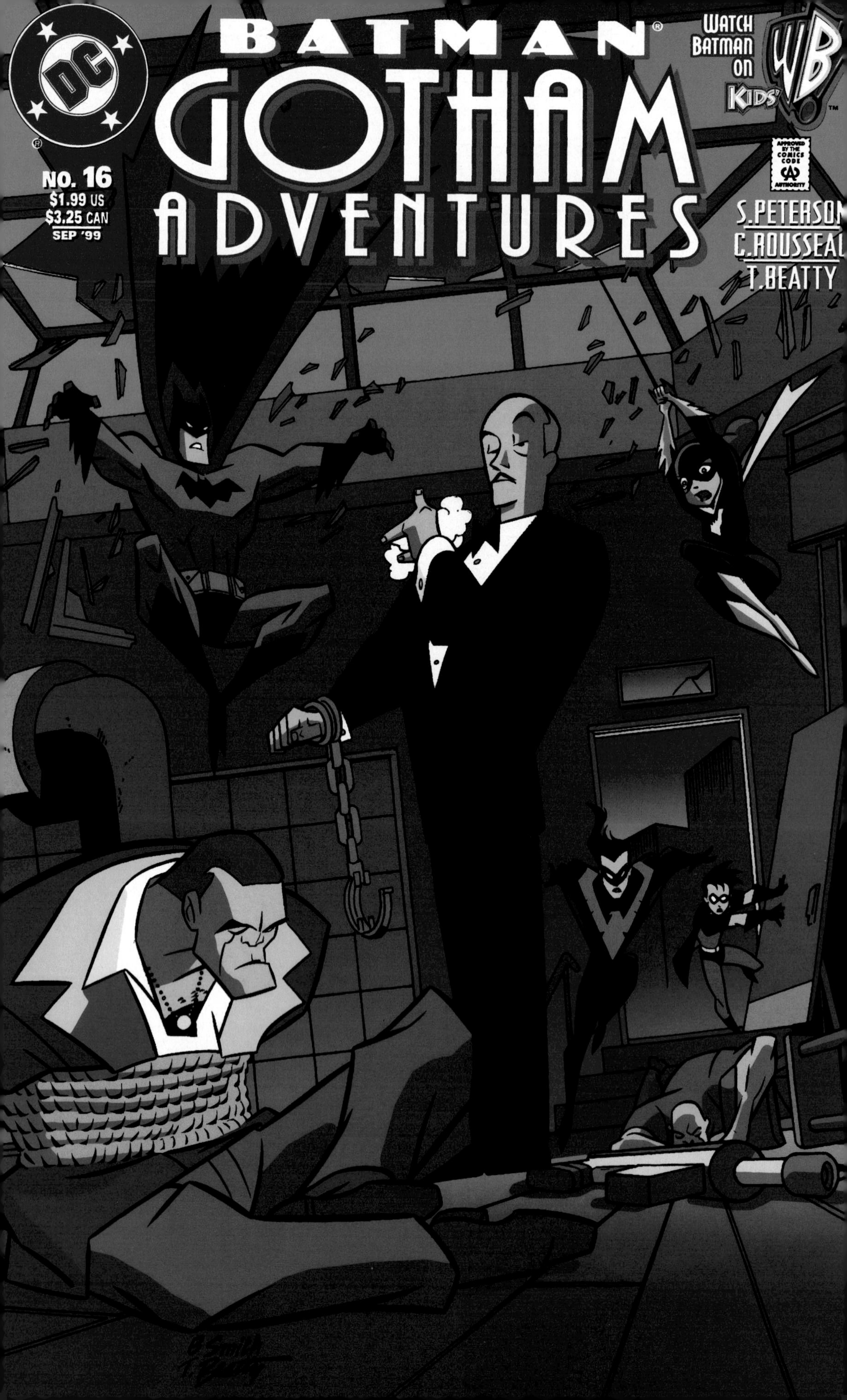

DC
BATMAN®
GOTHAM
ADVENTURES
NO. 16
$1.99 US
$3.25 CAN
SEP '99
WATCH BATMAN ON
KIDS' WB
APPROVED BY THE COMICS CODE AUTHORITY
S.PETERSON
C.ROUSSEAU
T.BEATTY

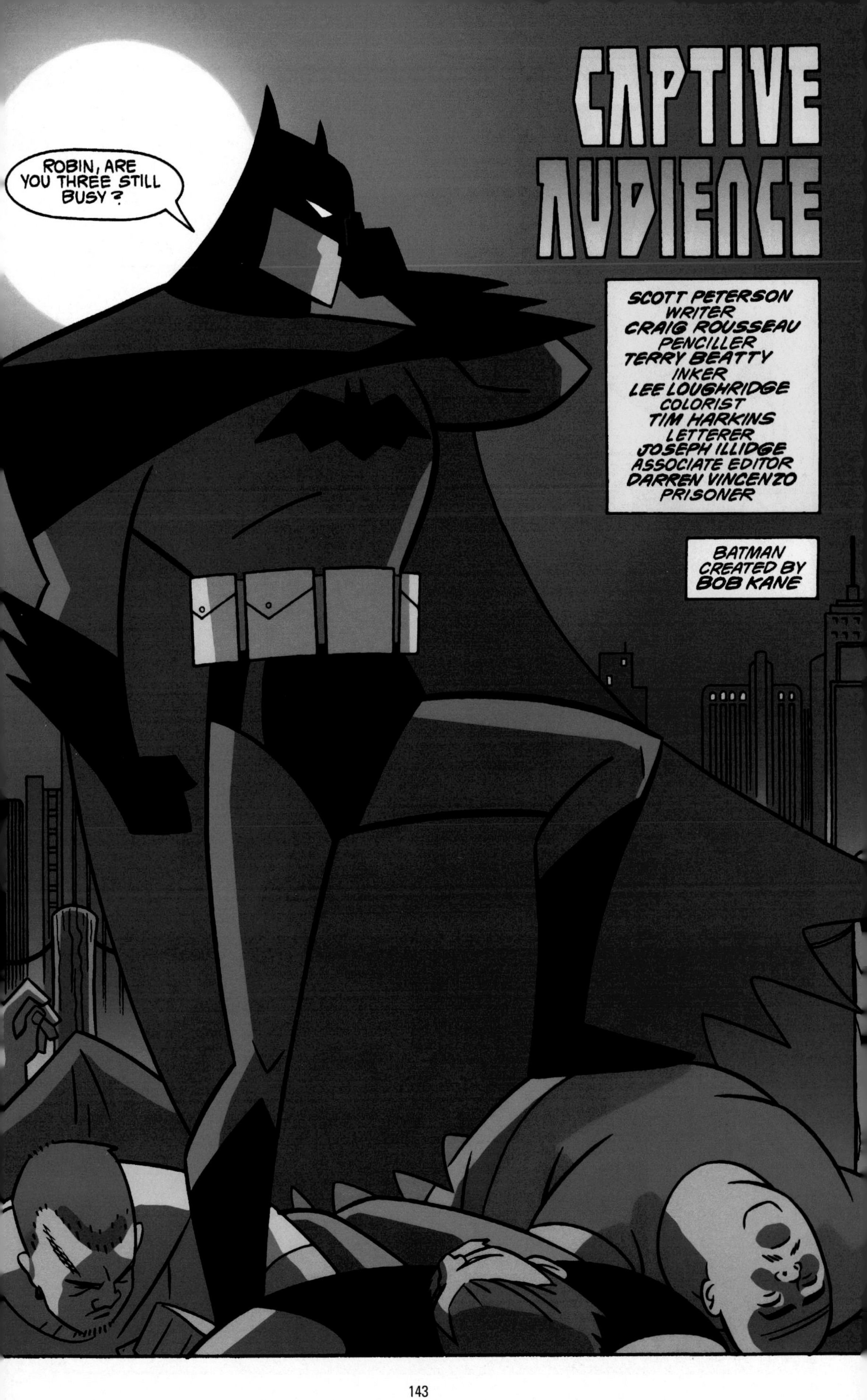

ROBIN, ARE YOU THREE STILL BUSY?
CAPTIVE AUDIENCE
SCOTT PETERSON WRITER
CRAIG ROUSSEAU PENCILLER
TERRY BEATTY INKER
LEE LOUGHRIDGE COLORIST
TIM HARKINS LETTERER
JOSEPH ILLIDGE ASSOCIATE EDITOR
DARREN VINCENZO PRISONER
BATMAN CREATED BY BOB KANE

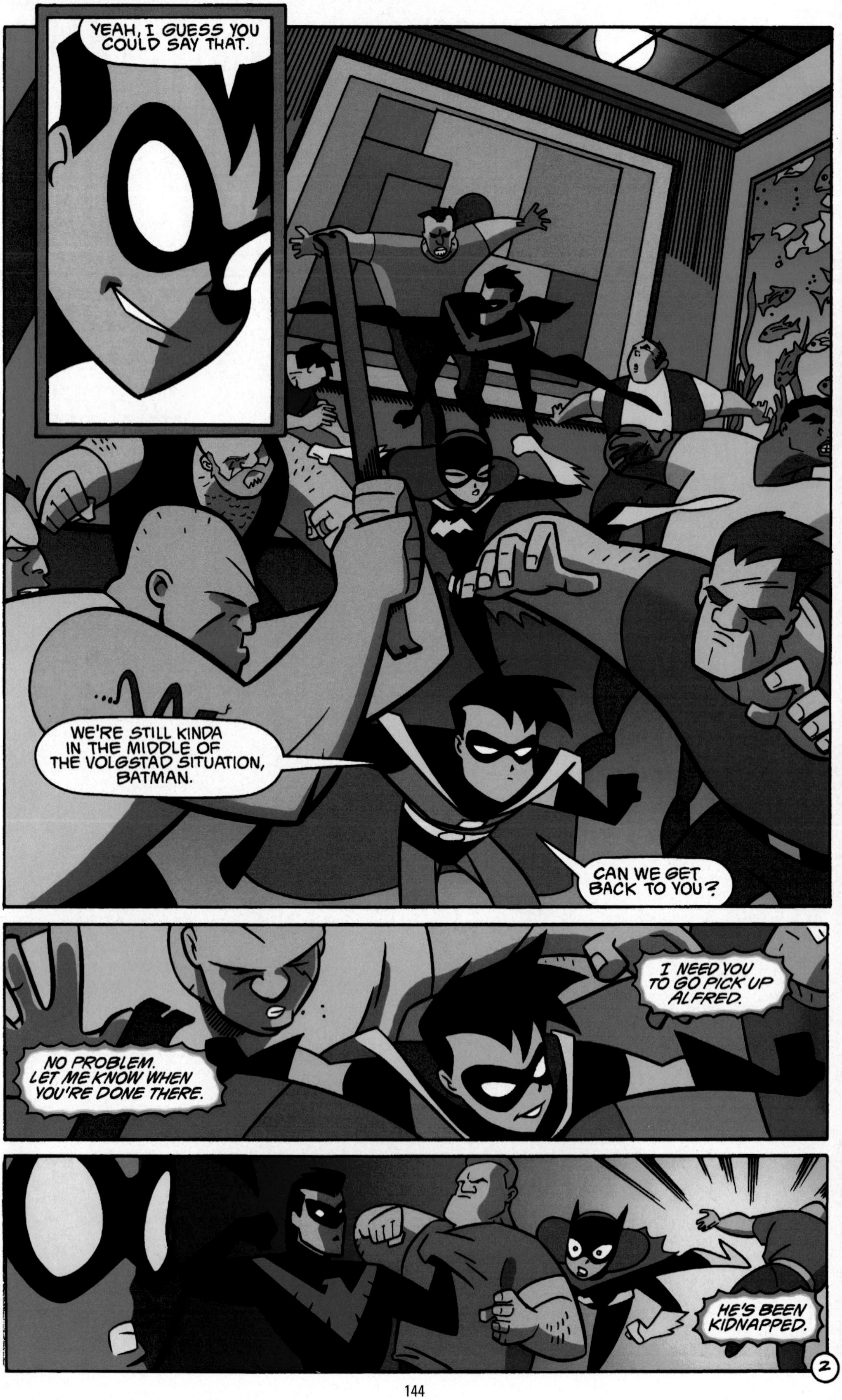
YEAH, I GUESS YOU COULD SAY THAT.
WE'RE STILL KINDA IN THE MIDDLE OF THE VOLGSTAD SITUATION, BATMAN.
CAN WE GET BACK TO YOU?
I NEED YOU TO GO PICK UP ALFRED.
NO PROBLEM. LET ME KNOW WHEN YOU'RE DONE THERE.
HE'S BEEN KIDNAPPED.
2

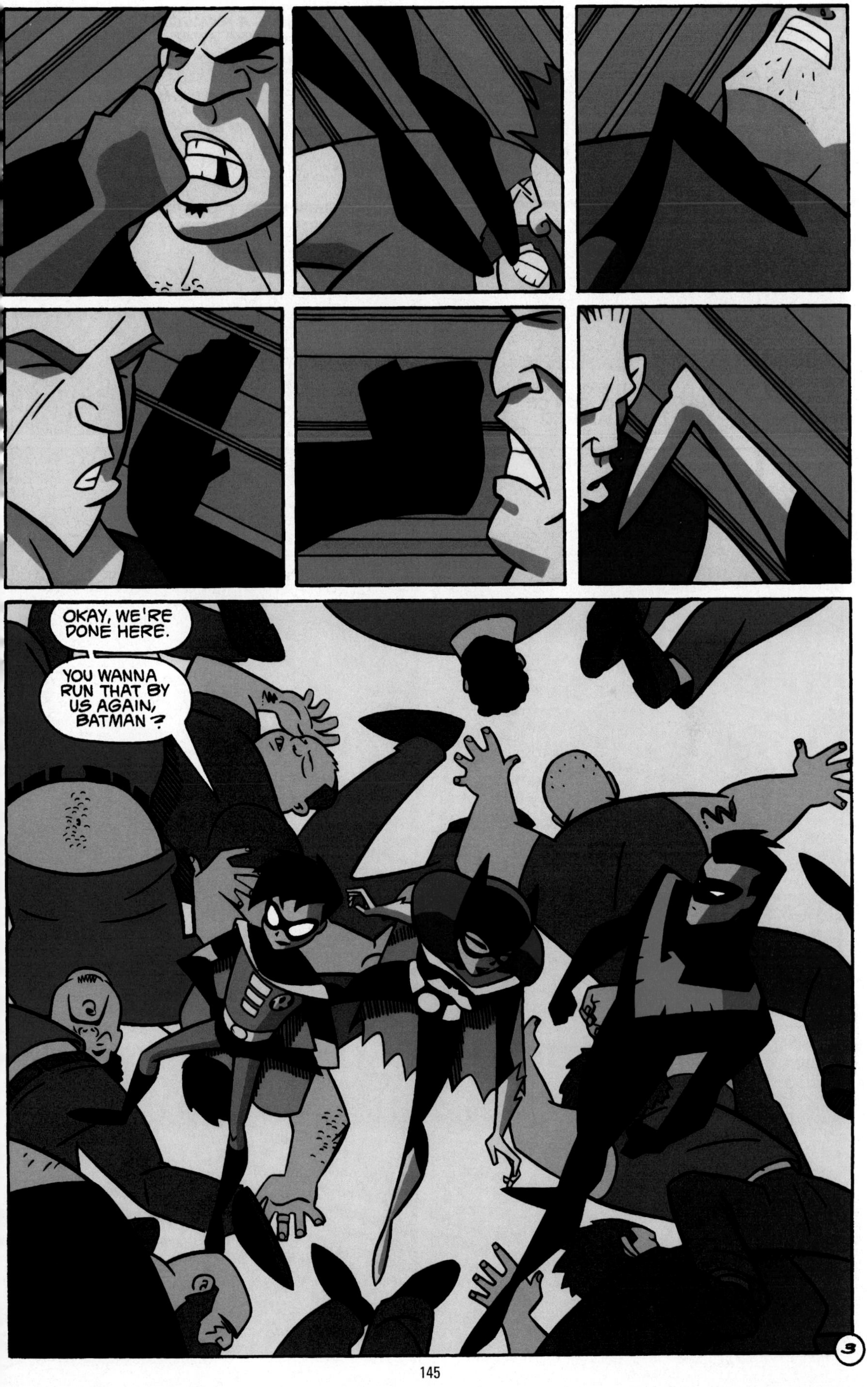
OKAY, WE'RE DONE HERE.
YOU WANNA RUN THAT BY US AGAIN, BATMAN?

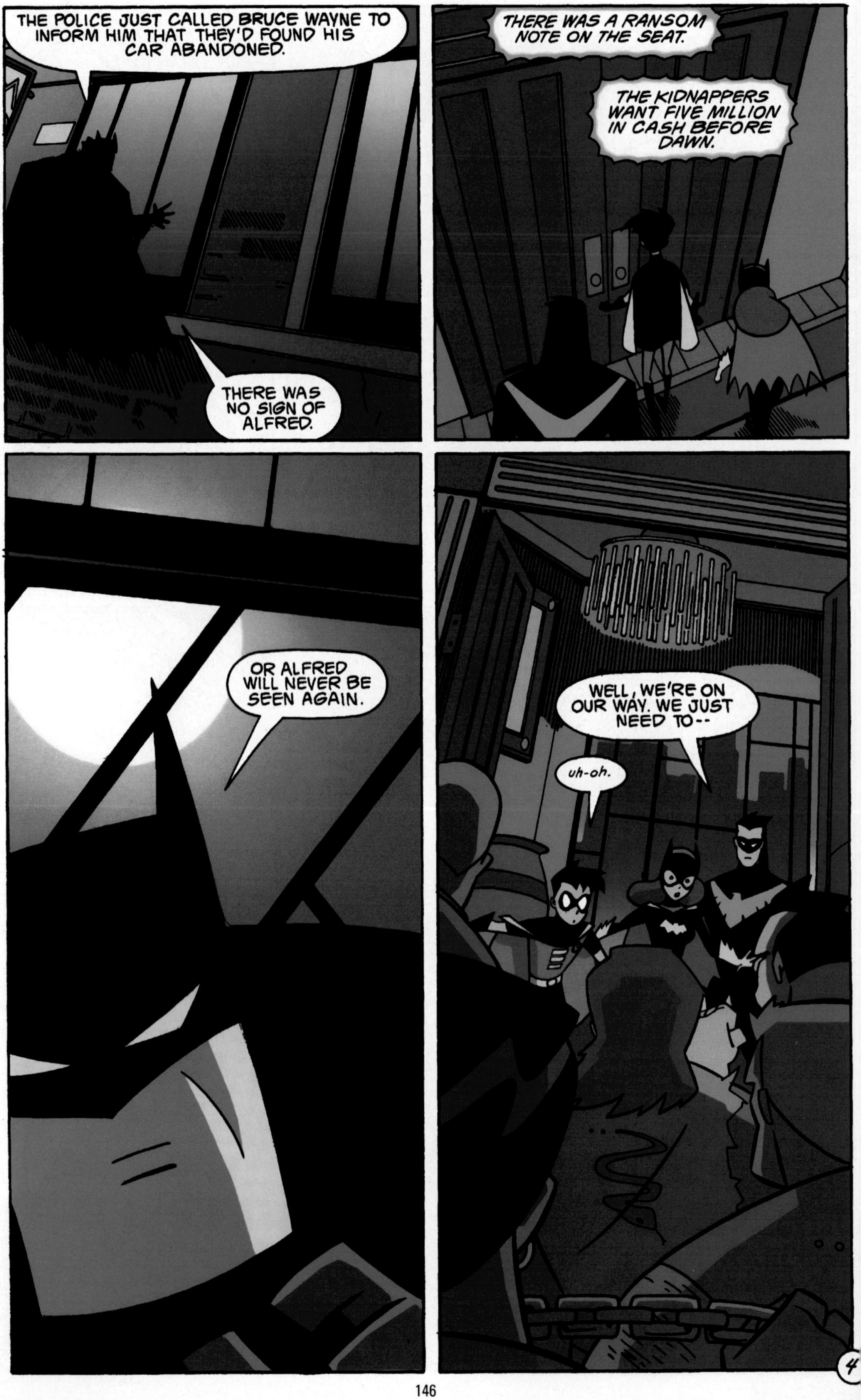

THE POLICE JUST CALLED BRUCE WAYNE TO INFORM HIM THAT THEY'D FOUND HIS CAR ABANDONED.
THERE WAS NO SIGN OF ALFRED.
THERE WAS A RANSOM NOTE ON THE SEAT.
THE KIDNAPPERS WANT FIVE MILLION IN CASH BEFORE DAWN.
OR ALFRED WILL NEVER BE SEEN AGAIN.
WELL, WE'RE ON OUR WAY. WE JUST NEED TO--
uh-oh.
4

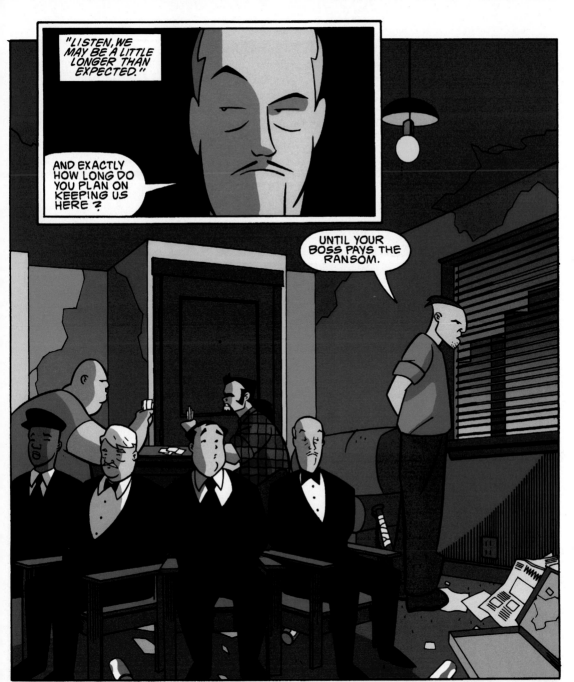

"LISTEN, WE MAY BE A LITTLE LONGER THAN EXPECTED."

AND EXACTLY HOW LONG DO YOU PLAN ON KEEPING US HERE?

UNTIL YOUR BOSS PAYS THE RANSOM.

I SEE. AND YOU WILL THEN ALLOW US TO GO?

UNLESS I'M IN THE MOOD FOR SOME FUN.

5

AND IF MISTER WAYNE REFUSES TO PAY?

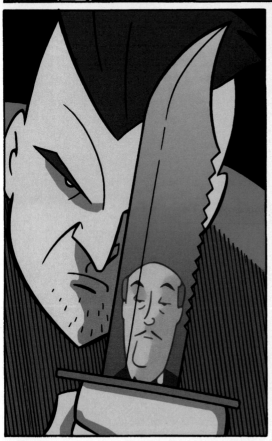

I SEE.

AND THESE OTHER WELL-DRESSED GENTLEMEN? HOW ARE THEY INVOLVED?

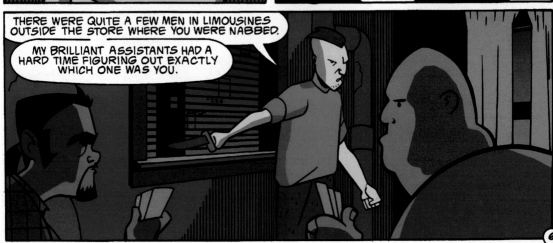

THERE WERE QUITE A FEW MEN IN LIMOUSINES OUTSIDE THE STORE WHERE YOU WERE NABBED.

MY BRILLIANT ASSISTANTS HAD A HARD TIME FIGURING OUT EXACTLY WHICH ONE WAS YOU.

6

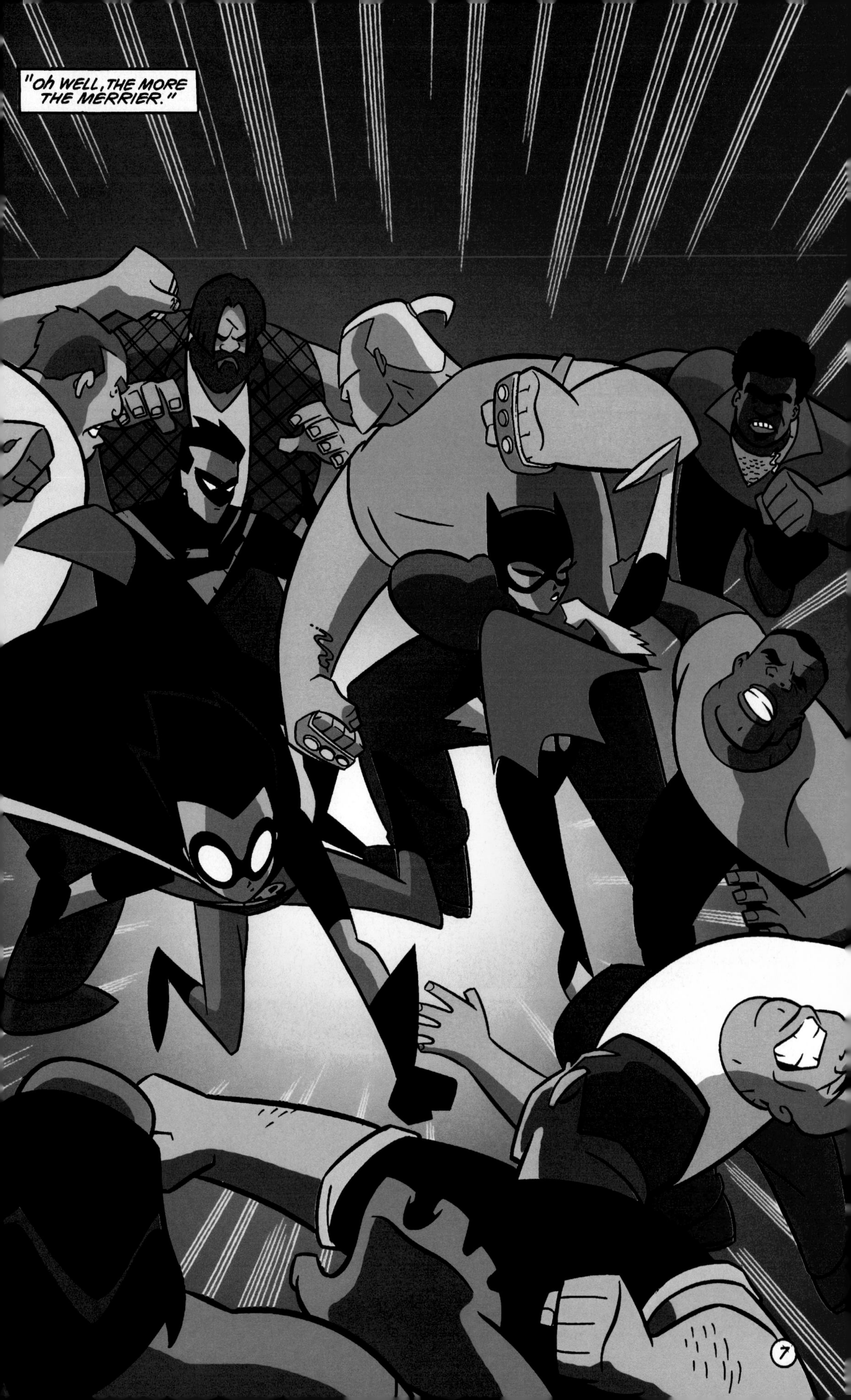
"Oh WELL, THE MORE THE MERRIER."

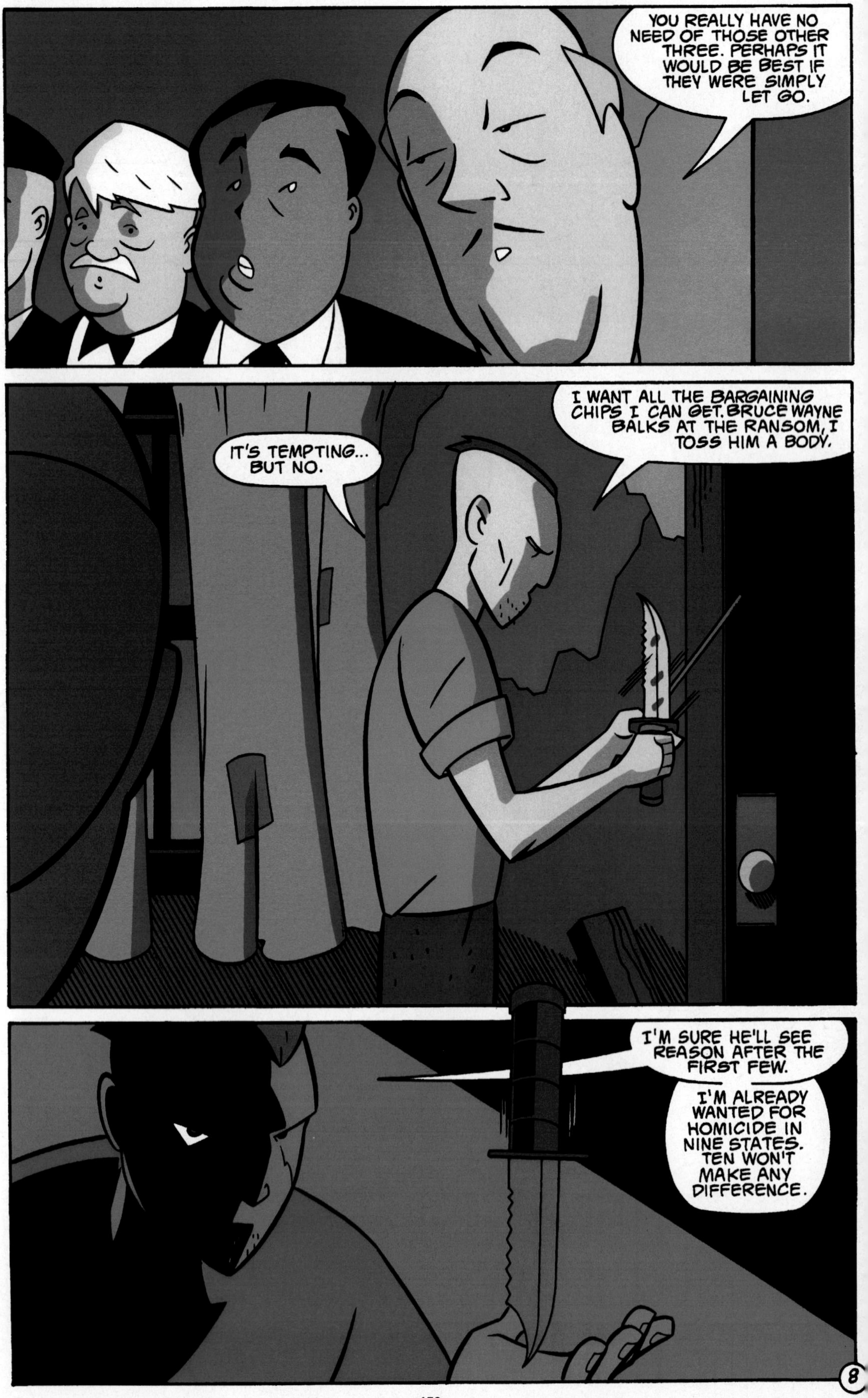
YOU REALLY HAVE NO NEED OF THOSE OTHER THREE. PERHAPS IT WOULD BE BEST IF THEY WERE SIMPLY LET GO.
IT'S TEMPTING... BUT NO.
I WANT ALL THE BARGAINING CHIPS I CAN GET. BRUCE WAYNE BALKS AT THE RANSOM, I TOSS HIM A BODY.
I'M SURE HE'LL SEE REASON AFTER THE FIRST FEW.
I'M ALREADY WANTED FOR HOMICIDE IN NINE STATES. TEN WON'T MAKE ANY DIFFERENCE.
8

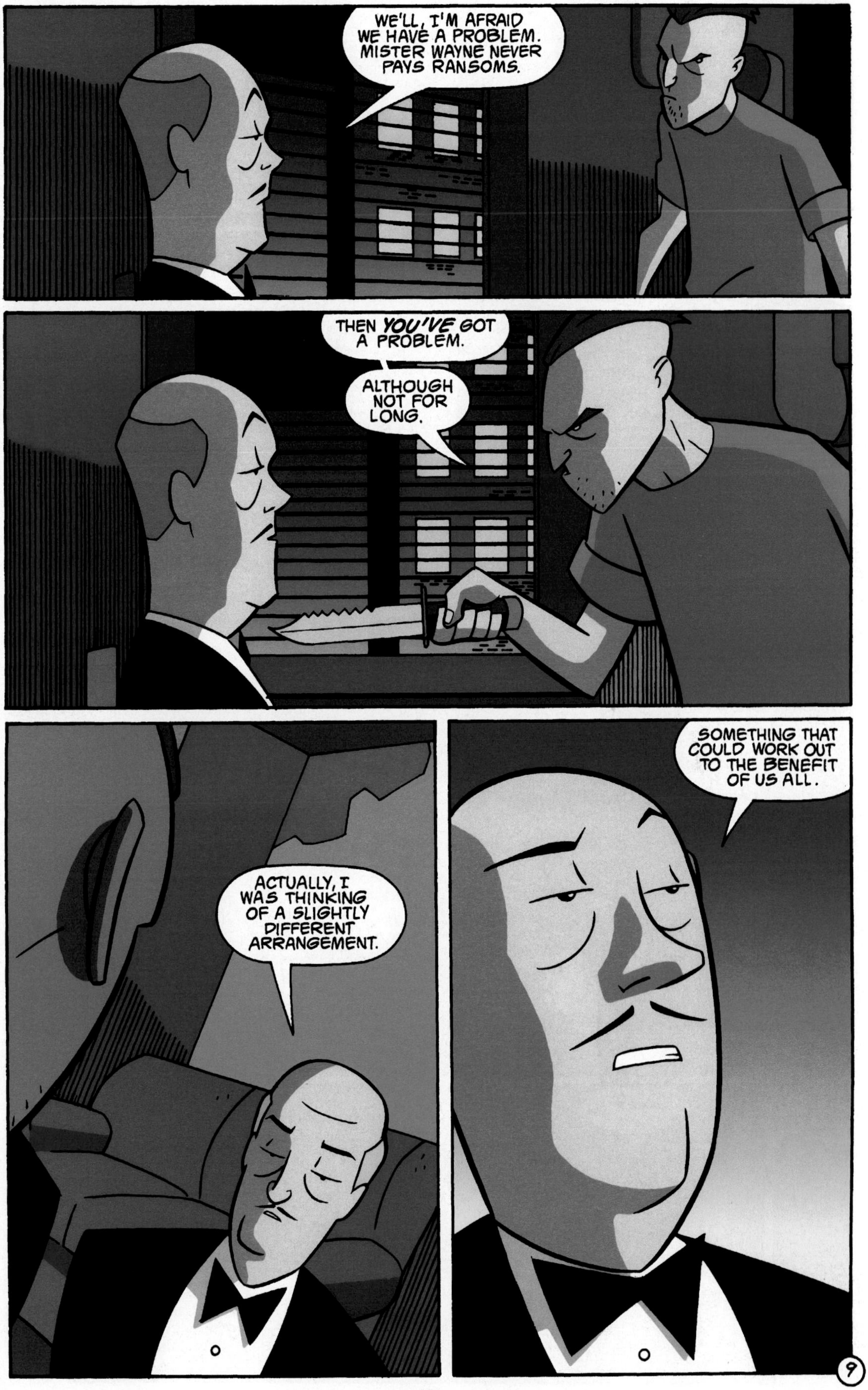
WE'LL, I'M AFRAID WE HAVE A PROBLEM. MISTER WAYNE NEVER PAYS RANSOMS.
THEN *YOU'VE* GOT A PROBLEM.
ALTHOUGH NOT FOR LONG.
ACTUALLY, I WAS THINKING OF A SLIGHTLY DIFFERENT ARRANGEMENT.
SOMETHING THAT COULD WORK OUT TO THE BENEFIT OF US ALL.
9

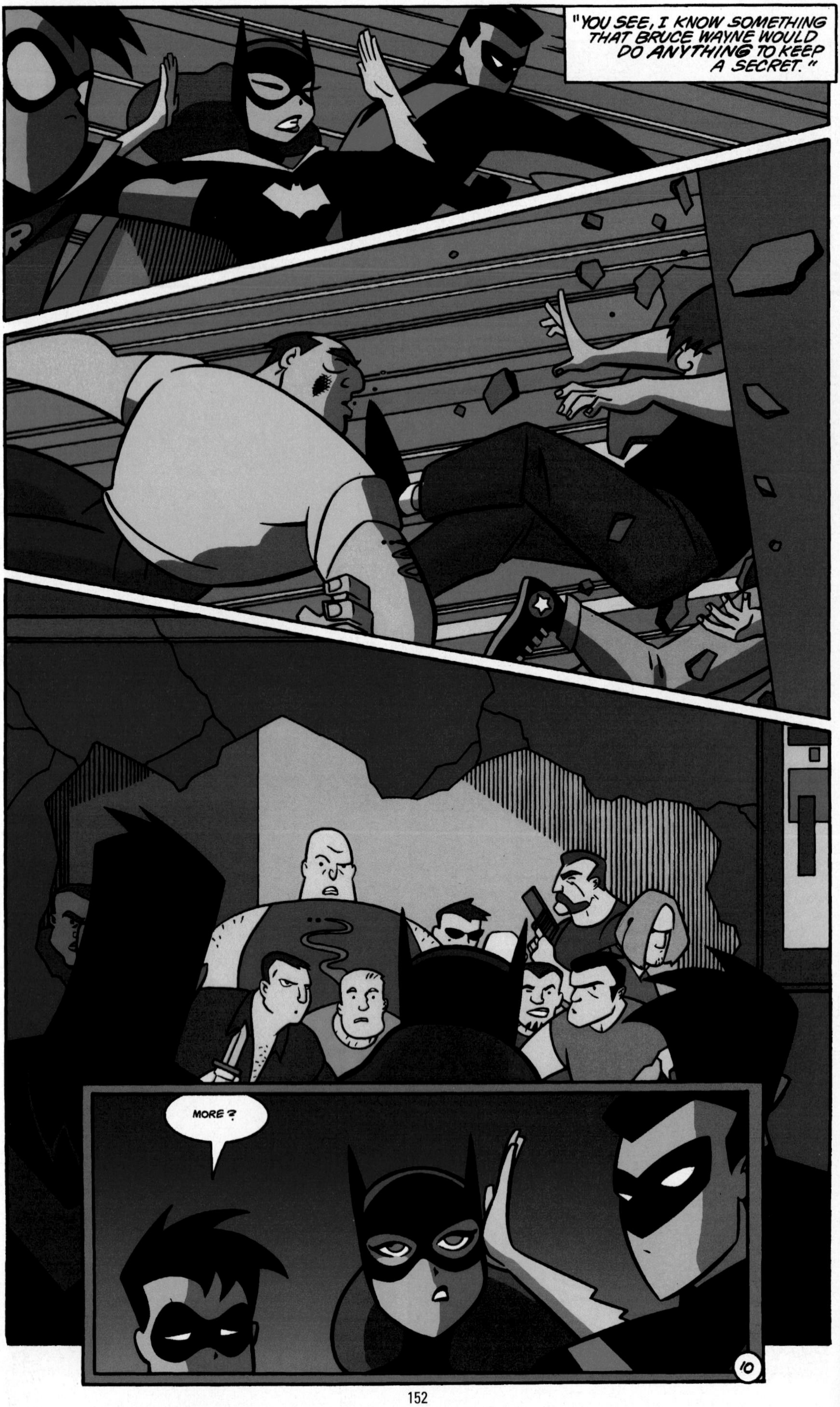
"YOU SEE, I KNOW SOMETHING THAT BRUCE WAYNE WOULD DO ANYTHING TO KEEP A SECRET."
MORE?
10

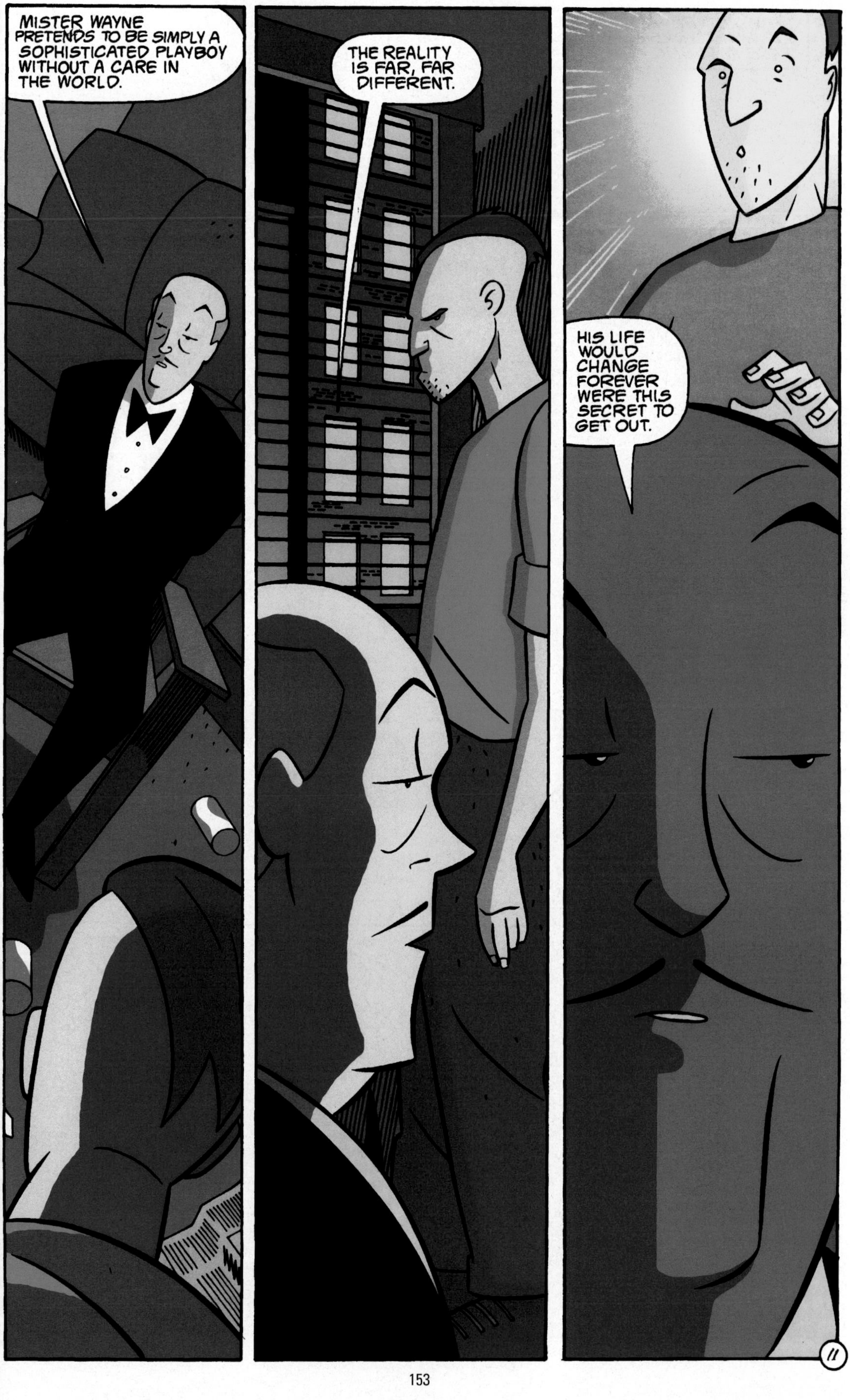
MISTER WAYNE PRETENDS TO BE SIMPLY A SOPHISTICATED PLAYBOY WITHOUT A CARE IN THE WORLD.
THE REALITY IS FAR, FAR DIFFERENT.
HIS LIFE WOULD CHANGE FOREVER WERE THIS SECRET TO GET OUT.
11

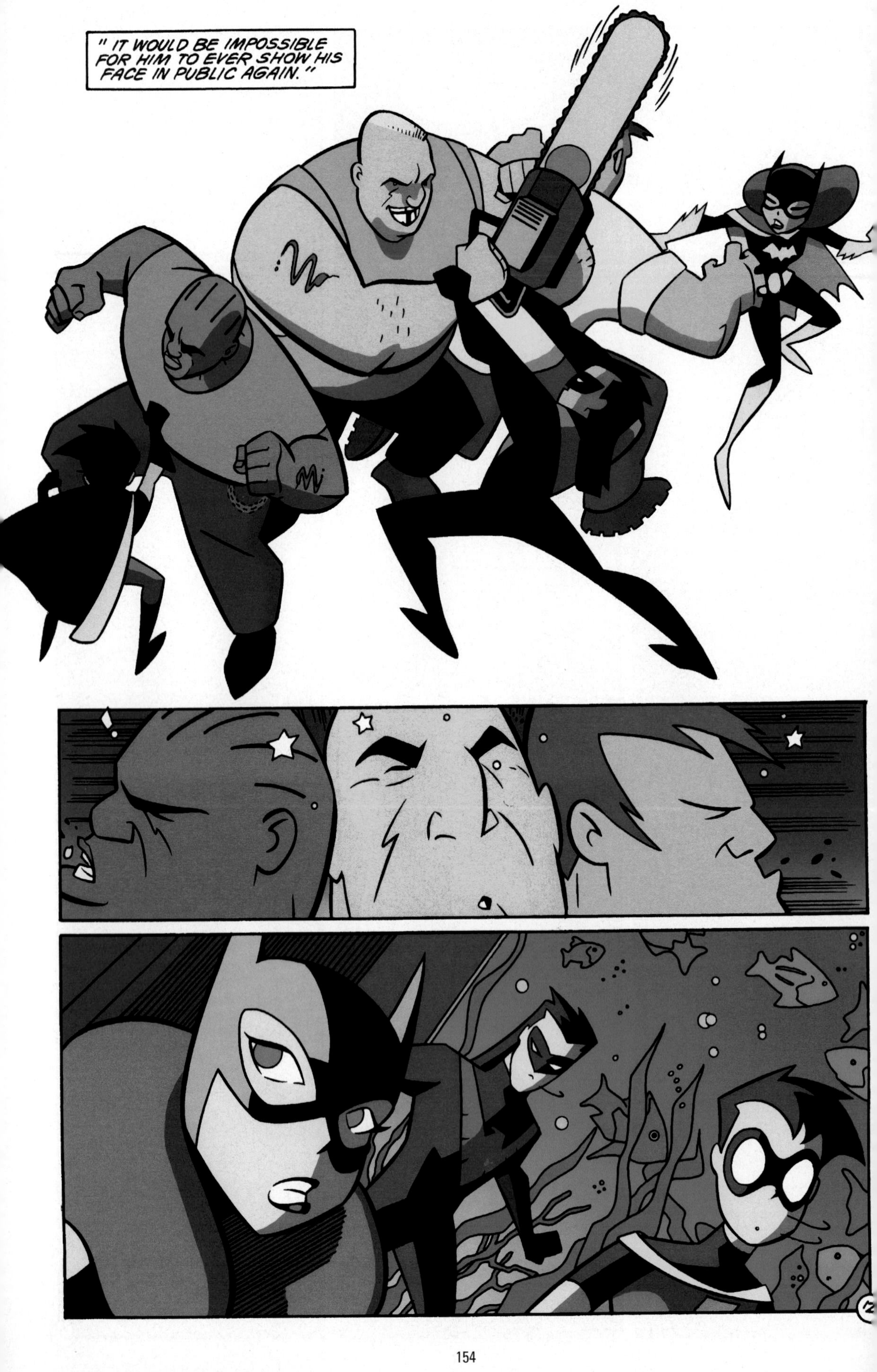
" IT WOULD BE IMPOSSIBLE FOR HIM TO EVER SHOW HIS FACE IN PUBLIC AGAIN."

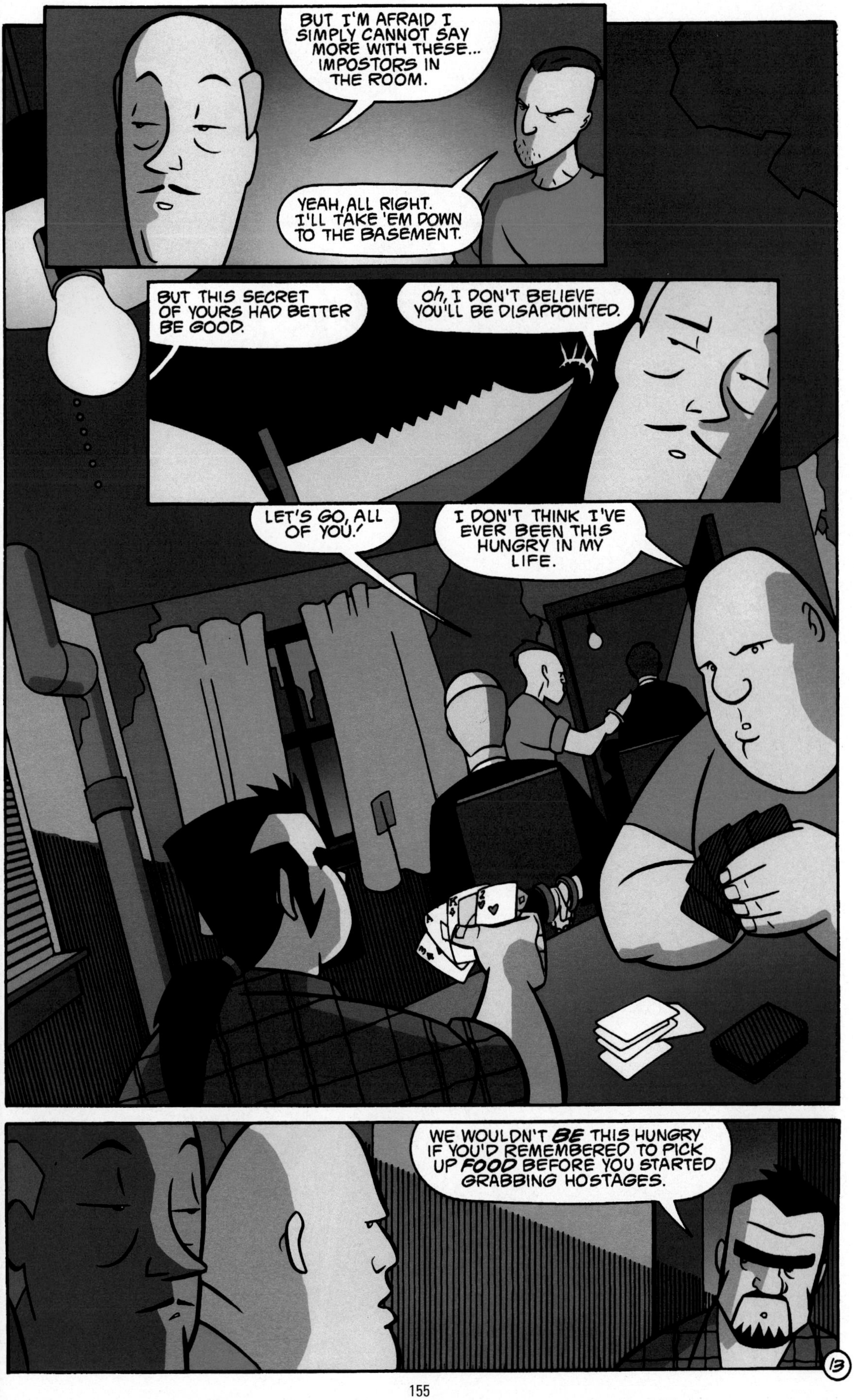
BUT I'M AFRAID I SIMPLY CANNOT SAY MORE WITH THESE... IMPOSTORS IN THE ROOM.
YEAH, ALL RIGHT. I'LL TAKE 'EM DOWN TO THE BASEMENT.
BUT THIS SECRET OF YOURS HAD BETTER BE GOOD.
Oh, I DON'T BELIEVE YOU'LL BE DISAPPOINTED.
LET'S GO, ALL OF YOU!
I DON'T THINK I'VE EVER BEEN THIS HUNGRY IN MY LIFE.
WE WOULDN'T BE THIS HUNGRY IF YOU'D REMEMBERED TO PICK UP FOOD BEFORE YOU STARTED GRABBING HOSTAGES.
13

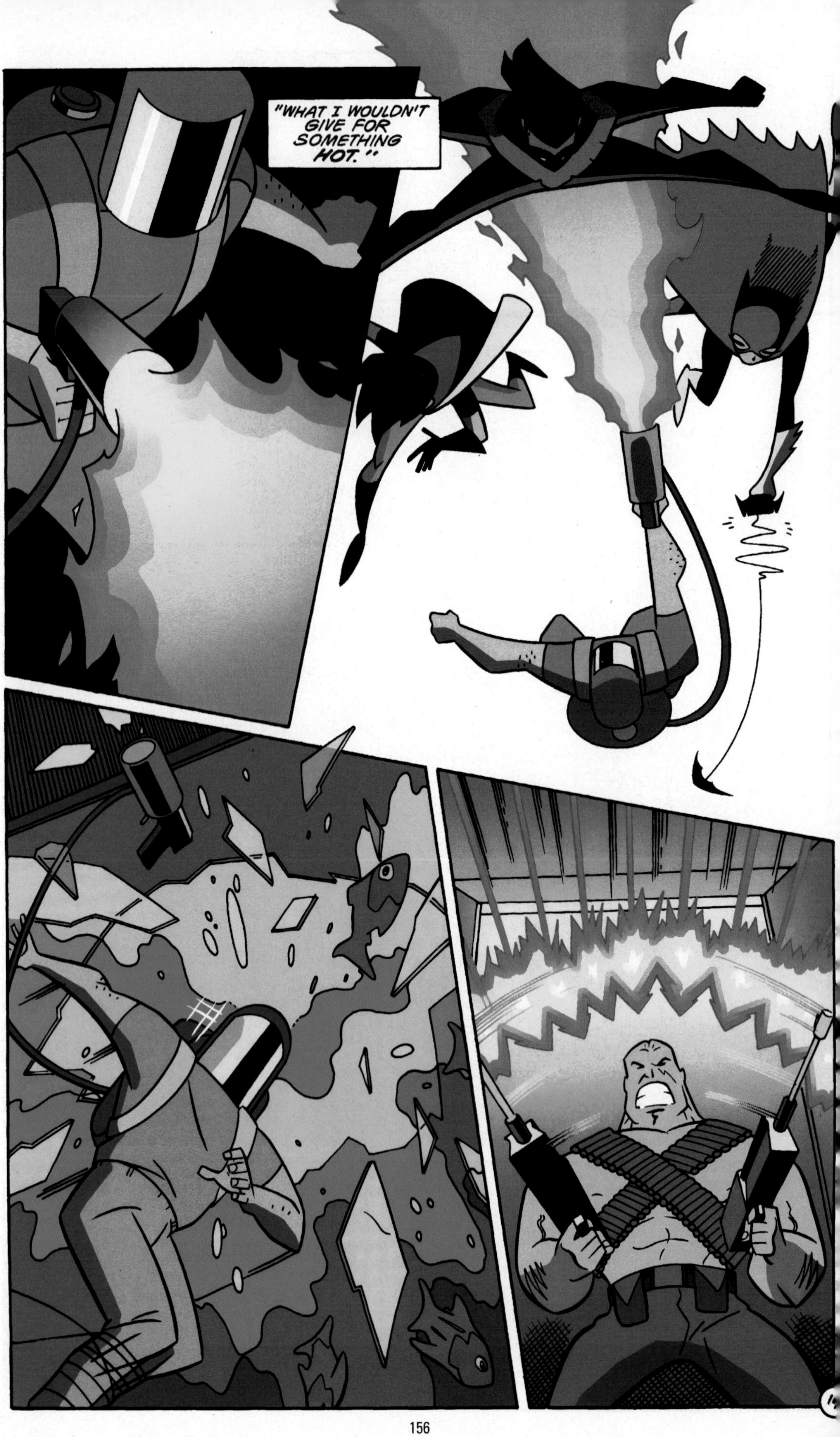
"WHAT I WOULDN'T GIVE FOR SOMETHING HOT."

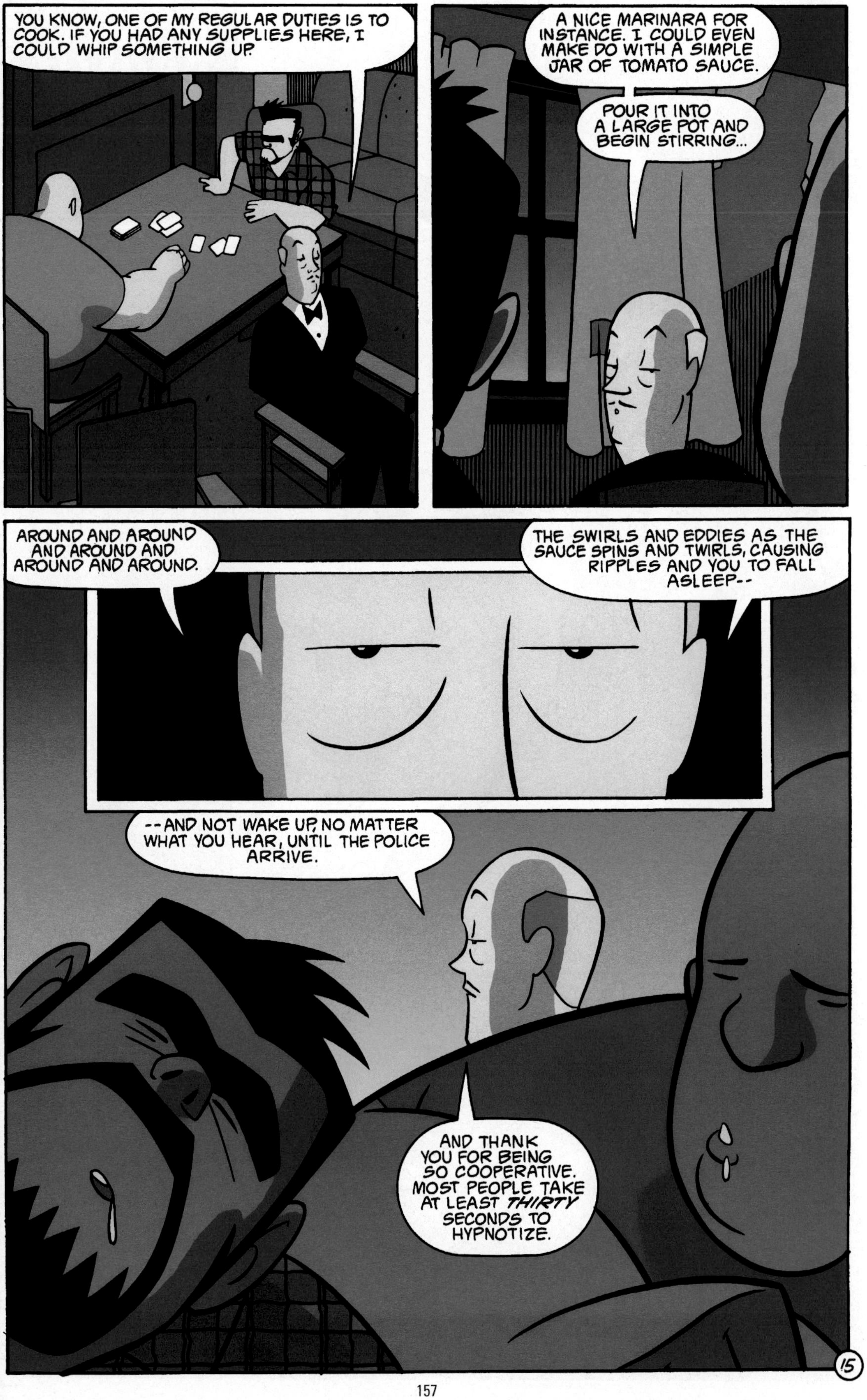
YOU KNOW, ONE OF MY REGULAR DUTIES IS TO COOK. IF YOU HAD ANY SUPPLIES HERE, I COULD WHIP SOMETHING UP.
A NICE MARINARA FOR INSTANCE. I COULD EVEN MAKE DO WITH A SIMPLE JAR OF TOMATO SAUCE.
POUR IT INTO A LARGE POT AND BEGIN STIRRING...
AROUND AND AROUND AND AROUND AND AROUND AND AROUND.
THE SWIRLS AND EDDIES AS THE SAUCE SPINS AND TWIRLS, CAUSING RIPPLES AND YOU TO FALL ASLEEP--
--AND NOT WAKE UP, NO MATTER WHAT YOU HEAR, UNTIL THE POLICE ARRIVE.
AND THANK YOU FOR BEING SO COOPERATIVE. MOST PEOPLE TAKE AT LEAST *THIRTY* SECONDS TO HYPNOTIZE.
15

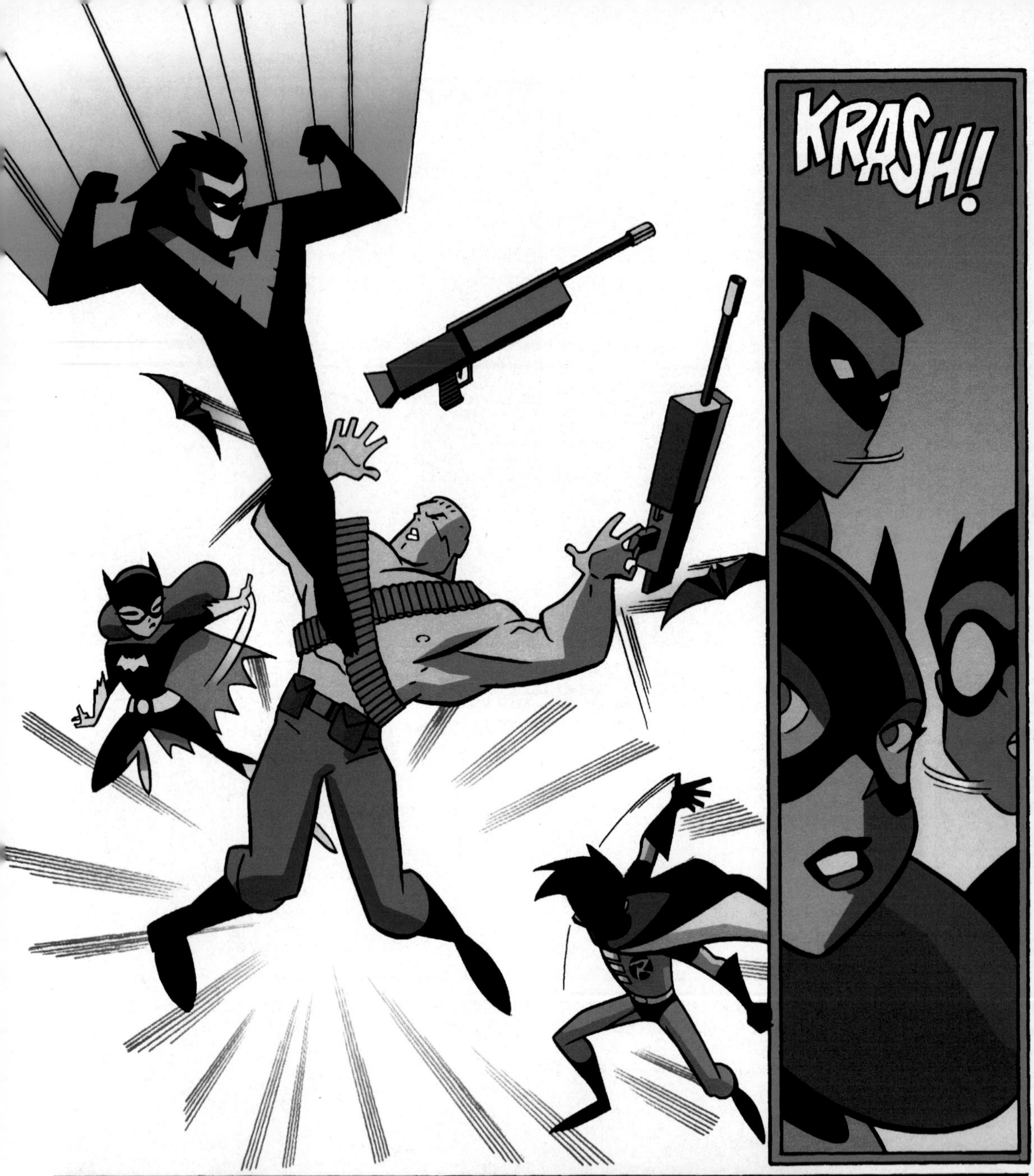
KRASH!

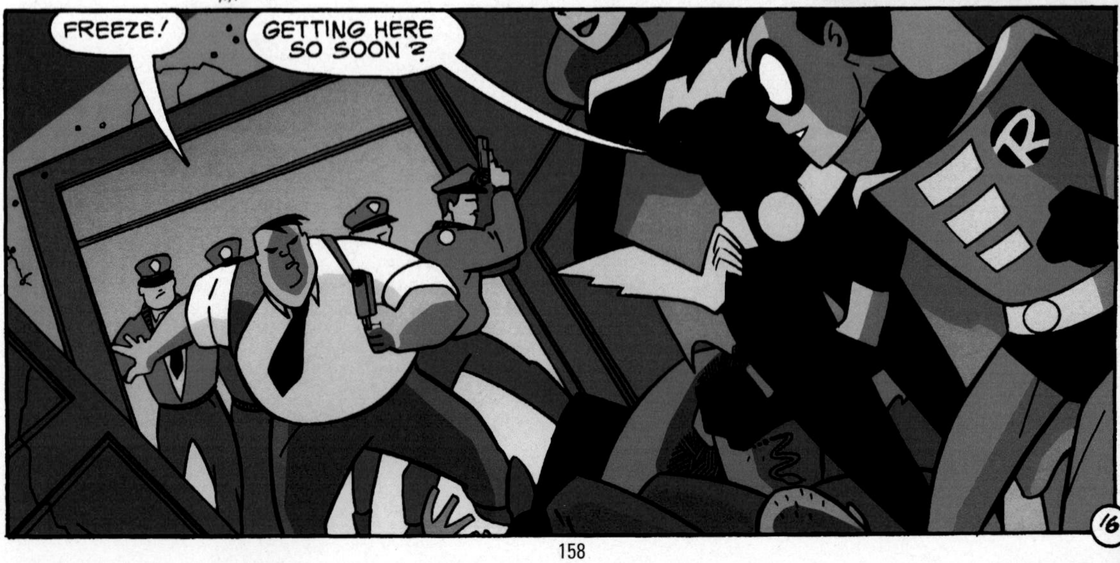
FREEZE!
GETTING HERE SO SOON ?
16

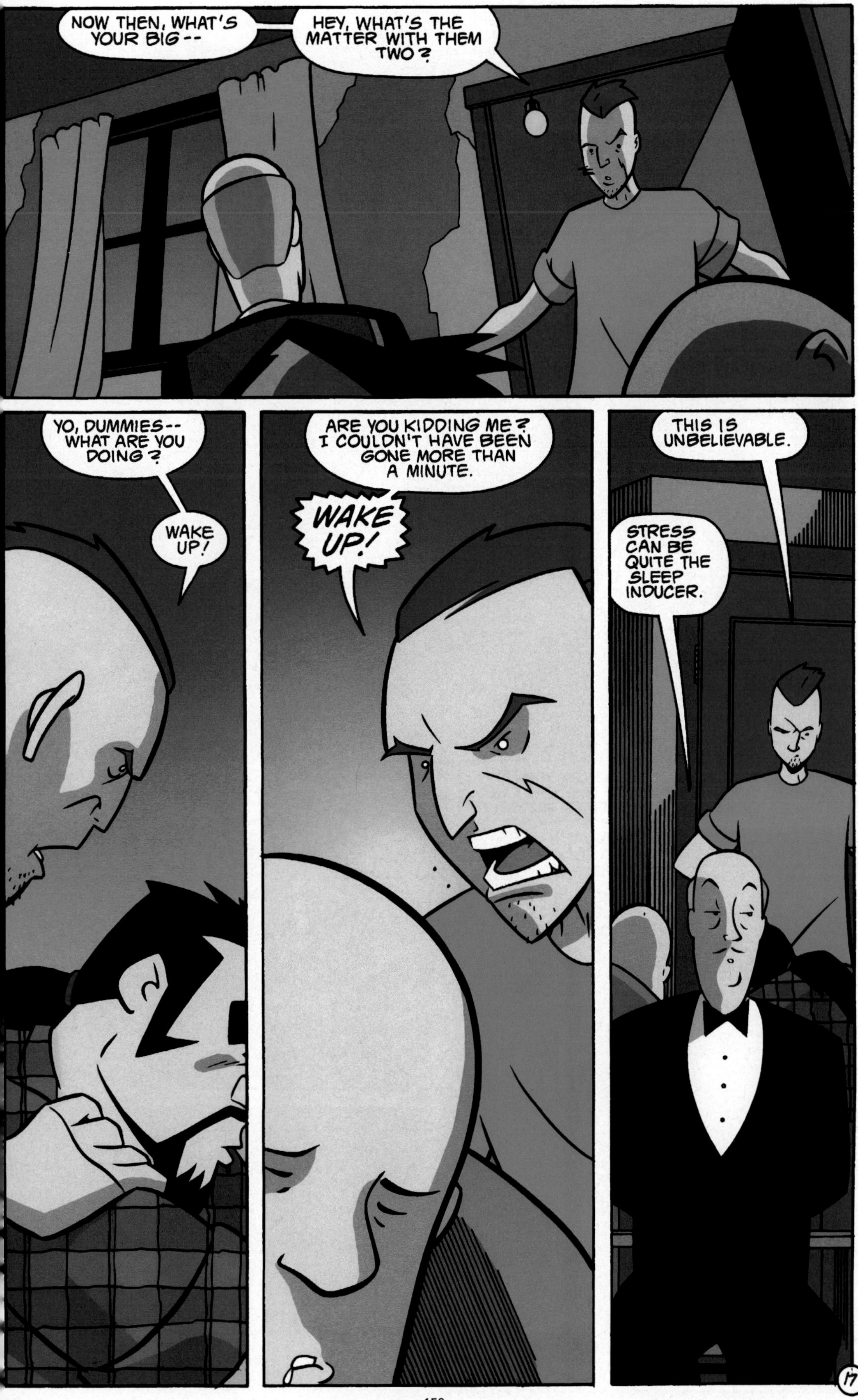
NOW THEN, WHAT'S YOUR BIG--
HEY, WHAT'S THE MATTER WITH THEM TWO?
YO, DUMMIES-- WHAT ARE YOU DOING?
WAKE UP!
ARE YOU KIDDING ME? I COULDN'T HAVE BEEN GONE MORE THAN A MINUTE.
WAKE UP!
THIS IS UNBELIEVABLE.
STRESS CAN BE QUITE THE SLEEP INDUCER.
17

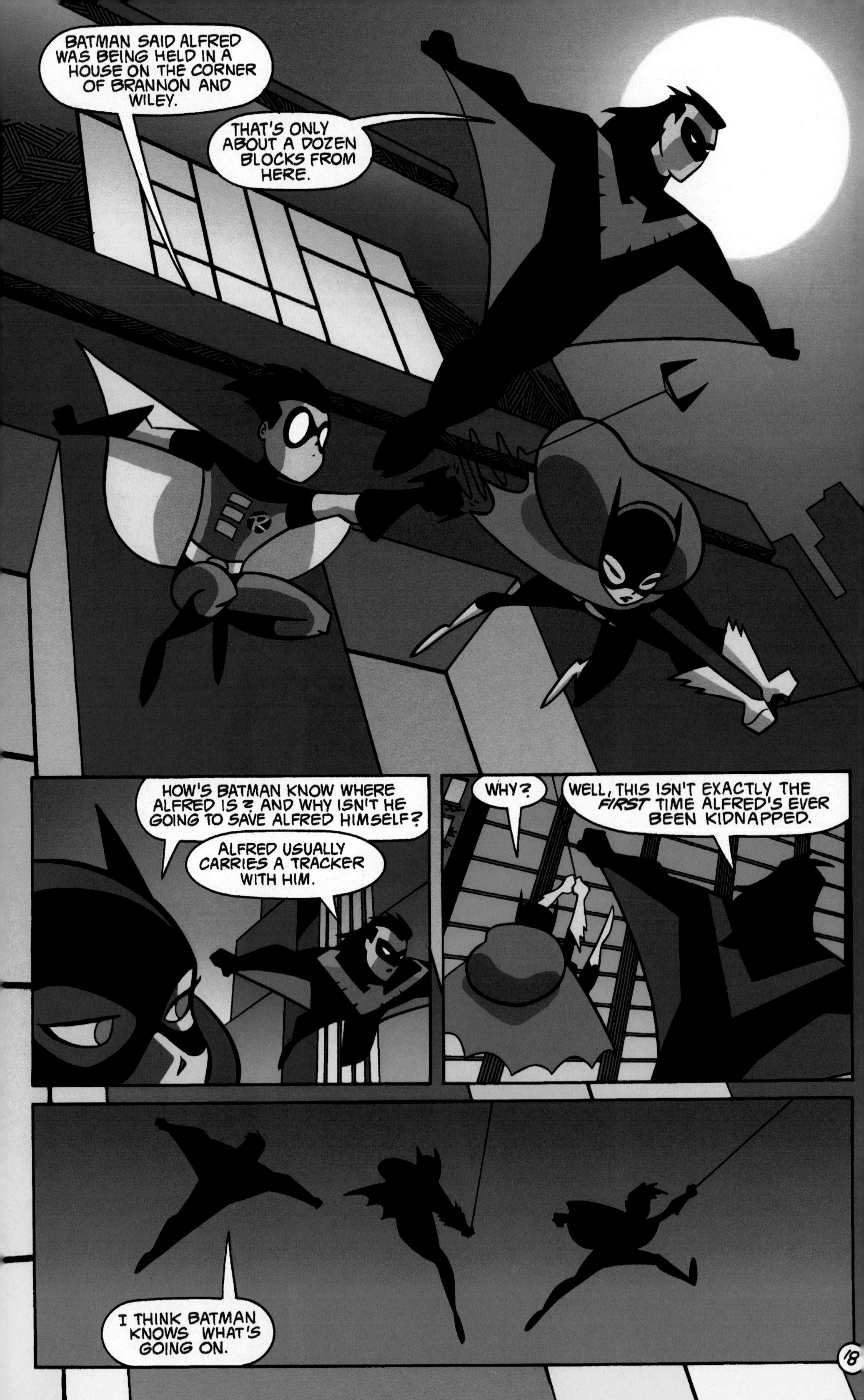
BATMAN SAID ALFRED WAS BEING HELD IN A HOUSE ON THE CORNER OF BRANNON AND WILEY.
THAT'S ONLY ABOUT A DOZEN BLOCKS FROM HERE.
HOW'S BATMAN KNOW WHERE ALFRED IS? AND WHY ISN'T HE GOING TO SAVE ALFRED HIMSELF?
ALFRED USUALLY CARRIES A TRACKER WITH HIM.
WHY?
WELL, THIS ISN'T EXACTLY THE *FIRST* TIME ALFRED'S EVER BEEN KIDNAPPED.
I THINK BATMAN KNOWS WHAT'S GOING ON.

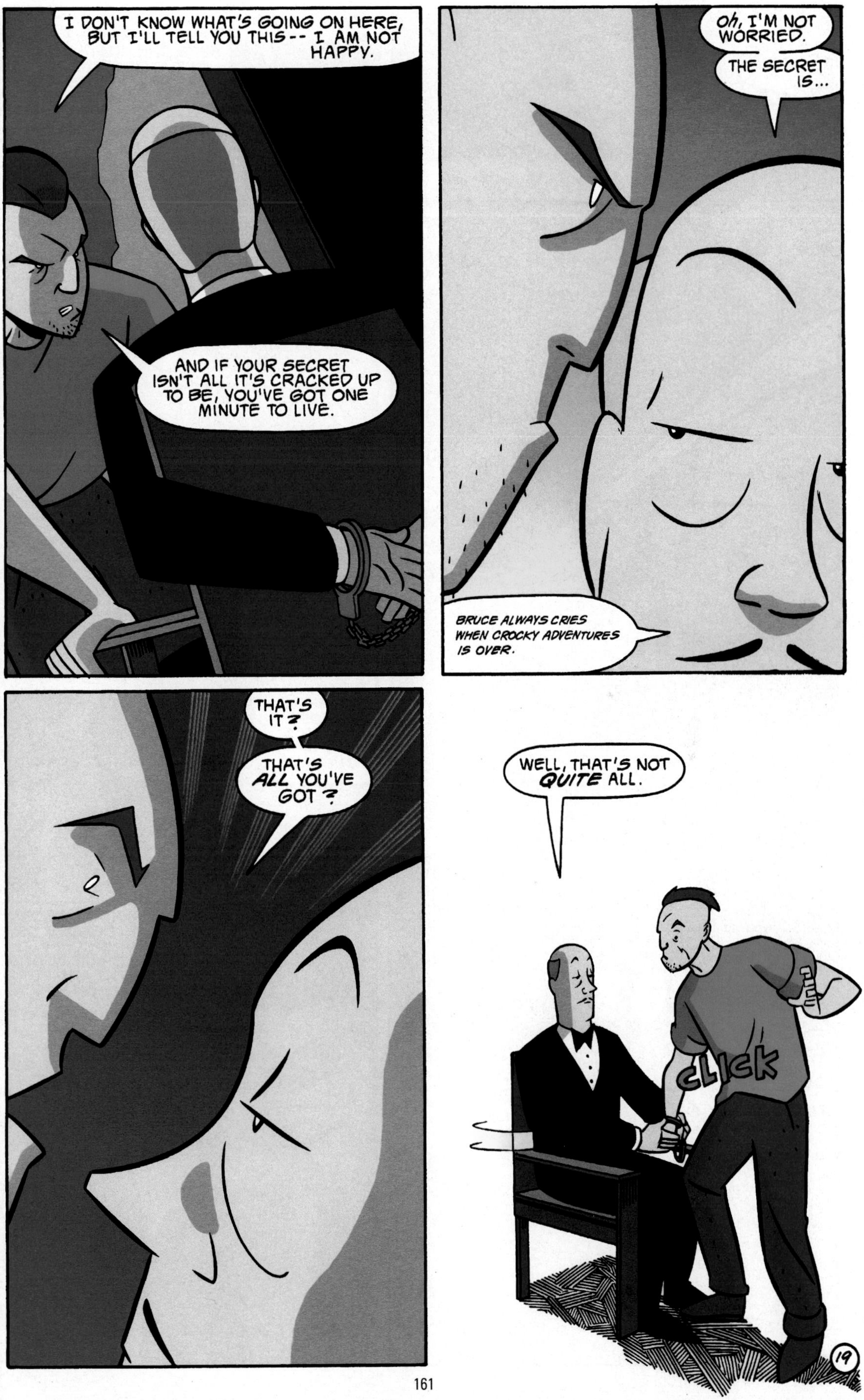
I DON'T KNOW WHAT'S GOING ON HERE, BUT I'LL TELL YOU THIS -- I AM NOT HAPPY.
AND IF YOUR SECRET ISN'T ALL IT'S CRACKED UP TO BE, YOU'VE GOT ONE MINUTE TO LIVE.
Oh, I'M NOT WORRIED.
THE SECRET IS...
BRUCE ALWAYS CRIES WHEN CROCKY ADVENTURES IS OVER.
THAT'S IT?
THAT'S ALL YOU'VE GOT?
WELL, THAT'S NOT QUITE ALL.
CLICK
19

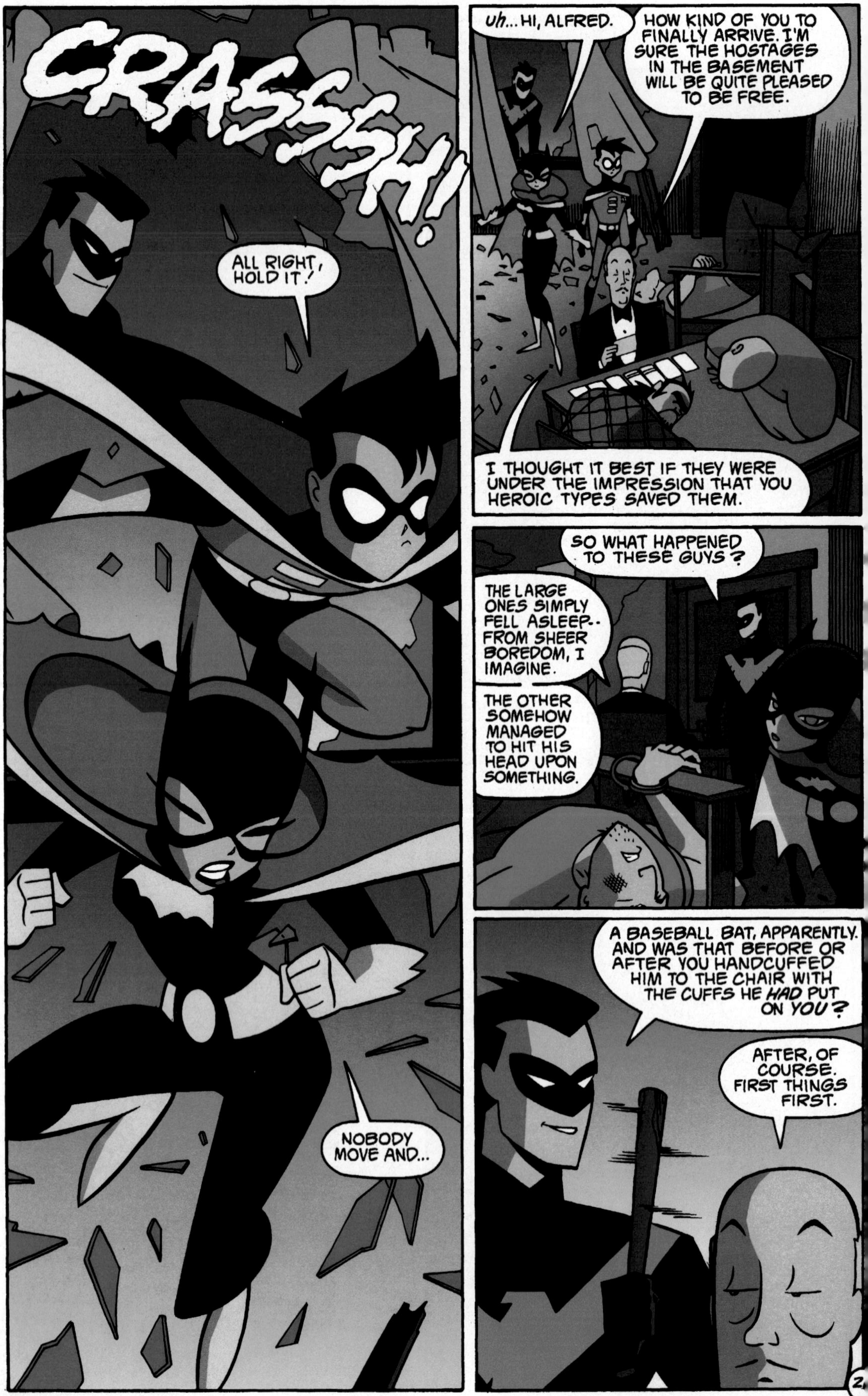
CRASSSH!
ALL RIGHT, HOLD IT!
NOBODY MOVE AND...
uh... HI, ALFRED.
HOW KIND OF YOU TO FINALLY ARRIVE. I'M SURE THE HOSTAGES IN THE BASEMENT WILL BE QUITE PLEASED TO BE FREE.
I THOUGHT IT BEST IF THEY WERE UNDER THE IMPRESSION THAT YOU HEROIC TYPES SAVED THEM.
SO WHAT HAPPENED TO THESE GUYS?
THE LARGE ONES SIMPLY FELL ASLEEP-- FROM SHEER BOREDOM, I IMAGINE.
THE OTHER SOMEHOW MANAGED TO HIT HIS HEAD UPON SOMETHING.
A BASEBALL BAT, APPARENTLY. AND WAS THAT BEFORE OR AFTER YOU HANDCUFFED HIM TO THE CHAIR WITH THE CUFFS HE HAD PUT ON YOU?
AFTER, OF COURSE. FIRST THINGS FIRST.

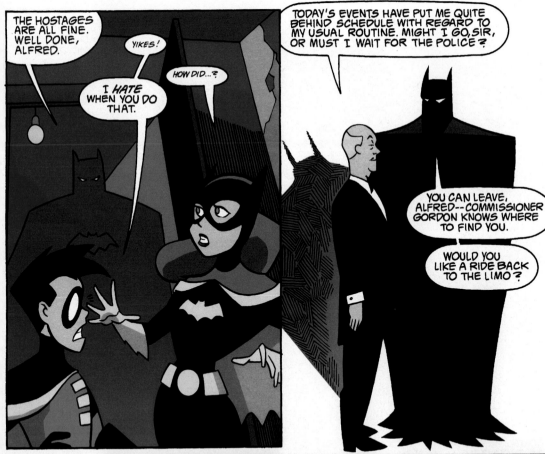

THE HOSTAGES ARE ALL FINE. WELL DONE, ALFRED.

YIKES!

I *HATE* WHEN YOU DO THAT.

HOW DID...?

TODAY'S EVENTS HAVE PUT ME QUITE BEHIND SCHEDULE WITH REGARD TO MY USUAL ROUTINE. MIGHT I GO, SIR, OR MUST I WAIT FOR THE POLICE?

YOU CAN LEAVE, ALFRED--COMMISSIONER GORDON KNOWS WHERE TO FIND YOU.

WOULD YOU LIKE A RIDE BACK TO THE LIMO?

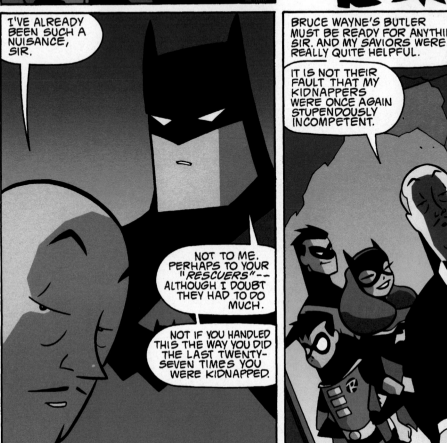

I'VE ALREADY BEEN SUCH A NUISANCE, SIR.

NOT TO ME. PERHAPS TO YOUR *"RESCUERS"*-- ALTHOUGH I DOUBT THEY HAD TO DO MUCH.

NOT IF YOU HANDLED THIS THE WAY YOU DID THE LAST TWENTY-SEVEN TIMES YOU WERE KIDNAPPED.

BRUCE WAYNE'S BUTLER MUST BE READY FOR ANYTHING, SIR. AND MY SAVIORS WERE REALLY QUITE HELPFUL.

IT IS NOT THEIR FAULT THAT MY KIDNAPPERS WERE ONCE AGAIN STUPENDOUSLY INCOMPETENT.

21

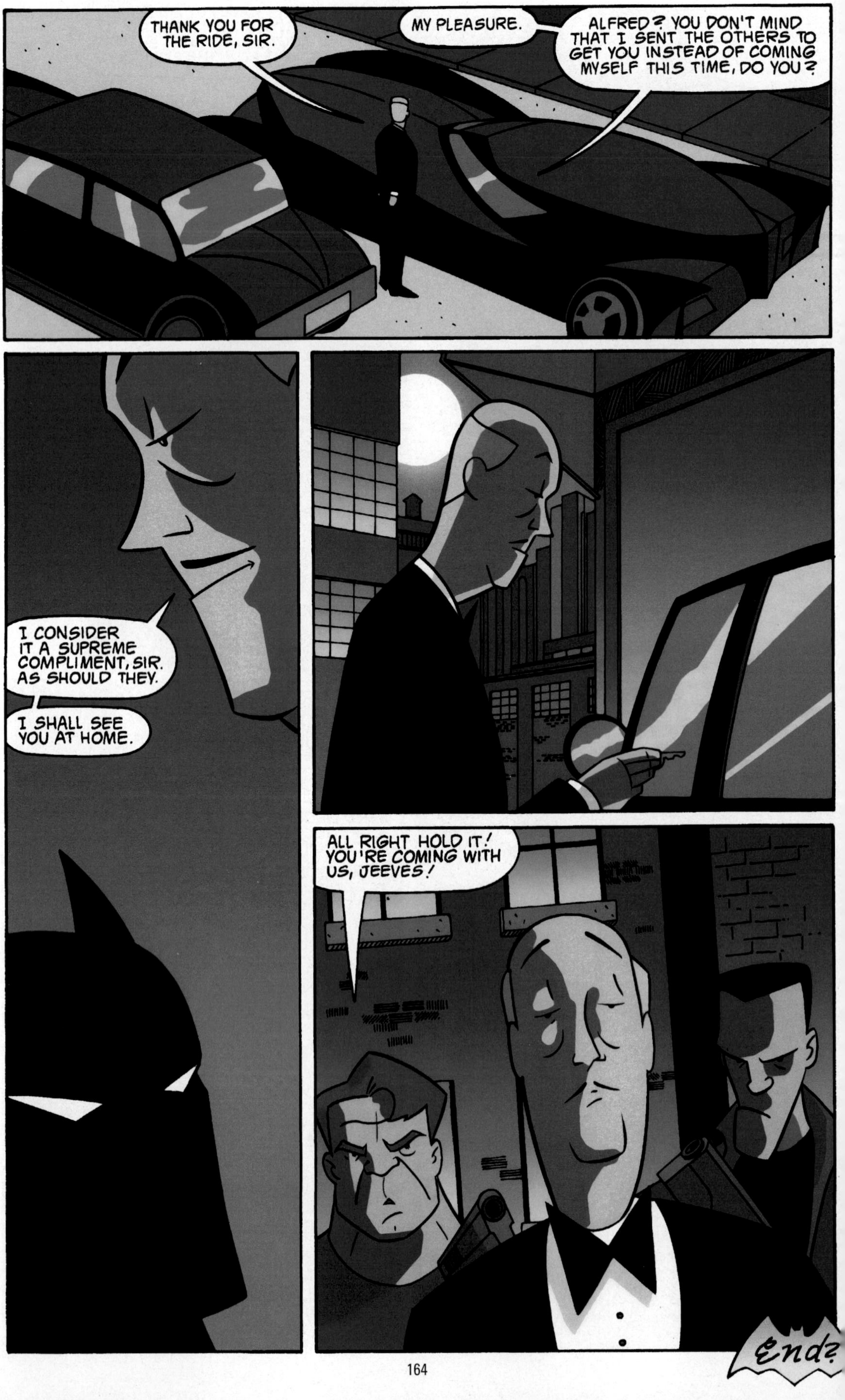
THANK YOU FOR THE RIDE, SIR.
MY PLEASURE.
ALFRED? YOU DON'T MIND THAT I SENT THE OTHERS TO GET YOU INSTEAD OF COMING MYSELF THIS TIME, DO YOU?
I CONSIDER IT A SUPREME COMPLIMENT, SIR. AS SHOULD THEY.
I SHALL SEE YOU AT HOME.
ALL RIGHT HOLD IT! YOU'RE COMING WITH US, JEEVES!
End?

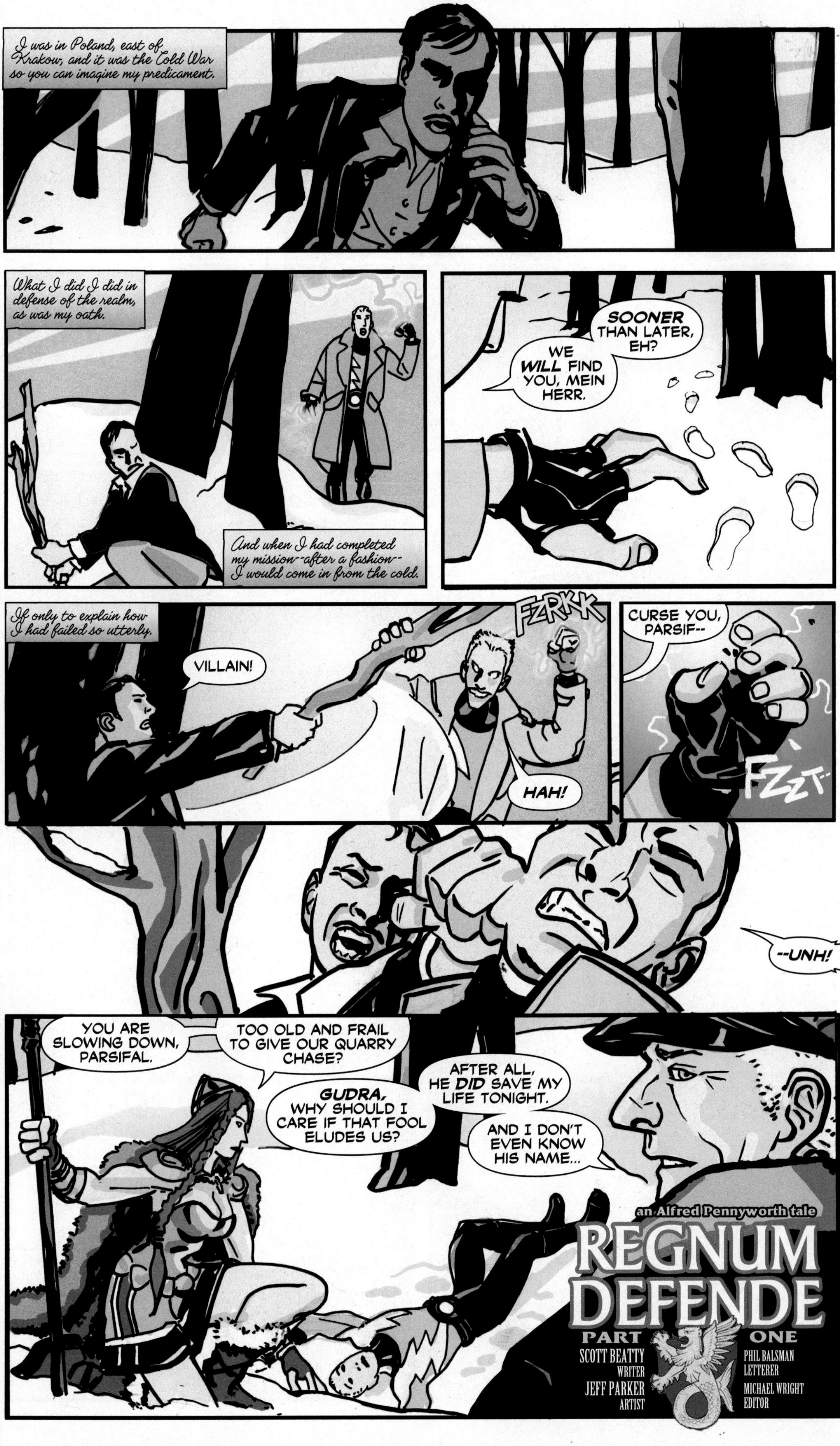

I was in Poland, east of Krakow, and it was the Cold War so you can imagine my predicament.
What I did I did in defense of the realm, as was my oath.
And when I had completed my mission--after a fashion--I would come in from the cold.
WE WILL FIND YOU, MEIN HERR.
SOONER THAN LATER, EH?
If only to explain how I had failed so utterly.
VILLAIN!
FZRKK
HAH!
CURSE YOU, PARSIF--
FZZT--
--UNH!
YOU ARE SLOWING DOWN, PARSIFAL.
TOO OLD AND FRAIL TO GIVE OUR QUARRY CHASE?
GUDRA, WHY SHOULD I CARE IF THAT FOOL ELUDES US?
AFTER ALL, HE DID SAVE MY LIFE TONIGHT.
AND I DON'T EVEN KNOW HIS NAME...
an Alfred Pennyworth tale
REGNUM DEFENDE
PART ONE
SCOTT BEATTY WRITER
JEFF PARKER ARTIST
PHIL BALSMAN LETTERER
MICHAEL WRIGHT EDITOR

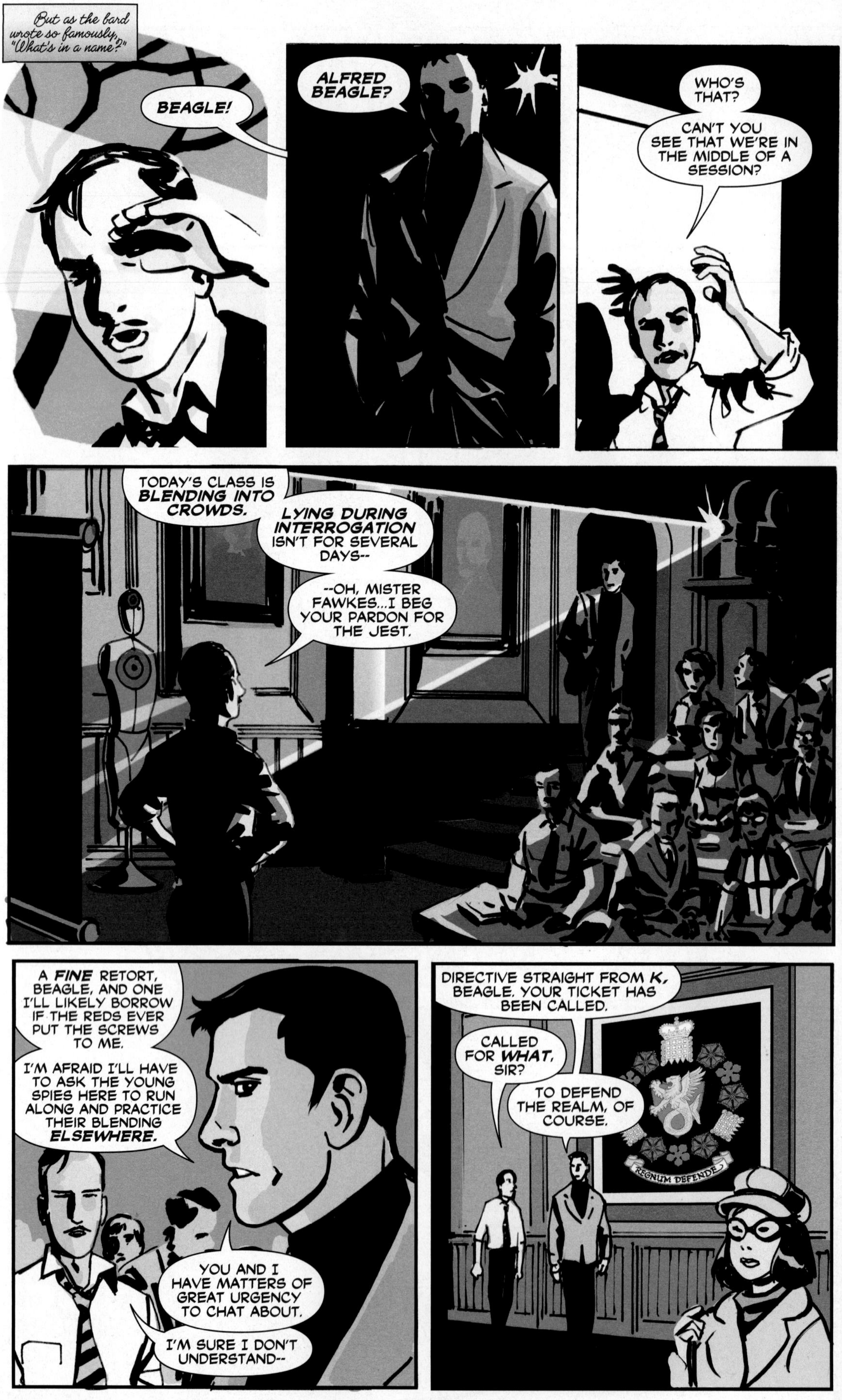
But as the bard wrote so famously, "What's in a name?"
BEAGLE!
ALFRED BEAGLE?
WHO'S THAT?
CAN'T YOU SEE THAT WE'RE IN THE MIDDLE OF A SESSION?
TODAY'S CLASS IS BLENDING INTO CROWDS.
LYING DURING INTERROGATION ISN'T FOR SEVERAL DAYS--
--OH, MISTER FAWKES...I BEG YOUR PARDON FOR THE JEST.
A FINE RETORT, BEAGLE, AND ONE I'LL LIKELY BORROW IF THE REDS EVER PUT THE SCREWS TO ME.
I'M AFRAID I'LL HAVE TO ASK THE YOUNG SPIES HERE TO RUN ALONG AND PRACTICE THEIR BLENDING ELSEWHERE.
YOU AND I HAVE MATTERS OF GREAT URGENCY TO CHAT ABOUT.
I'M SURE I DON'T UNDERSTAND--
DIRECTIVE STRAIGHT FROM K, BEAGLE. YOUR TICKET HAS BEEN CALLED.
CALLED FOR WHAT, SIR?
TO DEFEND THE REALM, OF COURSE.
REGNUM DEFENDE

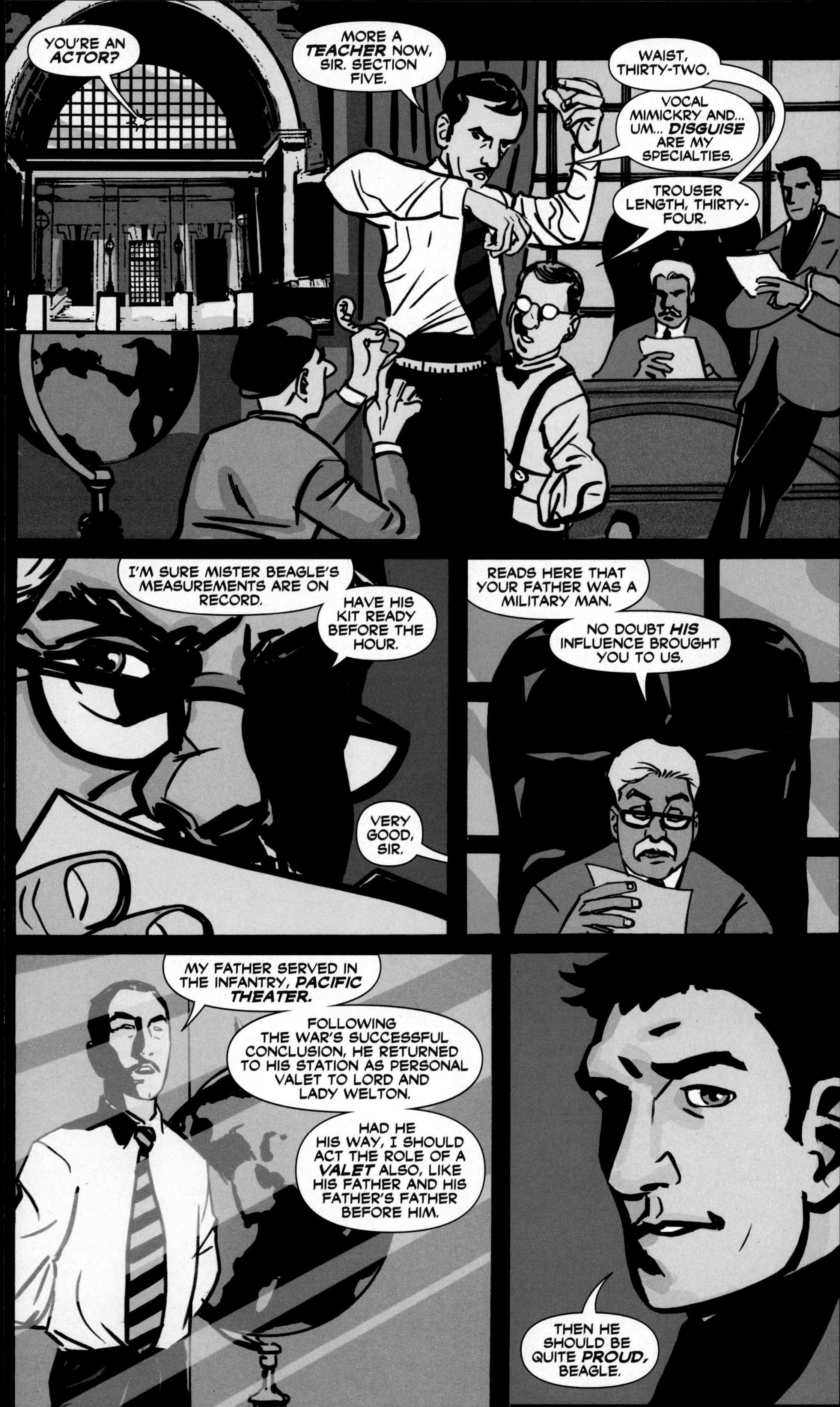
YOU'RE AN *ACTOR?*
MORE A *TEACHER* NOW, SIR. SECTION FIVE.
WAIST, THIRTY-TWO.
VOCAL MIMICKRY AND... UM... *DISGUISE* ARE MY SPECIALTIES.
TROUSER LENGTH, THIRTY-FOUR.
I'M SURE MISTER BEAGLE'S MEASUREMENTS ARE ON RECORD.
HAVE HIS KIT READY BEFORE THE HOUR.
VERY GOOD, SIR.
READS HERE THAT YOUR FATHER WAS A MILITARY MAN.
NO DOUBT *HIS* INFLUENCE BROUGHT YOU TO US.
MY FATHER SERVED IN THE INFANTRY, *PACIFIC THEATER.*
FOLLOWING THE WAR'S SUCCESSFUL CONCLUSION, HE RETURNED TO HIS STATION AS PERSONAL VALET TO LORD AND LADY WELTON.
HAD HE HIS WAY, I SHOULD ACT THE ROLE OF A *VALET* ALSO, LIKE HIS FATHER AND HIS FATHER'S FATHER BEFORE HIM.
THEN HE SHOULD BE QUITE *PROUD,* BEAGLE.

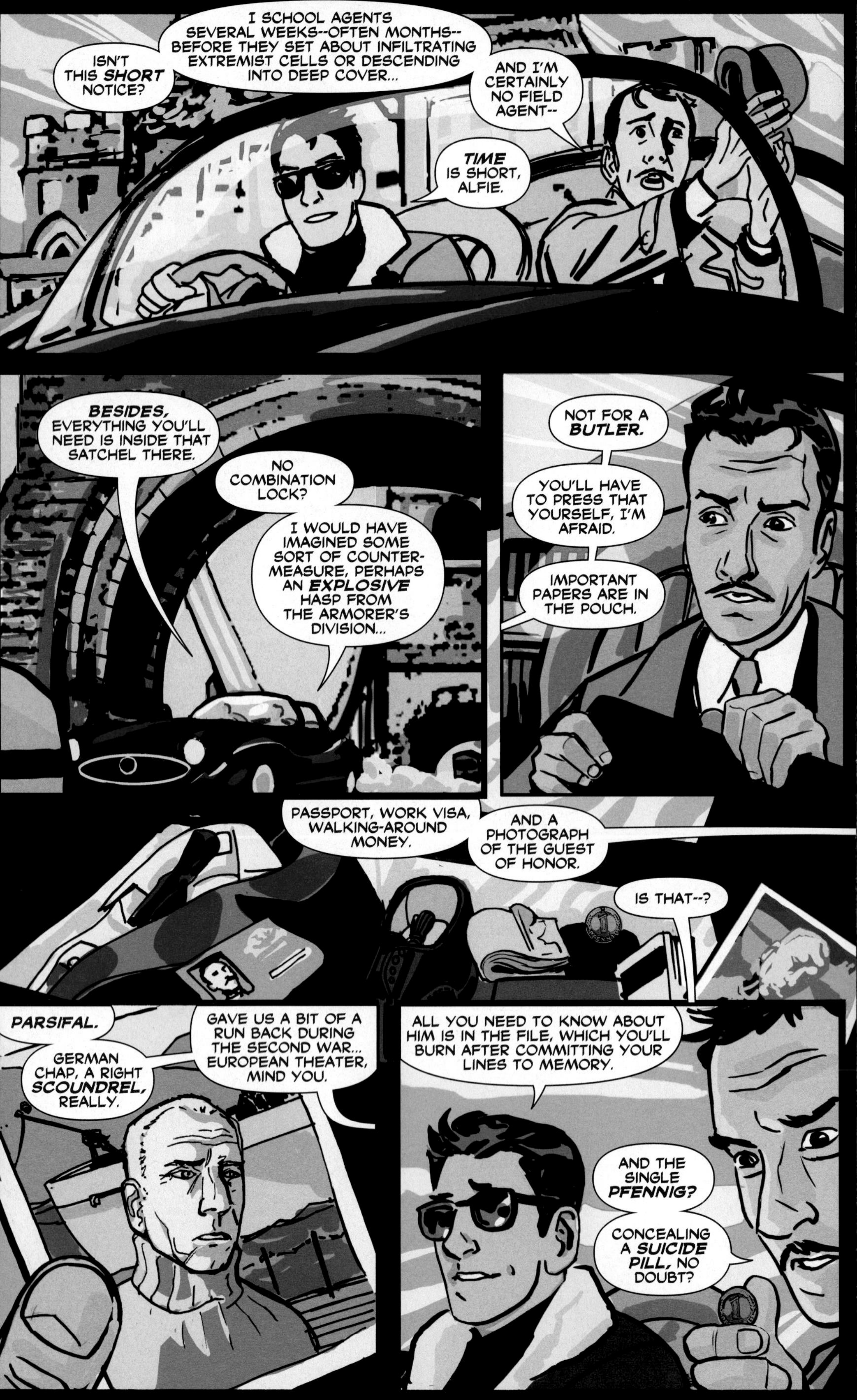
ISN'T THIS *SHORT* NOTICE?
I SCHOOL AGENTS SEVERAL WEEKS--OFTEN MONTHS--BEFORE THEY SET ABOUT INFILTRATING EXTREMIST CELLS OR DESCENDING INTO DEEP COVER...
AND I'M CERTAINLY NO FIELD AGENT--
*TIME* IS SHORT, ALFIE.
*BESIDES,* EVERYTHING YOU'LL NEED IS INSIDE THAT SATCHEL THERE.
NO COMBINATION LOCK?
I WOULD HAVE IMAGINED SOME SORT OF COUNTER-MEASURE, PERHAPS AN *EXPLOSIVE* HASP FROM THE ARMORER'S DIVISION...
NOT FOR A *BUTLER.*
YOU'LL HAVE TO PRESS THAT YOURSELF, I'M AFRAID.
IMPORTANT PAPERS ARE IN THE POUCH.
PASSPORT, WORK VISA, WALKING-AROUND MONEY.
AND A PHOTOGRAPH OF THE GUEST OF HONOR.
IS THAT--?
*PARSIFAL.*
GERMAN CHAP, A RIGHT *SCOUNDREL,* REALLY.
GAVE US A BIT OF A RUN BACK DURING THE SECOND WAR... EUROPEAN THEATER, MIND YOU.
ALL YOU NEED TO KNOW ABOUT HIM IS IN THE FILE, WHICH YOU'LL BURN AFTER COMMITTING YOUR LINES TO MEMORY.
AND THE SINGLE *PFENNIG?*
CONCEALING A *SUICIDE PILL,* NO DOUBT?

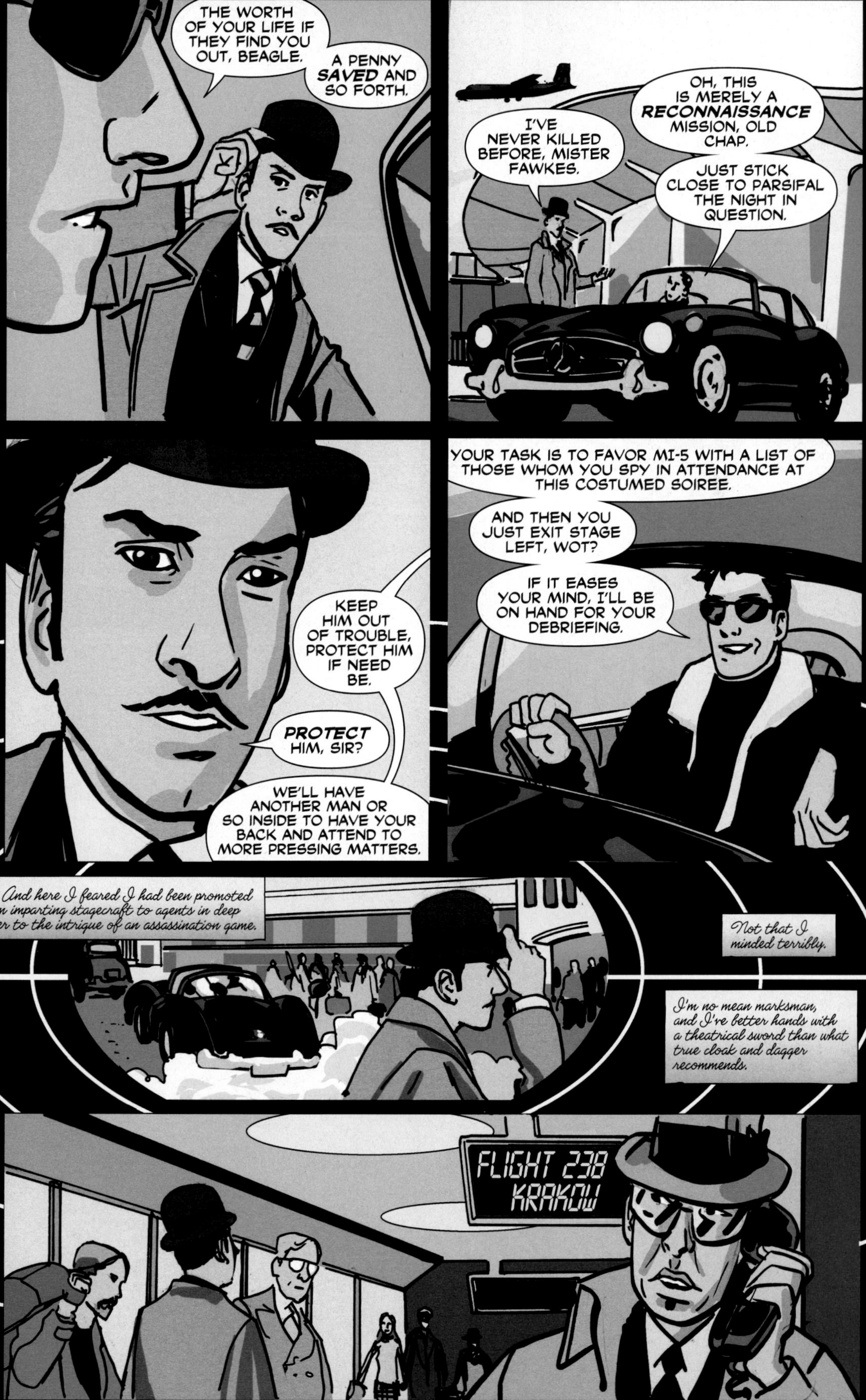
THE WORTH OF YOUR LIFE IF THEY FIND YOU OUT, BEAGLE.
A PENNY SAVED AND SO FORTH.
I'VE NEVER KILLED BEFORE, MISTER FAWKES.
OH, THIS IS MERELY A RECONNAISSANCE MISSION, OLD CHAP.
JUST STICK CLOSE TO PARSIFAL THE NIGHT IN QUESTION.
KEEP HIM OUT OF TROUBLE, PROTECT HIM IF NEED BE.
PROTECT HIM, SIR?
WE'LL HAVE ANOTHER MAN OR SO INSIDE TO HAVE YOUR BACK AND ATTEND TO MORE PRESSING MATTERS.
YOUR TASK IS TO FAVOR MI-5 WITH A LIST OF THOSE WHOM YOU SPY IN ATTENDANCE AT THIS COSTUMED SOIREE.
AND THEN YOU JUST EXIT STAGE LEFT, WOT?
IF IT EASES YOUR MIND, I'LL BE ON HAND FOR YOUR DEBRIEFING.
And here I feared I had been promoted om imparting stagecraft to agents in deep ver to the intrique of an assassination game.
Not that I minded terribly.
I'm no mean marksman, and I've better hands with a theatrical sword than what true cloak and dagger recommends.
FLIGHT 238 KRAKOW

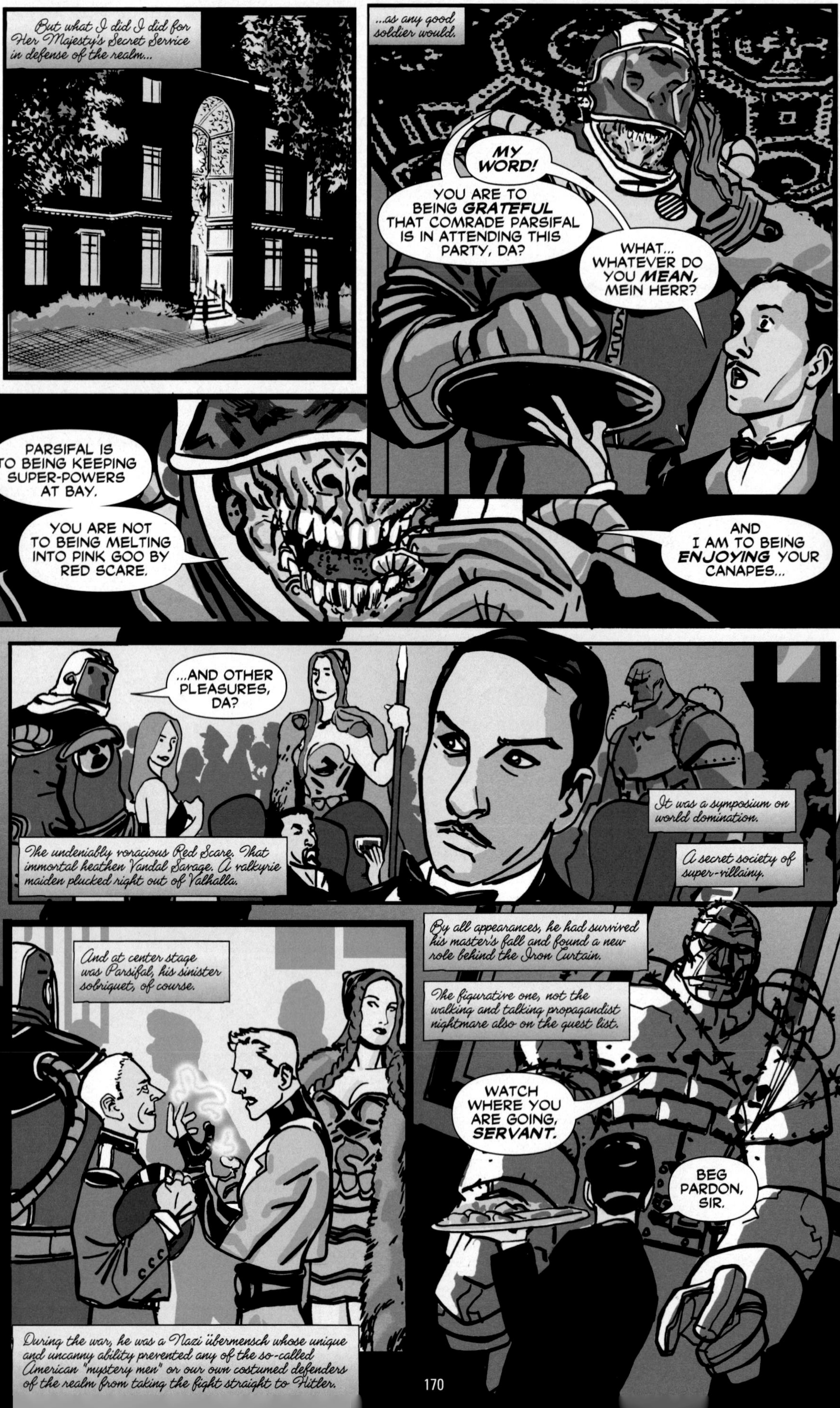
But what I did I did for Her Majesty's Secret Service in defense of the realm...
...as any good soldier would.
MY WORD!
YOU ARE TO BEING GRATEFUL THAT COMRADE PARSIFAL IS IN ATTENDING THIS PARTY, DA?
WHAT... WHATEVER DO YOU MEAN, MEIN HERR?
PARSIFAL IS TO BEING KEEPING SUPER-POWERS AT BAY.
YOU ARE NOT TO BEING MELTING INTO PINK GOO BY RED SCARE.
AND I AM TO BEING ENJOYING YOUR CANAPES...
...AND OTHER PLEASURES, DA?
The undeniably voracious Red Scare. That immortal heathen Vandal Savage. A valkyrie maiden plucked right out of Valhalla.
It was a symposium on world domination.
A secret society of super-villainy.
And at center stage was Parsifal, his sinister sobriquet, of course.
During the war, he was a Nazi übermensch whose unique and uncanny ability prevented any of the so-called American "mystery men" or our own costumed defenders of the realm from taking the fight straight to Hitler.
By all appearances, he had survived his master's fall and found a new role behind the Iron Curtain.
The figurative one, not the walking and talking propagandist nightmare also on the guest list.
WATCH WHERE YOU ARE GOING, SERVANT.
BEG PARDON, SIR.

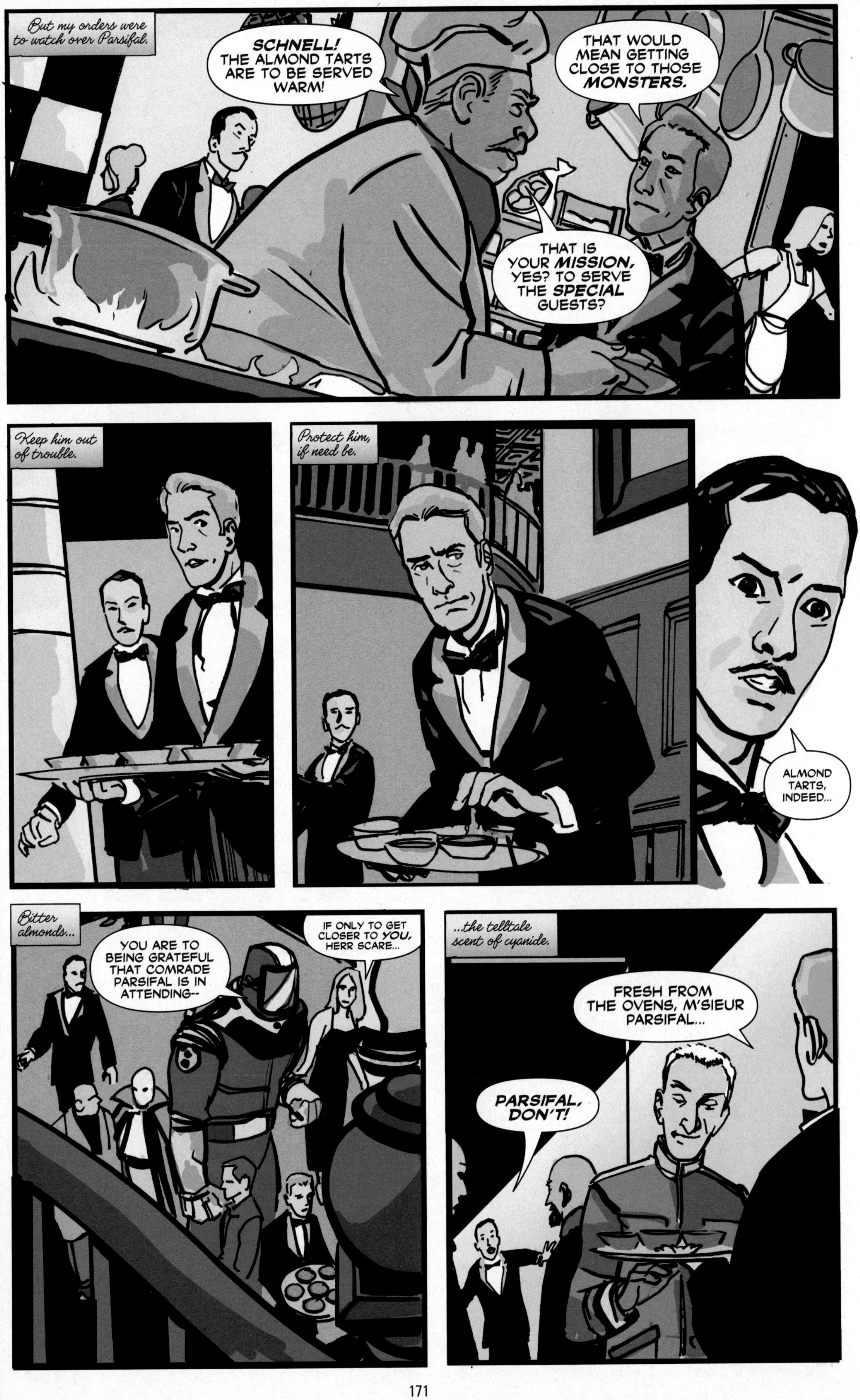
But my orders were to watch over Parsifal.
SCHNELL! THE ALMOND TARTS ARE TO BE SERVED WARM!
THAT WOULD MEAN GETTING CLOSE TO THOSE MONSTERS.
THAT IS YOUR MISSION, YES? TO SERVE THE SPECIAL GUESTS?
Keep him out of trouble.
Protect him, if need be.
ALMOND TARTS, INDEED...
Bitter almonds...
YOU ARE TO BEING GRATEFUL THAT COMRADE PARSIFAL IS IN ATTENDING--
IF ONLY TO GET CLOSER TO YOU, HERR SCARE...
...the telltale scent of cyanide.
FRESH FROM THE OVENS, M'SIEUR PARSIFAL...
PARSIFAL, DON'T!

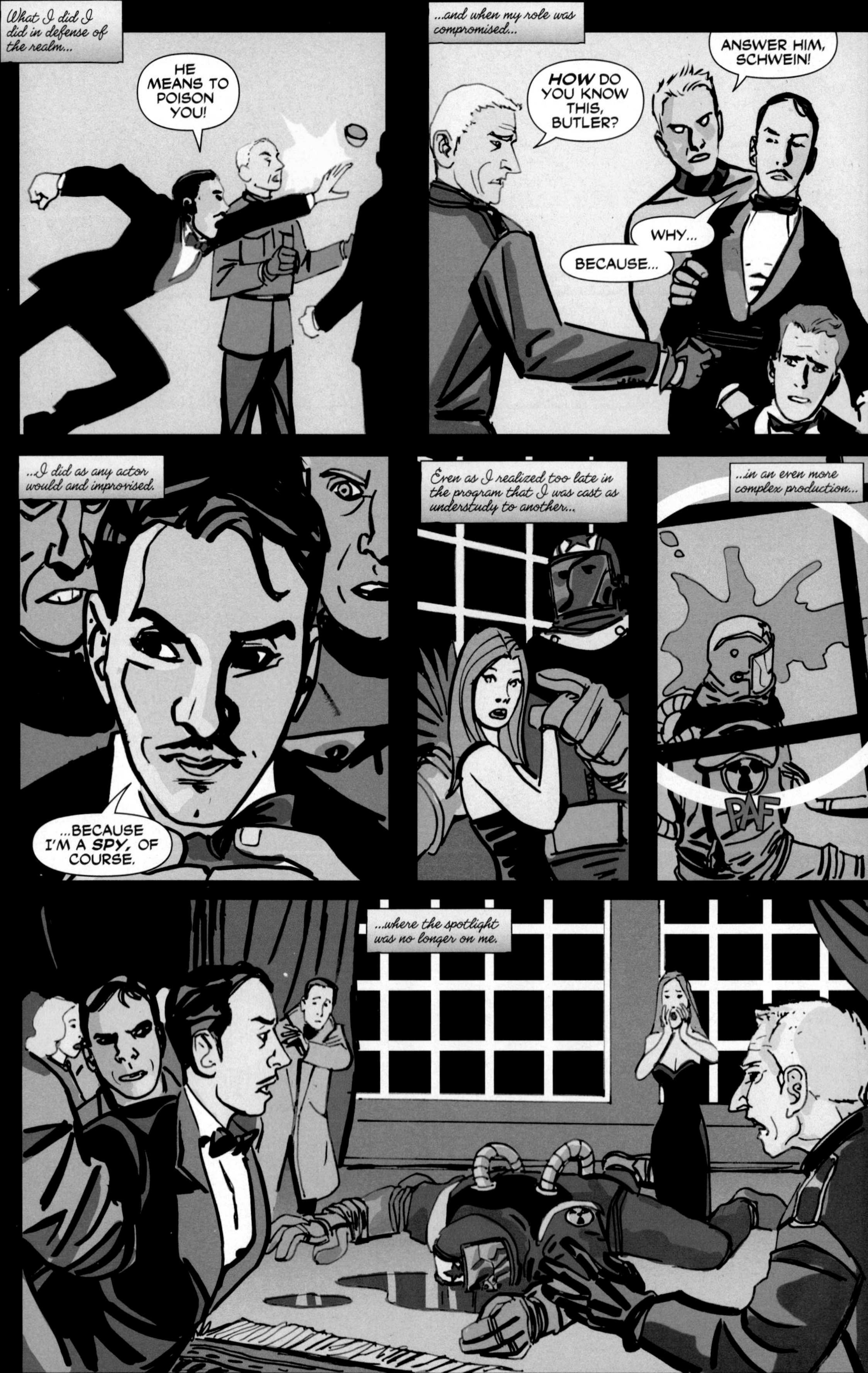
What I did I did in defense of the realm...
HE MEANS TO POISON YOU!
...and when my role was compromised...
HOW DO YOU KNOW THIS, BUTLER?
ANSWER HIM, SCHWEIN!
WHY...
BECAUSE...
...I did as any actor would and improvised.
...BECAUSE I'M A SPY, OF COURSE.
Even as I realized too late in the program that I was cast as understudy to another...
...in an even more complex production...
PAF
...where the spotlight was no longer on me.

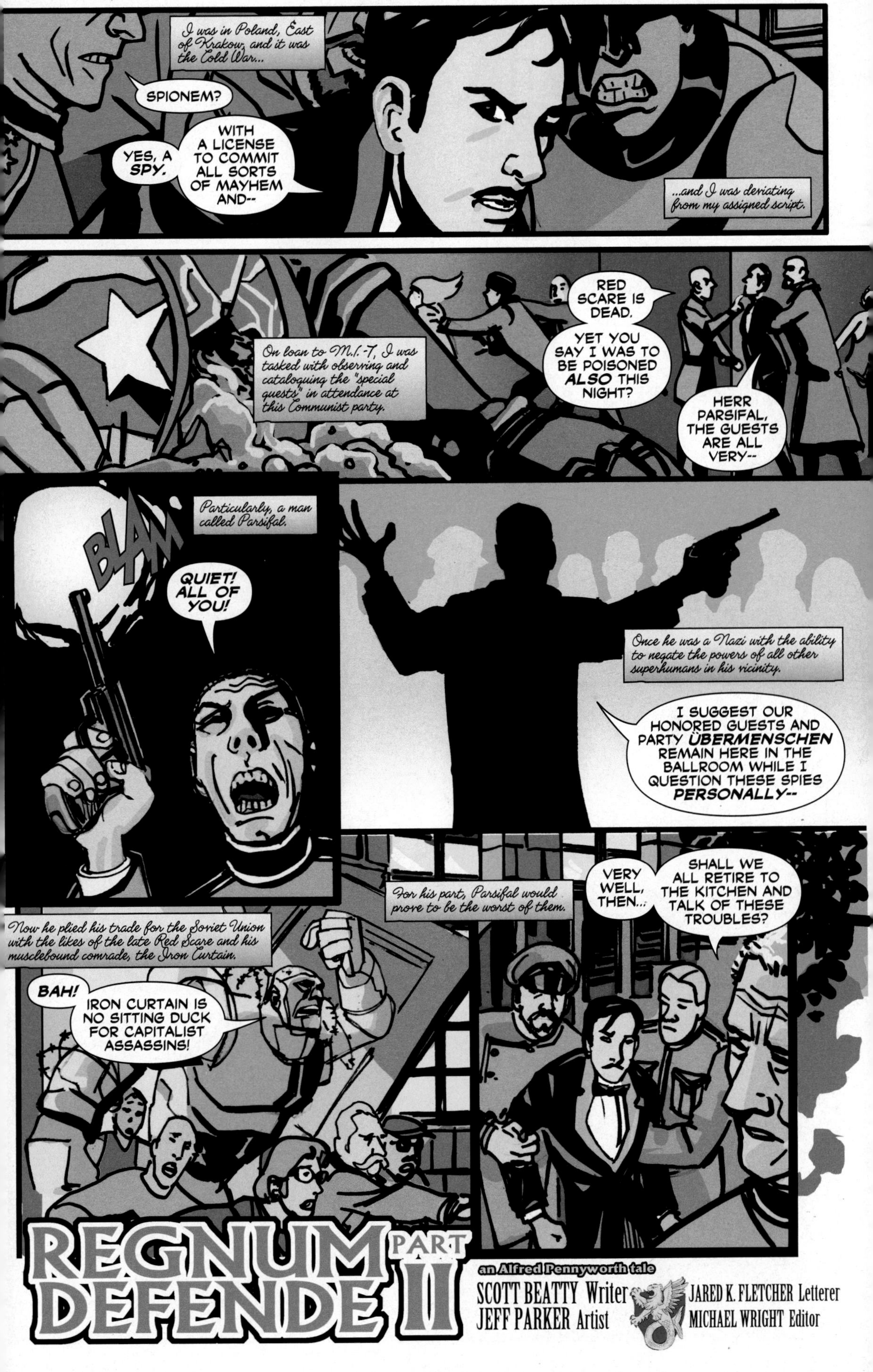
I was in Poland, East of Krakow, and it was the Cold War...
SPIONEM?
YES, A SPY.
WITH A LICENSE TO COMMIT ALL SORTS OF MAYHEM AND--
...and I was deviating from my assigned script.
On loan to M.I.-7, I was tasked with observing and cataloguing the "special guests" in attendance at this Communist party.
RED SCARE IS DEAD.
YET YOU SAY I WAS TO BE POISONED ALSO THIS NIGHT?
HERR PARSIFAL, THE GUESTS ARE ALL VERY--
Particularly, a man called Parsifal.
BLAM
QUIET! ALL OF YOU!
Once he was a Nazi with the ability to negate the powers of all other superhumans in his vicinity.
I SUGGEST OUR HONORED GUESTS AND PARTY ÜBERMENSCHEN REMAIN HERE IN THE BALLROOM WHILE I QUESTION THESE SPIES PERSONALLY--
Now he plied his trade for the Soviet Union with the likes of the late Red Scare and his musclebound comrade, the Iron Curtain.
BAH!
IRON CURTAIN IS NO SITTING DUCK FOR CAPITALIST ASSASSINS!
For his part, Parsifal would prove to be the worst of them.
VERY WELL, THEN...
SHALL WE ALL RETIRE TO THE KITCHEN AND TALK OF THESE TROUBLES?
REGNUM DEFENDE PART II
an Alfred Pennyworth tale
SCOTT BEATTY Writer
JEFF PARKER Artist
JARED K. FLETCHER Letterer
MICHAEL WRIGHT Editor

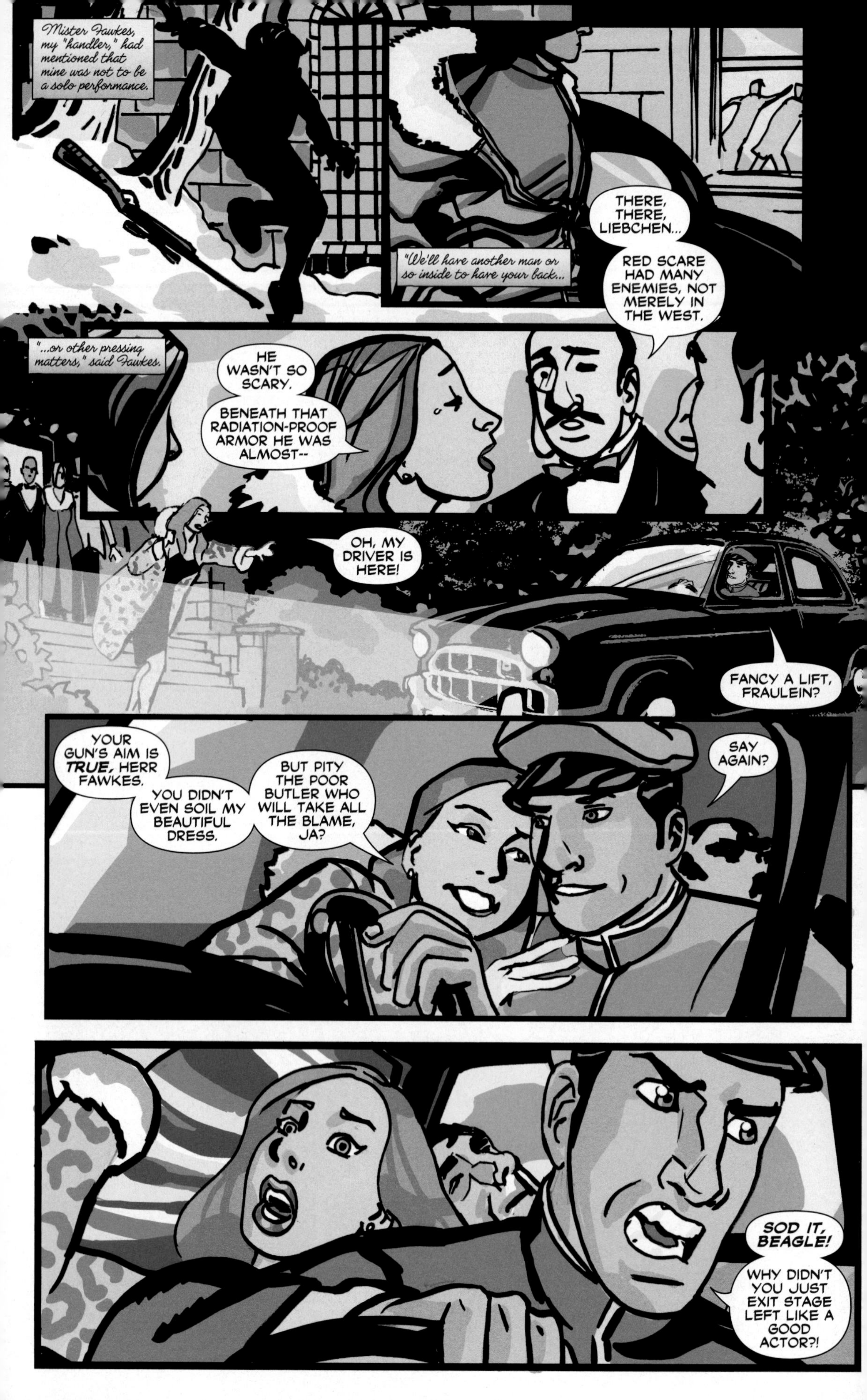

Mister Fawkes, my "handler," had mentioned that mine was not to be a solo performance.
"We'll have another man or so inside to have your back...
THERE, THERE, LIEBCHEN...
RED SCARE HAD MANY ENEMIES, NOT MERELY IN THE WEST.
"...or other pressing matters," said Fawkes.
HE WASN'T SO SCARY.
BENEATH THAT RADIATION-PROOF ARMOR HE WAS ALMOST--
OH, MY DRIVER IS HERE!
FANCY A LIFT, FRAULEIN?
YOUR GUN'S AIM IS TRUE, HERR FAWKES.
YOU DIDN'T EVEN SOIL MY BEAUTIFUL DRESS.
BUT PITY THE POOR BUTLER WHO WILL TAKE ALL THE BLAME, JA?
SAY AGAIN?
SOD IT, BEAGLE!
WHY DIDN'T YOU JUST EXIT STAGE LEFT LIKE A GOOD ACTOR?!

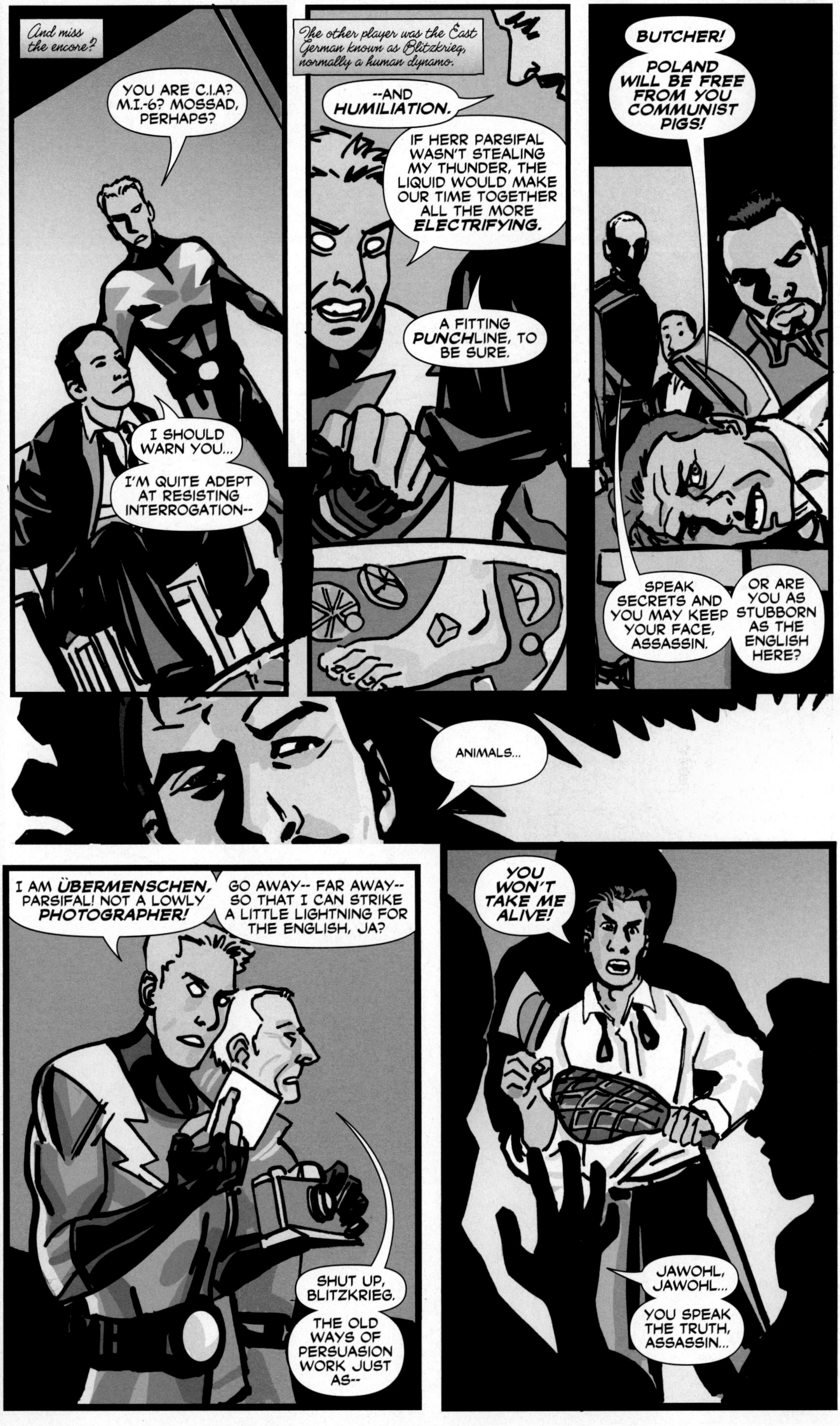
And miss the encore?
YOU ARE C.I.A? M.I.-6? MOSSAD, PERHAPS?
I SHOULD WARN YOU...
I'M QUITE ADEPT AT RESISTING INTERROGATION--
The other player was the East German known as Blitzkrieg, normally a human dynamo.
--AND HUMILIATION.
IF HERR PARSIFAL WASN'T STEALING MY THUNDER, THE LIQUID WOULD MAKE OUR TIME TOGETHER ALL THE MORE ELECTRIFYING.
A FITTING PUNCHLINE, TO BE SURE.
BUTCHER!
POLAND WILL BE FREE FROM YOU COMMUNIST PIGS!
SPEAK SECRETS AND YOU MAY KEEP YOUR FACE, ASSASSIN.
OR ARE YOU AS STUBBORN AS THE ENGLISH HERE?
ANIMALS...
I AM ÜBERMENSCHEN, PARSIFAL! NOT A LOWLY PHOTOGRAPHER!
GO AWAY-- FAR AWAY-- SO THAT I CAN STRIKE A LITTLE LIGHTNING FOR THE ENGLISH, JA?
SHUT UP, BLITZKRIEG.
THE OLD WAYS OF PERSUASION WORK JUST AS--
YOU WON'T TAKE ME ALIVE!
JAWOHL, JAWOHL...
YOU SPEAK THE TRUTH, ASSASSIN...

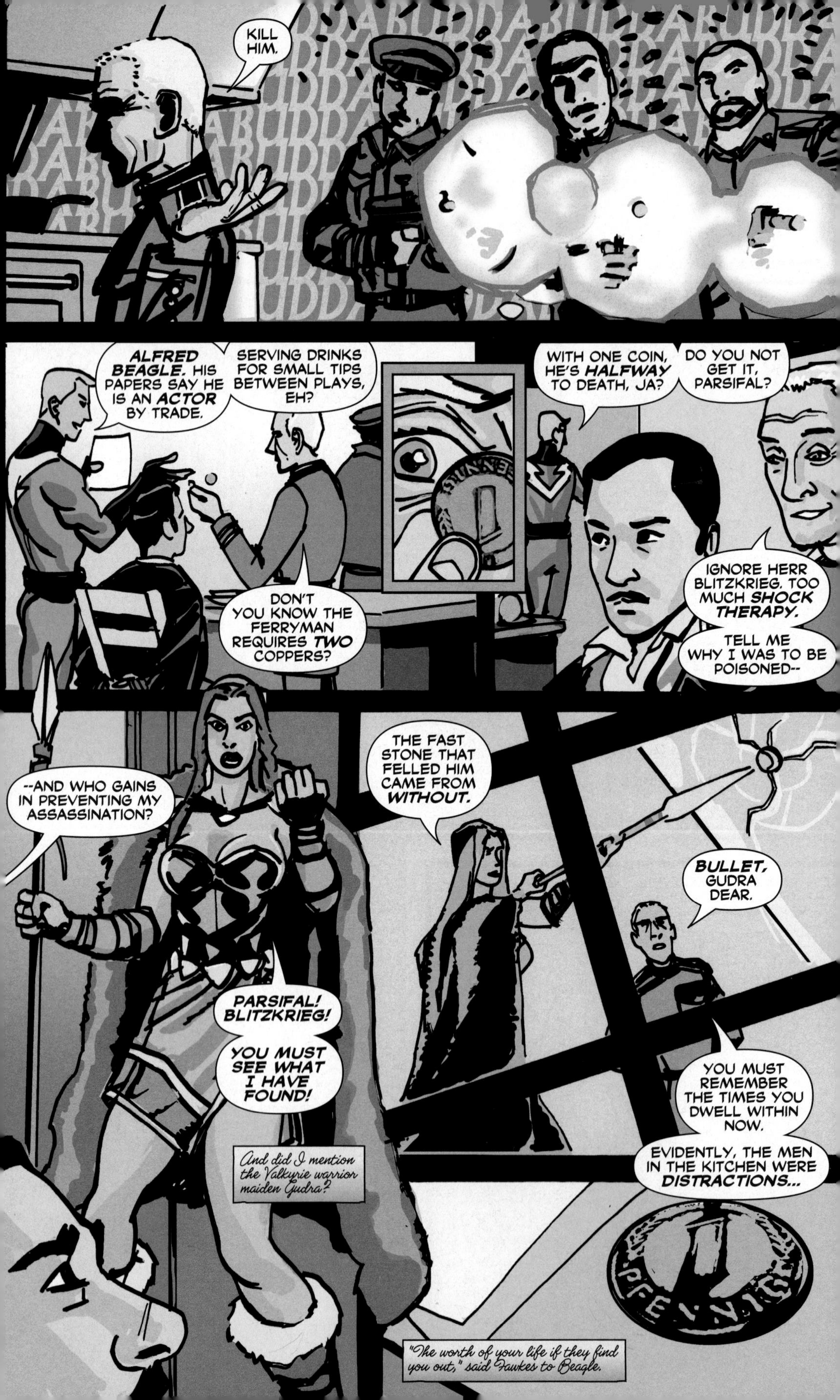
KILL HIM.
BUDDABUDDABUDDA
ALFRED BEAGLE. HIS PAPERS SAY HE IS AN ACTOR BY TRADE.
SERVING DRINKS FOR SMALL TIPS BETWEEN PLAYS, EH?
DON'T YOU KNOW THE FERRYMAN REQUIRES TWO COPPERS?
WITH ONE COIN, HE'S HALFWAY TO DEATH, JA?
DO YOU NOT GET IT, PARSIFAL?
IGNORE HERR BLITZKRIEG. TOO MUCH SHOCK THERAPY.
TELL ME WHY I WAS TO BE POISONED--
--AND WHO GAINS IN PREVENTING MY ASSASSINATION?
PARSIFAL! BLITZKRIEG!
YOU MUST SEE WHAT I HAVE FOUND!
And did I mention the Valkyrie warrior maiden Gudra?
THE FAST STONE THAT FELLED HIM CAME FROM WITHOUT.
BULLET, GUDRA DEAR.
YOU MUST REMEMBER THE TIMES YOU DWELL WITHIN NOW.
EVIDENTLY, THE MEN IN THE KITCHEN WERE DISTRACTIONS...
"The worth of your life if they find you out," said Fawkes to Beagle.

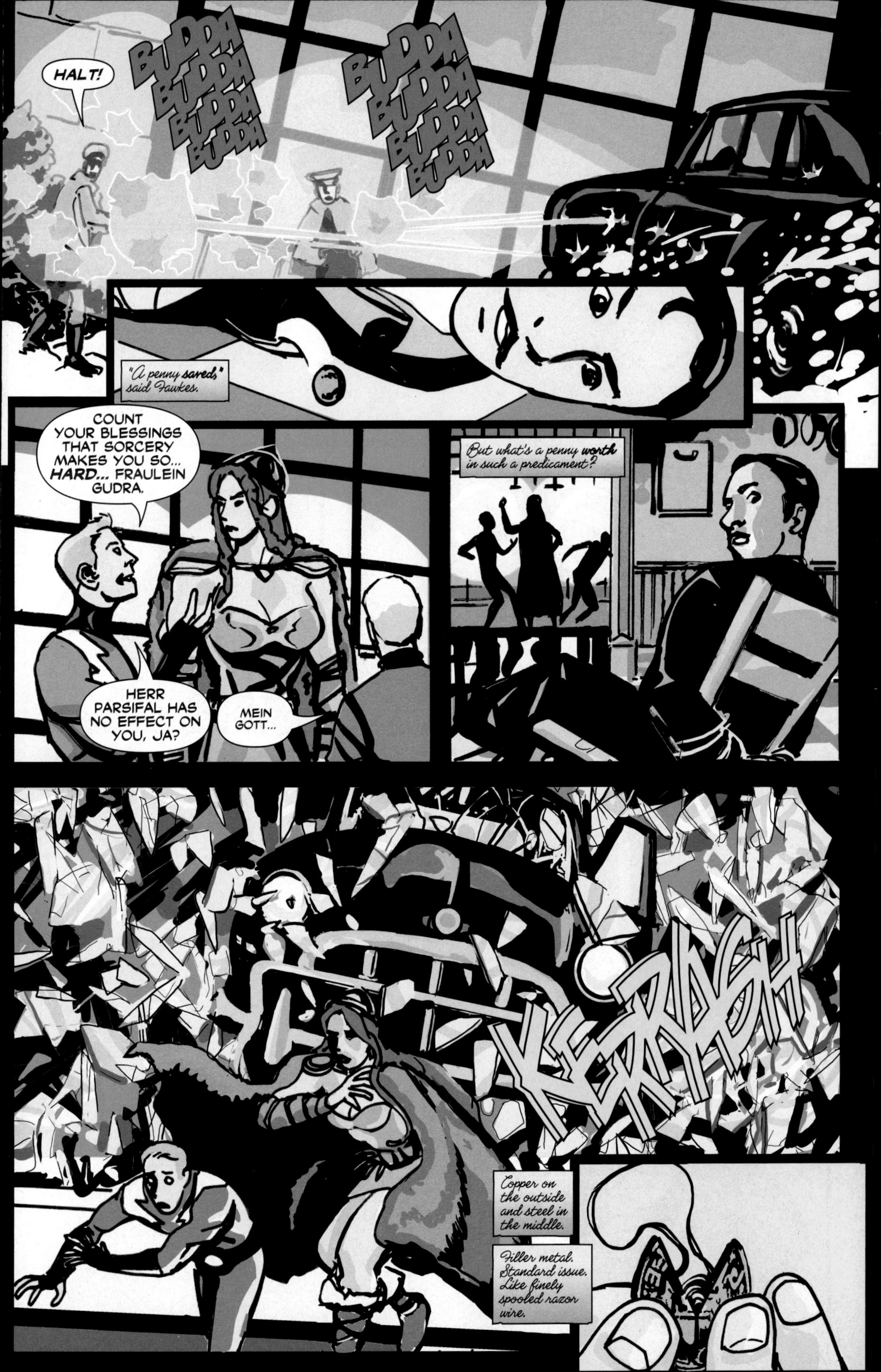
HALT!
BUDDA BUDDA BUDDA BUDDA
BUDDA BUDDA BUDDA BUDDA
"A penny saved," said Fawkes.
COUNT YOUR BLESSINGS THAT SORCERY MAKES YOU SO... HARD... FRAULEIN GUDRA.
HERR PARSIFAL HAS NO EFFECT ON YOU, JA?
MEIN GOTT...
But what's a penny worth in such a predicament?
KERRASH
Copper on the outside and steel in the middle.
Filler metal. Standard issue. Like finely spooled razor wire.

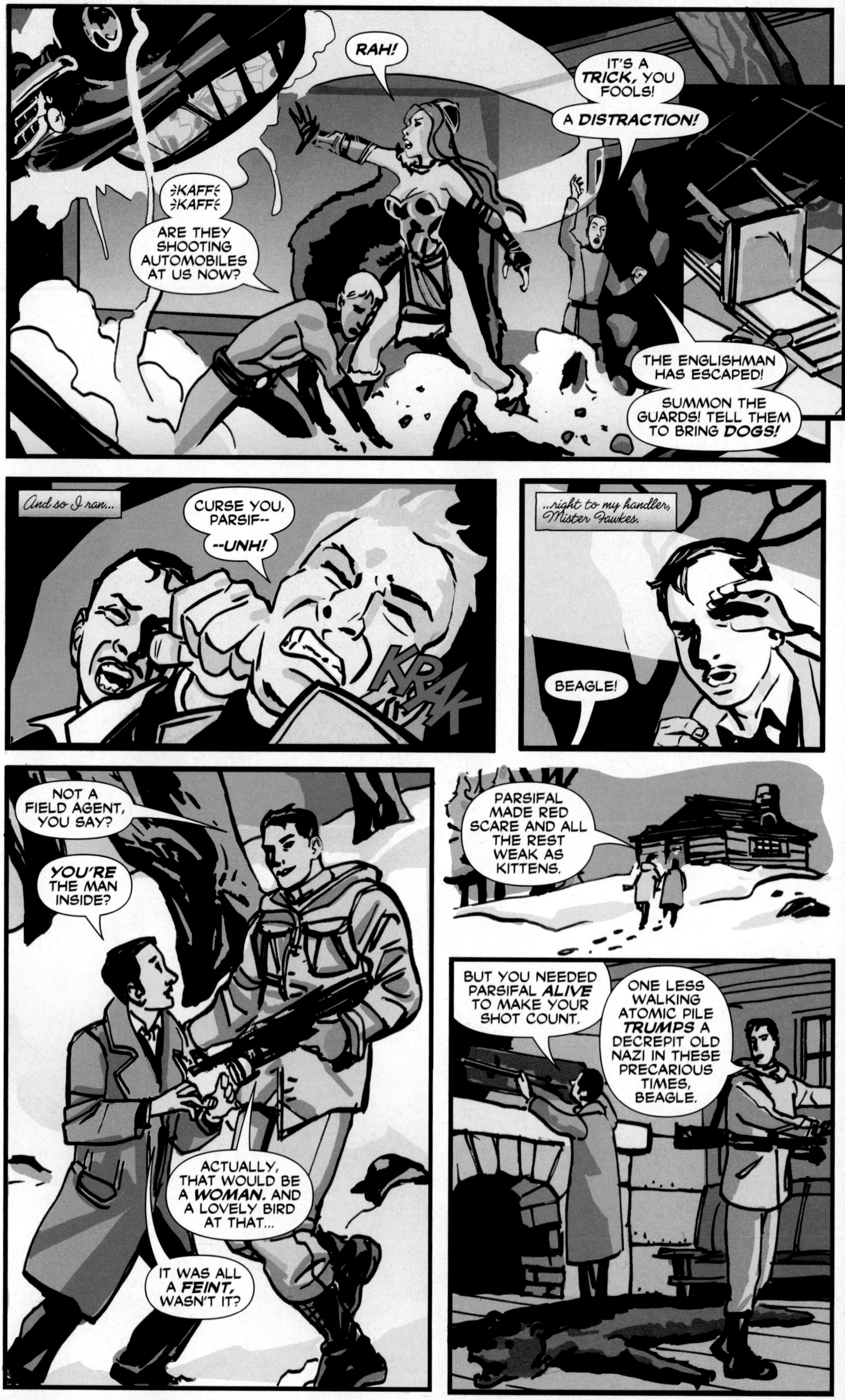
RAH!
IT'S A TRICK, YOU FOOLS!
A DISTRACTION!
KAFF KAFF
ARE THEY SHOOTING AUTOMOBILES AT US NOW?
THE ENGLISHMAN HAS ESCAPED!
SUMMON THE GUARDS! TELL THEM TO BRING DOGS!
And so I ran...
CURSE YOU, PARSIF--
--UNH!
KRAK
...right to my handler, Mister Fawkes.
BEAGLE!
NOT A FIELD AGENT, YOU SAY?
YOU'RE THE MAN INSIDE?
ACTUALLY, THAT WOULD BE A WOMAN. AND A LOVELY BIRD AT THAT...
IT WAS ALL A FEINT, WASN'T IT?
PARSIFAL MADE RED SCARE AND ALL THE REST WEAK AS KITTENS.
BUT YOU NEEDED PARSIFAL ALIVE TO MAKE YOUR SHOT COUNT.
ONE LESS WALKING ATOMIC PILE TRUMPS A DECREPIT OLD NAZI IN THESE PRECARIOUS TIMES, BEAGLE.

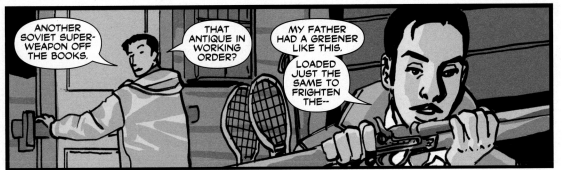

ANOTHER SOVIET SUPER-WEAPON OFF THE BOOKS.

THAT ANTIQUE IN WORKING ORDER?

MY FATHER HAD A GREENER LIKE THIS.

LOADED JUST THE SAME TO FRIGHTEN THE--

HAH! YOU ARE FOUND!

UNH!

WHAT WELL-DEVELOPED MUSCLES... MY DEAR... YOU MUST EXERCISE QUITE... VIGOROUSLY--

PUT HIM DOWN, MISS GUDRA...

HAH. I AM VALKYRIE.

YOUR FAST STONES WILL SCARCELY STING ONE SUCH AS ME.

THAT'S QUITE THE POINT, MISS GUDRA...

WHOOM

ROCK SALT?

WHAT BETTER WAY TO FRIGHTEN OFF A NASTY BIRD?

RAAAAHH!

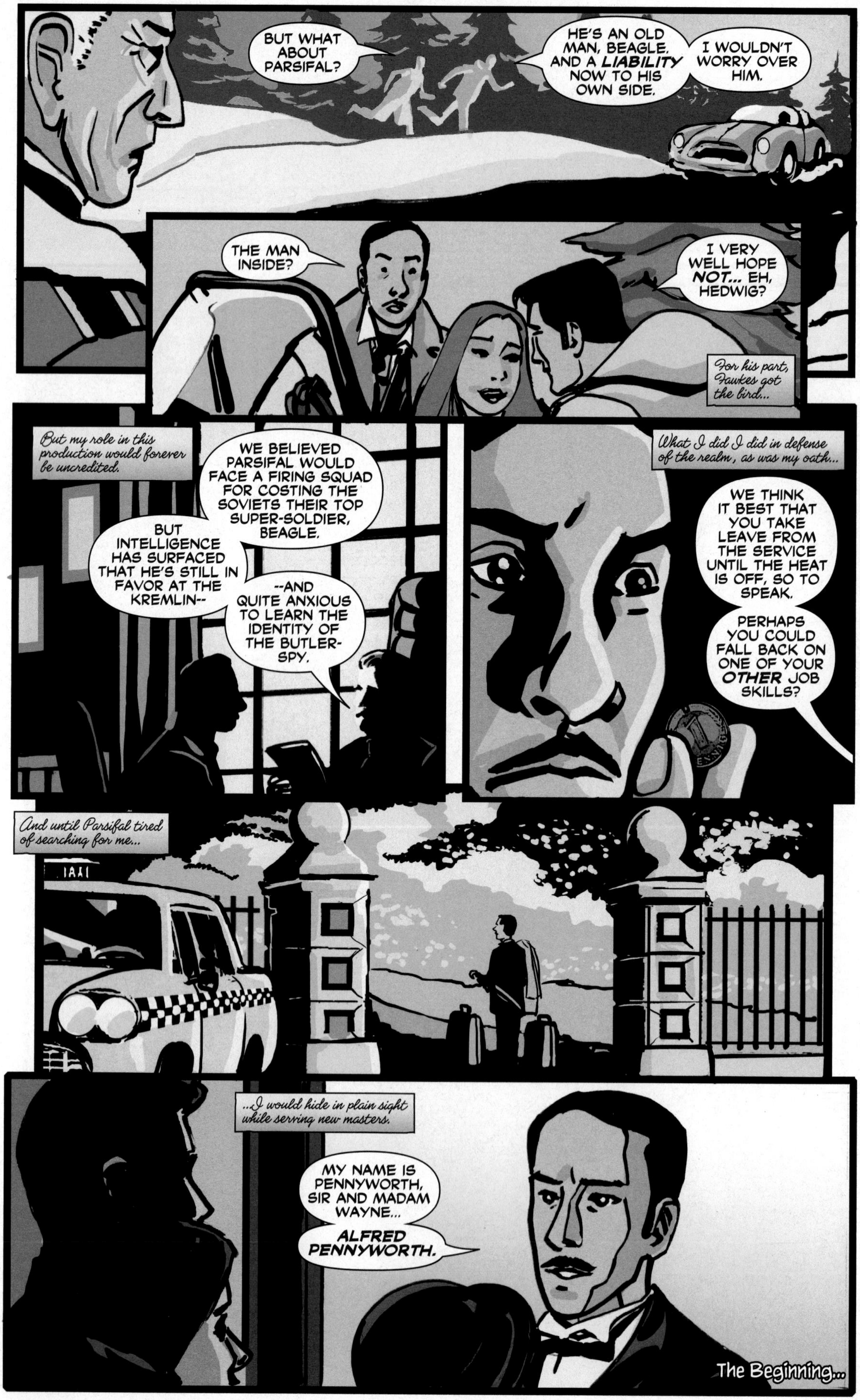
BUT WHAT ABOUT PARSIFAL?
HE'S AN OLD MAN, BEAGLE. AND A LIABILITY NOW TO HIS OWN SIDE.
I WOULDN'T WORRY OVER HIM.
THE MAN INSIDE?
I VERY WELL HOPE NOT... EH, HEDWIG?
For his part, Fawkes got the bird...
But my role in this production would forever be uncredited.
WE BELIEVED PARSIFAL WOULD FACE A FIRING SQUAD FOR COSTING THE SOVIETS THEIR TOP SUPER-SOLDIER, BEAGLE.
BUT INTELLIGENCE HAS SURFACED THAT HE'S STILL IN FAVOR AT THE KREMLIN--
--AND QUITE ANXIOUS TO LEARN THE IDENTITY OF THE BUTLER-SPY.
What I did I did in defense of the realm, as was my oath...
WE THINK IT BEST THAT YOU TAKE LEAVE FROM THE SERVICE UNTIL THE HEAT IS OFF, SO TO SPEAK.
PERHAPS YOU COULD FALL BACK ON ONE OF YOUR OTHER JOB SKILLS?
And until Parsifal tired of searching for me...
TAXI
...I would hide in plain sight while serving new masters.
MY NAME IS PENNYWORTH, SIR AND MADAM WAYNE...
ALFRED PENNYWORTH.
The Beginning...

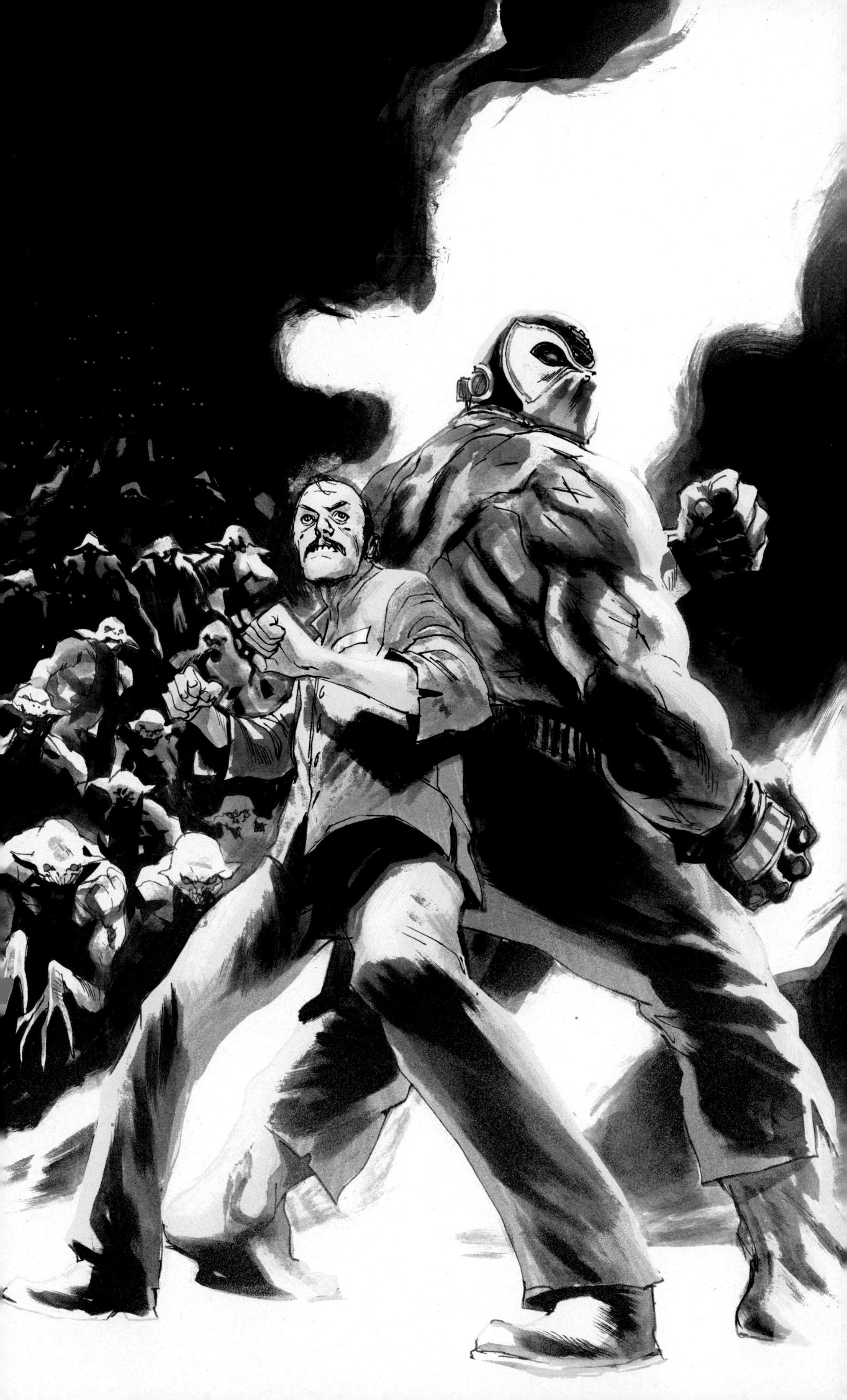

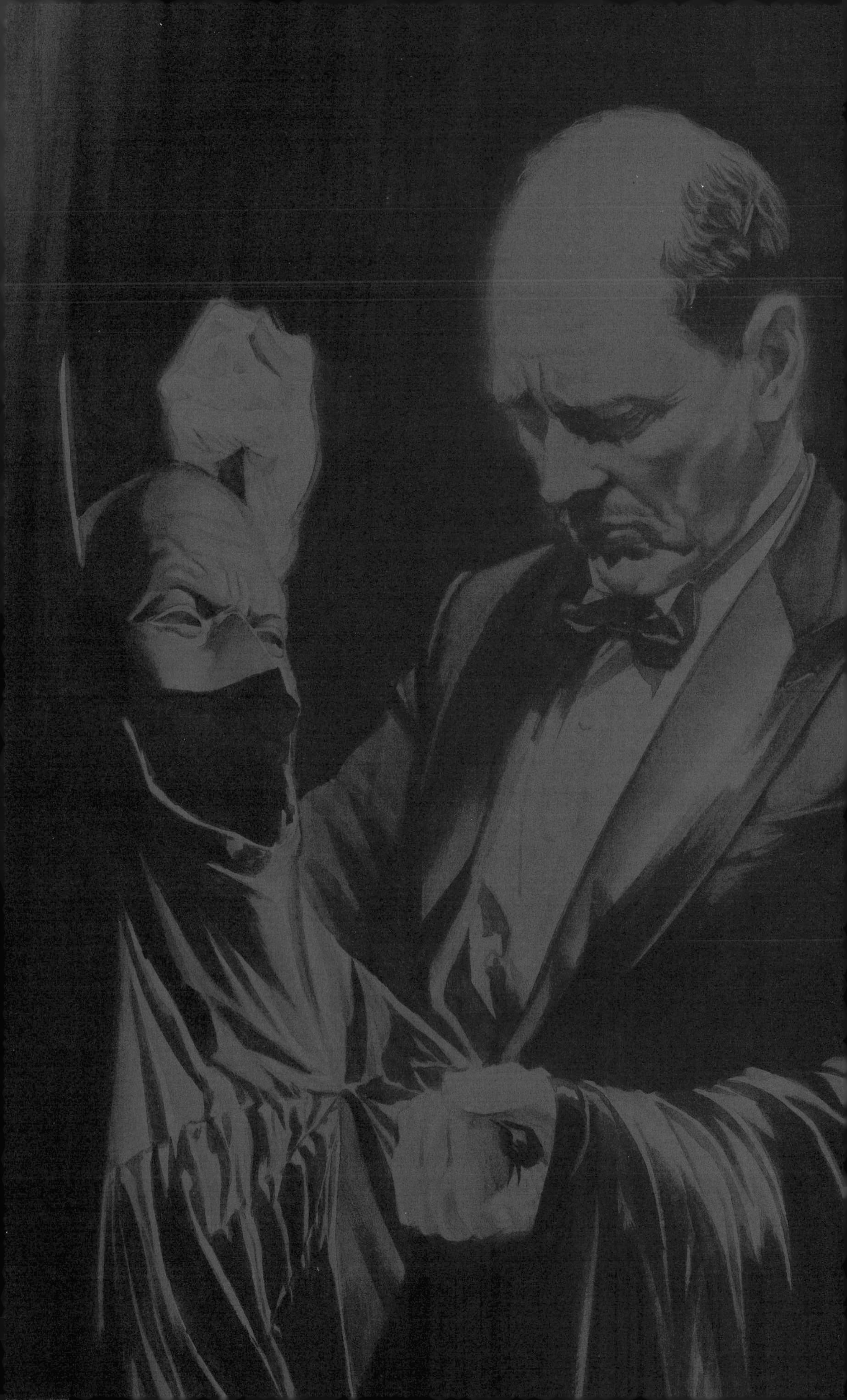

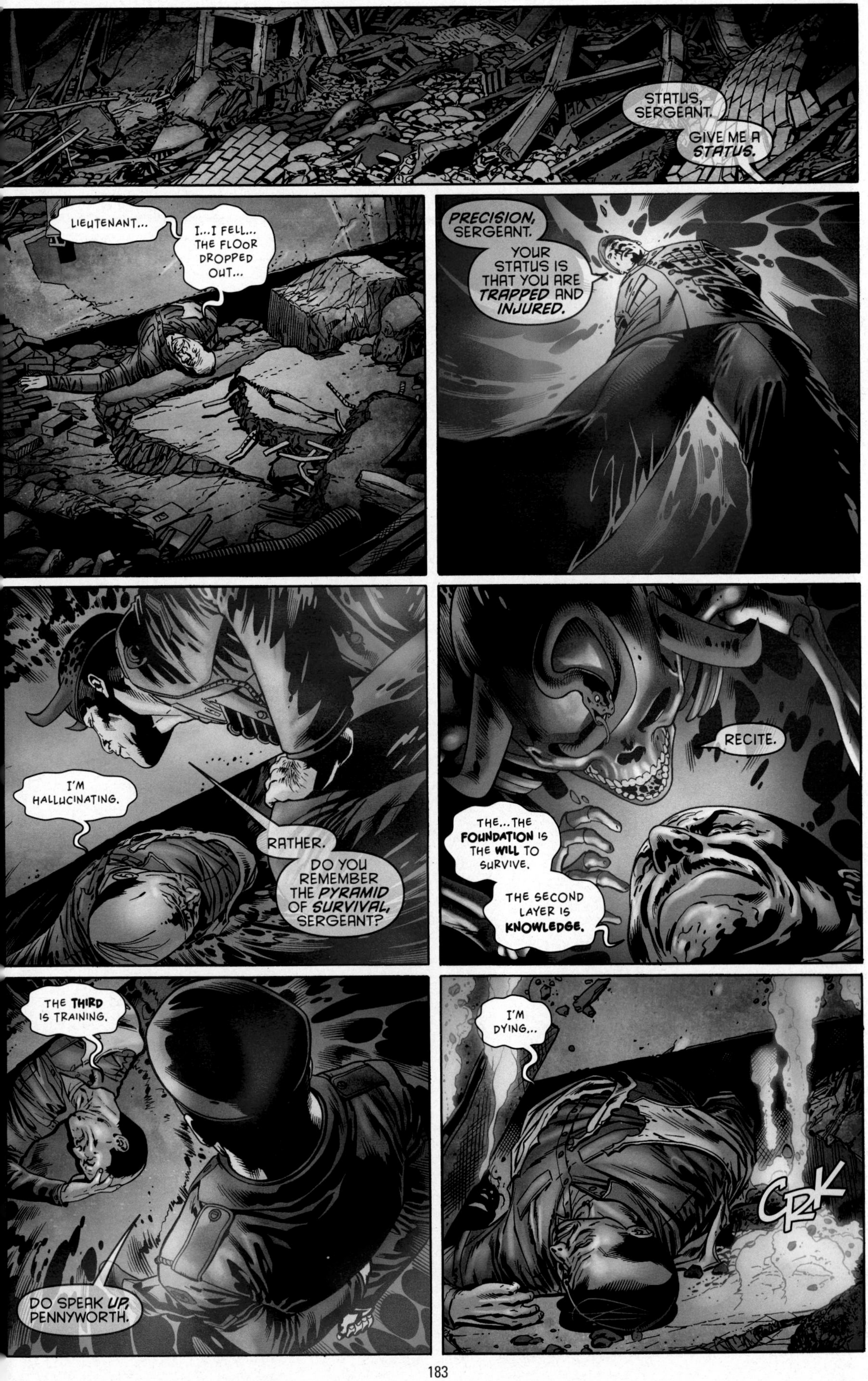
STATUS, SERGEANT.
GIVE ME A STATUS.
LIEUTENANT...
I...I FELL... THE FLOOR DROPPED OUT...
PRECISION, SERGEANT.
YOUR STATUS IS THAT YOU ARE TRAPPED AND INJURED.
I'M HALLUCINATING.
RATHER.
DO YOU REMEMBER THE PYRAMID OF SURVIVAL, SERGEANT?
RECITE.
THE...THE FOUNDATION IS THE WILL TO SURVIVE.
THE SECOND LAYER IS KNOWLEDGE.
THE THIRD IS TRAINING.
DO SPEAK UP, PENNYWORTH.
I'M DYING...
CRK

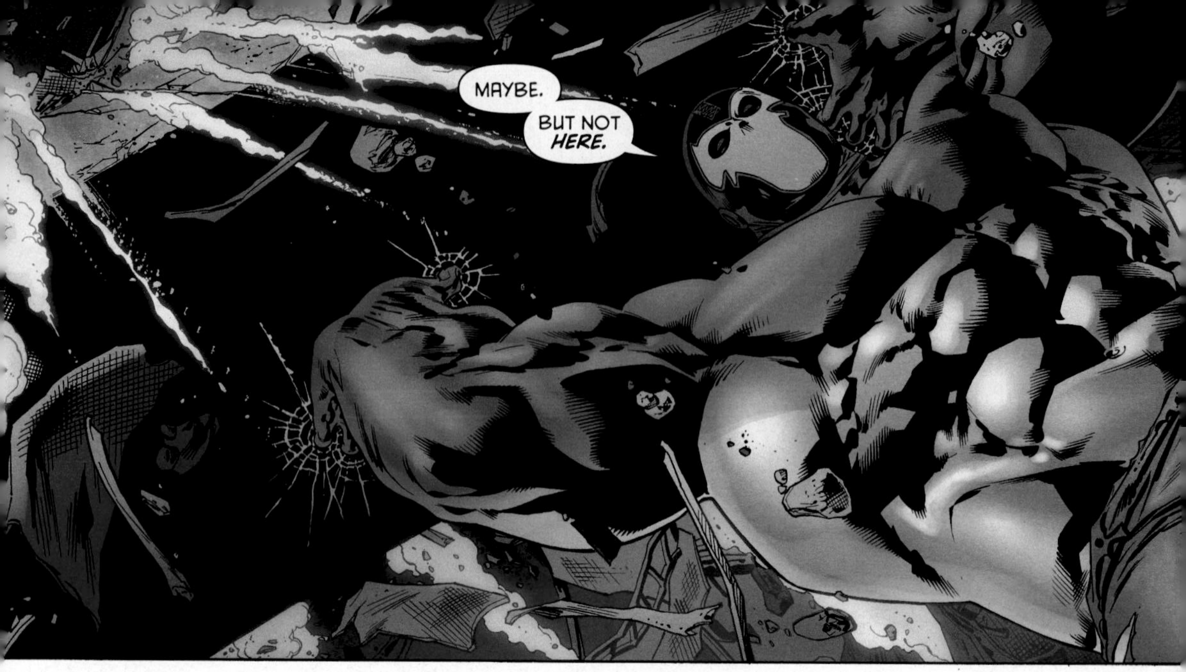
MAYBE.
BUT NOT *HERE.*

# BURIED DEEP

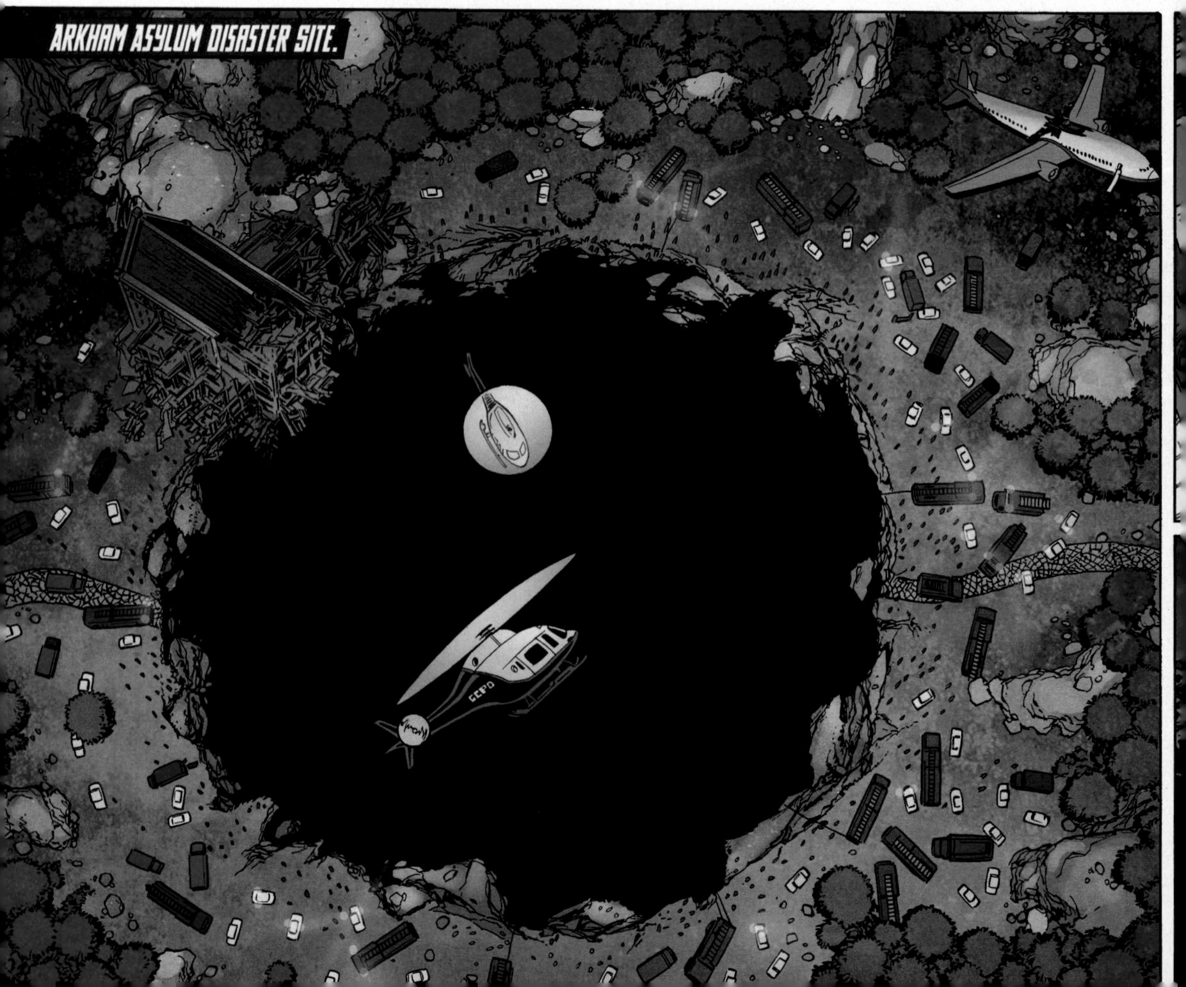
ARKHAM ASYLUM DISASTER SITE.
GCPD

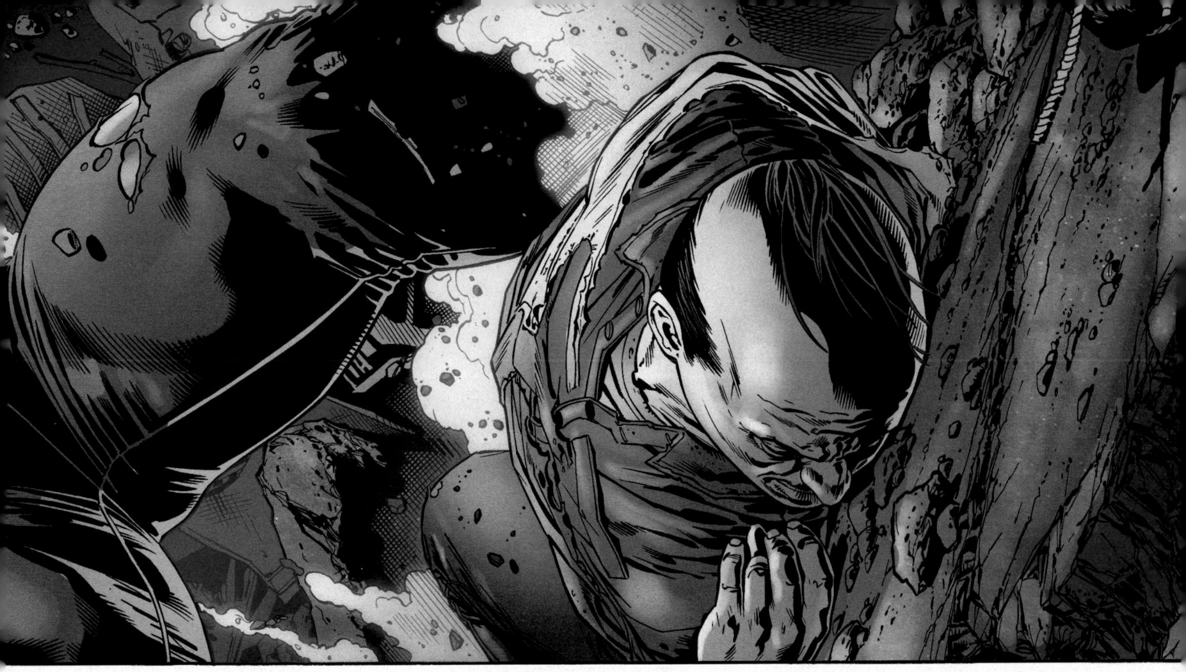

SCOTT SNYDER & JAMES TYNION IV STORY RAY FAWKES SCRIPT

KYLE HIGGINS & TIM SEELEY CONSULTING WRITERS FERNANDO PASARIN PENCILS

MATT RYAN INKS BLOND COLORS TAYLOR ESPOSITO LETTERS RAFAEL ALBUQUERQUE COVER

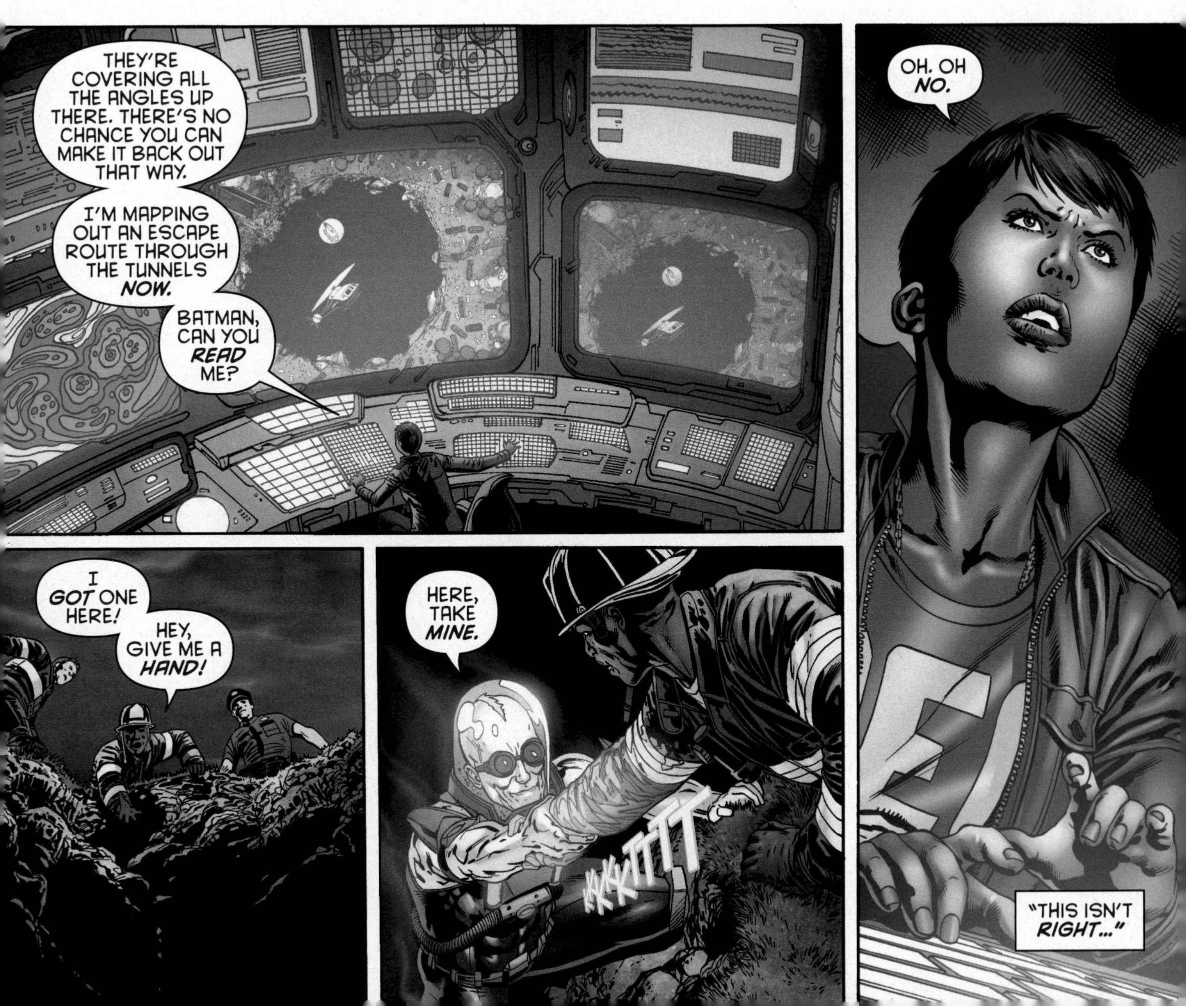

THEY'RE COVERING ALL THE ANGLES UP THERE. THERE'S NO CHANCE YOU CAN MAKE IT BACK OUT THAT WAY.
I'M MAPPING OUT AN ESCAPE ROUTE THROUGH THE TUNNELS *NOW.*
BATMAN, CAN YOU *READ* ME?
OH. OH *NO.*
I *GOT* ONE HERE!
HEY, GIVE ME A *HAND!*
HERE, TAKE *MINE.*
KKKKTTTT
"THIS ISN'T *RIGHT...*"

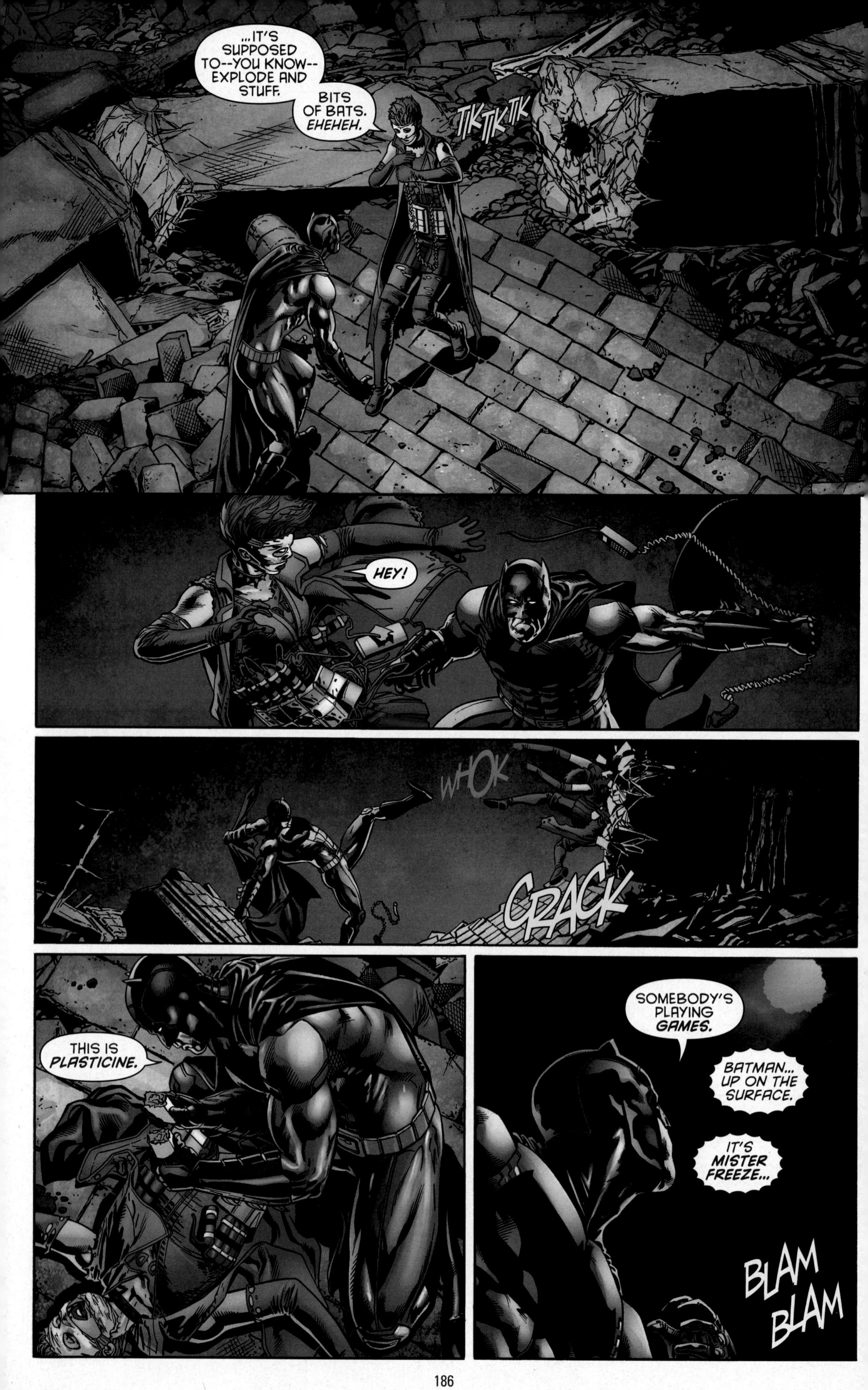
...IT'S SUPPOSED TO--YOU KNOW--EXPLODE AND STUFF.
BITS OF BATS. EHEHEH.
TIKTIKTIK
HEY!
WHOK
CRACK
THIS IS PLASTICINE.
SOMEBODY'S PLAYING GAMES.
BATMAN... UP ON THE SURFACE.
IT'S MISTER FREEZE...
BLAM BLAM

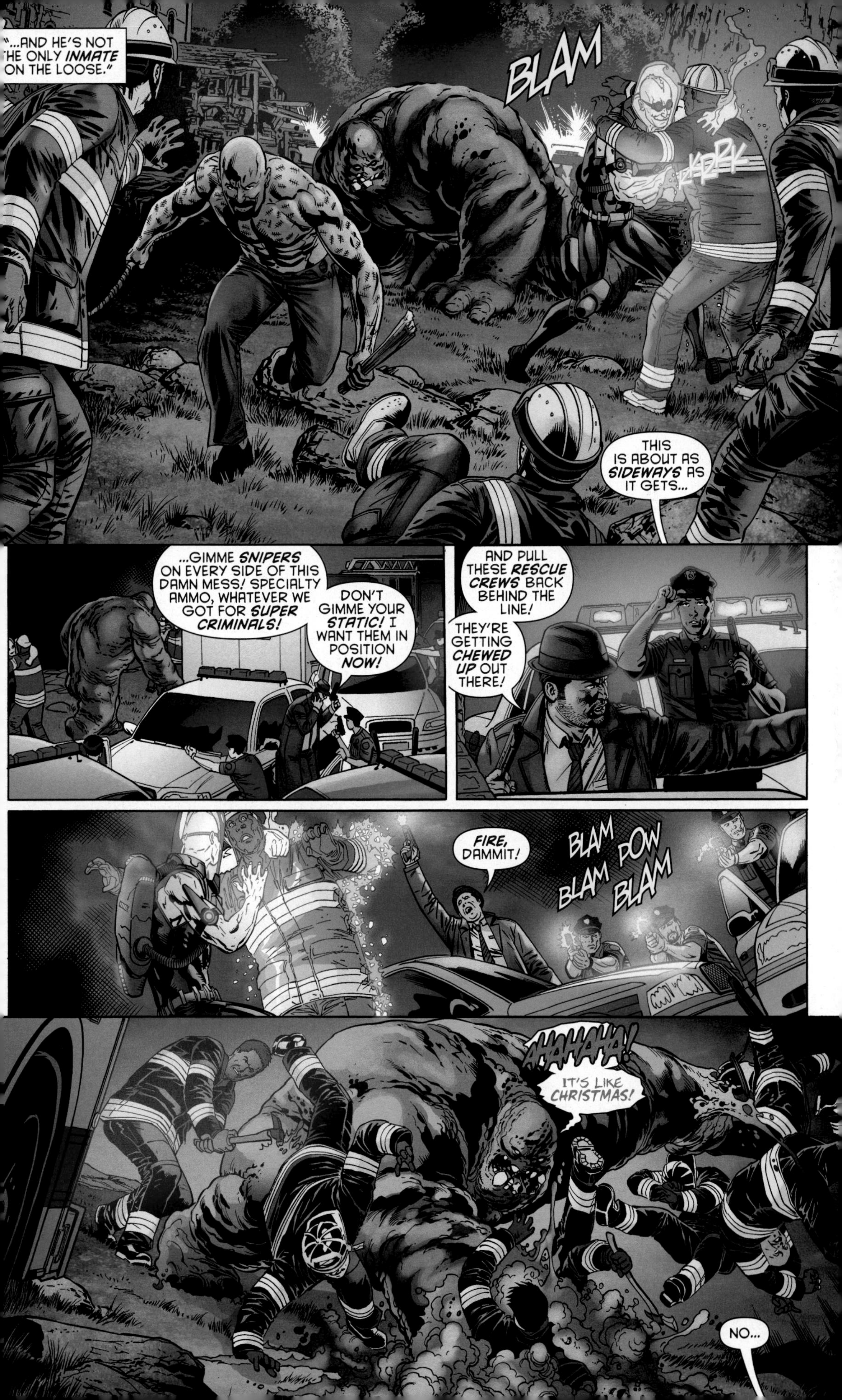
"...AND HE'S NOT THE ONLY INMATE ON THE LOOSE."
BLAM
KRZRK
THIS IS ABOUT AS SIDEWAYS AS IT GETS...
...GIMME SNIPERS ON EVERY SIDE OF THIS DAMN MESS! SPECIALTY AMMO, WHATEVER WE GOT FOR SUPER CRIMINALS!
DON'T GIMME YOUR STATIC! I WANT THEM IN POSITION NOW!
AND PULL THESE RESCUE CREWS BACK BEHIND THE LINE!
THEY'RE GETTING CHEWED UP OUT THERE!
FIRE, DAMMIT!
BLAM BLAM POW BLAM
AHAHAHA!
IT'S LIKE CHRISTMAS!
NO...

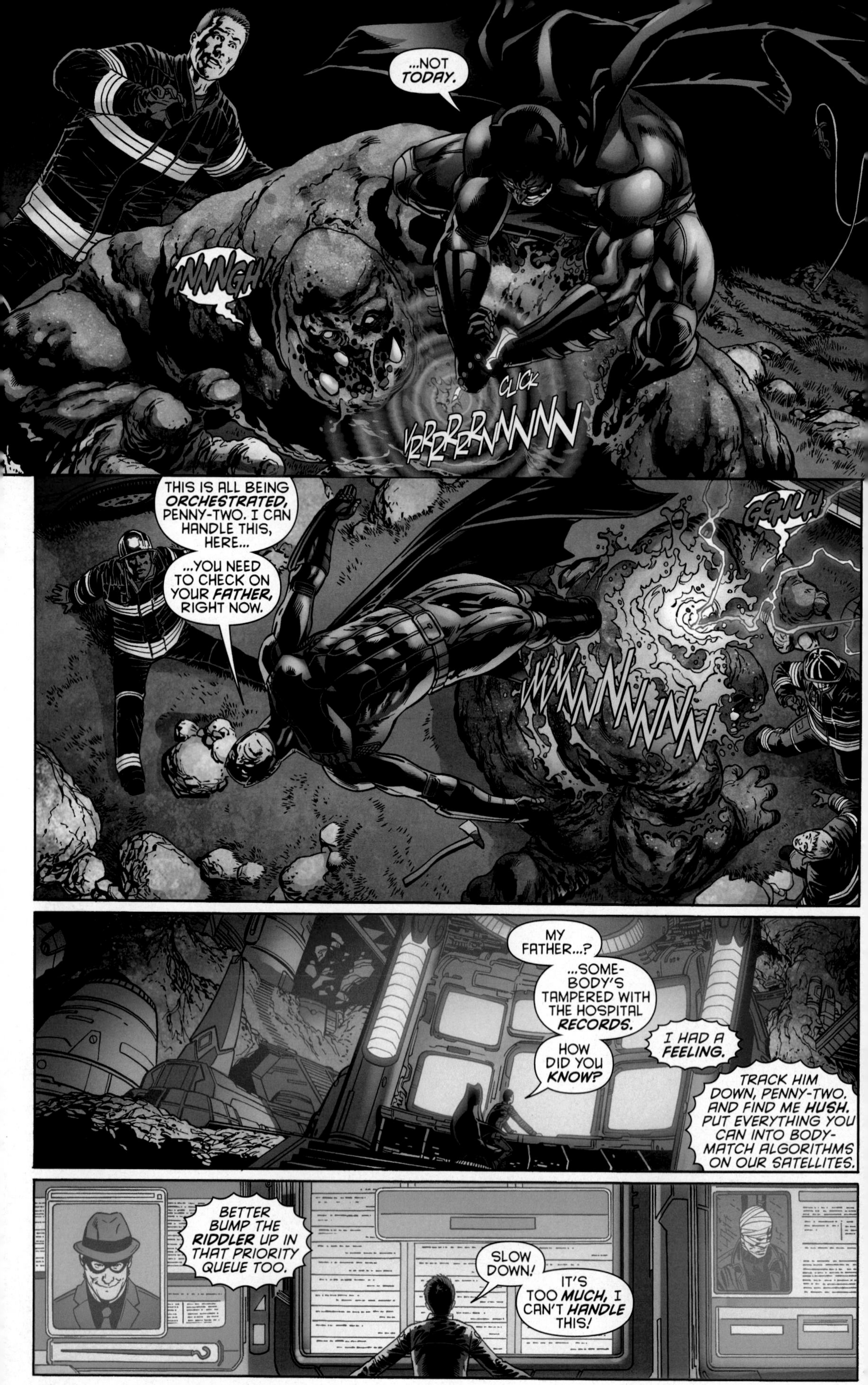

...NOT TODAY.
HNNNGH!
CLICK
VRRRRRRNNNNN
THIS IS ALL BEING ORCHESTRATED, PENNY-TWO. I CAN HANDLE THIS, HERE...
...YOU NEED TO CHECK ON YOUR FATHER, RIGHT NOW.
GGHUH
WWNNNNNNNN
MY FATHER...?
...SOMEBODY'S TAMPERED WITH THE HOSPITAL RECORDS.
HOW DID YOU KNOW?
I HAD A FEELING.
TRACK HIM DOWN, PENNY-TWO. AND FIND ME HUSH. PUT EVERYTHING YOU CAN INTO BODY-MATCH ALGORITHMS ON OUR SATELLITES.
BETTER BUMP THE RIDDLER UP IN THAT PRIORITY QUEUE TOO.
SLOW DOWN!
IT'S TOO MUCH, I CAN'T HANDLE THIS!

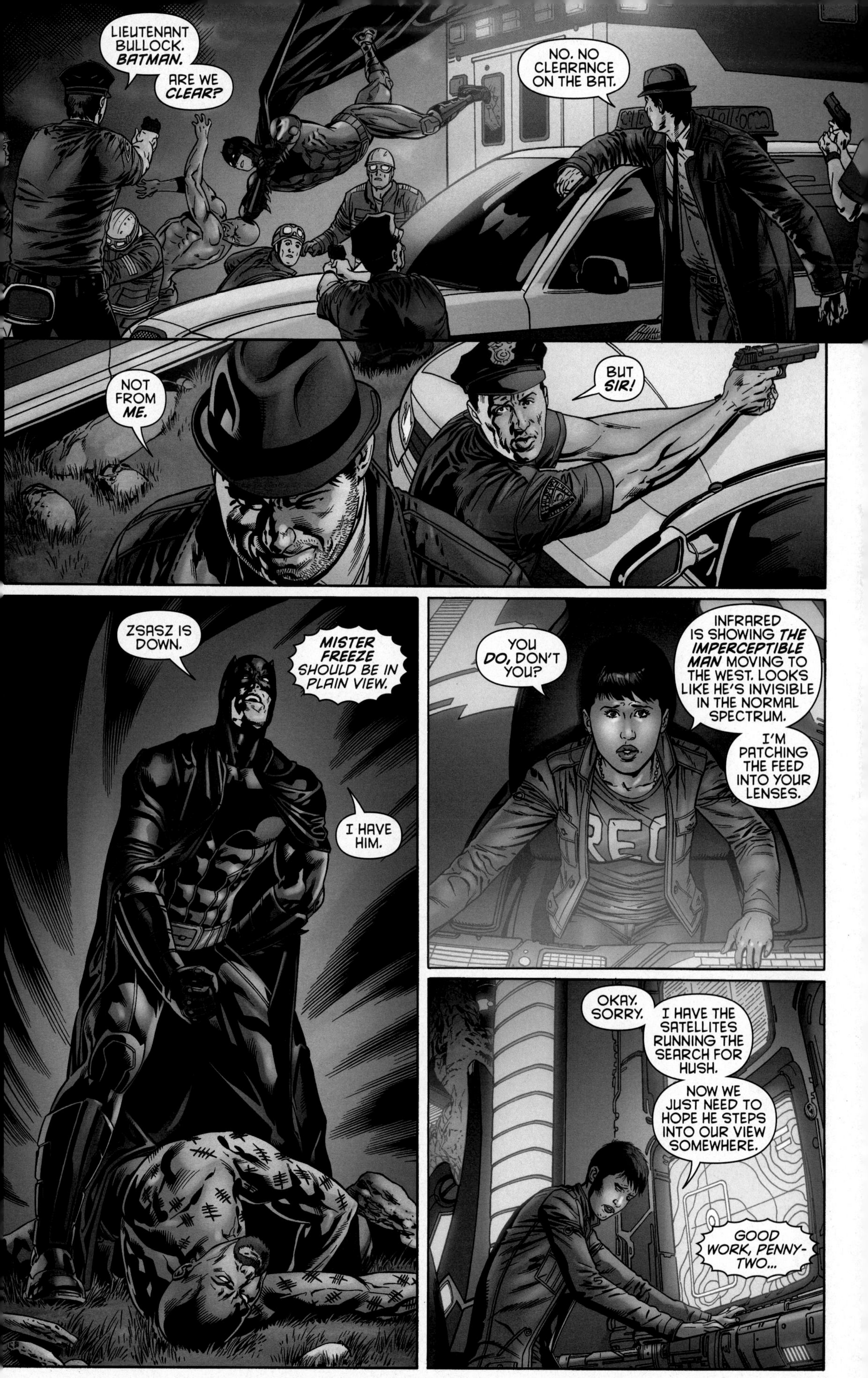
LIEUTENANT BULLOCK. BATMAN.
ARE WE CLEAR?
NO. NO CLEARANCE ON THE BAT.
NOT FROM ME.
BUT SIR!
ZSASZ IS DOWN.
MISTER FREEZE SHOULD BE IN PLAIN VIEW.
I HAVE HIM.
YOU DO, DON'T YOU?
INFRARED IS SHOWING THE IMPERCEPTIBLE MAN MOVING TO THE WEST. LOOKS LIKE HE'S INVISIBLE IN THE NORMAL SPECTRUM.
I'M PATCHING THE FEED INTO YOUR LENSES.
OKAY. SORRY.
I HAVE THE SATELLITES RUNNING THE SEARCH FOR HUSH.
NOW WE JUST NEED TO HOPE HE STEPS INTO OUR VIEW SOMEWHERE.
GOOD WORK, PENNY-TWO...

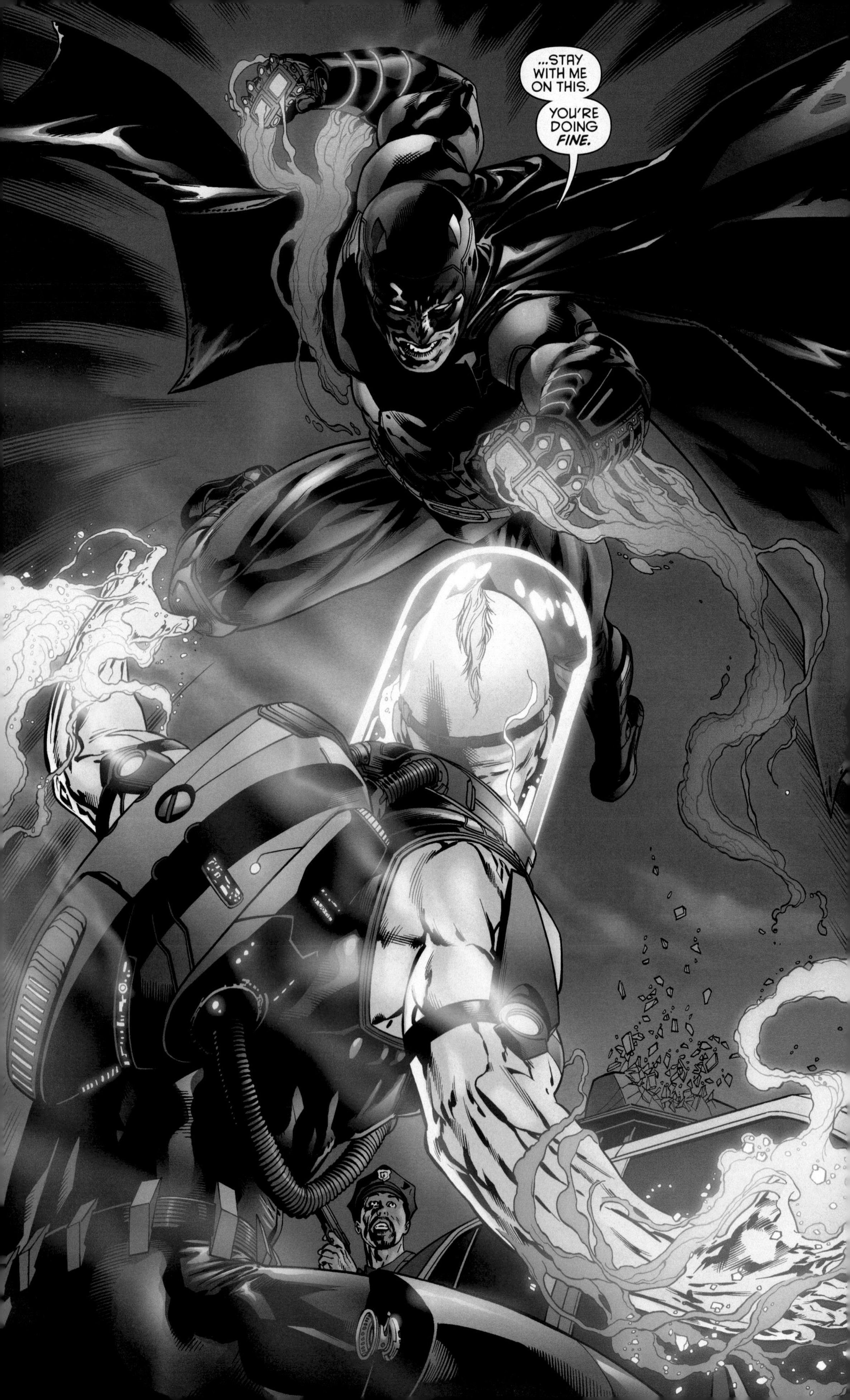
...STAY WITH ME ON THIS.
YOU'RE DOING FINE.

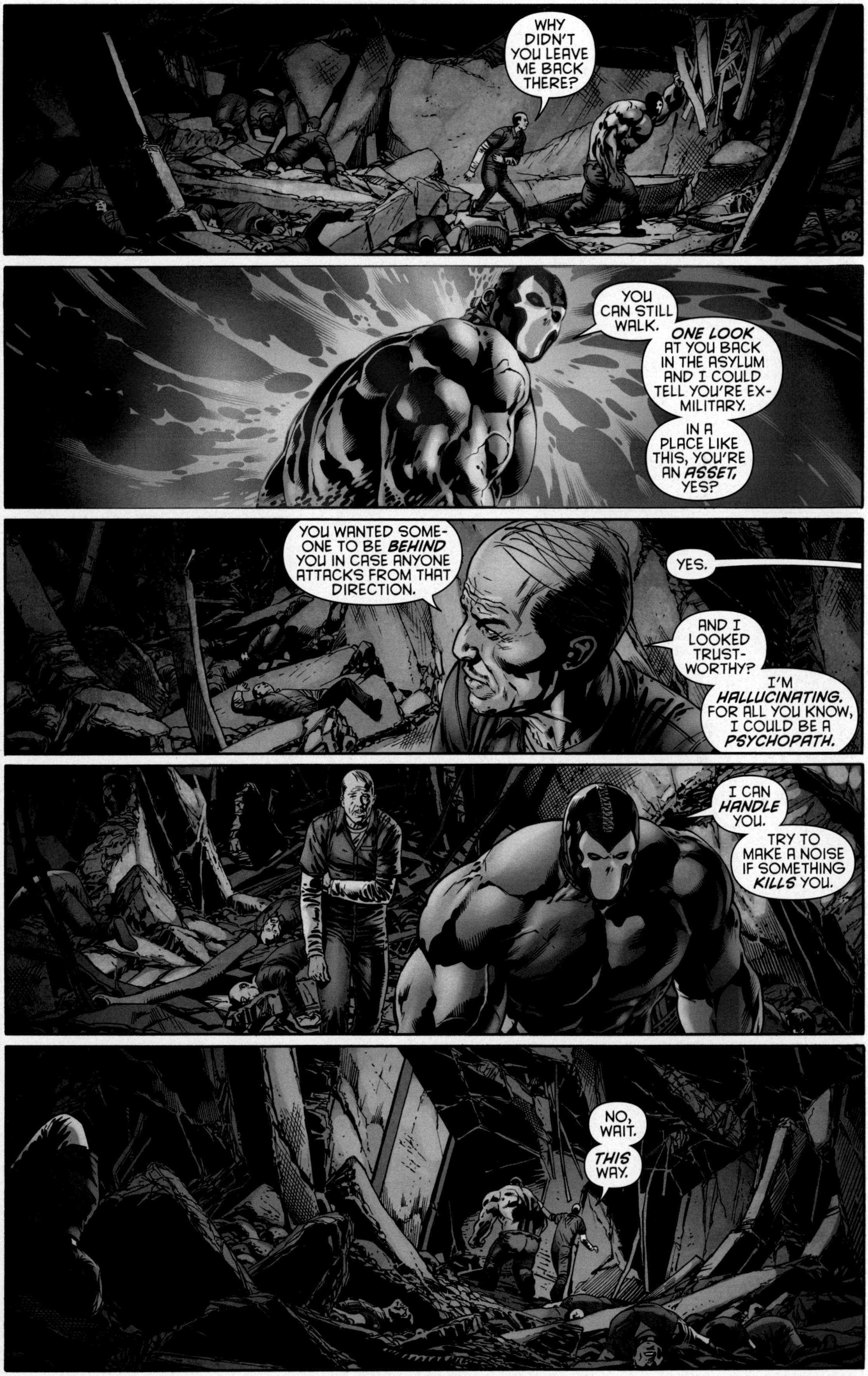
WHY DIDN'T YOU LEAVE ME BACK THERE?
YOU CAN STILL WALK.
ONE LOOK AT YOU BACK IN THE ASYLUM AND I COULD TELL YOU'RE EX-MILITARY.
IN A PLACE LIKE THIS, YOU'RE AN ASSET, YES?
YOU WANTED SOME-ONE TO BE BEHIND YOU IN CASE ANYONE ATTACKS FROM THAT DIRECTION.
YES.
AND I LOOKED TRUST-WORTHY?
I'M HALLUCINATING. FOR ALL YOU KNOW, I COULD BE A PSYCHOPATH.
I CAN HANDLE YOU.
TRY TO MAKE A NOISE IF SOMETHING KILLS YOU.
NO, WAIT.
THIS WAY.

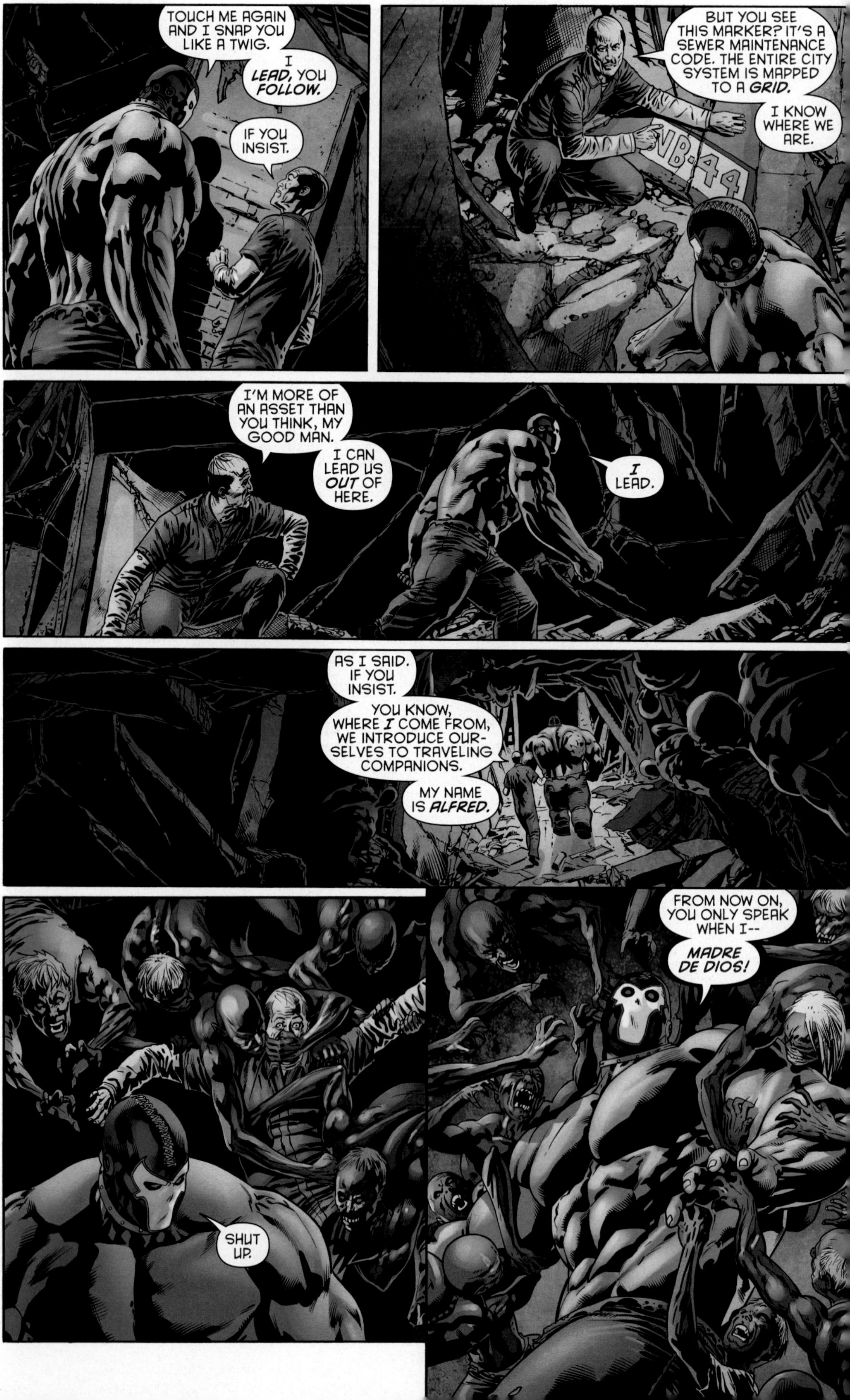
TOUCH ME AGAIN AND I SNAP YOU LIKE A TWIG.
I LEAD, YOU FOLLOW.
IF YOU INSIST.
BUT YOU SEE THIS MARKER? IT'S A SEWER MAINTENANCE CODE. THE ENTIRE CITY SYSTEM IS MAPPED TO A GRID.
I KNOW WHERE WE ARE.
VB-44
I'M MORE OF AN ASSET THAN YOU THINK, MY GOOD MAN.
I CAN LEAD US OUT OF HERE.
I LEAD.
AS I SAID. IF YOU INSIST.
YOU KNOW, WHERE I COME FROM, WE INTRODUCE OUR-SELVES TO TRAVELING COMPANIONS.
MY NAME IS ALFRED.
SHUT UP.
FROM NOW ON, YOU ONLY SPEAK WHEN I--
MADRE DE DIOS!

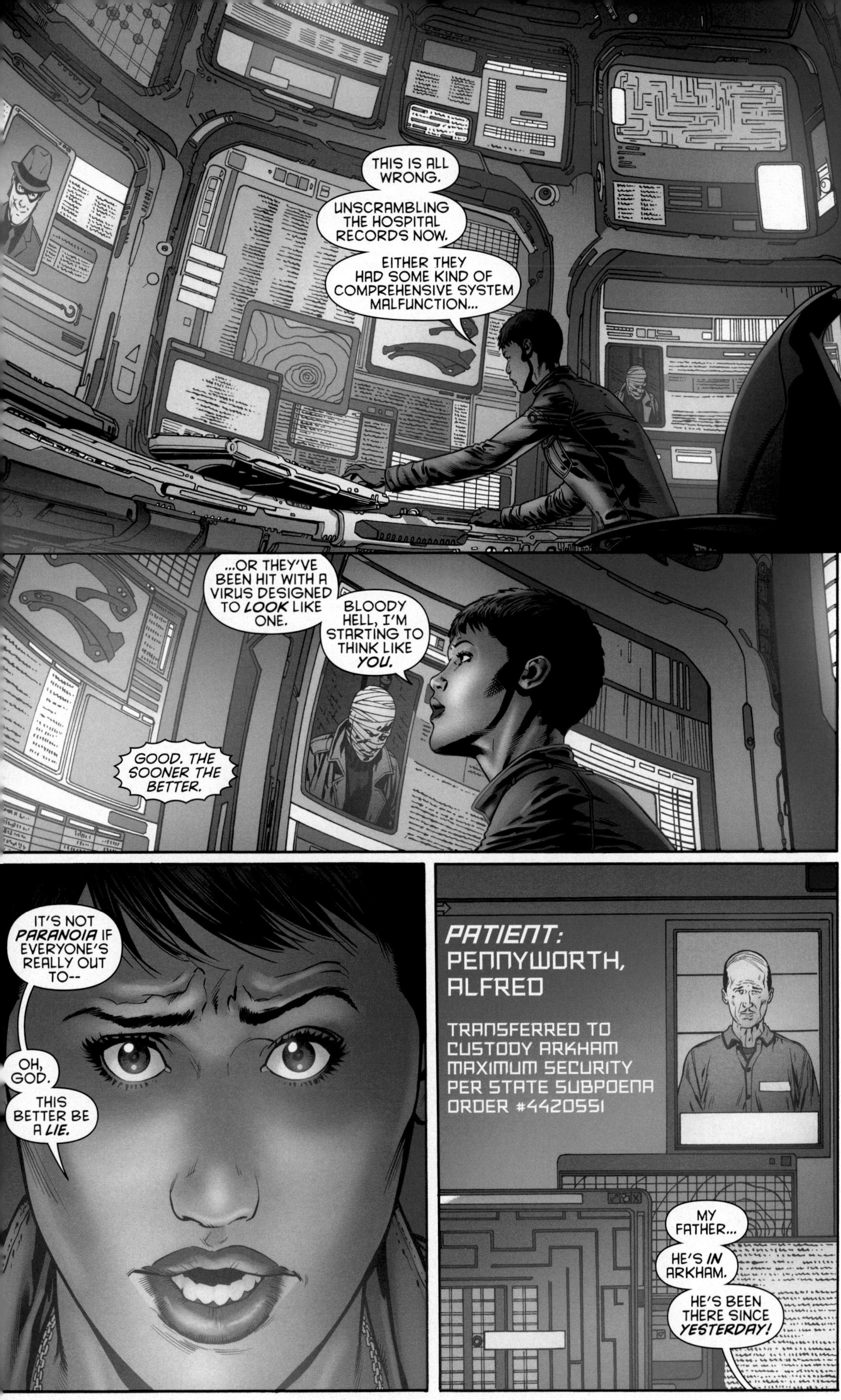
THIS IS ALL WRONG.
UNSCRAMBLING THE HOSPITAL RECORDS NOW.
EITHER THEY HAD SOME KIND OF COMPREHENSIVE SYSTEM MALFUNCTION...
...OR THEY'VE BEEN HIT WITH A VIRUS DESIGNED TO LOOK LIKE ONE.
BLOODY HELL, I'M STARTING TO THINK LIKE YOU.
GOOD. THE SOONER THE BETTER.
IT'S NOT PARANOIA IF EVERYONE'S REALLY OUT TO--
OH, GOD.
THIS BETTER BE A LIE.
PATIENT: PENNYWORTH, ALFRED
TRANSFERRED TO CUSTODY ARKHAM MAXIMUM SECURITY PER STATE SUBPOENA ORDER #4420551
MY FATHER...
HE'S IN ARKHAM.
HE'S BEEN THERE SINCE YESTERDAY!

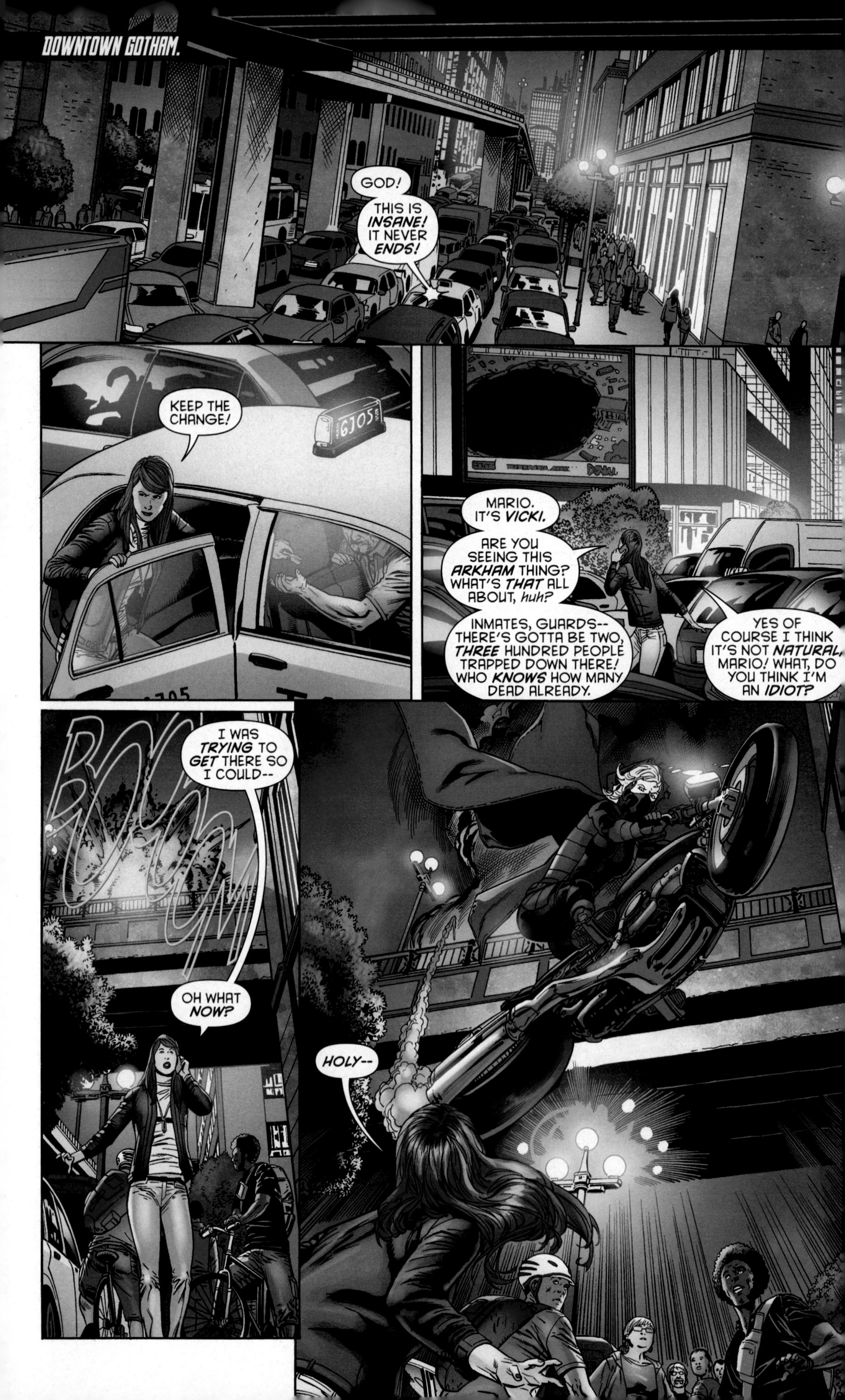
DOWNTOWN GOTHAM.
GOD!
THIS IS INSANE! IT NEVER ENDS!
KEEP THE CHANGE!
6J05
MARIO. IT'S VICKI.
ARE YOU SEEING THIS ARKHAM THING? WHAT'S THAT ALL ABOUT, huh?
INMATES, GUARDS-- THERE'S GOTTA BE TWO, THREE HUNDRED PEOPLE TRAPPED DOWN THERE! WHO KNOWS HOW MANY DEAD ALREADY.
YES OF COURSE I THINK IT'S NOT NATURAL, MARIO! WHAT, DO YOU THINK I'M AN IDIOT?
I WAS TRYING TO GET THERE SO I COULD--
BOOM
OH WHAT NOW?
HOLY--

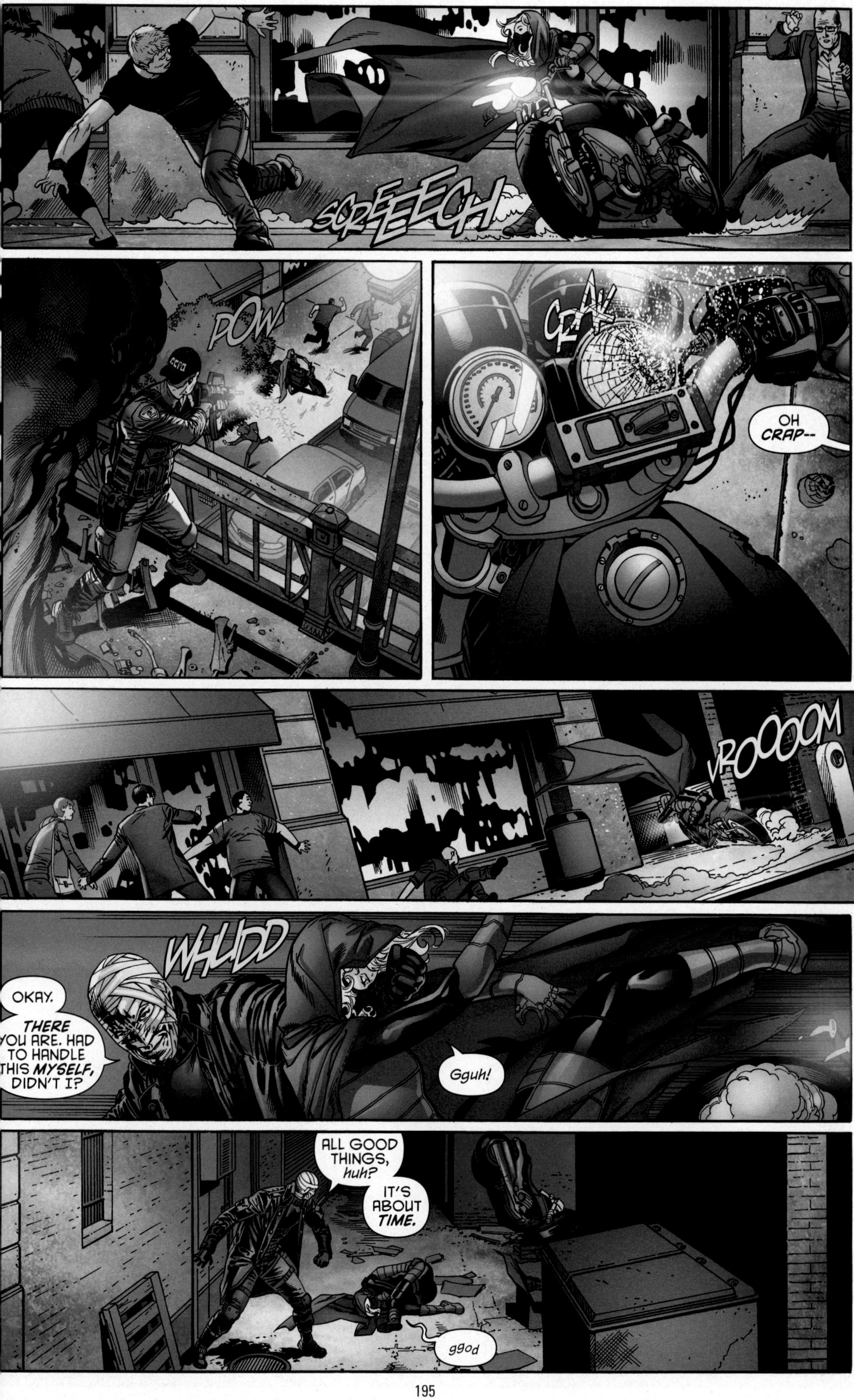
SCREEEECH
POW
CRAK
OH CRAP--
VROOOOM
WHUDD
OKAY. THERE YOU ARE. HAD TO HANDLE THIS MYSELF, DIDN'T I?
Gguh!
ALL GOOD THINGS, huh?
IT'S ABOUT TIME.
ggod

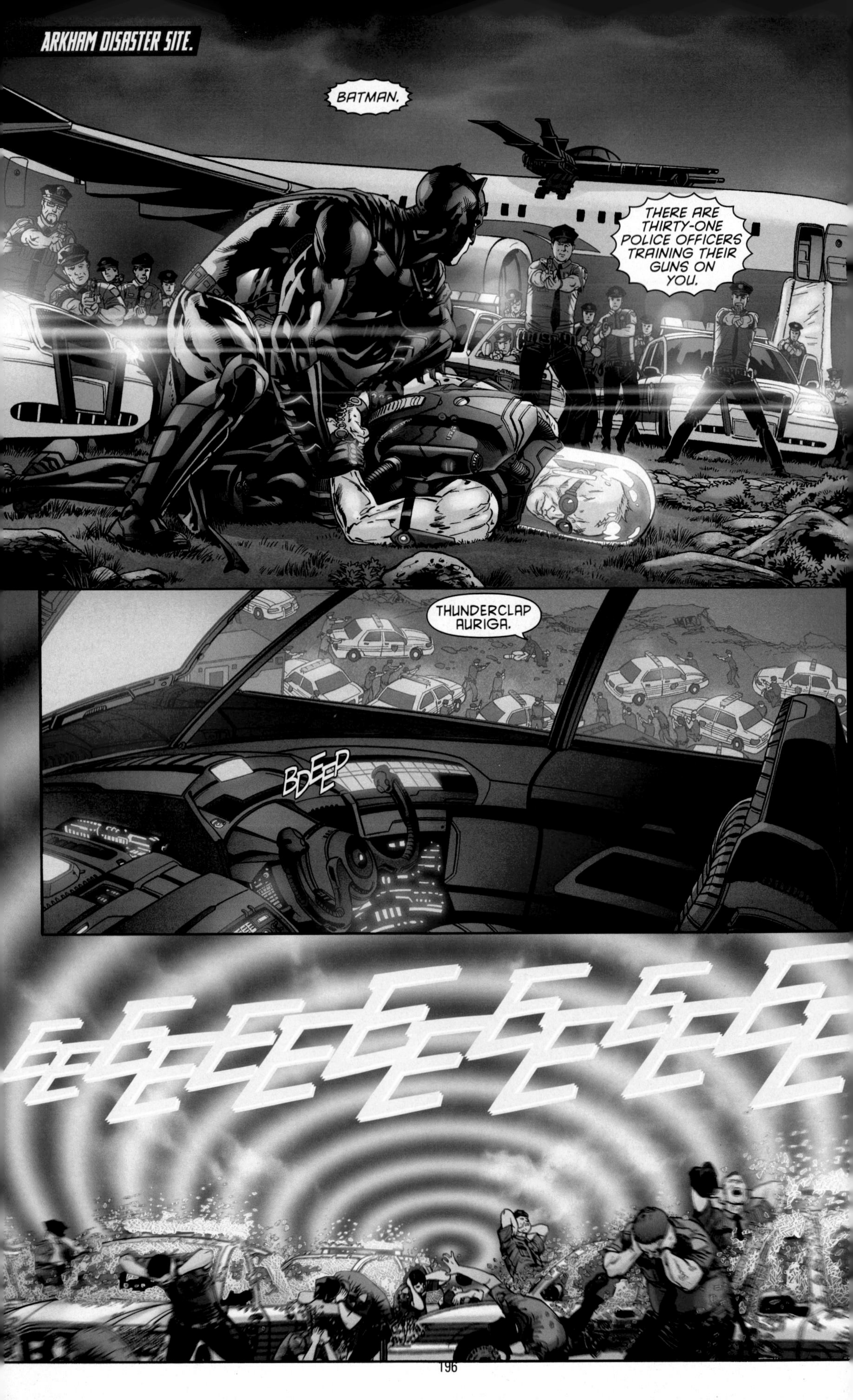
ARKHAM DISASTER SITE.
BATMAN.
THERE ARE THIRTY-ONE POLICE OFFICERS TRAINING THEIR GUNS ON YOU.
THUNDERCLAP AURIGA.
BDEEEP
EEEEEEEEEEEEEE

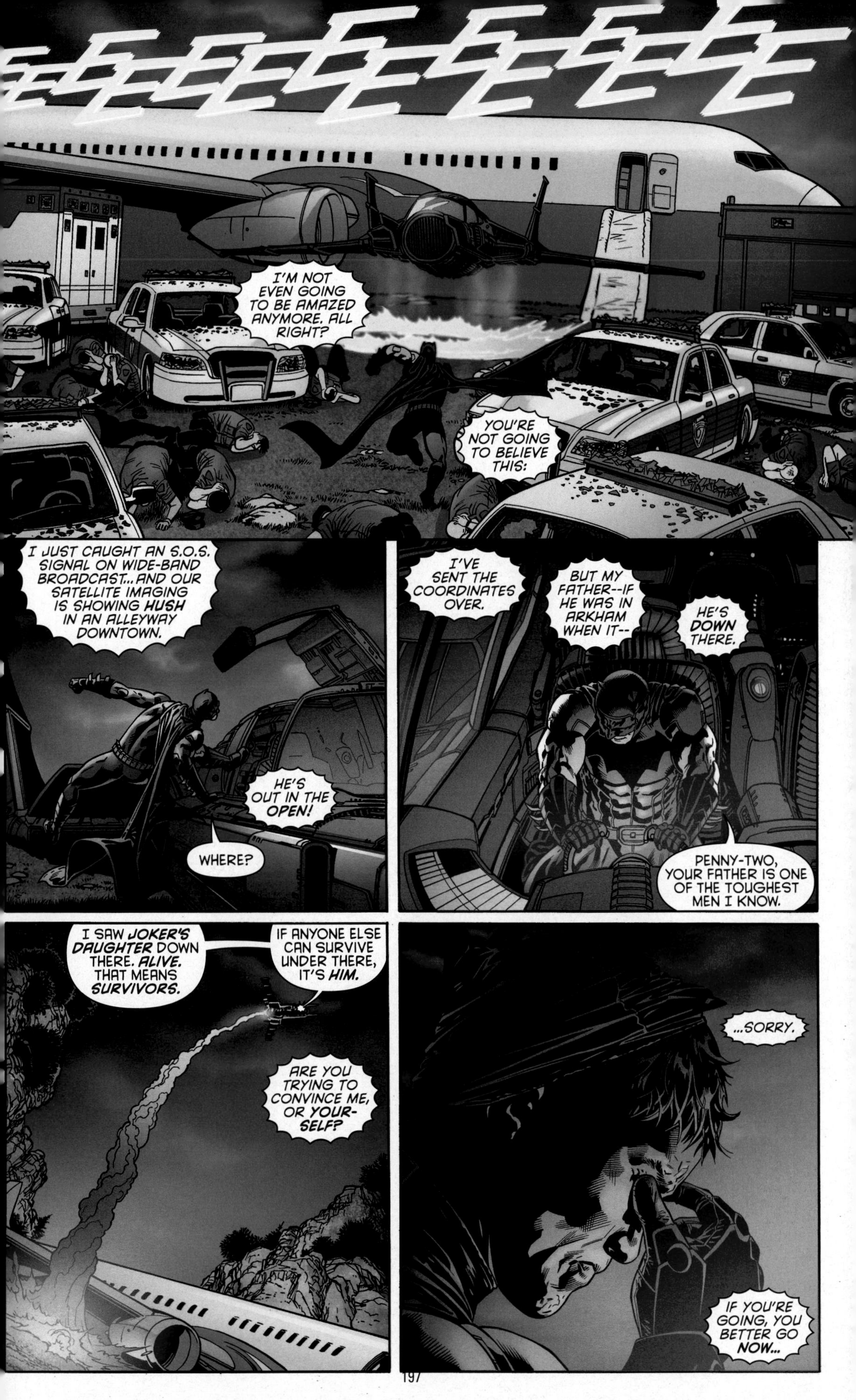
EEEEEEEEEEEEEEEEE
I'M NOT EVEN GOING TO BE AMAZED ANYMORE. ALL RIGHT?
YOU'RE NOT GOING TO BELIEVE THIS:
I JUST CAUGHT AN S.O.S. SIGNAL ON WIDE-BAND BROADCAST...AND OUR SATELLITE IMAGING IS SHOWING HUSH IN AN ALLEYWAY DOWNTOWN.
HE'S OUT IN THE OPEN!
WHERE?
I'VE SENT THE COORDINATES OVER.
BUT MY FATHER--IF HE WAS IN ARKHAM WHEN IT--
HE'S DOWN THERE.
PENNY-TWO, YOUR FATHER IS ONE OF THE TOUGHEST MEN I KNOW.
I SAW JOKER'S DAUGHTER DOWN THERE. ALIVE. THAT MEANS SURVIVORS.
IF ANYONE ELSE CAN SURVIVE UNDER THERE, IT'S HIM.
ARE YOU TRYING TO CONVINCE ME, OR YOURSELF?
...SORRY.
IF YOU'RE GOING, YOU BETTER GO NOW...

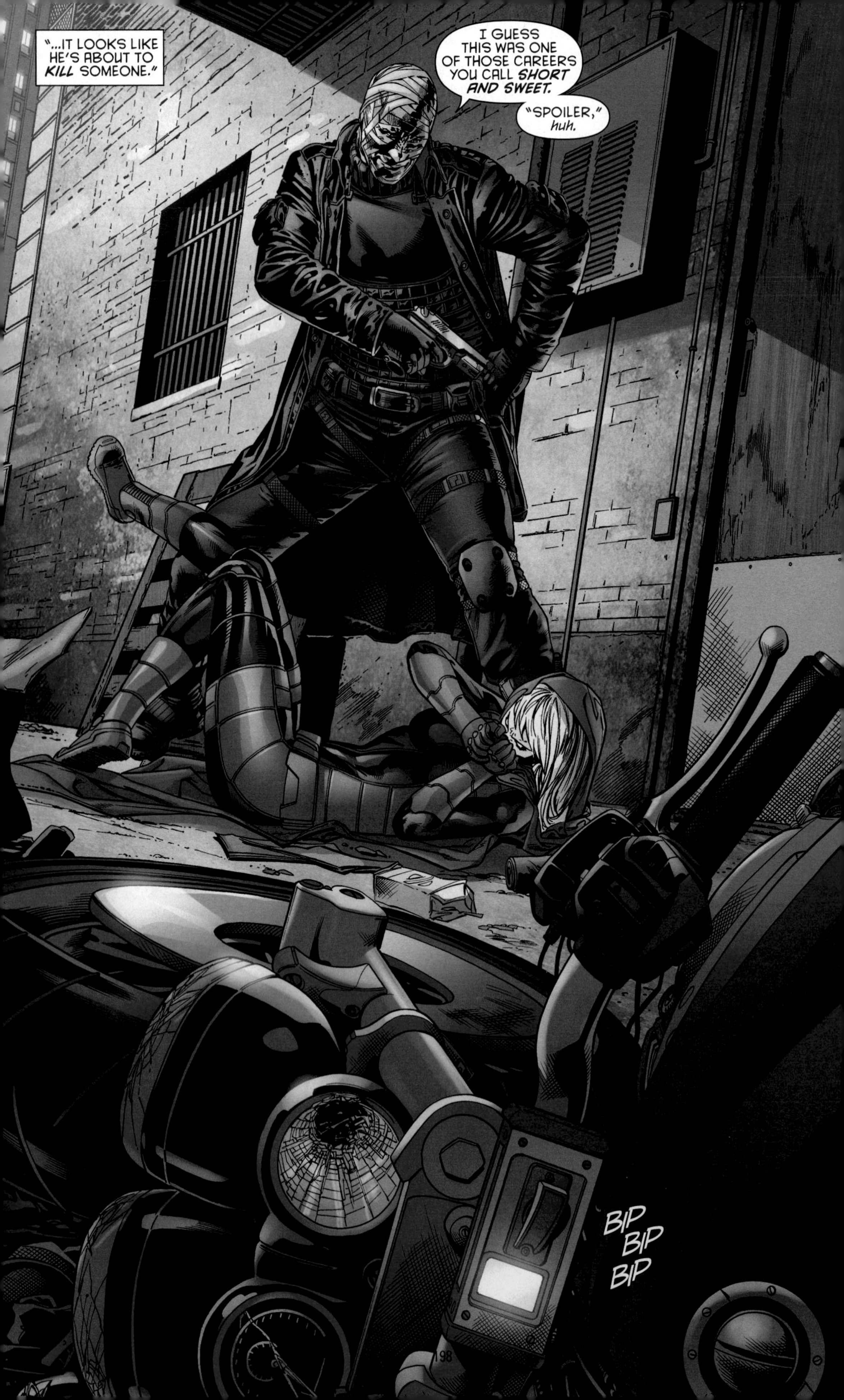
"...IT LOOKS LIKE HE'S ABOUT TO *KILL* SOMEONE."
I GUESS THIS WAS ONE OF THOSE CAREERS YOU CALL *SHORT AND SWEET.*
"SPOILER," *huh.*
BIP BIP BIP

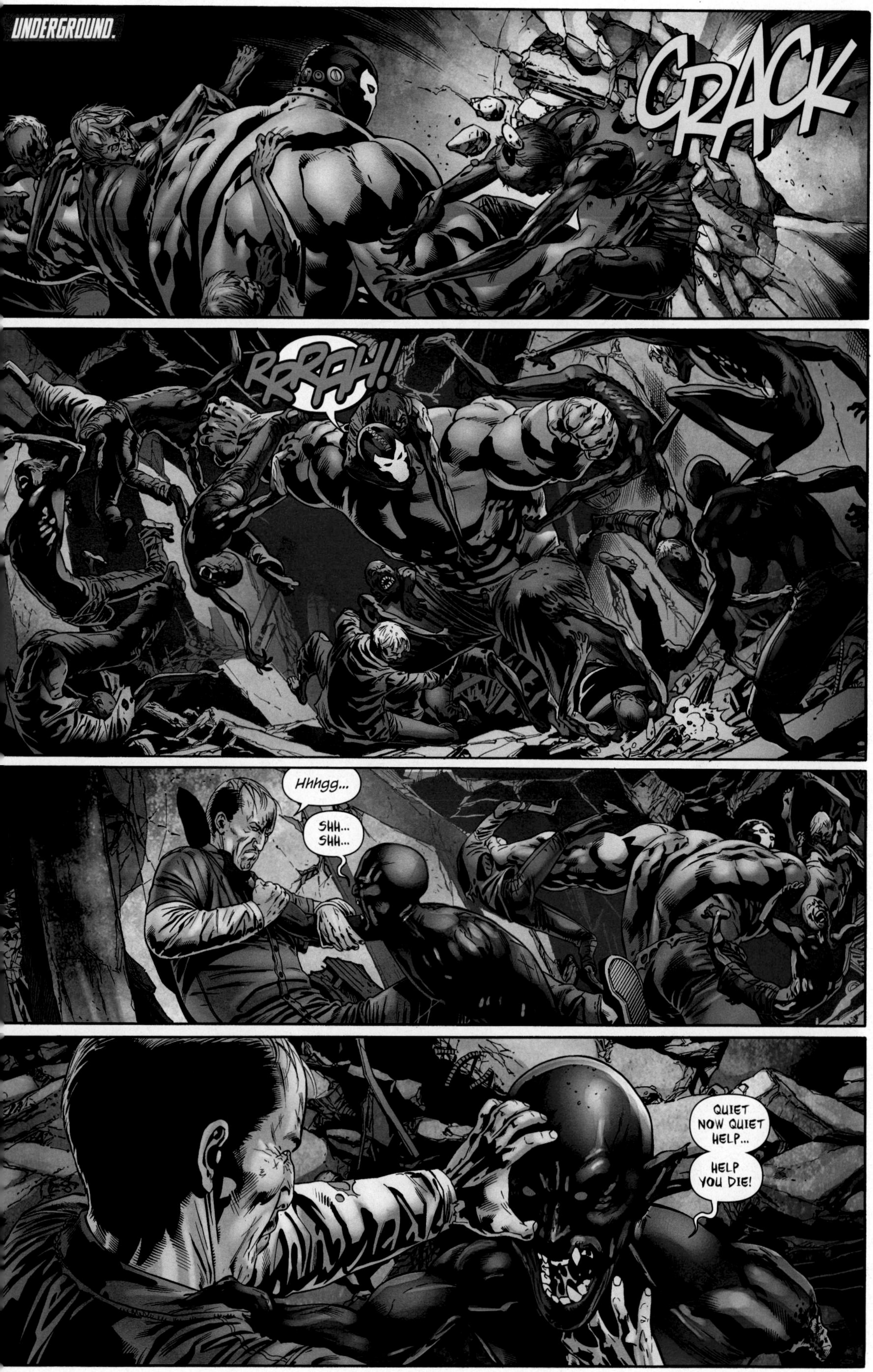

UNDERGROUND.
CRACK
RRRAAH!
Hhhgg...
SHH... SHH...
QUIET NOW QUIET HELP...
HELP YOU DIE!

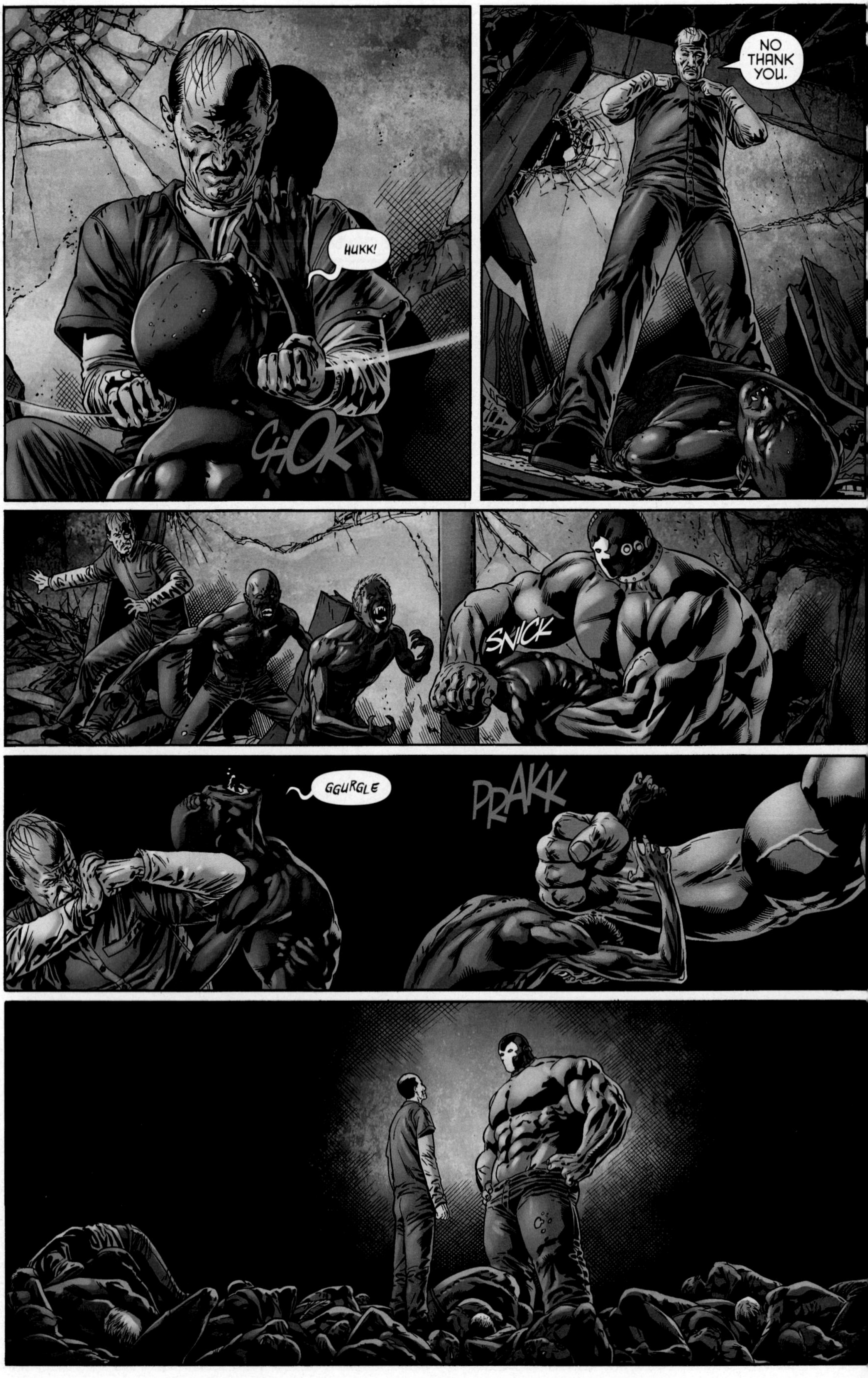
HUKK!
CHOK
NO THANK YOU.
SNICK
GGURGLE
PRAKK

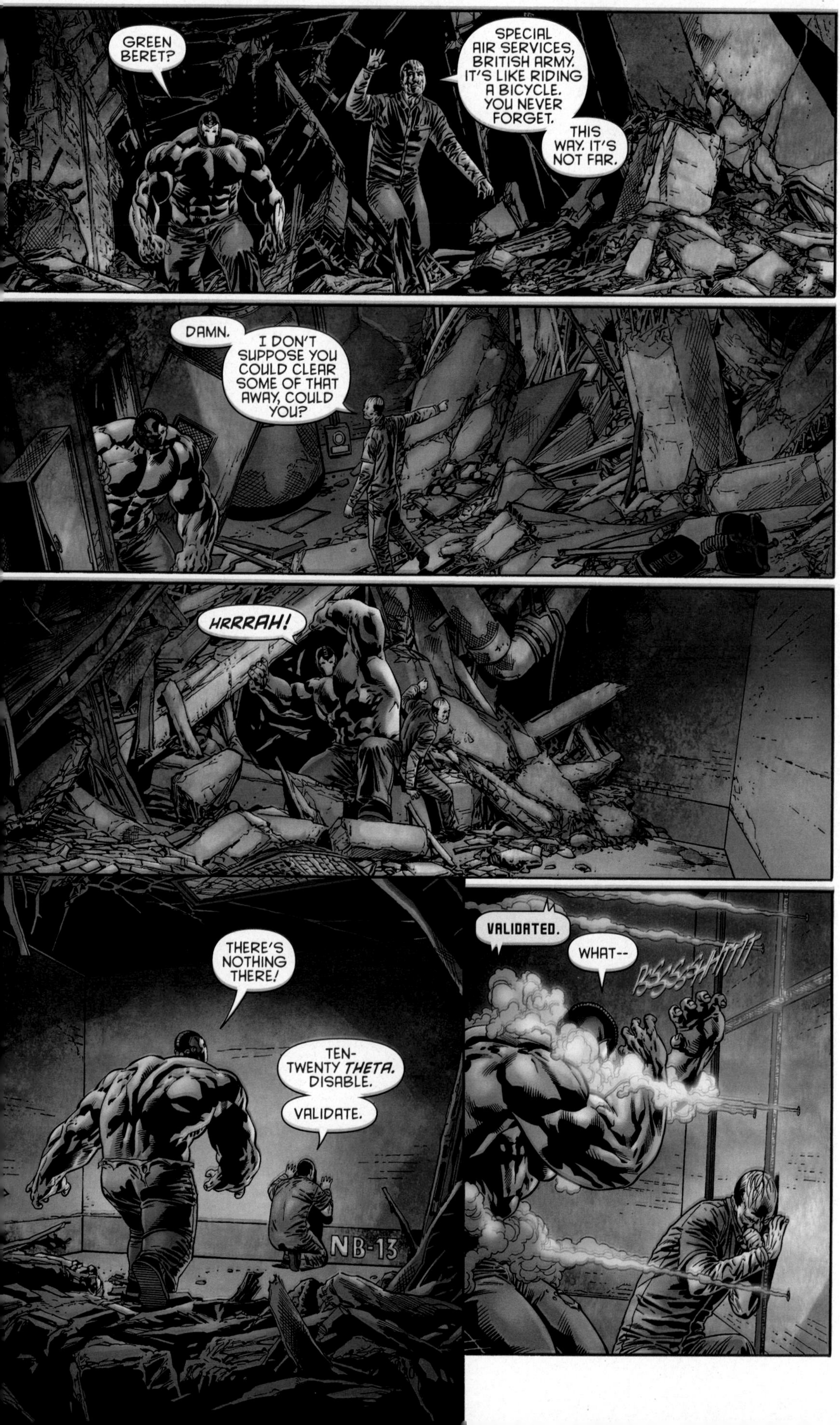
GREEN BERET?
SPECIAL AIR SERVICES, BRITISH ARMY. IT'S LIKE RIDING A BICYCLE. YOU NEVER FORGET.
THIS WAY. IT'S NOT FAR.
DAMN.
I DON'T SUPPOSE YOU COULD CLEAR SOME OF THAT AWAY, COULD YOU?
HRRRAH!
THERE'S NOTHING THERE!
TEN-TWENTY THETA. DISABLE.
VALIDATE.
NB-13
VALIDATED.
WHAT--

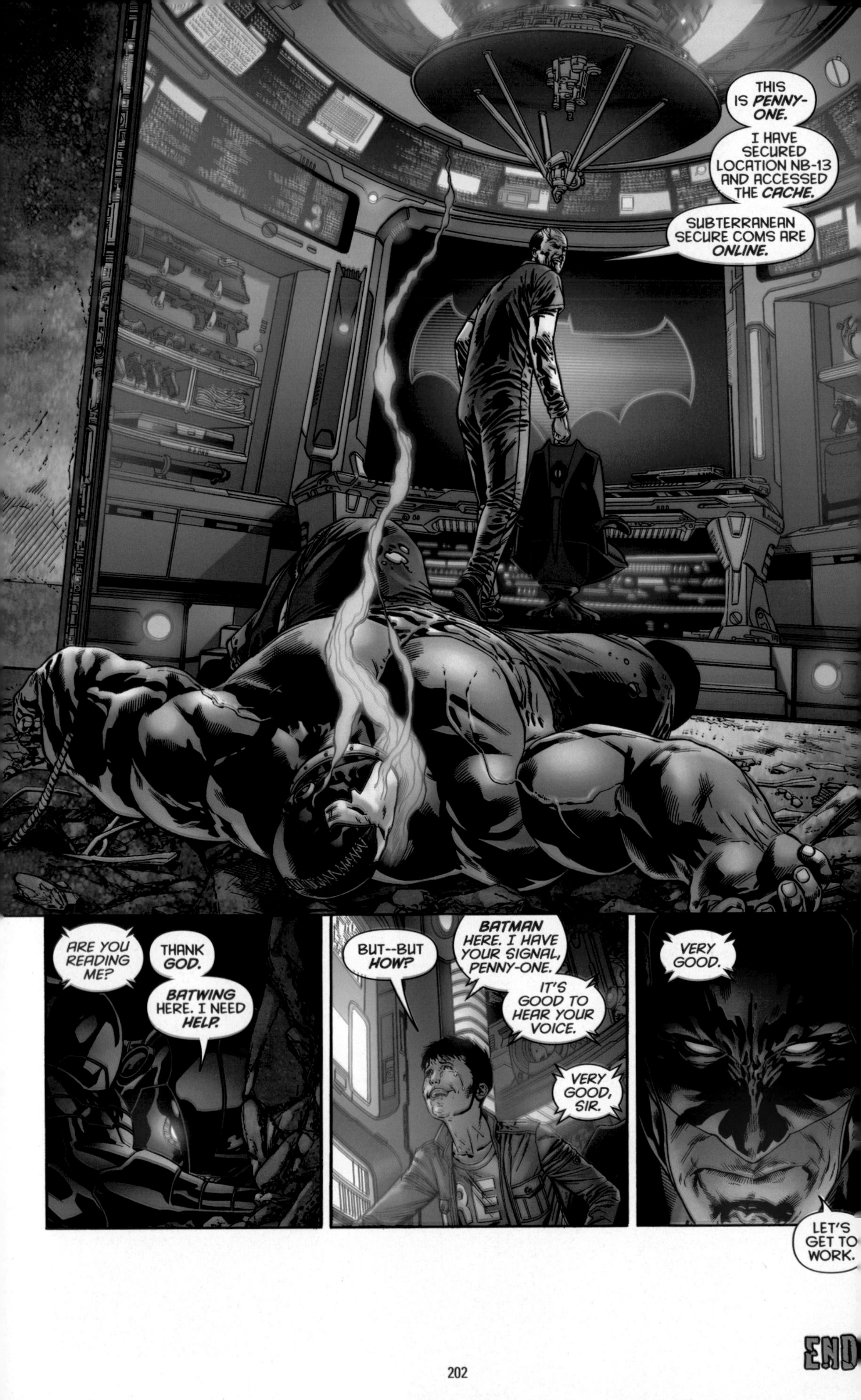
THIS IS PENNY-ONE.
I HAVE SECURED LOCATION NB-13 AND ACCESSED THE CACHE.
SUBTERRANEAN SECURE COMS ARE ONLINE.
ARE YOU READING ME?
THANK GOD.
BATWING HERE. I NEED HELP.
BUT--BUT HOW?
BATMAN HERE. I HAVE YOUR SIGNAL, PENNY-ONE.
IT'S GOOD TO HEAR YOUR VOICE.
VERY GOOD, SIR.
VERY GOOD.
LET'S GET TO WORK.
END

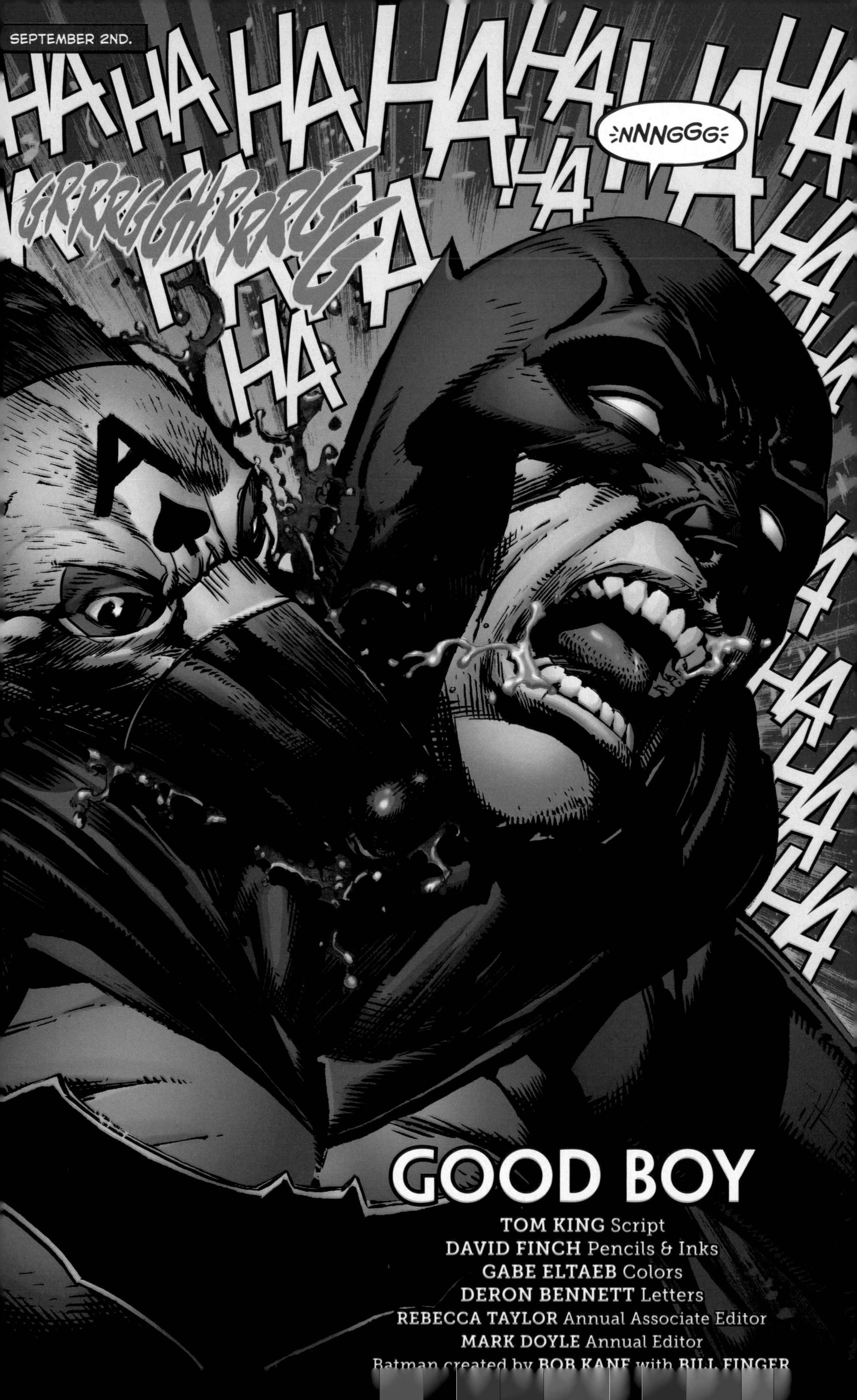
SEPTEMBER 2ND.
NNNGGG
GOOD BOY
TOM KING Script
DAVID FINCH Pencils & Inks
GABE ELTAEB Colors
DERON BENNETT Letters
REBECCA TAYLOR Annual Associate Editor
MARK DOYLE Annual Editor
Batman created by BOB KANE with BILL FINGER

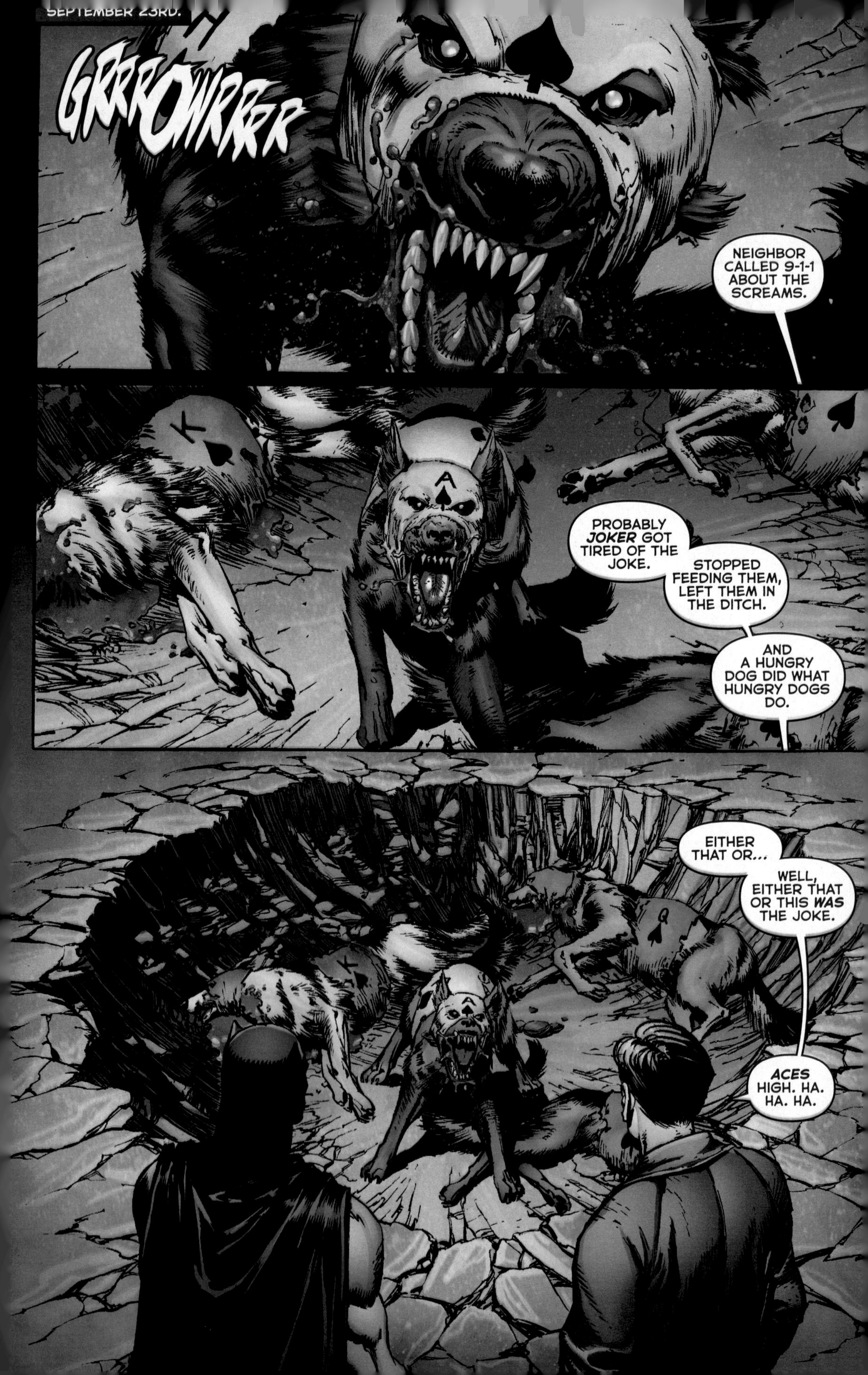
SEPTEMBER 23RD.
GRRROWRRRR
NEIGHBOR CALLED 9-1-1 ABOUT THE SCREAMS.
PROBABLY JOKER GOT TIRED OF THE JOKE.
STOPPED FEEDING THEM, LEFT THEM IN THE DITCH.
AND A HUNGRY DOG DID WHAT HUNGRY DOGS DO.
EITHER THAT OR...
WELL, EITHER THAT OR THIS WAS THE JOKE.
ACES HIGH. HA. HA. HA.

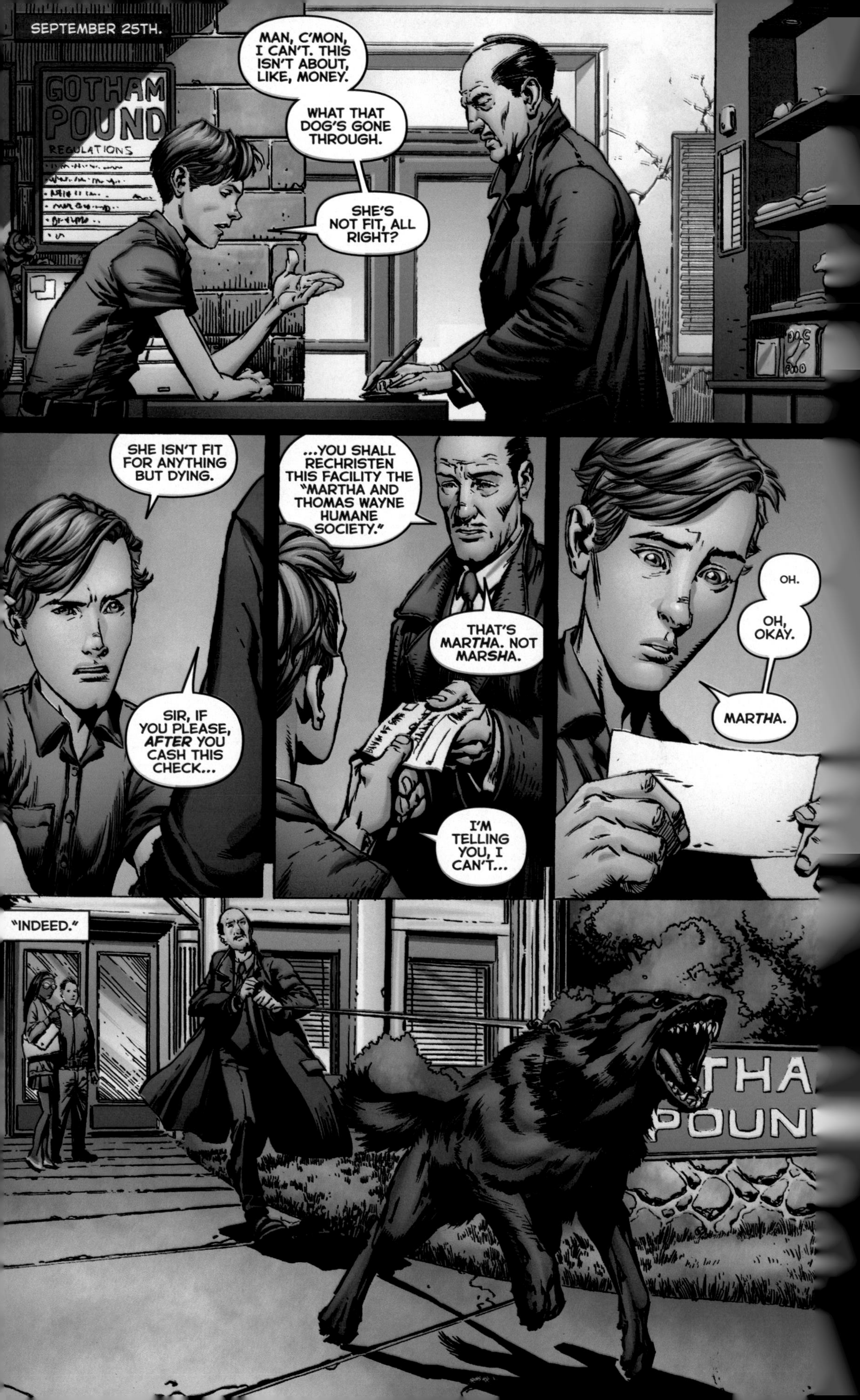

SEPTEMBER 25TH.
MAN, C'MON, I CAN'T. THIS ISN'T ABOUT, LIKE, MONEY.
WHAT THAT DOG'S GONE THROUGH.
SHE'S NOT FIT, ALL RIGHT?
GOTHAM POUND
REGULATIONS
SHE ISN'T FIT FOR ANYTHING BUT DYING.
SIR, IF YOU PLEASE, *AFTER* YOU CASH THIS CHECK...
...YOU SHALL RECHRISTEN THIS FACILITY THE "MARTHA AND THOMAS WAYNE HUMANE SOCIETY."
THAT'S MAR*THA*. NOT MAR*SHA*.
I'M TELLING YOU, I CAN'T...
OH.
OH, OKAY.
MAR*THA*.
"INDEED."

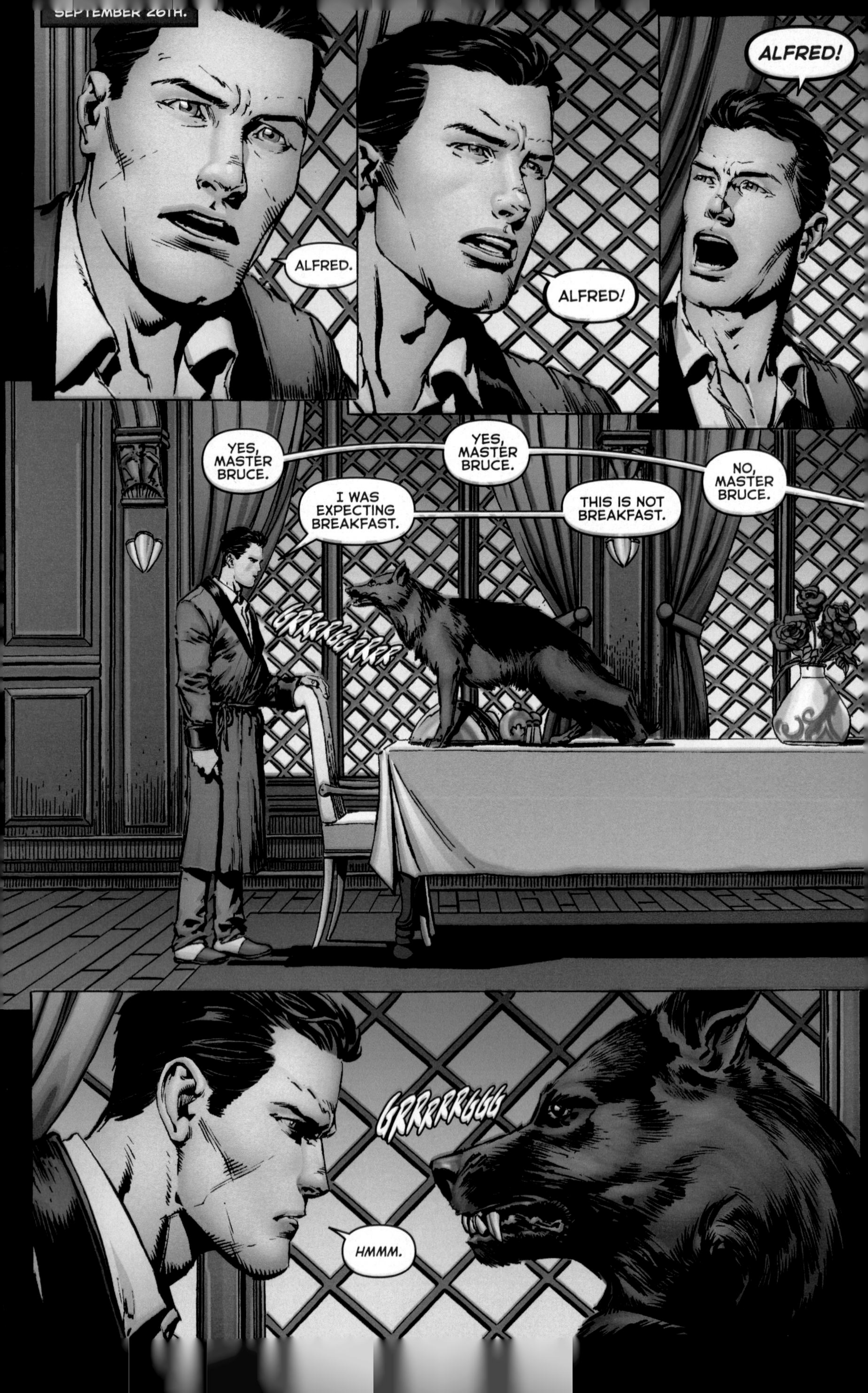
SEPTEMBER 26TH.
ALFRED.
ALFRED!
ALFRED!
YES, MASTER BRUCE.
I WAS EXPECTING BREAKFAST.
YES, MASTER BRUCE.
THIS IS NOT BREAKFAST.
NO, MASTER BRUCE.
GRRRRGGRRRR
GRRRRRGGG
HMMM.

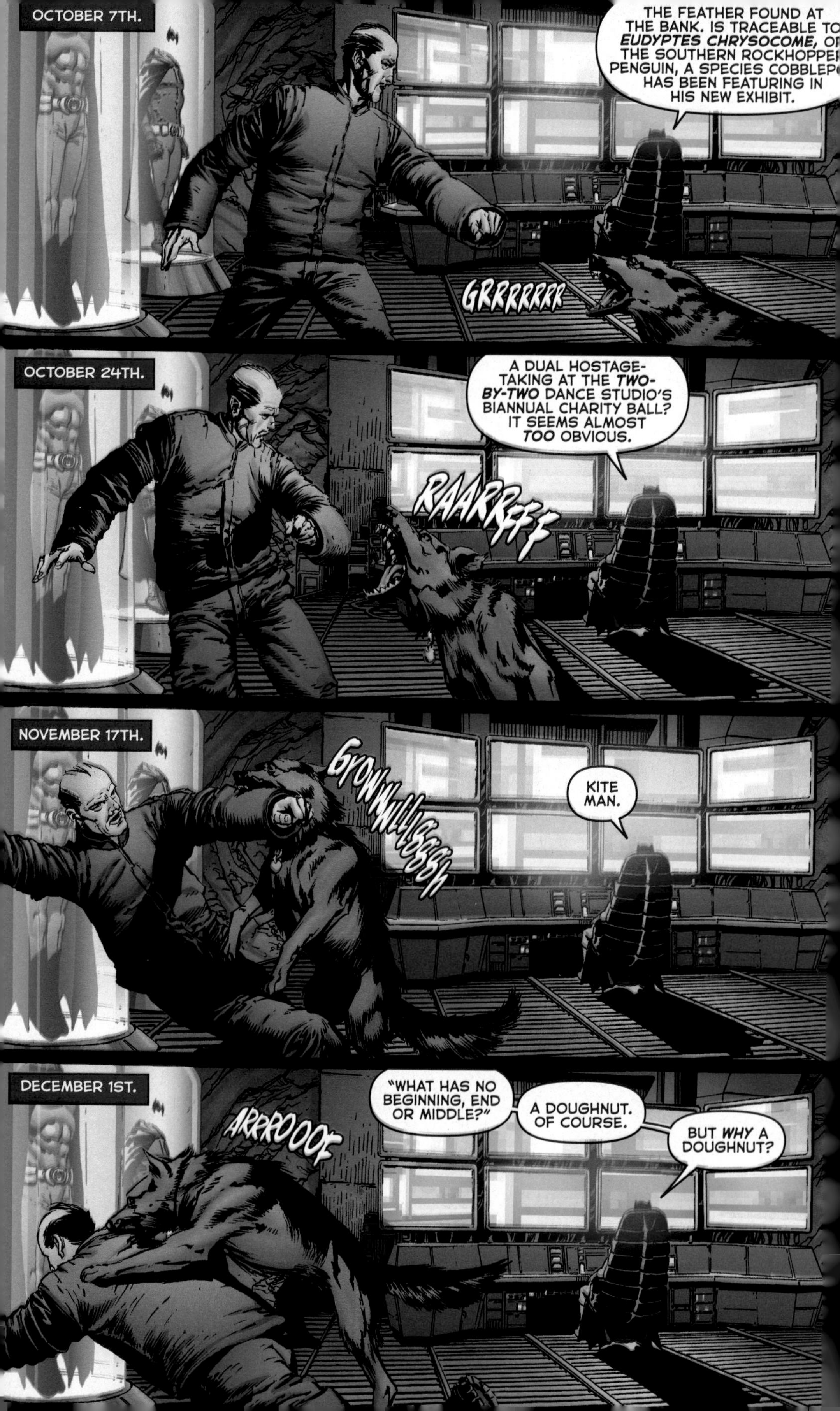
OCTOBER 7TH.
THE FEATHER FOUND AT THE BANK. IS TRACEABLE TO *EUDYPTES CHRYSOCOME,* O THE SOUTHERN ROCKHOPPER PENGUIN, A SPECIES COBBLEP HAS BEEN FEATURING IN HIS NEW EXHIBIT.
GRRRRRRR
OCTOBER 24TH.
A DUAL HOSTAGE-TAKING AT THE *TWO-BY-TWO* DANCE STUDIO'S BIANNUAL CHARITY BALL? IT SEEMS ALMOST *TOO* OBVIOUS.
RAARRFFF
NOVEMBER 17TH.
GROWWLLLGGGH
KITE MAN.
DECEMBER 1ST.
ARRROOOF
"WHAT HAS NO BEGINNING, END OR MIDDLE?"
A DOUGHNUT. OF COURSE.
BUT *WHY* A DOUGHNUT?

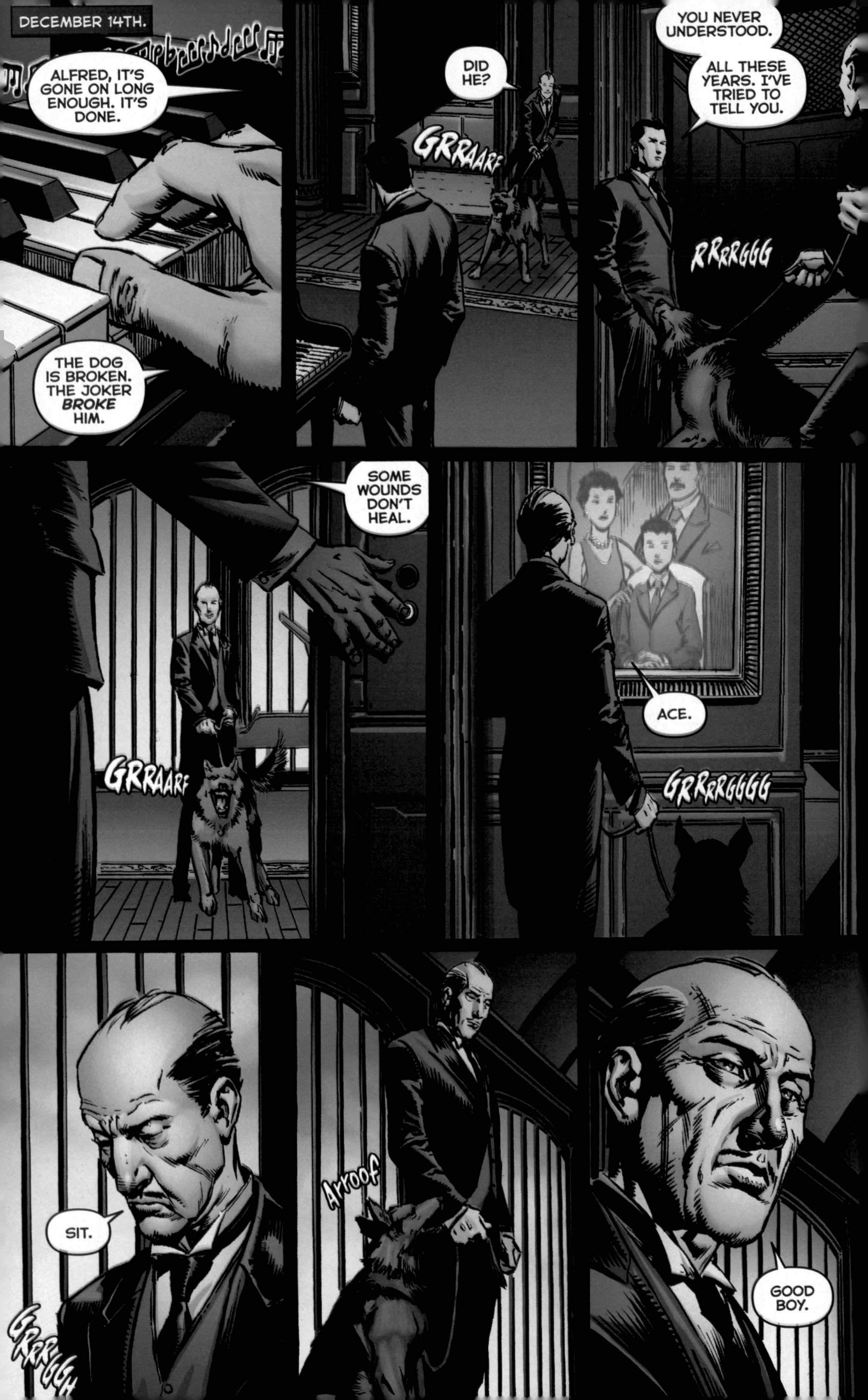

DECEMBER 14TH.
ALFRED, IT'S GONE ON LONG ENOUGH. IT'S DONE.
THE DOG IS BROKEN. THE JOKER *BROKE* HIM.
DID HE?
GRRAARF
YOU NEVER UNDERSTOOD.
ALL THESE YEARS. I'VE TRIED TO TELL YOU.
RRRRGGG
SOME WOUNDS DON'T HEAL.
GRRAARF
ACE.
GRRRRGGGG
SIT.
GRRRGGH
ARROOF
GOOD BOY.

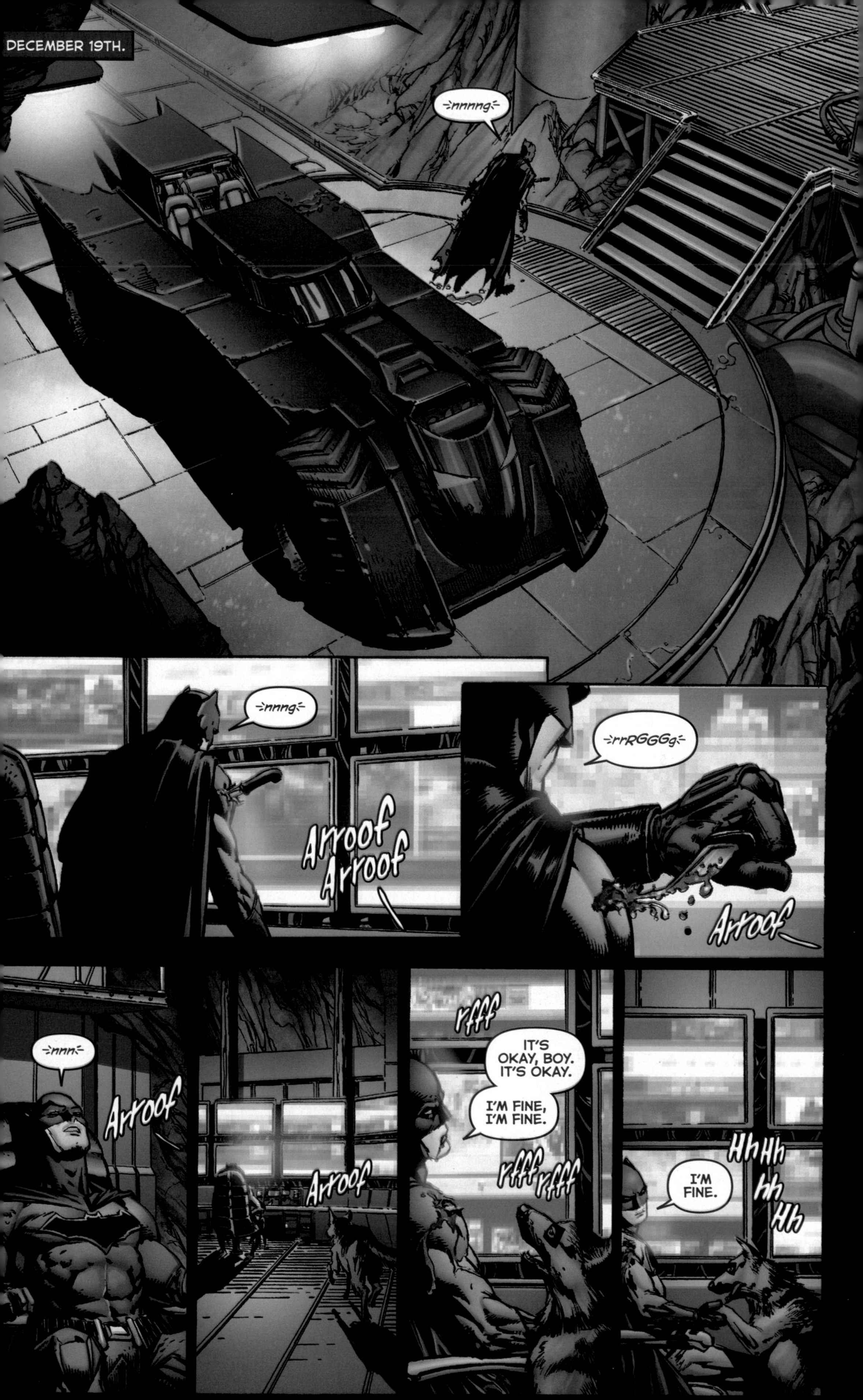
DECEMBER 19TH.
nnnng
nnng
Arroof
Arroof
rrRGGGg
Arroof
nnn
Arroof
Arroof
rfff
IT'S OKAY, BOY. IT'S OKAY.
I'M FINE, I'M FINE.
rfff rfff
I'M FINE.
Hh Hh
hh
Hh

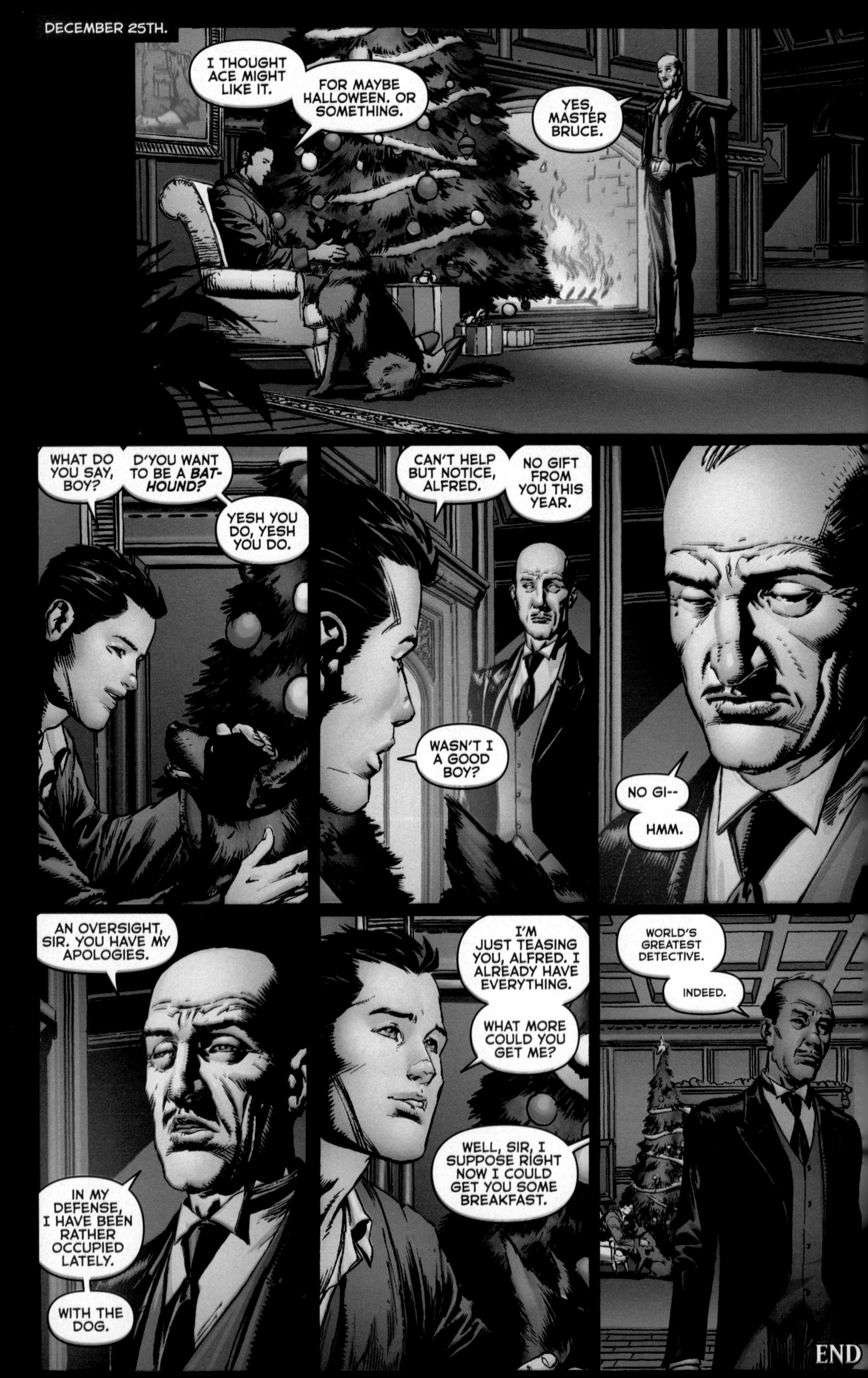
DECEMBER 25TH.
I THOUGHT ACE MIGHT LIKE IT.
FOR MAYBE HALLOWEEN. OR SOMETHING.
YES, MASTER BRUCE.
WHAT DO YOU SAY, BOY?
D'YOU WANT TO BE A *BAT-HOUND?*
YESH YOU DO, YESH YOU DO.
CAN'T HELP BUT NOTICE, ALFRED.
NO GIFT FROM YOU THIS YEAR.
WASN'T I A GOOD BOY?
NO GI--
HMM.
AN OVERSIGHT, SIR. YOU HAVE MY APOLOGIES.
IN MY DEFENSE, I HAVE BEEN RATHER OCCUPIED LATELY.
WITH THE DOG.
I'M JUST TEASING YOU, ALFRED. I ALREADY HAVE EVERYTHING.
WHAT MORE COULD YOU GET ME?
WELL, SIR, I SUPPOSE RIGHT NOW I COULD GET YOU SOME BREAKFAST.
WORLD'S GREATEST DETECTIVE.
INDEED.
END

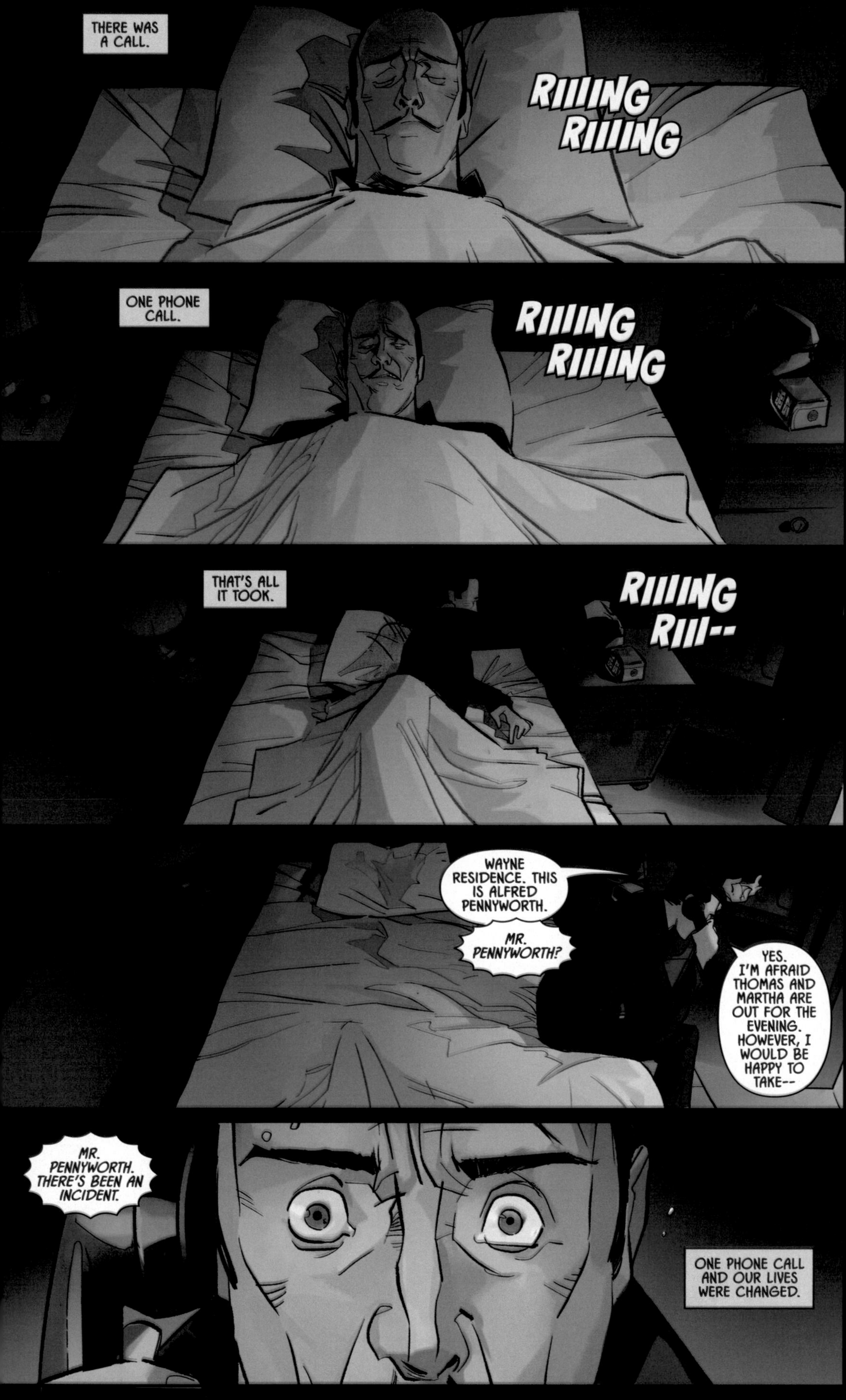

THERE WAS A CALL.
RIIIING RIIIING
ONE PHONE CALL.
RIIIING RIIIING
THAT'S ALL IT TOOK.
RIIIING RIII--
WAYNE RESIDENCE. THIS IS ALFRED PENNYWORTH.
MR. PENNYWORTH?
YES. I'M AFRAID THOMAS AND MARTHA ARE OUT FOR THE EVENING. HOWEVER, I WOULD BE HAPPY TO TAKE--
MR. PENNYWORTH. THERE'S BEEN AN INCIDENT.
ONE PHONE CALL AND OUR LIVES WERE CHANGED.

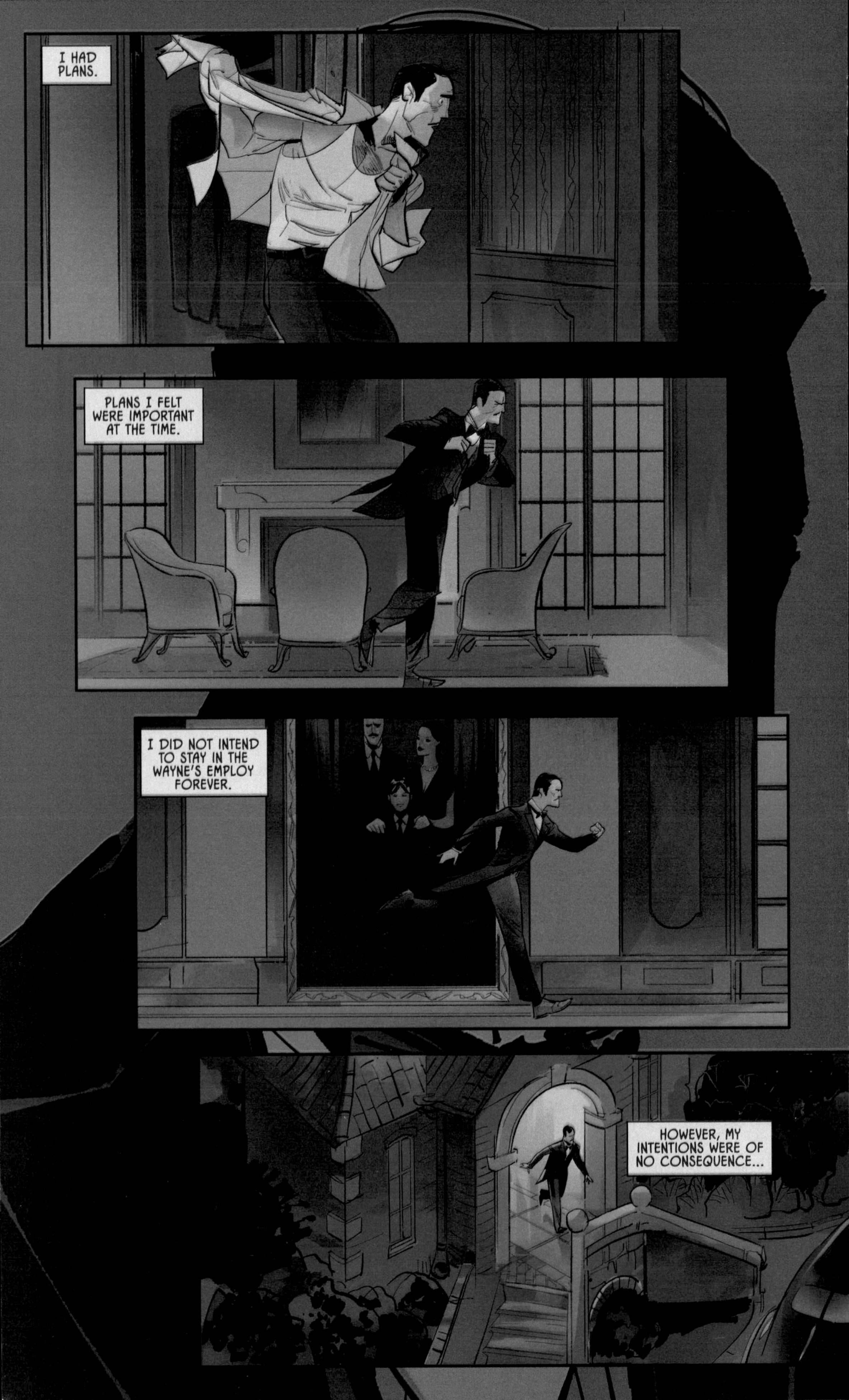
I HAD PLANS.
PLANS I FELT WERE IMPORTANT AT THE TIME.
I DID NOT INTEND TO STAY IN THE WAYNE'S EMPLOY FOREVER.
HOWEVER, MY INTENTIONS WERE OF NO CONSEQUENCE...

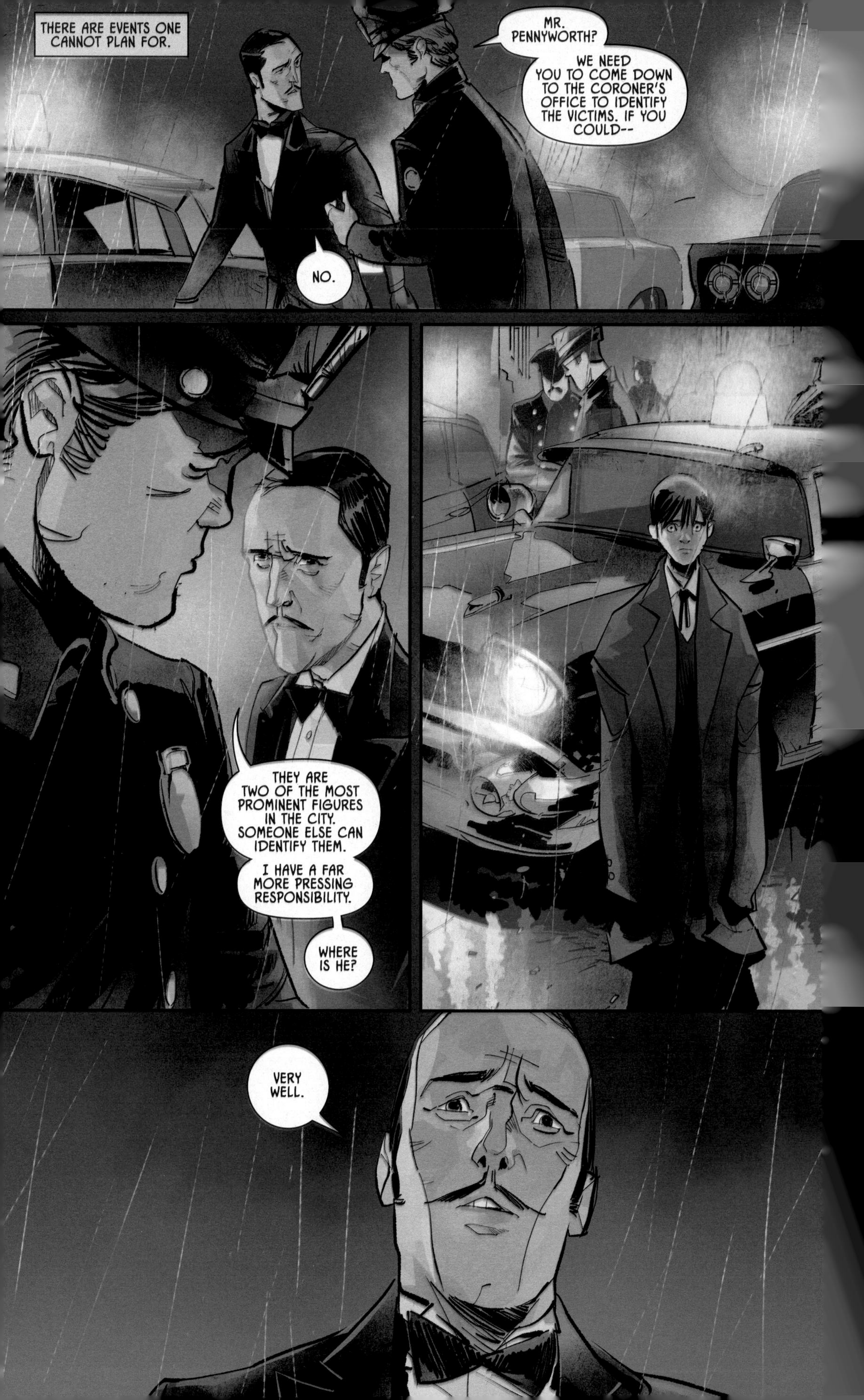
THERE ARE EVENTS ONE CANNOT PLAN FOR.
MR. PENNYWORTH?
WE NEED YOU TO COME DOWN TO THE CORONER'S OFFICE TO IDENTIFY THE VICTIMS. IF YOU COULD--
NO.
THEY ARE TWO OF THE MOST PROMINENT FIGURES IN THE CITY. SOMEONE ELSE CAN IDENTIFY THEM.
I HAVE A FAR MORE PRESSING RESPONSIBILITY.
WHERE IS HE?
VERY WELL.

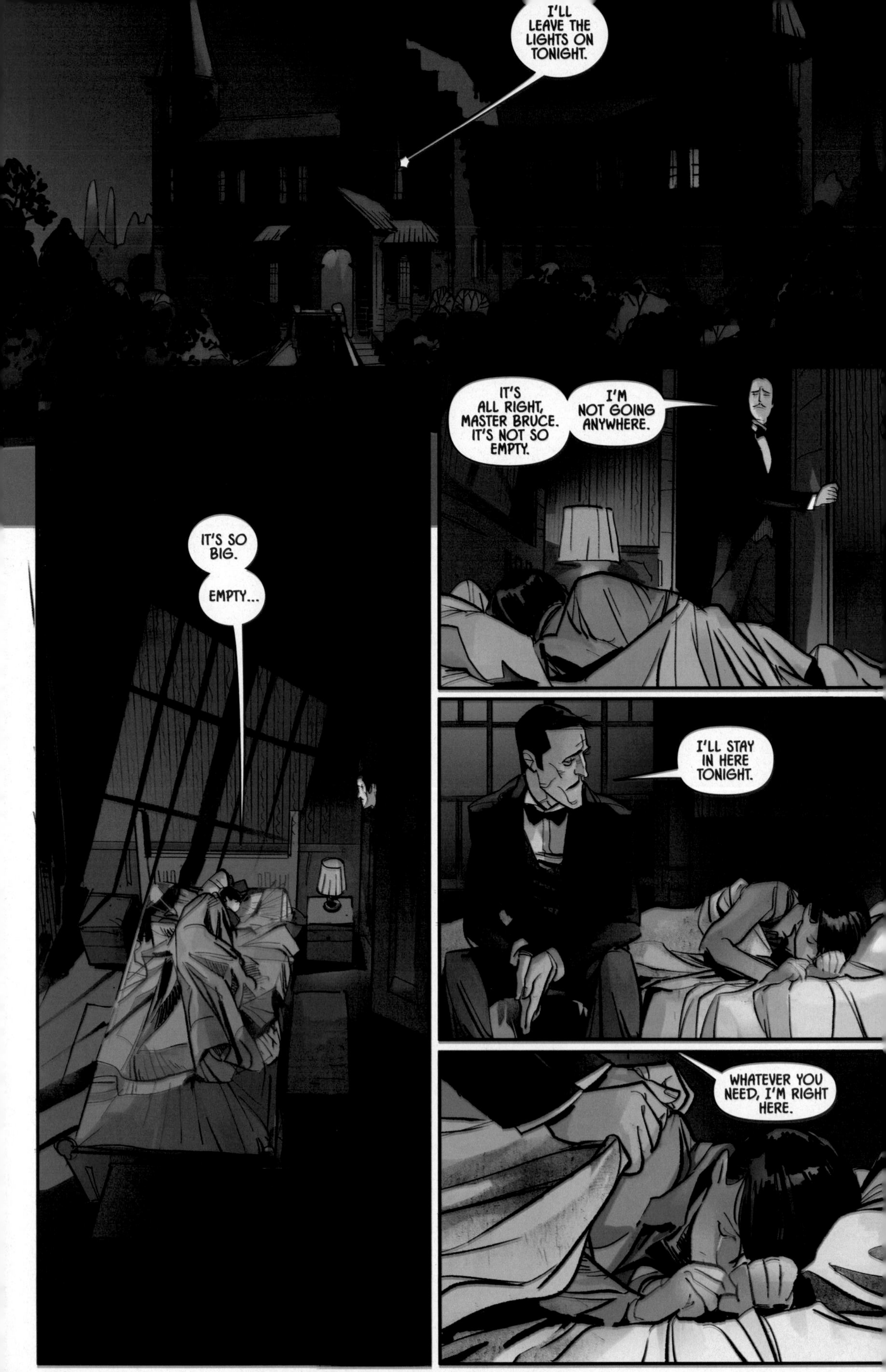
I'LL LEAVE THE LIGHTS ON TONIGHT.
IT'S SO BIG.
EMPTY...
IT'S ALL RIGHT, MASTER BRUCE. IT'S NOT SO EMPTY.
I'M NOT GOING ANYWHERE.
I'LL STAY IN HERE TONIGHT.
WHATEVER YOU NEED, I'M RIGHT HERE.

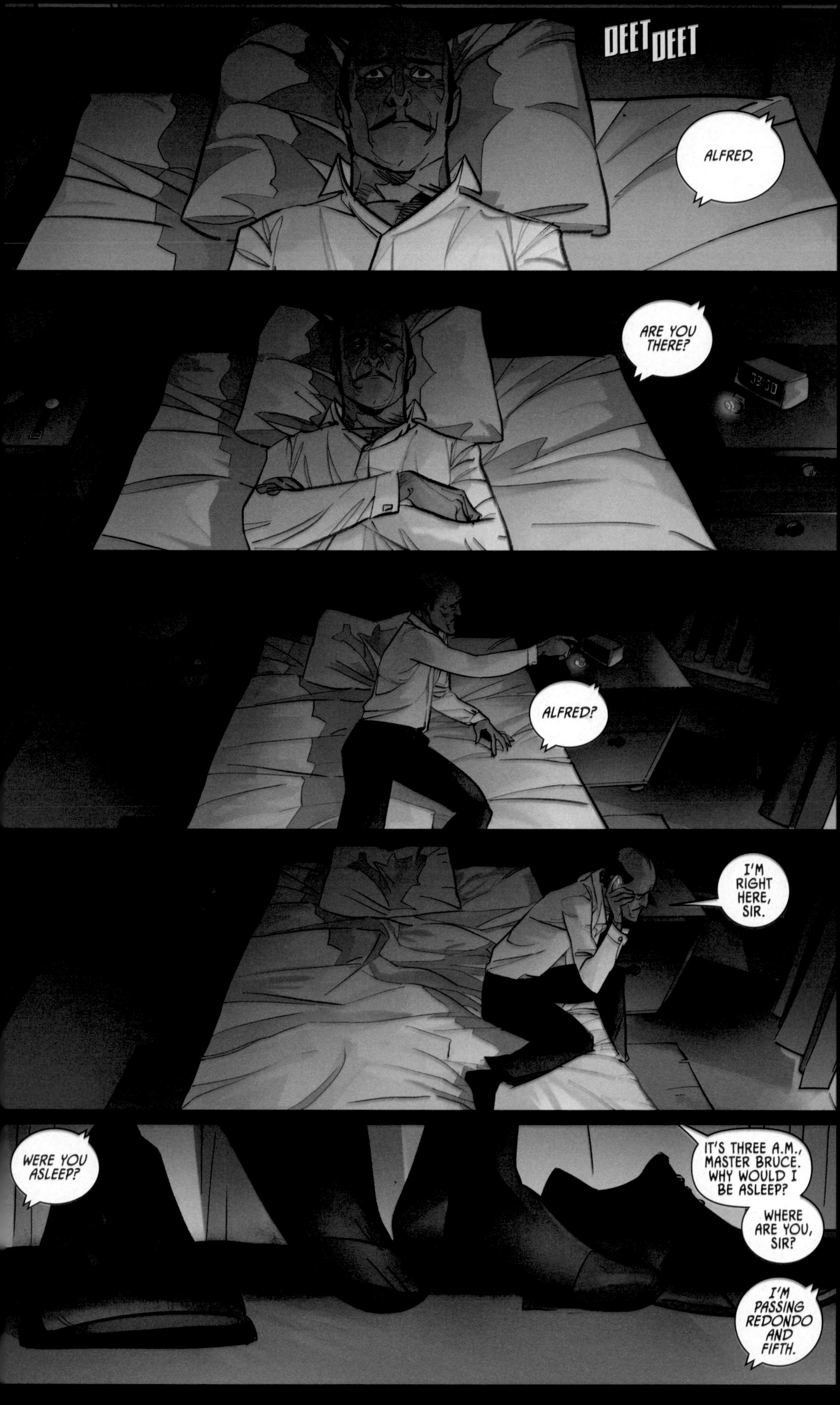
DEET DEET
ALFRED.
ARE YOU THERE?
ALFRED?
I'M RIGHT HERE, SIR.
WERE YOU ASLEEP?
IT'S THREE A.M., MASTER BRUCE. WHY WOULD I BE ASLEEP?
WHERE ARE YOU, SIR?
I'M PASSING REDONDO AND FIFTH.

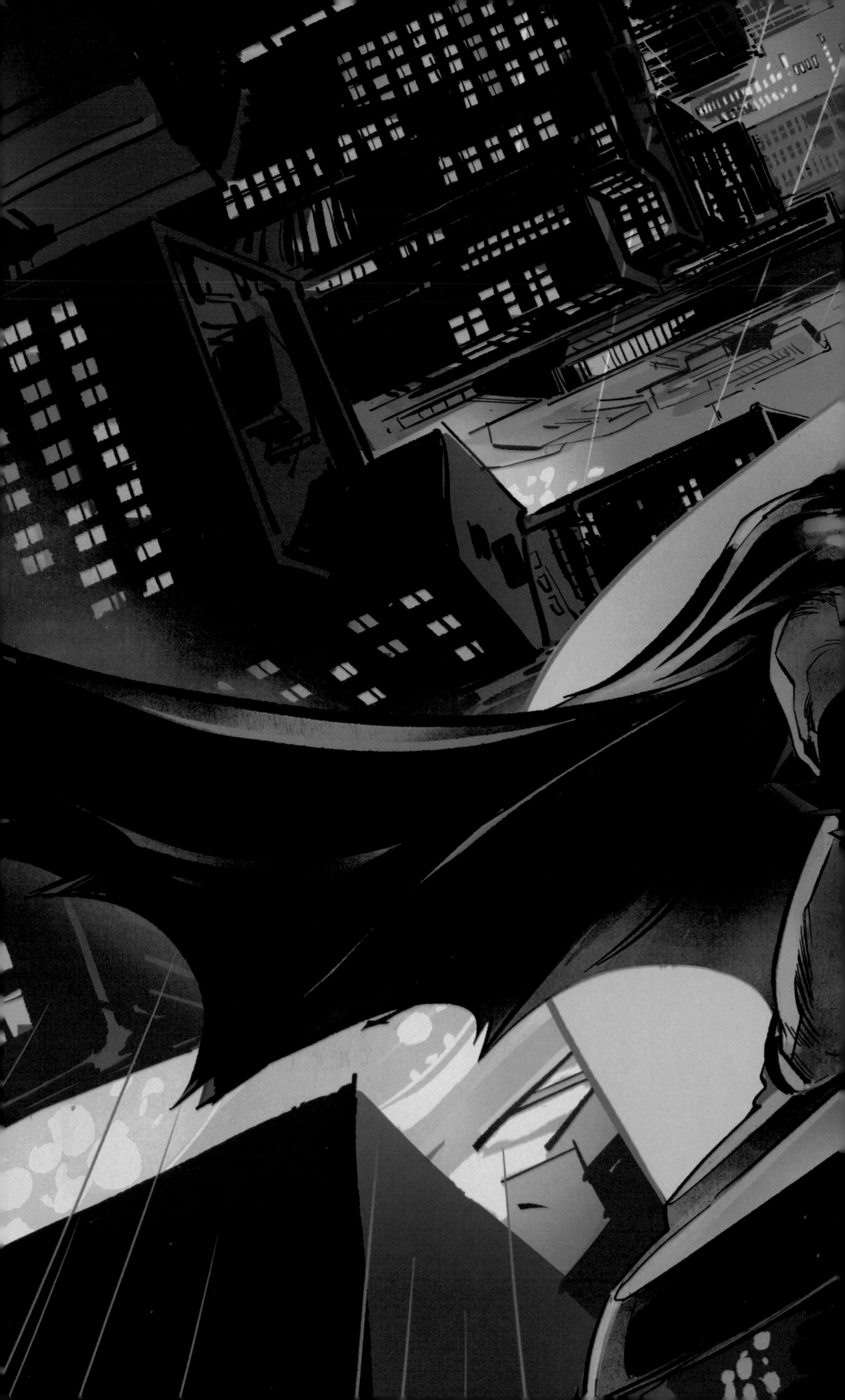

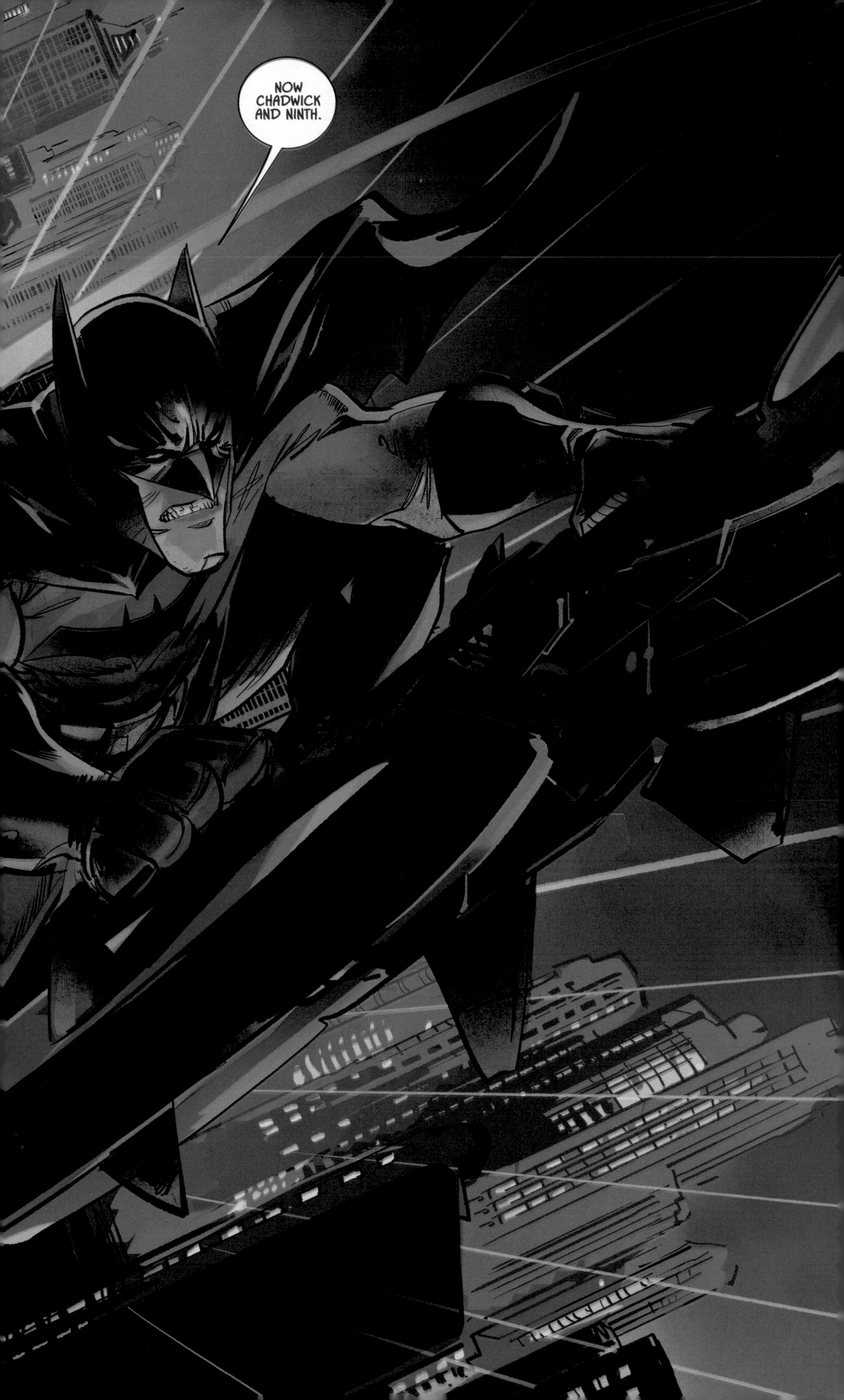
NOW CHADWICK AND NINTH.

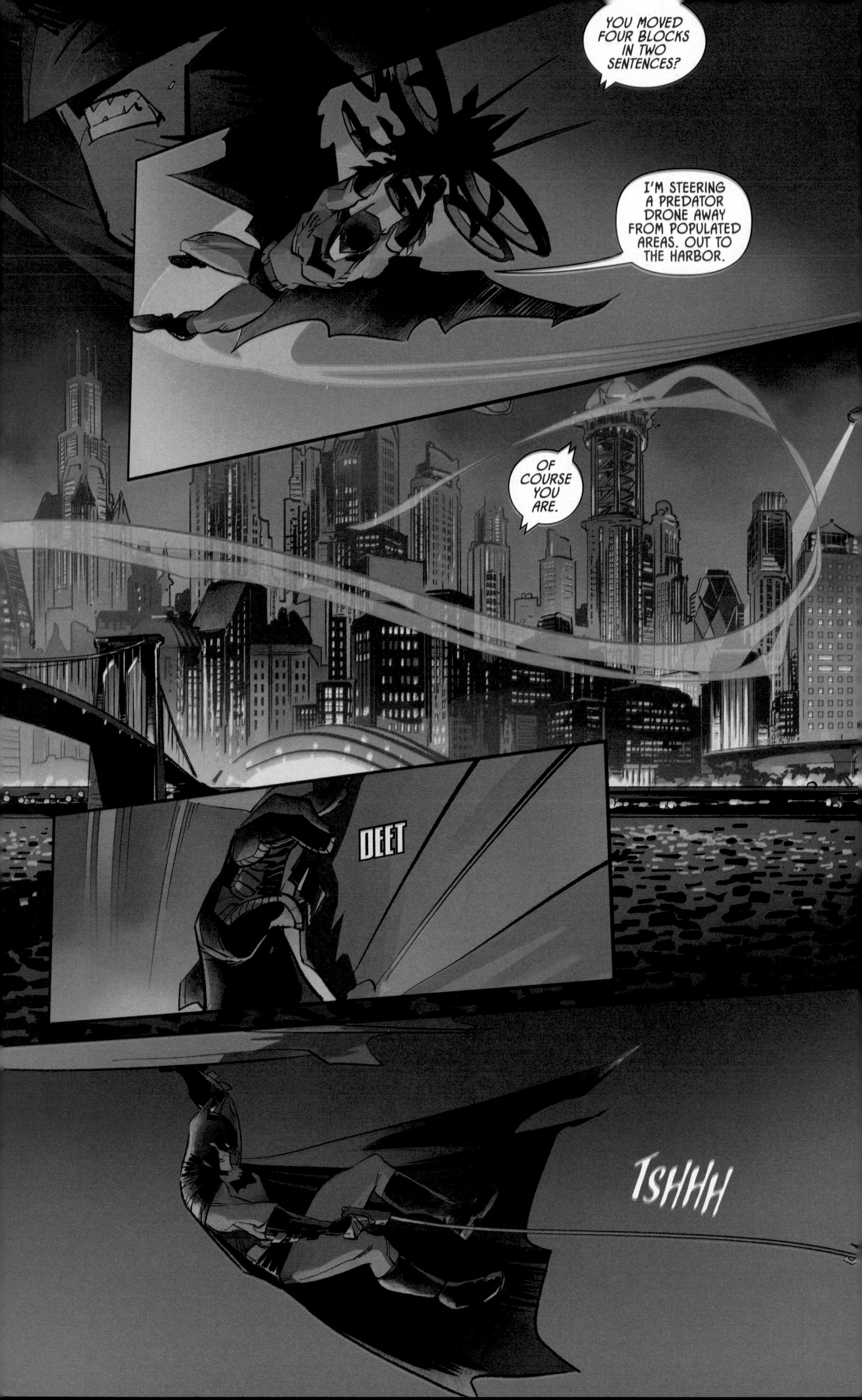
YOU MOVED FOUR BLOCKS IN TWO SENTENCES?
I'M STEERING A PREDATOR DRONE AWAY FROM POPULATED AREAS. OUT TO THE HARBOR.
OF COURSE YOU ARE.
DEET
TSHHH

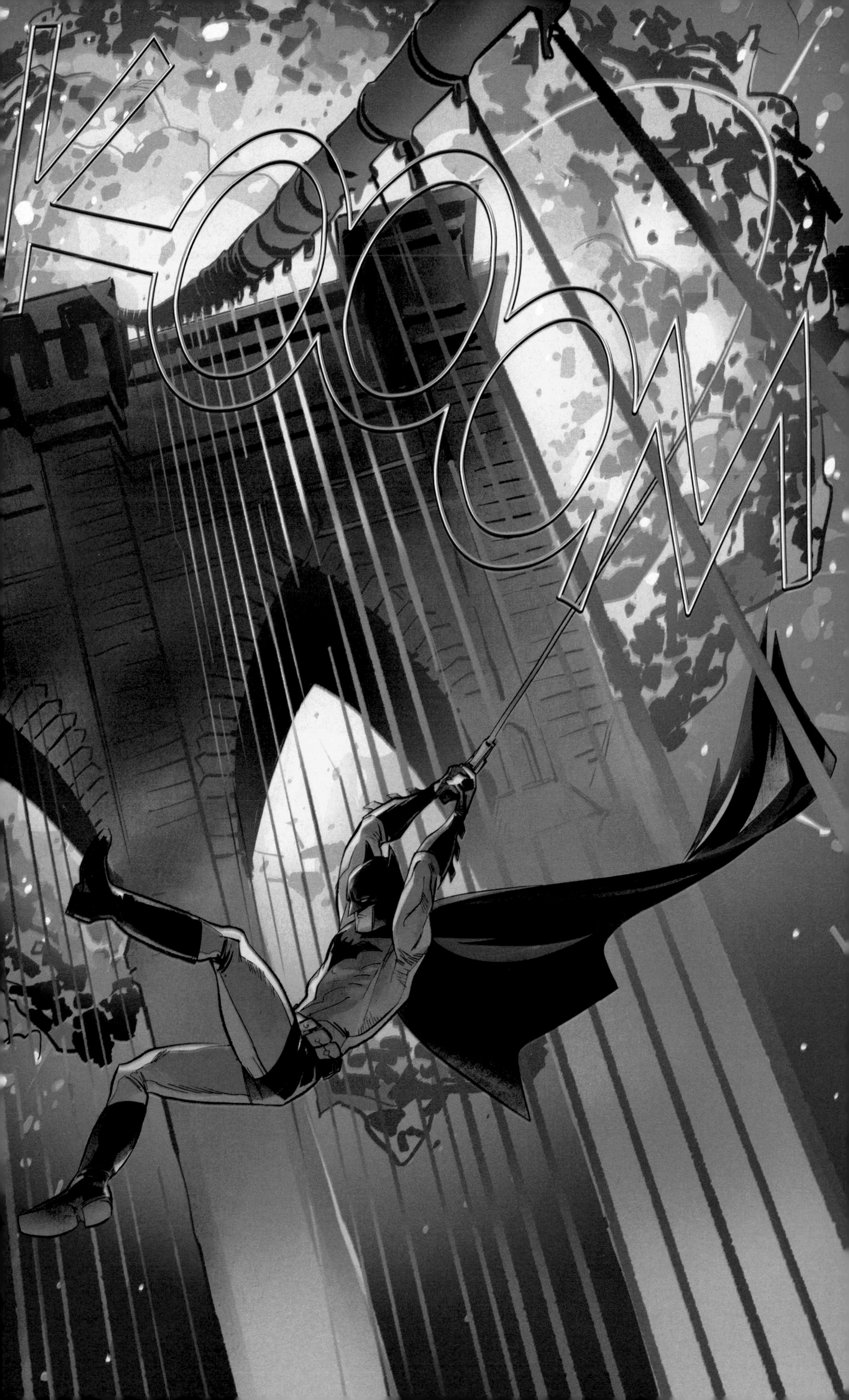
KOOOOM

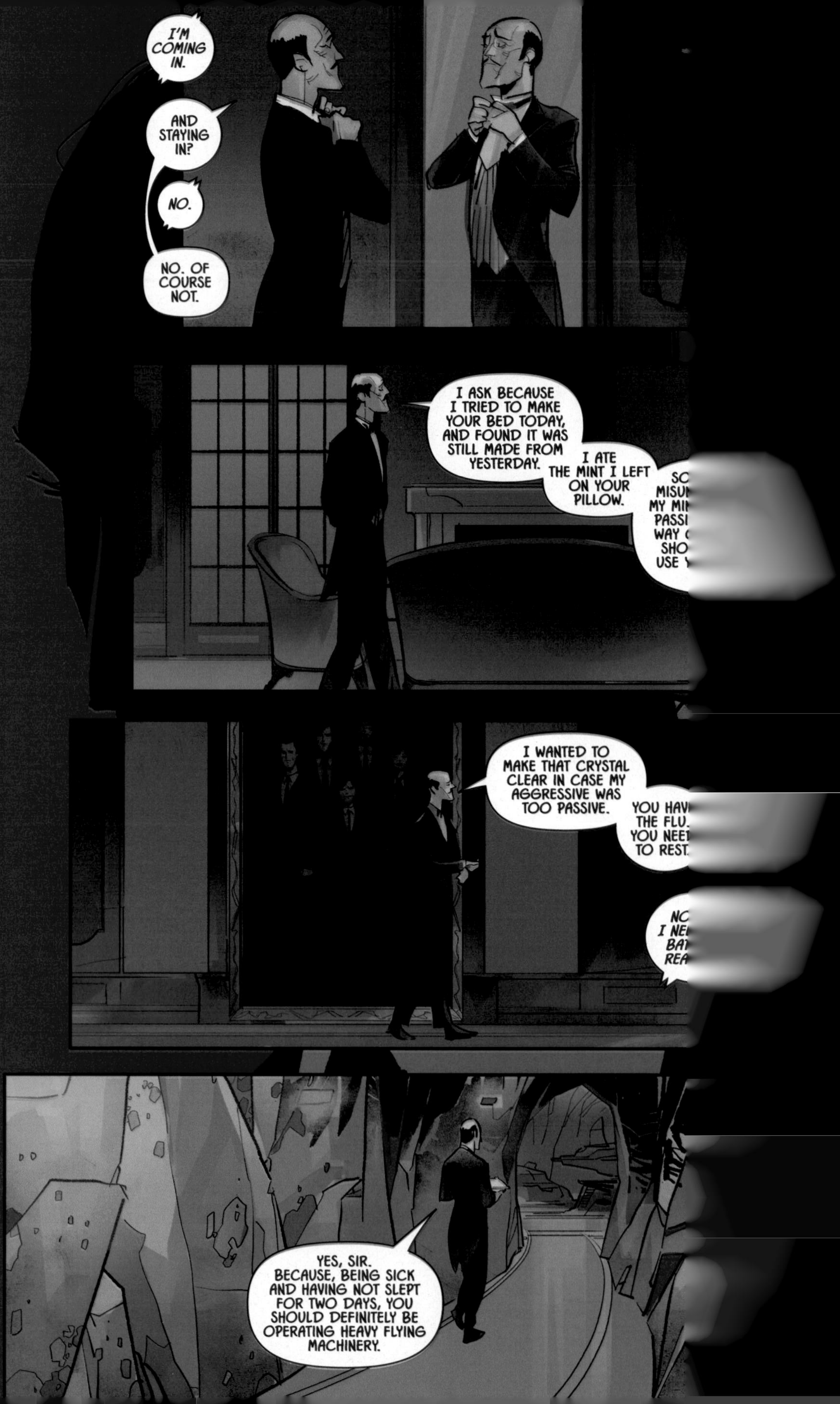
I'M COMING IN.
AND STAYING IN?
NO.
NO. OF COURSE NOT.
I ASK BECAUSE I TRIED TO MAKE YOUR BED TODAY, AND FOUND IT WAS STILL MADE FROM YESTERDAY.
I ATE THE MINT I LEFT ON YOUR PILLOW.
I WANTED TO MAKE THAT CRYSTAL CLEAR IN CASE MY AGGRESSIVE WAS TOO PASSIVE.
YES, SIR. BECAUSE, BEING SICK AND HAVING NOT SLEPT FOR TWO DAYS, YOU SHOULD DEFINITELY BE OPERATING HEAVY FLYING MACHINERY.

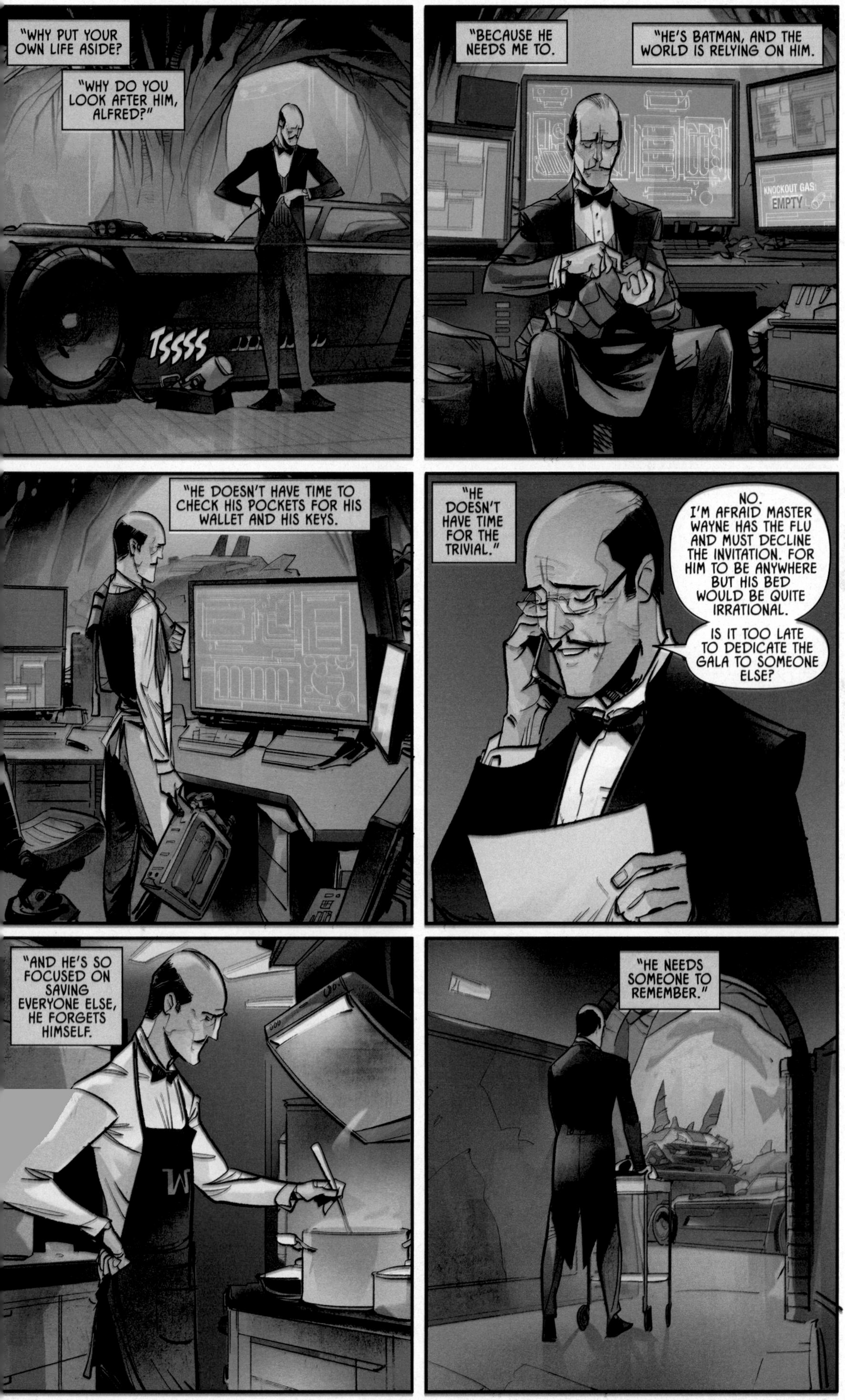

"WHY PUT YOUR OWN LIFE ASIDE?
"WHY DO YOU LOOK AFTER HIM, ALFRED?"
TSSSS
"BECAUSE HE NEEDS ME TO.
"HE'S BATMAN, AND THE WORLD IS RELYING ON HIM.
KNOCKOUT GAS: EMPTY
"HE DOESN'T HAVE TIME TO CHECK HIS POCKETS FOR HIS WALLET AND HIS KEYS.
"HE DOESN'T HAVE TIME FOR THE TRIVIAL."
NO. I'M AFRAID MASTER WAYNE HAS THE FLU AND MUST DECLINE THE INVITATION. FOR HIM TO BE ANYWHERE BUT HIS BED WOULD BE QUITE IRRATIONAL.
IS IT TOO LATE TO DEDICATE THE GALA TO SOMEONE ELSE?
"AND HE'S SO FOCUSED ON SAVING EVERYONE ELSE, HE FORGETS HIMSELF.
"HE NEEDS SOMEONE TO REMEMBER."

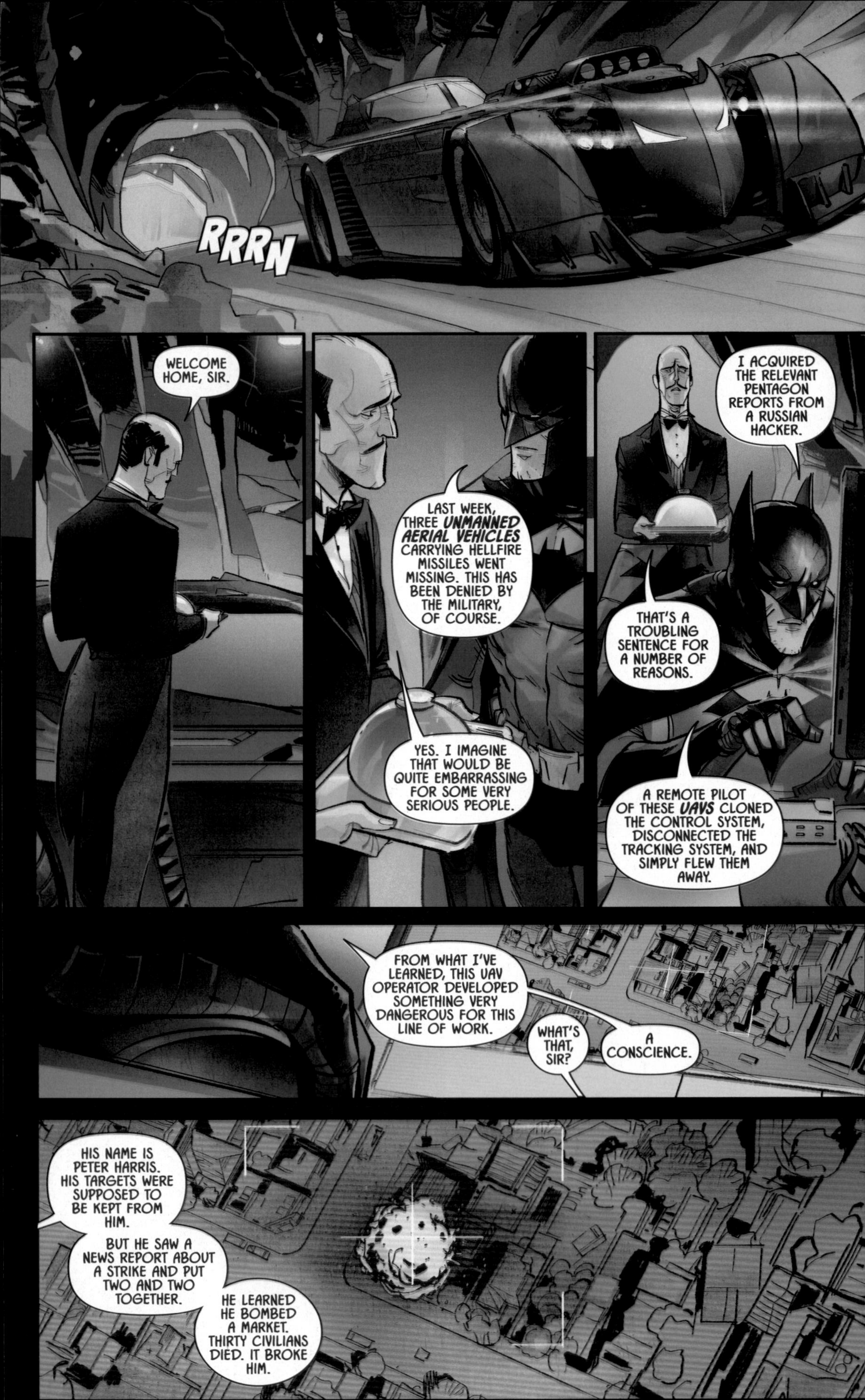
RRRN
WELCOME HOME, SIR.
LAST WEEK, THREE *UNMANNED AERIAL VEHICLES* CARRYING HELLFIRE MISSILES WENT MISSING. THIS HAS BEEN DENIED BY THE MILITARY, OF COURSE.
YES. I IMAGINE THAT WOULD BE QUITE EMBARRASSING FOR SOME VERY SERIOUS PEOPLE.
I ACQUIRED THE RELEVANT PENTAGON REPORTS FROM A RUSSIAN HACKER.
THAT'S A TROUBLING SENTENCE FOR A NUMBER OF REASONS.
A REMOTE PILOT OF THESE *UAVS* CLONED THE CONTROL SYSTEM, DISCONNECTED THE TRACKING SYSTEM, AND SIMPLY FLEW THEM AWAY.
FROM WHAT I'VE LEARNED, THIS UAV OPERATOR DEVELOPED SOMETHING VERY DANGEROUS FOR THIS LINE OF WORK.
WHAT'S THAT, SIR?
A CONSCIENCE.
HIS NAME IS PETER HARRIS. HIS TARGETS WERE SUPPOSED TO BE KEPT FROM HIM.
BUT HE SAW A NEWS REPORT ABOUT A STRIKE AND PUT TWO AND TWO TOGETHER.
HE LEARNED HE BOMBED A MARKET. THIRTY CIVILIANS DIED. IT BROKE HIM.

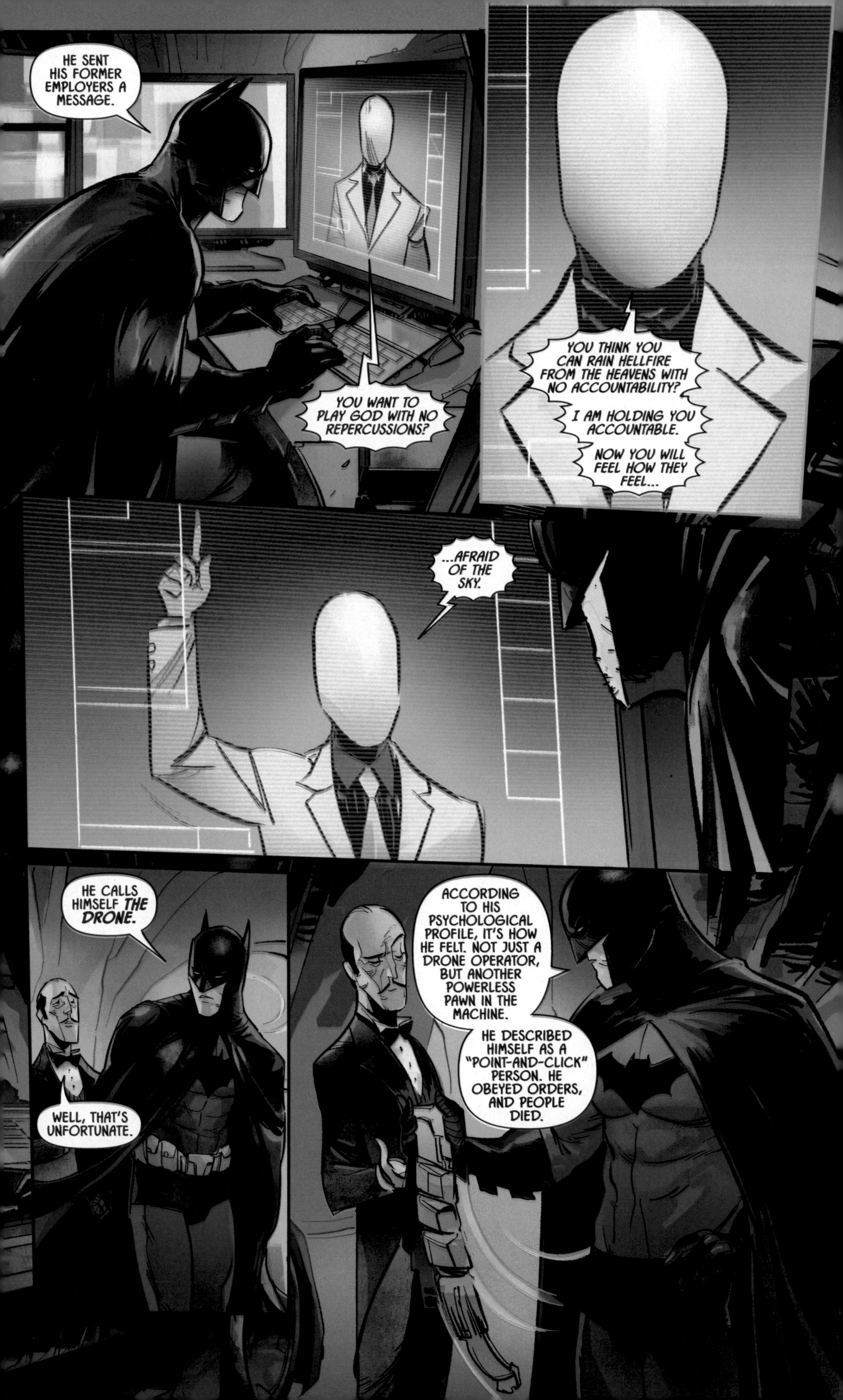

HE SENT HIS FORMER EMPLOYERS A MESSAGE.
YOU WANT TO PLAY GOD WITH NO REPERCUSSIONS?
YOU THINK YOU CAN RAIN HELLFIRE FROM THE HEAVENS WITH NO ACCOUNTABILITY?
I AM HOLDING YOU ACCOUNTABLE.
NOW YOU WILL FEEL HOW THEY FEEL...
...AFRAID OF THE SKY.
HE CALLS HIMSELF *THE DRONE.*
WELL, THAT'S UNFORTUNATE.
ACCORDING TO HIS PSYCHOLOGICAL PROFILE, IT'S HOW HE FELT. NOT JUST A DRONE OPERATOR, BUT ANOTHER POWERLESS PAWN IN THE MACHINE.
HE DESCRIBED HIMSELF AS A "POINT-AND-CLICK" PERSON. HE OBEYED ORDERS, AND PEOPLE DIED.

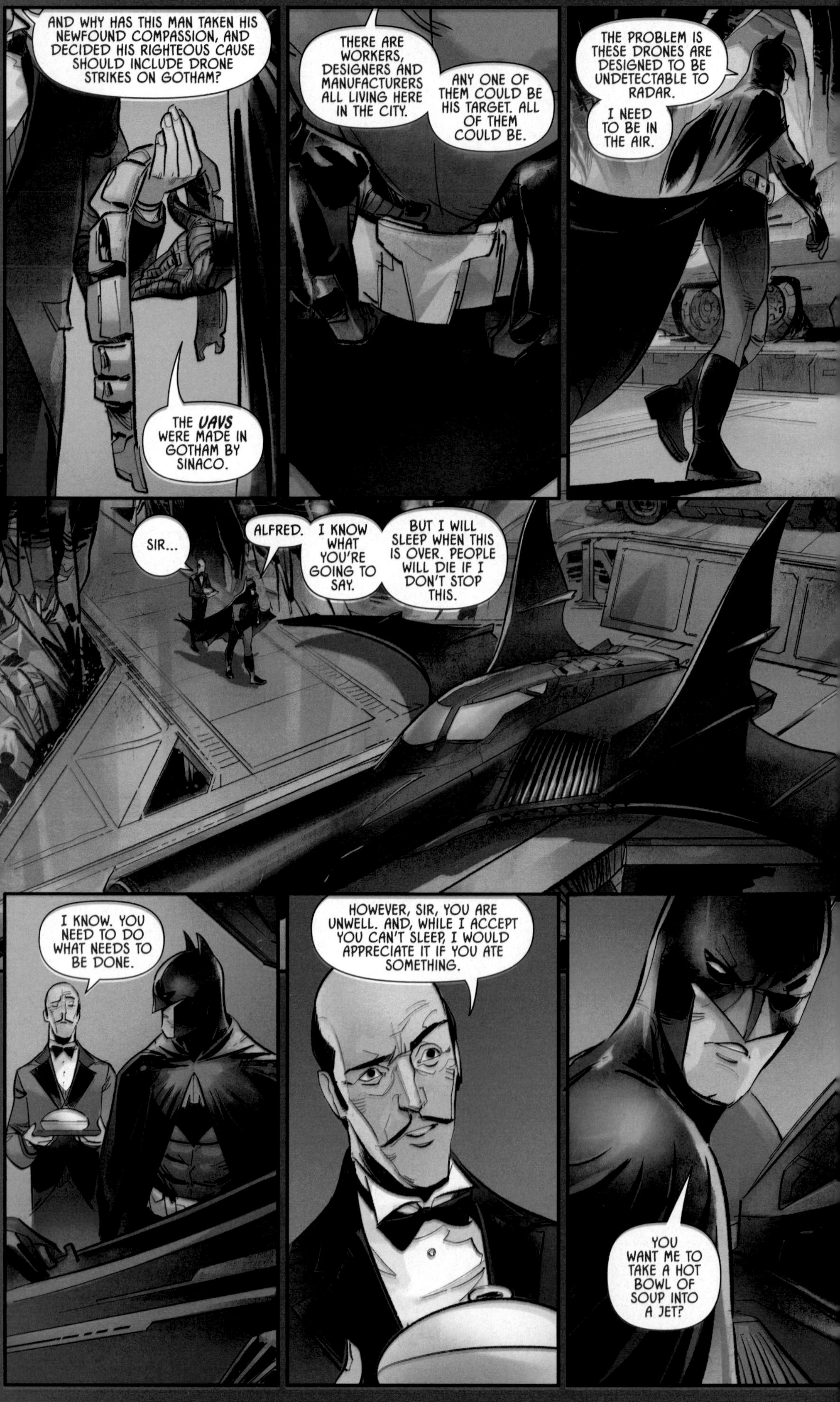
AND WHY HAS THIS MAN TAKEN HIS NEWFOUND COMPASSION, AND DECIDED HIS RIGHTEOUS CAUSE SHOULD INCLUDE DRONE STRIKES ON GOTHAM?
THE UAVS WERE MADE IN GOTHAM BY SINACO.
THERE ARE WORKERS, DESIGNERS AND MANUFACTURERS ALL LIVING HERE IN THE CITY.
ANY ONE OF THEM COULD BE HIS TARGET. ALL OF THEM COULD BE.
THE PROBLEM IS THESE DRONES ARE DESIGNED TO BE UNDETECTABLE TO RADAR.
I NEED TO BE IN THE AIR.
SIR...
ALFRED.
I KNOW WHAT YOU'RE GOING TO SAY.
BUT I WILL SLEEP WHEN THIS IS OVER. PEOPLE WILL DIE IF I DON'T STOP THIS.
I KNOW. YOU NEED TO DO WHAT NEEDS TO BE DONE.
HOWEVER, SIR, YOU ARE UNWELL. AND, WHILE I ACCEPT YOU CAN'T SLEEP, I WOULD APPRECIATE IT IF YOU ATE SOMETHING.
YOU WANT ME TO TAKE A HOT BOWL OF SOUP INTO A JET?

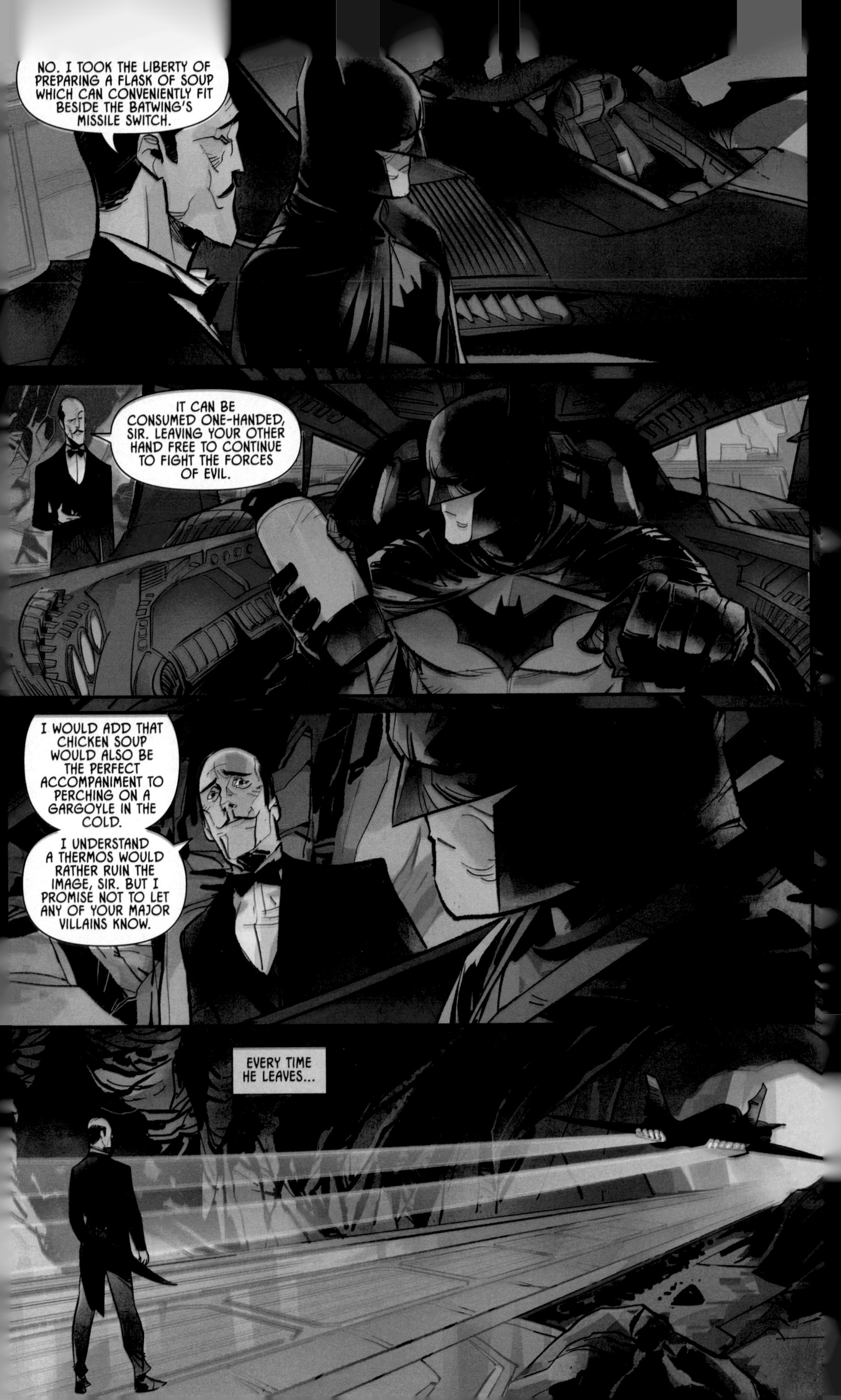

NO. I TOOK THE LIBERTY OF PREPARING A FLASK OF SOUP WHICH CAN CONVENIENTLY FIT BESIDE THE BATWING'S MISSILE SWITCH.
IT CAN BE CONSUMED ONE-HANDED, SIR. LEAVING YOUR OTHER HAND FREE TO CONTINUE TO FIGHT THE FORCES OF EVIL.
I WOULD ADD THAT CHICKEN SOUP WOULD ALSO BE THE PERFECT ACCOMPANIMENT TO PERCHING ON A GARGOYLE IN THE COLD.
I UNDERSTAND A THERMOS WOULD RATHER RUIN THE IMAGE, SIR. BUT I PROMISE NOT TO LET ANY OF YOUR MAJOR VILLAINS KNOW.
EVERY TIME HE LEAVES...

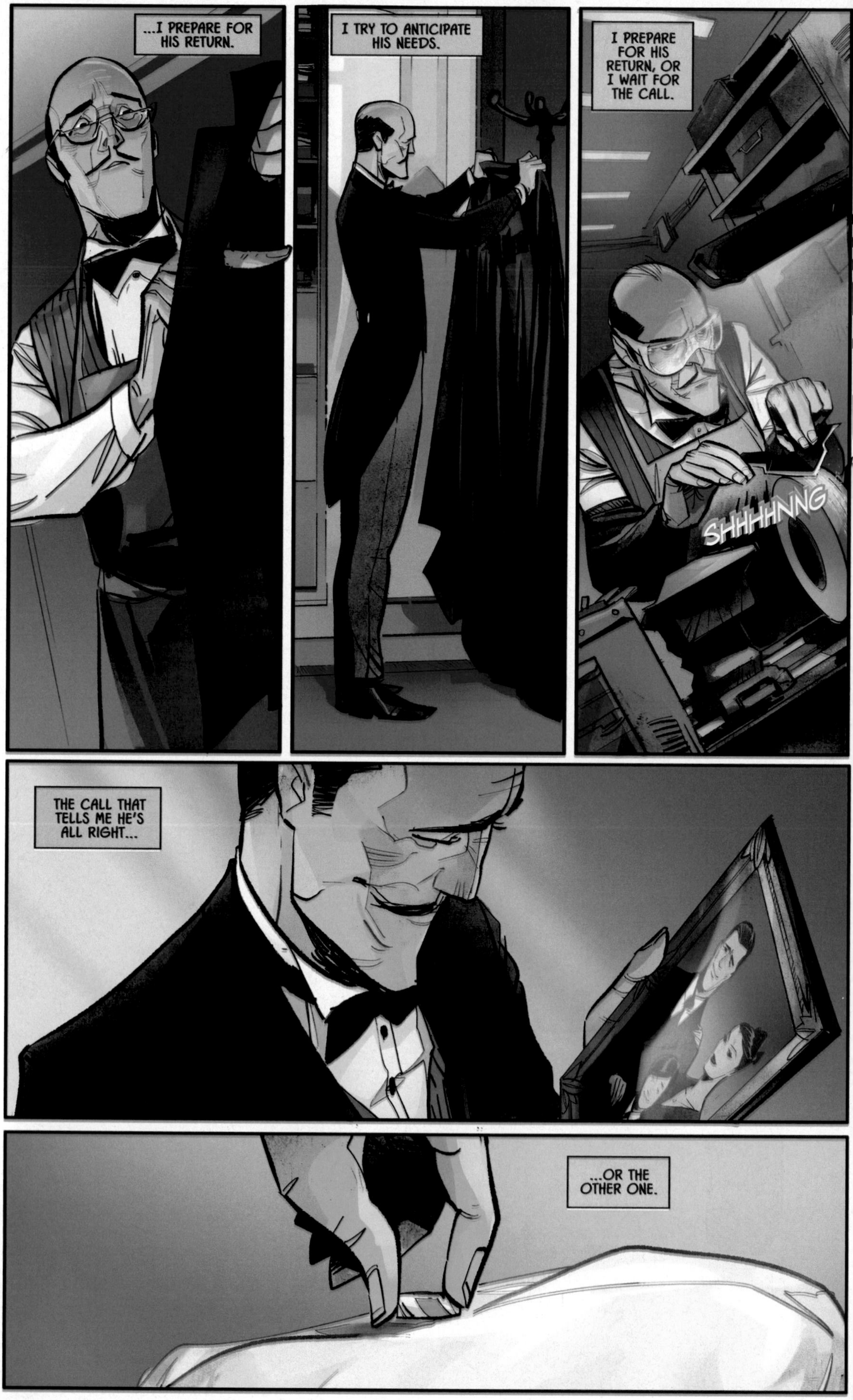
...I PREPARE FOR HIS RETURN.
I TRY TO ANTICIPATE HIS NEEDS.
I PREPARE FOR HIS RETURN, OR I WAIT FOR THE CALL.
SHHHHNNG
THE CALL THAT TELLS ME HE'S ALL RIGHT...
...OR THE OTHER ONE.

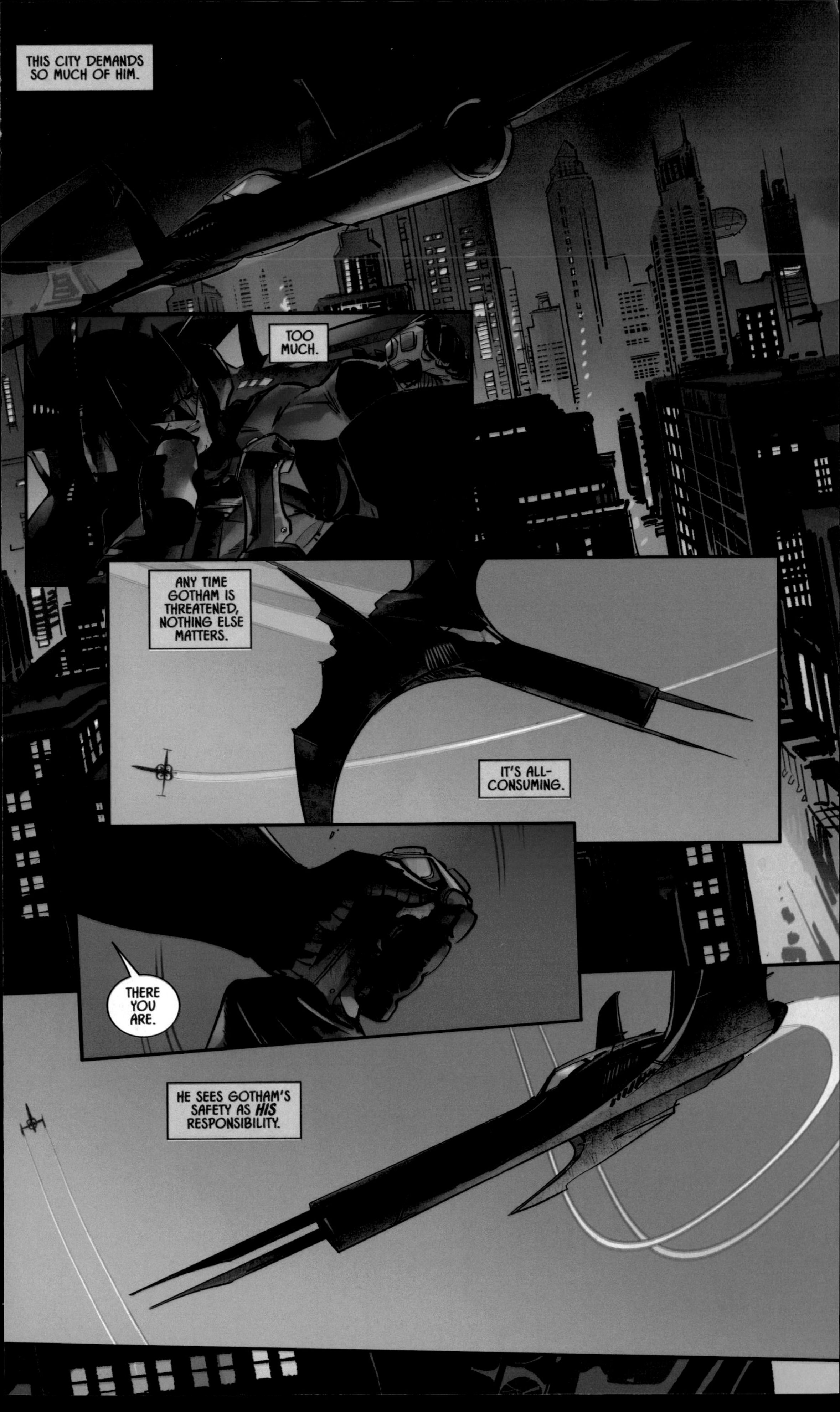
THIS CITY DEMANDS SO MUCH OF HIM.
TOO MUCH.
ANY TIME GOTHAM IS THREATENED, NOTHING ELSE MATTERS.
IT'S ALL-CONSUMING.
THERE YOU ARE.
HE SEES GOTHAM'S SAFETY AS HIS RESPONSIBILITY.

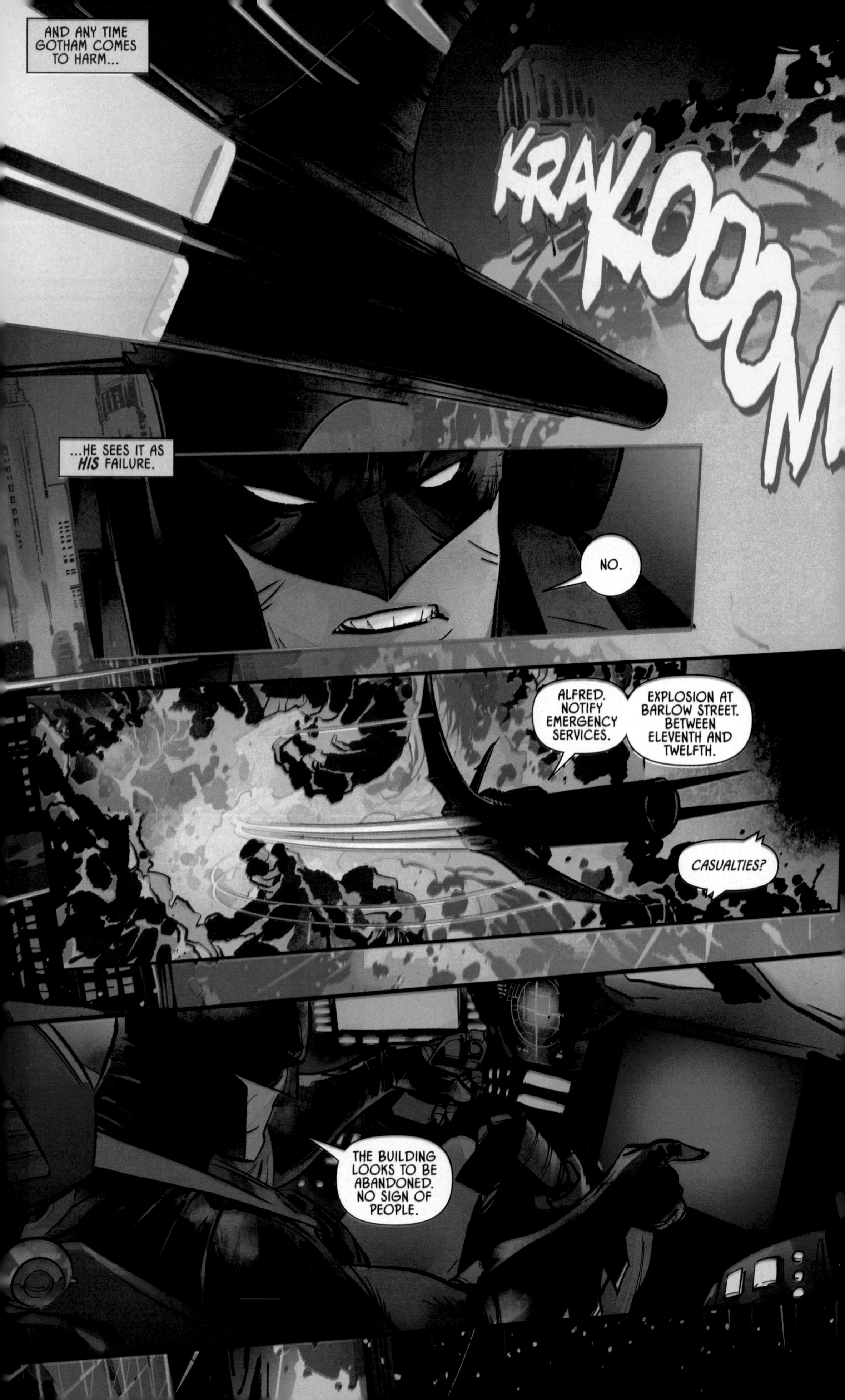
AND ANY TIME GOTHAM COMES TO HARM...
KRAKOOOM
...HE SEES IT AS *HIS* FAILURE.
NO.
ALFRED. NOTIFY EMERGENCY SERVICES.
EXPLOSION AT BARLOW STREET. BETWEEN ELEVENTH AND TWELFTH.
*CASUALTIES?*
THE BUILDING LOOKS TO BE ABANDONED. NO SIGN OF PEOPLE.

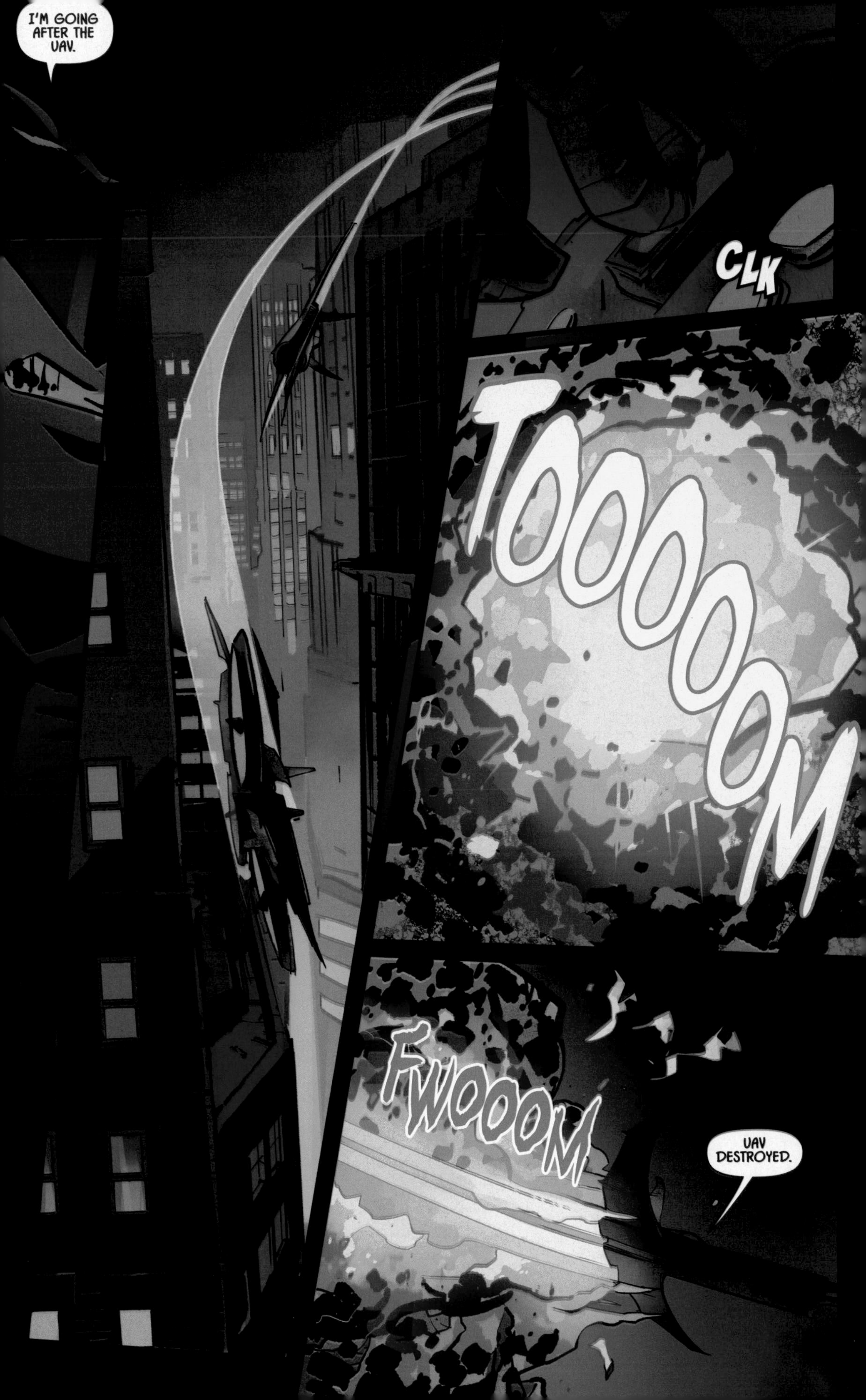
I'M GOING AFTER THE UAV.
CLK
TOOOOOOM
FWOOOM
UAV DESTROYED.

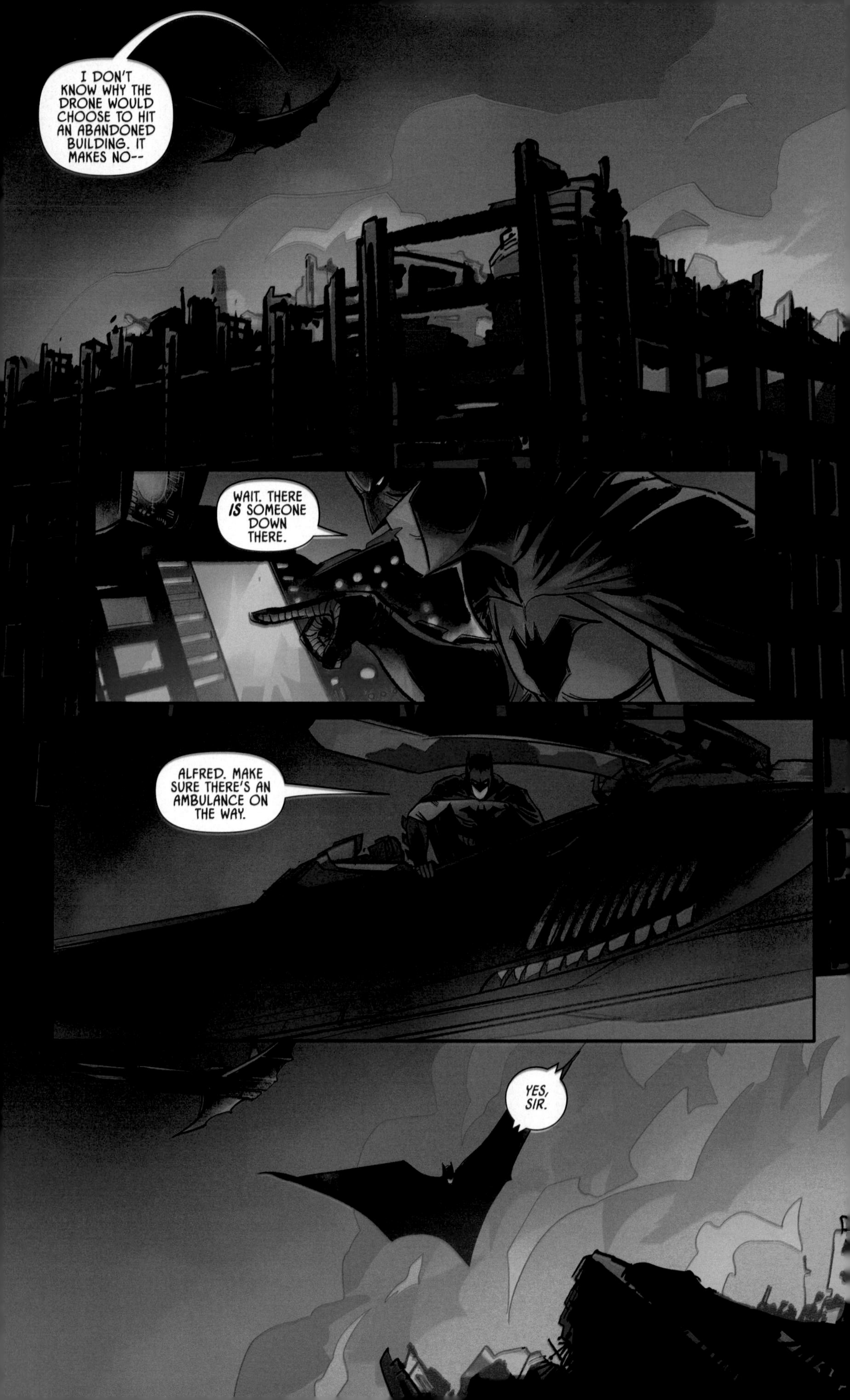
I DON'T KNOW WHY THE DRONE WOULD CHOOSE TO HIT AN ABANDONED BUILDING. IT MAKES NO--
WAIT. THERE IS SOMEONE DOWN THERE.
ALFRED. MAKE SURE THERE'S AN AMBULANCE ON THE WAY.
YES, SIR.

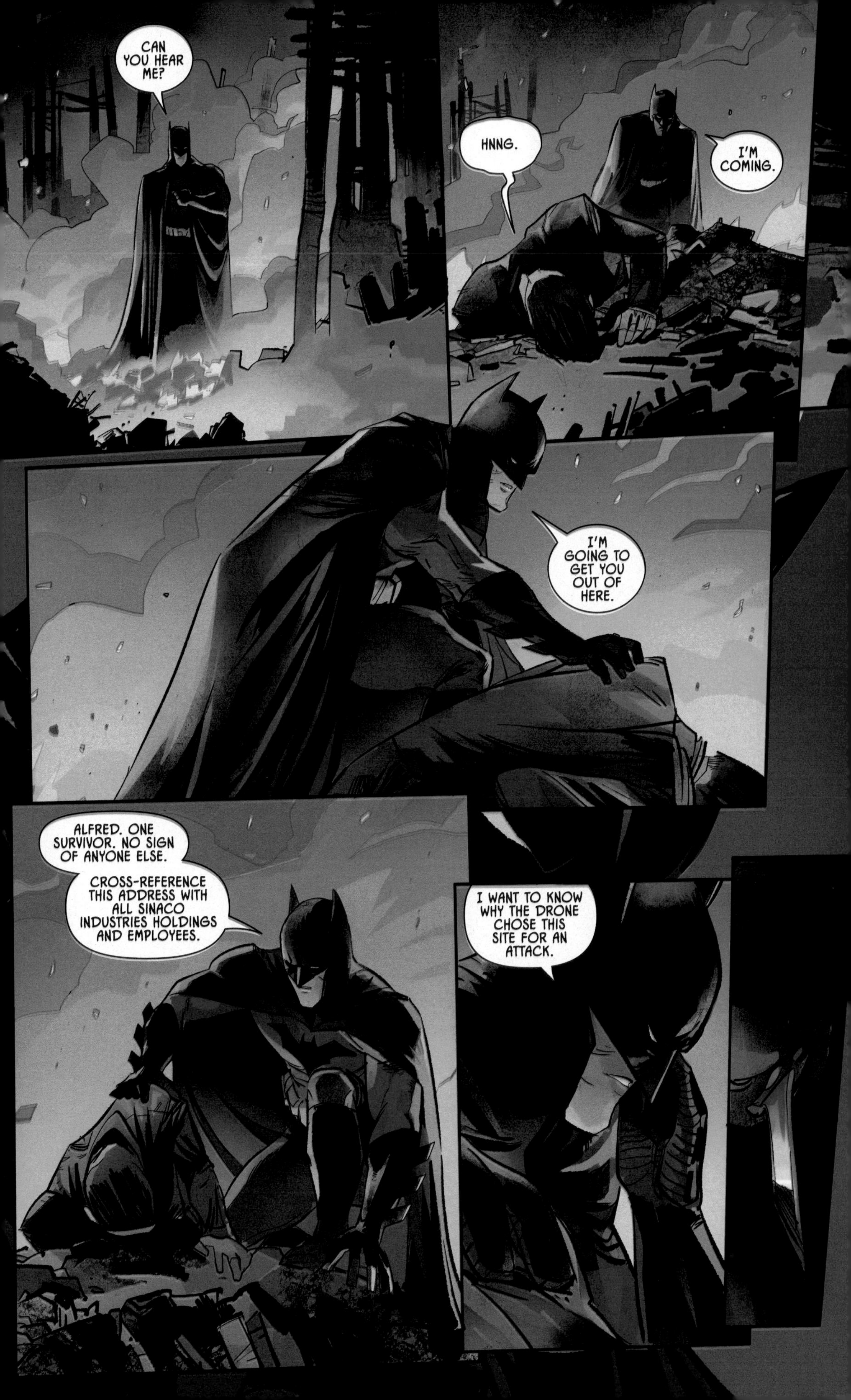
CAN YOU HEAR ME?
HNNG.
I'M COMING.
I'M GOING TO GET YOU OUT OF HERE.
ALFRED. ONE SURVIVOR. NO SIGN OF ANYONE ELSE.
CROSS-REFERENCE THIS ADDRESS WITH ALL SINACO INDUSTRIES HOLDINGS AND EMPLOYEES.
I WANT TO KNOW WHY THE DRONE CHOSE THIS SITE FOR AN ATTACK.

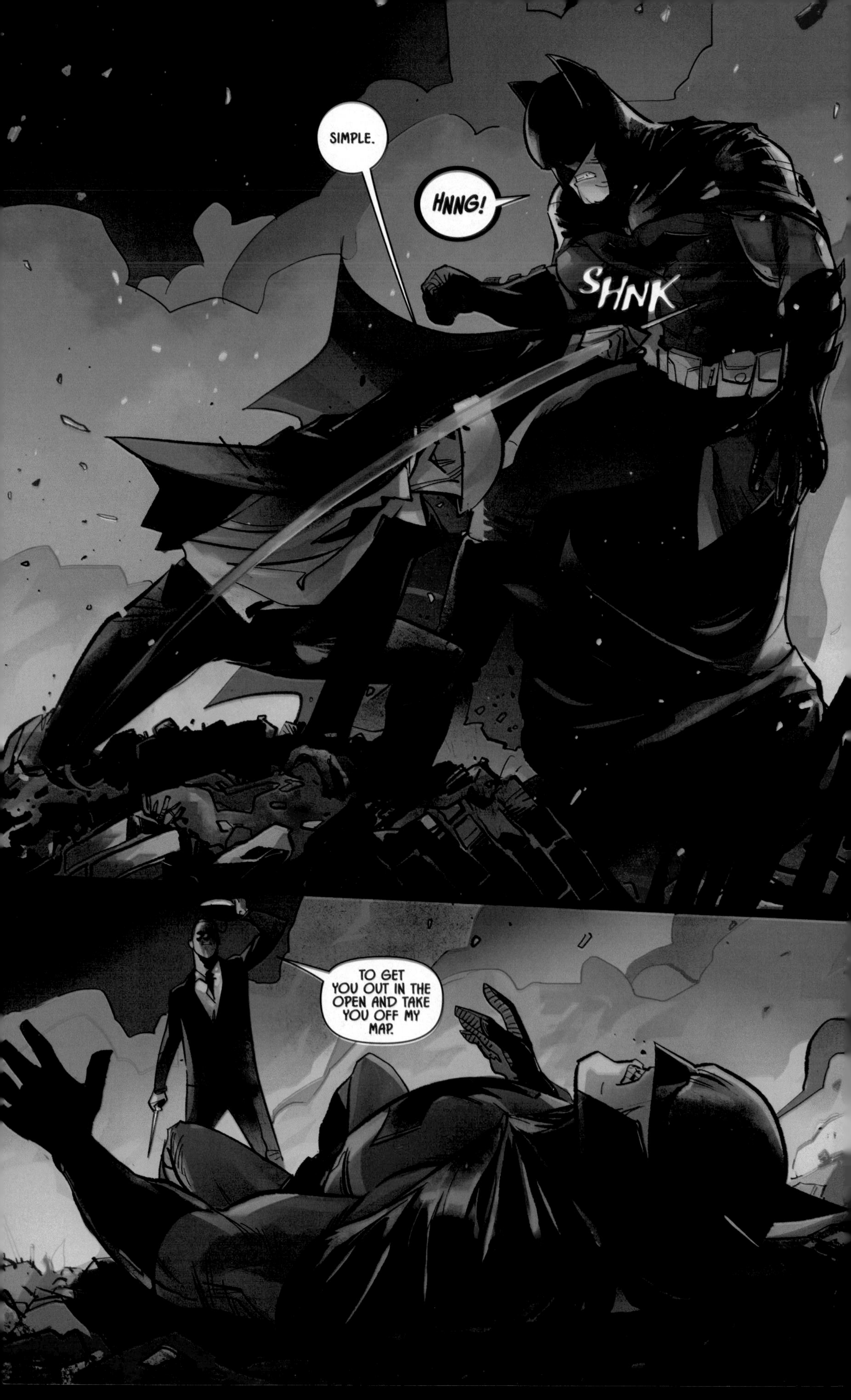
SIMPLE.
HNNG!
SHNK
TO GET YOU OUT IN THE OPEN AND TAKE YOU OFF MY MAP.

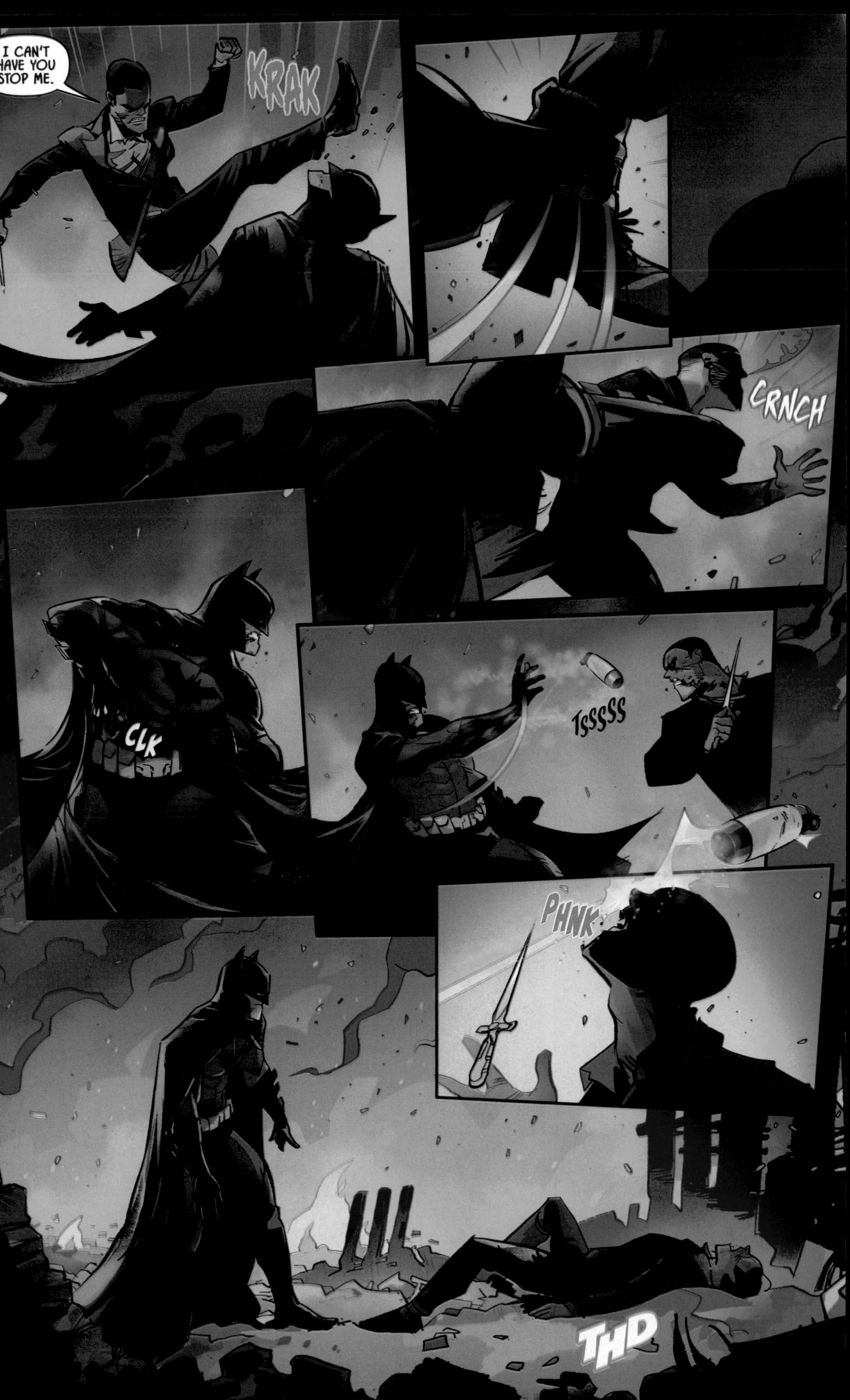
I CAN'T HAVE YOU STOP ME.
KRAK
CRNCH
CLK
TSSSSS
PHNK
THD

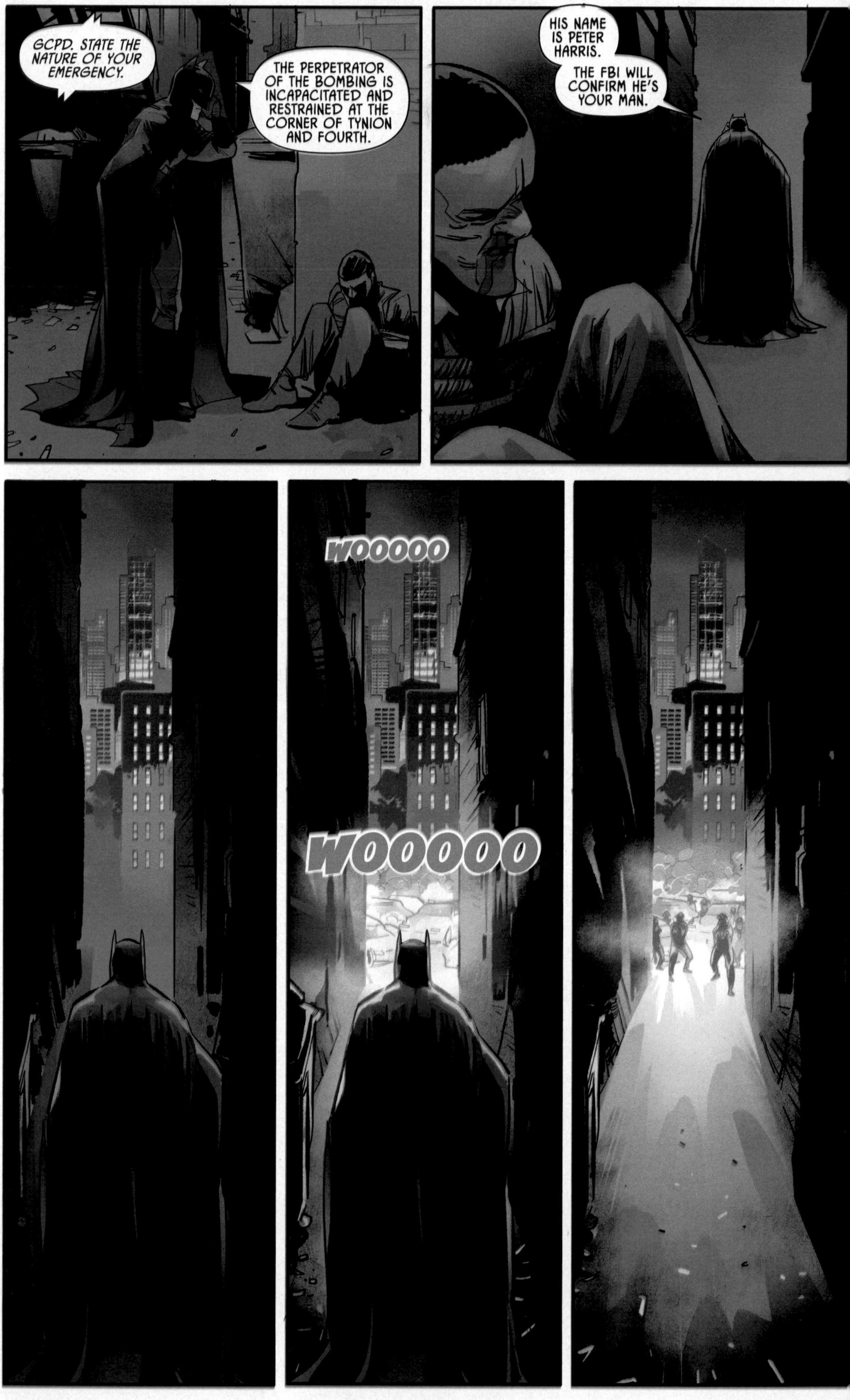
GCPD. STATE THE NATURE OF YOUR EMERGENCY.
THE PERPETRATOR OF THE BOMBING IS INCAPACITATED AND RESTRAINED AT THE CORNER OF TYNION AND FOURTH.
HIS NAME IS PETER HARRIS.
THE FBI WILL CONFIRM HE'S YOUR MAN.
WOOOOO
WOOOOO

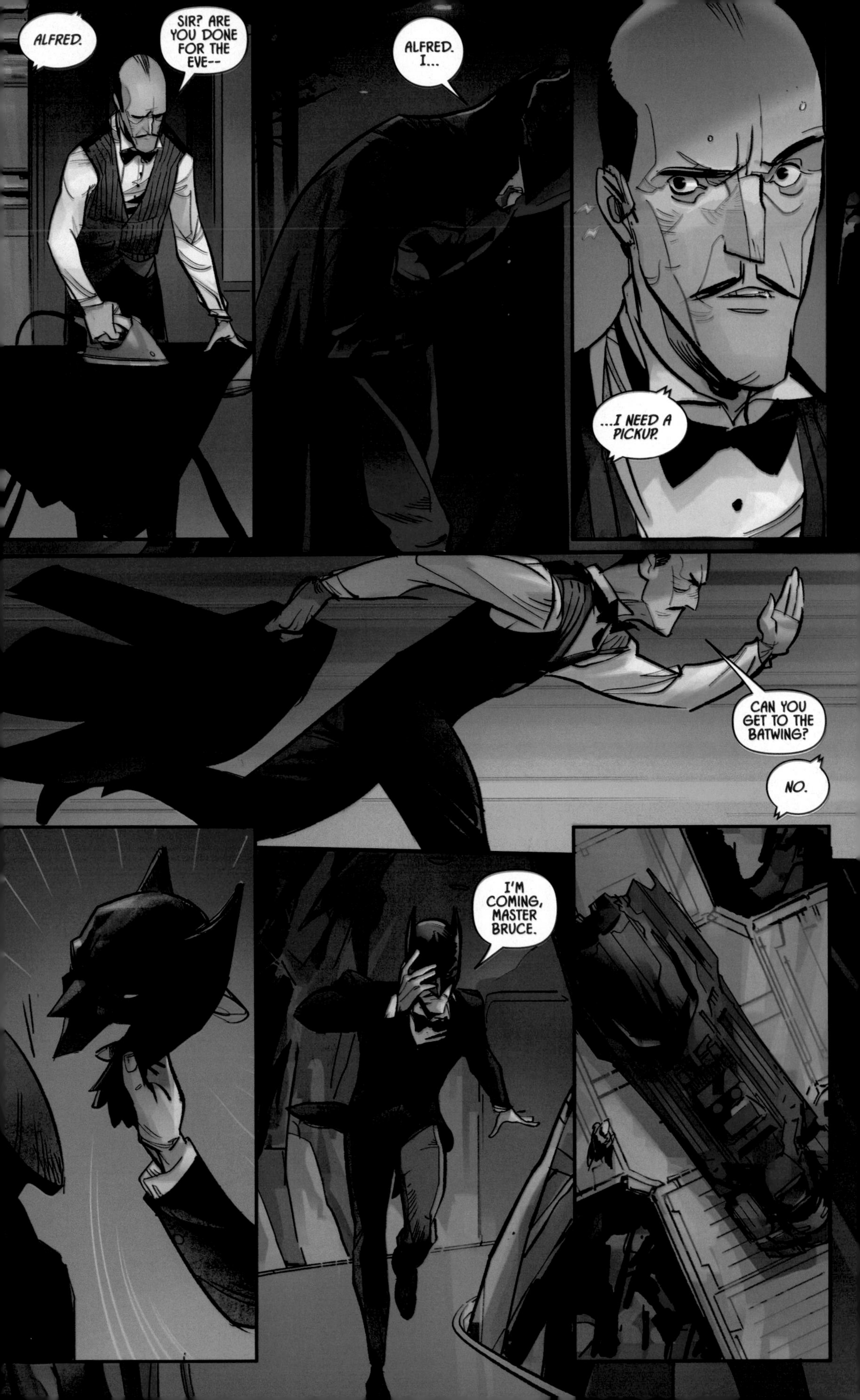
ALFRED.
SIR? ARE YOU DONE FOR THE EVE--
ALFRED. I...
...I NEED A PICKUP.
CAN YOU GET TO THE BATWING?
NO.
I'M COMING, MASTER BRUCE.

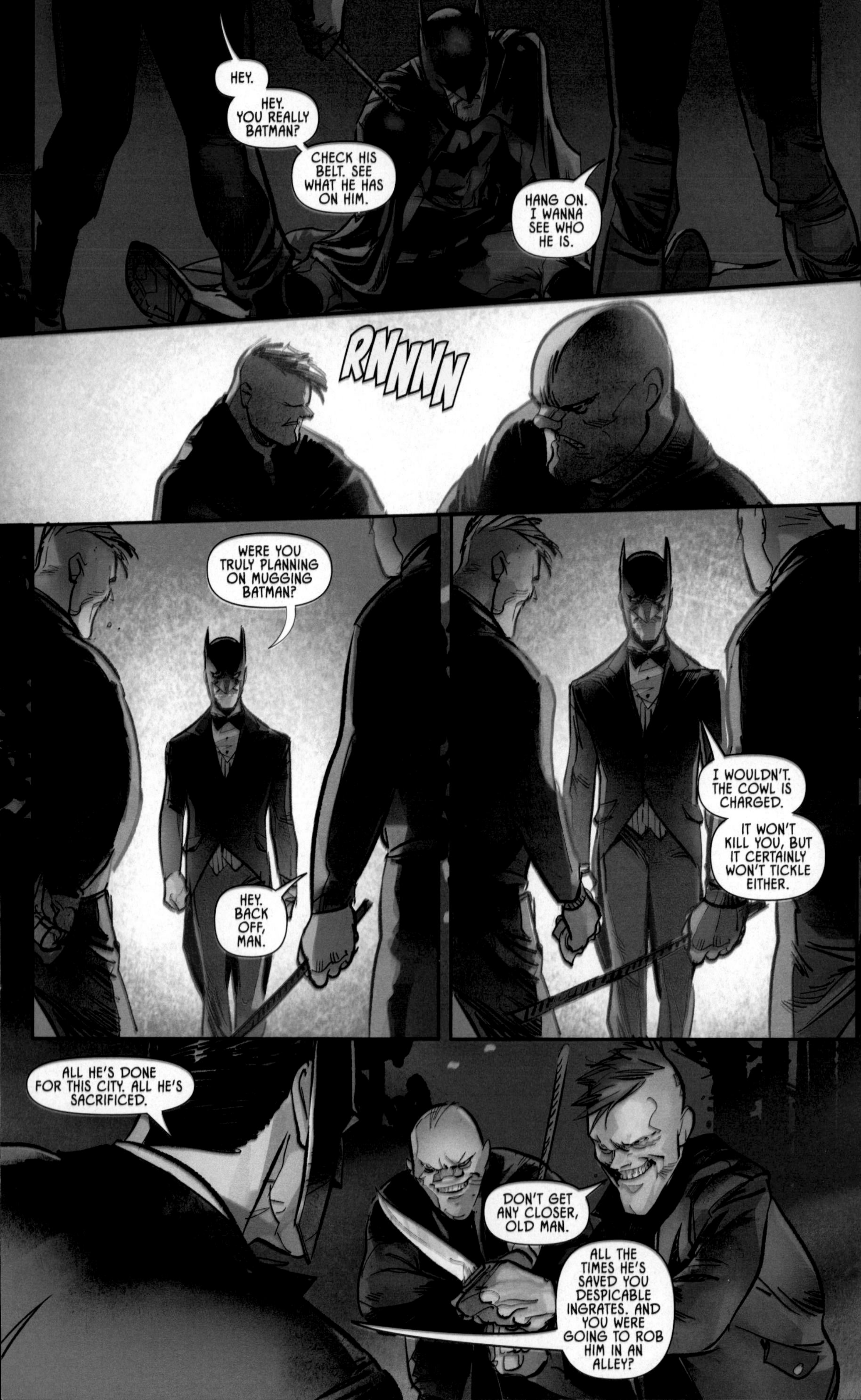
HEY.
HEY. YOU REALLY BATMAN?
CHECK HIS BELT. SEE WHAT HE HAS ON HIM.
HANG ON. I WANNA SEE WHO HE IS.
RNNNN
WERE YOU TRULY PLANNING ON MUGGING BATMAN?
HEY. BACK OFF, MAN.
I WOULDN'T. THE COWL IS CHARGED.
IT WON'T KILL YOU, BUT IT CERTAINLY WON'T TICKLE EITHER.
ALL HE'S DONE FOR THIS CITY. ALL HE'S SACRIFICED.
DON'T GET ANY CLOSER, OLD MAN.
ALL THE TIMES HE'S SAVED YOU DESPICABLE INGRATES. AND YOU WERE GOING TO ROB HIM IN AN ALLEY?

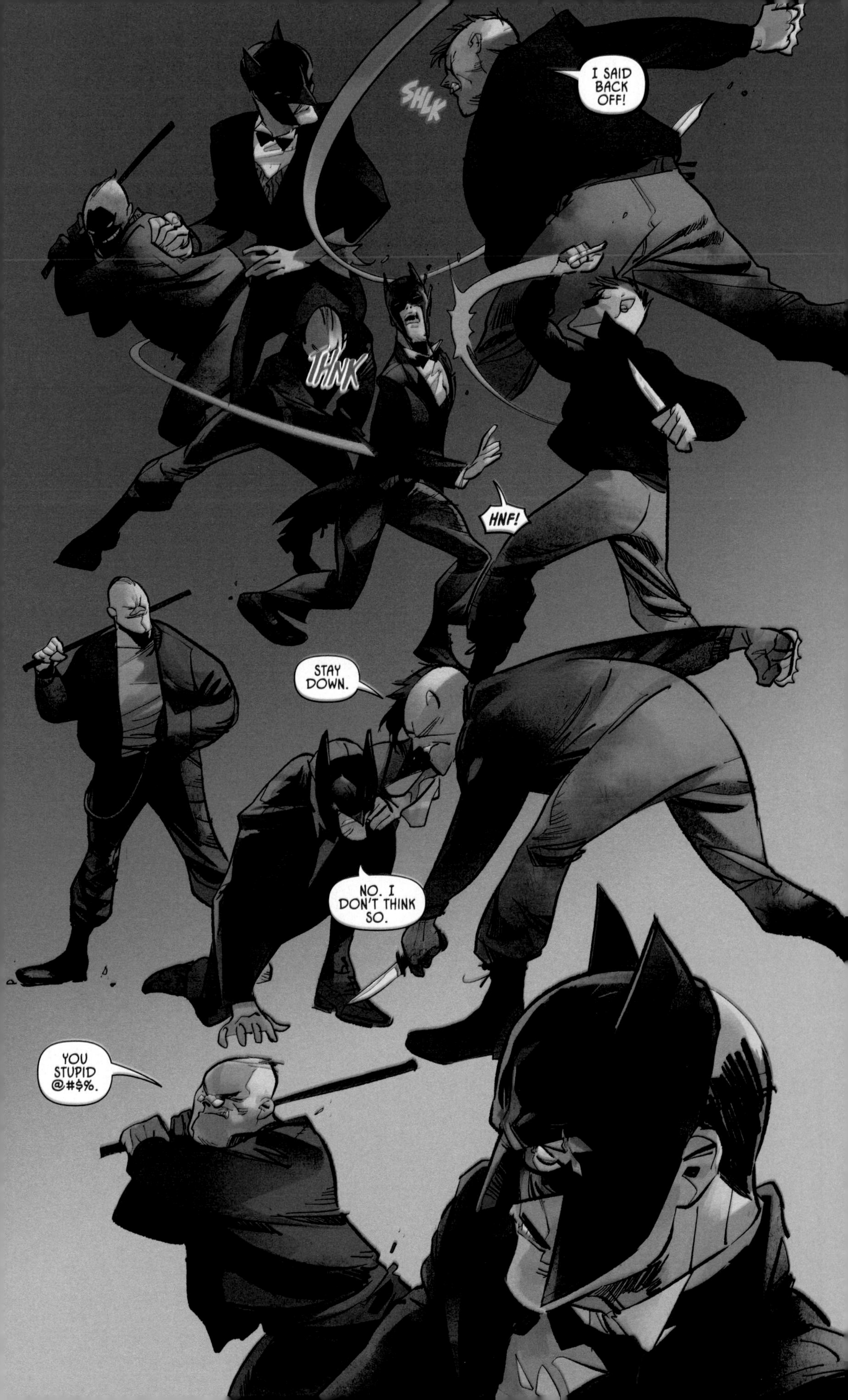
SHLK
I SAID BACK OFF!
THNK
HNF!
STAY DOWN.
NO. I DON'T THINK SO.
YOU STUPID @#$%.

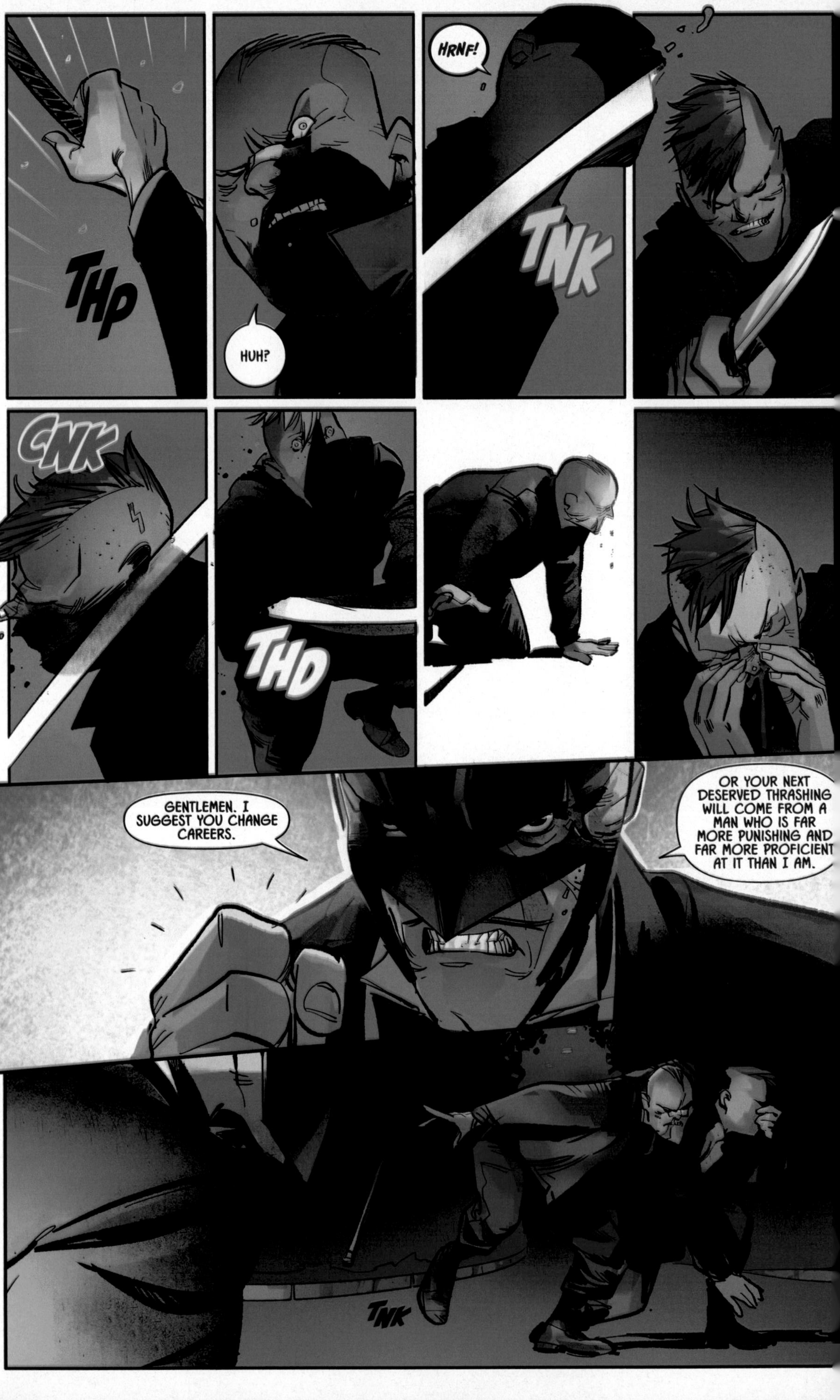
THP
HUH?
HRNF!
TNK
CNK
THD
GENTLEMEN. I SUGGEST YOU CHANGE CAREERS.
OR YOUR NEXT DESERVED THRASHING WILL COME FROM A MAN WHO IS FAR MORE PUNISHING AND FAR MORE PROFICIENT AT IT THAN I AM.
TNK

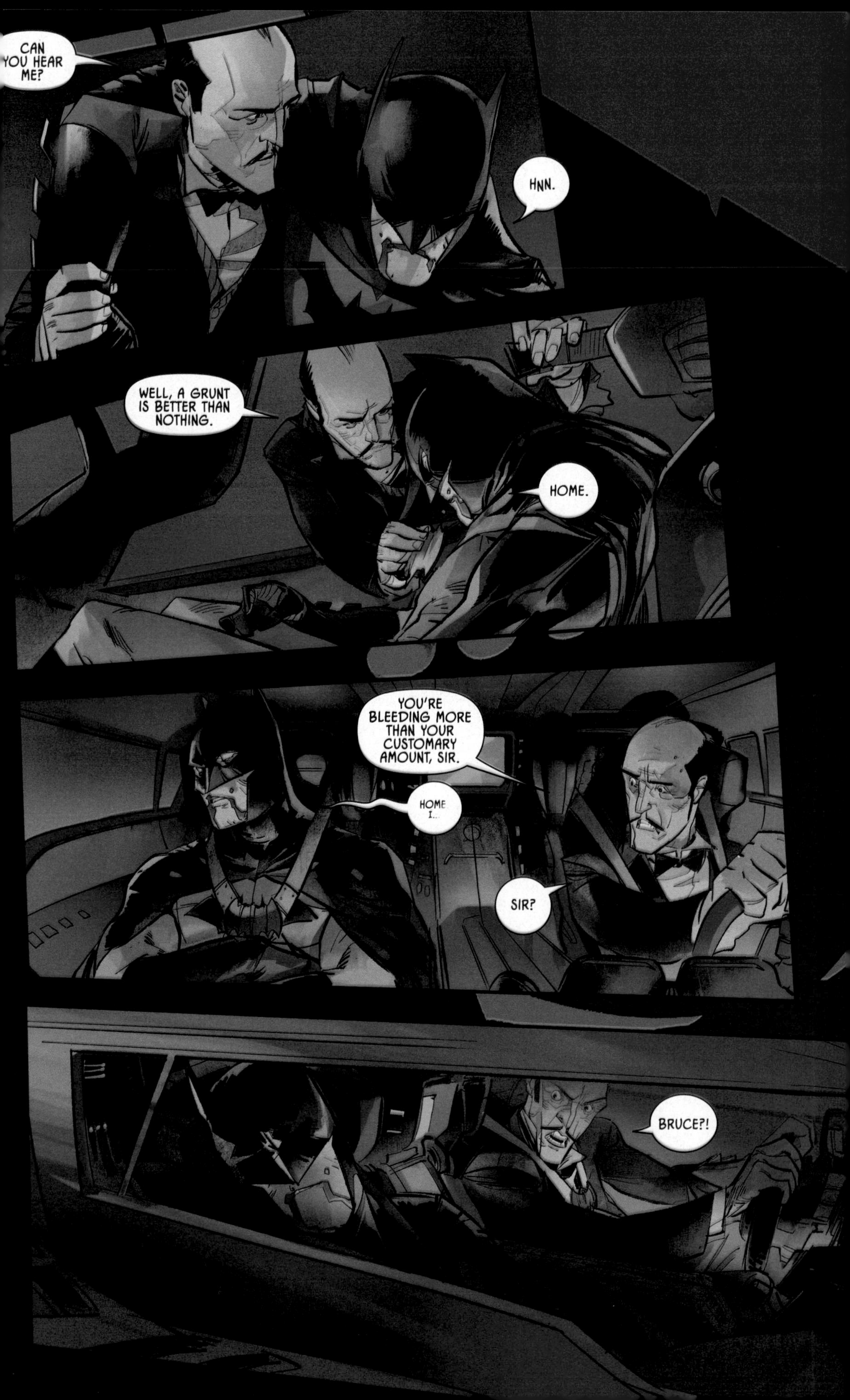
CAN YOU HEAR ME?
HNN.
WELL, A GRUNT IS BETTER THAN NOTHING.
HOME.
YOU'RE BLEEDING MORE THAN YOUR CUSTOMARY AMOUNT, SIR.
HOME I...
SIR?
BRUCE?!

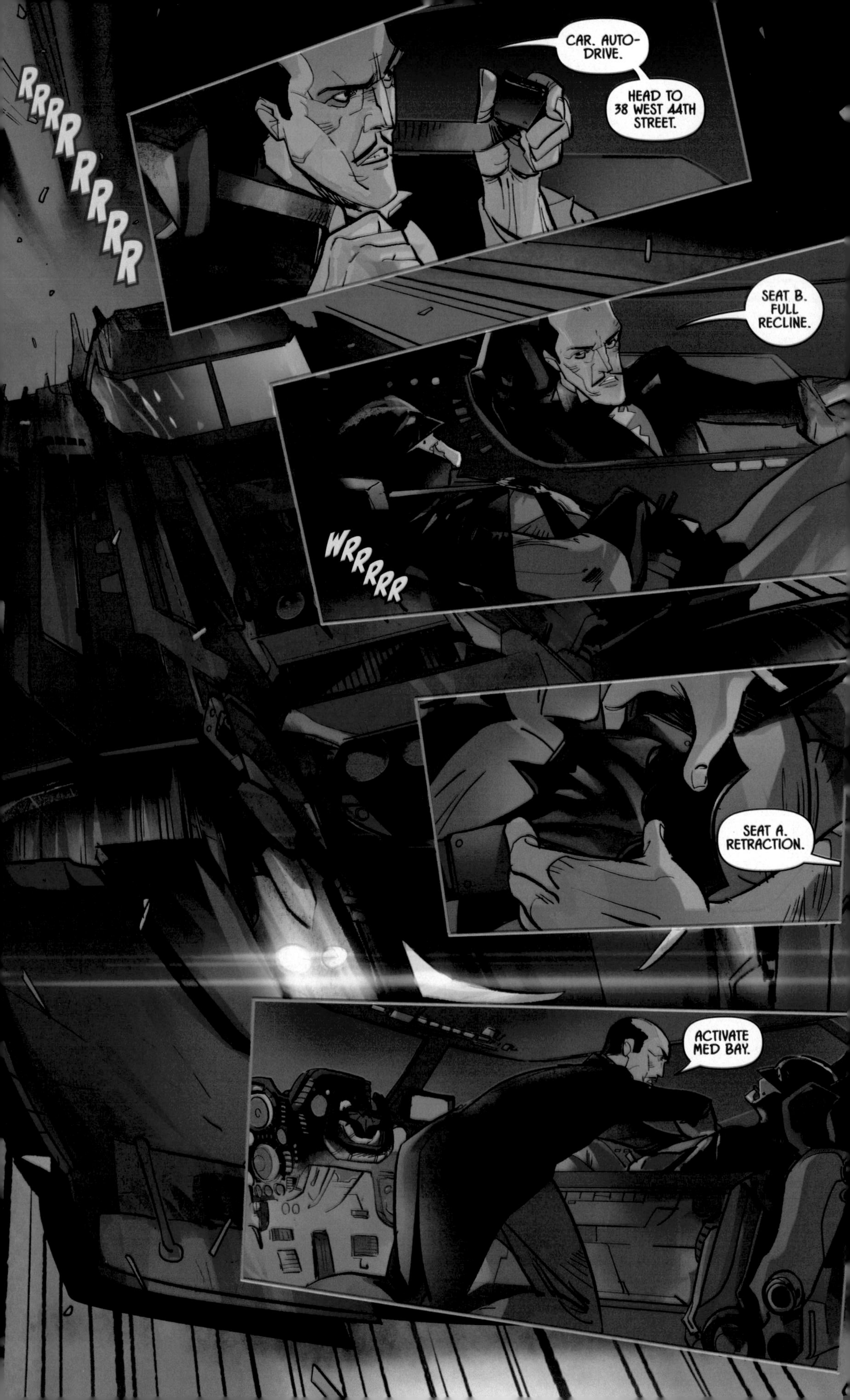
RRRRRRRR
CAR. AUTO-DRIVE.
HEAD TO 38 WEST 44TH STREET.
SEAT B. FULL RECLINE.
WRRRRR
SEAT A. RETRACTION.
ACTIVATE MED BAY.

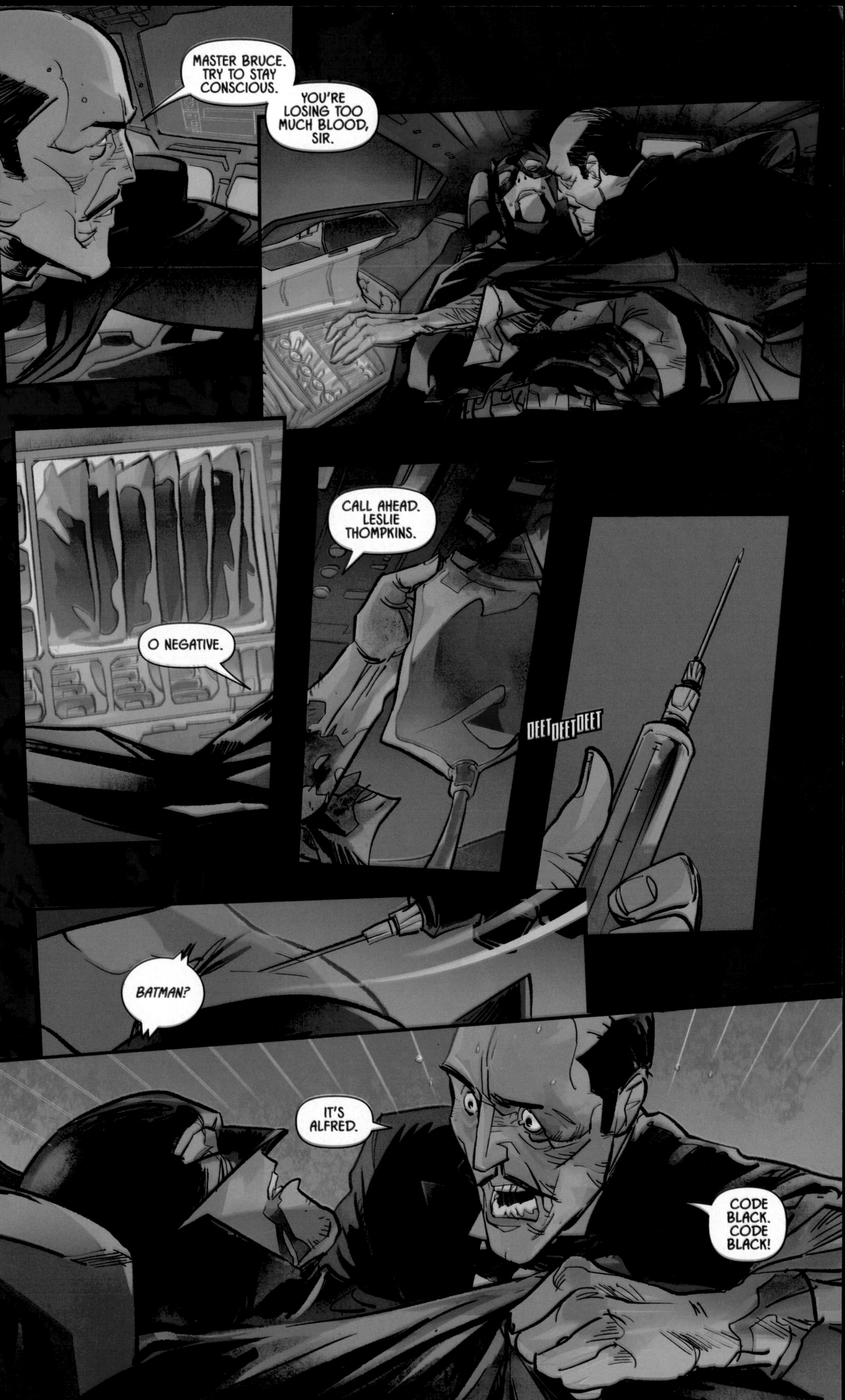
MASTER BRUCE. TRY TO STAY CONSCIOUS.
YOU'RE LOSING TOO MUCH BLOOD, SIR.
O NEGATIVE.
CALL AHEAD. LESLIE THOMPKINS.
DEET DEET DEET
BATMAN?
IT'S ALFRED.
CODE BLACK. CODE BLACK!

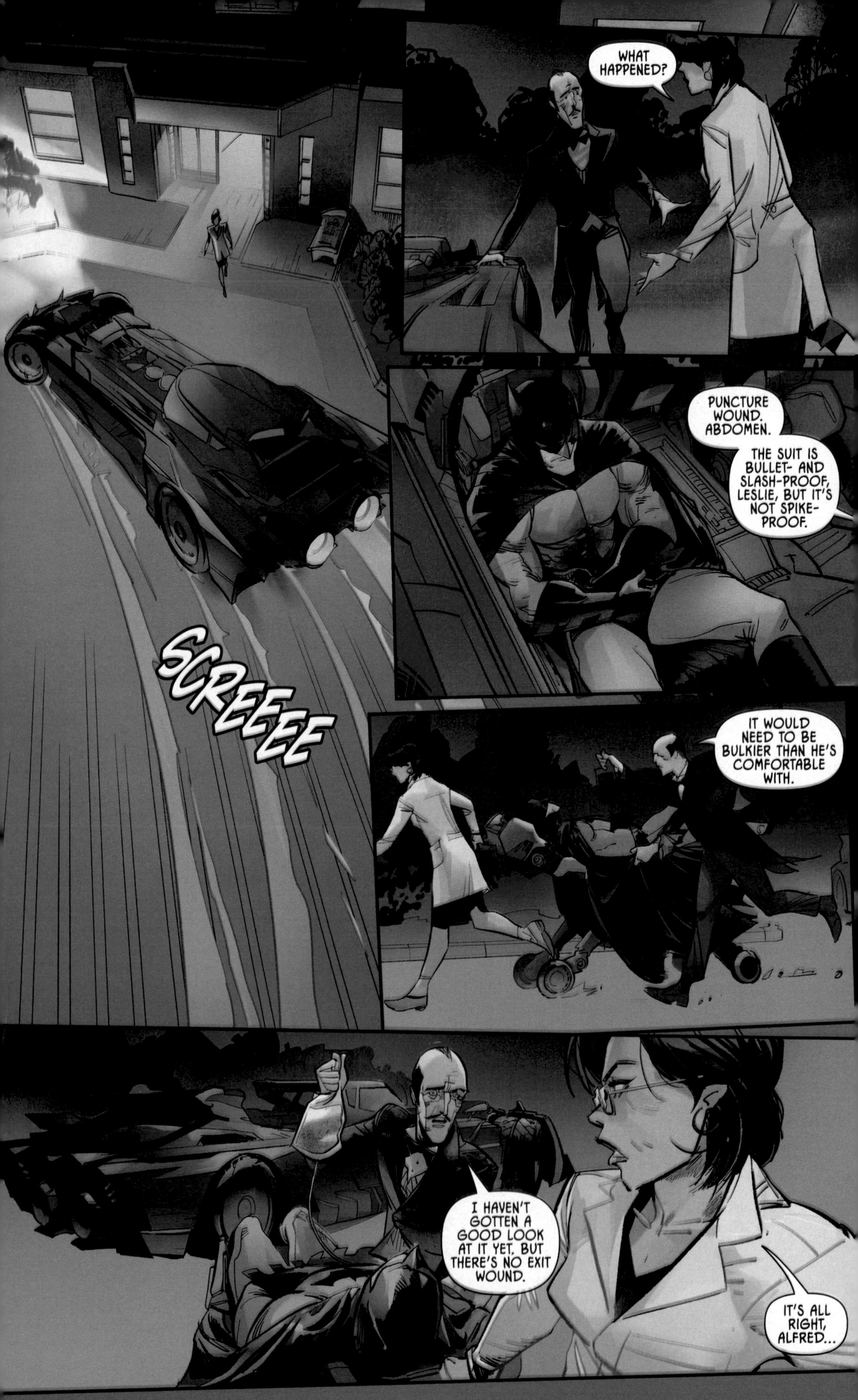

SCREEEEE
WHAT HAPPENED?
PUNCTURE WOUND. ABDOMEN.
THE SUIT IS BULLET- AND SLASH-PROOF, LESLIE, BUT IT'S NOT SPIKE-PROOF.
IT WOULD NEED TO BE BULKIER THAN HE'S COMFORTABLE WITH.
I HAVEN'T GOTTEN A GOOD LOOK AT IT YET, BUT THERE'S NO EXIT WOUND.
IT'S ALL RIGHT, ALFRED...

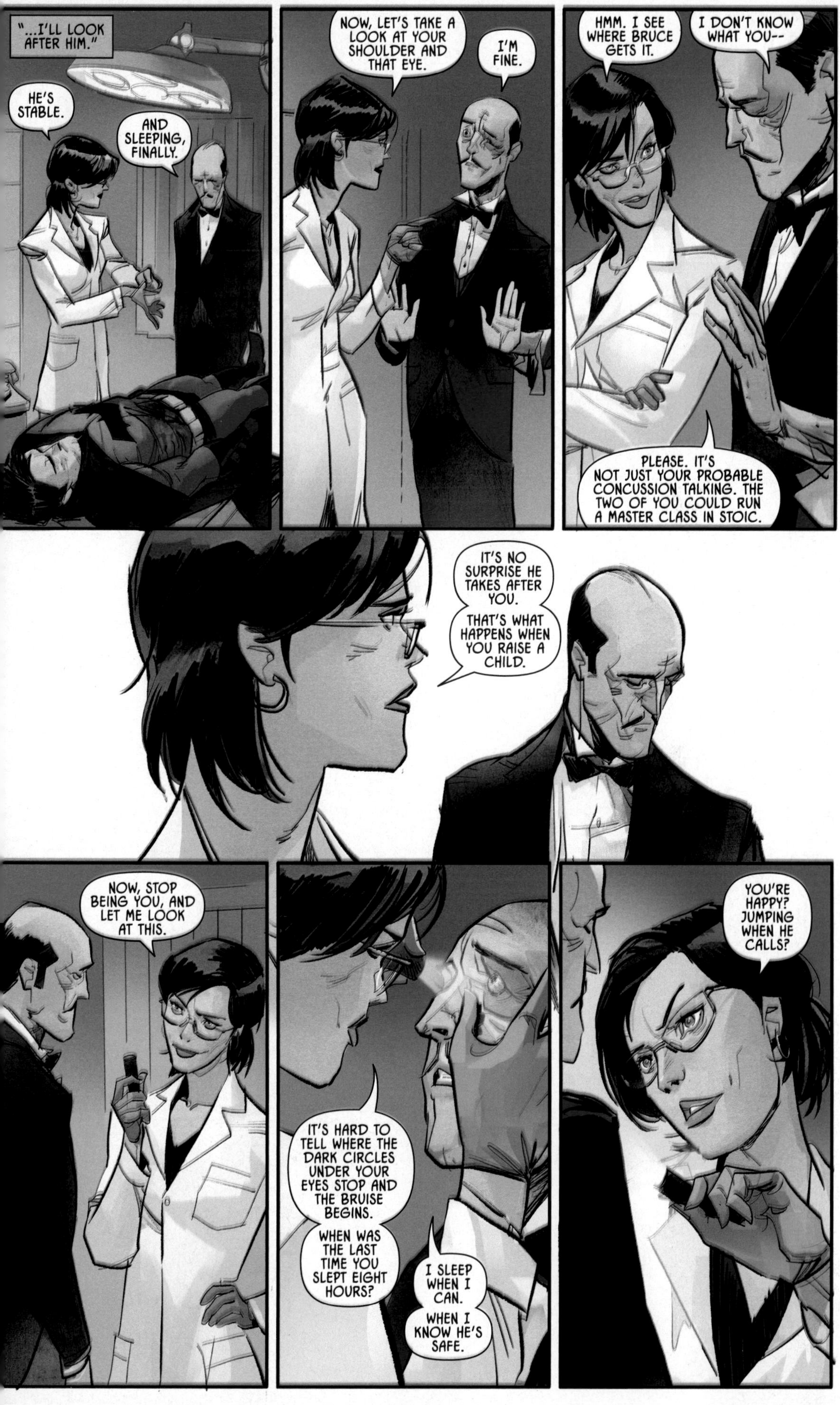
"...I'LL LOOK AFTER HIM."
HE'S STABLE.
AND SLEEPING, FINALLY.
NOW, LET'S TAKE A LOOK AT YOUR SHOULDER AND THAT EYE.
I'M FINE.
HMM. I SEE WHERE BRUCE GETS IT.
I DON'T KNOW WHAT YOU--
PLEASE. IT'S NOT JUST YOUR PROBABLE CONCUSSION TALKING. THE TWO OF YOU COULD RUN A MASTER CLASS IN STOIC.
IT'S NO SURPRISE HE TAKES AFTER YOU.
THAT'S WHAT HAPPENS WHEN YOU RAISE A CHILD.
NOW, STOP BEING YOU, AND LET ME LOOK AT THIS.
IT'S HARD TO TELL WHERE THE DARK CIRCLES UNDER YOUR EYES STOP AND THE BRUISE BEGINS.
WHEN WAS THE LAST TIME YOU SLEPT EIGHT HOURS?
I SLEEP WHEN I CAN.
WHEN I KNOW HE'S SAFE.
YOU'RE HAPPY? JUMPING WHEN HE CALLS?

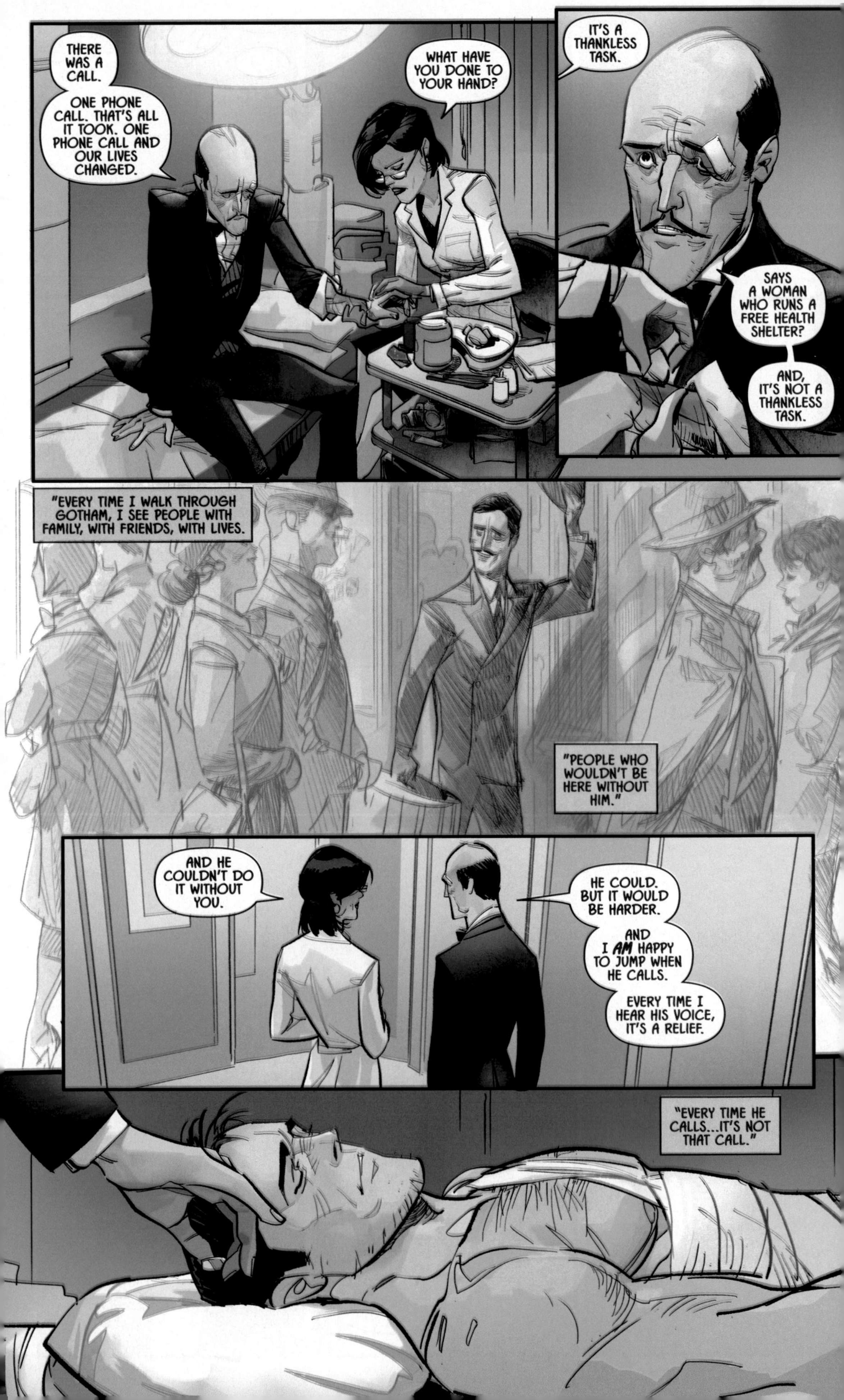

THERE WAS A CALL.
ONE PHONE CALL. THAT'S ALL IT TOOK. ONE PHONE CALL AND OUR LIVES CHANGED.
WHAT HAVE YOU DONE TO YOUR HAND?
IT'S A THANKLESS TASK.
SAYS A WOMAN WHO RUNS A FREE HEALTH SHELTER?
AND, IT'S NOT A THANKLESS TASK.
"EVERY TIME I WALK THROUGH GOTHAM, I SEE PEOPLE WITH FAMILY, WITH FRIENDS, WITH LIVES.
"PEOPLE WHO WOULDN'T BE HERE WITHOUT HIM."
AND HE COULDN'T DO IT WITHOUT YOU.
HE COULD. BUT IT WOULD BE HARDER.
AND I **AM** HAPPY TO JUMP WHEN HE CALLS.
EVERY TIME I HEAR HIS VOICE, IT'S A RELIEF.
"EVERY TIME HE CALLS...IT'S NOT THAT CALL."

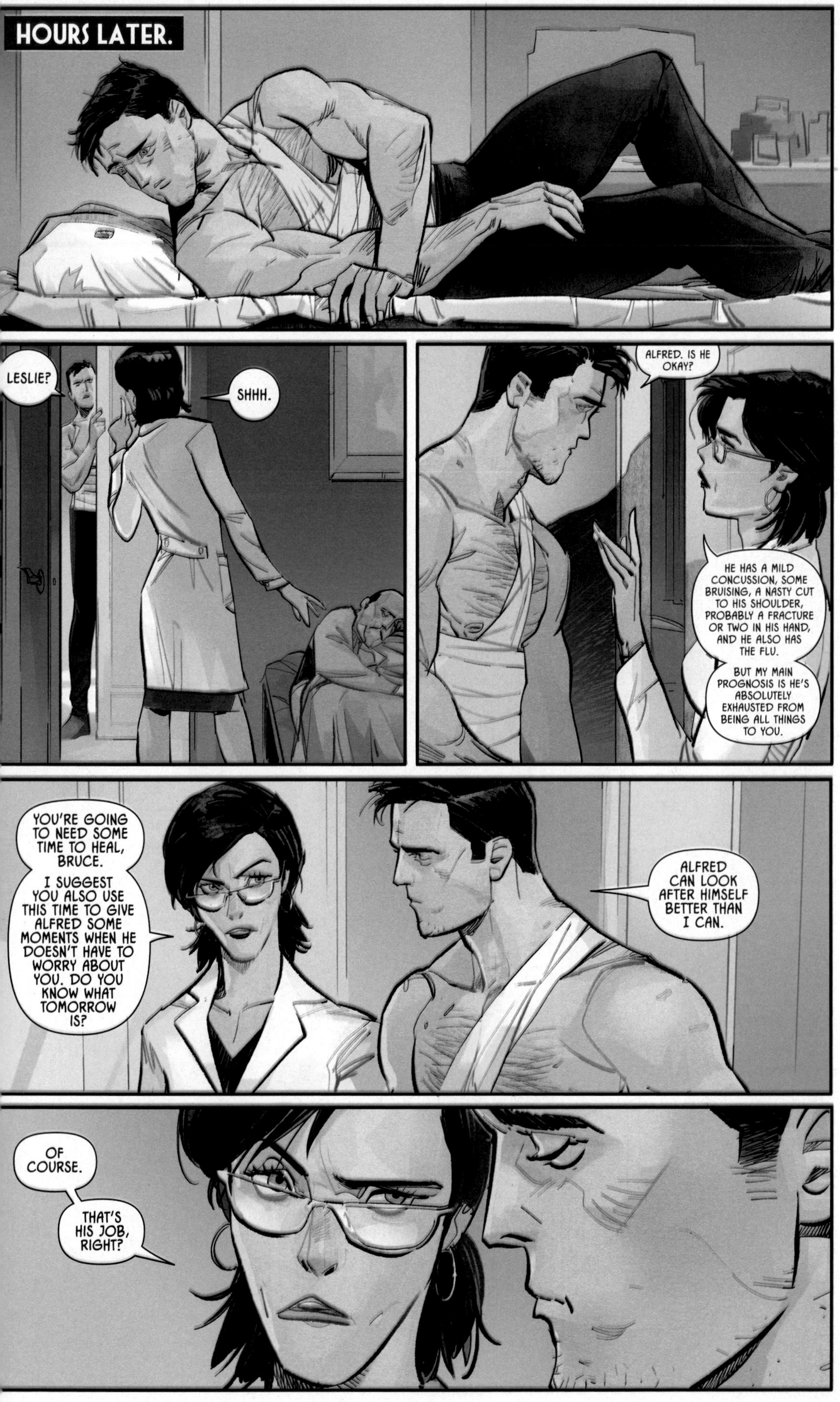
HOURS LATER.
LESLIE?
SHHH.
ALFRED. IS HE OKAY?
HE HAS A MILD CONCUSSION, SOME BRUISING, A NASTY CUT TO HIS SHOULDER, PROBABLY A FRACTURE OR TWO IN HIS HAND, AND HE ALSO HAS THE FLU.
BUT MY MAIN PROGNOSIS IS HE'S ABSOLUTELY EXHAUSTED FROM BEING ALL THINGS TO YOU.
YOU'RE GOING TO NEED SOME TIME TO HEAL, BRUCE.
I SUGGEST YOU ALSO USE THIS TIME TO GIVE ALFRED SOME MOMENTS WHEN HE DOESN'T HAVE TO WORRY ABOUT YOU. DO YOU KNOW WHAT TOMORROW IS?
ALFRED CAN LOOK AFTER HIMSELF BETTER THAN I CAN.
OF COURSE.
THAT'S HIS JOB, RIGHT?

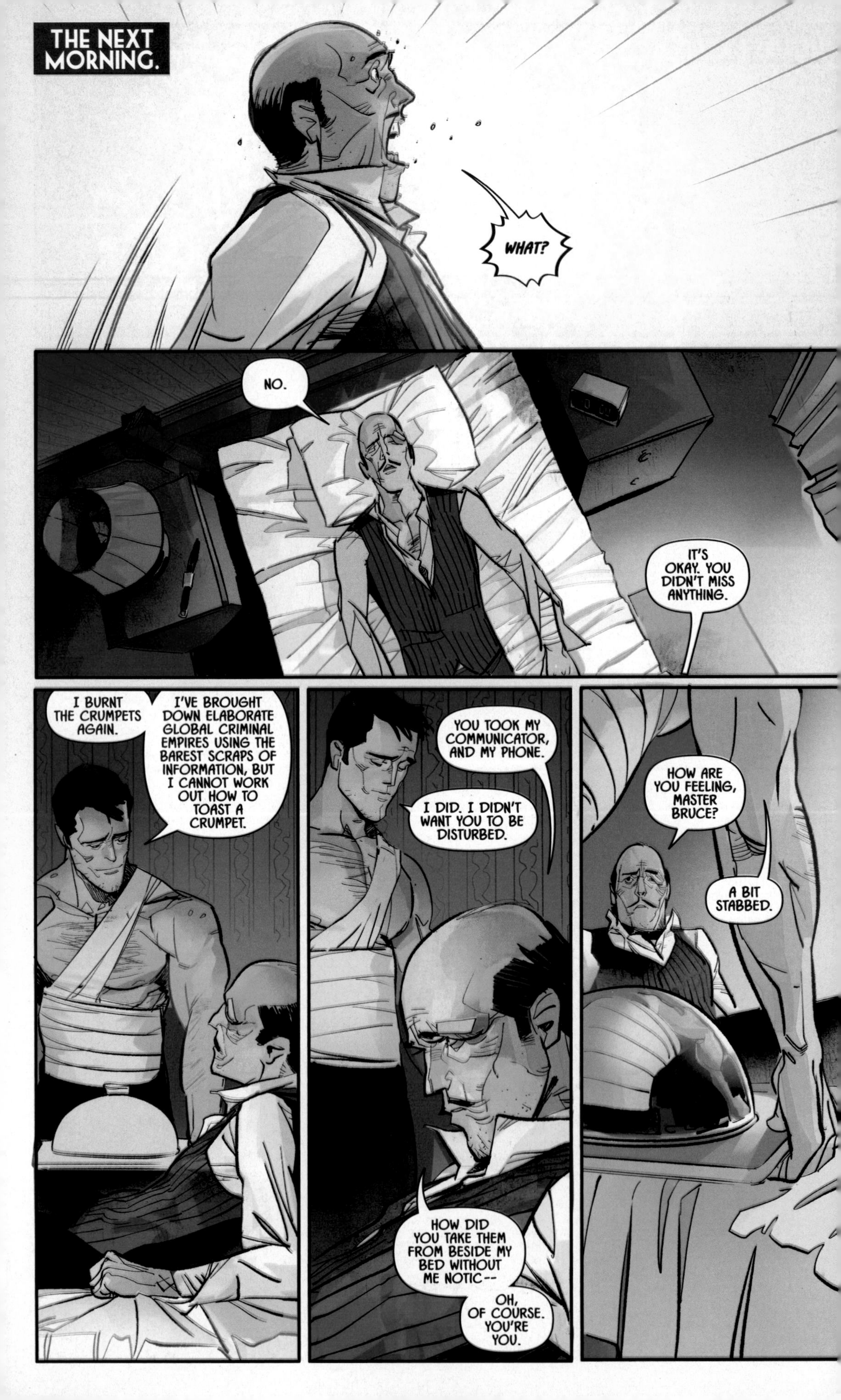
THE NEXT MORNING.
WHAT?
NO.
IT'S OKAY. YOU DIDN'T MISS ANYTHING.
I BURNT THE CRUMPETS AGAIN.
I'VE BROUGHT DOWN ELABORATE GLOBAL CRIMINAL EMPIRES USING THE BAREST SCRAPS OF INFORMATION, BUT I CANNOT WORK OUT HOW TO TOAST A CRUMPET.
YOU TOOK MY COMMUNICATOR, AND MY PHONE.
I DID. I DIDN'T WANT YOU TO BE DISTURBED.
HOW DID YOU TAKE THEM FROM BESIDE MY BED WITHOUT ME NOTIC--
OH, OF COURSE. YOU'RE YOU.
HOW ARE YOU FEELING, MASTER BRUCE?
A BIT STABBED.

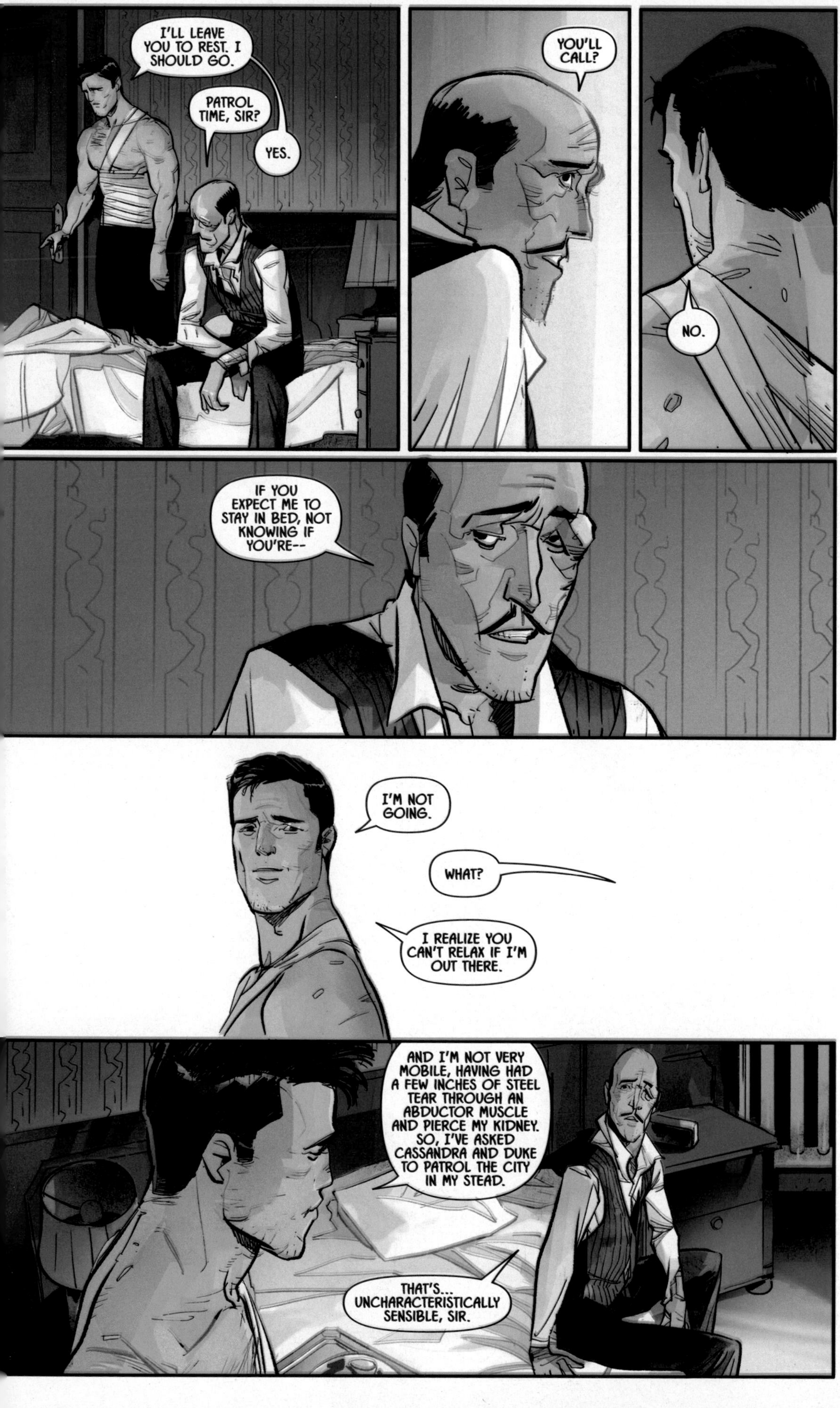
I'LL LEAVE YOU TO REST. I SHOULD GO.
PATROL TIME, SIR?
YES.
YOU'LL CALL?
NO.
IF YOU EXPECT ME TO STAY IN BED, NOT KNOWING IF YOU'RE--
I'M NOT GOING.
WHAT?
I REALIZE YOU CAN'T RELAX IF I'M OUT THERE.
AND I'M NOT VERY MOBILE, HAVING HAD A FEW INCHES OF STEEL TEAR THROUGH AN ABDUCTOR MUSCLE AND PIERCE MY KIDNEY. SO, I'VE ASKED CASSANDRA AND DUKE TO PATROL THE CITY IN MY STEAD.
THAT'S... UNCHARACTERISTICALLY SENSIBLE, SIR.

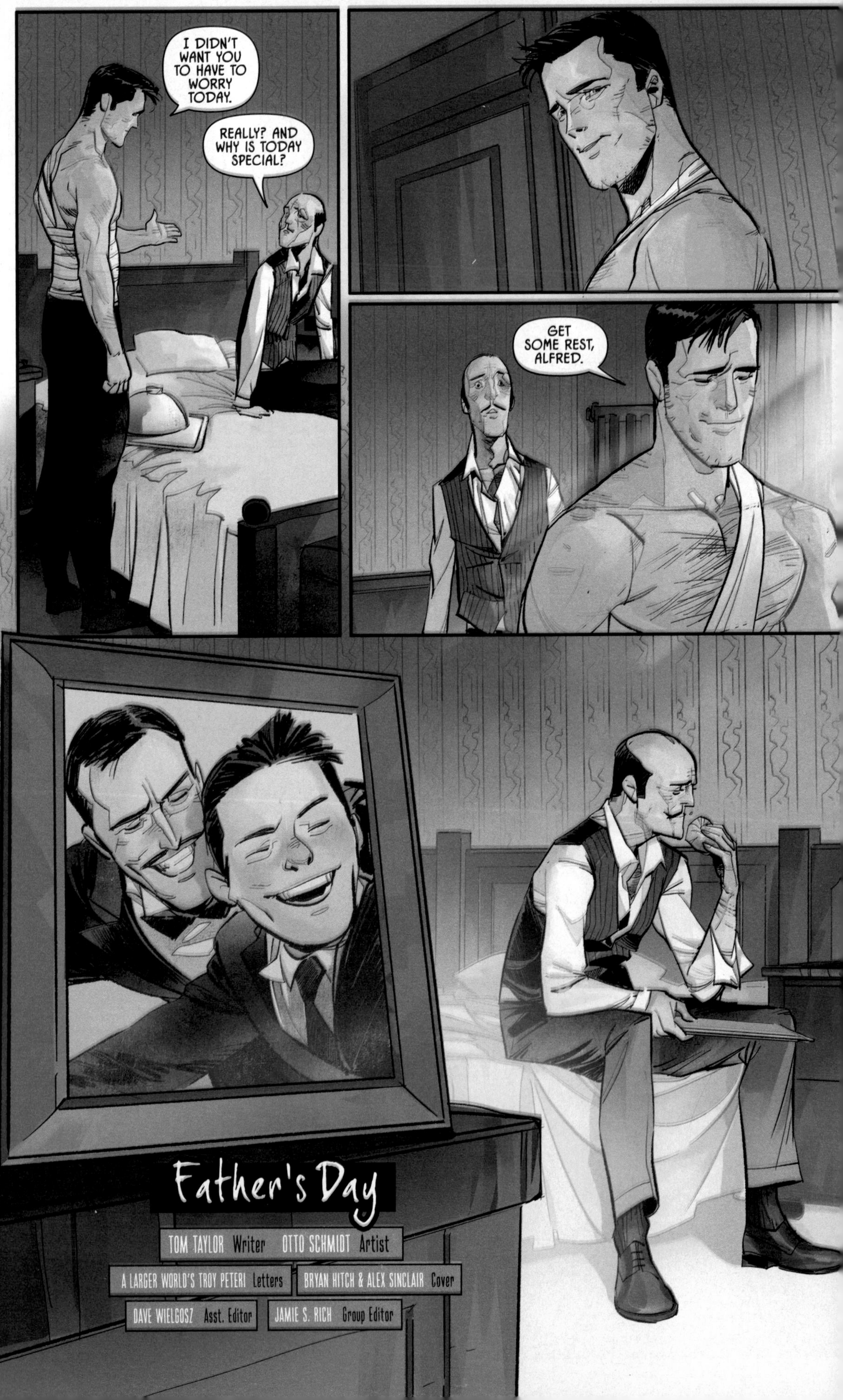
I DIDN'T WANT YOU TO HAVE TO WORRY TODAY.
REALLY? AND WHY IS TODAY SPECIAL?
GET SOME REST, ALFRED.
Father's Day
TOM TAYLOR Writer OTTO SCHMIDT Artist
A LARGER WORLD'S TROY PETERI Letters
BRYAN HITCH & ALEX SINCLAIR Cover
DAVE WIELGOSZ Asst. Editor
JAMIE S. RICH Group Editor